SURPRISE, KILL, VANISH

ALSO BY ANNIE JACOBSEN

Area 51: An Uncensored History of America's
Top Secret Military Base

Operation Paperclip: The Secret Intelligence Program
That Brought Nazi Scientists to America

The Pentagon's Brain: An Uncensored History of DARPA,
America's Top Secret Military Research Agency

Phenomena: The Secret History of the U.S. Government's
Investigations into Extrasensory Perception and
Psychokinesis

SURPRISE, KILL, VANISH

THE SECRET HISTORY OF
CIA PARAMILITARY ARMIES, OPERATORS, AND ASSASSINS

ANNIE JACOBSEN

BACK BAY BOOKS
Little, Brown and Company
New York • Boston • London

Back Bay Books / Little, Brown and Company
Hachette Book Group
1290 Avenue of the Americas, New York, NY 10104
littlebrown.com

Originally published in hardcover by Little, Brown and Company, May 2019
First Back Bay trade paperback edition, July 2020

Back Bay Books is an imprint of Little, Brown and Company, a division of Hachette Book Group, Inc. The Back Bay Books name and logo are trademarks of Hachette Book Group, Inc.

The publisher is not responsible for websites (or their content) that are not owned by the publisher.

The Hachette Speakers Bureau provides a wide range of authors for speaking events. To find out more, go to hachettespeakersbureau.com or call (866) 376-6591.

ISBN 978-0-316-44143-8 (hardcover) / 978-0-316-44141-4 (large print) / 978-0-316-44142-1 (pb)
LCCN 2018966018

Printing 7, 2023

LSC-C

Printed in the United States of America

For Kevin

I am tired and sick of war. Its glory is all moonshine. It is only those who have neither fired a shot nor heard the shrieks and groans of the wounded who cry aloud for blood, for vengeance, for desolation. War is hell.

—General William Tecumseh Sherman
(attributed, 1863)

CONTENTS

PART III

1981

PART IV

2001

AUTHOR'S NOTE ON SOURCES

This is a nonfiction book about complex individuals working in treacherous environments populated with killers, connivers, and saboteurs. In reporting this book I sat for hundreds of hours with sources who recounted to me situations of sheer pandemonium and chaos entwined with the human will to survive and the intellectual challenge of not giving up hope.

Some interviews took place in sources' homes, others in the anonymity of roadside diners. One interview took place on horseback up in the mountains, an off-the-grid location where that particular source felt comfortable speaking. Halfway into our outing, as we were riding along in the otherwise quiet forest, we heard screaming—unmistakably a woman's voice. A figure on horseback rounded the bend, the terrified rider hanging on for dear life as her horse galloped out of control, reins dangerously askew. My source, a Central Intelligence Agency (CIA) paramilitary operator, leapt off his horse, positioned himself in the wide path, and deftly grabbed the reins of the thousand-pound animal as it charged by. I knew he had a background with horses, but it was extraordinary to witness how quickly and intuitively he brought a dramatic and potentially dangerous situation under control.

"There you go, ma'am," my source said to the breathless rider, handing the reins back to her. He asked if she needed further assistance, which she declined. In the chaos of the action his shirt came untucked and I noticed he carried a SIG Sauer P320 semiautomatic pistol at his back, near his buttocks. He checked it for safety and climbed back on his horse, and we rode on.

Reporting a book about the shadow world of CIA covert-action operations requires determining first who can be trusted and then how to fact-check their stories. Covert action is, by its very nature, designed and orchestrated to remain hidden from public scrutiny. The majority of the covert-action operations around the world that I describe were orchestrated to be plausibly denied. And yet forty-two men and women with firsthand knowledge of these events allowed me to interview them for this book. Dozens of other individuals who played ancillary roles in the action were also interviewed.

Every primary source came to me by referral, which is how I've reported and written four previous nonfiction books. To verify facts, I reviewed sources' military service records, exceptional performance awards, medals, passports (real and pseudonymous), identification cards, journals, diaries, and more. How to fact-check sources' stories? The CIA and its intelligence community partners guard their secrets through a complex array of code words, cover stories, and operational names. Through Freedom of Information Act (FOIA) requests and preexisting declassification efforts, I accessed thousands of pages of documents from the CIA, the Departments of Defense and State, and other government entities, housed in the National Archives and elsewhere, cited in the notes and bibliography. And this book would not exist without the work of other journalists, scholars, and historians whose books, monographs, papers, and news articles I have duly cited.

Those interviewed for this book served thirteen presidents (seven Democrats, six Republicans) from Franklin Roosevelt to Barack Obama. They include two surviving members of the Office of Strategic Services (OSS); eight individuals who served the CIA at the Senior Intelligence Service (SIS) level, equivalent to an ambassador at the State Department or a general at the Defense Department;

eleven chiefs of station from countries on five continents; numerous chiefs of base who served in some of the world's most dangerous outposts, including in Sudan, Yemen, Iraq, and Afghanistan; nineteen operators from the Special Activities Division (SAD), Ground Branch; and an attorney at the CIA who wrote scores of classified Presidential Findings, starting with those on the Iran hostage crisis, and was uniquely helpful in clarifying Executive Office–level decision making. Every operation reported in this book, however shocking, was legal. Other sources shared information with me on background, to assist in my understanding of the subject matter but without direct attribution to them.

SURPRISE, KILL, VANISH

Some might say this is a book about assassination, but really it is a book about covert action, *Tertia Optio,* the president's third option when the first option, diplomacy, is inadequate and the second, war, is a terrible idea. All covert action is classified, designed to be plausibly denied, and because of this it is sometimes called the president's hidden hand. The most extreme of all hidden-hand operations involves killing a leader or prominent person, and this book focuses on that act.

The president's third option was born in the wake of World War II, and those who created it did so to avert World War III. With its ethos in unconventional warfare, the Central Intelligence Agency officers and operators who conduct covert action were originally called the president's guerrilla warfare corps.

The same legal construct that allowed national-security advisors for Presidents Eisenhower and Kennedy to plot to kill foreign leaders like Fidel Castro also allowed Presidents Bush and Obama to create a system in which prominent people can be placed on a kill-or-capture list, to be targeted and killed. This authority remains in effect today. Targeted killing is not limited to high-technology drone strikes. The president's guerrilla warfare corps kills enemies mano a mano, in close-quarters combat when necessary. The group that has the authority to conduct these lethal operations outside a war zone, on the ground, is the CIA's Special Activities Division. One of its most lethal components is called Ground Branch.

The origins of the Special Activities Division, including its Ground Branch, lie in the CIA's precursor agency, the Office of Strategic Services, and specifically its Special Operations (SO) Branch, a guerrilla warfare corps whose goal was to kill Nazis—to sabotage and subvert the Third Reich. The motto of one unit, the OSS Jedburghs, was "Surprise, Kill, Vanish."

The OSS was modeled after a wartime British organization, also classified, called Special Operations Executive (SOE). The idea that most people find hand-to-hand killing repugnant but mechanized killing somehow more palatable is central to this book.

From the early days of the OSS Special Operations Branch to the present-day activities of the CIA's Ground Branch, the most ruthless and risky lethal operations have evolved and transformed. Over the decades, killing a leader or prominent person under the rubric of covert action has been called many things by those who plan and oversee operations but never assassination, because assassination is illegal. Killing a leader or prominent person at the behest of the president is legal under Title 50 of the U.S. Code.

President Dwight Eisenhower's advisors discussed "eliminating" foreign leaders, and they set up a Health Alteration Committee to "neutralize" or "disable" certain people. They spoke in riddles to uphold the construct of plausible deniability, Congress later found. President John F. Kennedy's advisors formalized killing and called it Executive Action. To President Ronald Reagan the construct became "pre-emptive neutralization"—eliminating terrorists before they had a chance to strike again. Under President George W. Bush the term "lethal direct action" was used. Under President Barack Obama, killing terrorists became known publicly as "targeted killing." The question arises, how does killing any one person advance U.S. foreign policy objectives? This book aims to shine some light on how and why certain leaders and prominent people are targeted and killed.

In the early days of covert action there was no oversight; in the mid-1970s, after the Church Committee hearings produced a report called "Alleged Assassination Plots Involving Foreign Leaders," oversight was given to Congress, where it remains today. Covert-action orders are formalized by CIA lawyers in a Presidential Finding, or Memorandum of Notification (MON), to be signed by the president. John A. Rizzo, former chief legal officer for the CIA, who served seven presidents and wrote scores of these covert-action findings, including the Memorandum of Notification that authorized lethal direct action against terrorists as of September 17, 2001, which remains in effect today, goes on record in this book.

William D. Waugh, one of the oldest longest-serving covert-action operators in the United States and a highly decorated U.S. Army Green Beret, makes up the core of this book. His is an extraordinary life spent dedicated to perfecting the art of covert action. Covert action is assigned to the CIA in peacetime but run jointly by the Defense Department during war.

Because foreign governments, nonstate actors, and lone-wolf assassins regularly try to kill America's commander in chief, it is important to also understand how deterrence against assassination is the other side of the covert-action coin. This part of the narrative is told through the lens of Lewis C. Merletti, the nineteenth director of the U.S. Secret Service and a former member of the Counter Assault Team (CAT), the paramilitary force of the U.S. Secret Service. Like Waugh, Merletti's unconventional-warfare expertise comes from his combat experiences in Vietnam as a Green Beret.

I first started thinking about assassination in 2009, when I was working as a reporter for the *Los Angeles Times Magazine*. A source visited my home on the way back from the Middle East. He worked in counterterrorism; that was the extent of what he could say about his employment situation. I knew him to be an expert weapons handler; he almost always traveled with gun cases. And yet the commemorative medallion he showed me from his most recent travels read: "American Embassy: Kabul, Afghanistan." Nothing in his area of expertise was related to diplomacy, as far as I knew, but we both understood it was best to leave it at that.

My two sons were young at the time, and dozens of G.I. Joes— from the Revolutionary War era to the twenty-first century—filled our California house and yard. At the boys' request, the source pains- takingly identified G.I. Joes' unique weapons: Confederate rifles with bayonets, M1 Garands, AK-47s, M16 rifles. Later, the source asked if it was okay to show my boys two real firearms, for educational pur- poses. He was a licensed weapons safety instructor and had twice taken me shooting. I said yes.

Watching carefully as he showed my children a sidearm and a compacted sniper rifle, I noticed that there was one case he never opened. Later that evening, I asked him privately what was inside. He opened it, revealing a large serrated knife.

"What's that for?" I asked, almost immediately realizing my mis- take.

"Sometimes a job requires quiet," he said. He closed the case.

Neither of us said another word.

That was the moment I realized the obvious: the United States kills its enemies not only in high-technology drone strikes but also at close range. I later learned from another source that my houseguest worked for the CIA's Special Activities Division, Ground Branch.

This encounter stayed with me, as did the idea of close-quarters killing, and my reaction to it. I could imagine my houseguest killing an Al-Qaeda fighter using a sniper rifle, but the idea of him cutting someone's throat, or thrusting it in a man's ribs, gave me pause. Why? And why is all covert action secret, classified—designed for the pres- ident to deny and the public to never know?

My source never spoke of his work in the Middle East, not before he showed me the knife and not after. It was understood that his work was classified. Hidden programs are notorious places to cover up fail- ure, to conceal egregious mistakes. I wondered if dispatching para- military operators around the world to conduct lethal covert-action operations was all too often a recipe for disaster or, instead, mostly a weaponized strength.

Is killing a person decreed by the president to be a threat to U.S. national security right or wrong? Moral or immoral? Honorable or dishonorable? I found answers in writing this book. I hope readers find theirs.

PART I

1941

CHAPTER ONE

An Office for Ungentlemanly Warfare

It was the first Sunday in December 1941, and the boy selling popcorn behind the concession stand at the Strand Theatre in Bastrop, Texas, had just turned twelve. His name was William Dawson Waugh, but everyone called him Billy.

Shortly after 2:00 p.m., Sheriff Ed Cartwright walked into the theater with a terrible look on his face. He told Billy Waugh to run upstairs, have the projectionist shut off the film, and turn on the lights. Taking the stairs two at a time, Waugh did as instructed. From high above in the projectionist's booth he watched as the room full of moviegoers squinted and complained about the movie being interrupted. Then Sheriff Cartwright walked onto the stage and everyone fell silent.

"Listen up," the sheriff said. "The Japanese just attacked Pearl Harbor." The U.S. Pacific Fleet was destroyed and thousands of Americans were dead. What would happen next was anyone's guess, the sheriff said, but it would be foolhardy to rule out the possibility of another attack. Sheriff Cartwright told everyone to go home and cover their windows with blackout material. Listen to the radio and stay informed.

Billy Waugh stayed behind, watching the moviegoers file out. After he finished cleaning up, he went home to the house where he lived with his mother, Lillian, a part-time schoolteacher, and his older sister Nancy. The next day, Congress declared war on Japan. Three days after that, Adolf Hitler declared war on the United States, and Congress then declared war on Germany and Italy. With America at war around the world, Billy Waugh made a vow to himself: one day I'll go to war, too.

The day Pearl Harbor was bombed in a surprise attack remained imprinted on his mind. By that time, 1941, Billy Waugh knew more about war than most twelve-year-old boys. He'd been absorbing information from the newsreels that played before Strand Theatre films. Hitler's campaign, Blitzkrieg, or lightning war, astounded him. This idea of total war, of all-out victory at any human cost, was mindboggling and frightening.

"It is not right that matters, but victory," Hitler told his generals. "Act brutally!...Be harsh and remorseless...the success of the best [is] by means of force..."

Of all the tactics and techniques being used by the Nazis in the invasion of western Europe, it was the boldness of the paratrooper unit (Fallschirmjäger) that left Billy Waugh thunderstruck. Newsreel films showed Nazi commandos leaping out of airplanes and parachuting into the war theater to launch deadly surprise attacks. Then there was the paraglider attack at the Belgian fortress Eben Emael, once considered the most impenetrable fortress in the world. Seventy-eight Nazi paratroopers, piloting gliders and armed with flamethrowers, landed on the rooftop of the fortress, and overtook 650 Belgian defenders—a victory from which the Belgian Army never recovered. One month after the Nazis captured Eben Emael, the U.S. Army created its own paratrooper division in Fort Benning, Georgia, the first in American history.

Every spare moment Billy Waugh had, in between school and the three part-time jobs he worked—as a paperboy, stock boy, and popcorn popper—he gathered information about these U.S. paratroopers. The most important items for a successful parachute jump, he learned, were the boots. They were tall, to mid-shin, with rawhide laces and stitching across the toe. Billy Waugh became focused on owning a pair of his own. His alcoholic father had died of cirrhosis of the liver when Billy was ten. The money he earned from his after-school jobs went to his mother, to help pay for the family's living expenses. Now, with a clear goal in mind, he began skimming nickels and dimes off his earnings. When he finally saved up seven dollars, he hitchhiked thirty miles to Austin and bought himself a pair of paratrooper boots. Elated, he felt a step closer to one day becoming a U.S. paratrooper. The world was all right.

Across the Atlantic, war raged in Europe. It was May 27, 1942, and in the Czech town of Holešovice the Nazi general riding in an armor-plated Mercedes-Benz had been targeted for assassination. SS-Obergruppenführer Reinhard Heydrich was a Janus-like creature: blond, blue-eyed, and beautiful, his skin smooth and pale like that of a porcelain doll, but he was also a monster, cruel and sadistic beyond measure. His own boss, Adolf Hitler, described Heydrich as a man with an iron heart. A secret unit inside British intelligence sought to kill him. The assassination plot was called Operation Anthropoid.

Concealed on a hillside not far from where Heydrich was driving his Mercedes, two British-trained assassins lay in wait. Jan Kubiš and Josef Gabčík, both Czech nationals in their midtwenties, were members of a classified British commando unit that existed inside the British Secret Intelligence Services, Section 6—MI6. Only an elite few were aware that these commando units were part of an underground paramilitary army working under the bland-sounding cover name Special Operations Executive. Kubiš and Gabčík had been assigned to SOE's Division D, for destruction, and their work was based on unconventional-warfare tactics, also called guerrilla warfare.

The existence of SOE was a source of great controversy within the British military establishment. Most British generals believed war was first and foremost about chivalry and honor. That it must be fought in adherence to the laws of war. While no single document can be identified as the ancient source from which the laws of war have evolved, modern-day codes of conduct stem from the Lieber Code, a set of 157 rules written by lawyer and university professor Francis Lieber during the American Civil War. Issued on April 24, 1863, by President Abraham Lincoln as General Orders No. 100, these rules were to serve as a uniform code of conduct governing the behavior of the Union Army, the Confederate Army, and the armies of Europe. They were later expanded upon in Hague Convention resolutions of 1899 and 1907. Rule 148 of the Lieber Code explicitly prohibited assassination. "Civilized nations look with horror upon offers of rewards for the assassination of enemies as relapses into barbarism," Lieber wrote. Guerrilla fighters were labeled "insidious" enemies and therefore not entitled to the protections of the Laws of War.

War, like sport, was to be a gentleman's game. Guerrilla warfare was most ungentlemanly, based as it was on treacherous principles like sabotage and subversion. Sabotage during World War II meant blowing up trains, bridges, and production plants behind enemy lines—situations in which civilians would likely be killed. Subversion, or undermining the authority of an occupying force, required a host of dirty tricks and deceptive acts, including assassination. But Prime Minister Winston Churchill believed that SOE Division D was necessary, and he personally approved of every mission it undertook. Because guerrilla warfare in general, and SOE operations in particular, were considered ungentlemanly, the SOE became known as Churchill's Ministry of Ungentlemanly Warfare.

Commandos like Kubiš and Gabčík were trained to infiltrate enemy-occupied territory, perform hit-and-run operations, and then disappear. The short-term goal of their efforts was to create paranoia among Nazi officials and embolden underground resistance movements. The long-term goal of the SOE was to prepare the battlefield for an upcoming Allied invasion.

In Nazi-occupied Czechoslovakia, Obergruppenführer Reinhard Heydrich was in charge. He was also one of the most influential and powerful generals in the vast Nazi war machine. Heydrich reported directly to Heinrich Himmler, the ambitious, sadistic Reichsführer whose evil knew no bounds. Heydrich created and supervised the Einsatzgruppen, extermination squads whose 3,000 members shot and killed more than one million men, women, and children during the war. He served as one of the main architects of the Final Solution and personally initiated the deportation and mass murder of European Jews. In 1942, he was at the top of SOE's kill list.

At SOE, the Heydrich assassination operation was handled jointly by two men, Major General Sir Colin McVean Gubbins, a decorated World War I hero and SOE's director of operations, and František Moravec, the former chief of Czech military intelligence, then living in England in exile. As with most SOE commandos, Jan Kubiš and Josef Gabčík had been handpicked for bravery, cunning, and a willingness to ruthlessly kill. "The whole art of guerilla [sic] warfare lies in striking the enemy where he least expects it, and yet where he is most vulnerable," Gubbins instructed his men. "Inflict the maximum amount of damage in a short time and get away."

The SOE considered assassination a necessary dark art, a way to weaken the Nazis' impenetrable hold on power. A successful operation required months of planning by Gubbins and Moravec, followed by months of intense training and rehearsing by Kubiš and Gabčík. Much of the work took place in a classified SOE facility in Scotland code-named Training Center STS 25. Here, the assassins trained in guerrilla warfare tactics including hand-to-hand combat, sharpshooting, cover and concealment, and the manufacture of homemade bombs. They learned map reading and code deciphering. How to slit the throat of a sentry or guard without making a sound. Finally given the green light, Kubiš and Gabčík were flown in under cover of darkness by a British pilot and a crew of five. They jumped out of the aircraft over a village just east of Prague and parachuted in behind enemy lines. Safely on the ground, the two commandos met up with resistance fighters who hid them from discovery until they were ready to strike. On May 27, 1942, the moment arrived.

There, in Nazi-occupied Holešovice, Kubiš and Gabčík lay camouflaged in the grass. They'd arrived to the target area on bicycles, now stashed in a nearby grove of trees. Each man had a pistol in his pocket. Gabčík carried a Sten submachine gun. Kubiš held the assassination weapon: an antitank grenade that had been specially modified by British explosives expert Cecil Clarke. The small bomb needed to be powerful enough to shatter the armored plating on Heydrich's Mercedes, so as to kill him, but light enough to be accurately thrown by Jan Kubiš.

High on the hill above the assassins, a signal mirror flashed. Heydrich's Mercedes had been spotted by a local Czech accomplice, Josef Valčík. Soon the car would round the corner and approach where Kubiš and Gabčík were concealed. The planning had been meticulously mapped out. The geography of the land was such that at mid-hill, the road twisted in a hairpin turn, meaning Heydrich's chauffeur would be forced to brake and slow down. Kubiš and Gabčík would have a five-second window to kill Reinhard Heydrich and flee.

As the car made its way down the hill, the assassins could see that the top of Heydrich's Mercedes 320 Convertible B was open wide. Opportunity at hand, Gabčík stood up, released the catch on his Sten submachine gun, and rushed toward the sharpest point in the road's curve. As the Mercedes braked and decelerated, Gabčík took aim and fired, bracing himself for a powerful explosion of gunfire. Instead, a catastrophic misfire. Nothing but the impotent *click* of the weapon as it failed to fire. Gabčík, now standing there in the road, was mortally exposed.

Heydrich's driver screeched to a full stop. SS-Oberscharführer

Johannes Klein was an imposing Nazi chauffeur and bodyguard. Six foot three, he was trained in the art of tactical military driving. Had he followed Third Reich protocol, Klein would have accelerated and sped away. But Heydrich apparently ordered Klein to stop the car. With Gabčík still standing next to the Mercedes, Heydrich pulled his Luger from its holster, stood up in the convertible, and began shooting at Gabčík. What Reinhard Heydrich failed to realize was that a second SOE-trained assassin was nearby.

Jan Kubiš moved into action. Following protocols learned over months of SOE commando training, he stepped forward and hurled the incendiary device into Heydrich's Mercedes. In the chaos of the moment, he missed. Instead, the bomb exploded against the car's right rear fender, sending glass and metal shards flying through the air. Reinhard Heydrich was hit by debris. Not realizing he'd been wounded, Heydrich got out of the car and continued firing. Ditching his faulty submachine gun, Gabčík returned fire with his pistol. Enraged, Heydrich lumbered toward his assassin as Gabčík sought cover behind a telephone pole. As the smoke from the car bomb cleared, Kubiš emerged bleeding from a head wound. One witness described blood pouring down his forehead into his eyes. Klein exited the car and began firing at Kubiš. Improbably, the bodyguard's gun also jammed, affording Kubiš time to flee.

Gabčík remained pinned down behind the telephone pole, engaged in a lethal exchange of gunfire with Heydrich. But as Heydrich charged, still firing at Gabčík, he suddenly and dramatically collapsed in the road. The debris from the bomb had penetrated his skin and lodged in his organs. Adolf Hitler's powerful deputy lay stricken on the pavement, unable to move.

"Get that bastard!" Heydrich shouted at Klein, pointing in the direction of Gabčík as he fled. The chauffeur chased the assassins across a field, leaving Heydrich writhing in pain on the road. Kubiš and Gabčík escaped.

Heydrich was rushed to nearby Bulovka Hospital, where three

of the Nazis' most senior doctors came to his aid. Theodor Morrell, Hitler's personal physician, Karl Brandt, Nazi health commissioner, and Karl Gebhardt, chief surgeon of the Waffen-SS, concluded that Heydrich's diaphragm was torn and that grenade fragments were embedded in his spine—not necessarily life-threatening injuries. But the three physicians overlooked the fact that tiny bits of horsehair from the upholstered seats of the Mercedes had lodged into Heydrich's spleen. Just a few days later, on June 4, 1942, the man with the iron heart died from septicemia, or blood poisoning.

When Hitler learned of Heydrich's assassination, he became enraged. Privately, he blamed Reinhard Heydrich for his own careless death. "Since it is opportunity which makes not only the thief but also the assassin, such heroic gestures as driving in an open, unarmored vehicle or walking about the streets unguarded are just damned stupidity, which serves the Fatherland not one whit," Hitler said on the day Heydrich died. "That a man as irreplaceable as Heydrich should expose himself to unnecessary danger, I can only condemn as stupid and idiotic." Publicly, Hitler demanded revenge. That the assassins had been able to escape and go into hiding was an outrageous insult to the Third Reich. At Heydrich's funeral in Berlin, Hitler ordered his ministers in Prague to find the assassins, or else.

The reprisals were brutal, indiscriminate, and far-reaching. "The barbaric idea was to terrify the Czech people by completely destroying a village at random," said František Moravec, former chief of Czech military intelligence and the man who'd trained the assassins. Northeast of Prague, the Gestapo cordoned off Lidice, rounded up all 173 male inhabitants, and executed them in the village square. Three hundred women and children were sent to Ravensbrück concentration camp for extermination. The houses in the village were set on fire, then bulldozed over so no trace remained. "The operation was executed with such thoroughness that even the persons who happened to be absent from the village on the night of the destruction were gradually located and executed," said Moravec.

A reward of one million reichsmarks was offered for information on the assassins' whereabouts. A local Nazi collaborator named Alois Kral revealed that Jan Kubiš and Josef Gabčík were hiding in the basement of a Russian Orthodox church in Prague. Nazi commandos stormed the church, and when they determined that Kubiš and Gabčík were located in the tunnels below, they flooded the basement with water. Kubiš tried to fight his way out but was mortally wounded. Gabčík, knowing he would soon be killed or captured, swallowed a cyanide pill given to him by the SOE. Both men's bodies were recovered and buried in a mass grave.

The reprisals did not end in Lidice. Five days later, Nazis razed Ležáky after a shortwave radio transmission was found to have been sent from the village to the British. All thirty-three residents and their children were killed. The following week, 115 people accused of being members of the Czech resistance were executed. Heydrich's successor, SS General Kurt Daluege, boasted that in retaliation for killing Reinhard Heydrich, 1,331 Czech citizens were executed and another 3,000 Jews exterminated. Was it worth it? Five thousand Czechs "paid with their lives for the death of a single Nazi maniac," Moravec lamented after the war.

In 1945, after the Germans surrendered, Moravec returned to Prague to speak with Alois Kral, imprisoned and awaiting trial for Nazi collaboration.

"Greetings, brother," Kral said sarcastically to Moravec when the two men met.

"Brother?" asked Moravec, astonished.

"I killed two Czechs. You killed five thousand. Which of us hangs?" Kral asked.

It was Kral who was hanged; General Moravec watched the execution. By then, Czechoslovakia had become part of the Communist Soviet bloc. After the execution, as Moravec walked away, he stopped to ask a question of a communist functionary—a Czech national—a man familiar with the Heydrich case.

"Will you please tell me where Kubiš and Gabčík are buried?" Moravec asked.

"Nowhere," came the abrupt answer. "There are no graves. You foot-kissers of the British are not going to have that excuse to build a statue and hang wreaths. Czech heroes are Communists [now]."

And so it goes. Wars are fought. One side wins, the other side loses. Some go home. Others become casualties. Freed from Nazi rule, the Czechs lived under a communist-led government that answered to another tyrant, Josef Stalin.

For the second time in a decade, František Moravec fled his country, this time for America. There, the former head of Czech military intelligence took a job as an advisor to the U.S. Department of Defense, where he worked until suffering a heart attack in 1966. He died in the parking lot of the Pentagon, seated in the front seat of his car.

To the SOE, the assassination of Reinhard Heydrich was necessary and justified. The spectacle killing of a top Nazi general poked holes in the armor of the Nazi war machine. To the general Czech population, it made the strong appear weak. Inside the Third Reich, the meticulously planned and executed assassination operation gave rise to fear and paranoia among other Nazi officials. When Winston Churchill was briefed on Operation Anthropoid, he expressed approval. When U.S. President Franklin Roosevelt asked whether the British had a hand in Heydrich's assassination, Churchill is said to have winked.

In Washington, DC, a retired World War I general and recipient of the Medal of Honor named William J. Donovan had been trying for years to get President Roosevelt to authorize an unconventional-warfare organization modeled after SOE. Two weeks after Reinhard Heydrich's assassination, Donovan got his wish. As per Executive Order 9182, the Office of Strategic Services was born, a closely held secret at the time but now famously known as the wartime predecessor of the CIA. Under the authority of the Joint Chiefs of Staff, OSS would work in partnership with SOE. William J. Donovan was made director, and within days of its creation, recruiting for OSS was in full swing.

At Fort Polk in Louisiana, U.S. Army officer Aaron Bank, 40, was restless and bored. It had been seventeen months since the sneak attack on Pearl Harbor and the same amount of time since Bank had requested troop assignment. He was burning to see combat, but in the eyes of the U.S. Army, Aaron Bank was too old. And so instead, he'd been assigned to a railroad battalion, overseeing soldiers lay tracks connecting Fort Polk to Camp Claiborne, fifty miles away. "My spirits were low with such unrewarding duties," he told a friend.

One day in the spring of 1943, passing the adjutant's tent, Bank spotted a notice on a bulletin board. The army was looking for volunteers. The notice read: "Likelihood of a dangerous mission guaranteed." Knowledge of French or another European language was the only requirement, but volunteers would need to qualify as paratroopers.

"My pulse quickened," Bank later recalled, "a ray of hope appeared." Fluent in French and eager to jump out of airplanes, Bank signed up. A few days later, he received orders. He was to report to the Q Building in Washington, DC, wearing civilian clothes. Aaron Bank did not yet know it, but he'd been assigned to the OSS, to its Special Operations Branch, the American equivalent of SOE's Division D. The mandate of the Special Operations Branch was to "effect physical subversion of the enemy," in three distinct phases: infiltrate, prepare the battlefield, and conduct sabotage and subversion. Bank was assigned to the French Operational Group for Operation Jedburgh.

Initial training took place at a secret facility in Prince William Forest Park, in Virginia, that went by the code name Area B. Volunteers learned right away the kinds of commando operations they were being prepared for. "Either you kill or capture, or you will be killed or captured," the Jedburghs were told, an instruction that was emphasized by the Fairbairn-Sykes OSS stiletto knife issued to members. This double-edged weapon, designed exclusively for surprise attack and killing, resembled a dagger. Its foil grip and slender blade made for easy penetration into a man's rib cage. How best to use the now legendary Fairbairn-Sykes stiletto in hand-to-hand combat was taught to the Jedburghs by Lt. Col. William E. Fairbairn, one of the knife's designers. "In close-quarters fighting there is no more deadly weapon than the knife. An entirely unarmed man has no certain defense against it," Fairbairn explained. Of Fairbairn's training, a young recruit named Richard Helms had this to say: "Within fifteen seconds, I came to realize that my private parts were in constant jeopardy." Helms would one day serve as the eighth director of Central Intelligence.

In addition to the art of knife fighting, Jedburghs learned pistol shooting and grenade throwing. How to kill a man with a pencil to the throat, how to garrote an enemy with piano wire. In evade-and-escape training they practiced rope climbing and map reading, how to cross a raging river and scale a cliff. To master the art of sabotage, the Jedburghs learned to construct bombs powerful enough to blow up bridges, canal locks, and industrial plants. To infiltrate territory laced with land mines, they practiced on an obstacle course laced with small explosive charges and called Demolition Trail. Trainees were told to keep their heads down and stay low. The only injury recorded was sustained by a young officer who broke his jaw and lost several teeth in a small explosion. The injured commando, William J. Casey, would one day serve as the sixteenth director of Central Intelligence, under President Ronald Reagan.

The OSS trained its agents to work from a mind-set that was diametrically opposed to U.S. Army doctrine at the time. Conventional warfare was based upon frontal assault against an enemy's main line of resistance. On colossal tank battles, combined with air power, and army ground force assault. Guerrilla warfare—also called unconventional warfare and irregular warfare—was the opposite.

Close-quarters combat and throat slitting were par for the course. Whereas infantry soldiers followed strict orders within a chain of command, Jedburghs were trained in the art of self-reliance. They were volunteering for mysterious, often solo assignments involving improvisation on the ground. OSS chief William Donovan believed in the necessity of guerrilla warfare, a sentiment he conveyed to President Roosevelt, in a letter housed at the National Archives. "My observation is that the more the battle machines are perfected, the greater the need in modern warfare of men calculatingly reckless with disciplined daring, who are trained for aggressive action," Donovan said. "It will mean a return to our old tradition of the scouts, the raiders, and the rangers," he insisted in a reference to the unconventional-warfare tactics used during the American Revolution.

To understand and embrace OSS-style guerrilla warfare was to reject preconceived notions of honor, chivalry, and fair play as the gentleman's way of war. "What I want you to do is get the dirtiest, bloodiest, ideas in your head that you can think of for destroying a human being," SOE's founder, General Gubbins, educated the Jedburghs. "The fighting I'm going to show you is not a sport. It's every time, and always, fight to the death."

After six weeks, Aaron Bank and fifty-five American Jedburghs were sent to England for more advanced training, this time with their British, French, and Belgian counterparts. On the Scottish shores of Loch nan Ceall, at a Victorian lodge called Arisaig House, the Jedburghs learned how to operate under extreme duress, how to stay awake for days on end, hike one hundred miles, raid a building, seize a small town. Finally, in a last phase of training, the multinational Jedburgh teams were sent to a manor house in Cambridgeshire called Milton Hall. One of the largest private homes in England, the manor had been donated to the cause by Lord and Lady Fitzwilliam. Oil portraits of Fitzwilliam family ancestors dating back to 1594 hung on the walls. In the massive sunken gardens, the Jedburghs practiced martial arts. In the converted dairy barns they learned to decode cipher, feign deafness, use sign language, and transmit Morse code. In the manor's grand library they watched Nazi propaganda films, a way to become familiar with how the enemy moved, spoke, and dressed. Milton Hall served as a kind of finishing school for commandos, one of the last stops before embarking on dangerous missions that many would not survive. Jan Kubiš and Josef Gabčík trained at Milton Hall shortly before leaving on their mission to kill Heydrich.

The final phase of Jedburgh training involved parachuting infiltration techniques, taught in Altrincham, Manchester, at a facility code-named STS-51. This three-day educational course included three live parachute jumps. The first, in daylight, was out of a balloon flying 700 feet off the ground. The second was out of an airplane flying at an altitude of roughly 500 feet. The third served as a dry run for insertion behind enemy lines; in the dead of night, commandos jumped out of a plane flying at roughly 1,500 feet.

On June 5, 1944, the eve of the Normandy invasion, the first Jedburgh team, code-named Team Hugh, parachuted into Nazi-occupied France with instructions from Prime Minister Winston Churchill to "set Europe ablaze." Ninety-two Jedburgh teams would follow, including one led by Aaron Bank, now advanced to chief of guerrilla operations in France. The mission of these Jedburgh teams was to blow up infrastructure, kill Nazis, and disappear without a trace. In this way the official motto of the Jedburghs became "Surprise, Kill, Vanish."

In Texas, Billy Waugh learned about the Normandy invasion from the radio at his grandmother's house. Winnie Waugh lived directly across the street, and whenever Billy had the chance, he listened to programs like *GI Live* and *This Is Our Enemy*. On the afternoon of June 6, 1944, NBC Radio announced the D-Day invasion of Nazi-occupied France. Then came the newsreels of the Normandy invasion. The most amazing footage was of fifteen hundred airplanes dropping thousands of American paratroopers into France, their silk canopies filling the skies like balloons. To Billy, these operations were mythic, and when he heard that recruiting stations in Los Angeles, California, allowed boys of fifteen to pass for older and join the war, he decided to run away and become a combat soldier.

Billy Waugh packed a bag and hit the road, hitchhiking west out of Bastrop. He made it 650 miles, to Las Cruces, New Mexico, where he was stopped along Highway 80 by a police officer. When he failed to produce identification, he was arrested for truancy and put in jail. The police said they'd release him only if he could produce enough money to buy a bus ticket back home. With no choice but to call his mother, Billy Waugh picked up the phone. His mother agreed to wire him bus fare if he promised to finish high school. Billy kept his word. This war would end without him, but he was now determined to become a U.S. Army paratrooper first thing after high school.

In Europe, as part of a plan called Operation Foxley, the British Special Operations Executive conceived of ways to assassinate Adolf Hitler. One plot called for a sniper to shoot Hitler during his morning walk around the Berghof, his residence in the Bavarian Alps, using a Mauser Kar 98k with a telescopic sight. Another plan involved sending a single commando into Nazi Germany to poison Hitler's food with an unidentified toxin, code-named "I." In a third plot, commandos would attach a suitcase full of explosives under the Führer's train car. But the laws of war forbade assassination, and many British generals worried that such a high-profile assassination could open the door to a war crimes trial.

Not everyone agreed. On the pro-assassination side was Air Vice Marshal A. P. Ritchie, who told colleagues that the German people viewed Hitler as "something more than human." To Ritchie, it was "this mystical hold which [Hitler] exercises over the German people that is largely responsible for keeping the country together at the present time." In a bid for assassination, he argued, "Remove Hitler and there is nothing left." But Vice Marshal Ritchie was a minority voice. Decades earlier, in 1907, forty-four nations had met at The Hague to formalize the laws of war as had been originally written in the Lieber Code. In Laws and Customs of War on Land (Hague, IV), assassination was further defined to include any form of "treacherous killing." Wartime killing had sharp distinctions, the authors wrote, citing by example two contradictory ways to kill a general or king—one considered a treacherous war crime, the other a lawful killing. A soldier is forbidden to sneak into the tent of a general or king disguised as, say, a peddler. But if that soldier is in uniform, and is part of a small attacking force, then he is allowed and encouraged to kill the general or the king. One soldier is a "vile assassin," the other "a brave and devoted soldier," according to the Hague Convention. The reason for the distinction, the authors wrote, was to diminish the "evils of war."

And so—despite how arbitrary this and other prohibitions seemed to some—the British SOE's plans to assassinate Hitler were scrapped. There was no way an SOE commando could operate inside Nazi Germany wearing a uniform of the British Army, it was argued. But over at the Office of Strategic Services, the boldness of Operation Foxley inspired the OSS chief of secret intelligence for operations in Europe to devise a Hitler assassination plot of his own. The chief was a young American lawyer turned commando named William J. Casey, the same young man who'd broken his jaw and lost several teeth on the Demolition Trail while training for OSS Special Operations at Area B.

To Casey's eye, if OSS was going to defy the Laws and Customs of War on Land in order to assassinate Hitler, why stumble over a rule regarding uniforms? His audaciously deceptive plan, called Operation Iron Cross, was to insert an OSS commando team disguised as enemy soldiers wearing Nazi uniforms. To lead this five-man OSS team, which would be populated out by a battalion of turncoat Nazis, Bill Casey chose Aaron Bank. The two men had trained together back at Prince William Park in Virginia, at Area B.

After the war, Aaron Bank recalled Bill Casey describing Operation Iron Cross to him as the most important assassination operation of the war. The OSS had recently captured, turned, and trained 175 German POWs. These men, formerly avowed Nazis, were now willing to work for the OSS. In the winter of 1945 the plan was to have Aaron Bank, a four-man OSS team, and the captured Nazis parachute in behind enemy lines, posing as Wehrmacht soldiers. The team, called the OSS Iron Cross Mountain Infantry, would hike through the mountainous terrain, locate Hitler's Eagle's Nest hideaway, ambush the Nazi leader, and kill him. But to command such a unit deep in enemy territory involved extreme risk. The drop zone chosen would be deep within the Inn Valley, in Austria. There would be no backup air support, no infantry army to call. All it would take was one double-crosser, one Nazi POW still secretly loyal to Hitler, and the mission would unravel. In all likelihood, the OSS team led by Aaron Bank would be executed on the spot.

Setting aside worry over the Hague resolution against treacherous killing, Bill Casey was concerned about a certain rule of engagement (ROE) issued by Supreme Allied Commander General Dwight D. Eisenhower, to whom he was fiercely loyal. General Eisenhower had forbidden the U.S. Army and the OSS from recruiting and hiring Nazi POWs for any kind of mission. Casey, skilled lawyer that he was, appreciated loopholes. By encouraging the captured Nazis to "volunteer" for the Iron Cross Mountain Infantry mission, he created a legal go-around that allowed him to proceed.

As chief of OSS Special Operations in Europe, Bill Casey had authorized dozens of teams air-dropped into this area. But he remained cautious about inserting the Iron Cross Mountain Infantry, because he knew the area around Eagle's Nest to be heavily guarded by elite Nazi commandos. Still, Casey authorized Bank to begin preparing the team and await further instructions.

At an undisclosed European location, Bank led commando training, teaching Nazi turncoats new infiltration techniques, including how to extract individuals from armored cars and how to storm a mock-up of the target. The plot advanced to the point where Bank was given a large sum of cash with which to pay bribes, and a small gold ring to barter for his freedom in the event he was separated and captured. Each OSS operator was given a cyanide capsule, as Jan Kubiš and Josef Gabčík had been.

The prospect of killing Adolf Hitler caused Aaron Bank to lie awake at night thinking "wild thoughts, world shattering in scope," he later wrote. If Bank's OSS team succeeded in killing Adolf Hitler it would be the end of the war, because the German General Staff would surely surrender. With no one left to command the army, wrote Bank, "This would be the only time in [history] that five guys would be responsible for ending a major war."

Bank continued to train the Iron Cross Mountain Infantry. He and his men conducted a dangerous dry run over the drop zone, practicing reconnaissance and exfiltration techniques. Then he waited. And waited. The anticipation was excruciating. Storms hung over the Alps, first for days, then weeks. It was April 1945. Finally, Aaron Bank was flown to Supreme Headquarters Allied Expeditionary Force, in Paris, for a classified briefing with General Eisenhower. The U.S. Army had moved infantry soldiers into the Inn Valley. There were boots on the ground now, closing in around Eagle's Nest. Operation Iron Cross was canceled. Bank was devastated. To kill or capture Hitler was the opportunity of a lifetime. In a flash, it was gone.

On May 7, 1945, the Nazis surrendered at a brief ceremony inside a schoolhouse in Reims, France. General Walter Bedell Smith, Eisenhower's chief of staff, officiated the historic end of the Third Reich. Three months later, after the United States dropped two atomic bombs on Hiroshima and Nagasaki, Imperial Japan surrendered unconditionally to the Allies, ending World War II.

Six weeks later, on October 1, 1945, President Truman signed an order abolishing the OSS. Truman disliked William Donovan and his band of ungentlemanly warriors. In a curt memorandum, the president thanked Donovan for his service and wished him well. To President Truman's eye, America was the new standard-bearer of democratic ideals. The U.S. military was the mightiest in the world. Soldiers of a democracy do not fight guerrilla wars. Gentlemen do not slit throats.

In Bastrop, Texas, Billy Waugh took part in every victory parade. He'd stand on the corner when the parade began, waving his flag at the war heroes. Then he'd duck away from the crowds, race through an alleyway, and get back to the street, in advance of the marching men. He'd repeat this action all morning or afternoon until the parade ended. Two local marines wounded in the war were especially interesting to him. One had a wound to the head and the other wore a cast on his leg.

"Whenever I was near them," remembers Waugh, "in a street or a store, I felt awed to be in their presence. I admired their strength and nobility."

One month after graduating from high school, Billy Waugh joined the U.S. Army as a paratrooper. He was off to Fort Benning, in Georgia, to learn how to jump out of airplanes. His whole life was in front of him and it felt great.

CHAPTER TWO

Tertia Optio

Six months passed. One night in April 1946, America's ambassador to the Soviet Union, General Walter Bedell Smith, was riding in his chauffeur-driven limousine headed to the Kremlin, where he was set to meet with Josef Stalin. Tempered yet tenacious, the former general was a man well versed in military operations. During the war, Bedell Smith served as Eisenhower's chief of staff. Wartime colleagues called him "Ike's hatchet man." General Eisenhower called him "the greatest general manager of the war." An all-around intimidating figure, Bedell Smith was rarely one to express unease, and yet here he was, feeling apprehensive about what lay ahead. He served as President Truman's top diplomat now, and the issue at hand was how not to go to war with the Soviet Union.

"I believed myself more or less immune to excitement, but I must confess I experienced a feeling of tension as the hour for the interview approached," Bedell Smith later recalled. "I thought the meeting might be a stormy one." World War II had been over for less than a year, and already Stalin was the new nemesis of the Western world.

Stalin was paranoid and power-mad. As premier of the Soviet Union, he ruled by terror. Since his rise to power in the early 1920s, he'd starved and killed millions of his own people and personally oversaw the assassination of rivals who threatened him, including

Leon Trotsky, an early architect of the Soviet state, whom he had ordered to be killed in Coyoacán, Mexico, in 1940. Stalin assassinated writers and philosophers unwilling to peddle propaganda, and scientists and engineers who failed to solve his technology problems. In 1937, he had eight of his top army generals executed in the Great Purge. During World War II, he had been one of America's most powerful allies, which made it necessary to look beyond his crimes and win the war. Now, from the perspective of the State Department officials to whom Walter Bedell Smith reported, Josef Stalin was no longer behaving as a friend.

The U.S. embassy car moved quickly down Arbat Street through the soot-stained snow, the American flags attached to its antennae whipping in the night air. This route to the Kremlin was along one of the most heavily policed streets in the world, but because the car's occupants enjoyed diplomatic privileges, it never had to stop; all the traffic lights remained green as Bedell Smith's driver hurtled along.

Sitting alone in the backseat, the ambassador read and reread pages of notes prepared for him by the State Department. "Possible Points to Be Stressed in Conversation with Stalin," its header read. Just a few days prior, Bedell Smith's chargé d'affaires at the embassy in Moscow, a career diplomat named George Kennan, had advised President Truman on the threat posed by Stalin, in what would become known as the Long Telegram. Stalin knew only the "logic of force," Kennan said. The Soviets were on the move, devouring territory around the globe. The United States had only one option. Stalin had to be stopped.

Bedell Smith's mission was to find out how much more land Stalin intended to grab. To look at a map made the problem self-evident. Russia's human losses in World War II had been colossal, with some twenty million dead. But more troubling for the West were its territorial gains. During the war, Stalin's Red Army took possession of almost half of Europe, then kept much of it after the Nazis capitulated. In 1946, power came in numbers; military strength was still about a nation's potential army size. The U.S. population was around 140 million. Stalin ruled over 200 million Russians and another 100 million people living beyond the country's traditional borders in the land that had been grabbed. To make matters even more threatening, the Union of Soviet Socialist Republics (USSR) was getting bigger by the season. The question Bedell Smith needed answered was simple but uncomfortable: How much further was Stalin going to go?

The embassy car deposited Bedell Smith at the Kremlin's main gate, and the ambassador was taken inside to Stalin's personal office building. Bedell Smith was escorted up to the third floor, down a long, austere corridor, and into a high-ceilinged, wood-paneled conference room. There sat Stalin, his back to the wall, facing Bedell Smith as he entered. Behind the dictator hung massive oil portraits depicting the great Russian marshals, most of them on horseback. Bedell Smith spotted Suvorov and Kutuzov, "two military strategists noted for their expansionist views."

Once seated, Bedell Smith spoke first, through an interpreter. He discussed the most pressing issues from his State Department notes, watching Stalin as he took exaggerated draws on a long, thin cigarette. By the time Bedell Smith finished talking, Stalin had picked up a red pencil and begun writing—points to later debate, Bedell Smith first assumed. But upon closer inspection, it was clear that Josef Stalin was doodling. The ambassador was stunned. "His drawings, repeated many times, looked to me like lopsided hearts done in red, with a small question mark in the middle." Stalin entered the conversation by making a point about oil. Iranian oil.

"You don't understand our situation with regards to oil and Iran," Stalin said, suggesting that he could answer the ambassador's questions with a singularly cryptic point. "The Baku oil fields are our major source of supply. We are not going to risk our oil supply." The Soviet Union needed a greater share in the exploitation of the world's oil, Stalin said, and the competition for these resources was a significant point of contention between Russia and the United States. As Bedell Smith considered his response, Stalin took the opportunity to bring up a more personal matter. Lately, Great Britain and the United States had been "teaming up against Russia and placing obstacles in her path," Stalin said.

Bedell Smith was caught off guard. Did Stalin "really believe that the United States and Great Britain are united in an alliance to thwart Russia?" he asked.

"*Da*," Stalin replied in a long, slow breath. *Yes.*

"I must affirm in the strongest possible terms, that is not the case," the U.S. ambassador insisted. Except it was true. British prime minister Churchill had stated as much just one month before, during a speech at Westminster College in Fulton, Missouri. "An iron curtain has descended across the [European] Continent," Churchill famously declared. "[From] Warsaw [to] Berlin... all these famous cities, and the populations around them, lie in what I must call the Soviet sphere, and all are subject in one form or another not only to Soviet influence but to a very high and, in many cases, increasing measure of control from Moscow." Churchill had compared Stalin to a puppet master. This infuriated Stalin. Like most tyrants, he resented any person who suggested that his popularity was based not on adoration but fear.

Stalin had hated Churchill for decades. "In 1919... Churchill tried to instigate war against Russia, and persuaded the United States to join him in an armed occupation against parts of our territory," Stalin reminded Ambassador Bedell Smith, adding, "Lately he's been at it again." Stalin called the Westminster speech "an unfriendly act," and said that it was "an unwarranted attack upon the U.S.S.R." He pointed out that the United States would never stand by passively if such an insult was hurled in its direction. "But Russia, as the events of the past few years have proved, is not stupid," Stalin forewarned. "We can recognize our friends from our potential enemies."

Ambassador Bedell Smith was in a bind. He needed an answer

for President Truman, so he asked Stalin directly, "How far is Russia going to go?"

Stalin paused. Stopped doodling the red hearts and the question marks. Looking directly at Walter Bedell Smith, he replied in a monotone, "We're not going to go much further."

But what, exactly, did "much further" mean? That was the enigma of 1946. Stalin ended the interview and the ambassador was shown the door.

Eleven months later the United States drew a line in the sand, declaring communism the enemy of democracy. On March 12, 1947, in a dramatic speech to a joint session of Congress, President Truman warned the American people that Moscow had to be stopped. "It must be the policy of the United States to support free peoples who are resisting attempted subjugation," Truman said. Without American help, darkness and cataclysm would descend in the world, and "disorder might well spread throughout the entire Middle East." In a display of near-unanimous support, the members of Congress took to their feet. For two minutes President Truman enjoyed his first standing ovation since the end of the war. The speech marked the beginning of the Truman Doctrine, American foreign policy designed to confront and counter Soviet geopolitical expansion.

Congress passed the National Security Act of 1947, restructuring the U.S. military and intelligence agencies and creating a national-security apparatus for the modern era. The act officially established the Central Intelligence Agency and the White House National Security Council (NSC). And it gave way to an unconventional-warfare division for the president to command, on his authority and his alone. This unit was designed to be covert. George Kennan called it a guerrilla warfare corps for the commander in chief. Covert action would become the president's hidden hand, visible only to those in his inner circle.

The National Security Council directed the CIA to take control of these hidden-hand operations, officially called covert-action operations, under Title 50 authority of the U.S. Code. The Department of Defense would work under a separate authority called Title 10, which outlines the role of the armed forces. This distinction remains in effect today.

During a National Security Council meeting in December of 1947, the president's advisors clarified that the CIA's covert-action authority would include "preventative direct action through paramilitary activities" as a means of countering "the vicious covert activities of the USSR." "Direct action" would become a key phrase at the CIA, one that allowed its officers and operators Title 50 authority not available to anyone else in the United States unless expressly directed by the president.

The CIA's general counsel, Lawrence Houston, requested clarification. How much autonomy would the CIA have in conducting these covert-action operations? "Lack of such specific direction may be considered a weakness in the National Security Act of 1947 that deserves further consideration by the Congress," Houston wrote. The following month, National Security Council Directive 10/2 (NSC 10/2) provided the clarification Houston had sought. A new office was to be created inside the CIA, called the Office of Special Projects, where covert actions would be planned and executed in peacetime. In times of war, the CIA was to coordinate its covert operations with the Defense Department and the Joint Chiefs of Staff. "'Covert operations' are understood to be all activities… which are conducted or sponsored by this Government against hostile foreign states or groups," according to the directive, "…but which are so planned and executed that if uncovered, the U.S. Government can plausibly disclaim any responsibility for them." While the concept of willful ignorance has insulated countless commanders and kings from embarrassment and scandal, it was in this moment that the president's National Security Council made the concept of plausible deniability an official construct. Plausible deniability would hereafter allow U.S. presidents to say they didn't know.

For the first time in American history, the president had at his disposal a secret paramilitary organization, authorized by Congress, to carry out hidden-hand operations to protect U.S. national-security interests around the world. Before NSC 10/2, there were two ways in which U.S. foreign policy and national security were pursued. The first option was diplomacy; the second, war. Covert action was now the president's third option, or *Tertia Optio,* after diplomacy failed and a Title 10 military operation was deemed unwise. On September 1, 1948, the Office of Special Projects changed its name to the more innocuous-sounding Office of Policy Coordination (OPC) and got to work. "The new organization's activities might well enhance possibilities for achieving American objectives by means short of war," said George Kennan, co-architect of NSC 10/2 along with James Forrestal, the nation's first secretary of defense. According to a report written by the National Security Council, kept classified for fifty-five years, the CIA's Office of Policy Coordination would now be responsible for covert-action paramilitary operations including "guerrilla movements...underground armies...sabotage and assassination."

In its first two years of existence, the CIA's covert operations concentrated on anticommunist partisan groups in Europe and the Eastern bloc. Then, on June 25, 1950, the unthinkable happened. The army of North Korea, backed by Soviet tanks and Chinese intelligence, invaded South Korea, with the goal of reuniting the divided country under communist rule.

The entire Western world was caught off guard. The CIA had failed to foresee an attack that the U.S. national-security apparatus feared could be the opening salvo of World War III. The United Nations called upon the invading communist troops to cease fighting and withdraw to the 38th parallel. When the invaders refused, the UN Security Council looked to its members for help. "I have ordered United States Air and Sea forces to give the Korean government troops cover and support," President Truman announced from the White House press room. After just five years of peace, the country was at war again. Behind-the-lines paramilitary operations were needed to augment conventional forces. The CIA surged ahead with plans to take the lead.

CHAPTER THREE

Surprise Attack in Korea

That the nation's new intelligence agency had failed to anticipate the invasion of an ally by communist forces put the CIA in a compromised position. President Truman blamed leadership and decided that CIA director Admiral Roscoe Hillenkoetter had to go. To replace him, he called upon General Walter Bedell Smith, who was physically unwell. The stress of having served as ambassador to Moscow had left Bedell Smith with a severe ulcer, and he'd recently undergone major surgery at Walter Reed to have two-thirds of his stomach removed. President Truman had previously offered him the job as CIA director, a position he had graciously turned down. Now, with the United States at war in Korea, President Truman's request became an order, and Bedell Smith became the new director of the CIA.

With a formidable figure now at the helm, the CIA's credibility and access to resources dramatically expanded. According to CIA documents kept classified for nearly fifty years, "Korea became a testing ground for the support of conventional warfare with unconventional efforts," or black operations behind enemy lines. Walter Bedell Smith had no experience in covert operations, so he looked to outside experts. He chose them unwisely, he later learned.

★   ★   ★

With black operations now at the fore, the CIA called upon the experience and talents of the Office of Strategic Services, dismantled by Truman in October 1945. Its members had hardly disappeared from public service. At the start of the Korean War, one-third of the CIA's total personnel had previously served in the OSS. "I know nothing about this business," Bedell Smith confided to Admiral Sidney Souers, the CIA's first director. "I need a Deputy who does." For the job of deputy director of plans, a euphemism for director of covert operations, he chose veteran OSS officer and future CIA director Allen Dulles. In turn, Dulles filled the positions below him with veterans of the OSS.

Frank Wisner, formerly the OSS station chief in Romania, assumed responsibility for Office of Policy Coordination operations and staff. Wisner, or "Wiz," as he was known among colleagues, was a complex individual, obsessed with rolling back Soviet gains. A former Olympic runner, he was now overweight and out of shape from years of heavy drinking and womanizing. He was under pressure from the FBI for having had a wartime affair with a Romanian princess suspected of being a Soviet spy. His mercurial behavior was written off by colleagues and family alike as part of his personality. "He seemed to be only half with us, always pondering some insoluble riddle," said his son Graham. "Nevertheless, he dominated every conversation with an extraordinary mixture of wit, charm, humor, and southern power." What no one knew at the time was that Frank Wisner was in the early stages of mental illness and would eventually end his own life with a shotgun blast in the mouth. For now, he was in charge of planning and overseeing paramilitary action in Korea, sending hundreds, perhaps thousands, of good men to their deaths. The black mark he left on the Agency still haunts the CIA today.

Walter Bedell Smith mistrusted Frank Wisner, but he was stuck with him. In Korea, Wisner and his team began planning covert-action operations. One of the first was an operation to infiltrate an agent into Pyongyang to assassinate North Korea's communist dictator, Kim Il Sung. The operation was so sensitive it was personally handled by Wisner's deputy chief of CIA covert operations, a former OSS officer named Hans V. Tofte.

The enigmatic Hans Tofte was an American citizen born in Denmark. At first glance, he appeared highly qualified for the job. Fluent in Japanese, Russian, and Chinese, he had lived overseas in his twenties and been recruited by the British Secret Intelligence Services in the early years of the war. When the OSS was created, Tofte was assigned to its Special Operations division. He had trained Jedburgh candidates Bill Casey and Aaron Bank in guerrilla warfare at Area B. Inserted into the war theater by parachute, he fought the Nazis behind enemy lines, in Italy and Yugoslavia, with valor. The king of Denmark knighted him. But like Frank Wisner, something had happened to Hans Tofte in the five years since the end of World War II. His character transformed. By 1950, Tofte was a liar and a thief. Was it post-traumatic stress? Hubris? Too much booze? The danger of covert-action operations, and the plausible deniability construct in which they exist, was that it made it possible for ignoble actions to be easily concealed.

Like Frank Wisner, Tofte would ultimately experience a tragic downfall. Fired from the CIA for stealing classified information, he would die impoverished, his reputation in ruins. But for now, as deputy chief of CIA covert operations in Korea, Tofte was in charge of running the assassination plot to kill Korean president Kim Il Sung. To do this, he oversaw six CIA operators who worked out of a hotel room in Tokyo.

There were classified reasons why the CIA feared Kim Il Sung. To the intelligence community, he was the most dangerous kind of despot, a Soviet puppet. The CIA believed Kim Il Sung to be a "top-ranking traitor who isn't even who he said he [is]," according to a dossier entitled "The Identity of Kim Il Sung." The man's real name was Kim Sung-ju, analysts concluded. Orphaned as a child, he was said to have "killed a fellow student" while in high school. The circumstances of the murder were chronicled in his CIA file: "Needing money, he stole it from [a] classmate, was caught, [and] fearing possible disclosure, killed his classmate," the dossier read. It was around this time that the orphan Kim Sung-ju was identified by communist intelligence agents as someone the party could blackmail into use.

The real Kim Il Sung had been a genuine war hero, a courageous guerrilla fighter who'd battled Japanese invaders in the Paektu Mountain region of Korea during World War II. According to information in the CIA dossier, Stalin's assassins killed the war hero and "disappeared him." This enabled Stalin's minions to steal the war hero's identity and give it to the orphan boy, with a caveat. The impostor? Kim Il Sung would now act as Moscow's puppet.

In the fall of 1945, when Stalin appointed a man named Kim Il Sung to be secretary general of the North Korea Communist Party, the identity theft was complete. "Specific instructions [were] given to the leaders of that regime that there should be no questions raised about Kim [Il Sung]'s identity," the CIA learned. If the story were indeed true, North Korea's new leader was an exceptionally dangerous kind of tyrant, fundamentally beholden to the Kremlin. If Kim Il Sung did not do exactly as instructed by the Politburo, his background as a murderous orphan, not a war hero, could be revealed.

North Korea was one of the poorest countries in the world, and Kim Il Sung was dependent upon Russian patronage for his country's most basic needs. Everything he did was now in service to his communist masters, including the siege and subsequent land grab of South Korea. The CIA's Office of Policy Coordination put North Korean president Kim Il Sung at the top of one of its earliest known targeted kill lists.

Hans Tofte received a cable from Washington. An assassin had been chosen for the job. Tofte was to receive the CIA covert-action operator in Tokyo, then oversee his infiltration into Pyongyang.

"The man [was] a Cherokee Indian code-named Buffalo," Tofte told historian Joseph Goulden after the war. As had Reinhard Heydrich's assassins, Jan Kubiš and Josef Gabčík, Buffalo had volunteered for the job. "He'd been asked in Washington, 'How would you like to kill Kim Il Sung?' And he had accepted the mission with great pride," Tofte recalled.

Tofte received instructions to meet the assassin "near the wall of the Imperial Palace in Tokyo, at sunset" at a designated time, on a specific day. In keeping with the protocol of the day, Tofte, carrying a briefcase full of cash from his office's unvouchered funding authority, met with the assassin to turn over initial payment. In the event Buffalo killed North Korea's leader, he'd receive a "grand prize of a considerable amount of money." The mission failed and Buffalo was never heard from again.

The idea that a Native American Indian, an assassin for the CIA, could simply make his way to Pyongyang in the middle of a war and blend in among the locals there was ambitious and foolhardy. It also set a precedent for what would eventually become known as lethal direct action—targeted killing—directed against a specific person either in peacetime or war. While the Hague resolution prohibited assassination, Title 50 covert-action authority made targeted killing legal, intended to counter "the vicious covert activities of the USSR." The fabricated identity of Kim Il Sung was a case in point, a Soviet covert act of deception directed against the United States. Through North Korea's supreme commander, Stalin could entangle the United States in a war on the Korean Peninsula.

The Office of Policy Coordination began inserting CIA paramilitary teams deep inside Korea, behind enemy lines. The teams, led by Americans and made up of anticommunist Korean and Chinese nationals, were air-dropped into hostile territory to conduct sabotage and subversion, including hit-and-run assassinations, similar to what the OSS had done during World War II. The results were disastrous, as explained by the man assigned to lead the CIA's parachute infiltration efforts, a former OSS Jedburgh named John "Jack" Singlaub. In 2016, Singlaub, ninety-six, recalled these wartime tragedies with clarity and stoicism.

"One of the impossible imperatives of war in Asia was that Westerners could never simply disappear behind enemy lines into the civilian populations as we had [done] in Nazi-occupied Europe," Singlaub said. "This was a tremendous challenge in Korea and an equally difficult problem in Vietnam." He was referring to the future war in which he would also play a significant role, running covert-action operations for the CIA. Singlaub would rise to the position of U.S. Army major general.

In 1951, Jack Singlaub served as CIA deputy chief of station in Seoul. He and his colleagues worked out of the newly renovated Traymore Hotel downtown. Their cover was that they were with an advisory organization called the Special Operations Group (SOG), Joint Advisory Commission, Korea (JACK), 8132nd Army Unit. The cover name paid homage to the OSS Special Operations Branch, and the unit became known simply as JACK. JACK's first commander, Singlaub's boss, was the CIA's chief of station in Seoul, Ben Vandervoort, a legendary paratroop commander who'd lost one eye fighting Nazis in Holland. A month after Singlaub arrived, Vandervoort was called back to Washington, much to Singlaub's dismay. His replacement was a former CIA operative and army colonel named Albert R. Haney, a man whose integrity would also come under fire, as had Wisner's and Tofte's.

Following a blueprint created by the OSS, the CIA's Office of Policy Coordination sought to organize an anticommunist guerrilla force it could train and equip for partisan warfare behind enemy lines in Korea. OPC officers combed through refugee camps in South Korea looking for local fighters qualified for paramilitary service, including North Korean and Chinese nationals. Back in America, dozens of college graduates were being recruited by the CIA to lead these covert-action operations in the Far East. One of the young recruits was Donald P. Gregg, who was studying cryptanalysis—the study of hidden information systems—at a liberal arts college in Massachusetts. Gregg would eventually work for the CIA for thirty-one years.

Gregg and dozens of other new officers-in-training were sent to a clandestine irregular-warfare facility run by the CIA on the island of Saipan, a tiny dot in the Pacific Ocean 2,000 miles southeast of Seoul. There, hundreds of young male Korean and Chinese refugees recruited from war camps underwent weeks of training in guerrilla warfare tactics. "We were following in the footsteps of the OSS," says Gregg, who later became U.S. ambassador to South Korea.

But unlike veteran covert-action officer Jack Singlaub, Don Gregg had no experience fighting wars, let alone using unconventional-warfare tactics behind enemy lines. He'd only recently graduated from Williams College and barely knew where Korea was on the map. "We didn't know what we were doing," he says of his experiences on Saipan. "I asked my superiors what the mission was but they wouldn't tell me. They didn't know. We were training Koreans and Chinese and a lot of strange people," Gregg recalled. The problem facing the CIA in Korea was twofold: Who exactly were the indigenous forces the Agency was training, and could it be assumed that they, too, were in pursuit of American goals? A great majority spoke no English. An equal number were illiterate. How could the CIA identify a traitor under such circumstances? How would anyone know if a recruit or volunteer was in fact a spy sent by the North Korean People's Army or the Internal Security Forces?

Jack Singlaub had his own set of worries, more practical than theoretical. His OPC colleagues Frank Wisner and Hans Tofte were anxious to begin air-dropping teams of CIA operators and their local forces into North Korea, behind enemy lines. As the man overseeing air-insertion tactics, Singlaub felt this pressure. He also worried about getting the men safely into the war zone. "The Chinese were well aware of our airdrop operations and had learned to recognize [the sound] of low-flying transport planes that had an open door," he recalls. Singlaub felt it would be safer to air-drop the operators into enemy territory from higher up. This would give them a greater chance of successful clandestine insertion, he believed.

CIA covert-action operations were being run out of a forward operating base (FOB) on Yong-do Island in southwestern Korea, and it was there that Singlaub began testing his new idea. "Parachuting was my specialty from the OSS Jedburgh days," he recalls. He borrowed a B-26 light bomber aircraft from the air force, rerigged the bomb bay as a jump platform, and went out for a test. "I told the pilot to keep his airspeed close to normal for level flight, then jumped assuming the same position I'd used to jump into Nazi-occupied France." Once he was out of the aircraft, he pulled his parachute and floated down to the ground. "The test demonstrated we could use bombers for agent drops," he says. The success sparked another idea, a way to get a team in even more secretly. What if, he thought, instead of pulling his rip cord right away, he instead allowed his body to fall through the air, reaching terminal velocity—roughly 122 mph or 54 meters per second—and then pull? This was long before the days of skydiving, back when "the military had very clear protocols about how its paratroopers jumped," Singlaub clarifies. What he wanted to do now was free-fall, then pull his rip cord, say, one thousand feet above the ground. While inherently more dangerous than a static line jump, free-falling meant the enemy was less likely to see an agent's parachute as he floated to earth.

To test this idea, Singlaub borrowed an L-19 Bird Dog from the air force. Accompanied by airborne specialist Captain John "Skip" Sadler, he made a series of test jumps, leaping out of the aircraft and having Sadler record the time before his parachute blossomed. After each test, Singlaub waited longer on the next jump, thereby getting closer to the ground each successive time. "Objects on the ground came into sharp focus within a thousand or so feet. I watched an object on the road below change from a blurred dot to what looked like a child's toy, to an actual U.S. Army jeep with a white star stenciled on its hood. I pulled the rip cord." Singlaub's parachute opened and his feet hit the sand. "Neither of us realized at the time that we'd invented the concept of high-altitude low-opening (HALO) parachute drops, right there over the Han River in Korea." The HALO jump has since become the most effective means of inserting covert-action operators into denied territory and behind enemy lines. In 2019, it is still the method of choice.

In Washington, DC, a battle over covert-action operations was under way between the CIA and the U.S. Army. When war broke out on the Korean Peninsula, there was no special operations forces (SOF) capability at the Defense Department. "The military response was hesitant, skeptical, indifferent, and even antagonistic" with regard to all aspects of unconventional, or irregular, warfare, says retired colonel and U.S. Army historian Alfred H. Paddock Jr. Most military leaders at the Pentagon wanted no part of these ungentlemanly black operations. "Guerrilla warfare was frowned upon," says Singlaub.

There were two notable exceptions. Leading a small group of guerrilla warfare pioneers inside the military establishment in 1951 were General Robert A. McClure, former director of the Psychological Warfare Division during World War II, and Colonel Russell W. Volckmann, a former U.S. Army captain who'd led the only non-OSS guerrilla operations during the war, in the Philippines. What gave General McClure and Colonel Volckmann momentum in their efforts was that both men had the ear of their former boss, General Eisenhower, now serving as the U.S. Army chief of staff.

As per National Security Council Directive 10/2, covert action was to be the sole responsibility of the CIA during peacetime. Korea was different. This was war, McClure and Volckmann agreed. "To me, the military has the inherent responsibility [in] time of war to organize and conduct special forces operations," Volckmann told his commanding general. "I feel that it is unsound, dangerous, and unworkable to delegate these responsibilities to a civil agency"—that is, the CIA. General McClure took a similar position. "I believe the Army should be the Executive Agent for guerrilla activities," he told the army chief of staff. "I am not going to fight with CIA as to their responsibilities in those fields."

In an attempt to alleviate the conflict, the Joint Chiefs of Staff created an army organization to work with JACK, called CCRAK (pronounced "sea-crack"). In CCRAK documents located in the National Archives, the organization's original acronym is revealed: Covert, Clandestine and Related Activities in Korea, an on-the-nose description of the U.S. Army's secret guerrilla warfare unit in Korea. As happened at the CIA, the name was quickly changed to something more innocuous. CCRAK became Combined Command Reconnaissance Activities, Korea. An operations base was set up on Baengnyeong Island, off the coast of South Korea, near the Northern Limit Line. The unit assigned to work with the CIA's JACK was originally called the Guerrilla Section, 8th Army Miscellaneous, but this name was also deemed too revealing; it was changed to the United Nations Partisan Infantry Korea (UNPIK).

That the army was vying for power over covert operations infuriated the CIA's Frank Wisner. The CIA informed the Department of Defense of its displeasure. "Mr. Wisner, as head of OPC, would like it to be clearly understood that this understanding is reached on the assumption that the Army is creating a Special Forces Training Command for its own purposes and not at the request of CIA," Agency officials wrote, in a now declassified memo. Theirs was a temporary wartime gesture of cooperation. "The CIA [is] not going to place itself in the position of giving the Army an excuse to justify the creation of its own unconventional warfare capability." Once the war was over, Agency officials demanded that covert-action authority be returned to the CIA.

The aversion to risk was perhaps the single greatest discrepancy between the CIA and the Pentagon. The CIA was about taking chances. Its officers and operators were trained to act as the president's hidden hand. Covert-action operations are meant to remain forever hidden from public scrutiny. In the event one becomes known, plausible deniability becomes the goal. At the opposite end of the spectrum is the U.S. military, an organization that follows strict procedures and protocols. Its classified and clandestine operations might be kept secret for a period of time, but eventually they are meant to be revealed. "One of the biggest obstacles I faced in Korea," says Singlaub, "was the Pentagon's worry that these [paramilitary] units might be captured, broken by physical and psychological torture, and turned against us for propaganda purposes." Unlike CIA officers, the Pentagon's soldiers are not explicitly trained how to lie.

JACK and CCRAK's guiding principals were, however, ultimately the same. Each organization was born of the OSS, with foundations in guerrilla warfare. A manual entitled "Psy War 040 CIA" was given to both sets of operators to study and learn from. "Hit and run; these are the guerilla's [sic] tactics," its authors explained. "Primary objective; the killing and capture of personnel…sniping and demolitions. Initiative and aggressiveness tempered by calm judgement will be encouraged. Avoid trying to win the war by yourself."

Colonel Douglas C. Dillard, a twenty-six-year-old infantry officer from Georgia, was put in charge of delivery and resupply of these joint CIA-army airborne operations, code-named AVIARY. The missions were kept classified until 2009. Although some took place early in the Korean War, the scale of operations rose dramatically starting in February of 1952. "One of AVIARY's first missions ended in disaster," Colonel Dillard recalled in 2009.

It was the winter of 1952, a period of time known as the Second Korean Winter, now twenty months into the war. A dismal lull had settled over the battlefield, with fighting diminished to violent, small-unit clashes and struggles over key outpost positions along the front lines of Korea's hilly landscape. Hundreds of Americans had been captured and were being kept under brutal conditions inside POW camps. The joint CIA-army mission on the night of February 18, 1952, was designed to air-drop paramilitary operators who would gather reconnaissance on a POW camp and then exfiltrate by ground.

The missions were dangerous. Territory above the 38th parallel was notoriously inhospitable. Unlike with the OSS Jedburgh airdrops into France, there'd be a very limited greeting party on the ground, maybe one or two anticommunist partisan agents. Radio communication did not exist in the outer reaches of this landscape, so agents were dropped in with homing pigeons strapped to their legs. This was often their only means of communicating with their CIA and U.S. Army handlers in the south: a single homing pigeon to let the handler know they'd made it safely in. "The rate of return was incredibly low," recalls CIA historian John P. Finnegan.

New tradecraft techniques were constantly being developed and tested. On this mission the covert-action operators wore enemy uniforms and carried Chinese-made weapons. "They could impersonate enemy patrols and, if necessary, shoot their way back to UN lines," Dillard explained. But there was a much bigger problem facing the unit. "One everyone knew about and few wanted to discuss," says Singlaub. "How do you trust that the indigenous agents you are paying will not try and kill you?" A traitor in the ranks almost certainly meant death.

It was the early morning hours of February 19, 1952, and air force captain Lawrence E. Burger was piloting a C-47, south of Wonsan, North Korea. There were two missions on deck, both covert-action operations, both parachute infiltrations of American, Korean, and Chinese national paramilitary teams behind enemy lines. Given the limits on usable aircraft, it was common to run more than one mission per flight. Master Sergeant Davis T. Harrison stood in the door with the four anticommunist Chinese agents he was running, preparing them for a static line jump. The partisans had been culled from a refugee camp down south and trained for action by CIA paramilitary officers. They all stood in the doorway ready to jump.

Three of the Chinese guerrilla fighters were big; one was small. Each man stood the proper distance from the next, rip cords attached to the static line. It was best to have the smallest man jump first, Sergeant Harrison later told a military investigation board, "but this particular man made such a fuss about jumping out last," and the situation gave Harrison pause. But Harrison didn't speak Chinese, and the partisan agent didn't speak English—an ongoing problem with covert operations inside JACK. The general rule in these kinds of intense moments was to be flexible. Think fast.

Seated inside the aircraft, Sergeant Harrison observed Private First Class Dean H. Crabb, his fellow covert-action operator. Crabb was seated next to the four anticommunist guerrilla fighters working under his authority. This team would be making the next jump even deeper behind enemy lines, almost one hundred miles north of what was about to be the first airdrop.

It was 1:45 a.m., pitch dark outside and well below zero. Sergeant Harrison scanned the ground down below for a sign. The way signaling worked out there was that when anticommunist partisans on the ground heard the airplane approach, they would ignite small fires inside metal buckets to briefly illuminate the drop zone. Harrison stared down into the darkness below. The snow was fierce. There were big winds, freezing temperatures, and the threat of anti-aircraft fire from enemy forces on the ground. At last, he spotted a faint cluster of signal fires.

Harrison alerted the pilot, Captain Burger. This mission was now a go. Captain Burger banked the aircraft and made a wide circle, lowering his altitude as the CIA's AVIARY team prepared to jump. The first Chinese partisan moved to the door. Harrison gave the rebel fighter the go-ahead to jump and watched as the man leapt out into the air. The second man quickly jumped. When the third man hesitated, Harrison knew intuitively that something was terribly wrong. Instead of jumping, the man reached into his pocket and pulled out a grenade. He yanked the pin, rolled it into the seating area of the aircraft, and leapt out into the night air.

Davis T. Harrison was instantly blown out of the aircraft. Assistant jumpmaster Corporal George Tatarakis was also jettisoned from the burning plane. Dean Crabb and his team of four Chinese partisans were killed instantly by shrapnel and blast. Captain Burger struggled with the crippled aircraft, ordering his six-man crew to bail out while he worked to keep the aircraft steady. The men, later identified as Rowden, Layer, King, Dick, and Haley, somehow managed to bail out. Captain Burger stayed at the controls of the airplane until it crashed into a mountain range below.

Master Sergeant Davis Harrison and Corporal George Tatarakis, both wearing parachutes, pulled their rip cords before hitting the ground. Both landed safely, as did the five members of the crew. Everyone but Harrison was captured by the North Korean Army. Harrison evaded capture for twenty-four hours, sneaking into a house and asking for help. The family offered him sanctuary but, while he was sleeping, notified the North Korean Army, which came and took Harrison away. Each of the covert-action operators and the aircrew died or were killed in POW camps in the north. Harrison's body was repatriated after the war.

The mission was but one of dozens of disastrous operations, all kept classified for decades, the great majority of which amounted to a tragic intelligence failure. Thousands of anticommunist foreign fighters and their American handlers were dropped into North Korea, never to return. These were "suicide missions," concluded

Peter Sichel, CIA station chief in Hong Kong. Many of the operatives recruited by the Office of Policy Coordination from refugee camps turned out to be double agents.

If program organizers Frank Wisner, Hans Tofte, and Albert Haney were naive to the double cross in the beginning, declassified documents make clear that as early as eight months into the war, they understood what was going on. Their intelligence was thin, spurious, or feigned. But the trio continued winging it, sending volunteer operators to their graves. They reported mission success instead of abject failure. The result was the death of what the CIA now concedes amounted to hundreds, perhaps thousands, of men and women.

At the Pentagon, General McClure and Colonel Volckmann blew the whistle internally. But the damage could of course not be undone. The experience "transformed McClure's reservations into outright suspicions about the CIA's motives," wrote Alfred Paddock. Hans Tofte was replaced in Korea by career CIA officer John L. Hart. Upon reviewing classified documents that Tofte kept in his office, Hart became outraged and notified CIA director Walter Bedell Smith. "The results of our investigation surpassed our most pessimistic expectations," he later explained, countless intelligence reports merely "fabricated by people living in Seoul."

Bedell Smith sent his deputy, Loftus Becker, to Seoul to tell the CIA's John Hart that the Agency could not afford a scandal. With its reputation "not yet established," Becker told Hart the CIA "simply could not admit to other branches of government—least of all to the highly competitive U.S. military intelligence services—its inability to collect intelligence on North Korea." Hart's reports were classified. So were Operation AVIARY's catastrophic losses. Devastated by the deception, Loftus Becker resigned. The North Korean covert-action operations would remain a secret failure for decades.

Haney, Tofte, and Wisner moved on to a new covert-action operation, this time in Guatemala. The CIA had failed in Korea because it entered the game too late and had no reliable network of agents on the ground. In Guatemala, the plan was to be preemptive. Fix things before they happened. This doctrine would become known as regime change.

General McClure wrote to his commander, General Charles Bolte, with his analysis of the situation. "I would take the opportunity to bring you up to date on the Army/CIA relationship," McClure explained. "In recent conferences at CIA, I have heard [it said], 'Since we are now a fourth service many of the activities for which the Army was planning should be transferred to CIA, including the command of military forces designed for guerrilla warfare in time of war.' Needless to say I am very unhappy about it both because I question the ability of CIA and second, because I have never believed the Joint Chiefs intended to abrogate their responsibilities for the active command of military operations in time of war."

At the CIA, Walter Bedell Smith was also concerned. In a letter to Ludwig Lee Montague, his advisor on the National Security Council staff, Smith expressed fear that his covert-action deputies Allen Dulles and Frank Wisner could lead the CIA into "some ill conceived and disastrous misadventure." But the horse was already out of the barn. The CIA's covert-action operation budget had expanded to become three times the size of the Agency's budgets for intelligence and espionage combined. It was a Catch-22. The CIA needed to train and equip partisans in order to form a guerrilla warfare corps on the ground. This underground army was a necessary component in supplying the CIA with intelligence that would keep its agents from being killed. But in reality, the amount of intelligence that could be garnered from inside a totalitarian state like North Korea was close to nil. "The possibility of recruiting and running any such sources was as improbable as placing resident spies on the planet Mars," lamented former OSS officer Richard Helms, Frank Wisner's deputy and a future director of Central Intelligence.

Bedell Smith considered curtailing the CIA's covert-action operations. "Too many paramilitary operations [pose] a distinct danger to CIA as an intelligence agency," he told his staff. Something had to change, or, he feared, "the [covert action] operational tail will wag the intelligence dog." But Bedell Smith was fiercely loyal to the Agency that he was in charge of, and in a letter to the National Security Council, on the subject of covert action, he conveyed a far less dramatic position. "At certain times in the past we have been importuned by General McClure's people to provide them with detailed information concerning guerrilla groups of which we may have some knowledge," he wrote. "We have consistently declined to furnish this information to General McClure because the information requested impinges directly upon secret operations in which we are currently engaged and for which, at this time, we are solely responsible." In his summary, Bedell Smith played the secrecy card.

In a CIA analysis of its Korean War operations, kept classified for fifty years, the Agency made it clear that it understood its paramilitary operations to be "not only ineffective but probably morally reprehensible in the number of lives lost." The AVIARY missions were doomed from the start, it concluded. The CIA had no reliable way to discern its enemies from its friends. "The amount of time and treasure expended was enormously disproportionate" to that which was gained.

JACK's classified missions in Korea were water under the bridge. By the end of the war, the CIA's Office of Policy Coordination had built an organization "capable of executing covert action on a worldwide scale." An untold number of covert-action operations would now begin.

While JACK and CCRACK were running dangerous black operations behind enemy lines, a traditional war was also being fought by U.S. Army soldiers on the ground. The oft-cited example of this kind of warfare was demonstrated in the trenches of World War I. Korea had become a war of attrition, a military strategy whereby each side wears down the other side through continuous, relentless loss, grinding down the enemy's morale. Like stags fighting with their horns locked, neither side could win. The end foreseen becomes not victory but collapse.

One of the foot soldiers fighting the Korean war of attrition was Billy Waugh, now a twenty-one-year-old platoon sergeant with the 187th Airborne Regimental Combat Team. He'd earned his wings with the 82nd Airborne, just as he'd said he would. With his Browning BAR rifle over his shoulder and his army boots laced up tight, Waugh remembers the demoralizing monotony he felt, marching across the frozen land bored out of his mind. "I wanted action. I wanted to fight and I wanted America to win the war." But none of this was happening in his infantry platoon.

The war in Korea was not the kind Billy Waugh envisioned for himself. He wanted to win a glorious victory, like the one earned against Germany and Japan. In Korea, the first casualty of war Waugh remembers seeing was a half-frozen civilian lying faceup, dead along the side of the road. "We'd march up over one hill with great expectations of meeting the enemy and finally engaging in fierce combat," he remembers. "Instead, from the top of one hill we'd look down across a treeless landscape and all we'd see was the next hill. It was trench warfare. The worst, most baseless form of combat. War by grinding down. I wanted to see combat. To be brave under fire."

Soon Waugh would have his wish. During a chance encounter on a train, he'd learn about secret wars being conducted by the U.S. government as covert operations behind enemy lines, in what would become known as "denied areas." Billy Waugh would spend the next seven decades, until at least 2011, engaged in or training for direct-action, kill-or-be-killed, covert-action operations against America's enemies around the globe. He would train and equip guerrilla fighters, lead hit-and-run ambushes, conduct sabotage against enemy infrastructure, and assassinate. Trudging across Korea's stripped and frozen earth, he foresaw none of this. All he knew was that General Sherman seemed about right. The glory of war was moonshine. War, at least this wretched war of attrition in Korea, was hell.

CHAPTER FOUR

Special Forces

In 1953, Billy Waugh was transferred to a U.S. military base in Augsburg, Germany. Before he left, he saved up his army money and bought himself a car, a sharp-looking 1949 Chevrolet four-door sedan. It was his first car and he adored it. When he received orders to travel to Germany, he arranged to have it shipped across the Atlantic so he could drive it around on the autobahn. A few weeks after he arrived in country, his Chevy arrived. The army notified him to say that his automobile was in the port city of Bremerhaven, 475 miles away. On the train ride there, he noticed two U.S. Army sergeants wearing unusual patches, with a parachute and aircraft on their shoulders.

"Why are you wearing that patch?" Waugh asked.

The men said that they were part of a new outfit, in Bad Tölz.

"Where the hell is Bad Tölz?" he asked.

They said that it was about eighty miles southeast of the U.S. military base in Augsburg.

"What do you do there?" Waugh asked.

They couldn't tell him, they said.

Now they really had Waugh's attention.

"Do you have any vacancies?" Waugh asked.

"We need MOS Triple Ones," one of the men said. "Platoon sergeants."

Waugh pointed to his own shoulder, to a Combat Infantry Badge indicating that he was MOS 111–eligible. The mysterious men gave him contact information.

"I got my car, hightailed it back to Augsburg, and asked for a 1049, request for transfer. Within a week, I was transferred, badge and baggage, to Bad Tölz. I signed in at headquarters, went straight to the snack bar, and introduced myself to the six guys who were there," remembers Waugh.

"Welcome to the 10th Special Forces," one of them said. The group was a classified U.S. Army program that trained soldiers for unconventional warfare. The first of its kind. Just four months old, it had been named the 10th Special Forces so as to deceive the Soviets into thinking there were nine other Special Forces units ready to engage in sabotage, subversion, and other forms of guerrilla warfare. Waugh remembers feeling awestruck. "I'd found my true home."

If the U.S. Army went into the Korean War with no formal special operations capabilities, it came out with a plan for an unconventional-warfare unit for use in future wars. Outraged over its stalemate with the CIA regarding who controlled covert operations in Korea, General McClure went directly to the Joint Chiefs of Staff, determined to create for the army a Special Forces capability like no other in the world. But to achieve success, said McClure, the organization should start "modest and austere." McClure knew that unconventional warfare was frowned upon by most generals in the Defense Department. He didn't want to jeopardize the potential for success.

In its simplest terms, the army's vision for unconventional warfare was to support resistance movements in foreign lands—local guerrilla forces that shared America's pro-Western, anticommunist goals. Any resistance movement that the U.S. Army would engage with would likely already be militarized and semiorganized. But to say that unconventional warfare could ever be defined in simple terms was wishful thinking. Resistance movements were notoriously turbulent, almost always led by charismatic leaders with big personalities, some noble, others corrupt. For the U.S. Army to find success in training and equipping these foreign fighters, its Special Forces operators would have to be flexible, patient, and extremely disciplined. They'd have to be self-reliant, quick-thinking warriors capable of operating in openly hostile territory without the support of conventional military forces close by. In the winter of 1952, General McClure secured the necessary blessing of the Joint Chiefs of Staff. The 10th Special Forces Group would be a small and secret unit. Its soldiers would become known as Quiet Professionals.

Finding the right volunteers was a priority. McClure had his adjutant general prepare a roster of ex-OSS officers with commando, ranger, and guerrilla warfare backgrounds. He sent one of his officers to visit with retired general William Donovan at Donovan's law office in New York City. Donovan shared with McClure his personal files, containing the names and addresses of more than 3,900 former soldiers who'd served in the OSS during the war. The army sent out queries to hundreds of these individuals, some active-duty service members, others retired, to see if they were interested in volunteering for the clandestine unit. Volunteers had to be at least twenty-one years old, airborne-qualified (or willing to become so), and able to pass a series of physical and psychological tests. Enlisted men accepted into Special Forces had to commit to training in one or more of five specialty areas: operations and intelligence, engineering, weaponry, communications, and medical aid.

On June 19, 1952, the army activated its first unconventional-warfare unit at Fort Bragg, in North Carolina, consisting of one officer, one warrant officer, and seven enlisted men. The group's first commander was OSS Jedburgh, Colonel Aaron Bank. By the end of the month, 122 soldiers of all ranks were present for duty. In November of the following year, the 10th Special Forces Group (Airborne) received overseas orders and sailed for Europe. They arrived at Bremerhaven and then traveled by train to Bad Tölz. Their facility was a former Nazi training facility for the Waffen-SS.

The group's original mission was to conduct unconventional warfare behind enemy lines in the event of a Soviet invasion of Europe, modeled after what the OSS Jedburghs had accomplished in France. These small twelve-man units were called A-Detachments or A-Teams. Each was made up of two officers and ten noncommissioned officers, or NCOs. Every individual on the team had to pass months of training and a series of grueling tests to become Special Forces–qualified and wear the green beret. Each A-Team would be capable of infiltrating a target by air, land, or sea and exfiltrating stealthily. Each team, led by a captain, had members trained in weapons, demolition and engineering, medical, communications, and operations and intelligence. They would build their own bases, conduct their own perimeter defense, and be able to operate in hostile territory for an indefinite period of time. Everyone on the team was schooled in at least one foreign language.

The members of this new group called Special Forces prided themselves on being a certain breed of soldier with distinct temperaments and special abilities. "Hard-bitten troopers who were willing to take calculated risks and face challenges that conventional units need never be concerned with," said Bank. Men born of an "almost inhuman ability" to absorb any stressful situation and carry on into battle without letting mental concerns or emotions get in the way. Operators needed to be extremely competitive, self-reliant, stress-resistant, and stoic to the point of arrogant.

Major General Edward Partain, an early member of Special Forces, summed it up this way: "In the early fifties, Special Forces groups were not a recognized part of the Army. They were seen as outsiders, great warriors but they could not live comfortably within the peacetime regimental system. You had people of the sort that you wished you could deep freeze on the last battlefield and thaw out on the next battlefield of the next war. It was a rough group."

Billy Waugh recalls Special Forces operators being called "snake-eaters, miscreants, and rogues" by conventional officers in starched shirts. Many of those recruited for Special Forces in the early 1950s were soldiers who fought in World War II for foreign armies, in foreign countries. Men like Larry Thorne.

Larry Thorne (christened Lauri Törni in Finland) stands out as a Special Forces legend: fearless, driven, and recklessly daring. "He would have been at home with the Greeks who infiltrated Troy inside a wooden horse," said James Goodby, former U.S. ambassador to Finland, "the doomed protagonist in the mold of ancient Greek heroes." Thorne began his career as a captain in the Finnish Army Reserves, where he trained army ski troops. When the Soviet Union invaded Finland in November 1939, Törni served as unit commander. Under arduous conditions and in subzero temperatures, Törni and his unit were infiltrated behind enemy lines, where they engaged in hit-and-run operations, on skis, against Russian troops.

The Red Army had more than three times as many soldiers as the Finns, and what should have been clear Russian victories instead went to Törni's unit. "In reaction to Thorne's brave, devastating raids behind Soviet lines, the Red Army placed a price on his head, dead or alive, reputedly the only Finnish soldier so singled out for bounty," says his biographer, J. Michael Cleverley. For his leadership and bravery, Törni was awarded the Knight of the Mannerheim Cross, the country's highest commendation for valor and the equivalent of the U.S. Congressional Medal of Honor. Finland's relations with the Soviet Union changed several times during the war and when the country's leaders turned to Nazi Germany for military aid, Törni traveled to Austria for seven weeks of training with the Waffen-SS. He returned to Finland as a Finnish officer and was also recognized as a German Untersturmführer. In 1943 he commanded a guerrilla warfare unit called Detachment Törni. This seventy-man anti-Soviet strike force was a Finnish Waffen-SS battalion. As its commander, Lauri Törni wore a Nazi uniform and was awarded the Iron Cross.

After the war ended, he was arrested and charged with treason. Found guilty and sentenced to six years, he was incarcerated in Finland's notorious Turku prison. But the indomitable Lauri Törni escaped from prison three times, until he was transferred to Riihimäki prison, on a small island north of Helsinki. In December 1948 he was pardoned by Finnish president Juho Paasikivi and released. But when the threat of additional war crime charges resurfaced, Törni assumed the identity of a Finnish merchant sailer and fled to Venezuela under the alias Eino Morsky. From Venezuela he secured passage on a freighter headed to the United States. Just a few miles out from the shores of Mobile, Alabama, Törni leapt overboard and swam to shore, in a classic example of clandestine infiltration into a foreign target.

A fugitive in the United States, he made his way to New York City, changed his name to Larry Thorne, and worked as a carpenter in Brooklyn and Connecticut. It did not take long for the consummate warfighter to become restless and bored. In 1951, he sought out William Donovan, the former director of the OSS, and asked for his help joining an American unconventional-warfare unit. Donovan schooled Thorne on the newly instated Lodge-Philbin Act, which Massachusetts senator Henry Cabot Lodge Jr. had been instrumental in getting passed. It allowed foreigners to join the U.S. military and earn citizenship if they served honorably for the United States for at least five years. Larry Thorne breezed through U.S. Army basic training and was singled out as a prime candidate for the 10th Special Forces Group. Sent to Bad Tölz, he became an invaluable part of the unit. "Thorne is one of the most devoted and conscientious officers I have known," wrote his commander, "an aggressive officer who is at his best in a situation which demands physical exertion, direct action, and forceful leadership." In addition to his physical prowess and irregular-warfare skillset, he spoke English, German, Estonian, Swedish, Norwegian, and of course Finnish. Working alongside Larry Thorne, Billy Waugh was amazed by the soldier's breadth of talent, his discipline, stamina, and confidence.

At Bad Tölz, Thorne was participating in a third military command. He'd fought for the Finns, the Nazis, and now the United States. "He was what we called a total oner," explains Waugh. "Having engaged in clandestine ops for several nations in just about every environment known to man, he could adapt to stressful situations anywhere in the world. Mostly he preferred going at it alone." In Bad Tölz, Larry Thorne was made captain and became the quintessential Green Beret. He was exactly what the Special Forces were looking for in a warfighter.

One example of Thorne's skill and prowess involved the successful completion of a perilous mission in Iran. In 1957, a U.S. Army single engine Otter aircraft filled with classified military equipment crashed somewhere in the mountains of northern Iran, in uncharted territory. The rescue operation called for locating the crash site, getting a team in there, recovering the bodies and the classified equipment, and getting out undetected. Three previously orchestrated attempts had all failed when Captain Larry Thorne volunteered for the job. Thorne parachuted into Iran with a twelve-man team of Green Berets. The unit made their way up a 14,000-foot peak, recovered all the bodies and the equipment, then exfiltrated through Tehran.

Bad Tölz was not for everyone; but for the disciplined nonconformists who embraced unconventional warfare, it was home. Countless foreign languages could be heard spoken in the coffee shop and around the team rooms. Besides European languages — French, Polish, Czech — one heard Turkish, Arabic, Urdu, Farsi, and Pashto. The concept of training guerrilla fighters in other countries was at the core of the new U.S. Army Special Forces' capability. Partnership with special units of foreign armies was a primary goal. In service of this mission, Special Forces operators trained with teams in Norway, Germany, Spain, Italy, Turkey, Pakistan, Iran, Jordan, and Saudi Arabia. A team led by Major Joseph Callahan traveled to Jordan to establish the first airborne school for the Jordanian Army at the behest of King Hussein. A team led by Steve Snowden traveled to Turkey to train what would become known as the Turkish Special Forces. Another group went to Saudi Arabia and trained 350 officers and noncommissioned officers in a guerrilla force supported by King Faisal. Four teams traveled to Iran to train the Iranian Special Forces in mountain warfare. Another team trained Kurdish tribesmen in the mountains of Iran. One team went to Pakistan, where they trained with their special warfare warriors in desert warfare.

The 10th Special Forces Group remained a closely guarded secret until 1955, when the *New York Times* published a cryptic article about the men, describing them as a "liberation" force designed to fight behind enemy lines. A photograph showed members of the group wearing their green berets, their faces blacked out to keep their identities concealed.

The U.S. Army Special Forces began to grow. Hundreds, then thousands, of unconventional American warriors volunteered to join this elite group. They worked tirelessly, training and equipping guerrilla fighters around the globe so as to keep the threat of Soviet expansion in check. U.S. Army Special Forces soldiers would eventually fight secret wars alongside many of the foreign fighters they trained. Other times, they would find themselves fighting against them.

CHAPTER FIVE

Ruin and Rule in Guatemala

On the wild night of June 16, 1954, a charismatic twenty-six-year-old Argentine doctor named Ernesto "Che" Guevara stood staring out the window of an apartment in Guatemala City, listening to machine-gun fire and watching a fighter-bomber aircraft fire on civilians below. He sat down to pen a letter to his mother, a wealthy aristocrat whom he adored. He felt a rush, watching people die for a cause, he confided to her. "Even the light [aircraft] bombings have their grandeur...the sounds of its machine gun, and the light machine guns that fired back at it, [leave me] with the magic sensation of invulnerability." At the time, the young doctor had no idea that the jetfighter he observed was being flown by an American-trained mercenary pilot who was part of a covert-action operation for the CIA. The moment transformed him, he later said.

Like an inciting incident in a Shakespearean tragedy, the attack on Guatemala City catalyzed Che Guevara into action. Many men dream of leading a revolution, but Che Guevara would actually do it. His actions put him directly in the crosshairs of three U.S. presidents—Eisenhower, Kennedy, and Johnson. He would eventually be assassinated by CIA-trained fighters in the mountains of Bolivia in 1967.

Che Guevara had come to Guatemala to study medicine amid social revolution. When he first arrived, the country was in the throes of civil unrest. Guatemala, located just south of Mexico in Central America, had been plagued by violence and social upheaval since 1944, when university professor José Arévalo became the country's first democratically elected president. For the first time in its history, Guatemala got a constitution, an elected representative body, and a supreme court, but the violence was constant. President Arévalo survived twenty-five coup and assassination attempts in his six years in office. From the perspective of the White House, political instability of this magnitude made Guatemala a prime target for Soviet meddling, and in 1950 the U.S. State Department sent its top diplomat, George Kennan, to investigate.

After touring Latin America, Kennan took the hard-line view that Moscow was indeed making ominous inroads in the Western Hemisphere. "Here, as elsewhere," Kennan wrote in a secret report for the secretary of state, "the inner core of the [Soviet] communist leadership is fanatical, disciplined, industrious, and armed with a series of organizational techniques which are absolutely first rate." In all likelihood, Kennan warned, Moscow's first conquest in Latin America would be Guatemala, which it could then use as a beachhead to launch a takeover of the Americas. Kennan advised the secretary of state that communist influence in the Western Hemisphere had to be curtailed at any cost. Diplomacy was unlikely to work, and military intervention was not plausible, he wrote, which left covert action as the third and best option. "Now this gets us into dangerous and difficult waters, where we must proceed with utmost caution," advised the man who'd first proposed that the CIA develop a guerrilla warfare corps.

What choice was there? From Albania to Poland, seven governments in Eastern Europe were now being ruled by Stalinists, leaders who'd been emplaced by rigged elections and who maintained power through a devious partnership with Moscow's ironfisted state security services. Moscow's movement toward Latin America forecast only disaster. Kennan's report was reviewed by the president's National Security Council, whose members unanimously agreed. Covert action was the best way forward.

The following year, in March 1951, a liberal democrat named Jacobo Arbenz, son of a Swiss German father and a Guatemalan mother, was elected president. In his inaugural address, Arbenz promised to move Guatemala from "a backward country with a predominantly feudal economy into a modern capitalist state." The way he intended to do this, he said, was by limiting influence by foreign corporations. Guatemala was a poor nation with an agrarian-based economy. Two percent of the population owned 72 percent of the land. The largest landowner, also one of the country's largest employers, was the American-owned United Fruit Company, a banana farming concern. When President Arbenz instituted sweeping reforms in farm labor and called for the expropriation and redistribution of land, including 234,000 acres owned by United Fruit, President Truman's National Security Council took the position that these anti-American moves were being engineered by Moscow. The time had come for the hidden hand of the United States to intervene. "It [is] essential to our security that we fight fire with fire," Kennan observed.

President Truman created a powerful new advisory committee to determine the "desirability and feasibility" of covert-action operations. Called the Psychological Strategy Board (PSB), it included the director of Central Intelligence, the undersecretary of state, and the deputy secretary of defense, with a representative of the Joint Chiefs of Staff acting as principal military advisor. The informal structure of the PSB allowed for "problem solving" to occur outside the scope of normal bureaucratic channels, insulating the president from potential backlash through plausible deniability. "The working group should shy away from any thought of a 'Charter' which would require formal departmental concurrence," suggested Frank Wisner, then CIA deputy director of plans, in an early staff meeting. An agreement was reached to "develop a paper which would be informally accepted by the Board as indicating the general lines which [we] would probably follow." In the case of Wisner, who was simultaneously in charge of JACK operations in Korea, the construct of plausible deniability insulated him personally from consequence, as the historical record makes clear. Whether Wisner was aware of his outsized incompetence during this fateful time, willfully ignorant of it, or mentally ill remains the subject of debate.

What is clear is that the goal of the PSB was not only to devise and plan covert operations but to manipulate the public's perception of these hidden-hand events. "Our job is to influence the minds and wills of other people," board members agreed, not as in "word warfare" but through paramilitary actions that had real-world consequences. "[We] help shape events [to] include all elements of pressure and persuasion," PSB director Gordon Gray told the president.

The PSB's plan for Guatemala was to stage a coup d'état against President Arbenz and overthrow him, using a CIA-trained guerrilla fighting force. The Office of Policy Coordination was in charge, as in Korea. The man chosen by the CIA to lead the mutiny and be installed as Guatemala's new, pro-American president was a former Guatemalan military officer living in exile in Honduras, Carlos Castillo Armas. He was corrupt, right-wing, and militaristic, but the Office of Policy Coordination was willing to work with him because he had a decent-sized guerrilla force loyal to him, fighters who could be trained and equipped by CIA paramilitary officers with relative ease.

In January 1952, CIA headquarters began drafting its first-known assassination list, a compilation of individuals "to eliminate immediately" under the Agency's Title 50 covert-action authority.

This list was followed by at least two additional kill lists, one titled "Guatemalan Communist Personnel to be disposed of during Military Operations of Calligeris" (the code name for Carlos Castillo Armas) and the other under the heading "Selection of individuals for disposal by Junta Group." The targets, or "disposees" [*sic*], would be "neutralized" under a construct called "Executive Action." This euphemism, adopted by numerous future U.S. presidents, remains in effect as of 2019.

Whether President Truman was made aware of the assassination campaign remains a mystery. But the very next month, the subject of Soviet assassination capabilities was discussed by Gordon Gray in a Top Secret "Report to the President." "Throughout the world," Gray wrote, "[the Kremlin] has built up networks of agents who would move at the word of command to carry out an assassination or foment a civil war," a subtle suggestion that the PSB plans for assassination were but a necessary means of fighting fire with fire.

Assembling a list of individuals for assassination was a flawed and haphazard process. CIA officers first worked from a 1949 Guatemalan Army list of communists, augmented by information from the Directorate of Intelligence as it came in. Memos made public in 1997 show that the list included "top flight Communists whom the new government would desire to eliminate immediately in the event of a successful anticommunist coup" but quickly grew to include other Guatemalans. Clandestine service officers were queried to help decide who else should be included on a "final list of disposees," with one employee assigned the job of quality control, "to verify the list and recommend any additions or deletions."

The assassination list was sent to Carlos Castillo Armas for input. The illegitimate son of a farmer, Armas had spent much of his life engaged in guerrilla warfare. From 1948 to 1949, he'd served as the director of Guatemala's military academy. By 1952, he'd been involved in two previous coups d'état in Guatemala. He was a wanted man in his own country and his list of enemies was long. In September 1952, Armas added as many as fifty-eight names to the CIA's assassination list.

Things quickly got more complicated. That same month, in the Dominican Republic, the strongman Generalissimo Rafael Trujillo, called "the cruelest dictator in the Americas," got word of the CIA's assassination list and wanted in. Trujillo made a deal with Carlos Castillo Armas. In exchange for "the killing of four Santo Dominicans at present residing in Guatemala," he offered Armas his material support.

"Castillo Armas readily agreed," says CIA staff historian Gerald Haines. In addition to requesting that certain of his enemies be targeted and killed by the CIA, Trujillo offered to send his own assassins to participate in the action, "special [assassination] squads [that] were already trained." In a declassified Agency memorandum, these death squads were referred to as "Trujillo's trained pistoleros" and as "K" (presumably for "kill") groups. But after considerable debate, says Haines, the idea was vetoed by the State Department. Still, Armas continued to make side deals of his own, and the CIA learned that Armas intended to make "maximum use of the K groups," and would dispatch "Nicaraguan, Honduran and Salvadorian soldiers in civilian clothes to infiltrate Guatemala and assassinate unnamed Communist leaders" loyal to Armas. In Guatemala City, a local asset provided his CIA handler with a "hit list with the location of the homes and offices of all targets [that] had already been drawn up." Haines says records of what happened next were destroyed or lost.

The CIA did not create the Latin American propensity for assassination. Long before the Central Intelligence Agency existed, targeting killing was a well-established political tool throughout the region. These were the rules of the game for authoritarian regimes that ruled by force and corruption, not laws. In 1949, President Arbenz himself had benefited from the assassination of his political rival, Francisco Javier Arana. Arbenz had been one of only six men present when Arana, chief of the country's armed forces, was shot in broad daylight during an altercation on the Puente de la Gloria, outside Guatemala City. As president, Arbenz did little to solve the extrajudicial killing he'd personally witnessed. There was no investigation of the murder, and his rival's assassins were never apprehended. As of 2019, the killing remains a mystery.

As the CIA worked on its paramilitary operations and assassination plans, the president's Psychological Strategy Board oversaw a robust psychological warfare campaign intended to influence the minds and wills of the people—to wage a Nerve War Against Individuals, according to a declassified memo. The idea was to instill fear and paranoia in a core group of military officials close to Arbenz so they might become turncoats and participate in "a mass defection of the Guatemalan army." As the plans moved forward, the U.S. presidency changed hands. In January 1953, Dwight D. Eisenhower became the thirty-fourth president of the United States, and the PSB briefed the new commander in chief on its covert-action operations. "Cold War concerns convinced President Eisenhower to order the removal of the democratically elected leader by force," according to Haines.

Starting on April 13, 1953, top Guatemalan communists received "death notice" cards, some for as many as thirty consecutive days, the contents of which remain classified. Others received physical objects courtesy of the CIA, including small wooden coffins, hangman's nooses, and toy bombs. Communist leaders came home from work, or woke up in the morning, to find graffiti painted on the exterior walls of their homes. "Here Lives a Spy," one message read. Another threatened, "You have Only 5 Days."

The operation was gaining momentum. Declassified documents illustrate how quickly CIA officials at the highest level got on board with more advanced assassination, or "liquidation," plans. J. C. King, CIA chief of the Western Hemisphere Division, learned of the hit list and on August 28, 1953, suggested "possibly assassinating key

Guatemalan military officers if they refused to be converted to the rebel cause." The following month, King sent a memo to CIA director Allen Dulles stating his support for "neutralizing" President Arbenz.

To the CIA, assassination was an objective, an action to be carried out with the precision and detachment of a military operation. It was during this period that the CIA assembled its first known how-to instruction booklet on assassination as an instrument of foreign policy—as a political tool. "An extreme measure not normally used in clandestine operations." Titled "A Study of Assassination," the manual was organized into sections including "Planning," "Techniques," and "Classifications." The ideal assassin worked alone, always mindful of the fact that "no assassination instructions should ever be written or recorded." He or she would almost always report to just one person, with this same individual overseeing their infiltration to, and exfiltration from, the target area.

In addition to having all the qualities of a clandestine service agent, an assassin would have to be "determined, courageous, intelligent, resourceful and physically active." Knowledge of a variety of weapons, including knives, firearms, grenades, and small bombs, was imperative for success. "It is possible to kill a man with the bare hands, but very few are skilled enough to do it well," the CIA posited. "A human being may be killed in many ways but sureness is often overlooked by those who may be emotionally unstrung by the seriousness of the act they intend to commit." In a section entitled "Justification," the CIA warned its would-be assassins of the dark psychological territory into which they were heading. "Murder is not morally justifiable," and "assassination can seldom be employed with a clear conscience. Persons who are morally squeamish should not attempt it."

The unvarnished truth about assassination was that while some operations involved the objective detachment of a sniper rifle, a pistol, or a lethal dose of poison, an assassin must always be ready to kill his target mano a mano. For that, he had to be willing to make use of any real-world object that might be lying around. "Anything hard, heavy and handy will suffice," counseled the CIA, "a hammer or axe, fire poker or lampstand." Pushing a target off a bridge, down an elevator shaft, or out an open window was a wise course of action; the assassin could "play horrified witness" if questioned by police. Staged car accidents were not recommended because a lengthy investigation almost always ensued. But if an assassin could drug his target and push the man and his vehicle off a high point or into deep water, that tactic could be considered. If the target was an alcoholic, getting the man drunk and injecting him with a lethal dose of morphine before he passed out was always a viable option. Avoid explosives and demolition charges, assassins were told. They were unreliable and prone to accidents. Often, when used as a booby-trap with a time delay, these kinds of devices wound up killing the wrong man.

Most of all, the assassin had to accept that he was not judge, jury, or hangman. "Assassination of persons responsible for atrocities or reprisals may be regarded as just punishment," the authors forewarned, but to think of it as retribution for an offense was not what covert action was about. To kill a specific individual under Title 50 authority of the U.S. Code was about prevention, not revenge. "Killing a political leader whose burgeoning career is a clear and present danger to the cause of freedom may be held necessary," the authors of the CIA's assassination manual made clear.

On September 11, 1953, the CIA submitted its "General Plan of Action" for Guatemala, code-named Operation Success (PBSUC-CESS). President Eisenhower signed off on the operation, approving a $2.7 million budget for "psychological warfare and political action" as well as "subversion," to be conducted by the CIA. On December 23, 1953, the CIA's Office of Policy Coordination opened a classified forward operating base in Miami, Florida, where covert operations in Guatemala would be run.

All elements of covert actions had code names: people, places, operations, and locations. The PBSUCCESS headquarters building, code-named Lincoln, was located about ten miles from Miami, on the second floor of a shabby two-story structure in the corner of Opa Locka Airport, only ever to be referred to as Building 67. "Effective this date all addressee stations will constitute component elements of PBSUCCESS regional command with project headquarters at LINCOLN under Jerome Dunbar," Allen Dulles wrote. Jerome Dunbar was the code name for retired Colonel Albert Haney, former CIA station chief in Seoul. It was Haney, Frank Wisner, and Hans Tofte who had run the ill-fated JACK missions in Korea.

The CIA reached an agreement with rebel groups in Honduras, Nicaragua, and El Salvador to train and equip its guerrilla fighting forces inside these neighboring countries' borders. In these secret paramilitary training camps, deep in the jungle, the CIA trained and armed local commandos to act as the fighting brigade for Castillo Armas. Come "D-Day," this paramilitary army of foreign fighters would make an amphibious beach landing and carry out the CIA's coup d'état, in the style of the Normandy invasion. Declassified documents reveal that at least 1,725 foreign fighters were trained by the CIA, with another "2500 persons of lesser caliber and faith committed to joining the fighting force if called upon."

On January 5, 1954, Albert Haney requested a final list on the "liquidation of personnel." The following week, Lincoln requisitioned twenty suppressors for twenty .22-caliber rifles, which were sent from CIA headquarters. A small group of "key leaders" were then chosen for the assassination program. On January 13, cables were sent discussing training protocols for these "assassination specialists."

On April 17, 1954, Secretary of State John Foster Dulles (the CIA director's brother) gave PBSUCCESS the "full green light." The following month, perhaps sensing his end was near, President Arbenz offered to meet with President Eisenhower, to reduce tensions between the two countries. But it was too late. The CIA coup d'état was in motion.

On June 15, 1954, CIA-trained sabotage teams and invasion forces launched from Honduras, Nicaragua, and El Salvador and moved quickly into staging areas just outside the Guatemalan border. At 5:00 p.m. on June 18, President Arbenz held a massive rally at the railroad station. The gathering was buzzed by CIA planes. At dusk, Castillo Armas crossed the border with his personal strike force. Overhead, CIA planes strafed army troop trains. In Washington, DC, the PSB ordered the Matamoros fortress in downtown Guatemala City bombed. A hundred miles east of the capital, the city of Chiquimula fell to CIA guerrilla forces as an American F-47 flown by a mercenary pilot dropped bombs. Finally, on June 27, 1954, as Castillo Armas attacked the city of Zacapa, President Arbenz capitulated and resigned.

By June 30, the CIA decided that the coup had been a success. Now it was time for the hidden hand of the CIA to vanish. Frank Wisner sent a cable entitled "Shift of Gears," urging all CIA officers and operators to withdraw. On July 4, the CIA dispatched a recovery team to Guatemala City to collect 150,000 documents related to all communist activity, for future use. On July 12, the Lincoln office in Opa Locka was shuttered. Frank Wisner ordered Albert Haney to destroy all documents relating to Operation Success. A few survived.

The president asked the CIA to brief him on the operation. Allen Dulles, Frank Wisner, and J. C. King used maps and charts to narrate how the coup had unfolded. The president asked how many men had died. "Only one," a briefer lied. Eisenhower shook his head. "Incredible," he said.

"Indeed it had been incredible," writes CIA historian Nick Cullather. According to the Agency's own records, at least forty-eight rebel fighters were killed in the action. The CIA's perpetuation of the falsehood that it had been a success gave way to a decades-long

CIA myth that the Guatemala operation had been an "unblemished triumph." It was often cited as a model, a means of encouraging future presidents to authorize similar covert-action operations around the world.

On September 1, 1954, Castillo Armas declared himself the new president of Guatemala. Shortly after he took power, a group of junior army cadets, unhappy with the army's capitulation, staged a coup. It was quickly put down, leaving twenty-nine dead and another ninety-one wounded. Come October, so-called elections were held, but Castillo Armas was the only candidate. As his government was being installed, a second insurgency emerged. This new military junta came down hard on the resistance movement, quashing rebellions with murder and oppression. It left tens of thousands—some historians say as many as 200,000—killed, tortured, maimed, or missing.

Three years later, on July 26, 1957, Armas, the CIA's puppet dictator, was shot in the presidential palace by a member of his own guard. He died instantly. The assassin, Romeo Vásquez Sánchez, fled to another room in the palace and committed suicide.

The facts of the CIA's hidden-hand operations in Guatemala would remain secret until May of 1997, when the Agency's history staff "rediscovered" the allegedly lost records. Congress had been looking for them since at least 1975, when the Senate began its investigation into U.S. government–sanctioned assassination. Four years later, in 1979, a Freedom of Information Act lawsuit ordered the Guatemala documents be declassified, but the CIA was able to keep its records sealed on national-security grounds. As for the assassination programs and kill lists, CIA staff historians continue to insist that no one was actually assassinated. This is a doubtful claim. When the documents were finally declassified, the names of the people targeted for assassination were redacted, making it impossible to discern if any were killed before, during, or after the coup.

Extreme secrecy and illicit hiding are but two elements of plausible deniability, designed to keep the office of the president from being embroiled in controversy and disgrace. But there is so much more that results, including grave and unintended consequence the CIA can neither foresee nor control. In its hidden-hand operations in Guatemala in 1954, the CIA created a revenge-seeking monster intent on destroying its creator. It took the form of Che Guevara, the young doctor who watched the CIA-led coup through an open window in an apartment in Guatemala City.

Shortly after he wrote the letter to his mother expressing the magical sensation he felt watching violence and revolution unfold, Che Guevara set out onto the city streets to organize a resistance movement against the plotters of the coup. He teamed up with an armed militia organization called the Communist Youth, and expressed a desire to fight. Instead, the group's leaders assigned him hospital duty and instructed him to await further orders. Within a few days, martial law was declared across Guatemala and the Communist Party was disbanded. With its fighters being rounded up, Che Guevara sought refuge in the Argentine embassy.

There he learned that the heart of the Latin American communist movement was moving to Mexico City. He applied for a visa and made his way. It was there that he met a young Cuban-born revolutionary living in exile there, Fidel Castro. "He is a young man, intelligent, very sure of himself and of extraordinary audacity," Che Guevara wrote in his diary. "I think there is a mutual sympathy between us." Fidel Castro asked Che Guevara to join his guerrilla movement and serve as the rebel group's official doctor, and he accepted on the spot. In just five short years, the two revolutionaries would transform from complete unknowns to two of the highest-ranking enemies of the United States.

Back in Guatemala, as the CIA's cleanup group was sorting through files of the fallen Arbenz regime, CIA officer David Atlee

Phillips came across a single sheet of paper about the young doctor named Che Guevara and his communist ties.

"Should we start a file on this one?" Phillips's assistant asked his boss.

"Yes, I guess we better have a file on him," Phillips replied.

Soon the CIA would place Che Guevara on their kill list.

CHAPTER SIX

Kings, Shahs, Monarchs, and Madmen

Halfway across the world in the Middle East, the president's covert-action advisors also had their eyes on Iran. In these early days of the Cold War, the Middle East was awash in spectacle killings that the CIA saw as motivated not only by politics but also by religion and revenge. Assassination operations undertaken by religious fanatics were particularly dangerous, the Agency believed, "since a fanatic is unstable psychologically [and] must be handled with extreme care." In Iran, a group of these fanatics had recently succeeded in assassinating eight high-ranking members of the country's secular government. They called themselves Fedayeen-e Islam, Self-Sacrificers of Islam, Shiite fundamentalist Muslims whose declared mission was to rid Iran of "corrupting individuals" through assassination. In 1953, President Eisenhower's PSB met to discuss covert-action plans involving Iran's prime minister, Mohammad Mossadegh, who the CIA believed was at the top of Fedayeen-e Islam's kill list.

The assassination of a prominent government official creates a vacuum of instability, both actual and perceived. By 1953, when briefing Eisenhower on the assassination threat level in Iran, CIA director Allen Dulles, a member of the Psychological Strategy Board, told the president in no uncertain terms that if something wasn't done about the situation, Moscow would surely take advantage of it.

"A Communist takeover [of Iran] is becoming more and more of a possibility," Dulles told the president, and "the elimination of Mossadegh, by assassination or otherwise, might precipitate decisive events." The result would be a domino effect across all of the Middle East. "If Iran succumbed to the Communists there is little doubt that in short order the other areas of the Middle East, with some 60% of the world's oil reserves, would fall into Communist control." The CIA decided that its best bet for a covert-action partner to counter Soviet influence in Iran was the country's vain young king, Shah Mohammad Reza Pahlavi. The Fedayeen-e Islam had tried to kill the shah just a few years before.

It was a cool, crisp morning in 1949, in the capital city, and the twenty-nine-year-old king climbed out of his limousine and began making his way up the steps of Tehran University, waving to the crowd. A man pretending to be a photojournalist called out the shah's name. As Mohammad Reza Pahlavi looked his way, the assassin fired off five shots, hitting him. One bullet entered the shah's face through his open mouth, passing through his upper lip and exiting his face without hitting any bone. As he fell, a second bullet struck him in the backside, wounding him. The assassin fired off three more bullets, all of which hit the shah's hat, before police leapt on the man and killed him. As the assassin's dead body was pummeled by a vengeful mob, the shah was rushed to a nearby hospital, where he spoke with members of the press. "A few shots won't deter my duties to my beloved country," he told visitors gathered at his bedside.

The assassin's name was Fakhr-Arai, a member of the Fedayeen-e Islam. By the time he tried to kill the shah, the group had already succeeded in killing two prominent members of Iranian society:

Ahmad Kasravi, a historian, in 1946, and Mohammad Masoud, a newspaper publisher, in 1948. Both men had been writing and publishing antireligious pieces when they were assassinated. Their writings had deeply offended a central figure inside the Self-Sacrificers of Islam, a forty-nine-year-old cleric named Ruhollah Khomeini. Though relatively unknown outside religious circles at the time, in the decades to come this revolutionary cleric would become one of the most infamous villains in the Western world, known as Ayatollah Khomeini, the supreme leader of Iran.

Fedayeen-e Islam modeled their activities after history's original assassins, the Hashashin, an eleventh-century strike force of Shiite fundamentalist warriors led by the enigmatic holy man Hassan-i Sabbah, from whom the word "assassin" derives. Like its medieval predecessor, the modern Fedayeen-e Islam in Iran sought to target and assassinate those it deemed enemies of Shiite Islam. The assassins and their abilities, indeed the very mention of their name, bred terror. They were deadly and cunning, rumored to possess invisibility. One of the first known Western references to the assassins appears in a report written by Frederick I, the Holy Roman Emperor, in the year 1173. "They had a habit of killing [enemies] in an astonishing way," explains Bernard Lewis, professor emeritus at Princeton University, who first located the original reference (in 1967), "but it was the fanatical devotion, rather than the murderous methods" of the assassins that struck the imagination of Europe. Dormant for hundreds of years, the assassins were now at it again. The shah's political ideology, the Divine Right of Kings, was a Western concept the Self-Sacrificers of Islam vowed to destroy.

After the Shiite fundamentalists tried to kill the shah in 1949, and despite the group's clear allegiance to Islamic fundamentalism, the shah's secular government, led by a prime minister, instead placed blame on Iran's pro–Soviet Union communist party, the Tudeh Party, or Party of the Masses. As the shah recovered in the hospital, Iranian state police arrested more than two hundred Tudeh Party members and confiscated the group's assets in an effort to rid the country of communists. The remaining members of the Tudeh Party went underground.

In Western media outlets, the assassination attempt was reported as being linked to economics, not religion. "The assassination attempt came one day after 2,000 students marched around the Majlis (Parliament) building and demanded cancellation of the Anglo-Iranian Oil Company's concession [that is, exclusive rights] to take oil out of Iran," reported the United Press. Half a century earlier, in 1901, a British entrepreneur named William D'Arcy secured from the corrupt former shah of Iran, Mozaffar ad-Din Shah Qajar, the exclusive rights to pump oil out of the desert, on decidedly one-sided terms. D'Arcy's British oil company would keep 84 percent of the profits, while 16 percent would go to the monarchy for the king to disperse as he saw fit, which was mostly in his pocket. Now, forty-eight years later, the bogus terms of the oil deal had become a legitimate point of contention for many Iranians. But in 1949 it was not oil that was directly related to the assassination attempt on the corrupt and ineffectual Shah Mohammad Reza Pahlavi; it was religion.

In the Western media, the Soviet Union was cast as the villain in the Iranian situation. "Iran has been the scene of unrest since the end of the war," reported the Associated Press. "Its vast oil resources have been a bone of contention between the Soviet Union, which has demanded concessions, and the Western powers, which have resisted Russian entrance into the oil fields where they have long dominated." This was precisely what Stalin warned Ambassador Bedell Smith about, during their meeting at the Kremlin. Nine months after the Self-Sacrificers of Islam failed to kill the shah, they succeeded in assassinating his minister of the royal court, Abdolhossein Hazhír. In an attempt to keep order, the shah appointed a hardline anticommunist military general named Ali Razmara to be the new prime minister of Iran. In response, the Fedayeen-e Islam dispatched an assassin to kill him.

On March 7, 1951, Prime Minister Razmara was paying his respects at a funeral in the Shah Mosque, in Tehran, when a religious zealot named Khalil Tahmasebi stepped forward from the crowd and fired a bullet directly into his face, killing him instantly. The assassination garnered the world's attention. "Premier of Iran Is Shot to Death in a Mosque by a Religious Fanatic; Victim of Assassin," headlined the Associated Press. Just twelve days later, General Razmara's minister of education, Abdul Hamid Zanganeh, was shot and killed by the same group while standing on the steps of Tehran University, where Fedayeen-e Islam had almost killed the shah two years before. In response to the back-to-back assassinations, the shah declared martial law.

In Washington, DC, members of the CIA convened to discuss next steps. "The assassination of Prime Minister Razmara seriously worsens an already grave situation in Iran," warned a representative from the Office of Policy Coordination. "Political and economic insecurity combined with chauvinist and fanatical religious emotions [have] produce[d] an atmosphere extremely favorable to Soviet subversion." Alarmist or not, the perspective of the CIA was that the entire Middle East was on the brink of falling to communism. The successful assassination of a head of state can prompt copycat killings, raising the specter of chaos and instability, which is exactly what happened four months later, as a series of brutal assassinations swept across the Middle East. The first was in Lebanon.

As with most of its Arab neighbors, Lebanon had only recently gained independence from French colonial rule after the end of World War II. As per the terms of the United Nations Charter, the last French troops withdrew from Lebanon in December 1946. On July 17, 1951, Riad Al Solh, Lebanon's first prime minister, was gunned down at Marka Airport in Amman, Jordan. The killers, members of a group called the Syrian Socialist National Party, declared that theirs was a revenge killing for the execution of one of their own party's cofounding members. Three days later, on July 20, King Abdullah of Jordan was killed by a Palestinian assassin at the entrance to the Al Aqsa Mosque in Jerusalem. He was walking into Friday prayers. The king, age sixty-nine, died instantly from three shots to the head and the chest. "The King who made [Jordan] a nation is no more," a British newsreel proclaimed. "He was our friend. And for this he died."

Standing at the king's side when he was assassinated was his fifteen-year-old grandson, Prince Hussein, hit by bullet fragments. The prince's life was saved when the fragments bounced off a medal, pinned to his chest, that his grandfather had given him earlier that same day. The assassin was shot dead by bodyguards and a state of emergency was declared in Jordan. The king's eldest son, Prince Talal, took the throne. But Talal had a hidden history of mental illness and had been secretly treated for schizophrenia in a Swiss clinic the year before. After ruling Jordan for a year, he was removed from power by the parliament. Prince Hussein became King Hussein of Jordan, now age sixteen. He would rule Jordan for the next forty-five years. Having witnessed the assassination of his grandfather by a Palestinian fanatic made the teenage King Hussein forever cautious of those around him, he later said, and caused him to treat his fellow Arab rulers with a degree of skepticism. He is said to have always carried a gun when he left the palace and slept with a pistol within arm's reach.

After the death of King Abdullah of Jordan, the State Department sent a telegram to all its ambassadors in the Arab states and Israel, encouraging them "to counsel restraint and moderation" as it worked to shore up a secret partnership with the shah of Iran. The killing of other heads of state in the region "could promote a further weakening of Iran's internal stability," CIA analysts feared. And the result could be "a general sense of aimlessness, insecurity, and frustration...highlighting Iran's lack of capable leadership." Which is exactly what happened next.

In Tehran, riots broke out. To appease an angry public, the shah appointed Mohammad Mossadegh, an Iranian nationalist, to serve as prime minister, giving him authority over Iran's military forces. One of Mossadegh's first actions was to wrest control of the oil industry from the Anglo-Iranian Oil Company, which infuriated the British. Mossadegh imprisoned the founder of the Self-Sacrificers of Islam, Navab Safavi, which enraged the Fedayeen-e Islam, who put Mossadegh on their kill list.

Unable to kill Mossadegh, the Fedayeen went after the prime minister's loyal foreign minister, Hossein Fatemi. In what was sure to be a spectacular display of fanaticism and revenge, the Fedayeen engineered a plan to kill Fatemi while he was attending a commemorative event marking the assassination of newspaper publisher Mohammad Masoud. But at the exact moment the assassin was reaching into his front jacket pocket to pull out a gun, a local photographer just so happened to snap a photograph of the killer, an image that would be reprinted in newspapers around the world. Adding to the uncanny timing of the photograph was the fact that the killer wasn't a grown man but a young boy of fifteen. In 1952, the marriage of violence and Islamic fundamentalism was unfamiliar to most Westerners, and the idea that a teenage boy could be seduced into becoming an assassin in the name of religion was considered downright shocking. The teenager managed to get off only a single shot, hitting Iran's foreign minister in the stomach, wounding him. The boy was captured by the shah's state police, who took him back to police headquarters, where he confessed to being a member of Fedayeen-e Islam. In Washington, DC, President Eisenhower approved the Psychological Strategy Board's plans for a hidden-hand coup d'état in Iran.

A year passed. On March 4, 1953, the National Security Council convened to discuss Iran. Dulles repeated his thoughts on what the assassination of Prime Minister Mossadegh would mean for the United States. "If he were to be assassinated or otherwise to disappear from power, a political vacuum would occur in Iran and the Communists might easily take over." And if the communists moved on the Middle East and all its oil, it would mean the outbreak of war.

President Eisenhower was briefed on numerous plans. When he expressed a preference for U.S. financial support to Mossadegh instead of getting rid of him, representatives from State, Defense, and the CIA argued that to do so was useless. The days of propping up people who didn't like the United States were coming to an end, CIA director Allen Dulles advised. Charles Wilson, secretary of defense, agreed. "In the old days, when dictatorships changed it was usually a matter of one faction of the right against another, and we had only to wait until the situation subsided," Wilson told Eisenhower. "Nowadays, however, when a dictatorship of the right [is] replaced by a dictatorship of the left, a state could presently slide into Communism and [become] irrevocably lost to us." It was the same mantra that had allowed the CIA to garner covert-action authority in Korea and Guatemala. Diplomacy wasn't working, and military intervention was unwise. That left the president with his third option, the hidden hand.

The president told his advisors that the situation was "a matter of great distress" to him. That he could not understand why "we seemed unable to get some of the people in these downtrodden countries to like us instead of hating us." After listening to the president, the National Security Council secured authorization to proceed. The following month, on April 4, 1953, one million dollars was wired to the CIA's Tehran Station to bring about the downfall of Mohammad Mossadegh.

The CIA plot to overthrow Mossadegh, code-named Operation Ajax, took place the third week of August 1953. The details of the coup—even the basic questions like who hatched the plot and who carried it out—remain the subject of debate. Mossadegh was not assassinated but instead arrested and convicted of treason. He served three years in jail before being banished to house arrest. He died in 1967. A retired army general named Fazlollah Zahedi became the CIA's front man, retaining power as prime minister for two years. But the real goal for the United States was to quietly help the shah assume absolute power in Iran. With military and economic backing, by 1955, the CIA got its wish.

The Defense Department sent General McClure, founder of the U.S. Army 10th Special Forces, to Tehran, to serve as chief of the U.S. Military Mission in Iran. His job was to help Iran build up its conventional military forces, as well as a guerrilla warfare corps. In a letter to his liaison on the National Security Council, McClure relayed what he'd learned. "His majesty's first and most important problem was the morale of the armed forces. Something must be done immediately to provide min[imum] housing requirements for its officers and noncommissioned officers, many of whom [are] at present living in squalor," McClure wrote. Like a kid in a candy store, the shah's wish list was long. "He desires a highly proficient and technically trained small army with considerable mobility, which could be backed, in time of war, by large numbers of tribesmen armed as Infantry and trained to fight defensively until overrun and then resort to guerrilla tactics."

The shah insisted he needed an arsenal of weapons systems and artillery from the United States in order to exercise dominance in the region: "Three Battalions of Patton Tanks, an antiaircraft battalion to protect troops, steel mating for airstrips, 155 Howitzers and land mines," wrote McClure. The shah accepted the fact that it was "too early" to talk about being supplied with U.S. jet fighter aircraft. The shah's military reorganization was well under way, McClure wrote, the country's charter being rewritten to move military authority away from the prime minister so it was entirely under the shah's direction and control.

President Eisenhower expressed his approval for what was originally seen as a successful coup in Iran. The Soviets were at bay, at least for now. "The CIA carried out [a] successful regime-change operation," says CIA staff historian David Robarge. "It also transformed a turbulent constitutional monarchy into an absolutist kingship and induced a succession of unintended consequences." Not until the Iranian Revolution in 1979 would the most impactful of the unintended consequences be revealed. Scores of foot soldiers of the revolution seeking to overturn the shah were members of Fedayeen-e Islam. But in 1953, with the shah firmly installed as the American puppet, and order seemingly in place, CIA officers mistakenly believed they could control the Self-Sacrificers of Islam, maybe even work with them.

A new strategy for dealing with radical Islamic fundamentalists emerged. The communists were avowed atheists. The CIA and the National Security Council advised President Eisenhower that the United States should begin using the communists' irreligiosity against them. In September 1957, at a White House meeting with the president, Secretary of State John Foster Dulles, the CIA's Frank Wisner, members of the Joint Chiefs of Staff, and President Eisenhower agreed. "We should do everything possible to stress the 'holy war' aspect" endemic to the Middle East, Eisenhower said. Dulles suggested that the CIA create a "secret task force" through which the United States could deliver weapons, intelligence, and money to American-friendly monarchs including King Saud of Saudi Arabia, King Hussein of Jordan, and King Faisal of Iraq. It was an idea that would have grave unintended consequences. From these task forces a thousand monsters would be born.

As was the case with many Arab rulers in the 1950s, Egypt's Gamal Abdel Nasser came to power using assassination as a political tool, at least according to his successor, Anwar Sadat. In an interview with Arab television, Sadat said that Nasser conducted "a large-scale assassination campaign" starting in January 1952, an act that helped him secure power and respect. After trying, unsuccessfully, to machine-gun down a political rival during a military parade, Nasser led a successful military coup against King Farouk, which launched the Egyptian revolution. No one liked Egypt's King Farouk. He was corrupt and ineffectual, vilified for riding around the country in his private train consuming oysters while so many of his subjects suffered from poverty and hunger. Spared execution, King Farouk was forced to abdicate, and he lived out the rest of his life in Monaco and Italy. Nasser became president of Egypt in 1956.

The use of assassination as a political tool cuts both ways. In a region where assassination was as much about revenge as it was about politics and religion, once you tried to assassinate a rival, you could assume that your rivals were going to be coming after you. Two years after taking power, Nasser became the target of an assassination attempt by the Muslim Brotherhood, Egypt's Sunni fundamentalist group.

On October 26, 1954, Nasser was in Alexandria, delivering a speech to celebrate the British military withdrawal. The historic event was broadcast live on radios all across Egypt and the Arab world. As Nasser regaled the massive crowd of supporters who'd gathered in Mansheya Square, a member of the Muslim Brotherhood stood up and fired at President Nasser from just twenty feet away. Despite firing eight shots in all, the assassin missed Nasser entirely. Pandemonium erupted among the crowd while Nasser remained sublimely calm. He seized upon the moment for political advantage, addressing millions of Egyptians listening to his speech on the radio.

"My countrymen!" Nasser shouted out. "My blood spills for you and for Egypt!" Even though Nasser wasn't bleeding, the crowd went wild. "Let them kill me!" he cried. "It does not concern me so long as I have instilled pride, honor, and freedom in you. If Gamal Abdel Nasser should die, each of you shall be Gamal Abdel Nasser!" As the crowd erupted in cheers, Nasser continued shouting into the microphone. "Gamal Abdel Nasser is of you and from you, and he is willing to sacrifice his life for the nation," he repeated again and again. Nasser, already popular, was now also publicly adored across the Arab world. His vision for pan-Arabism, the desire to unify the Arab world from North Africa to West Asia, from the Atlantic Ocean to the Arabian Sea, could now take hold.

In neighboring Libya, a young Bedouin boy named Muammar el-Qaddafi listened to Nasser's Mansheya Square radio broadcast with supreme adoration. In school, Qaddafi would leap up onto his chair and recite Nasser verbatim. People thought he was odd. His classmates made fun of him. He didn't care. One day, he said, he'd prove all of them wrong. And he'd exact revenge on anyone who ever dared doubt him. Muammar el-Qaddafi would grow up, join the military, and seize power from Libya's corrupt King Idris. He would emulate Gamal Nasser, promote his ideology, and insist the two men become friends.

Two thousand miles away, in Iraq, a rebel group plotted to assassinate their king. On July 14, 1958, the last king of Iraq, his family, his advisors, and his prime minister were all killed in one of the most brutal assassination and coups d'état in modern history. The bloodbath was a terrifying mix of political killing and revenge murder, finalized and sensationalized in a sadistic display of mob rage. King Faisal II, born in 1935, became king of Iraq when he was just three years old, after his playboy father died in a car crash. During World War II, the boy lived with his mother, Queen Aliya, in England. As a teenager, he attended the British boarding school Harrow alongside his second cousin, Hussein, then serving as king of Jordan.

King Faisal was twenty-three and engaged to be married when on July 14 the military stormed the palace in Baghdad. One of the king's military commanders, a brigadier general named Abd al-Karim Qasim, ordered that the members of the royal family be lined up in front of a wall and machine-gunned to death. Prime Minister Nuri al-Said escaped the immediate carnage and the following day donned an abaya and sneaked out a back door of the palace. He was captured and shot, and his corpse "cut up by shawerma knives" by a vengeful mob. The mutilated corpses of the crown prince and the prime minister were then strung up outside the Ministry of Defense and hit with sticks. After the bodies were taken down, they were laid out in the street, where they were run over by an army vehicle. The corpses "resembled sausage," reported a Baghdad newspaper, which ran photographs of the bodies and the mayhem.

King Faisal II had been decidedly pro-Western, a friend of the State Department and a guest of the White House during a visit to DC. His 1958 assassination was a blow to the CIA's desire for regional control. The king had been a cornerstone partner in the Baghdad Pact of 1955, a five-nation alliance signed by Iran, Iraq, Pakistan, Turkey, and the United Kingdom, in support of Western democratic ideals. The alliance, known as CENTO, was modeled after NATO and promised mutual cooperation among its signatory nations. At its core, the Baghdad Pact was an agreement to contain the spread of communism and limit Moscow's influence in the already volatile Middle East.

After the murders, Allen Dulles was asked to meet with President Eisenhower to brief him on worst-case scenarios in Iraq and how the king's killing might affect the overall region. Dulles told Eisenhower that a chain reaction downfall could easily occur across the entire Middle East. The kings of Jordan, Saudi Arabia, and Iran were all extremely vulnerable to assassination, Dulles warned, and if they were murdered, their weak governments would surely fall.

Iraq's new leader, General Abd al-Karim Qasim, withdrew from the Baghdad Pact and began forging a partnership with the Soviet Union. In 1959, in keeping with the cycle of revenge, a six-man hit squad aligned with an underground resistance force tried to assassinate Qasim. One of the assassins was a foot soldier from the village of Tikrit named Saddam Hussein. During the ambush, Saddam

Hussein began shooting prematurely, drawing fire from Qasim's bodyguards and causing the plan to go awry. Qasim's chauffeur was killed, but General Qasim survived the attempt on his life. Believing they'd killed General Qasim, the members of the hit team fled.

Saddam Hussein vanished. When he resurfaced years later in Egypt, the world was a different place.

CHAPTER SEVEN

The KGB's Office of Liquid Affairs

Through the 1950s, the president's advisors continued to see the Soviets as the cause of anti–American acts and sentiment they could otherwise not explain. At the same time, Moscow remained hyperfocused on controlling the public's perception of communism. From 1954 onward, the CIA believed that the Kremlin was behind the recent spate of émigré kidnappings and assassinations in Eastern Europe. Too many community leaders who'd spoken out against the Soviet Union were winding up disappeared or dead. For the most part this was speculative. If only the CIA had hard evidence. The hit-and-run ambushes were brazen and bold, often occurring in broad daylight on city streets. Finally, in 1954, the CIA got the evidence it was looking for in the strange case of KGB assassin Captain Nikolai Evgenievich Khokhlov.

Captain Khokhlov was a shy man, quiet and unassuming. His first career, before the Second World War, was as a theatrical performer. His special talent was whistling. Now here he was, standing in a hallway in Frankfurt, Germany, a KGB assassin on a mission to kill. It was April 1954, and everything in Khokhlov's life was about to change.

He rang the doorbell above a small nameplate that read GEORGIY SERGEYEVICH OKOLOVICH. Russian by birth, Okolovich was an outspoken anti-Soviet émigré and chief of operations of the Popular

Labor Alliance of Russian Solidarists, a virulently anticommunist group in West Germany. The door opened. The two men stood face-to-face.

"Georgiy Sergeyevich?" Khokhlov asked.

"Da," said the man, "*Yes, I am he.*"

"I have come to you from Moscow," Khokhlov stated. "The Central Committee of the Communist Party of the Soviet Union has ordered your assassination. The murder is entrusted to my group. I cannot let this murder happen."

The target, Georgiy Okolovich, let the assassin, Nikolai Khokhlov, inside. Khokhlov sat down, presented his credentials, and went over the details of the plan. Then he begged for help. He couldn't go on like this, Khokhlov said, overseeing the deaths of people the Kremlin wanted killed. Khokhlov wanted to switch sides—to betray his country and defect to the West. If Okolovich were willing to help him, they both would live. And so assassination as a secret weapon in the battle between East and West moved out of the shadows and into the public eye.

One week later, on April 22, Captain Nikolai Evgenievich Khokhlov took to the podium at a press conference in Bonn, Germany. He announced to the world that he was an assassin for the KGB. A "crisis of conscience" had prevented him from killing, he said. The KGB was evil and had to be stopped, he warned. As proof, he revealed yet another Soviet covert-action operation that had been carried out the week before. While Khokhlov was being debriefed by U.S. intelligence agents in Bonn, a second assassination team dispatched by the KGB had succeeded in kidnapping and assassinating an anti-Soviet émigré named Aleksandr Trushinovich, Okolovich's counterpart at the Popular Labor Alliance of Russian Solidarists in Berlin.

At first, the CIA was suspicious of Khokhlov. His story sounded apocryphal. The more likely scenario was that Khokhlov was a double agent, a Soviet mole. But after a few days of questioning, Khokhlov's

American handler became convinced he was indeed a KGB assassin who had experienced a crisis of conscience that led to an ideological shift. In the Cold War battle between the United States and the USSR, most defecting was done from East to West, which made Russia look bad. The Soviet Union spent time and treasure trying to control the free world's perception of communism, which is why outspoken anti-Soviet émigrés like Georgiy Okolovich and Aleksandr Trushinovich were high on the assassination list. Now so too was Khokhlov.

Adding to the drama of his defection was the fact that he carried with him physical evidence of the Soviet-led assassination plot. The weapon the KGB had given him was a cunning little close-quarters killing machine, a poison dart gun disguised to look like a cigarette pack. At first glance, the two rows of tightly packed smokes appeared normal. But Khokhlov demonstrated how, with the press of a secret button, a four-inch-long dart gun sprang forth, capable of firing small, poison-tipped bullets into a victim. The weapon's delivery system was no louder than a snap of the fingers, Khokhlov demonstrated, and designed to be fired in a public space without notice.

In Khokhlov's debrief, the CIA learned quite a bit about the unusual man, code-named Whistler, including his intelligence activities during the war. When higher-ups in the KGB's predecessor organization, the NKVD (People's Commissariat for Internal Affairs), learned that the blond, blue-eyed Khokhlov spoke German and could whistle, they foresaw an excellent disguise for a wartime covert agent. In 1941, Khokhlov was recalled from a frontline infantry unit, indoctrinated by the NKVD, and sent for paramilitary training, where he learned assassination techniques behind enemy lines. He studied infiltration and exfiltration tactics, reconnaissance tradecraft, hand-to-hand combat skills, and the art of silent killing, training similar to OSS operators'. In the fall of 1943, Khokhlov had parachuted into Belarus under cover of night, where he linked up with Soviet partisans and oversaw the assassination of Nazi Generalkommissar Wilhelm Kube, the Butcher of Belarus. Khokhlov, it seemed, was the communist version of the Special Operations Executive's Jan Kubiš and Josef Gabčík, the commandos who assassinated SS-Obergruppenführer Reinhard Heydrich, the Butcher of Prague.

After the war, Nikolai Khokhlov went to work for Russian intelligence, posing as a German, a Pole, and a Romanian. In 1954, after the death of Stalin, the NKVD became the KGB and Khokhlov was called back to Moscow. He began to have second thoughts about being a professional assassin right around the time he was sent to Frankfurt to kill Georgiy Okolovich.

During Khokhlov's debrief, the CIA learned information it coveted. The KGB's assassination unit was called the 12th Department and was "divided into sections (*otdeleniye*) or directions (*napravleniye*), by countries or groups of countries, such as, for example, the United States ('the principal enemy'), England, Latin America, etc." According to Khokhlov, the 12th Department headquarters in Moscow maintained fifty to sixty experienced employees and was headed by a general named Nikolai B. Rodin, who, "under the alias Korovin, had previously been the KGB resident in Great Britain." Secrecy regarding assassination operations was maintained through careful selection of agents and the specialized training of Soviet personnel. "The officers do not discuss their experience among others; department documents are not circulated," Khokhlov's handlers learned. If an assassination plot were ever recorded, it would be kept track of under the code phrase Executive Action, within the KGB directorate of "liquid affairs" (*mokryye dela*), also known as "wet matters."

The 12th Department had two secret weapons laboratories whose scientists worked on weapons for Executive Action operations. One of these laboratories, code-named Laboratory No. 12, produced "special weapons and explosive devices." It was here that the Soviets engineered and prepared deadly tools of assassination, from "drawing up blueprints [to] melting and pouring bullets." A second lab, called Kamera, or the Chamber, "developed poisons and drugs for 'special tasks.'" Stalin personally oversaw the creation of the Kamera lab,

Khokhlov said, which was located in a suburb outside Moscow called Kuchino. The laboratory housed a torture chamber, a place where death-row prisoners were used as guinea pigs, injected with "different powders, beverages, and liquors…to test the effectiveness of various types of injections." One high-priority effort for the scientists and engineers at Kamera, Khokhlov said, was to create poisons that would be undetectable in an autopsy. Only a handful of high-level persons were ever allowed to enter this classified facility. Khokhlov had never been to Kamera, he said, but knew people who had.

All assassins were trained in the art of kidnapping, the preferred hit-and-run tactic of the 12th Department. The Russian strike-force units were called combat groups (*boyevaya gruppa*). Each consisted of a Soviet staff officer, like Khokhlov, augmented by a team of indigenous agents, local assets familiar with customs and terrain near where a target lived. On the mission to kill Georgiy Okolovich, Khokhlov had been assigned to work with two German-born KGB agents he identified as Hans Kukowitsch and Kurt Weber. All combat-group paramilitary operators were "armed and prepared to perform executive actions when required to do so, either in time of peace or war," Khokhlov said.

The list of Soviet targets for assassination was long, particularly among the anticommunist émigré community. The members of the Politburo guarded a reputation they constructed for themselves, and were determined to stamp out dissent. The best way to silence former citizens who threatened the facade was to kidnap and assassinate them. "The assassinations of some émigré leaders [are often] carried out so skillfully as to leave the impression that the victims died from natural causes," reads a declassified CIA report. The individuals who died were reportedly "victims of an apparent heart attack, suicide, fall, or traffic accident." Other émigré leaders were wanted for information they had. These people were targeted for kidnapping by a direct-action strike force called a Combat Action Team. The paramilitary team followed orders from the directorate of liquid affairs.

The CIA had a thick dossier of the disappeared émigrés, to which Khokhlov added several names. There was Walter Linse, president of the Association of Free German Jurists (lawyers), kidnapped off the streets of Berlin in July of 1952 by a thirteen-man KGB Combat Action team, never to be seen again. There was Bohumil Lausman, an outspoken anticommunist Czech who disappeared from Vienna in 1953 and was later reported to have been taken to a Soviet gulag, where he died. The Ukrainian national Valeri P. Tremmel was grabbed off the streets of Linz, Austria, in June 1954, never to be seen or heard from again.

For his high-profile defection to the West and his refusal to kill on moral grounds, Khokhlov was featured in *Time* magazine and *Life* magazine and in a four-part series in the *Saturday Evening Post*, "I Would Not Murder for the Soviets." When he testified for Congress, he made the Soviet Union sound downright diabolical. He spoke of Soviet death camps, brutal police tactics, and the machine-gunning of citizens who'd gathered to resist totalitarian rule. Under oath, he swore that while "members of the elite enjoy very good living conditions, the ordinary man in the Soviet Union is treated as a slave."

Embraced by the United States, Khokhlov soon became the target of the KGB. To assassinate their former assassin, the KGB ordered scientists in the 12th Department, now renamed the 13th Department, to develop a special toxin undetectable in an autopsy. They wanted a poison that would first disfigure him, then bring about a long, slow, excruciatingly painful death. Not as much for revenge but to send a clear message to anyone who might be thinking about betraying Russia. Three years passed.

In 1958, Khokhlov traveled to Germany to give a speech at a convention of anticommunist émigrés gathered at the Palmengarten conservatory in Frankfurt. During a break, he was sitting at a terrace café enjoying a cup of coffee when he became light-headed. There weren't many people around, he recalled, just a few beer drinkers. Sipping the coffee, he suddenly thought that it tasted funny. Never mind, he thought, and got up and went into the conservatory's concert hall to enjoy the opera being performed. His ears started ringing. He felt nauseated. His vision blurred. "Things began to whirl," he later told the CIA. Khokhlov staggered out to the parking lot, found the car he was driving, and somehow made it back to his hotel, stopping to vomit several times along the way. In the hotel foyer he collapsed and lost consciousness. Taken to Frankfurt University Hospital, he awoke to learn he'd been diagnosed with a basic case of gastritis.

But his condition quickly worsened, and worsened. Soon, his entire body turned a copper-colored red. "My mind began disintegrating," he recalled. He could not accurately determine if he was dreaming or awake. He lost the ability to count beyond ten. Days passed. A nurse came into the room, looked at him, and froze. Then she screamed and ran out. Looking in the mirror, Khokhlov saw that he was covered in black-and-blue marks. Patches of his skin were mottled brown. His pillowcase was covered in blood. "My face had turned into a mask reminiscent of [a] Boris Karloff monster," he remembered. When he reached up to touch his hair, huge tufts fell out.

In Washington, DC, the Pentagon received word of what had happened to Nikolai Khokhlov. The Defense Department swung into action, sending American military physicians to bring Khokhlov under their care. His white blood cell count had fallen from the normal level of 6,000–7,000 down to 700. Doctors took a bone marrow sample. His blood-building cells were dying off. The test samples came back: he'd been poisoned by some kind of radioactive isotope. Doctors gave him very little chance of recovery. Then, after a week of blood transfusions, Khokhlov somewhat miraculously recovered.

It was the CIA that concluded that Khokhlov had been poisoned with radioactive thallium, a deadly toxin, likely created by Soviet scientists in their Kamera lab. The poison had been engineered to work in a "diabolically clever" fashion, an analyst wrote, designed to produce an initial display of symptoms doctors would almost certainly misdiagnose as generic gastritis. The assassins, assumed to be from the KGB's directorate of liquid affairs, had probably posed as waiters at the Palmengarten conservatory terrace café, where one of them had slipped a few drops of radioactive thallium into Khokhlov's coffee cup.

Just one week after Nikolai Khokhlov was released from the American military hospital in Frankfurt, the directorate of liquid affairs struck again. This time they succeeded in poisoning a high-profile anticommunist Ukrainian politician named Lev Rebet, killing him. The assassination occurred in Munich, Germany, in the stairwell of a newspaper office where Rebet had been working with a reporter to expose Kremlin-sponsored assassinations. In World War II, Rebet was the leader of the Ukrainian government until he was arrested by the Gestapo in 1941. He'd survived imprisonment at Sachsenhausen concentration camp, only to be killed by a KGB assassin with a poison dart gun in an office-building stairwell.

Initially, Lev Rebet's death was reported as being from natural causes. The autopsy that followed his collapse in the stairwell stated the cause of death as a heart attack. But four years later, in 1961, a second KGB assassin, Bohdan Stashinsky, defected to Berlin, surrendering himself to West German authorities who turned him over to the CIA. At a U.S. facility in Frankfurt, Stashinsky spent weeks in the custody of the CIA, interrogated by an officer named William Hood. Stashinsky told Hood that he was assigned to the directorate of liquid affairs and that he'd assassinated Lev Rebet with a specially crafted poison gun, a tiny weapon with which he'd sprayed atomized hydrogen cyanide directly into Rebet's face. He described watching Rebet crumple over and die right in front of him.

Unlike Nikolai Khokhlov, Bohdan Stashinsky did not experience a crisis of conscience. He was a double agent. In 2011, at the age of eighty, he revealed in an interview with Ukrainian journalist Natalya Prykhodko that he was always a committed communist and had been sent by the Kremlin to turn himself in, win the good graces of the CIA, and continue his work as a Soviet mole.

Bohdan Stashinsky served eight years in a German prison for the murder of Lev Rebet. This light sentence was likely a result of the lie he propagated—that he couldn't bear to be an assassin and instead turned himself in. After Stashinsky's release in 1966, he went to Washington to work with the CIA. But "they suspected a double game," he says, and he was sent to a backwater post in Panama. After a few years with no access to anything important, Stashinsky was "extracted and transported to Paraguay" by the KGB. He went to Africa, had plastic surgery (so the CIA couldn't find him), and returned to the USSR in 1970. The CIA's files on Bohdan Stashinsky remain classified.

In Moscow, the KGB opened two new divisions inside its directorate of liquid affairs. Department T (for "terrorism") oversaw assassinations by "shooting, poisoning, blowing [things] up and subversion." Department V (for "victory") kept track of its assassins' successes. The new name for work being done by Department T was now "direct action," declassified CIA documents reveal.

CHAPTER EIGHT

Green Light

It was the fall of 1960, and Billy Waugh stood in the open air, on the inky black sea, near the jackstaff of the nuclear attack submarine USS *Grayback*. As the sub slid through the water off the east coast of Okinawa Island in the Pacific, Waugh and three team members prepared for a Top Secret wet-deck launch—a subsurface infiltration technique mastered by a small, elite group of U.S. Special Forces operators called a Green Light Team. The training mission was to emplace a tactical nuclear weapon into the target area, arm the device, and exfiltrate without detection. The submarine's motto, *De Profundis Futurus,* was indicative of these perilous Cold War times. Here now, in the last year of the Eisenhower administration, if the United States went to war, the battle cry would likely be nuclear.

"It was an atomic weapon we were carrying," remembers Waugh. "Not a mock-up. The army had us train with an actual nuclear device. We had to be battle-ready, and we were." The tactical nuclear weapon Waugh and his teammates were carrying was a W54 Special Atomic Demolition Munition, or SADM. It weighed ninety-eight pounds and had a projected yield of between one and seven kilotons. This weapon was designed to be carried on a man's back or chest, or in pieces, to be assembled on the battlefield. Built by Sandia laboratory in New Mexico, the portable atomic weapon was capable of entirely destroying an area roughly one mile in diameter. "Few humans, buildings [or] structures in the kill radius" would survive, according to material declassified by the Department of Defense. Green Light operators who trained with an actual SADM device — who parachuted with it, and swam with it strapped to their bodies — understood the profound responsibility. The blast from a one-kiloton atomic weapon was equivalent to 20,000 pounds of TNT. But as Green Berets, Waugh and the men he was with had been trained to operate under extraordinary pressure, entrusted to handle a device capable of death and destruction on an unimaginable scale, whose power was contained inside a small aluminum vessel the size of a kitchen garbage can.

Waugh strapped the components of the heavy and cumbersome nuclear weapon to his chest. "As team leader, I carried two of the four plutonium rings," he remembered in 2016. "Two of the other team members each carried a single ring." The rings were attached to his body with cloth ties and secured with metal clips. Waugh pulled his infrared device for night viewing down over his eyes, scanned the surface of the water, and climbed down off the submarine's stanchion. Skillfully, as trained, he lowered himself into the 15-man rubber boat (RB-15) and assumed position. Were the inflatable boat to strike the jackstaff, it could mean disaster. If the RB-15 flipped, the submarine's powerful propellers would likely suck the Green Light Team members into its wake. But the four men on Waugh's team boarded the boat without incident, and the submarine sunk down below the surface and disappeared. "We paddled four hundred meters to shore. Quiet. Silent. No motor, no sound," recalls Waugh.

Once on the shore, the Green Light Team deflated the rubber boat, buried it, and covered their tracks with sand and foliage. "We walked to the target area. Once we got there, we assembled the device, set the timer for four hours, and armed it. It took two of us to do it. That was the fail-safe." No single team member could arm the nuclear device alone. "When it was time to exfiltrate, we started walking out. Used commo to relay our position." The effort to communicate was successful, and finally the team was picked up by helicopter and taken back to base. "To Camp Hardy," says Waugh, "for a debrief." Camp Hardy was a U.S. military installation on the northeast coast of Okinawa, halfway between the villages of Higashi and Arakawa. That Top Secret Green Light Team atomic weapons training missions took place here, starting in 1960, has never been officially acknowledged by the Department of Defense.

Strategically located 910 miles from Tokyo, Japan, Okinawa had a blood-soaked history. In the spring of 1945, a final showdown between the United States and Japan took place here, the last stepping-stone before the mainland. More than 140,000 people died on Okinawa between April and June 1945, in the largest sea-air-land battle of World War II. More than 12,000 Americans were killed and 36,000 wounded. By June 22, when the fighting ended, 110,000 Japanese soldiers had been killed, and 160,000 Okinawan civilians had been sacrificed by the Japanese Army or killed by U.S. military personnel.

After the Japanese surrender, Okinawa became a protectorate of the United States, technically no longer part of Japan. The U.S. military constructed bases for its army, air force, and navy here, including at Naha and Kadena, and Torii Station. In 1950, with the outbreak of war on the Korean Peninsula, Okinawa became a strategic foothold for U.S. military and intelligence operations in Asia, a place from which the army and navy launched conventional-force operations. But the need for unconventional-warfare bases was now expanding, for classified units like the Green Light Teams and others. In June 1957, the U.S. Army activated the 1st Special Forces Group (Airborne) on Okinawa, tasked with the responsibility for Pacific theater guerrilla warfare operations. As for Billy Waugh, after being singled out for parachute and weapons handling skills back at Fort Bragg, he'd been sent to Okinawa as a member of Company A, 1st Special Forces Group, for live-action SADM training.

The role of a Green Light Team was to carry a nuclear device into battle, behind enemy lines, where it could be used as a tactical weapon. SADM was designed for sabotage: to blow up fortified enemy infrastructure, including tunnels, viaducts, and mountain passes. The small nuclear weapon could also be placed just inside the enemy's front line and detonated there. In addition to killing significant numbers of enemy soldiers, a nuclear explosion near the main line of defense would force an army to spend precious resources caring for what would likely be tens of thousands of mortally wounded soldiers, casualties of small-scale atomic warfare.

To be selected for a Green Light Team was a rare and private honor. Team members worked under pseudonyms and wore fatigues with no military markings or insignia. "The unit was classified, and you didn't go around discussing it or talking about it at the mess hall," says Waugh. Being chosen meant you'd demonstrated an ability to perform flawlessly, with laser focus under great stress. Flexible and rigorous in equal measure. Initial training was at the U.S. Army Engineer Center at Fort Belvoir, in Virginia, where Green Light Team members learned infiltration techniques including parachute drops onto land, wet-deck launches from subs, and a combination of parachute drops into the ocean accompanied by underwater infiltrations, in scuba gear.

To parachute a tactical nuclear weapon out of an aircraft required meticulous attention to detail. "Timing was everything," remembers Waugh. "You all had to jump quickly—you couldn't afford to be spread out when you landed on the ground." The disassembled device was placed into a breakaway bag made of canvas, sealed with a heavy rubber band, and attached to the team leader's parachute harness. A jumper's rigging was engineered in a way that once out of the aircraft, the nuclear component would fall to the end of a seventeen-foot lowering line. According to declassified Defense Department material, "By separating the munition from the jumper, the impact shock on water entry would be decreased. It also keeps the weapon from free-falling and prevents loss in night missions or heavy seas." But accidents happened, as Waugh recalls. "A Green Light crew on Okinawa lost a nuclear device. It slipped out of its harness and fell into the mud on the sea floor. Every asset in the U.S. Navy was involved in finding the missing SADM. Eventually we found it. These kinds of mishaps are always resolved." The Defense Department has never confirmed the incident.

The nuclear weapons work of the Top Secret Green Light Teams on Okinawa was a product of President Eisenhower's limited nuclear war doctrine, officially called the New Look. The concept of a limited nuclear war was a paradox, a seeming contradiction of Eisenhower's military doctrine of Mutual Assured Destruction, or MAD.

Mutual Assured Destruction presumed that opposing sides would each build an arsenal of nuclear weapons so massive, the capability alone would serve as a deterrent, or disincentive, for ever starting a nuclear war. Neither side would be crazy enough to launch a nuclear strike against the other side, the theory went, because all-out nuclear warfare guaranteed complete annihilation of both sides.

But what about smaller wars? So-called limited nuclear wars? To satisfy this question, Eisenhower's National Security Council created the New Look limited war strategy, which gave birth to thousands of tactical nuclear weapons in the late 1950s and early 1960s, including the SADM. These small-sized nuclear weapons were designed for actual use on the battlefield, not for deterrence. Nuclear weapons were miniaturized, to fit into artillery shells, surface-to-air missiles, air-to-air missiles, short-range missiles, as truck-portable weapons, man-portable weapons, as atomic land mines and depth charges. But the very possibility of limited nuclear war presented an obvious problem. It was like asking a dying man to fight with a butter knife when there's an ice pick within reach.

"The way to deter aggression is for [America] to be willing and able to respond vigorously at any place and with means of its own choosing," Secretary of State John Foster Dulles told the Council on Foreign Relations in January 1954, in his first public speech promoting the use of strategic nuclear weapons to win small wars directed by Moscow. These atomic munitions could be used "in the Arctic and in the Tropics; in Asia, the Near East, and in Europe; by sea, by land and by air," Dulles warned. With this New Look doctrine in play, the United States promised it could, and if it wanted to would, respond to a conventional threat anywhere in the world with a precision nuclear strike.

But just four months after Dulles's 1954 speech, its hollow bluster became clear, in the tiny Southeast Asian country of Vietnam. There, on a small mountain outpost on the Vietnamese border near Laos, a ferociously fought battle came to a brutal climax, stunning the world. The event, now long forgotten by most, was the Battle of Dien Bien Phu, a fifty-seven-day armed conflict between the communists of North Vietnam and the far more technologically advanced French Union Army and its air force. It is one of the most significant unconventional-warfare battles of the modern era.

At Dien Bien Phu, 42,000 guerrilla fighters, aided by more than 114,000 Vietnamese civilians, put a decisive end to one hundred years of French colonial rule. The success of the battle belonged inarguably to two men: the group's charismatic leader, Ho Chi Minh, and the general of his army, Vo Nguyen Giap. Just nine years earlier, during World War II, these two men had been trained by an OSS Special Operations team to fight Japanese invaders inside Vietnam. Called the OSS Deer Team, the unit was the Vietnamese equivalent of the French Jedburghs. In September 1945, Colonel Aaron Bank, leader of one of these teams, spent a day personally driving around Vietnam with Ho Chi Minh after Bank's OSS car broke down.

In the modern history of unconventional warfare, General Giap's battle tactics at Dien Bien Phu remain remarkable. In addition to the guerrilla fighters, trained in tactics taught to General Giap by the OSS Dear Team, the 114,000 civilians who showed up proved invaluable to the cause. Men and women of all ages and abilities walked to the remote mountain outpost of Dien Bien Phu from across North Vietnam, transporting supplies and heavy weapons from hundreds of miles away. Among the weapons hauled through the treacherous terrain were roughly 500 American-made howitzers, left behind by U.S. forces in Korea and appropriated by the Chinese.

To get to Dien Bien Phu, General Giap's army of civilians built roadways and footpaths through deep mud, dense jungle, and mountainous terrain with shovels carried on their backs. Once they reached the battle area, they hand-dug a trench around the 14,000 French forces holding ground there. Ho and Giap's revolutionaries set up their Soviet- and Chinese-made antiaircraft guns they'd pulled up the mountain, using ropes. They used these gifts of their communist benefactors to fire at French fighter-bombers, shooting down scores and making resupply impossible. Entrenched and surrounded, the French lost the ability to fight. On May 7, 1954, after a nearly two-month-long siege, French forces surrendered. Some 1,600 French troops were dead, 5,000 wounded, 1,600 missing. Over 8,000 French soldiers were captured by the communists, called Viet Minh, and marched off to prison camps, some as far as 500 miles away. Fewer than half of these POWs survived.

In the final days of the Battle of Dien Bien Phu, the United States did not come to the aid of its ally, France. In the aftermath of the French capitulation, President Eisenhower was forced to consider anew the national-security challenge that was Vietnam. A delegation of U.S., French, British, Soviet, and Chinese diplomats met in Switzerland and agreed to divide Vietnam into North and South, as had been done in Korea at the end of World War II. Ho Chi Minh and the Viet Minh were given control of the north. Emperor Bao Dai and a new prime minister named Ngo Dinh Diem were assigned control in the south.

The situation was the best the United States could hope for in Vietnam in 1954. In a classified memorandum to the president, CIA director Allen Dulles relayed a simple truth. "The evidence [shows] that a majority of people in Vietnam supported the Viet Minh rebels," Dulles wrote. "The victory in the Battle of Dien Bien Phu has tremendously boosted Ho's popularity." And right behind Ho in popularity was General Giap.

In the North, in Hanoi, Ho Chi Minh made General Giap his vice premier and defense minister, and the commander in chief of the Vietnam People's Army. General Giap wrote a handbook on guerrilla warfare, *People's War, People's Army,* which was aggressively studied within the CIA. "Giap shares with Premier Khrushchev a conviction that the future holds many 'just wars of national liberation,'" one analyst wrote. Giap's book provided guidance for regular citizens who wanted to join the underground movement and participate in sabotage and subversion against the south. "[G]uerilla [*sic*] war must multiply," wrote Giap. It was time for the movement to "develop into mobile warfare," he commanded, "[to] wear out and annihilate bigger enemy forces and win ever greater victories." At the CIA, plans for covert-action operations against Ho Chi Minh and General Giap moved to the fore.

In an effort to diminish Ho and Giap's rising popularity, and to bolster Emperor Bao Dai and Prime Minister Diem, the CIA established a secret presence in Saigon, in the south. With clandestine offices tucked away inside the U.S. Embassy there, the CIA dispatched a retired air force colonel named Edward Lansdale to serve as chief of covert operations. Within weeks of his arrival Lansdale reported back to DC, describing the situation in Saigon as chaotic and ungovernable. Bandits and roving gangs controlled the streets. A criminal gang called Binh Xuyen held power over the riverboats. Animist-based religious sects, including the Hoa Hao and the Cao Dai, sold protection against violence and crime in the form of trinkets and magic spells. But Lansdale believed America could work with President Diem, he told his superiors. Diem was an avowed anticommunist, and espoused admiration for everything the West represented. Diem dressed like a British dilettante and spoke fluent English, having studied Catholicism at a Maryknoll seminary in New Jersey for almost a year. He seemed easy enough to control.

Using CIA cash, Colonel Lansdale paid off the criminal gangs to cease and desist, then bribed Diem's opposition leaders to step down. In 1955, also with CIA funds, he helped rig an election that got rid of the increasingly unpopular and corrupt Emperor Bao Dai. Lansdale encouraged Diem to unify the disparate groups of people who populated South Vietnam, including the urban elite, the rural peasants, and the tribal hill people. This was what the communists were doing up North, through heavy-handed, Soviet-style coercion. But the North was unified, Lansdale told Diem, and without unification, the communists would be more likely to succeed in dividing and conquering the south with their mobile guerrilla warfare plans. Declassified documents from CIA archives indicate Lansdale tried repeatedly to get Prime Minister Diem to unify and strengthen civil society through education and infrastructure programs for people in the south, ones the CIA was ready and willing to pay for. But Diem would have none of it. President Eisenhower had called him the "miracle man in Asia" during Diem's visit to America, and apparently Diem thought that made him invincible. He was wrong.

Lansdale began working on covert actions that did not require Diem's cooperation. Operation Passage to Freedom, disguised as a humanitarian effort by the U.S. Navy, was a covert-action operation run by the CIA. Under the catchy slogan "God Has Gone South," the effort drew the world's attention to the plight of religious Vietnamese being persecuted by God-hating communists. With help from the U.S. Navy's 7th Fleet and nongovernmental organizations (NGOs), the CIA engineered the exodus of 1.25 million Vietnamese Catholics from the north to the south. "U.S. officials wanted to make sure that as many persons as possible, particularly the strongly anticommunist Catholics, relocated in the south," Lansdale later recalled.

But how to get people to uproot their families and move hundreds of miles? Lansdale, a master of propaganda, devised a plan. He had CIA artists create pamphlets showing Hanoi with three nuclear mushroom clouds superimposed on a map. He infiltrated CIA assets into the North to spread rumors of a possible U.S. nuclear strike against Hanoi. The way to avoid death by nuclear holocaust was to move south. The public remained naive as to Lansdale's efforts, and the compaign was a success, lauded by the international press. But it damaged Ho Chi Minh's reputation as a liberator, at least temporarily. And it infuriated the Politburo, which fired back with a brutal covert-action assassination campaign against South Vietnam.

Ho Chi Minh and General Giap did not have a powerful navy at their disposal, but what they did have were assassins. Starting in 1959, they began developing an entire mobile warfare army of singleton killers—men and women willing to travel south and assassinate pro-Western South Vietnamese officials, teachers, policemen, and intellectuals. By the time the CIA was wrapping up Operation Passage to Freedom, hundreds of Hanoi's assassins had been emplaced below the 17th parallel. Aided by a partisan support network of communist sympathizers in the south, these groups, called special activity cells, were trained by a security operations officer named Nguyen Tai. Nguyen Tai's story did not become public until 1990, after his memoirs were published in Hanoi. He served in the Ministry of Public Security, North Vietnam's espionage and security organization modeled after the KGB. "His father, Nguyen Cong Hoan, was one of Vietnam's most famous authors," says former CIA operations officer Merle L. Pribbenow. Tai's rise to power came after he helped the government build a case against his own father for "anti-regime statements." To betray one's family in the name of the communist party was rewarded as loyalty.

In 1959, assassins trained by Nguyen Tai and his Security Operations Officers succeeded in the hit-and-run killings of more than

1,200 South Vietnamese officials. The assassins would run up to a target, point a pistol at the person's head, pull the trigger, and disappear. The ease with which the assassins were able to strike, then vanish, bred paranoia, chaos, and fear. The following year, in 1960, the number of close-contact assassinations more than doubled, with upward of 3,500 district officials, rural police, village chiefs, local teachers, and others murdered in the south. "This covert war was a difficult, dirty, no-holds-barred struggle that employed assassination and terror as its stock-in-trade," says Pribbenow.

Eisenhower was in an untenable position. Diplomacy was out of the question and military action was deemed unwise. The president's third option in South Vietnam, covert action, was having little effect. The president's advisors suggested Eisenhower take action in Vietnam's neighbor to the west, the kingdom of Laos, where a new communist insurgency was beginning to take hold. These guerrilla fighters, who were allied with Ho Chi Minh's forces in North Vietnam, were called the Pathet Lao. The result was a CIA-led covert-action program in Laos, first called Operation Ambidextrous, renamed Operation Hot Foot, and finally known as Operation White Star. The man in charge was Colonel Arthur D. "Bull" Simons, a hard-charging unconventional-warfare specialist from World War II operations in the Philippines.

CIA officers and U.S. Army Green Berets disguised as land surveyors with the National Geodetic Survey association were sent to Laos to train Royal Lao soldiers in unconventional-warfare techniques. The 107 Green Berets who participated in the operation were assigned to units called Mobile Training Teams. One of these operators was Billy Waugh.

One morning during SADM training on Okinawa Island, Waugh received his unusual orders. His papers stated that he was going on a six-month Temporary Duty Assignment (TDY) to Vietnam, when in fact he was going to Laos as a member of Operation White Star. Waugh and a twelve-man Special Forces A-Team traveled from

Okinawa to the Philippines, to Bangkok, and then to Vientiane, Laos. From there, the A-Team took army vehicles to Pakse, Laos, located in the western part of the country near its border with Thailand. The Green Berets wore civilian clothing and carried Defense Department civilian identification cards. When the White Star team arrived at what would be their training center for the next six months, they found nothing but an isolated village of thatched huts. Everything the Green Berets needed to set up training operations was air-dropped in from Okinawa—food, weapons, construction materials, even two trucks and a bulldozer.

Laos was an impoverished country living in a preindustrial age. When Waugh first arrived there, the landlocked nation didn't have a single paved road, railroad, or newspaper. Its estimated two million people were more likely to identify themselves as Hmong and Meo tribesmen than as citizens of Laos. "Most of the [White Star] trainees were illiterate, and many did not know that Laos was an independent nation or that it possessed a standing army," says Defense Department command historian Ken Finlayson. "White Star advisors faced an almost insurmountable task in trying to instill a sense of urgency and purpose in the Laotian soldiers, to implement rigid training schedules," and to prepare them for battle with the Pathet Lao.

The intention of White Star was to train Laotian troops to a level of competence that would enable them to fight the communist Pathet Lao. This proved to be a daunting task, if not an impossible one. "The Laotian commander of our unit drank a lot and drove his Mercedes around," remembers Waugh. "The concept of discipline or physical training did not exist." White Star advisor Colonel Alfred Paddock recalls that "an astonishing fifteen soldiers were killed by their own mines during our stay." How to train a rebel army in the developing world in keeping with U.S. Army standards? The same conundrum has plagued the U.S. Army from World War II to the present day.

But there was a far more dangerous problem unfolding, one that neither the CIA nor the Defense Department foresaw. Hanoi was using Laos as a supply route, a way to move weapons, fighters, and supplies from North Vietnam into South Vietnam. This passageway would become known as the Ho Chi Minh Trail. It consisted of more than 1,500 miles of interconnected pathways and roads, some wide and sturdy enough for trucks, others meant for elephants, foot soldiers, and bicyclists. A Top Secret National Security Agency (NSA) report declassified in 2007 called the Ho Chi Minh Trail "one of the great achievements in military engineering of the twentieth century." Thanks to the triple-canopy jungle that stretched across much of Laos and Vietnam, the construction of the trail was happening right under the CIA's nose.

It was a communist-led covert-action operation of epic proportions—viciously effective and so easy to plausibly deny. Historians agree: the Ho Chi Minh Trail was a primary factor in America's losing the Vietnam War.

CHAPTER NINE

The Special Group

During the last year of Eisenhower's presidency, in a radical escalation of hidden-hand operations, a small group of the president's principal advisors began openly discussing among themselves plans to assassinate foreign leaders. This new group was called the Special Group.

It was not uncommon for the president's covert-action advisory board to change names. The National Security Council remained the official oversight board, and smaller ancillary groups were often created to deal with the most incendiary and potentially scandalous covert operations. First there was the Psychological Strategy Board, formed in 1951, as we have seen. During the Guatemala coup d'état, in 1953, the PSB was reorganized as the Operations Coordinating Board (OCB). After the issuance of a new directive, Covert Operations NSC 5412/2, in 1955, the Planning Coordination Group (PCG) was created. Some months later, the Special Group emerged, with requirement for membership a rank of assistant secretary or above.

The word "assassination" was never used and certainly not committed to paper. Instead, a Senate investigation later found, the president's advisors used "secrecy, compartmentation, circumlocution, and the avoidance of clear responsibility" to maintain plausible deniability around assassination schemes. The president's inner circle discussed the pros and cons of "eliminating" or "neutralizing" certain individuals, and "getting rid of" or "disposing of" foreign leaders, so as to advance U.S. foreign policy goals. "Speaking in riddles to each other" became commonplace, Senate investigators found.

On February 25, 1960, members of the Special Group convened to discuss "eliminating" General Qasim, the prime minister of Iraq—the man who had ordered the machine-gun killing of the king of Iraq, his family, and his prime minister in 1958, and whom Saddam Hussein had tried to kill the following year. A stenographer took notes as the Special Group discussed setting up a Health Alteration Committee to poison Qasim. "We do not consciously seek subject's permanent removal from the scene; we also do not object should this complication develop," said the CIA's Near East Division chief. After deliberation, the Special Group agreed that the prime minister should be mailed a monogrammed handkerchief laced with poison. For this, the CIA's new deputy director of plans, Richard Bissell, brought the Agency's top poison expert, Sidney Gottlieb, on board. The plan never materialized because Prime Minister Qasim's internal enemies killed him first. "[He] suffered a terminal illness before a firing squad in Baghdad (an event we had nothing to do with)," a Special Group memo sarcastically clarified.

Other assassination plans discussed by the Special Group in 1960 involved Patrice Lumumba, prime minister of Congo. "[We] agree that planning for the Congo would not necessarily rule out 'consideration' of any particular kind of activity which might contribute to getting rid of Lumumba," members agreed on August 25, 1960, a prime example of Special Group circumlocution. Killing Rafael Trujillo, president of the Dominican Republic, was also discussed. But the most intense focus during Eisenhower's last year as president was on eliminating Fidel Castro, Che Guevara, and Raul Castro. In less than a year, these three revolutionaries had emerged from virtual anonymity to establishing a Soviet foothold on the island nation of Cuba, located just ninety miles off the coast of Florida.

"Unless Fidel and Raul Castro and Che Guevara could be eliminated in one package," J. C. King warned the Special Group on March 9, 1960, the situation in Cuba would likely be "a long, drawn-out affair." Admiral Arleigh Burke, chief of naval operations, agreed. "Any plan for the removal of Cuban leaders should be a package deal, since many of the leaders around Castro [are] even worse than Castro." In March the Special Group reached unanimity: "Fidel and Raul Castro and Che Guevara should disappear simultaneously."

In the six years that had passed since Che Guevara witnessed the CIA-directed bombing of Guatemala City, he'd become a hard-core guerrilla fighter and an enterprising revolutionary. After leaving Mexico and secretly arriving in Cuba in 1956, Che Guevara, Fidel Castro, and a band of guerrilla fighters set up a training camp in the Sierra Maestra and began preparing for revolution. Their rebel army numbered between twelve and two hundred men at any given time, and with so few fighters in their ranks, loyalty was everything. This world was black-and-white; you were friend or enemy. If you were enemy, you were targeted and killed.

"Desertion, insubordination and defeatism," wrote Che, were punishable by death. When a rebel fighter named Sergio Acuña was caught trying to run away, he was tortured, shot, and hanged. In his journal Che called the incident "sad but instructive." When Che learned that a guide named Eutímio Guerra had sold information about their group to the Batista regime, he executed him on the spot. "The situation was uncomfortable for the people and for Eutímio so I ended the problem by giving him a shot with a .32 pistol in the right side of the brain," Che wrote in his diary.

After two and a half years of training in the mountains, on January 1, 1959, the rebel fighters began making their move on the capital city. Che Guevara led a column of guerrilla fighters out of the mountains and into Havana, while Fidel Castro and a separate column of revolutionaries marched on the south. By the end of the day, in an astonishing display of giving up without a fight, President Batista's

40,000-man Cuban army laid down their arms en masse. Batista fled to the Dominican Republic, allowing the revolutionaries to assume control. "The tyranny has been overthrown!" Castro declared. "The people won the war!" Fidel Castro was the leader of Cuba now.

Within weeks of taking power, he began executing people perceived to be leftovers from the Batista regime. He named Che Guevara commander of Havana's La Cabaña prison, where war crime tribunals were hastily set up. Those pronounced guilty were lined up against the prison wall and executed by firing squad. In the days that followed the revolution, more than one hundred and fifty pro-Batista Cubans were shot dead. When asked by the foreign press about the summary executions, Che fired back, "To send men to the firing squad, judicial proof is unnecessary." Besides, he said, the concept of justice was a hypocritical creation of Western capitalists. "These procedures are an archaic bourgeois detail," Che insisted, "this is a revolution. . . . A revolutionary must become a cold killing machine, motivated by pure hate."

The executions were about revenge as much as they were about redress, said Raul Castro. In an interview with the Associated Press, he called the men being executed "Batista's assassins" and cited their responsibility for what he said were "6,000 Batista-era assassinations, in Oriente Province alone." Cuba was not experiencing a peaceful transfer of power. There was no swearing-in ceremony; power was being conveyed through bullets, not ballots.

As it was in Vietnam, the CIA was deeply troubled by the majority support these radical revolutionaries garnered from the people. At a rally in Havana on January 21, 1959, Fidel Castro asked an estimated half-million-person crowd if they supported his policy of execution by firing squad. "I am going to ask the people something," Castro announced from his podium. "Those who agree with the justice that is being carried out, those who agree that the [Batista] henchmen should be shot, raise your hands." A sea of hands went up, followed by nearly two minutes of applause. "Batista is our Hitler!"

Castro exclaimed, drawing a comparison between the Nuremberg trials and the executions being overseen by Che. "The allied powers punished the war criminals after the Second World War, and they have less right to do so than we have, because they meted out punishment under the ex post facto legislation, while we are punishing the war criminals under legislation passed before the crime, in public trials, in courts made up of honest men." Castro's background as a lawyer was not lost on the CIA.

In no time, Fidel Castro began severing ties with American businesses, oil consortiums among them, ending fifty years of bilateral trade. He delivered firebrand anti-American speeches, rallying against capitalism and the West. When he signed a deal with the Soviet Union to buy their oil in return for military and economic aid, the Sovietization of Cuba officially began. Che started learning Russian and hosting Marxist study groups. He wrote and published a book, *Guerrilla Warfare,* its title an homage to Chairman Mao's *On Guerrilla Warfare.* Santa Claus was outlawed in Cuba, English no longer allowed. The Chaplin Cinema in downtown Havana was renamed the Carlos Marx.

In Washington, DC, the Eisenhower White House shuddered to think of all that could go wrong. "Castro's Cuba raised the specter of a Soviet outpost at America's doorstep," a Senate report read. The State Department's Bureau of Intelligence and Research, the oldest civilian intelligence element in the U.S. government and a direct descendant of the Office of Strategic Services Research Department, sent its director of the American Republics, a man identified in declassified documents as Mr. Hall, to Cuba to assess the situation. What Mr. Hall discovered and reported back to the State Department laid the seeds for a series of Title 50 hidden-hand operations, including assassination, in Cuba over the next four years.

"The hypnotic hold Fidel has over the mob is frightening," Hall reported. "He can raise it to a bloodthirsty pitch then cool it to an obedient ardor. Hitler was never as good, although it must be admitted he worked on a better educated element," Hall wrote on November 18, 1959. "Fidel gave one the impression of a complete hysteric with a Messianic complex, if not a manic-depressive," he observed. But Mr. Hall expressed an even greater sense of foreboding when speaking of Che. "Che Guevara did not rave nor rant, spoke in the tone of a man who knows what he wants and how to get it and, as the best educated of the lot, is a truly sinister character. All gave us the devil."

What to do? In Mr. Hall's assessment, "[Fidel's] hold on the lower class and on at least half of the middle class is complete. There is an atmosphere of terror prevalent and for all purposes a police state exists in Cuba. People are not only afraid to speak before strangers, but persons disappear as in the time of Batista...." To Mr. Hall's eye, the devil we knew, General Batista, was gone, and the new devils Che and Fidel were far more menacing than previously realized.

Which is when the Special Group began actively discussing the pros and cons of assassinating Fidel Castro, Che Guevara, and Raul Castro, at a meeting on January 23, 1960. The following month, the State Department approved a $4.4 million budget to get rid of the three. "Possible removal of top three leaders is receiving serious consideration at HQS," according to declassified minutes of the meeting. A follow-up memo discussed "arranging an accident." But the State Department's Mr. Hall warned against such action. "The assassination of Fidel would bring about looting and a bloodbath such as Habana [sic] has never known," cautioned Hall. Over the next four months, various means of assassination were considered. Then, in July 1960, Allen Dulles vetoed the idea. Dulles favored a covert action to invade Cuba with an "exile army" and force a coup d'état. Styled after what the CIA had done in Guatemala, this was meant to be a hidden-hand operation. Instead, it would become known to the world as the most inglorious CIA debacle of all time, the failed invasion of Cuba at the Bay of Pigs.

★   ★   ★

The invading paramilitary force would be drawn from anti-Castro refugees living in Miami. After Fidel Castro and Che Guevara took power in 1959, some 100,000 Cuban refugees fled the country, a great majority of them landing in Miami. The U.S. government set up resettlement programs, offering housing and jobs to this new diaspora. The CIA began setting up its hidden-hand operations for Cuba inside a nondescript building on the University of Miami campus, code-named Building 25. For a period of time in the 1960s, the CIA's Miami Station was the largest CIA intelligence operation facility in the world. Case officers assigned to Operation JM/WAVE began keeping track of Cuban émigrés, creating profiles and databases, and ultimately figuring out who best to approach for its forthcoming covert action.

In the summer of 1960, the CIA began recruiting assets from a pool of young anti-Castro dissidents of fighting age to make up a paramilitary force code-named Brigade 2506. What started out as twenty-eight men in a south Florida jungle training camp would eventually grow to more than 1,400 paramilitary operators, spies, saboteurs, and pilots trained by the CIA and U.S. Army Green Berets. One among them was a nineteen-year-old architecture student named Felix Rodriguez.

Well-educated, determined, and nationalistic, Felix Rodriguez was born into a ruling-class family in Sancti Spiritus, in central Cuba, in 1942. When he was twelve, Rodriguez's wealthy Uncle Toto, who served as President Batista's minister of public works, paid for him to attend an American boarding school in Pennsylvania. When the revolution happened in 1959, Felix Rodriguez and his family were vacationing in Mexico. There they received word that the Castro regime had seized their properties and turned them over to the state. The family never returned to Cuba, instead moving to Miami.

Exiled from his homeland, the young Felix Rodriguez became fiercely anti-Castro. His parents begged him to accept what was, he says—to move on and embrace their new situation. They bought him an Aston Martin convertible and enrolled him in the University of Miami. But Felix Rodriguez wanted none of it. "I was more interested in joining an anti-Castro organization than I was in continuing my education," he explains. In the fall of 1960, while preparing to begin freshman classes at the university, he was approached by a clandestine service case officer with the CIA.

"I knew the mission was to overthrow the government of Fidel Castro," Rodriguez explained in 2017. "But I had no idea I was being recruited by the CIA." In those days, he guesses, not one in a thousand Cubans had ever even heard of the Central Intelligence Agency. Rodriguez believed the cover story he and the other recruits were told, that the man paying for the paramilitary action was a wealthy sugar-mill baron whose property in Cuba had also been confiscated by the Castro regime.

Felix Rodriguez was thrilled to be chosen for a commando operation against the Castro regime. In September 1960, he learned the mission was a go. "We were told we were going to a secret location not in the U.S.," Rodriguez recalls. He and a group of young Cuban exiles were driven to an airport in Opa Locka, Florida, the same airport the CIA used for its Guatemala coup d'état. "Our clothes and personal possessions were taken, we were strip-searched to make sure we weren't carrying any forbidden articles, like a compass. Our watches were confiscated so we wouldn't know how long we flew." The truck drove into a closed hangar, where the men disembarked, only to be greeted by U.S. Immigration and Naturalization Services (INS) officials, who gave each of them a form to fill out. It dawned on Rodriguez that "if we were leaving the country, we were apparently doing it with the approval of the U.S. government." Dressed in army fatigues and a khaki shirt, the rebel fighters were loaded onto a C-54 aircraft, its windows painted black, then flown for several hours, landing just before dawn. "After we landed, a jeep drove up and I noticed immediately that it had Guatemalan plates." The CIA's paramilitary army was in Guatemala City as guests of President Roberto Alejos Arzu, a friend of the CIA.

The CIA's anti-Castro covert-action training camp was located eighty miles northwest of Guatemala City, in the countryside of Retalhuleu, code-named Camp Trax. At this abandoned coffee plantation, owned by a business associate of President Arzu, U.S. Army Green Berets trained the Cuban émigrés in guerrilla warfare techniques including pistol shooting, map reading, and hand-to-hand combat but also more ambitious tactics, like how to land an amphibious craft on a rocky beach, and how to use explosives powerful enough to take out a bridge. Conditions were grim, Rodriguez recalls. It was humid beyond measure; poisonous insects and alligators were a constant threat. But morale was high, thanks to the camp's enthusiastic commanding officer, Colonel Napoleón Valeriano.

Colonel Valeriano was an unconventional-warfare legend among commandos in training. As a young army soldier in World War II, Valeriano had been infiltrated into the Philippines by submarine. There, he led guerrilla warfare operations against the Japanese alongside Colonel Volckmann, one of the original founders of the U.S. Army Special Forces, with General Robert McClure and Colonel Aaron Bank. Valeriano's staff of trainers at Camp Trax were Ukrainian-born Green Berets, beneficiaries of the Lodge-Philbin Act, called Lodge-billers, many of whom trained with the 10th Special Forces at Bad Tölz. These Green Berets taught the Cuban exile army how to shoot Thompson submachine guns, 57mm recoilless rifles, and .45-caliber pistols, remembers Rodriguez, an eighteen-year-old novice at the time. They gave us "instructions in explosives, communications, jungle survival, and escape and evasion techniques. We learned how to judge the distance of the enemy from sound and muzzle flash."

Four months into the training, the group was flown to the Panama

Canal Zone, to the U.S. Base, Fort Clayton, for a New Year's Eve party. "Our instructors provided Heineken beer and wine so we could celebrate." Shortly before midnight, Rodriguez remembers being struck with "a truly inspired idea," he explains, "an operation that would shorten the war and save lives." He volunteered to assassinate Fidel Castro. "And the CIA took me up on the idea," he says.

One week later, Felix Rodriguez was flown to Miami, where he was taken to a safe house in the Homestead area outside the city. "I was given a rifle and told to wait." Soon, he'd be infiltrated into Cuba by boat, his handler told him, then taken to Havana, where local partisans working with the CIA would assist him. In Havana, he would go to the upper floor of a predetermined building, set up his high-powered rifle in an open window, and assassinate Fidel Castro as Castro rode by, during a parade on the street below.

While the CIA was training Brigade 2506 for a paramilitary invasion of Cuba, the Special Group approved another covert-action operation inside Cuba's Caribbean island neighbor the Dominican Republic, five hundred miles to the east. The plan was to assassinate the nation's corrupt unelected leader, General Rafael Trujillo.

For three decades Trujillo, kept in power by American allies, had ruled the country by terror. Trujillo was power-mad and masochistic. Historians hold him responsible for tens of thousands of extrajudicial killings, including those in 1937 in the border region with Haiti, which would come to be known as the Parsley Massacre. "Few bullets were used," according to a UN Security Council report on the mass killing. "Instead, 20,000–30,000 Haitians were bludgeoned and bayonetted, then herded into the sea, where sharks finished what Trujillo had begun." For reasons that remain murky, suddenly in winter of 1960 President Eisenhower's Special Group decided the United States would end its support of Trujillo. Ambassador Joseph Farland remembers appealing to Trujillo's daughter Flor, during a visit to her home outside the nation's capital. "I drove out to her house in a Volkswagen that I had and said...your father is going to be assassinated. There is no question in my mind whatsoever about that...we want him to retire and leave this country." When Trujillo refused an offer of exile, the Special Group agreed it was time to eliminate him.

"He kept law and order...and he didn't bother the United States. So that was fine with us," said the State Department's Henry Dearborn, in a 1991 oral history interview. Dearborn served as chargé d'affaires at the embassy in Santo Domingo, which had been renamed Ciudad Trujillo, or Trujillo City. "Something had to be done about this man," Dearborn recalled. On March 16, 1961, "matters took an active turn," according to a CIA document marked Top Secret, later reviewed by a Senate Intelligence Committee. "They [the CIA] developed an assassination plot which, because of my close relationship with them, I was fully aware of," Dearborn testified.

Dearborn served as liaison between the CIA and the assassination team, which was made up of seven anti-Trujillo partisans. "I carried out the contacts with the opposition reporting to CIA," Dearborn clarified. "We were using all these weird means of communication because we didn't want to be seen with each other. Things like notes in the bottom of the grocery bag, rolled up in cigars."

Richard Bissell, then working as CIA station chief in Santo Domingo, oversaw plans on the ground. On March 22, he requested that headquarters send him "three .38 calibre revolvers and ammunition." In a separate cable, Dearborn wrote, "Plans for Trujillo's assassination coming to a head." The following week, Bissell briefed Dearborn: a shipment of four machine guns and 240 rounds of ammunition was en route to the U.S. embassy, which he was to give to the assassins in a clandestine manner. Separately, three carbine rifles were being dropped off at the U.S. embassy by a navy contact, Bissell said. Dearborn kept the assassins in the loop through a liaison, or cutout, so as to ensure he never had direct contact with the killers. "I had a different typewriter on which I typed out my messages to the opposition so that it wouldn't be traced to Embassy typewriters," Dearborn recalled, but in truth, "I had told the [State] Department via CIA communications...all about the plan."

Dearborn's job was to maintain plausible deniability should anything go wrong. "I knew how they were planning to do it, I knew, more or less, who was involved. Although I was always able to say that I personally did not know any of the assassins, I knew those who were pulling the strings." Until then, he had a facade of diplomacy to uphold. "There had to be a certain set of circumstances when they could put their plan into action." For now, he was ordered to wait.

Meanwhile, in Miami, the lethal covert-action operation in which Felix Rodriguez would assassinate Fidel Castro was given the green light. It was the second week in January 1961, Rodriguez recalls, "just days before John F. Kennedy took office as president." Late one night, a handler picked up Felix Rodriguez from the safe house outside Miami where he'd been staying. Rifle case in hand, he was driven to a small beach in the Florida Keys. "The driver flashed the lights and a small boat came ashore," he recalls. Rodriguez climbed into a small rubber boat that ferried him out to a much larger yacht waiting about a half mile out at sea.

"The captain was an American," Rodriguez remembers, "but the crew were all Ukrainians. Tough-looking SOBs who carried Soviet bloc automatic weapons." Back at the safe house, Rodriguez was told he wouldn't have to sight the rifle when he arrived in Cuba. "It had already been zeroed in. The resistance army [in Cuba] had obtained a building in Havana, facing a location that Castro frequented at the time, and they'd managed to presight the rifle," says Rodriguez.

Under the cover of night, the yacht sped across the ocean to infiltrate Cuba near Varadero Beach on the north coast. "We showed up at a predetermined location," recalls Rodriguez, but the rendezvous boat failed to show and the group returned to Miami. Days later, another attempt was made. Arriving at the target area this second time, Rodriguez recalls seeing a hundred-foot-long ship, "clearly far too large for a clandestine op. It looked like a ghost ship. We couldn't see anybody on board."

The group aborted the mission a second time and again returned to Miami. On a third infiltration attempt, the yacht suffered hydraulic failure. Back in Miami the vessel was met by a case officer who asked Felix Rodriguez for the rifle and ammunition. "They said they'd changed their minds about the mission," Rodriguez recalls.

In Washington, DC, President Eisenhower and his staff prepared to leave the White House. The baton would now pass to the handsome young senator from Massachusetts, John F. Kennedy. The day before Kennedy's inauguration, he met with President Eisenhower in the Oval Office. Partially declassified records from this meeting, on January 19, 1961, indicate that the outgoing and incoming presidents discussed the most critical covert-action operations being planned by the Special Group: in Cuba, Vietnam, and Laos. The incoming president was struck by the idea of covert action — of a hidden-hand power to be wielded at the sole discretion of the commander in chief. One of his first actions as president was to meet with the Special Group to learn more.

Just eight days after taking office, the CIA's Edward Lansdale briefed President Kennedy on the dire situation in Vietnam. Ho Chi Minh and General Giap's mobile warfare campaign was as aggressive as it was ruthless, assassinating an average of eleven civil servants every day. "Vietnam is in a critical condition and [we] should treat it as a combat area of the Cold War, as an area requiring emergency treatment," Lansdale told the president.

Kennedy appealed directly to Congress, bringing to its attention the assassination campaign. In a speech called "Urgent National Needs," he warned of Soviet hidden-hand operations in Vietnam and elsewhere, of the existential threat communism posed to the free world.

"Their aggression is more often concealed than open," Kennedy said. "They have fired no missiles; and their troops are seldom seen. They send arms, agitators, aid, technicians and propaganda to every troubled area. But where fighting is required, it is usually done by others—by guerrillas striking at night, by assassins striking alone—assassins who have taken the lives of four thousand civil officers in the last twelve months in Vietnam alone."

Vietnam, Laos, Cuba. President Kennedy inherited complex hidden-hand operations in each of these three tiny countries from his predecessor. He also inherited President Eisenhower's Special Group, to which he quickly added his brother, U.S. attorney general Robert F. Kennedy. It was an unusual arrangement, with far-reaching consequences. As chairman of the Special Group, Attorney General Robert Kennedy—the most senior Justice Department official in the United States—was now in charge of overseeing the CIA's covert operations, most of which the majority of Americans would consider illegal. Assassination was at the top of the list.

PART II
1961

CHAPTER TEN

An Assassination Capability

O n the morning of February 24, 1961, in the residential Miramar district of Havana, Che Guevara left his home on Eigh-
teenth Street and walked with his bodyguards down the
pretty, tree-lined street, headed to his car. As he climbed in the
driver's seat, four or five assassins emerged from where they'd been
hiding in the bushes and opened fire. A violent gun battle left one of
Che's neighbors, a man identified as Mr. Salinas, dead in his car. As
Che sped away, his bodyguards continued firing. Inside the house,
Che's wife, Aleida, heard the intense gunfire. She grabbed their
three-month-old daughter, Aledita, and with their nanny rushed to
hide under the stairwell.

In Havana, there was a news blackout on the attempted assassination. (Aleida Guevara kept the story secret for thirty years, sharing
it with Che's biographer, Jon Lee Anderson, after she left Cuba for
Spain to live in exile.) Because Cuba is a police state, very little
unflattering news ever leaves the island. That such an important
leader as Che Guevara would be vulnerable to assassination was not
a message the Castro regime wanted to convey. Instead, a semioffi-
cial cover story emerged, purporting that the dead man, Mr. Salinas,
had been having an affair and that the killing was an illicit romance
gone awry. In a country where possession of an illegal firearm was a

capital offense, the cover story seems implausible. Was the CIA involved? Or were the assassins really anti-Castro Cubans acting on their own? Further news was repressed, not surprising given Che Guevara's views of the press. "Newspapers are instruments of the oligarchy," he told the Cuban people. "We must eliminate all newspapers; we cannot make a revolution with free press." As of 2019, the mystery remains unsolved. But in response to the assassination attempt against him, Che Guevara is said to have kept a grenade in the cigar box he often carried.

After three failed attempts to assassinate Fidel Castro, in late January or early February 1961, Felix Rodriguez was reassigned to the CIA's Brigade 2506. He was emplaced on a five-man direct-action paramilitary team called a Gray Team. The Gray Teams would be infiltrated into Cuba in advance of an assault by Brigade 2506, at Bahía de Cochinos, the Bay of Pigs. Assassination plans aside, the CIA was now moving forward with a covert-action amphibious invasion followed by a coup d'état.

The CIA was relying on its Gray Teams to locate, train, and equip pockets of previously identified resistance fighters, similar to what the OSS Jedburghs had done shortly after Allied forces stormed the beaches at Normandy. But in France, ninety-three Jedburgh teams had been air-dropped in behind enemy lines. In Cuba there were just seven teams, each made up of five men. "It was high-risk," Rodriguez remembers. "Thirty-five [of us] went to Cuba, only fifteen survived."

On February 28, 1961, Rodriguez and the members of his Gray Team left an isolated beach in Key West bound for Cuba. This time, instead of a yacht they rode in a twenty-five-foot Zodiac boat, "filled to the gunwales with weapons and explosives." Four and a half hours later, the team made a stealth beach landing at Arcos de Canasi, forty miles east of Havana. It was Rodriguez's first time back to Cuba since he was a schoolboy. "We had our weapons and backpacks but we also had to land two tons of equipment, explosives, grenades, machine guns, ammunition, and communications equipment." To be caught likely meant summary execution. Rodriguez and his Gray Team members were met on the beach by anti-Castro partisans, local farmers and sugar mill workers who were members of a group called Movimiento de Recuperación Revolucionaria (MRR), a pro-U.S. resistance movement. The MRR had already been partially armed; CIA Air Branch pilots had managed to covertly air-drop bundles of World War II–era M3 submachine guns and .45 pistols. (In addition to the CIA's Ground Branch, there is Air Branch, which is the aviation wing of the Special Activities Division, and Maritime Branch, for amphibious operations. There's also a political action arm, which interfaces with all three branches.)

From the beachhead at Arcos de Canasi, Felix Rodriguez was driven to Camaguey, where he met with the head of the Cuban resistance, a young man who went by the code name Francisco. "Seeing him on the street, you'd mistake him for a student," recalls Rodriguez. Francisco was an eloquent, soft-spoken engineering student. "He naturally inspired people," Rodriguez said. The popularity of Francisco's movement made him the number-one target of Castro's intelligence services, and meeting with him was a tense affair.

Over the next few weeks, Felix Rodriguez moved from safe house to safe house around Havana, meeting individually with leaders of the underground. In mid-March, he was called back to Miami to resupply. There he was told that he'd be reinserted again soon. The invasion would be happening any day now.

Finally word came. "I was driven to the Keys by a lanky Texan who went by the code name Sherman," Rodriguez recalls. "He presented me with something special to take to Cuba. A mini-flamethrower. It fit very comfortably in one hand, yet it threw a fifteen-foot-wide column of white phosphorous flame." The Texan told Rodriguez that the weapon was highly classified, "but he wanted me to have it anyway." This time he was inserted near

Morón, on the central coast. There, he was met by another member of the underground and driven to Havana in an old Buick, "the flamethrower hidden underneath the dashboard." Rodriguez was dropped off at a safe house in El Vedado, and told to lay low and await orders.

In its Bay of Pigs invasion planning, the CIA pulled yet again from its own history, as we have seen. Modeling the invasion and coup on the Guatemala operation was ironic, given that those operations had radicalized Che Guevara. But Cuba in 1961 was a very different environment in which to operate than Guatemala had been in 1954. President Arbenz commanded an army of 10,000 men. Fidel Castro allegedly had a million soldiers on call. Arbenz, a socialist, did not run Guatemala as a military dictatorship; Castro controlled the people of Cuba with absolute power, using Soviet tactics of repression and fear. Most significant of all, Arbenz did not have a direct line to the Kremlin the way Castro did. In hindsight, the CIA's disastrous covert-action Bay of Pigs operation was born of wishful thinking.

As with all military dictatorships, spies in Cuba were ubiquitous. For the CIA, the threat of a double agent was a constant source of concern. Unknown to the Agency, Castro had managed to infiltrate its ranks long before the invasion was given the green light. In Miami, the CIA had recruited Benigno Pérez Vivancos, a former lieutenant in Castro's army, thinking he was an anti-Castro émigré. Vivancos stood out as brave and reliable and became the seventy-eighth fighting-age male recruited for Brigade 2506. In fact, he was a Castro loyalist, sent by Havana to spy.

The actions of this double agent proved deadly. On the night of April 1, 1961, not long after Felix Rodriguez arrived in Havana with his mini-flamethrower, Castro's G-2 intelligence conducted a raid on a house outside Havana and captured Francisco, whose real name was Rogelio Gonzalez Corso. Tried and found guilty, he was immediately executed. Based on information provided by Vivancos, Castro's government rounded up thousands of people it identified as possible members of the resistance. "[Castro] herded them into theaters, stadiums and military bases to squelch the possibility of a spontaneous uprising to overthrow his regime," says a CIA inspector general report.

Unaware of the compromise, Rodriguez waited for word of the invasion. On April 13, at CIA headquarters, Brigade 2506 was given the green light to set sail from Guatemala. On the morning of April 15, eight B-26 bombers, supplied by the CIA and flown by Cuban émigré pilots, attacked military airfields in Cuba in the first move of the covert operation. In response, Castro played an ingenious and unforeseen political card: he ordered his foreign minister, Raul Roa, to call the United Nations Political and Security Committee, in New York City, and demand that an emergency session be held. The request was honored, the session attended by the U.S. ambassador to the United Nations, Adlai Stevenson. Cuba's foreign minister rightly decried the United States for having attacked a sovereign nation unprovoked. "This was bad news for President Kennedy whose number one priority was hiding the hand of the U.S. Government," lamented an anonymous CIA staff historian in an Agency report, kept classified for decades. "Lying to the UN had serious consequences and a second [air] strike would put the United States in an awkward position internationally." The result meant disaster for Brigade 2506. President Kennedy's "political considerations trumped the military importance of a 'D-Day' air strike."

Without a second strike, the amphibious assault had no chance for success. And the element of surprise was no longer there. Shortly before dawn the following morning, with Brigade 2506 just hours away from landing at the Bay of Pigs, President Kennedy canceled the second round of air strikes. Pilots who'd been sitting on the runway awaiting orders for takeoff were told to stand down. As the sun rose on the morning of April 17, 1,311 members of Brigade 2506 made an amphibious landing. But instead of accomplishing a stealth infiltration, the CIA's paramilitary army of Cuban exiles were met on shore by Castro's military, whose forces far outnumbered and outgunned them.

In Havana, Felix Rodriguez learned about the Bay of Pigs invasion while listening to the radio. "All the Cuban radio stations were broadcasting the same emergency network," he remembers, saying the same thing: that the Americans had tried to launch a coup d'état and had failed. Peering out the window, Rodriguez watched in horror as a sea of military vehicles moved through the streets, each one overflowing with Castro's soldiers. On Cuban state TV, news footage showed members of Brigade 2506 as they were captured on the beach and marched off into the woods, their fates unknown.

Four members of Felix Rodriguez's Gray Team were picked up and arrested. Rodriguez fled the safe house and made a run for the Venezuelan embassy. He was aware of a treaty that allowed political refugees safe passage out of Cuba. After weeks of hiding inside the embassy, he was finally loaded onto a bus of refugees and driven to the airport. In a bitter twist of fate, the bus drove first through Miramar, passing Che Guevara's home on Seventeenth Street, where, two months earlier, the assassination attempt against him had failed. It continued on past Uncle Toto's once grand home, on Fifth Avenue and Twenty-Eighth Street, where Felix had enjoyed so many happy childhood memories. "It had been turned over to the state," says Rodriguez. Like all private property, it would be divided up among the people. "Later I would learn five Soviet families were living there," he recalls.

The Bay of Pigs was an extraordinary political embarrassment for President Kennedy. In the Dominican Republic, Consul General Henry Dearborn, the U.S. State Department's chargé d'affaires at the embassy in Santo Domingo, was woken in the middle of the night and told to cancel the CIA's plan to assassinate Trujillo. "I recall a frantic message from the [State] Department, I guess signed off on by President Kennedy," Dearborn remembered in 1991. It was "saying, in effect, 'Look, we have all this trouble with Castro; we don't want any more trouble in the Caribbean. Tell these people to knock it off'"—meaning the assassination plot. Dearborn followed orders, he says. "I communicated to the opposition people that Washington was very much against any attempt at assassination. The answer I got back from them was, 'Just tell Washington it is none of their business. This is our business. We have planned it and we are going to do it and there is nothing you can do about it.' I relayed this to Washington," said Dearborn.

The plan to assassinate Trujillo went ahead despite Washington's eleventh-hour attempts to call it off. On the night of May 30, 1961, Trujillo was seated in the backseat of his chauffeur-driven 1957 Chevrolet Bel Air, traveling down a country road outside the capital, when he was ambushed by a group of seven assassins brandishing weapons provided to the rebel group by the CIA. "We started shooting," recalled one of the killers, General Antonio Imbert, in an interview with the BBC in 2011. President Trujillo and his chauffeur were both armed, and they began shooting back. Trujillo managed to get out of the car. "Trujillo was wounded but he was still walking, so I shot him again" and killed him, said General Imbert. "We put him in [our] car and took him away." The assassins drove the dictator's dead body to a safe house belonging to the partisans, where it was later discovered by state police.

Dearborn remembered hearing the news. He was out in the suburbs, at a country club. "The Chinese Ambassador was giving some kind of a money raising thing [for] charity, to which I went." After the event ended, Dearborn and a colleague left together in a State Department car. "We started back around 11:00 p.m. and ran into a roadblock along the ocean highway." The state police were stopping cars and conducting searches. "They looked in trunks, pulled up rugs, etc. I had a CIA fellow in the car—along about January the CIA had sent a couple of people into the consulate—and I said, 'Bob, this is it. I am sure this is it.'" The state police wouldn't let the men continue down that road. "When we [finally] got to the

Embassy, where I had been living for about a year, the telephone rang and one of my main contacts of the opposition said, 'It is over, he is dead.' I knew immediately what happened and went down to the office and sent off a message to Washington."

For the CIA, the assassination of President Trujillo had been an inadvertent success. The killers got away, although they were soon to be betrayed by co-conspirator General José Román. Hundreds of people suspected of being complicit in Trujillo's assassination were rounded up, detained, and tortured, in a move that echoed what happened in Czechoslovakia after Reinhard Heydrich's assassination by the British Special Operations Executive. Six of the seven Trujillo assassins were caught and executed. Only General Antonio Imbert got away. Decades later, the consensus in the Dominican Republic is that killing Trujillo was a heroic act, a textbook example of tyrannicide, the justified killing of a tyrant. "We Dominicans react very negatively when the people who killed Trujillo are called assassins," says Bernardo Vega, a former ambassador to the United States. Killing the cruelest dictator in the Americas, says Vega, "was a good thing to do."

The week after General Trujillo was buried, the U.S. State Department's Henry Dearborn was notified of a plan for his assassination. Dearborn was ordered to pack up his things, drive to the airport, and leave at once. He hurried to his office and loaded all the secret files into a burn barrel to destroy. Now, in good conscience, he said, he could leave. In a State Department oral history, he relayed "a funny incident" that drew to a close his three years as America's top diplomat in the Dominican Republic. "I had my shirt, tie, shoes and socks on but couldn't find my pants," he remembered. "I said [to my administrative assistant], an officer's wife, 'where are my pants?' She said, 'Oh, my god, I packed them.' [She] had to go back down to the car outside and unpack my pants so that I could leave the country with dignity."

Upon landing in the United States, Dearborn was called to

Washington, DC, to participate in a briefing of the president of the United States. John F. Kennedy, himself intensely interested in covert action, had asked to be briefed on the Trujillo assassination by those involved. In declassified Senate testimony, Dearborn later recalled, "One enlightening part of the discussion occurred when I interrupted [Kennedy] and said: 'I think that—.' The President interrupted me and said, 'We already know what you think.'" In his oral history, Dearborn made clear what President Kennedy's statement meant to him. "That showed clearly enough that he had been reading my cables," Dearborn said.

Dearborn's remembrance is notable given an official Department of Justice summation "with respect to Trujillo's assassination." In giving testimony for the attorney general's official report—that would be Attorney General Robert Kennedy, chairman of the Special Group—the CIA officials who were interviewed stated that they had "no active part but had a faint connection with the groups that in fact did [assassinate]" the president. Henry Dearborn knew otherwise. "When the meeting [with the president] broke up he shook hands with me and said, 'You did a good job down there.'"

Dearborn stood by his actions and those taken by the president's Special Group advisors, the State Department, and the CIA. "It is my firmly held view that those who killed Trujillo and those who backed them up would have acted if there had never been a CIA. They were only waiting for a favorable domestic and international atmosphere to give them the required courage," Dearborn stated on the record, in 1991. He died in 2013, at the age of one hundred.

Shortly after Rafael Trujillo was assassinated, President Kennedy's Special Group formalized assassination as a foreign policy tool—a program it called Executive Action Capability but which Congress later determined was "an assassination capability." Declassified testimony given to Senate investigators by CIA deputy director of plans Richard Bissell suggests that the person who authorized the assassination capability was President Kennedy. The Special Group (Augmented) had received its "orders from National Security Advisor McGeorge Bundy and [Deputy National Security Advisor] Walt Rostow," Bissell told Senate investigators behind closed doors, but these presidential advisors "would not have given such encouragement unless they were confident that it would meet with the President's approval."

Moving forward under the Kennedy administration, assassination operations acquired new euphemisms, including "direct positive action," "neutralization operations," "an accident plot," and "the last resort." Under the impossibly unsubtle cryptonym ZR/RIFLE, the CIA's Executive Action Office was staffed with an array of people, from senior managers to case officers, even a "principal agent with the primary task of spotting agent candidates," operatives willing to carry out "and to conceal the 'executive action capability.'" The CIA's Technical Services Division provided covert-action operators with whatever items they might need, from disguises to weapons to poisons. The Directorate of Support handled financial and administrative matters. The Office of Security made sure overseas clandestine facilities remained secure.

"Assassination was [now] an acceptable course of action," Congress learned, made possible through the establishment of plausible deniability: "The chairman of the Special Group was usually responsible for determining which projects required presidential consideration and for keeping him abreast of developments." According to Bissell, after President Kennedy appointed his brother chairman of the Special Group (Augmented), the construct became almost impenetrable. In this way, a system of "plausible denial" was fortified, said Bissell, a series of obfuscations that "served as 'circuit breakers' for presidents," preventing the Oval Office from being dragged into a scandal should a hidden-hand operation be revealed.

The president's assassination capability was intended to serve as a means of bringing order to the increasingly volatile situations unfolding in Cuba, Laos, and Vietnam. Instead it created mayhem, chaos, and collapse. But the real question, the riddle wrapped inside a mystery inside an enigma, was and remains: By allowing the use of assassination as a hidden-hand foreign policy tool, did President Kennedy become an easier target to assassinate?

CHAPTER ELEVEN

JFK, KIA

President John F. Kennedy was outraged with the CIA over the failure at the Bay of Pigs, which stained his first one hundred days as president. He'd campaigned on an anticommunist plank, singling out Cuba as a "hostile and militant communist satellite [receiving] guidance, support and arms from Moscow and Peking." To have failed so publicly, so early in his presidency, infuriated him.

Adding insult to injury, Che Guevara personally expressed his gratitude to the young president for the spectacular defeat, using White House emissary Richard Goodwin to relay his sarcastic message. "Guevara said...he wanted to thank us very much for the invasion," Goodwin told the president, "that it had been a great political victory for them—enabled them to consolidate—and transform [Cuba] from an aggrieved little country to an equal."

In response, President Kennedy made a move so shocking it upended covert-action operations in a way not seen since the creation of Title 50 and National Security Council Directive 10/2 (NSC 10/2). He gutted the existing paramilitary authority at the CIA, making "any large paramilitary operation [that was] wholly or partially covert [now] the primary responsibility of the Defense Department, with CIA in a supporting role."

"The fiasco at the Bay of Pigs...changed everything," says CIA staff historian John L. Helgerson. CIA director Allen Dulles asked to meet with the president, who refused. The president's mind was made up. "There [is] no point in the DCI [Director of Central Intelligence] discussing the matter directly with the President as that would be counterproductive," presidential advisor General Chester Clifton curtly informed the CIA. For the first time since 1947, the Pentagon was now in charge of the president's guerrilla warfare corps. "I can't overemphasize the shock—not simply the words—that procedure caused in Washington: to the Secretary of State, to the Secretary of Defense, and particularly to the Director of Central Intelligence," said Colonel L. Fletcher Prouty, chief of special operations for the Joint Chiefs of Staff under Kennedy. "Historians have glossed over that or don't know about it," Prouty said in 1989.

Kennedy lost the battle for a democratic Cuba in a most humiliating and public way. Now he was unwilling to experience a loss in Vietnam. It wasn't that the new president opposed hidden-hand paramilitary operations; he opposed the CIA's handling of them. In a series of meetings with his national-security advisors, he ordered covert-action operations to be accelerated in Vietnam, only now they would be led by U.S. Army Special Forces. This maverick move would have far-reaching consequences—not just in Vietnam but around the world, and not just in 1961 but for decades to come. By their very definition, paramilitary operations exist outside formal military operations (*para* means "distinct from"). To have the Defense Department now engaging in nonofficial military operations inside a foreign country during peacetime was a radical move into uncharted territory.

Immediately after the Bay of Pigs, President Kennedy asked top advisor General Maxwell Taylor to review all U.S. paramilitary capabilities and advise on next steps. Taylor submitted a report recommending that the president broaden the scope of classified covert operations in Vietnam. Kennedy authorized three Top Secret National Security Action Memorandums in succession, significantly widening a war that technically did not exist. To oversee operations in theater, the Joint Chiefs of Staff created a new office inside the Pentagon called the Special Assistant for Counterinsurgency and Special Activities (SACSA), to be run by a military general and his staff. SACSA would now function as the CIA's Office of Policy Coordination had during Korea. The man chosen to run SACSA was a marine corps general named Victor "Brute" Krulak.

A legend among his men, Brute Krulak was famous at the Pentagon for the risky, nighttime amphibious raids he'd led on islands across the Pacific during World War II. On one of these raids, he was leading thirty commandos on an ambush when their vessel hit a reef and began to sink. Facing certain death, they were rescued by a torpedo boat crew commanded by a young lieutenant named John F. Kennedy. The president and the general had history, and now Krulak was entrusted with a highly classified, highly unorthodox new job at the Department of Defense: to oversee quasi-military operations inside a sovereign nation against a belligerent force of guerrilla fighters, without a formal declaration of war. One of SACSA's first questions was, what to do about Laos?

President Eisenhower left John F. Kennedy with a muddled, complicated, and intractable situation in Laos. Laos was a victim of geography, Kennedy's Special Group advisors told him. "Hardly a nation except in the legal sense." But to lose Laos would be "the beginning of the loss of most of the Far East," Eisenhower forewarned. In an effort to contain the communist insurgency within Vietnam's borders, President Kennedy decided to pursue diplomacy in Laos. He canceled Operation White Star and instructed his advisors to negotiate a neutralization treaty. In July 1962, the governments of the United States, the Soviet Union, North Vietnam, and numerous other nations all signed the Declaration on the Neutrality of Laos, agreeing to leave Laos alone. "They all did," says scholar Richard Shultz, "except for the NVA," the army of North Vietnam. Insurgents do not honor borders or treaties. This reality continues to plague the Defense Department in 2019.

The Laos neutralization treaty of 1962 was a colossal deception, and a huge strategic win for North Vietnam. By the time the treaty was signed, Hanoi had already spent three long years building a clandestine transportation route and logistical system from Hanoi through Laos and into the south. Eventually, it also would include trails through Cambodia. This was the Ho Chi Minh Trail, the secret supply route Hanoi used to move fighters and weapons into territory it sought to control in the south. While the United States felt bound by honor to adhere to the neutrality declaration, Hanoi escalated its prohibited use of the trail. This gave the communists extraordinary momentum and new advantage at a critical time in their revolution.

Blind to the realities of the trail, the month after the Laos treaty was signed Secretary of Defense Robert McNamara called a meeting in Honolulu, Hawaii, bringing together the Defense Department, the Pacific Command, the CIA, and the State Department. McNamara presented Operation Switchback, a robust covert-action program designed to "inflict increasing punishment upon North Vietnam." One of the first orders of business was to create a new guerrilla warfare corps for the president, to carry out the punishment promised by the secretary of defense.

Now in a subordinate role, the CIA merged its existing paramilitary program, the Civilian Irregular Defense Group (CIDG), into the Defense Department's Military Assistance Command, Vietnam (MACV). Billy Waugh was an early member of the group and became one of the first Green Berets sent to Vietnam in this capacity. Waugh's group trained President Diem's soldiers in paramilitary tactics, "in everything from sabotage and assassination, to evade and escape," Waugh recalls.

The goal of the CIDG program was to create direct-action strike-force units made up of South Vietnamese peasants from indigenous hill tribes led by U.S. Army Green Berets and CIA advisors. This was a grander, more ambitious version of what the OSS Special Operations groups, including the Jedburghs, had accomplished during World War II. Waugh and his fellow trainers were to arm the rebels and teach them how to sabotage, subvert, and assassinate the communist infiltrators coming down from the north.

The effort was astonishing. Unlike the CIA, whose access to military resources had been limited, SACSA had the Defense Department to call upon, with its resupply capacity that seemed to know no bounds. Through a CIDG support office on Okinawa, warfighting supplies were air-dropped into Vietnam by the ton. Each month an average of 740 tons of weapons and supplies were delivered to Special Forces units set up in remote villages across South Vietnam. By the end of 1962 there were over 33,300 South Vietnamese peasants being paid by the Defense Department to participate in the CIDG program. Assigned American military–style titles, the participants were broken down by number: 6,000 Direct Action Strike Force Troops; 19,000 Village Defender Militia; 2,700 Mountain Scouts; 5,300 Popular Forces troops, and 300 Border Surveillance guards. Twelve months later, the number skyrocketed again. There were now more than 87,000 peasants on U.S. taxpayer payroll. But the program was grossly ineffective. When the NVA and Vietcong attacked a village, the strike force just ran away.

"This is not to say that they were afraid," wrote Colonel Francis J. Kelly, an unconventional-warfare expert for the Pentagon and the man who later commanded all Special Forces in Vietnam. "Most had seen a great deal of fighting. They were just not interested in, or even remotely enthusiastic about, the program. From the point of view of the Vietnam Special Forces and the government the CIDG program was an American project."

For Ngo Dinh Diem, the American-supported president of South Vietnam, what was happening in remote areas of the country meant very little. His own situation in Saigon had become dire. The Americans were beginning to lose faith in his leadership, and his military generals were plotting to overthrow him. The people of South Vietnam hated him. He persecuted Buddhists and liberal democrats in equal measure, arresting monks and nightclub owners, banning boxing matches and beauty pageants. He could barely control the unrest that was building in the cities, in Saigon and Hue. When people gathered to protest, Diem dispatched military police to beat them into submission.

By the spring of 1963, Diem's presidency was on the brink of collapse. The Kennedy White House now viewed the colonialist in the white three-piece suit as a losing horse. The only person in South Vietnam more hated than President Diem was his brother Ngo Dinh Nhu, chief of the secret police and commander of army special forces. In a last-ditch effort to salvage Diem's presidency, the White House wondered if perhaps the real problem wasn't Nhu. Through State Department channels, President Diem was told to consider getting rid of his brother. Word came back: never.

The tipping point came in June 1963 when, in protest of Diem's policies, a Buddhist monk named Thich Quang Duc set himself on fire in the middle of a busy Saigon street. The self-immolation was photographed, and the image of a human being on fire was reprinted in newspapers around the world. While the international community was shocked by the horror and tragedy of the monk's self-sacrifice, the Diem regime publicly mocked him. This led to what would become known as the Buddhist uprisings. In August 1963, after Diem declared martial law, the White House decided that it would no longer support President Diem.

The CIA dispatched Lieutenant Colonel Lucien Conein to gather intelligence. Conein served the CIA as the Saigon station liaison between Henry Cabot Lodge, then serving as U.S. ambassador to Vietnam, and South Vietnam's top military generals, a job Conein did well owing to a unique history with several of Diem's generals.

Back in 1945, the French-speaking Conein served as a member of the OSS Deer Team, the American group that armed and trained Ho Chi Minh, General Giap, and several hundred of their Viet Minh guerrilla fighters. During that time period Conein befriended many young Vietnamese officers, some of whom now served as generals under President Diem. In an effort to determine what was happening at the palace, Conein met with several of Diem's generals, using a dentist's office for these clandestine meetings.

Conein learned that the generals were planning to overthrow President Diem. The leader of the insurrection was General Duong Van Minh—"Big Minh," as he was known. Conein relayed this information to the president and his advisors. In turn, Conein was told to tell the generals that the White House supported this idea. "[We] will not attempt to thwart" this action, President Kennedy told Conein, trying to sound officially uninvolved.

On the morning of November 1, 1963, Lucien Conein awoke, changed into his military uniform, and prepared himself for the coup d'état that was about to begin. He tucked an ivory-handled .375 magnum revolver into his waist and filled a bag, meant for Big Minh, with three million Vietnamese piastres, roughly $40,000, in cash. Years later, Senate investigators asked Conein if he knew that the generals he was giving this money to planned on killing President Diem. "The majority of the officers... desired President Diem to have an honorable retirement," Conein swore. Regarding his brother and other powerful figures in the regime, "the attitude was that their deaths... would be welcomed."

With Green Berets guarding his family, Conein picked up a secure telephone given to him by Big Minh and called the CIA with a secret code: "nine, nine, nine, nine, nine..." The coup d'état against President Diem was about to begin. Conein kissed his wife and children good-bye, climbed into an army jeep waiting in the driveway, and headed off to headquarters, near the airport.

At 1:30 p.m., scores of Big Minh loyalists burst into army offices, police headquarters, and radio stations around Saigon, holding people at gunpoint and informing them that if they resisted they'd be shot. Military trucks loaded with artillery surrounded the palace. President Diem and his brother slipped out the back and disappeared. Diem's loyal bodyguards had no idea that their president had fled, and dozens of these men died defending the palace and Diem's honor. By 3:00 a.m. the palace was overrun, and soon looters were running through the streets with President Diem's possessions: gilded furniture, fine whiskey, American adventure magazines.

At 6:00 a.m. President Diem reached out to Big Minh from inside the Catholic church in Cholon where he and his brother were hiding. Diem offered to surrender, provided he was given the full honors due a departing president. When Big Minh refused, Diem settled for unconditional surrender and gave up his location at the church. Big Minh dispatched an American-made M113 armored personnel carrier and four jeeps filled with soldiers to retrieve the deposed president and his brother.

On the drive back to the palace, alongside a train crossing, Diem and Nhu were executed, shot with automatic weapons inside the armored vehicle. Their bullet-riddled bodies were photographed and then buried in an unmarked grave adjacent to the Saigon residence of U.S. ambassador Henry Cabot Lodge.

For all the euphemism and convoluted language behind and around President Kennedy's assassination program, there was absolutely nothing vague or indirect about the assassination that took place just three weeks later, on November 22, 1963, in Dallas, Texas. From the perspective of U.S. Secret Service agent Clinton J. Hill, killing a leader is a visceral and sickening reality.

Clint Hill, age thirty-two, had been on the Presidential Protective Detail since the Eisenhower administration, when he guarded the president's mother-in-law, Elivera Mathilda Carlson Doud. During the Kennedy White House he served as the special agent in charge of Jacqueline Kennedy, overseeing her safety at all times. On this day in Dallas, the president had made a protocol change. He didn't want Secret Service agents, including Clint Hill, to be standing on the running boards of the open-topped presidential limousine. Instead, Hill was now riding in a car directly behind the president and Mrs. Kennedy. He had weapons at the ready: a pistol at his waist, an AR-15 automatic rifle on the seat beside him, and a shotgun in the compartment near the jump seats.

When the first shot rang out, Clint Hill leapt out of the vehicle he was traveling in and ran to the president's limousine, using the rear running board to climb onto the trunk area and reach for Mrs. Kennedy, who was reaching out to him. He watched as the president grabbed his throat and lurched forward. A second shot rang out, blasting off a portion of the president's head.

As Clint Hill covered Mrs. Kennedy with his body, he observed the president. "The right rear portion of his head was missing. It was lying in the rear seat of the car. His brain was exposed. There was blood and bits of brain all over the entire rear portion of the car," Hill told the Warren Commission.

As the limousine raced to the hospital, a sobbing Mrs. Kennedy tried to make sense of the carnage.

"My God, they have shot his head off," she told Clint Hill. Then, to her dead husband, she implored, sobbing: "Jack, Jack, what have they done to you?"

At the hospital, doctors determined that a piece of the president's skull was missing. "The next day we found the [missing] portion of the President's head," Clint Hill told investigators. "It was found in the street."

Years later, in an interview for the *New York Times,* former CIA director Richard Helms made a provocative statement. Helms began his intelligence career with the OSS in 1942 and retired in 1973, having served Presidents Johnson and Nixon as director of Central

Intelligence. Under the Kennedy administration, he served as CIA deputy director of plans, which put him in charge of the president's Executive Action capability. In this capacity Helms oversaw the Kennedy administration's assassination program, including more than twenty now-declassified plots to kill Fidel Castro—with an exploding cigar, a contaminated diving suit, poison botulism-toxin pills, and other schemes, all of which failed.

"If you kill someone else's leaders," Helms told David Frost on national television in 1978, "why shouldn't they kill yours?"

Within a year and a half, the covert war became an overt war. The United States increased its military forces in South Vietnam and in March began bombing Hanoi in Operation Rolling Thunder. The governments of Russia and China increased support to Hanoi, providing men, weapons, and guerrilla warfare expertise to the communists. In Washington, DC, in an effort to define U.S. Defense Department goals inside Vietnam, John McNaughton, assistant secretary of the department, used a percentage calculus in a memo for national-security advisor McGeorge Bundy: "70%—to avoid a humiliating U.S. defeat; 20%—to keep SVN [South Vietnam]… territory from Chinese hands; 10%—to permit the people of SVN to enjoy a better, freer way of life." In South Vietnam, Joint CIA/ Defense Department hit-and-run ambush operations by the Civilian Irregular Defense Group continued full-bore, unleashing bloodshed and chaos on an increasingly divided civilian population while achieving little of the Pentagon's percentage-based goals.

Now it was dawn on June 17, 1965, and Billy Waugh was leading a ninety-man CIDG team on an ambush against an enemy camp inside a village called Bong Son. The camp, believed to house 200 to 300 communist fighters, was located in South Vietnam but was under the control of communist forces. Of ninety CIDG men, one was CIA, three were Green Berets, and eighty-six were indigenous villagers. The mission was to sneak up on the enemy soldiers while they were sleeping, kill as many of them as possible, and get out without loss. Surprise, kill, vanish.

The CIDG men had left their Special Forces A-Team camp at 1:30 that morning. Waugh was the point man, now leading the team silently on a narrow trail that snaked along the An Lao River. Just seventeen kilometers inland from the coast, the terrain was dense jungle. It was hot and humid, already 85 degrees. After roughly an hour of walking, the team came upon an NVA soldier who was supposed to be keeping guard but had fallen asleep. Waugh instructed one of the indigs to cut the man's throat.

"Examining the dead soldier's possessions," remembers Waugh, "we noted the modern gear he carried: a shiny Chinese pistol, a Russian AK-47, brand-new jungle boots, and an excellent radio." Inside the soldier's medicine kit was an array of supplies almost identical to what Special Forces medics carried, and Waugh remembers noting the odd symmetry involved. The kill-or-be-killed rule of unconventional warfare. "We took his gear and continued on."

The three other Americans on the team were Captain Paris D. Davis, the highest-ranking commissioned officer in the group; Sergeant Robert D. Brown, a medic; and Staff Sergeant David Morgan, the team's liaison to the CIA. "Captain Paris Davis, a blue-eyed black man from Washington, DC, had never been in combat before," says Waugh, and the same went for Sergeant Robert Brown, "an all-American kid from Montana who would soon be dead with a bullet in his head." The CIA operator David Morgan, like Waugh "battle-tested and sharp-witted, unafraid of fierce combat or hard work," had already served multiple tours in Vietnam.

Each of the Special Forces soldiers wore green battle fatigues and carried an M16 rifle and twenty-five magazines of .223-caliber ammunition, which meant each of them had five hundred rounds. Each soldier had twenty-eight grenades of various types: fourteen regular grenades, ten frag grenades, two white phosphorus grenades (an incendiary weapon meant to ignite cloth, fuel, ammunition, and more), and two smoke grenades. Rescue gear consisted of a signal mirror, a compass, and a bright red emergency panel. In his left pocket, Waugh carried hard candy for energy.

As they moved along the riverbank, Billy Waugh began to worry about the communications gear. If the operation went bad and they needed air support, the radio was their lifeline. It had been decided early on that the PRC-25 FM radio was to be carried by one of the eighty-six indigs, but now Waugh was having second thoughts. "Most of the indigs were poor farmers," he says. "Now they were mercenaries, paid to fight someone else's war." This was the first time any of them had been in combat. Waugh had trained the group in small arms and unconventional-warfare techniques, just as he'd trained hundreds of others like them, and he knew that the indigs might not stick around once shots started firing. On the other hand, he thought, there was nothing quite like a quick, successful ambush to bolster the confidence and competence of a mercenary. Either way, there was no guarantee. By nightfall all but fifteen of the indigs would be dead or gone.

Approaching the camp, the group divided into four units, each with a Green Beret or CIA officer in the lead. A few hundred meters outside the target, Waugh suddenly found himself just feet away from a man and a woman, hunched over. By the time they looked up at him, Waugh had his weapon on them. They were NVA cooks, collecting firewood. Hard at work in these predawn hours, preparing breakfast for soldiers who'd soon be awake. Behind a fence, Waugh spotted pots of food cooking over an open firepit. As the man reached for the pistol on his hip, Waugh took a swift step forward, grabbed him around the shoulders, and pushed his knife into the man's throat. The woman came at him with a stick, striking him and making noise. Waugh slit her throat and set her body down on the jungle floor. All was quiet again.

He knew instantly that the pace of the raid had to quicken. The noise could have alerted a sentry. Soon, all hell could break lose. He passed word down the line. From here on out, the men would communicate using hand and arm signals, no sound. Rounding a bend, Waugh caught sight of the enemy camp. The bamboo hooches, or sleeping barracks, were wide and low, with ceilings no more than three feet tall. Each hut was roughly forty feet wide and lined with platforms, three soldiers to a bed. Doing the math quickly in his head, he figured there were 250 men here.

He gave the signal to attack. The CIDG soldiers raised their M16s and opened fire. The gunfire led to chaos and pandemonium, with empty magazines dropping to the jungle floor. As the NVA soldiers leapt up from sleeping, a relentless barrage of firepower cut them down. Next Waugh and the others began hurling grenades, observing dispassionately as men and their barracks caught on fire. Waugh recalls watching enemy soldiers drop to the ground and roll, trying to stop from being burned alive. Some fighters returned fire, but mostly they fled. Then suddenly, unexpectedly, it got quiet. The battle was over. Waugh estimated that 150 NVA were dead. The rest appeared to have run off into the jungle.

"For about fifteen minutes we congratulated each other," remembers Waugh. "We were celebrating. Patting ourselves on the back. Examining the Russian weapons left behind when they fled." Waugh remembers thinking how satisfying it was that the raid had been a success. But war is nothing if not full of surprises.

From deep inside the jungle there was a sharp, distinct sound. A bugle call. Unmistakably a military command. "Bugles meant soldiers," explains Waugh. "NVA regulars." The NVA had called in the infantry using a signal instrument favored by American soldiers during the Revolutionary War. What none of them had realized was that the three sleeping hooches they'd just ambushed were the first three of several dozen hooches stretching deep into the jungle. Each held roughly sixty enemy soldiers. The Defense Department later estimated that there had been as many as three thousand soldiers at Bong Son. The bugle call had just woken them all up.

Waugh ran into the jungle, firing at anything that moved. He threw hand grenades and let off two flares, signaling to the team to disperse and retreat. The sound of boots was everywhere around him. The clattering of men. Commands yelled in Vietnamese. There was heavy automatic weapons fire coming at him, and green tracers likely from RPD rifles. The North Vietnamese Army had begun a massive counterattack, and Waugh was running out of ammo fast.

Racing through the jungle, he headed toward the rally point, an old cemetery on the high ground 650 feet to the west. Moving as fast as his legs could carry him, he suddenly found himself in an impossible situation. Directly in front of him there was nothing but a wide-open rice-paddy field. He'd run out of jungle, his only means of defense. Behind him was a battalion of battle-ready NVA. He had nowhere to go but across the open field.

He ran fast, his jungle boots sloshing through the wet grass. Concentrating hard on how to make it to the cemetery. There was commo hidden there, and commo meant an ability to call in air strikes. Rounds buzzed past his head. He was now out of ammunition and grenades. He saw a green tracer headed his way. Before he could react, *baamm!* He got hit in the right knee.

The impact knocked him over. He lay facedown in the wet grass. He pulled himself up on all fours and began to crawl. Finally, he spotted an embankment, a dirt irrigation berm running along the edge of the rice paddy. Concealed for the moment, he looked around to assess who was where. Sergeant Robert Brown, the young medic from Montana, had taken a bullet to the head and lay bleeding out in the grass. He counted twenty-five, maybe thirty mercenaries dead in the open field, cut down by NVA firepower as they tried to escape.

Waugh kept crawling. After another hundred or so feet he came upon a hole in front of him, as if someone had dug a pit. A foxhole in a rice paddy? How strange. He pulled himself down into the darkness. It was wet inside, about four feet wide—he couldn't determine how long. As he dragged himself down, he felt a flash of relief. He'd managed to escape from the enemy. He could hide here. Then he realized that there was someone or something down here in the hole with him. He couldn't see much in the dark. He heard breathing. He moved down the hole a little farther until he was staring into the flaring nostrils of a water buffalo. He could make out the animal's sharp horns and its dark black skin. There were whiskers on its nose. The animal jerked its head and snorted, as if to charge. Waugh wondered if he might die here, eviscerated by a water buffalo. But the animal was stuck in the mud, just as he was. Waugh might have laughed, except that he was soaking wet, bleeding heavily, and possibly losing consciousness. He could feel leeches crawling into his open wounds, eating their way into the space that used to be his right knee. Outside, on the field, he heard enemy machine-gun fire.

His brain struggled to figure out a next move when suddenly David Morgan, the CIA operator, appeared alongside him in the hole. Morgan looked at the water buffalo, then at Waugh. The NVA knew they were here in this hole, Morgan said. They had to move out. But Waugh was unable to move, and Morgan couldn't carry him. Waugh told Morgan to try to get to the cemetery alone. From there, he could call in air strikes to lay down suppressive fire and force the NVA to disperse. Waugh could still get out of here on his own.

David Morgan took off running. Waugh pulled himself up out of the hole and started crawling across the field. He made it about ten feet when he was hit again, this time worse than before. The round smashed into the bottom of his foot, tearing through his boot and ripping apart his toes before exiting his body just above the ankle bone. He knew enough about the body to know that this most likely meant his military career was over. Facedown in the mud, he strained to breathe. Tracers hit the dirt around him. He figured the enemy was 150 feet away. He needed to keep going, keep crawling despite the pain. His right leg wasn't working. He looked down and saw exposed bone. "My foot had been almost entirely torn off," Waugh recalled. "There were leeches covering the wound and I could see my exposed foot and ankle bones, white as snow."

Keep going, he told himself. Stop and you're dead. When he took a shot to the left wrist, part of his brain tried having a conversation with him about what it would be like if he lost his leg and never walked on two feet again. Another part of his brain said, *Don't think about that,* he recalls. The pain was intense, and he figured soon he'd lose consciousness. If the enemy got ahold of him, he was dead. Waugh reached into his rucksack. He pulled out his field syringe and morphine bottle, gave himself three quick shots. He waited for the drugs to take effect. A slight warm feeling came over him, but mostly he felt intense pain.

Ahead, Waugh could see CIA operator David Morgan at the rallying point. He'd made it. Damn. This was a good sign, quickly followed by a bad one. David Morgan's hand signals indicated that the radio had been shot to pieces. There was no way to call for rescue or air strikes. Waugh looked up. My God, he thought, was he hallucinating? Was this really Captain Paris D. Davis, coming to get him? Waugh remembers staring into Davis's eyes and how incredibly blue they were. He normally didn't notice things like this, and it jerked him back into reality. Neither man had any way to radio for help. The situation was dire. They tried discussing what to do next. Davis had his right hand up, pointing at something, when he got shot in the hand. The ends of his fingers were sheared off. Waugh watched blood spurt into the air between them. Davis howled and swore. He was right-handed, he said. Now he couldn't even shoot.

No commo. No ammo, thought Waugh. No way to communicate, no ability to shoot. Their only hope was rescue. The sun was coming up. Waugh pulled out his emergency panel and signal mirror. Davis made a run for the cemetery. An aircraft flying overhead, searching for the team, spotted what was happening and notified headquarters. The full fighting force of the U.S. Army and the air force was now coming to the rescue. It wasn't over yet.

Lying helpless in the rice paddy, Waugh looked up and watched the sky. He saw Navy F-8s and U.S. Air Force F-4C Phantom jets come in fast and low, dropping bombs and napalm on the battlefield. For a moment he had hope. Then suddenly he took a bullet to the right side of his head. Most likely a ricochet, it sliced a two-inch section of skin and bone off his forehead. The wound was not deep enough to kill him, but it was enough to knock him unconscious.

When Waugh awoke, the sun was high in the sky. Hours had passed and he was baked in a thick mud shell, like a crust. Warm rays beat down on him and he looked at his watch to see what time it was. No watch. He was naked. The NVA must have mistaken him for dead. Stripped him naked and taken his watch. After a few minutes, he heard the sounds of a helicopter. He couldn't believe he was alive. *Thwaap, thwaap, thwaap,* went the rotor blades. He watched as the helicopter landed. Out leapt a Special Forces soldier he knew, Sergeant First Class John Reinburg, a weapons expert. Was Reinburg really running toward him? He was pretty sure it was Reinburg, running in his jungle fatigues, crossing some 250 feet of open terrain. Or maybe the situation wasn't real. Maybe Waugh was imagining things. Now Reinburg was standing over him, talking. He told Waugh he was here to get him out of this mess alive. In the distance Waugh eyed the helicopter that Reinburg said was going to medevac him to a MASH hospital not far away. It was a UH-1D; he could see people climbing inside.

Reinburg told Waugh he was going to carry him the 250 feet across the open field to the helicopter, because Waugh's right knee and left leg were useless. The blood had dried, but the bones were exposed and there were leeches eating at his flesh. Reinburg hoisted

Waugh up from behind, holding him under his armpits, dragging him toward the helicopter. Across the field, he spotted Paris Davis, alive, crawling toward the helicopter. Then he heard the terrible sound of RPG tracers all over again.

"We're gonna make it," Reinburg promised as he dragged Waugh across the rice paddy. "We're gonna make it." He lugged Waugh's body five or six feet at a time. And just when Waugh started to believe he might come out of this disaster alive, Reinburg took a bullet to the chest. "The bullet hit him just above the heart," remembers Waugh. "And as he started to fall, a second bullet impacted his body, this time six inches lower down." Reinburg's lung collapsed and he struggled to breathe. "In that instant, Reinburg went from being strong and heroic to being in worse shape than me."

Another Green Beret came rushing out of the helicopter and began running across the open field. He was young. He grabbed Reinburg and started dragging him toward the helicopter. Maybe someone grabbed Billy Waugh, or maybe he and Paris Davis continued crawling toward the helicopter on their own power. Later, in debriefs, neither man could clearly recall. Special Forces training teaches its soldiers what needs to be done to stay alive: crawl, stay low, get to the helicopter no matter what.

Now the helicopter was just a few yards away. Waugh could see David Morgan and a few of the mercenaries waiting inside. The helicopter-door gunner was laying down suppressive fire, trying to keep Waugh and Davis from being fired upon by NVA soldiers hiding in the trees. Waugh was inside the helicopter now. As the aircraft started to lift up off the ground, a green tracer flew into the cabin and hit the door gunner, shearing off part of his arm. Waugh watched the gunner stare at what remained of his limb as the helicopter took off and they flew away.

When Billy Waugh awoke, he heard screaming. He was in a field hospital a few kilometers from Bong Son. Beside him, in the next bed over, John Reinburg was howling in pain as the nurses worked to debride him, removing damaged tissue and foreign objects—dirt, debris, and insects—from his gaping chest wounds. Waugh realized he was screaming, too, and that the nurses were doing the same thing to his leg.

A few days later, General William Westmoreland, commander of all U.S. forces in Vietnam, stopped by the field hospital and pinned a Purple Heart on Billy Waugh's uniform. Reinburg was awarded the Distinguished Service Cross.

Then came a U.S. Army doctor with grim news. Waugh was being sent back to the United States, to the lower-extremity amputation ward at Walter Reed.

CHAPTER TWELVE

The Studies and Observations Group

The Walter Reed amputee ward was a devastating sight to behold. Billy Waugh was now one of its patients, his right leg in a cast. The infection wasn't getting any better, and the doctor said part of his leg would likely need to be amputated, cut off below the knee. Day in and day out, Waugh watched fellow soldiers in the ward come and go. They'd get wheeled away to surgical rooms and return without an arm or a leg.

The way Waugh saw it, there were two categories of amputees. Some soldiers became a shell of their former selves after they lost a limb. Others somehow managed to keep things light, like the sergeant major in the next bed over who recently had his lower leg removed. Waugh went with him to the Friday night dance.

"Watch this," the sergeant major said, unhooking his prosthetic leg and putting it on backward, so the foot faced in reverse. The soldier with the prosthetic asked a pretty girl to dance and she said sure, but while they were dancing, she looked down at his backward foot, screamed, and ran away. The sergeant major howled with laughter. Waugh didn't know which was worse: to lose a limb or to find humor in it.

Soon enough, Dr. Arthur Metz, chief of lower-extremity amputation surgery, came to give Billy Waugh the bad news. Despite two surgeries and four weeks of antibiotics, the infection in his right leg had gotten worse. Dr. Metz proposed amputating the foot from the ankle down. If it got any worse, they might have to take the bottom half of the leg. Waugh could not bear the thought. "I had it in my mind to return to combat," he says. "In 1965, you couldn't fight without a foot."

Billy Waugh pleaded with Dr. Metz to be discharged. He wanted to go heal at his sister's house in Texas. Dr. Metz agreed and wrote him convalescent leave orders. Waugh was thrilled at first, but as he prepared to travel to Texas, hope gave way to misery. He missed being a soldier and the intensity of war. Something came over him and, penicillin bottle in hand, he decided to hitchhike to Vietnam, as a standby passenger on military aircraft. It seemed the pilots felt sorry for him with his long cast on his right leg, and he never had to wait long. In less than a week he made it from Washington, DC, to Travis Air Force Base, outside San Francisco, to the Philippines, and finally to Tan Son Nhat Airport in Saigon.

Saigon was a busy city in the summer of 1965. Waugh checked into the Hotel Majestic and headed to the Tu Do bar down the street, the place where soldiers went for rest and relaxation. It didn't take long for Waugh to spot two friends from Special Forces, Billy Kessinger, a medic, and Danny Horton, a communications man. Seated at a corner table, the trio of Green Berets began chatting. After a few beers, Kessinger and Horton hinted to Waugh about a highly classified direct-action unit that was just now expanding. An elite unconventional-warfare group that was secreted inside MACV. No one outside the unit knew about it; it was a special-access covert program called the Studies and Observations Group (SOG), named to deceive people into thinking its members were Ivy League–type analysts reading reports. In reality, the missions were so dangerously insane, Kessinger and Horton said, the acronym was translated to

Suicide on the Ground by some guys. Kessinger and Horton were already in SOG and they showed Waugh their credentials: a photo, a few coded letters, and a telephone number that you could call 24/7 if you ever needed anything. SOG members had unprecedented authority. They could go anywhere in South Vietnam, at any time of the night or day—no getting stopped by military police (MP). If you were in SOG, you were authorized to carry a firearm at all times. Kessinger and Horton called the creds a WoW pass, because you could walk on water with it.

Sitting and drinking at the Tu Do bar, the men talked late into the night, past curfew for American soldiers. When an American MP approached the table and asked for identification, Kessinger and Horton flashed their WoW passes. Waugh pulled a piece of paper from his pocket, unfolded it, and showed the MP his convalescent leave orders.

"What the hell are you doing on convalescent leave in Vietnam, Master Sergeant William D. Waugh?" the MP asked, reading from the papers.

"I'm visiting with my amigos," said Waugh.

The MP was not certain what to make of the situation, so he called his commanding officer, who asked if Master Sergeant Waugh was causing problems. The MP said he wasn't. The commanding officer said convalescent leave orders were good and Waugh could be left alone. The night ended without incident.

A week later, Waugh returned to America, more determined than ever to get himself assigned to this classified unconventional-warfare unit called SOG.

In Washington, DC, he traveled to the Pentagon to meet with the assignments officer for Special Forces, a woman named Billie Alexander. Seated across from her, Waugh pleaded to be assigned to MACV-SOG.

"All she could do was laugh," he recalls. "She said I could barely walk, how did I expect to ever fight again?"

Waugh proposed a challenge. If he was able to convince Dr. Metz to reassign him to Special Forces at Fort Bragg, and if he could last there for a month of training, would Billie Alexander recommend him for SOG?

"Perhaps she felt sorry for me," Waugh remembers, "because she looked at me for a while and then she said yes."

Waugh met with Dr. Metz, who rejected his idea. His lower leg was beyond salvage, Metz said, and required amputation. Waugh begged to undergo one last exploratory surgery. The doctor agreed. During the surgery, Dr. Metz went far up into the leg, near the knee, where he located a tiny sliver of Waugh's army boot lodged inside the tibia. This was the likely source of the months-long infection. Once it was removed, the final round of penicillin took hold and Waugh began to heal. The following month, he returned to Fort Bragg. In his second week back in Special Forces he received new orders. He was being sent to Vietnam as part of MACV-SOG.

The reason for SOG's highly classified nature was that it violated the Geneva Agreement of 1962, the Declaration on the Neutrality of Laos, which forbade U.S. forces from operating inside the country. But at the Pentagon, after almost two years of reading reports from intelligence assets in the field, the Defense Department was coming around to the idea that Laos was the key to the insurgency and the Ho Chi Minh Trail the locus of the problem. Now President Johnson needed convincing. The initial job of SOG reconnaissance men would be to sneak into Laos, take photographs of activity on the trail, plant listening devices, and get out alive with the evidence. Eventually they would be assigned cross-border missions into Cambodia as well.

"Nobody knew with certainty what was in Laos," says John Plaster, a former member of the classified unit. "Learning what was there was SOG's new operation." Plaster is considered one of the most competent snipers out there, and his experiences in MACV-SOG would later serve as the basis for part of the video game *Call of Duty: Black Ops*.

SOG's first chief was Colonel Donald Blackburn, the former leader of Operation White Star, and he prepared his fighters for battles in Laos that would be decidedly ungentlemanly. Blackburn was a master of guerrilla warfare. During World War II he led kill-or-be-killed missions in the Philippines, where the tribesmen he organized into a guerrilla fighting force turned out to be headhunters. Blackburn's wartime diary became a bestselling book, in 1955, called *Blackburn's Head-hunters*. In Laos, SOG operators would need to employ ruthless unconventional warfare tactics with unmerciful intensity. To direct SOG operations on the ground, Colonel Blackburn chose another guerrilla warfare legend, the Finnish-born Larry Thorne.

MACV-SOG started with just sixteen volunteers, all Green Berets who'd been training on Okinawa. The men worked out of a forward operating base in Kham Duc, a border village located sixty miles southwest of Danang. Similar to the Civilian Irregular Defense Group program, and the OSS Jedburghs before that, each SOG team was made up of two or three American soldiers and nine tribesmen. Initially the tribesmen were Nung, an ethnic Chinese minority; later they included Montagnards, indigenous people from Vietnam's Central Highlands whom the Americans called Yards.

"[We] Americans had advanced technology, such as helicopters, and the tribesmen had ancient techniques, such as silent ambush," explains John Plaster. The tribesmen helped the Green Berets understand the tactics that were being used by the NVA guerrilla fighters, things not found in any manual. For example, Nung tribesmen demonstrated how, by digging a four-foot hole into a hillside, a fighter could see and feel the vibrations of an advancing aircraft long before his ears registered the engine sound.

Shared tricks of the trade went both ways. Tribesmen were also recruited to watch and count enemy troops and supplies being moved through the jungle. Because most could not read or write

English or Vietnamese, the CIA's technical staff developed a nonliterate system of conveyance. Instead of words, the counting devices given out to recruits featured tiny pictograms representing men, weapons, vehicles, even elephants—a common means of transport in the region. When the recruits activated a toggle switch on the device, their data was transmitted to CIA aircraft, flying overhead.

Unlike the CIDG program, the bond between the tribesmen and the SOG operators was reported to be strong. "The Nung and Yards could have cared less about South Vietnam as a country," recalls Plaster. "They felt no allegiance to some abstract paymaster like the United States. But they were ready to die for their recon teammates, American and Yard alike."

SOG's first cross-border mission into Laos occurred on October 18, 1965. U.S. ambassador William Sullivan forbade SOG from using helicopter insertions into the supposedly neutral country, so the first team to go in, Reconnaissance Team (RT) Iowa, was inserted by helicopter on the Vietnam side of the border. They walked through the jungle into Laos. The team leader, or One-Zero, was Master Sergeant Charles "Slats" Petry; the assistant team leader, or One-One, was Sergeant First Class Willie Card. Together, these two Americans led seven Nung mercenaries and one lieutenant from the South Vietnamese Army (ARVN) to gather reconnaissance of enemy activity along the Ho Chi Minh Trail. Rather than oversee the mission from Kham Duc, Larry Thorne flew with his men in the helicopter, circling overhead until he received word they'd successfully crossed over into Laos.

Each SOG team wore Asian-made uniforms with no labels or insignia. They carried sterile weapons, meaning they came with no identifying marks, such as the Swedish K submachine gun; and they smoked Chinese cigarettes. If anyone got captured in Laos, no one could identify them as Americans. SOG operators were issued unmarked SOG Bowie-style knives with six-inch blades, designed by Ben Barker on Okinawa and secretly manufactured in Japan. Not since the days of the OSS had the U.S. military issued stiletto knives.

Overhead air support was critical to the success of every mission. The H-34 Kingbee helicopter was SOG's signature aircraft, a bubble-nosed workhorse able to withstand a hail of automatic weapons fire and keep flying. The Kingbees were flown by South Vietnamese air force pilots trained in Texas by the CIA. With radio call signs like Cowboy and Mustachio, these pilots saved countless SOG men from capture or death, performing radical jungle infiltration, exfiltration, and rescue operations day after day. "All gave some, some gave all," says SOG operator John Stryker Meyer of the Kingbee pilots. Cessna aircraft were also used regularly on missions, and flying on the first mission in a Cessna 0-2 spotter were U.S. Air Force major Harley Pyles and U.S. Marine Corps captain Winfield Sisson. If anything went wrong, the U.S. Air Force and the U.S. Navy were on standby, ready to send in covert air support in the form of overhead air strikes.

RT Iowa was inserted successfully, and after a few hours they radioed Larry Thorne to say they'd crossed the border into Laos. Thorne radioed Kham Duc to say he was now heading back to base. He was never heard from again.

"In the first few minutes of SOG's classified border operations, the program swallowed up one of its finest officers and a whole Kingbee" helicopter, says John Plaster. "That afternoon, the Cessna carrying Major Pyles and Captain Sisson disappeared." On SOG's first mission, three men went missing in action (MIA), never to be seen again. It was an indication of the kind of catastrophic loss SOG would face over the next six years. The great majority of such cases are either still classified or lack records, said to have been lost. Over the next eight months, five SOG recon teams working out of Kham Duc conducted forty-eight cross-border missions. In the winter of 1966, MACV headquarters opened a second SOG base up north, at Khe Sanh, closer to the demilitarized zone (DMZ). Still limping from five gunshot wounds to the leg, Billy Waugh arrived there in May.

★　★　★

Located in the northwest corner of South Vietnam, Khe Sanh was the most remote American military facility in all of the south, a strip of flat land surrounded by 4,000-foot mountains and treacherous ravines. Much of the activity centered around Co Roc Mountain, a 2,000-foot limestone peak visible from the base, as were Hill 1050 and Hill 950, veritable beehives of NVA activity. The geography here was unlike anything in the United States, endless karst-limestone outcroppings that looked like giant vine-covered chimneys. The base camp, under the control of the U.S. Marine Corps, was strategically located just fourteen miles south of the DMZ and twelve miles east of the border with Laos. For SOG, this meant that Khe Sanh was within striking distance of key enemy bases along the Ho Chi Minh Trail.

The SOG base at Khe Sanh was a Special Access facility, partitioned behind concertina wire, surrounded by blast walls, and built mostly underground. SOG operations were classified, which meant that even Khe Sanh's marine commander, Colonel David E. Lownds, wasn't privy to its activities. In 1966, when Waugh arrived, the new SOG chief was Jack Singlaub, the former OSS Jedburgh who ran covert CIA airdrop operations during the Korean War, under the cover name Joint Advisory Commission, Korea, or JACK. "There was no rest at SOG," remembers Billy Waugh, "only war, recon, rescue, sleep."

International law meant nothing to the enemy out here on the border region between Vietnam and Laos, a concept SOG men were regularly forced to grapple with. Despite the covert nature of their missions, Special Forces soldiers operated under the U.S. military chain of command and were bound by the laws of war. Ever since the Lieber Code of 1863, the execution of captured prisoners and the mutilation of dead soldiers' bodies on the battlefield were expressly forbidden. The 1949 Geneva Conventions updated these protocols for the modern era. And yet look at what the NVA had done to Sergeant Donald Sain, thought Billy Waugh, as he flew over Co Roc Mountain in a SOG observation aircraft.

It was June 1966. RT Montana had been ambushed three days before, with two SOG men captured and executed, and seven indigs killed in action (KIA) or missing in action (MIA). One-Zero Henry Whalen made it back to Khe Sanh and gave the ambush location coordinates to SOG commanders. Waugh was put in charge of a rescue-or-retrieval mission, which is why he was across the border in Laos now, searching for dead bodies from the Cessna. When he spotted Sergeant Donald Sain's body in a jungle clearing, he felt contempt and disgust.

Don Sain was a twenty-three-year-old kid from Santa Clara County, California, who'd worn a white tuxedo and a bow tie to prom just a few years before. Now he was not just dead but had been mutilated and put on display by the NVA. Sain's captors had killed him and arranged him in a spread-eagle position with his legs staked to the earth and his arms tied to a tree. Maggots were crawling around the gunshot wounds that Don Sain had taken to the chest. Once vibrant and full of life, he was now carrion.

It was 9:00 a.m. and Waugh assessed the situation. "I'd been in combat long enough to know Sain's body was not only displayed so we could see it, but it had to be booby-trapped as well," he recalls.

Waugh instructed the pilot to head back to the SOG base at Khe Sanh. There, he briefed his commanding officer. After putting together a Bright Light rescue team, the SOG men returned to the clearing in the jungle. The team included Danny Horton, the communications man from the Tu Do bar, Sergeant First Class James Craig, a medic, and Major Gerald "Jerry" Kilburn, the most senior officer in the group and a POW during the Korean War.

Flying the H-34 Kingbee was South Vietnamese air force pilot Nguyen Van Hoang, call sign Mustachio, so named after the Clarke Gable–style mustache he wore. Once, during a rescue operation and under heavy fire, Mustachio was struck in the neck with a bullet while piloting a Kingbee over a target. He plugged the bullet hole with his fingers and got the crippled helicopter twenty kilometers back to Khe Sanh, flying with only one hand.

With Mustachio at the controls, the Kingbee hovered over Sain's body. While Waugh tried to figure out how to get ahold of it without being hit by grenade frag, Mustachio searched for a landing zone. NVA were everywhere, and time was critical. Body retrieval was the perfect time for an ambush. Mustachio circled around a few times before setting the Kingbee down, roughly one hundred meters from the body. The rescue team hopped off.

Approaching the body, Billy Waugh felt the anger and disgust return. The stench of rotting flesh was hard to bear. He grabbed a climbing rope and told Major Kilburn his plan. "I decided to tie one end of the rope to the wheel of Mustachio's helicopter and the other end around Sain's leg. That way we'd move the body and let the booby traps explode harmlessly," Waugh recalls. The team looked at Waugh like he was crazy.

"There was no manual for this kind of horrid shit," he says. "The rope was the fastest and most efficient way to achieve the objective."

Waugh tied the rope to the helicopter wheel and instructed Mustachio to hover over Sain. Delicately, so as not to set off the grenades, he tied the rope around Sain's leg.

"Let's move out," he told the team. Everyone stepped back a few yards.

Using the helicopter, Mustachio pulled the body off the ground. Three or four booby-trap grenades started going off around Sain.

"Sain was hovering above us by his leg," remembers Waugh. "The fluids and maggots and crap from his body poured out as he was being lifted up and away. And as it did, Kilburn got sprayed with debris." Kilburn, a highly decorated combat veteran, had sustained three years of torture at the hands of his communist captors in the Korean War. But this was too much for him. When the fluids hit Kilburn, he screamed.

Mustachio lifted Sain's body and set it down. Kilburn finished screaming. Everyone got quiet. Sain's body had been recovered, but there was more work to do. A second SOG man from RT Montana was still missing, a kid from Missouri named Sergeant Delmer Lee "Outlaw" Laws. The Bright Light team searched the area, trying to find a blood trail and maybe find Laws. The SOG men divvied up ground, each man assigned a quadrant to scour. This part of the jungle was hostile and unforgiving, filled with poisonous snakes like the two-step snake—if it bit you, you had two steps left in you before you died. Waugh found himself waist high in wait-a-minute bushes, prickly plants with claws the sharpness of a cat's that hooked into your skin when you passed by. If you got snagged, you had to wait a minute to unhook yourself, or get torn to shreds. After several hours of searching, everyone's fatigues were ripped up, arms and faces scratched up and bleeding, but no one was ready to stop yet. They intended to find Outlaw.

Danny Horton called out. He'd found a blood trail.

Waugh saw Horton emerge from the woods, looking ill. In one hand he carried an American jungle boot. Something grotesque was sticking out of the shoe, recalls Waugh, as he figured out he was looking at part of Delmer Laws's leg. Danny Horton took the group to where he'd found it. "He'd been mostly eaten by a tiger," says Waugh.

The ride back to the SOG base was quiet. Beneath the helicopter, Sain's body was swinging from a rope. Delmer Laws's leg was lying on the floor of the helicopter in a plastic body bag.

Once they landed on the tarmac at Khe Sanh, Billy Waugh climbed out of the helicopter carrying Laws's leg in the bag. "My clothes were shredded, I was filthy, covered in horrible things. My arms and face were scratched, I smelled," he recalls. Standing there on the tarmac waiting for the SOG Bright Light team was an officer from the 5th Special Forces, "taking a break from his desk duties at MACV headquarters in Nha Trang," remembers Waugh. "He asked me to come inside."

Waugh followed his superior officer into the SOG base. The officer began yelling at him.

"Goddamnit, Waugh," he said. "You're filthy, you smell, and you're out of uniform. You're a disgrace. All of you."

Waugh set the plastic bag on the table. He took a moment before he spoke. Every soldier knows chain of command. Every soldier respects authority. Your superior officer is always correct. But Waugh could not contain himself. He took Laws's leg out of the body bag and set it on the table.

"How about him?" Waugh asked, pointing. "Is he a disgrace?"

The officer stared at the jungle boot and the bloody stump.

"What the hell is that?" he asked.

"It's Sergeant Delmer Lee Laws's leg," said Waugh. "The rest of him got eaten by a tiger. Is he out of uniform, sir?"

The officer grew quiet, apologized, and left.

The following week, a box arrived at Khe Sanh, from headquarters in Nha Trang. Inside, there were three boxes of crisp new jungle fatigues. No markings, of course. No one could know SOG operators were violating the Declaration on the Neutrality of Laos.

CHAPTER THIRTEEN

Kill or Capture

After the assassination of President Kennedy in November of 1963, President Johnson renamed the Special Group (Augmented) the 303 Committee. Assassination plots against foreign leaders appeared to have been toned down, or at least the president's inner circle of advisors stopped allowing the minutes of meetings in which they were discussed to be recorded. The exception was with plans to kill Fidel Castro and Che Guevara, which moved ahead full-bore. In 1967 the CIA inspector general ordered an internal report on its assassination capability, the working papers of which were then destroyed on the orders of CIA director Richard Helms.

At least one significant assassination plan was likely part of the destroyed cache: an extraordinarily sensitive mission to kill General Giap, the indomitable leader of the North Vietnamese Army. Giap was to visit an NVA command center in supposedly neutral Laos, a sovereign nation. The group chosen to kill him was MACV-SOG. One of the first two men to the target area was to be Billy Waugh.

It was June 2, 1967, and Billy Waugh was summoned to a briefing inside SOG headquarters at Khe Sanh. Something unprecedented was about to happen, he was told, a direct-action operation so important that all the other air-supported missions across Vietnam would come to a halt. Over the previous twenty-four hours, the CIA and the Pentagon had intercepted roughly 1,500 communiqués between Hanoi and an NVA stronghold located just a few miles from Khe Sanh, inside Laos. The area had been given the code name Oscar Eight. Analysis of the intercepted messages confirmed that Oscar Eight was the secret NVA field headquarters the CIA had been trying to locate for months.

The CIA sent its U-2 spy planes overhead in search of photographic intelligence. Images confirmed enemy traffic along the lower portion of the Ho Chi Minh Trail was being diverted to Oscar Eight. Then came a reconnaissance coup d'état: signals intelligence intercepted by the U.S. Army indicated that General Giap himself was headed to Oscar Eight for a meeting.

Billy Waugh would act as forward air controller, in charge of observation and relay for the mission. At 4:00 a.m. the next morning he'd fly in over the target in a Cessna and circle overhead for the duration of the mission—high enough to avoid NVA antiaircraft fire, but low enough to watch through binoculars what was unfolding on the ground. It would be Waugh's job to relay information to the various parties involved, via SOG's communication system, serving as a kind of battle coordinator in the sky.

The mission plan was succinct. Nine B-52 bombers would fly in over the target to drop 900 bombs, each 200 pounds—a means of inflicting massive damage on the enemy camp and obliterating its capacity to respond. Fourteen minutes later, two marine helicopter gunships would strafe the area, clearing a landing zone (LZ). Next, two troop transport helicopters, piloted by marine corps pilots, would deposit two teams of SOG Hatchet Forces, large thirty- or forty-man units used in big operations. Air support would come from two Skyraider aircraft, propeller-driven workhorses that were slow but effective. Two Kingbee helicopters would insert two nine-man SOG teams, experienced operators tasked with locating and killing General Giap. Finally, four fast-flying F-4 Phantom fighter jets would provide close air support. SOG had seven hours to kill or capture General Giap and get out.

But Oscar Eight was a defender's dream. The bowl-shaped valley was surrounded by hills on three sides, forming a strategic ridge-shaped horseshoe. On earlier recon missions, SOG teams reported seeing 12.7mm antiaircraft artillery, called triple-A, scattered on hilltops and platforms in the jungle canopy, like hunting blinds.

Now it was dawn at Khe Sanh. Billy Waugh climbed into the Cessna O-2 spotter aircraft, into the seat beside the pilot, James Alexander, an air force major. They flew eight miles out from Khe Sanh, over the jungle canopy and into Laos, becoming the first to survey the Oscar Eight target area. Waugh had been in combat missions in Vietnam off and on since 1961, and he thought to himself, *This day could change the war.* The Pentagon had determined General Giap to be an even greater source of morale to fighters than Ho Chi Minh himself. Killing Giap could end the war.

Through binoculars, Waugh spotted cook fires down below, soldiers up early preparing breakfast for the fighters, he surmised. Major Alexander moved the Cessna roughly fifteen miles to the south, where he began to circle overhead, in anticipation of the B-52 bombers soon to arrive. Waugh checked his watch. It was 4:45, the sun was coming up, and the sky was purple and orange. Above and in the distance, Waugh spotted the contrails of the B-52s. Like clockwork, at 6:00 a.m., nine B-52 bombers passed over Oscar Eight, inundating the target area with 200-pound bombs. It was a colossal attack, one that left the surrounding valley seemingly destroyed. Waugh observed how the land below was now pock-marked with hundreds of apartment-building-sized bomb craters, burned-out, smoking holes. Through binoculars, he watched weapons depots explode and burn. Grass sleep shacks had been set ablaze and scores of enemy fighters were rushing out from makeshift buildings, hurrying to put out fires. He watched fighters remove weapons from burning boxes and roll gasoline barrels out of the way.

Overhead, as the B-52s made a second pass, suddenly something entirely unexpected happened: the ridges around Oscar Eight lit up. NVA soldiers down below were firing back with a barrage of anti-aircraft fire. *How could this be,* thought Waugh. The camp had been heavily bombed, and yet the NVA air defenses appeared to be entirely intact. The B-52 bombers flew too high for the NVA to hit with antiaircraft fire, but the SOG helicopters that were about to come in would be vulnerable to direct fire. Concerned with the speed and aggression of the NVA gunners' response, Waugh picked up the radio and called the marine helicopter gunship pilots who'd soon be heading into the target area. They needed to turn around immediately.

"Abort this mission!" Waugh shouted. "Abort!"

No answer. Nothing but silence over the comms.

Waugh tried again. Then he tried contacting the marine pilots who were flying the CH-46 troop transport helicopters, each one packed with thirty SOG Hatchet Forces.

No answer. Silence. Shit.

"Did everybody switch VHF channels?" Waugh asked Major Alexander.

Major Alexander shook his head and tried his own commo. Nothing but radio silence on his, too.

Waugh checked his watch. The helicopters delivering the Hatchet Forces were scheduled to arrive fourteen minutes after the first B-52 bombing run, which meant any minute now. Desperate to get in touch with someone, Waugh kept trying his radio, but it was too late. Below and to the east, he spotted two marine helicopter gunships flying in fast and low. They began strafing the target area, clearing the LZ for the Hatchet Forces to land. Waugh and Alexander watched in horror as one of the gunships was picked off by NVA ground fire. Then the second helicopter was hit. The two helicopters each began to wobble and spin, then crashed into the landing zone almost side by side.

The sight of the twin helicopter crashes sent adrenaline coursing through Waugh's body. He had to get the CH-46 on the radio. Those Hatchet Forces could not land. It was suicide, he thought. He tried the UHF radio, then the VHF radio again.

"Do not land!" he shouted. "Abort. Hatchet Forces, do not land!"

All this high technology and nobody could hear anything. But the landings were now in progress, and Waugh watched helplessly as the CH-46s entered the target area. Double rotors spinning, one in front, one in back, like two school buses in the sky, he thought. Based on the angle at which they were flying in, the CH-46 pilots would be unable to see the crashed helicopters until after it was too late.

Waugh and Alexander were both shouting into their radios, "Abort! Abort!"

The helicopters were now roughly seventy feet above the ground, side by side over the landing zone. Through binoculars, Waugh could see into one of them. The door was open and dozens of men were inside, amped up and ready to deploy. He'd been in that position countless times, standing in the doorway before the helicopter even landed, waiting to hit the ground running. He knew precisely how charged they had to be when, hovering now only fifty feet above the ground, the helicopter was hit with antiaircraft fire. It appeared to split in half. Waugh watched as the SOG men tumbled out of the aircraft and began falling like stones to the ground. It was impossible to survive that kind of fall. Waugh felt ill.

The second helicopter was now forty feet over the landing zone when it, too, was hit with antiaircraft fire and split open. Waugh watched some of the men inside fall out and down. Others hung on to anything they could. The helicopter spun and maintained some of its lift, crash-landing in a way that left Waugh thinking there might be survivors. Straining to see through the binoculars, he counted nine, possibly ten men alive. He watched as they scrambled out of the burning aircraft and ran. Training taught them to take cover in the jungle, to evade and escape.

In came the two H-34 Kingbee helicopters carrying the SOG teams assigned to kill Giap. One was raked with enemy gunfire. Waugh watched as it burst into flames, then crashed into the ground. Through binoculars he saw three crew members scramble out of the burning helicopter and take cover. One SOG operator was shot dead as he ran, but the other two appeared to have made it into the jungle. Waugh kept his eyes on the SOG men as they evaded capture. They were definitely alive and definitely running for cover, he noted. The second helicopter appeared to have landed. As Waugh strained to see, Major Alexander moved the Cessna up to 4,000 feet, where the comm channels might be better, and as he did, Waugh briefly lost sight of what was happening on the ground.

Up at 4,000 feet, the radio worked and Waugh reached Major Kilburn at the SOG facility at Khe Sanh. Kilburn knew nothing about what was happening at the target area.

"We got a real problem here at Oscar Eight," Waugh said, and he relayed the dire situation as quickly and succinctly as he could.

The mission to kill or capture General Giap was now a rescue mission, Kilburn said. The goal was to try and get anyone trapped inside Oscar Eight out of there alive.

As Waugh discussed the situation with Major Kilburn, two Phantom fighter jets screeched in over the valley at Mach 2. Waugh watched, stunned, as antiaircraft fire hit one of the fast-moving jets in the right wing, near the fuel tank. The silver Phantom exploded in the air.

"Come on, parachute," Waugh wished out loud as the jet spiraled down. No parachute. The Phantom jet crashed into the hillside and exploded.

"Skyraiders coming in," someone said over the comms, startling him. "They think they can take out the triple-A."

Waugh shook his head. This was suicide. He and Major Alexander watched as two A-1E Skyraider propeller aircraft came in low and slow. Skyraiders fly 110 mph, and in this scenario they were sitting ducks. With an explosion of fire, each of them was hit by antiaircraft guns and crashed violently into the hillside below.

"It's a graveyard down there," Major Alexander said.

Through binoculars, Waugh watched as enemy fighters on the ground swarmed to the downed aircraft. He tried again to make radio contact with any of those who'd gone down, but no one responded to his calls. The Cessna was running low on fuel. Soon they'd have to turn back. Waugh called over the radio again. Nothing. Not a sound.

Then, suddenly, Waugh's radio crackled to life.

"This is Hatchet Force. On the ground," a faint voice said over the comms.

Incredible, thought Waugh. "Hatchet Force, where are you?" he asked.

"See the two red panels at the edge of the crater?" the SOG Hatchet Force operator asked.

Through binoculars, Waugh scanned the ground until he located a group of SOG men and Yards, gathered inside one of the bomb craters made by the B-52s just an hour or so earlier.

"We need air support," the soldier said. "We're twenty-five alive."

Unbelievable!

But the men in the bomb crater were surrounded on all sides by hundreds of NVA. As Billy Waugh and Major Alexander returned to Khe Sanh to refuel, they pondered the question: *How do you get twenty-five men out of a target area when you can't get any aircraft in?*

In the jungle outside Oscar Eight, SOG operator Sergeant First Class Charles F. Wilklow crawled along on his belly, leaving behind a trail of blood as he went. Wilklow had been badly injured in the CH-46 helicopter crash, along with two other SOG men, four aircrew, and thirty Montagnards, all of whom were now either killed or missing.

After surviving the initial helicopter crash, Wilklow took cover inside a bomb crater with SOG operators Billy Ray Laney and Ron Dexter and roughly twenty indigs. The soldiers' injuries ranged from compound fractures to chest wounds and at least fifteen of them required immediate evacuation. From the crater, they watched as two SOG Kingbee helicopters came in, preparing to load the most grievously injured onto the helicopters to get out.

The first Kingbee helicopter that was coming in took fire, crashed, and exploded in a fireball. But the second managed to land, Wilklow observed. The SOG operators who'd been assigned to kill General Giap jumped out while the injured soldiers from the bomb crater were loaded inside. Wilklow crawled to the helicopter and climbed aboard before it took off. Under heavy fire, the Kingbee lifted up and began to fly away. Hundreds of NVA bullets punched through the skin of the aircraft as it ascended. Then, just as the pilot got up over the jungle canopy, he took a bullet to the forehead and died. The helicopter lurched into a violent spin. For the second time that morning, Charlie Wilklow found himself in a helicopter crash.

The chopper spun and landed in the trees, the thick jungle canopy keeping it from hitting the ground. Wilklow looked around. He was alive but there were dead bodies everywhere. Pushing past the dead, and despite grievous injuries, he climbed down from the trees and began running. That's when an NVA bullet caught him in the leg. He crawled into hiding, out of view. For now. Through the bushes, he saw that SOG operator Billy Ray Laney was dead from a shot to the chest. He watched Ron Dexter be captured and executed on the spot. A third SOG operator, Frank Cius Jr., was also captured, but for some reason the NVA soldiers didn't kill him. They blindfolded Cius and marched him away.

Wilklow lay silent in the bush. He was light-headed from blood loss and without a weapon, having lost his CAR-15 in the second helicopter crash. He could hear the NVA searching for him, but he'd found a place to hide. Finally, he passed out. When he woke up, he saw an NVA soldier in the trees, staring down at him. The man had a

12.7mm machine gun trained on him and was smoking a cigarette. Wilklow passed out again. When he woke up the second time, there were a group of NVA soldiers around him. He figured he was done for.

Back at the SOG base at Khe Sanh, Staff Sergeant Lester Pace was at work on the tarmac, loading and unloading men as they came in. He watched Billy Waugh climb out of the Cessna and hurry down into the SOG bunker. Major Kilburn was holding a briefing inside. He quickly related the facts: twenty-five SOG men were alive in a B-52 bomb crater at Oscar Eight, fighting to hold back an untold number of enemy forces. They would not last long without resupply, Major Kilburn said. He decided to have *himself*, with weapons and as much ammo as possible, inserted into the bomb crater immediately, by Kingbee helicopter so he could personally take charge of the situation and direct tactical air strikes. Together with the twenty-five alive, Kilburn would hold off the NVA until a rescue operation could be launched, which would have to wait until after dusk.

Waugh reported what he'd seen: several SOG men had escaped into the jungle and were likely still alive. He volunteered to put a Bright Light rescue team together to search for anyone alive. Kilburn decided that sending in additional aircraft at this time of day was suicidal. Only the cover of darkness would change the calculus. It was barely 9:00 a.m. Waugh would have to wait until dusk to launch a rescue operation.

Mustachio volunteered to fly Kilburn in to the bomb crater at Oscar Eight. Lester Pace loaded up the aircraft for the two men. It was a radical, risky infiltration operation, which Mustachio pulled off flawlessly. In what an after-action report listed as occurring in less than ninety seconds, Kilburn leapt out into the bomb crater, the SOG men unloaded the weapons and ammo, then loaded the five worst-wounded indigs onto the helicopter, and, finally, signaled for Mustachio to get out. Back at the SOG base, the question on everyone's mind was, Could the men left in the bomb crater last until dusk?

In the jungle, Charlie Wilklow was awake again, thirsty beyond description, maggots crawling around his gaping leg wound. The group of NVA soldiers stood over him, staring down, a few with guns trained on him. The soldiers dragged Wilklow to a small camp adjacent to the Oscar Eight bowl. They assigned a guard to him, a strange-looking man whose face had been disfigured, leaving him with no nose, just two nostrils above the top lip. Every time Wilklow passed out, he experienced a terrible nightmare about his captor and his mutilated face.

After depositing Kilburn in the bomb crater, Mustachio made it back to base with five gravely wounded Yards. While Lester Pace unloaded the helicopter, Billy Waugh asked Mustachio how long until he was ready to go searching for missing SOG operators. Mustachio said he was ready now. It was 10:00 a.m. That's close enough to dusk, thought Waugh.

Mustachio and Waugh headed back to Oscar Eight, flying over it, outside the range of antiaircraft fire, desperately searching for a sign of anyone who might be alive. Any combat soldier who has evaded capture and awaited rescue will tell you that there is nothing like the sound of helicopter rotor blades to sharpen the will to survive. "These rescue operations were critical to morale," says John Plaster. The thought that your fellow "SOG men would never give up a chance to look for you" was why so many SOG operators were willing to keep running into battle despite highly unfavorable odds.

Meanwhile, on the jungle floor outside Oscar Eight, the group of NVA soldiers who'd captured Charlie Wilklow decided to use him as bait. Wilklow's lower leg was nearly destroyed. He was not going anywhere, so they laid him down in an open clearing and spread out his red rescue panel on his chest, hoping the SOG helicopter flying overhead would see him and come for him. But the jungle was endless, a sea of green trees, and neither Waugh nor Mustachio spotted Charlie Wilklow spread out on the ground with a signal panel on his chest. After dusk, Kilburn and the men in the bomb crater were all extracted alive. But there were no survivors beyond that. Twenty-four hours passed.

The next day, Waugh and Alexander continued searching. Nothing. Forty-eight hours passed, then seventy-two. Still searching, still no missing men found. On the fourth day, on a pass over the western edge of the horseshoe ridge, Waugh noticed an unusual color on the jungle floor: red. He asked Major Alexander to fly in closer.

My God, he thought, that's a red signal panel.

There was a body down there, with a signal panel across the chest. Waugh was certain of it.

Waugh used the FM radio to call back to Khe Sanh. He requested two SOG men and a helicopter for a rescue mission, but all the SOG recon men were out on new missions. The only SOG man on base was Lester Pace, working resupply. Didn't matter. Waugh knew Pace to be a dedicated SOG man who also happened to be endowed with "hellacious strength."

"I told him I needed him for a rescue mission," remembers Waugh.

Pace said he was just about to leave for some rest and relaxation in Hong Kong.

"No, you're not," said Waugh.

"Of course I was going to go on the rescue mission," Pace recalled in an interview for this book. "I'd already served my time in the jungle. Spent six or seven months on a SOG recon team. I knew everyone on base. Now in resupply, I'd get the guys anything they needed to complete a mission. I saw them go out, and I was [aware] who didn't return."

Not wasting any time, Waugh briefed Pace on the rescue mission over the radio. He'd need to rappel down out of a hovering Kingbee wearing an extraction rig and carrying a second one. "When you reach the man on the ground," said Waugh, "hook him to yourself, give the pilot the thumbs-up, and both of you will lift off." Pace said he understood.

The helicopter pilot flew Lester Pace to the target area, loitering over the jungle canopy where the man and his red panel were last seen. "I sensed nothing but danger," Pace recalled. "All the danger in the world. The NVA were like the Tasmanian devil. They swarmed. They hid. They were everywhere. My gut feeling was, 'Wow this might be the end for me.'"

With the pilot hovering over the target, Lester Pace leaned out of the helicopter for a better look. He saw the SOG man move. The man was definitely alive. Pace gave the pilot the signal he was going to go, then rappelled down toward the body. He hooked the soldier to the second rig, then gave the pilot the thumbs-up. The pilot lifted the two men up off the ground and moved fast out of enemy territory.

"Wilklow grabbed and hugged me," remembers Pace. "He said, 'I don't believe this. I'm supposed to be dead.'" The pilot made it safely back to base. When they landed at Khe Sanh with Charlie Wilklow, "everyone just grabbed and hugged him," Pace recalls.

Sergeant First Class Charlie Wilklow had survived two deadly helicopter crashes, been captured by the NVA, held as a POW, forgotten about, and then rescued—all against impossible odds. The NVA had set Wilklow up as bait and had prepared to ambush and kill or capture the SOG rescue team. But apparently after three and a half days the NVA gave up on Wilklow being rescued and instead left him out in the open to die. Maggots that had infested Wilklow's wounds saved his leg and probably his life; the insects ate away the dead tissue and kept him from developing blood poisoning.

After the war, Pace recalls driving on base at Fort Bragg. He saw a man walking along the side of the road and recognized him to be Charlie Wilklow. "I rolled down my window and introduced myself. Told him who I was," remembers Pace. "He couldn't believe it. He invited me back to his place. His wife cooked a nice dinner and he told her the whole story about how I saved his life."

Pace retired from the U.S. Army Special Forces, moved to Brooklyn, New York, and worked as a schoolteacher for twenty-five years. He never told his family about any of his classified SOG missions. Lester Pace's son, Bakari Pace, found out about his dad's past in 2011, after the existence of SOG was finally declassified by the Defense Department and SOG members started sharing their experiences in forums online. Charlie Wilklow was the only captured SOG operator to ever be rescued during the entire Vietnam War.

The CIA had been watching Che Guevara's moves closely for eight years. Yet in the spring of 1967, he'd disappeared. Despite the CIA's reach and resources, they had no idea where he was. In Cuba, things had ended badly for Che Guevara. In a speech in 1965, he'd attacked the Soviet Union, calling its leaders "state-run profiteers." He'd expressed outrage over the fact that the Soviet Union wasn't doing more to support small wars of liberation around the globe. Castro was unable to control Che's pro-war rhetoric, which included a call for "nuclear war should it come about." Moscow put pressure on Fidel Castro to do something about him. The CIA intercepted a communiqué from Leonid Brezhnev warning that "the activities of Ernesto 'Che' Guevara... were harmful to the true interests of the communist cause."

Under pressure from his Soviet benefactors, Fidel Castro sent Che Guevara to Africa, to start a revolution in Congo, which failed. In November 1966, Che Guevara left for Bolivia to try to start a revolution there. The handsome revolutionary was one of the most recognizable figures in the world, so he disguised himself as a middle-aged Uruguayan economist, wearing thick glasses and a skullcap that made him look bald. Before he left Cuba this last time, Che gave his wife, Aleida, a letter to read to their children should he never return. "Grow up to be good revolutionaries," Che implored. "Remember that the Revolution is what is important and that each one of us, on our own, is worthless."

Now it was the summer of 1967, and a deathly ill Che Guevara was holed up in the Bolivian mountains with a small band of Marxist revolutionaries who were in equally bad shape. Like men shipwrecked on an island, Che and his guerrilla fighters had barely anything to eat. When a local peasant shared his food with them, cooked pork, they were unable to digest the meat and got sick. Eventually they slaughtered their own horses and mules. Emaciated from diarrhea, and without asthma medicine, Che hadn't taken a bath in six months. The will to go on withered from him, he wrote in his diary. He felt depressed. The Bolivian Army was after him. So was the CIA.

In June 1967 in Miami, Florida, Felix Rodriguez received a call from his CIA case officer. Rodriguez had continued to work for the Agency on contract operations ever since he was first recruited for Brigade 2506, the Bay of Pigs operation in 1961.

Then came a mysterious call. "Are you willing to go to Bolivia and lead a mission?" a man asked cryptically. Rodriguez learned that the job he was being offered required unconventional-warfare skills, that it was an anti-guerrilla operation, a mission so highly classified it had been authorized by the president of the United States. The U.S. ambassador to Bolivia set forth a stipulation: that the man chosen by the CIA to lead the covert operation needed to be a non-U.S. citizen. Felix Rodriguez was still a Cuban national.

"What's the mission?" Rodriguez asked.

"Train Bolivian Army Rangers in unconventional warfare and go get Che Guevara," he was told.

Rodriguez was flown to Bolivia, where he worked alongside a Special Forces A-team, commanded by Major Ralph Shelton, training army rangers in unconventional-warfare techniques. By the first week of October, the CIA's network of assets had finally honed in on where Che Guevara was hiding out. He was holed up in the mountains, in a remote village called La Higuera, in Vallegrande Province. Two days later, Rodriguez was installing an aircraft antenna in an airplane at the general headquarters of the 8th Division of the Bolivian Rangers when the coded message came over the radio.

"Papá cansado," the message said. "Dad is tired." The rangers trained by Rodriguez had captured Che Guevara alive.

Rodriguez notified his CIA handler. That same night, President Johnson received a memo from national-security advisor Walt Rostow saying that Che Guevara had likely been captured. "The Bolivian unit engaged is the one we have been training for some time," Rostow told the president. "This tentative information that the Bolivians got Che Guevara will interest you. It is not yet confirmed."

In the morning, Felix Rodriguez and Bolivian colonel Joaquin Zenteno Anaya flew by helicopter to the one-room schoolhouse in the mountains where Che was being held captive. Rodriguez asked to see the prisoner alone. Che Guevara was on the floor, his arms tied and his feet bound. His clothes were torn, his hair was matted, and in place of shoes he wore pieces of leather tied with cord. There in the schoolhouse, with the prisoner looking on, Felix Rodriguez set up his radio and transmitted a coded message to the CIA station in La Paz, to be retransmitted on to headquarters at Langley, in Virginia. Rodriguez photographed Che's diary and confiscated his belongings: besides the diary, there were some pictures, Che's address book, and a roll of microfiche.

Rodriguez says he spoke to Che alone for over an hour and that he told him he was Cuban and had been part of the CIA's Brigade 2506. "I said that in the aftermath of the CIA invasion at the Bay of Pigs, he had personally executed several of my friends."

"Ha," Che said in response. Nothing more.

"I don't know what he was thinking at the moment and I never asked," Rodriguez recalls. He says he told Che that he was working for the CIA and that the Agency wanted him alive, not dead.

Shots rang out in the room next door. A fighter named Aniceto had just been executed, and Rodriguez recalls hearing the man's body fall to the floor.

Rodriguez received a radio call from the Bolivian High Command, he later told the CIA's inspector general, with a coded message—"the code numbers 500 and 600 as orders"—to execute the prisoner Che Guevara. He knew that this was a violation of the Geneva Conventions. Rodriguez maintains that the Bolivian Army was in charge of the operation, not the CIA. He stared at Che, a condemned man.

"We embraced," Rodriguez says. "It was a tremendously emotional moment for me. I no longer hated him."

Rodriguez walked out of the room, passing two Bolivian soldiers he says looked drunk. He asked them not to shoot Che Guevara in the face. He walked to a hilltop and stood there. When he heard shots ring out, he noted the time on his Rolex watch. It was 1:10 p.m.

After a few minutes, one of the soldiers came out carrying Che Guevara's watch, a Rolex like his own. Rodriguez asked to see it. When the soldier wasn't looking, he says, he swapped out Che's Rolex for his own.

It was time to move out. Using a canvas tarp, the soldiers loaded Che Guevara's body into the helicopter. But balancing the corpse inside the small helicopter was challenging, and a decision was made to strap the body to one of the helicopter's skids. Rodriguez struggled with the task. Looking down, he noticed he had Che Guevara's blood on his hands.

Back at Bolivian Army headquarters, Felix Rodriguez briefed Chief of Staff General Alfredo Ovando Candia on the events of the day. At one point during the conversation, the general ordered a subordinate to cut off Che Guevara's hands, remembers Rodriguez. "The hands were sent to Cuba, to Fidel [Castro], as proof that Che was dead," Rodriguez stated in an interview for this book. "I know for certain from sources that they are kept in preservatives, in Havana, in a secure facility there." Rodriguez says that on occasion, Che's amputated hands are ceremoniously brought out and shown to anti-American revolutionaries as a physical reminder of the dirty work done by the United States and the Central Intelligence Agency.

★   ★   ★

On February 24, 1969, Felix Rodriguez became a citizen of the United States. He told his CIA handler that he wanted to volunteer for U.S. government service in Vietnam. He was assigned to the Phoenix program, one of the most controversial programs of the Vietnam War.

"Phoenix was one of several pacification and rural security programs that CIA ran in South Vietnam during the 1960s," says Colonel Andrew R. Finlayson, an officer in the Phoenix program. "The premise of pacification was that if peasants were persuaded that the government of South Vietnam and the United States were sincerely interested in protecting them from the Vietcong and trained them to defend themselves, then large areas of the South Vietnamese countryside could be secured or won back from the enemy without direct engagement by the U.S. military."

This is not what happened. When so-called pacification was not realized, as the numbers of Vietcong in the south went up as opposed to going down, the program was expanded. Whereas the Civilian Irregular Defense Group program focused on armed defense, the Phoenix program was intelligence-based. The CIA created a network of roughly one hundred local intelligence committees across South Vietnam. These committees, says Colonel Finlayson, collected information on the Vietcong and then disseminated it to local police. When this didn't work, the CIA-funded program became even more aggressive. "Essentially, these committees created lists of known VCI [Vietcong] operatives. Once the name, rank, and location of each individual VCI member became known, CIA paramilitary or South Vietnamese police or military forces interrogated these individuals for further intelligence on the communist structure and its operations."

These CIA paramilitary teams were called Provincial Reconnaissance Units (PRUs). Felix Rodriguez was the deputy field advisor for the PRU in the village of Bien Hoa. His boss was a CIA officer named William Buckley, who, in due time, would become the central figure in President Ronald Reagan's decision to construct a foreign policy tool called "pre-emptive neutralization." But that was far in the future. For now, every day with the PRU was about trying to quell the communist insurgency enveloping the south.

Every field advisor assigned to a PRU paramilitary team worked undercover. Rodriguez's cover was that he was a civilian advisor for the U.S. Army. CIA internal memos described the Provincial Reconnaissance Units as the "investigatory [and] para-military-attack" teams that would support the Phoenix program in the field. Witnesses say that the program used torture, murder, and assassination to try to rid the south of the Vietcong. U.S. officials have long disputed this claim. A similar program was developed in Afghanistan forty years in the future. What would begin as a program of pacification in Afghanistan, in September 2001, would be transformed into the first U.S. government targeted killing campaign to be publicly acknowledged by an American president.

CHAPTER FOURTEEN

Green Berets

The Special Forces A-Team camp at Thanh Tri was located in Kien Tuong Province in the Mekong Delta, strategically positioned just three miles from Vietnam's border with Cambodia. What happened there in the summer of 1969 would become an international scandal known as the Green Beret Affair, a tragic conundrum that would raise complex questions about murder versus assassination, about the mysterious relationship between the CIA and the Green Berets, and about the laws of war. Most important to this story, the Green Beret Affair of 1969 demonstrates how the construct of plausible deniability shields the U.S. president from wrongdoing while exposing operators who carry out euphemistic orders vulnerable to prosecution and jail time.

As per the terms of the 1954 Geneva Conference on Indochina, fighting in Cambodia was prohibited. By 1967, intelligence indicated that the communists had expanded the Ho Chi Minh Trail down into Cambodia, to a terminus point on the border just thirty miles from Saigon called the Parrot's Beak. Starting in the spring of that same year, MACV-SOG began running secret cross-border operations into Cambodia under the code name Daniel Boone. Detachment B57 of the 5th Special Forces (Airborne) at Thanh Tri provided intelligence for those and other missions under the CIA code name

Project Gamma. Like so many other Green Beret paramilitary units across Vietnam, the one at Thanh Tri was a hybrid of Special Forces soldiers, CIA personnel, and local indigenous soldiers. Detachment B57 was made up of six Green Berets, three CIA operators, and as many as 450 indigenous fighters. The unit was commanded by one of the CIA operators, a twenty-seven-year-old former insurance sales-man named Robert F. Marasco. He went by the cover name Captain Martin.

By the winter of 1968–69, Marasco had assembled a network of twenty indigenous assets who spied for him around the Parrot's Beak. His most valuable spy, called a principal asset, was a thirty-one-year-old native of the north named Thai Khac Chuyen ("Chew-win"). Chuyen's official position was S5 interpreter, or terp, in military speak.

Chuyen had been recruited by CIA case officer Sergeant Alvin Smith Jr., who went by the cover name Peter Sands and who reported to Marasco at Thanh Tri. Smith was an enigmatic CIA case officer, older than Marasco by fifteen years. He was also a veteran of uncon-ventional warfare, having led covert operations behind enemy lines in Korea. According to his file, Alvin Smith once served as the only American in a battalion of 1,400 Korean and Chinese indigenous troops as part of a JACK mission that has never been fully declassified.

For better or for worse, Alvin Smith was known for becoming friendly with his assets. At the nearby support base in Moc Hoa, he'd sometimes stay up late into the night drinking whiskey with Chuyen. How Chuyen spoke such good English irked Smith. Chuyen said he grew up reading books in English and that he'd worked for the U.S. military in Saigon. When pressed, Chuyen was vague about the details, claiming the missions were all classified.

Now it was March 1969, and there'd been an unusual number of mortar attacks on Moc Hoa, an indicator that a bigger attack might be coming. Marasco sent a unit out on a recon mission, led by a Green Beret from Kentucky named Terry McIntosh. Just nineteen at the time, McIntosh was one of the youngest Green Berets assigned to the war. He'd already been in Vietnam for seven months.

"It was me, Chuyen, and ten indigenous troops on the mission," McIntosh recalled in an interview for this book. "A little before dawn, I spotted enemy movement along the tree line," indicating an ambush. McIntosh fired a grenade launcher in the direction of the troops and watched the fighters disperse. He handed the scope off to Chuyen. "He looked through it. I remember that he smiled. I thought that was strange but dismissed it," remembers McIntosh, who then tried calling the A-Camp for support. But the radio was dead. "Ground-to-ground comms were usually excellent out here," he recalls. That the radio didn't work was strange to him. Suddenly, a volley of fire erupted from all sides, as if the Vietcong had foreknowledge that the team was coming, says McIntosh. A massive firefight ensued, with McIntosh firing his assault rifle until he was out of ammunition. "Chuyen was on my left, and the others to my right, but I noticed that Chuyen wasn't firing his weapon," he remembers. "He was fiddling with it, and later claimed that it jammed. At the time, I accepted his explanation without reservation."

Back at A-Camp, the commander heard artillery fire and ordered a mortar attack based on the unit's last known position. The firefight ended without any fatalities from Detachment B57, and the men returned to Thanh Tri. McIntosh, a radio specialist, and a teammate examined the gear. "It had been tampered with," McIntosh recalls. He told Marasco, who became concerned. One of Marasco's other assets told him he'd heard Chuyen was a communist spy.

Marasco ran a search in the MACV database, but there was no record of Chuyen. As a CIA employee, Marasco had access to classified information that others did not. That no record on Chuyen appeared likely meant that he was lying about having ever worked on classified missions in Saigon. Fearing he was a double agent, Marasco radioed headquarters at Nha Trang and asked that both men, Smith and Chuyen, be reassigned. Smith was moved over to the 5th Special

Forces headquarters and Chuyen returned to Saigon, where his family lived.

A few weeks later, a Special Forces recon team recovered photographs of a high-level North Vietnamese Army general meeting with his local Vietcong spies. In one of the photographs, there was Chuyen—standing right next to the North Vietnamese general, smiling. Robert Marasco was sure it was Chuyen. Alvin Smith was also shown the photograph and had the same response: it was Chuyen. Their principal asset was a spy for the north.

On June 9, CIA headquarters instructed Alvin Smith to bring Chuyen in, under the guise of a covert operation. For five days, Chuyen was interrogated. He repeatedly failed the polygraph, all the while insisting the person in the photograph was not him. The transcript of what he actually said has never been declassified, but according to reports leaked to the press, he cursed the Americans and said they'd lose the war to the communists in the north.

What to do with the double agent Chuyen? He couldn't be sent to local law enforcement; the police around the Parrot's Beak were notoriously corrupt and rife with double agents. Chuyen knew the identities of all the undercover CIA officers, operators, and assets at Thanh Tri. Alvin Smith suggested they try to turn Chuyen into a triple agent, someone who could work for the CIA again.

Marasco contacted the CIA station in Nha Trang and asked what he should do. He was told to kill him. "[Chuyen] was my agent and it was my responsibility to 'eliminate him with extreme prejudice,'" Marasco later told the *New York Times*. Marasco said these were "oblique yet very, very clear orders." He explained further that everyone working covert operations for the CIA and Special Forces knew that the phrase "eliminate with extreme prejudice" was a euphemism for kill.

Marasco reached out to the commander of the U.S. Army Special Forces, Colonel Robert B. Rheault, asking for his orders on the matter. Colonel Rheault told Marasco that the group was "to proceed." The CIA officers and U.S. Army Green Berets agreed on a cover story. They'd say Chuyen had been assigned to a covert mission and then disappeared. Everyone involved agreed to proceed—except Alvin Smith, who refused to participate.

Agent Chuyen was told he was needed for a highly classified mission. On June 20, 1969, the CIA officer and the Green Berets drugged Chuyen with morphine, drove with him to a remote beach near Nha Trang, and loaded him into a boat. They took the boat out into deep waters in Nha Trang Bay, where Marasco shot Chuyen in the head with a .22-caliber pistol, equipped with a suppressor, while Chuyen was still unconscious. The men loaded Chuyen's body into a mail sack, weighted it down with chains and tire rims, and threw him overboard into the South China Sea.

The following day, a cable came in from CIA headquarters. "Killing is no solution," it read.

Paranoia gripped CIA case officer Alvin Smith. He went to his CIA superior in Nha Trang and asked for asylum in exchange for information. With immunity in place, he told his superior officer that his colleagues at Thanh Tri had killed Chuyen and that now Smith feared for his own life. Things moved fast. The CIA officer notified the U.S. Army, which sent the information up the chain of command, all the way to the U.S. commander in Vietnam, General Creighton Abrams Jr.

General Abrams summoned Colonel Rheault to his office and asked what had happened to Chuyen. Rheault told the general that the asset was away on a secret mission, when in fact he'd already been killed. When General Abrams learned he'd been lied to, he exploded with rage. The following day, Colonel Rheault, Robert Marasco, and six Green Berets were arrested, handcuffed, and sent to the Long Binh Jail outside Saigon. They'd be tried for conspiracy to commit murder and murder in the first degree, Abrams said.

The military imposed a gag order on those who knew about the case, but reporters quickly learned of the arrests and the details of their imprisonment. That American Green Berets were being held in solitary confinement, in tiny 5' × 7' cells with just a cot and a bare lightbulb, seemed outrageous. How could the U.S. Army treat its own soldiers like this? Most shocking of all, the secretary of the army said that if the men were convicted, their punishment would be "life in prison, not a firing squad." Firing squad? The press cried absurd. Despite the growing antiwar movement across America, a majority of civilians sided with the Green Berets, calling them scapegoats of the Pentagon war machine.

More mysterious details emerged: double agents, triple agents, Green Berets, the CIA. Then came the rumor that the Green Berets were operating across the border in Cambodia, this at a time when the Nixon White House had already insisted that a *New York Times* reporter who'd revealed that the United States was dropping bombs on Cambodia was a liar. When someone leaked to the press the photograph of Chuyen standing next to the North Vietnamese Army general, smiling, citizens and congressmen alike began to ask questions. How could killing a Vietcong spy in a war zone be considered a war crime? *Life* magazine interviewed Colonel Rheault's eleven-year-old son, Robert Jr. "What's all the fuss about?" asked the fifth grader. "I thought that's what Dad was in Vietnam for—to kill the Vietcong."

Henry Rothblatt, defense attorney for the Green Berets, made a brilliant move. He deposed the CIA. Marasco's identity as a CIA officer remained classified (Marasco revealed his identity to the *New York Times* in 1971). Rothblatt was betting that there was no way the White House would allow the CIA to testify in court. Between its ongoing assassination programs, the Phoenix program, the classified MACV-SOG missions into Laos and Cambodia—these were but a few of the president's hidden-hand programs that surely needed to remain that way. The president's inner circle would never allow the CIA to testify about its operations in Vietnam. The White House had far too much to lose.

President Nixon had a last-minute idea, a double cross of CIA director Richard Helms, whom Nixon disliked. In a note to Henry Kissinger, his national-security advisor, Nixon wrote, "K—I think [Richard] Helms should be made to take part of the rap." While there's no record of Kissinger's reaction, based on actions taken it is likely he advised the president against throwing Helms under the proverbial bus. Instead, the following morning, on September 29, 1969, the U.S. Army unexpectedly dropped all charges against the eight men involved in the Green Beret Affair. The U.S. Department of Justice concluded that a fair and impartial trial was not possible. Further details of the CIA's refusal to testify remain classified, but under pressure, the Nixon White House was forced to acknowledge that the president had been involved in the decision to drop all murder charges.

Decades later, after MACV-SOG was declassified, a fascinating detail emerged. On August 25, a month after the CIA officers and the Green Berets were arrested but before the Nixon White House dropped the murder charges, a SOG recon team called RT Florida was sent on a Top Secret cross-border mission into Cambodia. There the team was pursued by a squadron of NVA soldiers using dogs to track them. In the process of evading capture, the SOG operators shot and killed two NVA officers. One of the dead men turned out to be a high-ranking intelligence officer. Inside the large leather satchel he carried was a gold mine: a cache of documents, one of which was a partial roster of double agents and spies operating for Hanoi inside South Vietnam. One name on the roster "was the double agent executed by order of Colonel Rheault," writes scholar Richard Shultz.

"War is never pleasant," says Terry McIntosh. "War is bigger than the individual soldier. For the record, as tragic as it was for all parties, I salute Marasco and others who were charged. They were soldiers under orders. There were no good options for them. The job fell to them. The moral issues are still unresolved."

It was into this highly charged environment that a young Green Beret named Lewis C. Merletti volunteered to go to Vietnam.

Lew Merletti stood in the green grass on the side of Interstate 95 North in Fayetteville, North Carolina, with his thumb out. It was 1969, he was twenty-one years old, and he was hitching a ride to the Pentagon to volunteer for service in Vietnam. His whole life was in front of him, including his plans, dreams, and aspirations—of doing great things for himself, his family, and his country—but he also felt he could not do any of this in good conscience if he skipped out on Vietnam.

"This war was going on, and I knew a lot of guys my age that were being drafted and didn't want to go and they were going anyway," recalls Merletti. "I really felt like, 'Hey, it's not right, I have to contribute to this. I can't be sitting back here safe [in the United States] if these guys are going over there fighting this war.' It just didn't seem to me to be fair." In 1969, the young Lew Merletti had no way of knowing what his immediate future included. He certainly had no idea that one day he would serve on the Presidential Protective Detail of three U.S. presidents, or that he would become the nineteenth director of the U.S. Secret Service—a law enforcement agency created by President Abraham Lincoln and signed into law on the morning of April 14, 1865, the day of Lincoln's own assassination.

The journey to war for Lew Merletti began two years earlier, when he signed up for military service as an airborne infantryman. At the end of his first week of jump school, a very confident, very focused, physically fit young man showed up in full military dress to speak to Merletti's group of roughly three hundred soldiers-in-training. The man wore the green beret. "He gets up on this platform in front of us and says, 'Gentlemen, I'm gonna be honest with you, Special Forces is losing men and we need volunteers,'" Merletti recalls. He volunteered.

Training lasted forty-two weeks. "You learn how to treat gunshot wounds, perform surgeries and amputations. It's basically like becoming a highly trained paramedic," Merletti explains. The U.S. Army Special Forces also wanted some of its medics to speak Vietnamese — they would be treating a lot of citizens in country — and so Merletti was sent to the language school, at Fort Bragg. Over the course of the next five months, for eight hours a day, he was taught Vietnamese by a lively young woman originally from North Vietnam. By the time he finished training, he had less than one year on his three-year enlistment. "I was told I didn't have to go to Vietnam," he remembers. It was too close to the end of his tour. "Unless I volunteered." This is why he was hitchhiking to the Pentagon, in Washington, DC, that spring day in 1969.

Merletti had been standing on the side of the road in full dress uniform with his green beret for about five minutes when a man in a VW bug pulled up, slowed to a stop, and rolled down the window.

"Where are you going?" the man asked.

"The Pentagon," Merletti said.

It was the height of the Vietnam War. It was also the height of the anti–Vietnam War movement. The country was terribly divided. Lew Merletti had a feeling that the outcome here — with the driver of the VW bug — could go either way.

"The Pentagon. Are you kidding me?" the man asked, incredulous.

Lew said he was not kidding. That he was going there to volunteer for combat service in Vietnam.

"Well, if you're going to the Pentagon," the driver said, "I'll take you straight there." And he did. Nearly fifty years later, Merletti vividly remembers being dropped off in the parking lot of the Pentagon, and he still thinks about the anonymous man who drove him there, the man's willingness to help do his part, however incremental.

There in Washington, DC, inside Defense Department headquarters, Merletti located Mrs. Billie Alexander, just as Billy Waugh had sought out and found Mrs. Alexander when he wanted to get assigned to SOG. "Everyone knew Billie Alexander was in charge of assigning volunteers to Special Forces in Vietnam," remembers Merletti, and, as she had for so many others, she approved his request. "You'll be in Vietnam in August," she said.

To get to Vietnam, Merletti first flew from his hometown of Pittsburgh, Pennsylvania, to Chicago, Illinois, where he had a layover. He traveled in his Class A dress uniform and green beret. "You really stood out as a soldier back then," Merletti recalls. "No one else in the entire military was authorized to wear a beret. There was only the Green Beret." Then, to his surprise, as he approached the gate, Merletti spotted a fellow Green Beret. But it wasn't just anyone—it was his very good friend from Special Forces training, 7th Group: Mike Kuropas. "He was saying good-bye to his family, so I kind of held back," he remembers. Eventually Mike Kuropas spotted Merletti, and introduced him to his family, a group of whom had come to the airport to see him off to war. "I met everybody and then it was time to go, to get on the plane," recalls Merletti. To go fight the war in Vietnam.

On the airplane a strange thing happened. Merletti and Kuropas were sitting together in the front of the plane. The flight attendants began to serve lunch, Merletti recalls. "They put a meal in front of me and then they said to Mike, 'We'll get you a meal in a minute.'" Five or so minutes passed before the flight attendant returned. "She says, 'We're really sorry, but we don't have any meals left. But here's a little voucher so the next time you fly, you'll get an upgrade or something like that.'" Mike Kuropas looked at the voucher. "He looks at me," remembers Merletti, "and he says, 'You know this is a bad omen,' and I say, 'What do you mean?' He says, 'I'm not coming back.' I say, 'Mike, don't say that. Don't say that at all.' I said, 'You know, we all have those thoughts, but don't go there, just don't do it.'"

Mike Kuropas looked squarely at Lew Merletti and said, "No, I know I'm not coming back."

When they arrived in country, Merletti, Kuropas, and the rest of the Green Berets were taken to the island facility of Hon Tre, off the coast of Vietnam. There, Special Forces soldiers coming from the United States for insertion into the battlefield generally spent several days getting a refresher course in shooting, using hand grenades, setting off claymore mines, and using of mortars. When the training on Hon Tre was over, the group traveled to Special Forces headquarters in Nha Trang. "They tell us, 'Okay, everybody fall out, you have your orders.' We lined up, and we're standing at attention and they begin calling names off and telling you where you're going."

Merletti heard the sergeant say his name: "Merletti, A-502." This meant he'd been assigned to Detachment A-502 of the 5th Special Forces Group. The detachment's mission was to advise and assist the Vietnamese Special Forces in the joint CIA-Pentagon program, the Civilian Irregular Defense Group. Lew Merletti remembers thinking to himself, "Hey, that's not a bad assignment." Then he heard Mike Kuropas's name being called out, and the assignment he'd been given: "Kuropas, CCC." Merletti remembers thinking to himself, "Oh, God."

Everyone knew that CCC was part of MACV-SOG. The acronym CCC stood for Command and Control, Central, one of what were now three SOG bases in South Vietnam. Special Forces soldiers who were new to the program knew SOG was the place where hard-core warriors with extensive combat experience fought direct-action missions behind enemy lines. SOG was where Special Forces legends like Larry Thorne, Ed Wolcoff, and Billy Waugh fought and thrived—some until they died. But for newcomers, for initiates into combat, SOG was dangerous. It was Suicide on the Ground. Merletti tried to make light of Kuropas's assignment but found the reality of the situation difficult to accept.

"I volunteered for Vietnam," he recalls, "I don't think Mike Kuropas had. I believe he'd received orders to go. I knew he didn't want to go to SOG, to CCC," remembers Merletti. "But I knew he'd give it his best."

The sergeant in charge announced that helicopters would be arriving momentarily to take everyone to their specific destinations. "The formation breaks up," says Merletti, "and Mike, who was standing maybe two people down from me, he steps over and he put out his hand and he says, 'Hey, thank you for your friendship and everything, it's been wonderful.' He said, 'I really appreciate you being my friend but this is it. It's over.' And I said, 'Please, Mike, don't say that.' And he says, 'No, no, no, it's gonna happen, it's gonna happen. It's alright.'"

Lew Merletti got on one army helicopter and Mike Kuropas got on another army helicopter. Either right before the birds flew away or as they were taking off, Merletti either said out loud to Mike Kuropas or he said to himself: *No, I'll meet you back here in one year.*

Lew Merletti was sent to a small village called Trung Dong in the Central Highlands, a remote area at risk of being dominated by the Vietcong. He lived in a Special Forces A-Camp there, built earlier by Green Berets. His team consisted of twelve Americans and a unit of indigenous mercenaries, called CIDG strikers, being paid by the Department of Defense to defend their village and to stop the enemy from gaining further control of the area.

"I had not been exposed to combat," Merletti remembers, and on the very first night, there was an ambush. In the ensuing firefight, six Viet Cong were killed and one of the mercenaries was bitten by a poisonous snake, which Merletti treated in the field before having the man medevaced out, thanks to the guidance, he says, of teammate Sergeant John Deschamps. Some weeks later, he and the team were out on patrol in the dense jungle when the CIDG striker standing right next to him was shot in the head. "My immediate reaction," says Merletti, "was, I've got to get help! Then I realized *I was the help.*" After a few intense and shock-riddled moments, Merletti's Special Forces medical training kicked in. "I knew exactly what to do," he recalls. "I said to myself, 'I can do this, I was trained for this.'" And he did. He stopped the bleeding, wrapped the wound, and again oversaw the medevac.

For the better part of the year, Merletti served in combat as part of a Special Forces A-Team. "Every time you go out on patrol, you have a lump in your throat," he recalls. "You wonder, 'Is this it?' Every footstep you take, you know it could be your last footstep." To stay focused and not let his mind wander, when he went out on patrol, Merletti learned to pay attention to minute details. Every detail mattered. If he wasn't paying attention, he could cross a trip wire or step on a land mine or make a noise that might alert the enemy. "You couldn't let your mind drift. You couldn't think, Man I wish I were at the ballpark. I wish I had a cold lemonade or a beer in my hand." Do that and you're dead. "You learn to look at the ground in front of you, to look at your flank. Pay attention to every single detail, every moment of every day."

Merletti's one-year tour of duty was scheduled to come to an end on May 30, 1970. But in the spring of 1970, the Defense Department announced it was reducing troop numbers in Vietnam, at President Nixon's request, and all soldiers were being given what was called a thirty-day drop. And so, in the first week of April 1970, Lew Merletti learned he was scheduled to leave Vietnam on April 28. All across Vietnam, Green Berets received this same news, and that included Mike Kuropas—who for ten straight months now had been fighting intense direct-action missions on a recon team for SOG, CCC.

On the morning of April 15, 1970, trouble began near a Special Forces A-Camp at Dak Seang, in the Central Highlands, ten miles from the border with Laos. Intelligence showed a massive buildup of NVA forces was under way, positioned to overtake the camp and surrounding valley. The plan was to insert a battalion of Special Forces soldiers and their ARVN counterparts on top of the mountain to protect the camp and all it stood for. One of the soldiers who fought there described this hilltop as "little more than a bald knob with craters," but it was a strategic position, with a vantage point over the surrounding valley. The U.S. Army and the North Vietnamese Army each wanted to control it. Designated LZ Orange, the Defense Department would initiate an offensive move to control it.

"So it was that at 0430 in the morning of April 15th, the flight-line at Kontum Air Field came alive with pilots, crew chiefs, and gunners busying themselves with their preflight checks, mounting weapons and loading rocket pods," recalled Donald Summers, a member of the 170th Assault Helicopter Company. He was about to be inserted. As the sun rose, the offensive began. As at Oscar Eight, helicopter gunships cleared LZ Orange while two troop transport helicopters ferried in South Vietnamese soldiers and their U.S. Special Forces commanders. The first helicopter landed, and its crew charged out. Then, in a move perfected by the North Vietnamese Army, as the second helicopter hovered fifty feet over the landing zone, it was rocketed out of the air, killing nine of the twelve men on board. On the ground, there were eight South Vietnamese soldiers and five American soldiers who'd survived, including one pilot, one copilot, a door gunner, a pathfinder, and the crew chief.

U.S. Air Force fast fliers came in screeching overhead, laying down suppressive fire. Over the past several hours, the losses in the area had been staggering: four helicopters shot down, seven helicopters hit, fate unknown. One of the A-1E Skyraiders was last seen losing altitude above a ridge line, its engine on fire. It was at this point in the operation that the U.S. Army and the U.S. Air Force command assessed the operation, from headquarters, and decided a rescue mission was not possible without "an unacceptable further loss of life." Which is when a SOG Bright Light team operating out of Kontum was asked to volunteer for a rescue mission. Like firefighters running into a burning building, Staff Sergeant Mike Kuropas, Staff Sergeant Dennis Neal, and six Montagnard mercenaries volunteered for the job. The operational plan was to insert the Bright Light team onto LZ Orange to rescue the men trapped on the hill. Bill McDonald, of the 170th Assault Helicopter Company, volunteered to pilot the team into the target area.

Helicopter pilot Donald Summers was one of the men bleeding out and dying on the hill. He later recalled seeing the helicopter carrying the SOG Bright Light team on its approach. Roughly half a mile out from the landing zone, pilot Bill McDonald dropped his SOG helicopter into a deep dive and headed down to the valley floor. He had to fly in "low and fast, up the side of the mountain to the LZ," Summers recalled, or he would have been shot down long before he got anywhere near the hill. "He was taking extensive fire from 360 degrees, but he pressed on." Crippled from enemy gunfire but still flying, Summers watched, horrified. "The bird slammed into the landing zone." Fuel poured out of a large hole in the fuel cell. A rocket had lodged near the tail but not exploded.

Under a barrage of small arms fire, Summers and the other survivors ran toward the helicopter. Summers remembered reaching the aircraft and looking inside. There, SOG Bright Light team leaders Mike Kuropas, Dennis Neal, and the six Montagnards lay dead on the floor, shredded from multiple gunshot wounds. Summers climbed into the crippled helicopter, and by some strange aviation miracle, Bill McDonald was able to fly the helicopter away.

Thirteen days later, on April 28, Lew Merletti completed his service in Vietnam. He was helicoptered down from the A-Team camp at Trung Dong to Special Forces headquarters in Nha Trang. The first action he took was to walk up to the bulletin board and search for Mike Kuropas's name. He found it.

It read: "Michael Vincent Kuropas, Killed in Action, April 15, 1970."

Merletti felt crushing loss. "Standing there, I became overwhelmed with emotion," he recalls. "The reality set in. I thought about Mike and I still think about all the guys who died in Vietnam. Each one of them. They were alive one moment and then they got shot. There's no anesthesia on the battlefield. You get shot. It's incredibly painful to get shot. You bleed out before you die," Merletti says. Standing in front of Mike Kuropas's name, Merletti made a vow. "I wanted to try to live up to certain expectations of myself, for him. For Mike." Merletti vowed that moving forward in his life, were he to perceive something in front of himself as difficult, he would stop and think of Mike Kuropas. He would acknowledge that whatever problem he was having, he was having the problem because he was alive. Mike Kuropas would not have the luxury of problems. Mike Kuropas, age just twenty-two, was dead.

By the end of 1970, the war was all but lost, the human losses too great to bear. The mighty U.S. Defense Department could not win the war. There were no front lines. The enemy swarmed like bees, like ants crawling, or fish swimming, just as Mao Zedong warned in *On Guerrilla Warfare* and General Giap had echoed in his own manifesto. The communists dominated the geography of every environment. For much of the war, the Defense Department believed its helicopters could tip the balance of power, but by 1971 helicopter losses were insurmountable, too. The precise number of helicopters shot down during the Vietnam War remains classified as of 2019.

Still, the Defense Department was not ready to accept their loss, and several eleventh-hour attempts were made within SOG, before 1971, to develop new tactics to win a guerrilla war. Billy Waugh was at the locus of one of these new ideas: insertion by parachute in an unorthodox manner. It was to be called a HALO jump. This involved exiting an aircraft above 10,000 feet, free-falling to roughly 2,000 feet or even lower, then gliding to the earth using a steerable parachute. During the Korean War, General Jack Singlaub had practiced this tactic himself, as a possible insertion technique to use in the covert air operations he was in charge of for the CIA. But the tactic was never used in Korea.

In 1970, the HALO jump remained untested in war. Since World War II, paratroopers had always jumped into battle using static lines that would open the parachutes automatically, predictably, one after the next, so a large group of jumpers could land in a pattern on a drop zone. Vietnam was different. SOG recon teams knew the NVA didn't keep watch over landing zones at night because no one ever parachuted in the darkness. Until now.

Waugh was in charge of selecting the world's first combat HALO team, then overseeing all SOG HALO training, including of the indig fighters assigned to operations. The units practiced on a tiny islet just a few miles off the northwest coast of Okinawa called le Shima Island. There, SOG operators practiced jumping out of aircraft at 30,000 feet, in full combat gear, then performing a military free fall for 27,500 feet, reaching terminal velocity before pulling the rip cord and landing in the ocean. The attempt to train their indig counterparts was a tall order, remembers Waugh. The Green Berets were all airborne-qualified. Some, like Waugh, had been jumping out of airplanes for more than twenty years. None of the indigs had ever left Vietnam, let alone jumped out of an airplane with a parachute. "Half of our indigs had never seen the ocean before," recalls Waugh. "One of our guys got spooked and pulled his parachute right after he jumped. He missed the target by about ten miles. By the time we got to him in the rescue boat he'd already consumed about a gallon of seawater. He got very, very sick."

On November 28, 1970, SOG's first HALO team, RT Florida, jumped into Laos. The unit was led by Staff Sergeant Cliff Newman, Sergeant First Class Sammy Hernandez, and Sergeant First Class Melvin Hill, accompanied by an officer with the ARVN and two Montagnard mercenaries "who had no experience jumping, but did just fine," remembers Waugh. RT Virginia conducted five days of reconnaissance behind enemy lines and were exfiltrated without incident. This was the first known HALO combat jump in the history of warfare. Seven months later, on June 22, 1971, Billy Waugh led the third HALO jump team into combat, also in Laos. Teammate Madison Strohlein was captured and killed. The vertical wind tunnel at the John F. Kennedy Special Warfare Center and School at Fort Bragg was named in his honor.

But no amount of new thinking, and no number of unusual infiltration tactics, could salvage this unwinnable war. The following year, on May 1, 1972, SOG was disbanded. American citizens were fed up with violence and warfare. In January 1973, the Paris Peace Accords were signed, bringing an end to the Vietnam War, with the country to remain divided between the north and the south. With 58,000 Americans killed in Vietnam, guerrilla warfare was a dirty word. Across the military and intelligence communities, budgets were slashed. Across the CIA and the Defense Department, covert-action programs were disbanded.

The U.S. Army in general, and the U.S. special operations forces in particular, suffered a black eye. Four of the army's six Special Forces groups were inactivated. The two small units that remained were assigned to a program called SPARTAN (Special Proficiency at Rugged Training and Nation-Building). To stay active, its soldiers worked with Indian tribes in Florida, Arizona, and Montana helping to build roads and medical facilities. The U.S. Army vowed to concentrate on conventional warfare—to stay out of ungovernable places like the jungles in Southeast Asia and to instead prepare for infantry and tank warfare on the flatlands of central Europe.

Men like Billy Waugh, and the skills they possessed, were not needed by the U.S. military or intelligence services anymore. The army offered Waugh a desk job at Fort Devens, Massachusetts. Waugh knew, after more than ten years of covert action and direct-action combat operations, that office work was not for him. In lieu of a retirement ceremony, he and six Green Berets HALO-jumped out of an aircraft over Fort Bragg, pulling their parachutes 800 feet above parade grounds. They landed, packed up their parachutes, and spent the afternoon drinking beer in honor of their dead friends. Then they went home.

Back from Vietnam, Lew Merletti enrolled at Duquesne University, in Pittsburgh, Pennsylvania. He would earn his four-year degree in a little over three years. One day before he graduated, he was walking through the student center when he caught sight of a notice on a bulletin board. "NSA hiring," the notice read. He took the test being offered to new recruits, aced it, and was called in for an interview. Inside the foyer of a fancy building, he followed instructions that took him up an elevator to the thirty-fifth floor.

"I walked around. There didn't seem to be anyone in any of the offices, but eventually I located the correct room," Merletti recalls. Seated behind a desk was a man. After some small talk, the man spoke candidly.

"We're an intelligence-gathering agency," he said. "We're larger than the CIA. We want to offer you a job."

Merletti asked why the NSA, an intelligence agency, was interested in recruiting him, a former Green Beret. "After an exchange of words, I realized the recruiter was interested in my language capabilities, that I spoke Vietnamese."

The man told Merletti that if he were to work for the NSA, it would be a solid career. But a job with an intelligence agency was not what Lew Merletti had in mind for his future. "The war was over," he remembers thinking. "How long were we going to be spying on the Vietnamese?"

Merletti told the recruiter that he was interested in finding a long-term and fulfilling career. The NSA recruiter asked Merletti what it was he wanted to do.

"I feel that I'm really good at protecting people and saving lives," Merletti recalls telling him. "That's what I'd like to do."

"You should join the Secret Service," the man said.

Lew Merletti had never considered a career with the U.S. Secret Service. But it made sense. He had the skills of a Special Forces soldier and the heart and soul of a protector. After two interviews with the Secret Service, he was hired. He thought about how awesome it felt to work for the agency that protected the president of the United States. Assassination was as old as warfare and would never go away.

★   ★   ★

For Billy Waugh, the transition to a civilian career was not easy. In need of a paycheck, he took a job at one of the few federal institutions that was hiring combat veterans without prejudice: the U.S. Postal Service. In the fall of 1972, he reported for duty at a post office in Austin, Texas, twenty miles from where he was born. Waugh rose up through the ranks. With the discipline of a Green Beret and a desire to excel, he moved from mail carrier to the person who oversaw the automated mail-sorting machine.

"Let's face it," recalls Waugh, "for a person like me, post office work was worse than death."

Billy Waugh was forty-three. He'd spent twenty-five years of his life as a soldier, half of them in combat. In an interview in 2017, he shared a rare emotional moment about what he was thinking at that time.

"I do not ever recall feeling fear, not up to that moment in my life. Not in combat before, and not anywhere since. But there in the post office, I feared my life was over," he remembers. "That I would wind up some old man drinking at the end of the bar."

For five long years, Billy Waugh continued to work for the Postal Service, until one night, in July 1977, the telephone rang. He answered it and recognized the voice on the other end of the line. It belonged to a covert-action operator he had worked with in SOG, in Vietnam. The man asked Billy if he was ready for action, if he wanted back in.

Waugh said yes.

The OSS Jedburghs, predecessor of the CIA. Their motto was "Surprise, Kill, Vanish." *(Central Intelligence Agency)*

During the Korean War, CIA parachute infiltration efforts were led by former OSS Jedburgh John "Jack" Singlaub. The men worked under the cover name Joint Advisory Commission, Korea (JACK), 8132nd Army Unit. Thousands of Americans and indigenous fighters trained and equipped by the CIA vanished without a trace in this effort. *(Collection of John K. Singlaub)*

Near the end of World War II, Vietnamese revolutionaries Ho Chi Minh (goatee) and General Vo Nguyen Giap (tie) were trained in guerrilla warfare by the OSS. By the early 1960s both men were on the CIA's kill-or-capture list. *(Central Intelligence Agency)*

An early helicopter used by the CIA's Air Branch during the Korean War. *(Central Intelligence Agency)*

After the assassination of King Abdullah of Jordan in 1951, the CIA and the Defense Department built a secret partnership with the shah of Iran. The arrangement lasted twenty-eight years. *(Dwight D. Eisenhower Presidential Library, Museum, and Boyhood Home)*

CIA South Building in the old E Street complex, circa 1960. Located at 2430 East Street, NW, this was the original CIA headquarters—a facility taken over from the OSS. *(Central Intelligence Agency)*

President Kennedy and U.S. Ambassador Henry Cabot Lodge spent hours in the Oval Office discussing the covert war in Vietnam. After South Vietnamese president Diem and his brother Nhu were executed by military subordinates, their bullet-riddled bodies were photographed and buried in an unmarked grave adjacent to the Saigon residence of Ambassador Lodge. *(John F. Kennedy Presidential Library and Museum, photograph by Abbie Rowe)*

Billy Waugh as a young Green Beret master sergeant, 1964. *(Collection of William D. Waugh)*

The CIDG program was a direct-action strike force made up of indigenous Vietnamese. Green Berets and CIA advisors taught them to sabotage, subvert, and kill Vietcong communists, but the program failed. "From the point of view of the Vietnamese...the CIDG program was an American project," unconventional warfare expert Col. Francis Kelly warned the Pentagon. *(Collection of Terry McIntosh)*

In 1965, Billy Waugh received the Silver Star for gallantry when he was still a patient in the lower-extremity amputation ward at Walter Reed. Soon he was back in Vietnam, assigned to MACV-SOG—a unit so dangerous it was informally called Suicide on the Ground. *(Collection of William D. Waugh)*

President Lyndon B. Johnson being shown a relief map of Khe Sanh firebase by national security advisor Walt Rostow. The classified MACV-SOG base there was Special Access only, surrounded by concertina wire and located partially underground. *(Lyndon B. Johnson Presidential Library, photograph by Yoichi Okamoto)*

Billy Waugh on board a SOG helicopter in 1967, shortly before being dropped behind enemy lines on a recon mission in Laos. *(Collection of William D. Waugh)*

MACV-SOG conducted the first-ever wartime HALO missions into Laos starting in 1970. Waugh, twenty years older than many of his teammates, was in charge of training. Seen here on the night of the third jump are SOG warriors J. D. Bath (left), Waugh, and Jesse Campbell (right). Shortly after successful infiltration, teammate Madison Strohlein was captured and killed by enemy forces on the ground. *(Collection of William D. Waugh)*

CIA paramilitary operations officer Felix Rodriguez with Cuban revolutionary Che Guevara and CIA-trained Bolivian Army Rangers shortly before Che's execution. Rodriguez told Che that he was working for the CIA and that the agency wanted Che alive. *(Collection of Felix I. Rodriguez)*

Robert F. Marasco commanded CIA Detachment B57, part of a Special Forces camp on the Vietnam-Cambodia border. After the unit discovered that one of their indigenous assets was a spy, the man was killed. The international scandal became known as the Green Beret Affair. *(Collection of Terry McIntosh)*

Members of Detachment B57 believed that the man in the hat—shown here in a photograph beside a North Vietnamese general (obscured)—was their asset, Thai Khac Chuyen. In this U.S. Army–issued photo, Chuyen is shown next to his Defense Department identification photograph. The story raised complex questions about morality, the rules of war, and the mysterious relationship between the CIA and the Green Berets. *(Collection of Terry McIntosh)*

Lew Merletti volunteered for Vietnam, becoming a medic with the Green Berets. He would later become the nineteenth director of the U.S. Secret Service, and the first to have served as a member of its secretive paramilitary unit, the Counter Assault Team. *(Collection of Lewis C. Merletti)*

President Nixon and CIA director Richard Helms had a complex relationship. Helms had overseen Kennedy-era assassination plots but cautioned against the act: "If you kill someone else's leaders, why shouldn't they kill yours?" *(Central Intelligence Agency)*

The expansive grounds of the new CIA headquarters as seen from the air. *(Library of Congress, Carol M. Highsmith Archive)*

Nixon and Henry Kissinger in the Oval Office. Kissinger knew that PLO chairman Yasser Arafat ordered the murder of U.S. ambassador Cleo Noel and U.S. chargé d'affaires George "Curt" Moore in Khartoum, Sudan, but encouraged the CIA to use Arafat's terrorists as assets. *(Richard M. Nixon Presidential Library and Museum)*

During the Church Committee investigations into White House–level assassination plots, Kissinger warned President Ford that if certain revelations became public, "the CIA would be destroyed." Ford met with Chief of Staff Donald Rumsfeld and Deputy Chief of Staff Dick Cheney to discuss how to keep secrets and restore presidential power. *(Gerald R. Ford Presidential Library, photograph by David Hume Kennerly)*

Billy Waugh in Libya in 1978 with Libyan dictator Muammar Qaddafi's military commanders. Waugh went to Libya to work for an American weapons dealer doing business with Qaddafi; no one could know that he was also working for the CIA. *(Collection of William D. Waugh)*

While cultivating relationships with Qaddafi's military commanders in the late 1970s, Waugh secretly photographed classified Libyan military facilities, including one at Jebel Akhdar, the Green Mountain. Thirty-three years later the CIA sent Waugh back to Libya during the revolution that overthrew Qaddafi. His mission was to locate Qaddafi's former military contacts. Waugh was eighty-two years old. *(Collection of William D. Waugh)*

The CIA that Bill Casey took over in 1981 had been rocked by the Church Committee hearings, then decimated by the Ford and Carter administrations. Insiders call it the Time of Troubles. Casey, the former OSS officer behind the plot to assassinate Hitler, vowed to bring change—and he did. *(Ronald Reagan Presidential Library and Museum, photograph by Michael Evans)*

CIA clandestine service lawyer John Rizzo was traveling in the Middle East, in 1985, when this surveillance photograph—taken without his knowledge— was slipped under his hotel room door, "apparently just to let me know that my movements were being watched," says Rizzo. *(Collection of John Rizzo)*

After lone-wolf assassin John Hinckley Jr. tried to kill President Reagan, the Secret Service Counter Assault Team began shadowing the president 24/7. Lew Merletti was its seventh member. He is shown here in 1986 accompanying President Reagan to the Reykjavik summit to meet with Mikhail Gorbachev, the last general secretary of the Soviet Union. *(Ronald Reagan Presidential Library and Museum, photograph by Pete Souza)*

In April 1993, assassins tied to Iraq attempted to kill former president George H. W. Bush with a powerful car bomb during a state visit to Kuwait. Citing America's legal right to self-defense, President Clinton responded with a cruise missile attack on Baghdad, leveling much of the Iraqi intelligence headquarters and killing a night watchman. This was not an attempt to kill Saddam Hussein, President Clinton said, but a means to prevent future attacks. *(George H. W. Bush Library Center, photograph by Susan Biddle)*

President Clinton and Lew Merletti on the White House lawn. "The assassination of the President of the United States is, quite literally, a cataclysmic event in world history," Merletti told the Justice Department, adding that Secret Service agents must always have the trust and confidence of the presidents they protect. *(William J. Clinton Presidential Library and Museum, collection of Lewis Merletti)*

In 1994, Lew Merletti traveled with President Clinton to Israel, Syria, Egypt, Jordan, Saudi Arabia, and Kuwait. The focus of the trip was peace in the Middle East, but all Merletti could think about were assassination attempts and potential mass casualty attacks against his protectees. *(William J. Clinton Presidential Library and Museum, photograph by Bob McNeely)*

After the assassination of Israeli prime minister Yitzhak Rabin by Jewish law student Yigal Amir, President Clinton insisted on attending the funeral. The request put Merletti in charge of security for three living presidents and nearly the entire line of presidential succession. The group, seen here on board *Air Force One,* listens to a security briefing. *(William J. Clinton Presidential Library and Museum, Collection of Lewis Merletti)*

Yitzhak Rabin's state funeral at the Mount Herzl Cemetery in Jerusalem was a solemn affair. Here, Merletti stands directly behind President and Mrs. Clinton. *(William J. Clinton Presidential Library and Museum, photograph by Bob McNeely)*

During a covert operation in the North African desert, two men from the CIA's Special Activities Division, Ground Branch, work fast to fix a broken-down vehicle—prime time for an ambush. *(Private Collection)*

After laying siege to OPEC headquarters in Vienna in 1975, terrorist-for-hire Carlos the Jackal lived on the run. On assignment for the CIA in 1994, Billy Waugh took one of the first known photographs of the terrorist, in Khartoum, leading to his capture a few months later. Credit was given to the French intelligence service, DGSE, not the CIA. *(Collection of William D. Waugh)*

This surveillance photograph of Carlos the Jackal was taken by Billy Waugh using a 140-pound Questar lens secreted into Khartoum via diplomatic pouch. *(Collection of William D. Waugh)*

In six decades of covert operations for the CIA, Billy Waugh worked in sixty-four countries around the globe. Seen here in Cairo in 1997, he poses as a tourist while conducting surveillance. *(Collection of William D. Waugh)*

An unidentified team in an unidentified country, chasing "tangos," or targets, of a CIA covert operation. *(Private Collection)*

After 9/11, President George W. Bush agreed that the CIA, not the Defense Department, was best suited to wage the unconventional warfare campaign in Afghanistan. CIA operators were on the ground within weeks. Here, CIA director George Tenet briefs the president and his senior advisors on October 7, the day the Defense Department joined the war effort with a massive air bombing campaign. The president's decision put Secretary of Defense Donald Rumsfeld at odds with the CIA. *(George W. Bush Presidential Library and Museum, photograph by Eric Draper)*

In its global terror campaign, Al-Qaeda leadership relied upon bomb makers, weapons traders, money-men, recruiters, trainers, commanders, and radical imams. Senior Intelligence Service officer Enrique "Ric" Prado's idea was to widen that list and focus on mid- to upper-level terrorists. Prado discussed his plan with Vice President Dick Cheney, who agreed. Prado is seen here as a young Pararescue operator during a training operation in 1974. *(Collection of Enrique Prado)*

For the covert war in Afghanistan, Ken Stiles built the CIA's three-dimensional Geographic Information System, lauded at the White House as the Magic Box. In this way Stiles became the first targeting officer in CIA history. Sent into the war theater, he is shown here with indigenous fighters at a classified CIA facility in Afghanistan. *(Collection of Kenneth L. Stiles)*

For its Afghan campaign, the CIA sent roughly a hundred Special Activities Division officers and operators to lead the charge. They were later joined by 2,000 Special Operations Forces in the war theater. Waugh, one of the first men in, was inserted into Logar Province, southeast of Kabul. He is seen here with Operational Detachment Alpha (ODA) 594. *(Collection of William D. Waugh)*

Christmas in Afghanistan, 2001. The pink toilet paper was parachute-dropped in. The gifts around the tree are courtesy of the CIA and U.S. Army Special Forces. Waugh celebrated his seventy-second birthday in Afghanistan, his third war after Korea and Vietnam. *(Collection of William D. Waugh)*

Waugh arrived in Afghanistan with an M4 carbine, an AK-47 assault rifle, a Heckler & Koch 40mm grenade launcher, and a suitcase with $6 million in cash. Seen here inside an Afghan fortress in Gardez, he holds a silenced MP5. *(Collection of William D. Waugh)*

In the summer of 2002, as the Pentagon secretly prepared to begin its war in Iraq, the CIA conducted covert-action operations in the northern part of the country designed to train and equip indigenous forces. Here, the CIA's Charles "Sam" Faddis stands in a field south of Erbil, counting Iraqi soldiers alongside the Peshmerga commanders whose forces would augment CIA Ground Branch operations. *(Collection of Charles Faddis)*

Undergirding the narrative during the war in Iraq was revenge-based justice: *lex talionis,* the law of retaliation, as it was called in the ancient world. Special Activities Division, Ground Branch teams were regularly targeted for assassination by Shiite militia. Among the most dangerous assassins were those trained by Hezbollah chief of operations Imad Mugniyah. *(Private Collection)*

Billy Waugh's missions in Iraq remain classified. In this photo, taken in 2004, he stands in front of the former palace of Saddam Hussein's son Uday. The CIA took over the building and ran Ground Branch operations from there. *(Collection of William D. Waugh)*

Members of a Special Activities Division, Ground Branch, team in Afghanistan, with their indigenous force partners, at Torkham gate on the Afghan-Pakistani border, near the Khyber Pass. *(Private Collection)*

In Afghanistan, the program to take indigenous soldiers on kill-or-capture missions is modeled after the CIDG program in Vietnam. In Afghanistan, many commandos are poorly trained and often high on opium. In this photograph, the Afghan commando (at left) holds his weapon as if it were a film prop. But the indigs were and remain a White House mandate, meant to serve as the "Afghan face." *(U.S. Department of Defense)*

President Obama's decision to revoke enhanced interrogation of captured terrorists, and to accelerate targeted killing, had a profound effect on the age-old concept of assassination as a foreign policy tool. He is seen here with his inner circle of advisors (including Ambassador Susan Rice, the incoming National Security Advisor, and Jeff Eggers, Senior Director for Afghanistan and Pakistan), with whom he regularly discussed drone strikes—working "vigorously to establish a framework that governs our use of force against terrorists." President Obama told Americans, "Doing nothing is not an option." *(Barack Obama Presidential Library, photograph by Pete Souza)*

Billy Waugh in Hanoi in 2017, seen here with his former enemy Colonel Bon Giong, age ninety-two. In the Vietnam War, Giong commanded hit-and-run assassination strikes against operators like Waugh during MACV-SOG's Top Secret cross-border missions into Laos. *(Photograph by Finley Jacobsen)*

Colonel Giong, Vo Dien Bien (General Vo Nguyen Giap's son), and Billy Waugh discussing nuclear weapons, arguably the reason all covert-action operations remain a national security necessity. *(Photograph by Finley Jacobsen)*

Billy Waugh discusses war and ideology with Ernesto Guevara, son of Che. They are shown with Ernesto's friends in Havana in 2017. "Remember that the Revolution is what is important and that each one of us, on our own, is worthless," Che wrote to his children, in a letter to be read to them in the event of his death. "Grow up to be good revolutionaries." Ernesto is a lawyer and aspiring businessman. *(Author Collection)*

Lew Merletti and Billy Waugh, friends since Vietnam, in Waugh's home office in 2017. After leaving the military, Merletti spent the rest of his career protecting presidents of the United States from assassination—national security defense. Billy Waugh spent the rest of his life conducting covert-action operations for presidents of the United States—national security offense. The two work hand in glove, like yin and yang, or shadow and light. *(Author Collection)*

CHAPTER FIFTEEN

Revenge

I t was just after 7:00 p.m., March 1, 1973, and darkness had fallen in Khartoum, Sudan. Outside the Saudi Arabian embassy compound, small groups of diplomats stood around saying good-bye to one another after a successful cocktail party. The American guests of honor were George "Curt" Moore, the chargé d'affaires, and Cleo A. Noel Jr., the ambassador. They were getting ready to head over to the presidential palace to have dinner with President Gaafar Nimeiry of Sudan and Haile Selassie, the emperor of Ethiopia, when all hell broke loose.

A Land Rover screeched to a halt in front of the embassy's plate-glass doors, and out leapt eight masked gunmen, each with a dagger attached to his belt. One of the gunmen shot an embassy guard in the head; another raked a wall with automatic machine-gun fire. A bullet tore into the leg of Belgian chargé d'affaires Guy Eid and he fell to the ground, bleeding. Ambassador Noel got hit in the ankle and he, too, went down.

"Run, run, run for your lives!" shouted Jan Bertens, the Dutch chargé d'affaires, the only diplomat to make it to the street before the terrorists locked the gates and took everyone hostage. Inside a reception hall, each diplomat was forced to identify himself by nationality. The terrorists released all but three: Moore, Noel, and

Eid. The gunmen identified themselves as members of the Palestinian terrorist organization Black September. Founded in 1963, it had since become the most feared terrorist organization in the world.

Through local journalists, the terrorists made their demands known. They wanted Sirhan Sirhan, the Palestinian who'd assassinated Senator Robert Kennedy in 1968, freed from a California jail. And they wanted one hundred Black September operatives released from prisons in Israel and Jordan. At the White House, President Nixon was notified of the hostage situation by Henry Kissinger. The men sat down and discussed what to do next.

Twenty-six hours later, the president held a news conference. "The Sudanese government is working on the problem," Nixon said. He said of the hostages: "We will do everything that we can to get them released, but will not pay blackmail." The policy, which was not written down and which Nixon had made up three months earlier, during a hostage scenario in Haiti, would play a profoundly consequential role in the decades to come.

Just a few hours after hearing this news, the Black September terrorists in Khartoum received a phone call from their commanding officer in Beirut. Since President Nixon wasn't going to agree to the terrorists' demands, the commander said, the American diplomats were useless and the gunmen should "finish them off."

In Khartoum, Robert E. Fritts, the new deputy chief of mission, had just arrived at the American embassy, where he'd been sent to replace Curt Moore. The embassy staff was in a state of shock; the fate of their superior officers hung in the balance. But the mission of the U.S. State Department was unwavering: diplomacy must go on. Khartoum was a lawless town, fueled by anti-American sentiment, and this was a fact every Foreign Service officer knew and accepted. Islamists were fighting Marxists and tribal warlords in the streets. There had been two bloody coups in four years. This majority Arab nation had severed all diplomatic relations with the United States after the 1967 Six-Day War, and only recently had relations been rekindled, largely due to the diplomatic efforts of Curt Moore. Now he was being held at gunpoint inside the Saudi embassy, along with Cleo Noel and Guy Eid.

As deputy chief of mission, Fritts recalled the devastation he felt, trying to bring order to the chaos he was walking into. "The embassy occupied the upper floors of a commercial office building adjoined by others on the main street," he recalled. An intense dust storm called a haboob had kicked up, and the power was out. "Dust and grit were everywhere, in your eyes and teeth.... I climbed five or six floors up the back steps, carrying my suitcase and my garment bag over my shoulder."

Fritts made his way through the darkness into the embassy, where he caught sight of Sandy Sanderson, an administrative officer, standing in the dim light with his glasses on a string around his neck. "I couldn't quite see his face," said Fritts. "He was backlighted by the emergency lamps, but I could tell he was crying."

"We've heard there was gunfire in the Saudi embassy," Sanderson sobbed. "They may be dead. You're in charge."

Sandy Sanderson was right. Moments before their death, Eid, Moore, and Noel were allowed to write letters to their wives. "Cleo and I will die bravely and without tears as men should," was the last sentence Curt Moore wrote. These were not bullet-to-the-head assassinations. The men, blindfolded with their hands bound, were peppered with gunfire starting at the ankles with a barrage of bullets leading up to the head. Sadism was Black September's trademark, and its members were notorious for inflicting the maximum amount of pain and suffering on their victims. For Black September assassination was about revenge, about righting a wrong—the theft of the Palestinian homeland by the Jews. Documents kept classified for decades reveal the Black September gunmen were told by their handler that Curt Moore was the CIA's top man in the Middle East, that he worked for the Israelis and had personally directed the killing of Palestinians, none of which is known to be accurate.

But perhaps the most chilling details of the tragedy are tethered to the United States—in particular, to Henry Kissinger. Behind many hidden-hand operations lie secret deals and dark bargains. Just days before the assassinations in Khartoum, an NSA listening post in Cyprus picked up a radio transmission indicating that a major Black September operation was about to be carried out. "The exhibits arrive on the Egyptian plane Wednesday morning," a man in the PLO's Beirut headquarters told a colleague in the Khartoum office, deciphered as code for a coming attack. The "exhibits," the State Department later confirmed, were seven gunmen from Black September, four disassembled AK-47s, and eight hand grenades, all of which arrived on an Egypt Air flight from Cairo on February 28, the day before the killings. Why the State Department failed to properly warn its top diplomats in Khartoum of a suspected imminent attack would take decades to come to light.

Although it was not known in 1973, Black September was the brainchild of Yasser Arafat, chairman of the Palestinian Liberation Organization (PLO). That the Black September terrorists took direct orders from Arafat, who planned and ordered the murder of the two American diplomats in Khartoum, was known only to a select few presidential advisors at the time. This information was kept classified by the State Department until 2006, until after Arafat—by then a Nobel Peace Prize recipient—had died. Bruce Hoffman, one of the world's foremost experts on terrorist organizations, explains: Black September "had been formed as a deniable and completely covert special-operations unit of [the PLO group] al-Fatah by Arafat and his closest lieutenants." Its fighters were assigned hard-core terrorist operations that included bombings, ambushes, hijackings, kidnappings, and assassinations. "It was the most elite unit we had," one of al-Fatah's former commanding generals told Hoffman. "[Our] members were suicidal—not in the sense of religious terrorists who surrender their lives to ascend to heaven—but in the sense that we could send them anywhere to do anything and they were prepared to lay down their lives to do it. No question. No hesitation."

Black September's original mission was to foment regional violence and provoke Israel into bloody engagements, forcing its Arab neighbors from a passive to an active stance in its anti-Israel, anti-West campaign of violence. How Black September and the PLO worked together, in secret, is its own complex narrative. What is important to this story is that Arafat chose a man of contradictions, Ali Hassan Salameh, to serve as commander of the special operations unit. Salameh was the son of the martyred Sheik Hassan Salameh, commander of the Palestinian Holy War Army in the war against Israel, who died in battle in June 1948. But unlike his pious father, he was a playboy who drove around Beirut in expensive cars, ate at fancy restaurants, and dated models. Married, with two sons, he flaunted his girlfriend around town; she was a former Miss Universe named Georgina Rizk. Mossad gave him the insulting code name the Red Prince.

The terrorist organization took its name from the so-called Black September conflict. In September of 1970, Arafat's guerrilla warfare corps hijacked four international aircraft and forced them to land in the Jordanian desert, at Dawson's Field. Jordan's King Hussein used his army against the terrorist group, expelling all members from the kingdom. In revenge, Yasser Arafat secretly ordered the Red Prince to oversee the assassination of Wasfi al-Tal, Jordan's prime minister, during the Arab League summit in Egypt the following year. As Tal entered the foyer of the Sheraton Cairo Hotel, a Black September gunman stepped forward and shot him in the chest at point-blank range.

"They've killed me!" Tal cried out as he fell to the floor bleeding. "Murderers! They believe only in fire and destruction."

As Jordan's prime minister lay dying on the floor, the assassin got down on his hands and knees and licked the blood flowing across the marble floor. This was exactly the image of his Black September killers that Arafat wanted to portray, while keeping his hidden-hand role secret from the world. The *Times* of London ran a photograph of this blood-licking act, an image that was reprinted in newspapers around the world.

What Arafat also wanted, at least initially, was American passivity. As the United States withdrew its forces from Vietnam, Arab terrorist organizations started cropping up across the Middle East, inspired by the U.S. military's inability to defeat a much smaller guerrilla army. "Create Two, Three, Many Vietnams," Che Guevara had instructed his fellow revolutionaries around the world, calling the Middle East "a volcano...threatening eruption in the world, today." Even after his death, Che Guevara's words lived on.

After successfully killing the prime minister of Jordan, in 1972 Yasser Arafat endorsed the massacre of Israeli athletes at the Munich Summer Olympics, with operational command assigned to Ali Hassan Salameh. Eleven Israeli Olympic team members were murdered sadistically; one of the Olympians, weightlifter Yossef Romano, was castrated as his teammates looked on. Others were beaten and burned to death. Israel kept the most horrific details hidden from the public, knowing that this kind of violence opened the door to copycat operations. In response to the Munich massacre, Israeli intelligence launched Operation Wrath of God, with the goal of killing every Black September member involved.

Immediately following World War II, before the Nuremberg trials and other forms of procedural justice addressed the killing of millions of Jews, a small group of Holocaust survivors tracked down Nazi war criminals for assassination. They called themselves Nakam,

Hebrew for Avengers. The group used an underground intelligence network to learn where individual Nazis lived so that they could kill them. These assassinations were rarely reported in the media, because what country wanted the notoriety that came with a revelation that it had been harboring a Nazi war criminal? After Israel became a nation-state, a program of revenge killing was refined and developed by Mossad, Israel's equivalent of the CIA, which was founded in December 1949. Soon, in certain situations, assassination would be Mossad's weapon of choice.

Mossad's assassination program was officially classified, but unofficially it was an open secret. The logic was, "If you don't punish for one crime, you will get another," says Dina Porat, chief historian at Israel's Yad Vashem, or Holocaust, memorial. "This is what was driving [the Avengers], not only justice but a warning—a warning to the world that you cannot hurt Jews in such a manner and get away with it." In its first two decades of statehood, Mossad became the undisputed masters of assassination, overtaking even the KGB in ruthlessness, cunning, and effectiveness. The department inside Mossad responsible for assassination was named Caesarea, after the ancient Roman city built by Herod the Great. And inside Caesarea there was an even more secret, more elite assassination unit called Kidon, Hebrew for bayonet. After Black September murdered the eleven Israeli athletes in Munich, Mossad unleashed Kidon on them.

Mossad's targeted assassinations of Black September operatives were equally brutal; this, too, was revenge. Wael Zwaiter was shot eleven times at close range (allegedly one bullet for each murdered Israeli athlete) in his Rome apartment. Mahmoud Hamshari was blown up in his Paris home after a bomb, hidden inside his telephone receiver, was detonated by Israeli assassins from across the street. A Black September operative in London was expertly pushed under a fast-moving bus. More than a dozen Operation Wrath of God murders followed, including that of an innocent man named

Ahmed Bouchiki, in Lillehammer, Norway, a case of mistaken identity. Kidon operatives believed that the Norwegian waiter was the Red Prince.

As the cycle of violence escalated, Black September fought back with a plan to assassinate Israel's prime minister, Golda Meir, during a visit with Pope Paul VI. Relations between Israel and the Vatican had been strained since Israel's founding. Mossad legend has it that in 1948, in exchange for diplomatic relations, the Vatican asked Israel to hold a mock trial of Jesus and reverse the original biblical death verdict of Christ. Israel declined, and no prime minister had been invited to the Vatican since. Golda Meir was not about to cancel this historic trip because of a death threat by Black September.

In Rome, Mossad learned that the Red Prince intended to shoot down Meir's airplane with Russian-made SA-7 guided missiles as it landed at Rome's Leonardo da Vinci Airport. Using a network of sleeper agents, Mossad disrupted the plot with just minutes to spare, according to sources familiar with the case. After failing to kill Golda Meir in Rome, Yasser Arafat assigned the Red Prince an even more incendiary job: oversee the assassination of two U.S. diplomats in Khartoum, Sudan.

The cold-blooded, in-plain-sight assassinations of American diplomats inside another sovereign nation's embassy in Khartoum demanded a formidable response. Except most Americans had zero appetite for getting involved in terrorist disputes overseas. Five hundred ninety-one American POWs held in North Vietnam were still in the process of being brought home from Hanoi. Diplomacy with armed revolutionaries did not work; military force was not an option. The stage was set to handle the situation with the president's third option, the hidden hand.

After the Black September terrorists killed Curt Moore, Cleo Noel, and Guy Eid in the basement of the Saudi Arabian Embassy in Khartoum, the killers called their PLO commander in Beirut and asked what to do next. Yasser Arafat instructed them to surrender to Sudanese authorities.

"Your mission has ended," Arafat said, in a communication that was intercepted by Mossad and shared with Henry Kissinger, but which the State Department kept secret until 2006. "Explain your just cause to [the] great Sudanese masses and international opinion. We are with you on the same road," Arafat said.

The next morning the eight gunmen surrendered themselves. Two were released, the remaining six tried for murder. During the trial, the leader of the group said that they'd acted "under the orders of the Palestine Liberation Organization and should only be questioned by that organization."

The assassins were convicted by a Sudanese court, but just a few hours later President Nimeiry commuted their sentences and put them on a plane to Cairo, where they were turned over to the PLO. When pressed by the State Department, President Nimeiry defended his actions by saying that other states handed over Palestinian terrorists after "far less action," and that America needed to face the "political facts of life." President Nimeiry said that he "had Sudanese and Arab opinion to consider." Three decades later, in June 2006, the State Department quietly posted online a 1973 CIA Summary of the Assassinations in Khartoum. "The Khartoum operation was carried out with the full knowledge and personal approval of Yasser Arafat, Chairman of the Palestine Liberation Organization," it stated.

Robert Fritts recalled the fallout at the U.S. embassy in Khartoum. "The embassy [staff] was shattered, absolutely shattered. . . . The U.S. government pressured the Egyptians not to release them. They were put under loose house arrest in a Nile mansion. Eventually, they evaporated"—tacitly allowed to disappear. "It was a travesty," lamented Fritts. Henry "Kissinger [was] cited as having a bigger picture in mind."

That bigger picture Henry Kissinger had in mind was dark and complex. In late 1973, in addition to serving as the president's national-security advisor, Kissinger was now secretary of state, meaning he was at the top of the chain of command of all U.S. diplomats. Instead of bringing the killers to justice, the better play, Kissinger decided, was to make a deal with Yasser Arafat to use the Red Prince, Ali Hassan Salameh, as a clandestine asset.

At the CIA, the plan had been three years in the making. It began with a CIA case officer and expert on Middle East affairs named Robert Ames. Salameh and Ames were like two sides of a coin. Ames, thirty-five, looked like an insurance salesman, with his 1950s haircut and wide tie. A devoted husband and father of five, Bob Ames was frugal, rarely drank, and sported a small potbelly. Salameh roamed around Beirut in open shirts with chest hair spilling out, his playboy reputation preceding him. A fourth-degree black belt, the Red Prince chain-smoked, drank expensive Scotch, listened to Elvis Presley, and worked out regularly in the Continental Hotel gym. The cryptonym Bob Ames chose for Salameh was MJ/TRUST/2. MJ was the code for Palestinians/PLO; Ames allegedly chose the root word "trust" because he trusted Salameh; the number two designated him as the second CIA asset in a cluster. MJ/TRUST/1 was Yasser Arafat.

Perhaps it is impossible to understand how and why Bob Ames chose to trust a man who'd orchestrated the murder of eleven Israeli athletes in Munich, and two U.S. diplomats and a Belgian in Sudan, plus scores of others, but what is clear is that by 1974, Bob Ames's relationship with Salameh had warped. Ames had overstepped the unwritten case officer–asset rules in dangerous ways. In a letter to his wife, Yvonne, Ames called Salameh his "important friend." The two men exchanged gifts. After Salameh gave Ames a set of golden prayer beads, Ames wanted to give his friend a gift of equal significance. Salameh walked around Beirut with a pistol on his right hip (Beirut's *As-Safir* newspaper published photographs of him like this), and Ames thought it would be a great idea to give Salameh a gun as a gift. Before he did, he sought approval from CIA headquarters.

His superior, CIA director Richard Helms, expressed outrage. "This crossed some invisible ethical line," writes Ames's biographer, Kai Bird. "The Agency could have dealings with a terrorist but it would be unseemly to make a gift of a gun." Ames wouldn't give up, says his former analyst colleague Bruce Riedel, so headquarters suggested a compromise. They told Ames, "Okay, why don't you give him a replica of a gun?" Ames, insulted, rejected the idea. Former CIA case officer Henry Miller-Jones has an interesting take: "They tell you in the CIA never to fall in love with your agent. But everyone does."

For a while, the arrangement between the CIA and Ali Hassan Salameh suited the CIA. That arrangement was to now leave U.S. diplomats and CIA officers out of the Black September bull's-eye. "The Red Prince wrote and signed a 'non-assassination guarantee' for all U.S. diplomats in Lebanon," wrote British journalist Gordon Thomas. In Beirut's intelligence circles, the joke was, "It pays to live in the same building as American diplomats because the PLO security is so good." But the arrangement would only last as long as Salameh was alive. And Mossad had every intention of assassinating the Red Prince.

It would take a covert team of Mossad assassins five years to kill Salameh, with a car bomb exploded on a Beirut street on January 22, 1979. Four of his bodyguards and three innocent passersby were also killed in the targeted assassination. Before Salameh was blown up, Bob Ames was able to give to him the ultimate gift he longed for, a trip to the United States. With a CIA handler driving Salameh around, the Black September operations chief and his new bride, Georgina Rizk, visited CIA offices in Virginia, Hawaii, New Orleans, and California, where they also visited Disneyland. The Agency handler, code-named Charles Waverly, went out of his way to make Salameh comfortable, going so far as to teach the Red Prince how to eat oysters and scuba dive. His January 1979 assassination was a turning point in the Middle East for the CIA and would impact U.S. national security for decades to come. Twenty thousand people, including Yasser Arafat, attended Salameh's funeral.

Why did Henry Kissinger, as secretary of state, encourage the CIA's use of Ali Hassan Salameh, a known terrorist, as an ally? Why choose covert action, the president's third option, over diplomacy, the first? This decision likely had to do with Kissinger's proximity to a series of scandalous events that were unfolding in Washington, DC. In the spring of 1973, Congress began investigating what would become known as Watergate. "For the first time in its history, the [CIA] allowed investigators from Congress to review documents from its files and interview its employees," says former CIA inspector general L. Britt Snider. As it turned out, all five of the men arrested for burglarizing the offices of the Democratic National Committee at the Watergate Hotel in June 1972 had connections with the CIA. Here began a series of events and missteps within the CIA that would bring the Agency to the most dramatic turning point in its history. It was the closest the Agency has ever come to being disbanded.

Nixon's CIA director, James Schlesinger, was preparing to leave the Agency to become secretary of defense. Before he left, Schlesinger sent a memo to all CIA employees ordering them to reveal to him any illegal activity they might have been involved in since the Agency's creation twenty-five years before. The instruction prompted a flurry of written reports, which were then compiled into a 700-page document that would become known as the "Family Jewels." The action was unprecedented; the CIA had never compiled its hidden-hand operations before.

Three weeks later, the *New York Times* broke a story revealing that Kissinger had authorized the FBI and the CIA to illegally wire-tap reporters, White House officials, and even his own National Security Council staff. Mindful that a major scandal was brewing in Washington, DC, the CIA's new director, William Colby, felt the best move was to lock the Family Jewels inside the safe in his office. Over the next fifteen months, the Watergate scandal—about a different illegal wiretapping—consumed the news media and the public. The Family Jewels remained locked in Colby's safe. On August 8, 1974, President Nixon resigned and Vice President Gerald Ford assumed the presidency.

But the press was unrelenting, and the focus now swung to yet another CIA scandal that had previously remained hidden, raising alarms across the Ford White House. In December 1974, Colby, who had run the Phoenix program in Vietnam, sent Kissinger a note explaining some of the contents of the Family Jewels. Kissinger drafted a five-page memorandum for the president summarizing the contents of what was there. Some of the actions "clearly were illegal," Kissinger said; others "raise profound moral questions." The most incendiary material covered the CIA's role in the assassination of foreign leaders, Kissinger warned. He said that if these revelations became public, "the CIA would be destroyed." It was a stunning concept—that the CIA could actually be considered expendable. President Ford met with his chief of staff, Donald Rumsfeld, and his deputy chief of staff, Dick Cheney, to discuss the next move. They decided to invite editors from the *New York Times* to the White House for a discussion, in the spirit of transparency.

During a luncheon at the White House on January 16, 1975, *New York Times* reporters asked President Ford why the Family Jewels was not going to be declassified. Ford blundered. It contained explosive material that would "blacken the eye of every President since Truman," Ford said defensively.

"Like what?" one of the editors asked.

"Like assassination," answered Ford.

Everyone went silent. The comment was made off the record, the president insisted, but it was too late. The cat was out of the bag.

CBS News reported the bombshell. "President Ford has reportedly warned associates that if the current [Family Jewels] investigations go too far, they could uncover several assassinations of foreign officials involving the CIA." Across the nation and in Congress, there was uproar. Moral outrage. The White House vowed to create a commission to investigate, ultimately turning the matter over to Congress.

Starting in the spring of 1975, the Senate Select Committee to Study Governmental Operations with Respect to Intelligence Activities, chaired by Idaho senator Frank Church, held sixty days of closed hearings. Seventy-five witnesses were called to the stand, including many of the most senior officers at the CIA. Among the findings, the Church Committee learned that the CIA had conducted more than 900 "major projects" and "several thousand" smaller operations, "three-quarters of which had never been reviewed outside the Agency." The assassination plots against Rafael Trujillo, Fidel Castro, the Ngo brothers, and others were made public for the first time. Senator Church called the CIA "a rogue elephant raging out of control." Exotic weapons used in assassination plots were shown on TV, including a gun that shot poison darts. The investigation lasted six months.

That the CIA even had a paramilitary capacity shocked most Americans. That it engaged in plans to assassinate foreign leaders was perceived as morally outrageous. But what's notable is how blame fell almost entirely on the CIA, when a comprehensive read makes clear that the orders were coming from the office of the president. The House Select Committee had its own investigation going on, chaired by Otis Pike, a Democrat from New York. The Pike Committee interviewed many of the same individuals as the Church Committee and found that the White House was to blame, far more so than the CIA. "The CIA does not go galloping off conducting operations by itself," Congressman Pike wrote. "The major things which are done are not done unilaterally by the CIA without approval from higher up the line.... We did find evidence, upon evidence, upon evidence where the CIA said: 'No, don't do it.' The

State Department or the White House said, 'We're going to do it.' The CIA was much more professional and had a far deeper reading on the down-the-road implications of some immediately popular act than the executive branch or administration officials.... The CIA never did anything the White House didn't want. Sometimes they didn't want to do what they did."

As the committees prepared to release their reports, there was a stunning move from the White House. President Ford met with his advisors Rumsfeld and Cheney, who told him the reports had to be suppressed. "Any document which officially shows American involvement in assassination is clearly a foreign policy disaster," Rumsfeld said. "We are better off with a political confrontation than a legal one." Dick Cheney advised him that the White House should object to the release and attempt to block the reports on grounds that it compromised national security. President Ford agreed.

A new team of presidential advisors was needed, Rumsfeld told the president, leading Ford to dismiss several key members of his cabinet. Schlesinger was let go as secretary of defense, replaced by Rumsfeld; Cheney became White House chief of staff; CIA director William Colby was replaced by George H. W. Bush; Henry Kissinger retained his position as secretary of state but was replaced by Brent Scowcroft in the role of national-security advisor. Later, Ford expressed regret for taking these actions. "I was angry at myself for showing cowardice in not saying [no] to the ultraconservatives," he said. "It was the biggest political mistake of my life. And it was one of the few cowardly things I did in my life."

Despite considerable efforts, Ford's new team of advisors failed to keep the Church Committee report classified, with Congress asserting its right to override the president. The Church Committee report, "Alleged Assassination Plots Involving Foreign Leaders," was released in November of 1975. In a note all but lost to history, the Ford White House was able to suppress the Pike Report. Months later, parts of it were leaked to the *Village Voice,* but the public's mind was already made up. The CIA, not the White House, was to blame.

In undated notes located in files at the Gerald Ford Presidential Library, Dick Cheney advised President Ford on the imperative to restore the authority of the executive branch. It had been unduly diminished by Congress in the wake of the Watergate scandal, Cheney said, and by the congressional reports. The advice was significant, as it foreshadowed Cheney's own use of presidential authority twenty-six years later, when he served as vice president.

"As vice president, Cheney would participate in Presidential Findings and MONs that dictated covert action," says John Rizzo, the CIA's long-serving clandestine service legal officer, in an interview for this book. As vice president in the George W. Bush White House, Dick Cheney served in the inner circle of presidential advisors and was "present at most covert-action meetings," Rizzo clarifies, "not something you usually saw from a vice president." Rizzo was hired at the CIA in 1976 and served seven presidents, including as the CIA's top lawyer during the "war on terror." The remarkable construct of presidential authority, says Rizzo, is that the president of the United States "can listen to whomever he wants."

The year after the Church Committee published its report, President Ford issued Executive Order 11905, a decree to govern covert-action operations, and this included a prohibition on assassinations. "No employee of the United States Government shall engage in, or conspire to engage in, political assassination," it read. Senator Frank Church objected, stating that a presidential decree could easily be changed by decree, by another president. That by having an executive order on assassination and not a new law passed by Congress, the door was left wide-open for new liberties in interpretation when a more conservative president took the helm. Which is exactly what happened starting in 1981 when President Ronald Reagan and his advisors began exploring a new executive order allowing for preemptive neutralization of people who wanted to harm the United States.

As Americans were reading the Church Committee report, learning about the dark underbelly of hidden-hand operations and rogue actors, one of the most outrageous hostage-taking events of the twentieth century unfolded halfway across the world, in Vienna, Austria. On December 21, 1975, the Organization of the Petroleum Exporting Countries (OPEC) was holding a Conference of Ministers at its headquarters, in the Texaco building on Dr. Karl Lueger Ring, when six individuals, five men and a woman, casually walked up to the guard at the front desk and asked to be directed to the proceedings. They looked reasonable enough, wearing raincoats and carrying gym bags. At least one in the group spoke German. But then, reaching into their bags, they pulled out submachine guns and began shooting, killing three people.

The gunmen stormed the OPEC conference hall and corralled sixty people as hostages, including ten of the world's eleven oil ministers, whose countries controlled 80 percent of the world's oil. Never before, and not since, have so many government officials, from so many different nations, been taken hostage all at once.

Austria's head of state, Chancellor Bruno Kreisky, was out skiing in the Alps. When he learned the news from his ministers, he rushed back to Vienna to deal with this first-of-its-kind crisis. In a press conference, Kreisky said that his government did not know who the terrorists were and that their organizational demands were not clear. As chancellor, however, he had granted the terrorists permission to fly out of the country with the ten oil ministers, and others, as hostages. Kreisky neglected to say that he'd negotiated the release of the Austrian hostages, in exchange for meeting the terrorists' demands. In hindsight this course of action appears absurd, but in 1975, Austria, like most other nations, was unequipped to deal with a hostage crisis. "We were pressured into this decision by the fear that the hostages' lives would be taken," Chancellor Kreisky later said. "You cannot [stamp] out terrorism by retaliation because terrorism has its own laws."

At 7:00 the following morning, forty-one hostages were loaded onto a municipal bus, driven to the airport, and flown to Algeria, North Africa, in an Austrian Airlines DC-9 with a volunteer crew. At a second press conference, an Iraqi man acting as an intermediary said that the hostage-takers called themselves the Arm of the Arab Revolution and that their leader went by the nom de guerre Carlos the Jackal. His real name was Ilich Ramirez Sanchez. He was a twenty-five-year-old terrorist and assassin for hire. Born into a wealthy family in Venezuela, Ilich Ramirez Sanchez was sent by his Marxist father to Moscow to study at the Patrice Lumumba University, a breeding ground for a wide variety of terrorists-in-training. After getting expelled for reasons unknown, he transformed himself into Carlos the Jackal, hiring himself out to Arab terrorist organizations like Black September. By the time of the OPEC siege, the Venezuelan-born terrorist had killed at least seven people and was wanted by the British, French, and Israeli intelligence services.

In Algiers, Ilich Ramirez Sanchez met privately with President Houari Boumediene, and an agreement was reached. Five oil ministers and thirty-one hostages were released, while five oil ministers and ten civilians would be kept as hostages. The aircraft left Algeria, this time headed for Tripoli, Libya. Here, he met privately with President Muammar Qaddafi, and a secret agreement was reached. After this meeting, Ilich Ramirez Sanchez returned to the aircraft and instructed the pilots to fly back to Algiers, where the remaining five oil ministers and ten hostages were freed. He met with Boumediene a second time, flew to Baghdad, and vanished for more than a decade. It was later revealed that in Libya, he had been paid fifty million dollars in cash. Instead of sharing the money with his revolutionary comrades, he kept the money for himself. Carlos the Jackal would live off the cash for the next eighteen years.

The CIA now had a watchful eye on Libya, and on Muammar Qaddafi, and a list of questions it wanted answered. Who was this man who called himself Carlos the Jackal, and where was Arab terrorism headed next? Would non-Palestinians like Ilich Ramirez Sanchez remain committed to the Palestinian cause if there weren't millions of dollars to be made? To learn the answers to these questions would require covert operations, but for now the CIA's hands were tied. Alternative options needed to be explored, and they would be.

CHAPTER SIXTEEN

Colonel Qaddafi's Libya

For Billy Waugh, the years spent working for the U.S. Postal Service, 1972 to 1977, were misery incarnate. Then came the mysterious call, on July 20, propelling him back into the world of covert-action operations.

"The location is overseas," the caller said.

"Fine by me," said Waugh.

If Waugh was in, the man on the phone said he'd arrange for a down payment to be wired into his bank account.

"I'm in," said Waugh.

More details would be forthcoming, but in the meantime, Waugh needed to travel to northern Virginia and check into a specific hotel at 3:00 p.m. on July 25, just a few days away. Waugh agreed to the meeting at the hotel.

Forty-eight hours later, a large sum of money appeared in Waugh's bank account. The down payment was twice as much as the post office paid in a year. The overseas job was guaranteed for six months but might continue for years, he was told. All travel and living expenses would be paid by the client, whose identity was to remain hidden for now.

"Bring clothes to last for a year in a very warm climate," the man said. "The location is Africa."

Waugh considered the situation. "My instinct and intuition told me this was a CIA operation," he recalls. "That the Agency was forming some kind of ground team for a covert operation in Africa. I figured this was how the CIA worked, now that covert-action operations had been curtailed."

The next day at the post office, Waugh told his supervisor that he was resigning his position.

"You're a good worker, and the post office is a good job," Waugh recalls the man saying. "Why are you leaving?"

Waugh said he wasn't cut out for post office work.

At home, he packed a small bag. On the assigned day, he flew to Washington, DC, and took a cab to the hotel in northern Virginia.

At the 3:00 p.m. meeting he was not surprised to see the faces of three Green Berets from SOG, soldiers he'd worked with during the Vietnam War. Based on the skill sets of the team members, it was clear to Waugh that the job was paramilitary in nature. This four-man team included a medic, a communications man, a handheld weapons instructor, and Waugh—an expert in intelligence, surveillance, reconnaissance, and heavy weapons. During the meeting, a fifth man showed up and identified himself as "the client's lawyer." The team would be traveling to Libya, the lawyer said. Their job was to train soldiers who were part of Colonel Muammar Qaddafi's elite special forces. In addition to being its president, Qaddafi served as the country's commander in chief.

The former SOG operators were escorted to the Libyan embassy and issued travel visas. "We were told our flight was leaving late the next day," remembers Waugh.

Back at his hotel room, Waugh considered the facts and his suppositions. "In order to ensure plausible deniability," he guessed, "the CIA was using paramilitary contractors, and hiring them in a roundabout way." The situation presented an excellent financial opportunity for him. Still, his intuition said, *Make a few calls*.

Waugh reached out to several CIA contacts he had in Washington.

Not one of the people he spoke with had any knowledge of this Libyan operation. He called the client's lawyer and asked if the mission was a covert operation for the CIA. The lawyer said it was not. "He assured me it was all aboveboard and there was no legal risk," Waugh says. "That we were going to be training the Libyan special forces in basic infantry tactics only." Waugh asked to know the name of the client. The lawyer said the man's name was Edwin P. Wilson, and that he was a former CIA officer.

The client's lawyer said that while en route to Africa, the team would stop in Geneva for a briefing. There, they'd meet Edwin Wilson himself, who'd pay them directly and give them the names of their contacts inside the Libyan military. It was a sensitive job, the lawyer said, which was why the money was so good. Not everyone in Libya was pro-American, so it was imperative that the operators keep their identities hidden—for example, by always wearing a balaclava, the lawyer said—whenever they were on a military base. Colonel Qaddafi's friends included Fidel Castro and Idi Amin, the president of Uganda. Qaddafi didn't want anyone to know he also had American friends, the lawyer explained.

Waugh hung up and considered the situation. While he was sitting there thinking about what all this meant, the telephone rang. The caller addressed Waugh by name. Waugh did not recognize the man's voice; nor did the caller identify himself. Instead, he told Waugh that the two of them had mutual friends, and he mentioned two names, both of whom Waugh recognized as CIA. The man asked Waugh to meet him at a restaurant in Arlington, Virginia, in an hour. It was important, the man said. Waugh should come right away.

"The meeting is about your upcoming travel plans to Africa," the caller said cryptically.

At the restaurant, the man showed Billy Waugh his credentials, which identified him as working for the CIA. He said that his name was Pat.

About the upcoming trip to Libya: "It's not an Agency operation," Pat said.

Pat pulled out a briefcase and set it on the table between them. He opened up the case and removed a Pentax 35mm camera and several rolls of black-and-white film. He slid everything across the table to Billy Waugh.

"Pat said that I could assist the Agency and myself by taking photographs of the various military facilities I'd be visiting in Libya," Waugh recalls. Of particular interest to Pat was an area forty miles inland from the Gulf of Sidra called Jebel Akhdar, the Green Mountain, where there was a classified Libyan military facility. Satellite images indicated that surface-to-air missile sites were set up there, Pat explained, protecting the airspace around Benghazi. The missiles were Russian. Pat said that the CIA wanted photographs of them.

Waugh considered what he was being told. There was a loophole in the U.S. Neutrality Acts. While it was illegal to enlist in a foreign army, it was not illegal to "advise" a foreign army. That said, training a terrorist organization in explosives and munitions was treason. Libya was not yet a designated state sponsor of terrorism, but only because the State Department had not yet created its official list. However, Muammar Qaddafi was under the watchful eye of the CIA. To understand Qaddafi's actions, the CIA relied on open source intelligence and some human intelligence, mostly from Arab locals, whose trustworthiness was anybody's guess. The CIA wanted Billy Waugh to act as its eyes and ears on the ground, Pat told Waugh. In training Qaddafi's commandos, he'd be part of Qaddafi's inner circle. The risks were great, but the rewards could be huge.

Pat slid a small piece of paper across the table. On the paper was written a telephone number. This was to be Waugh's contact, Pat said. He gave Waugh a phrase-and-reply code, tradecraft for CIA assets in the field, and said Waugh should use both elements of the code in the event a problem arose in Libya. Waugh was told not to mention this assignment to anyone. Not to his team members in Libya, and not to the man financing the operation, Edwin P. Wilson. Finally, Pat said, if the photographs were decent, Waugh would be compensated for his efforts.

Pat asked Waugh if he understood the request, and if he accepted the assignment. Waugh said yes. Waugh was going to Libya to work for an American entrepreneur who was doing business with Qaddafi. No one outside Waugh's Agency contacts could know that he was also working for the CIA.

As Waugh headed to Benghazi in August of 1977, Libya inhabited a peculiar spot in the geopolitical landscape. For those living in Libya, life had already become a living hell, but on the international stage, the country was still considered a tinderbox waiting to catch fire. CIA analysts watched Qaddafi's every move, and its Libyan desk hummed with timely reports. Soon, they would include Libyan military secrets passed on from Billy Waugh.

Muammar Qaddafi had seized power in a military coup eight years before, in 1969, overthrowing the monarchy of King Idris. Qaddafi, then a military captain, made himself a colonel and declared his political party, the Revolutionary Command Council, to be the highest authority in Libya. He immediately imprisoned those who'd served the previous administration, many of whom would never be seen or heard from again. He tried King Idris in absentia and sentenced him to death. Much as Che Guevara and Fidel Castro had promised for Latin America—unity and harmony among a group of people who live in a certain region—so Qaddafi promised a beneficent solidarity for all Arab nations. Like his idol, Egyptian president Gamal Abdel Nasser, Qaddafi espoused a pan-Arab nationalism, the revolutionary brand.

Within a year of assuming power, Qaddafi expelled from the country all American and British military advisors and shut down their military facilities, calling them "bases of imperialism." The Italians, Libya's former colonizers, fared worse. Twelve thousand Italians were banished, told to exhume the bones of their dead relatives and take them back to Italy. The event was televised on Libyan state TV. Qaddafi promised reform for the people, including the nationalization of state oil.

To promote a pan-Libyan identity, Qaddafi created something called the Arab Socialist Union, which fizzled. After the death of Nasser in September 1970, Qaddafi tried to assume the position of Arab unifier, but that endeavor also failed. He then worked to create an Arab federation with Egypt, Syria, and Sudan. They all received sizable financial grants, thanks to the vast wealth Libya enjoyed through its oil, and had no choice but to go along. But this, too, failed. When, in 1973, Qaddafi learned of a coup being plotted against him, his grip tightened. He created a militia "to protect the revolution" and began a systematic purge of the educated class. Death squads terrorized the population. Political parties were outlawed. Under the draconian Law 75, dissent became illegal. The state took control of the press. There were no legal codes or a legal system; justice was arbitrary. Constitutional law was suspended and replaced with sharia—Islamic law.

For his first few years in power, Qaddafi was vocal in his disdain for the two superpowers, the United States and Russia, referring to each as "a plague." They were together engaged in a conspiracy to harm the third world, Qaddafi said. Privately, he bought MiG fighter jets, antiaircraft guns, and heavy weapons systems from the Soviet Union. Libya's neighbors, most notably Egypt and Sudan, grew suspicious and then alarmed. Qaddafi was no reformer; he was a megalomaniacal despot. Then, Egypt's new president, Anwar Sadat, began making inroads toward an alliance with the United States.

A turning point in public perception came in 1977, when Fidel Castro arrived in Libya for a ten-day visit as a guest of Qaddafi.

"We are all revolutionaries," Castro told the Libyan Congress. "The revolution must continue!" To a standing ovation, Castro praised Qaddafi. "Comrade al-Qaddafi has struggled for the sake of unity of the Arab world like no one else has done," Castro said. "[His] struggle for prosperity, man's dignity, freedom against exploitation bind us together. We highly admire what you are doing." Castro insisted that the greedy imperialists needed to be fought to the death, by any means necessary. There was only one way. One path. He ended his speech with a call to arms against the United States: "The country of death!" It was into this incendiary climate that Billy Waugh landed in Tripoli, Pentax camera in hand, a covert-action operator for the CIA.

At the airport in Tripoli, Waugh and the others were met by a man who went by the name Mohammad Fatah, likely an alias. The team was escorted through Libyan customs, then to a hotel on the beach. In the morning, they met with Qaddafi's minister of intelligence, Major Abdullah Hajazzi. He spoke in Arabic, which Billy Waugh was able to understand with some help from an interpreter: back in 1956, during U.S. Army Special Forces training, he'd been sent to Monterey for a five-month course in Arabic. He was rusty now, but soon he'd be almost fluent.

The team split up into their areas of expertise. Waugh was taken to Benghazi, roughly six hundred miles to the east, on the coast. It did not take long for Waugh to figure out that Edwin P. Wilson had several teams of former Green Berets inside Libya, doing an assortment of jobs. All were related to weapons training. Wilson, said to be a close personal friend of Qaddafi, owned a seaside villa on the north shore of Libya, near Tripoli, and ran his operations from there.

In Benghazi, Billy Waugh was set up in a room at the Omar Khayamm Hotel under the watchful eye of Libyan handlers. Each day, a woman in a black abaya sat in the hallway outside his room, taking notes. "The only thing visible was her eyes," remembers Waugh. "She was so hidden by a black robe, she could have been a man. Who knows."

For several months at a time, Waugh trained Libyan commandos in small arms, heavy weapons, and explosives. How to ambush a target, conduct hit-and-run operations, sabotage. "Most of the soldiers were unqualified and lazy," he recalls. "Many of them were Qaddafi's friends, or people he owed a favor. Most of them ignored training or flat-out refused to be told what to do."

Sometimes the consequences were lethal. Qaddafi wanted his own version of the U.S. Navy SEALs and assigned Waugh to lead training. During a training exercise on the Gulf of Sidra, one of the commandos in a boat ahead of Waugh leapt out of the craft and into the water and drowned. "He didn't know how to swim," recalls Waugh. "He thought the scuba suit worked like a life preserver" and would keep him afloat. In a post-accident debriefing, Waugh learned only two of the twenty-two commandos knew how to swim.

Things were heating up across the Middle East and North Africa, with Colonel Qaddafi playing the role of central provocateur. In the summer of 1977, Qaddafi's forces carried out a tank raid on the Egyptian border town Sallum. In response, Anwar Sadat sent three Egyptian Army divisions to its border with Libya, overpowering the Libyan brigades and pushing them back. The Egyptian air force attacked Libya's Gamal Abdul El Nasser Air Base, near the border. State Department officials feared Qaddafi wanted to provoke a war with Egypt. "LARG [Libyan Arab Republic government] anticipates military attack from Egypt, which it hopes to exploit and cause overthrow of Sadat," Robert Carle, the U.S. embassy chargé d'affaires in Tripoli, wrote in a classified cable. The U.S. urged restraint, and the border war lasted just three days.

But the feud between Qaddafi and Sadat would not dissipate. The CIA had intelligence indicating that Qaddafi was plotting to have Sadat assassinated. In November 1977, the Pentagon provided Sadat with an armored helicopter, a Sikorsky CH-53E. The White House sent a U.S. Secret Service team to Cairo; they taught evasive driving techniques to Sadat's bodyguards. The CIA set up a secure communication system in the palace so that the president's moves couldn't be anticipated. Anwar Sadat was America's best hope for an Arab partner in the Middle East, and he needed to stay alive.

In November 1977, Sadat stunned the world by announcing his intention to visit Jerusalem and speak before the Knesset, Israel's national legislature. For the first time in three decades, an Arab nation was acknowledging the nation-state of Israel. Sadat's ground-breaking three-day visit to the country was a first step in what would become the Camp David Accords, but the move infuriated Arab leaders. Qaddafi called for Sadat's death. No one was more outraged than an Islamic extremist group inside Egypt called the Muslim Brotherhood. They, too, began plotting to assassinate President Anwar Sadat.

It was in this extraordinarily volatile environment that Billy Waugh operated over the next two years, reporting to Qaddafi's minister of intelligence, Major Abdullah Hajazzi, and developing a close working relationship with a Libyan special forces captain who went by the name Mohammad al Faraj bin Ageby. Taking photographs without drawing suspicion was difficult at first, but over time Waugh became a trusted presence.

"I discovered that the commandos loved having their picture taken, and I took advantage of this," he says. He began taking photographs of extremely sensitive military sites. Flying in a helicopter to the military facility at the Green Mountain, he photographed surface-to-air-missile sites set up in a ring around Benghazi. The CIA had long suspected that Qaddafi was getting these defense missile systems from the Soviet Union. Waugh's photographs provided proof.

As one of the favored trainers of Qaddafi's special forces, Waugh was now the highest-placed CIA paramilitary asset in Libya, with direct access to Qaddafi's most sensitive military facilities. On one occasion, he was invited to attend a small air-power demonstration with Qaddafi and a guest of honor, Idi Amin. During the event, Waugh photographed Russian airplanes that the Soviets were supplying to Libya. Every action now had a dual purpose. While training Qaddafi's commandos how to HALO-jump out of aircraft over the desert, Waugh mapped regions previously uncharted by U.S. intelligence agencies.

The information that Waugh provided to his CIA handler was sensitive, as well as dangerous to his own livelihood, always marked "TS/SCI [Top Secret, Secret Compartmented Information] NOFORN [no foreigners] NOCONTRACT [no contractors] ORCON [original source controlled]"—to keep Waugh, as a source, compartmentalized. What Billy Waugh did not know at the time was that in addition to gathering intelligence for the CIA on Qaddafi, he was also gathering intelligence for the CIA on Edwin P. Wilson. The U.S. Department of Justice (DOJ) and the CIA were building a case against Wilson, who, the DOJ believed, was illegally selling heavy weapons and high-powered explosives to Libya.

Every few months, Waugh would travel back to Washington, DC, file reports, turn in his film, then return to Libya with his Pentax camera and a new supply of 35mm film. In the spring of 1979, he arrived in Benghazi and received unusual news. His Libyan counterpart, Mohammad al Faraj bin Ageby, said they were going to drive six hours into the desert to meet with Ageby's boss, Colonel Fatah.

"In a country where the president was a colonel, being a colonel was big-time," remembers Waugh. "This was not an inconsequential event, and it took me by surprise." Without further explanation, Waugh was driven to Tobruk, not far from the border with Egypt. There, he was brought to meet with Colonel Fatah.

"We notice you are good with a camera," Waugh recalls Colonel Fatah telling him. The comment sent a chill up his spine. Had he been discovered? Did Libyan intelligence know he was working for the CIA?

"We'd like you to cross over into Egypt and take photographs of the Egyptian armed forces set up there," Colonel Fatah said. From the tone of the colonel's voice, it sounded like an offer Waugh was not supposed to refuse. His mind worked quickly, thinking through a scenario. He told the colonel that he flat-out couldn't do that.

"Why not?" the colonel asked.

"If the U.S. found out about it, I'd be charged with spying for a foreign country," Waugh said. Treason.

Colonel Fatah told Waugh he didn't see the logic. Waugh tried explaining, but Colonel Fatah wasn't interested. After that, Waugh says, he felt his relationship with the Libyan command structure cool.

For a while, he was assigned to a remote military base on the northeast coast, at Darnah; then he was sent back to the facility outside Benghazi. Across the Arab world, things were getting worse for American workers. On base Waugh mostly wore his balaclava, but a lot of the time it was off. He was tan from the intense sunshine, but everyone knew he was the American with sandy-blond hair. In November, a group of students stormed the U.S. embassy in Tehran and took more than sixty American hostages. Hostilities toward Americans escalated from there. On December 2, Waugh received a call from Mohammad al Faraj bin Ageby. Something was happening, Ageby said. Qaddafi was furious with the Americans and Waugh needed to leave the country immediately or he'd be arrested.

In Saudi Arabia, local Sunni terrorists had seized the Grand Mosque in Mecca. They'd taken hundreds of worshippers hostage and laid siege to Islam's holiest site. As fierce gun battles raged inside the mosque, Iran's Ayatollah Khomeini took advantage of the chaos and unleashed a black propaganda campaign against Israel and America. The real culprits behind the mosque siege, Khomeini declared, were the Zionists and the Great Satanists of the United States. The siege was in fact led by a group of Islamic fundamentalists called al-Ikhwan, the Brethren, but Iran's supreme leader was pushing a fictional story, that Israeli and American commandos had parachuted into the mosque disguised as Muslims and committed the attack against Islam. Khomeini encouraged revolutionaries to go out and attack U.S. embassies in the Middle East and Africa as a response. His followers obeyed, and the U.S. embassy in Tripoli was now under siege.

Waugh caught a taxi and headed to the airport, leaving everything behind, including the clothes in his hotel room and the money in its safe. On a television in the airport, state TV showed footage of a violent mob outside the U.S. embassy in Tripoli chanting, "Death to America!" Demonstrating solidarity with the Iranian Revolution, some two thousand Libyans had attacked the embassy and set it on fire. Twelve Americans were trapped inside, locked in a walk-in vault. Waugh caught a flight to Frankfurt. By the time he landed, the embassy siege was over and American officials were saying that everyone had "escaped without harm." It would be thirty-two years before Waugh returned to Libya for the CIA, in October 2011, in the days immediately before Qaddafi was killed and disfigured by a violent mob.

In December 1979, U.S. dealings with Qaddafi were far from over. On the twenty-ninth, the U.S. State Department created its first official State Sponsors of Terrorism list, with four countries, including Iran and Libya. Qaddafi responded with one of the most bizarre international assassination campaigns in modern history. He publicly announced a state-sponsored targeted killing program, which he officially called Physical Liquidation of the Stray Dogs.

Qaddafi said that his targeted killing program extended to any

Libyan dissident who spoke out against his government. In a fiery speech broadcast on state radio, he called for "the physical liquidation of the enemies of the revolution abroad." While it sounded like bluster, it was not. Over the next several months, four anti-Qaddafi Libyan émigrés were assassinated: Mohammad Mustafa Ramadan and Mahmoud Abu Salem Nafa in London, and Abdul Aref Ghalil and Mohammad Salem Rtemi in Rome.

Come spring, the U.S. State Department ordered the expulsion of four Libyan diplomats in Washington whom President Carter described as "would-be assassins." On May 1, 1980, the *Financial Times* reported that police departments in the United States, Britain, France, Italy, and West Germany had been alerted by Interpol to guard against a possible wave of assassinations by Qaddafi's hit teams. Qaddafi issued a "final warning" to antigovernment Libyan exiles living abroad. "This is their last hope," he said. "Either they return to Libya where they would be safe and sound or they will be liquidated wherever they are."

When a Libyan émigré living in Fort Collins, Colorado, ignored Qaddafi's threats, Qaddafi sent one of his assassins to Colorado. The assassin was a former Green Beret named Eugene Tafoya.

It was 7:30 on the night of October 14, 1980, and a Fort Collins police officer named Ray Martinez answered a call on his radio. There was a woman named Farida Zagallai on the other end. She was hysterical. Her husband, Faisal, had been shot in the head and was lying on the floor of their apartment in a pool of blood, she said. Officer Martinez needed to come over to 1917 South Shields Street right away.

Officer Martinez recognized the name. Six months earlier, Faisal Zagallai, a Libyan graduate student, had applied for and received a permit to carry a concealed weapon, a 9mm semiautomatic pistol. Zagallai's reason for needing the weapon was unheard-of, certainly for a city like Fort Collins: he claimed to be on a hit list of people Colonel Muammar Qaddafi of Libya intended to assassinate as part of his Physical Liquidation of the Stray Dogs campaign. Back then, it sounded downright fictional.

Officer Martinez hurried over to the apartment and rushed inside. There on the floor, he found Faisal Zagallai lying in a pool of blood, two bullets in his head. The first .22-caliber bullet entered the eye socket, severed the optic nerve, and lodged in Faisal Zagallai's mouth. The second bullet sheared off part of his ear before entering his head through the cheek. The furniture in the living room was knocked over; clearly there had been a struggle. There was blood everywhere, on the carpet and the walls. There were bloody handprints on the doorframe. The assassin, it seemed, had vanished.

Officer Martinez interviewed two witnesses from the apartment building. One helped a sketch artist draw a composite of the suspect. The second witness described a man with a pockmarked face and a clip-on necktie who was carrying a silver-and-blue handgun. Detectives drove to the Denver airport and circulated the suspect sketch. A shuttle bus driver said he recognized the man and gave the FBI a few more clues. After a few days, there was a remarkable lead. The FBI received news of an English-language broadcast from a Libyan revolutionary group that was taking credit for what it called "a physical liquidation." This was part of "the final stage in the revolutionary conflict" between Libya and the imperialist United States, the group said. "A member of the World Revolutionary Committee [has] liquidated one Faisal Zagallai." It looked like Libyan leader Muammar Qaddafi was behind this assassination attempt—that his reach had extended into the United States.

Despite having been shot twice in the head, at close range, Zagallai was still alive. He'd been blinded in his right eye, but lived to tell the tale. Farida Zagallai had already told the FBI everything she knew and could remember. The couple had been out of work, she said, when they received an unsolicited phone call from a woman who identified herself as a recruiter for an insurance company looking for people who spoke Arabic. Farida Zagallai said the job interested her. The insurance company arranged to send someone to the house for an interview; it turned out to be the assassin. The man was strange and had alcohol on his breath, Farida Zagallai told the FBI. She went into the kitchen to make drinks, and when she came out, the assassin and her husband were engaged in hand-to-hand combat.

"He began striking me in rapid-fire karate blows," Faisal Zagallai told the FBI from his hospital bed. Faisal remembered raising his arms up to protect himself when the assassin reached for his gun. Faisal reached for his own gun, which he said he kept hidden under the couch cushions. The assassin's gun went off. "I felt I was shot in my head and I felt blood, but I kept struggling with him so I could take his gun," Zagallai testified. "We struggled from one end of the apartment to the other."

The FBI took over, but the case went cold. Then, as circumstance would have it, months later, two local boys on bicycles happened upon a .22-caliber blue-and-silver handgun lying in a ditch along a country road. The FBI traced the weapon to a retired dog warden living in a trailer park in the Florida Keys. The man, named Tully Strong, said he'd sold the gun to an old friend from Vietnam named Eugene Tafoya, a former Green Beret who'd been decorated with the Bronze Star for heroism.

The FBI learned that Tafoya lived in Truth or Consequences, New Mexico. With a bomb squad at the ready, they secured the perimeter, and in a ruse to lure Tafoya from the home without a struggle, they cut the power to his house. When Tafoya came out, they arrested him. Inside, the FBI located a trove of incriminating evidence: drawings of the Zagallais' apartment complex, a stack of Libyan currency, and a tape recording of a phone conversation from someone offering to pay Tafoya to take care of "someone who should quit breathing…permanently."

The FBI arrested Eugene Tafoya. Tafoya said the man to blame was Edwin P. Wilson, an American CIA agent living in a seaside villa in Tripoli, Libya. Tafoya said his intention was to rough up Faisal Zagallai, not kill him. Tafoya told the FBI he believed he was working for the CIA.

After a sensational jury trial, Eugene Tafoya was convicted of third-degree assault and conspiracy to commit third-degree assault but was acquitted on the more serious charges of attempted first-degree murder and conspiracy to commit first-degree murder. The jurors' verdict indicated that they believed that Tafoya was in fact acting on someone else's behalf, despite the fact that no evidence about the third party was introduced during the trial.

"Obviously we felt there was another party," the jury foreman, Gary Thornberg, told the *New York Times.* "But it didn't matter for our purposes who that [third party] was." Eugene Tafoya was sentenced to two years in prison.

Depending on whom you ask, the FBI and the CIA had been building a case against Edwin P. Wilson for years. In 1982 Wilson was arrested, tried, and convicted of illegally selling weapons to Libya. This included 42,000 pounds of military-grade C-4 explosives, which rivaled the U.S. military's domestic stockpile at the time. Wilson had them manufactured in Southern California. Edwin Wilson was sentenced to fifty-two years in federal prison. He served twenty-two years, much of it in solitary confinement. Then, in 2004, in a bizarre twist, a Texas judge overturned Wilson's conviction and he was set free.

His lawyers had gathered enough evidence to demonstrate to a judge that he'd been "informally" working for the CIA at the time of his arrest. The lawyers produced eighty instances of contact between Wilson and the CIA. In a legal briefing, Judge Lynn Hughes wrote that the U.S. government had "deliberately deceived the court" about Edwin Wilson's continuing contacts with CIA officials, thereby "double-crossing a part-time informal government agent." Decades later, it came to light that Wilson had initially gone to Libya on behalf of the CIA, in 1976, to locate Carlos the Jackal. He'd gone rogue, eventually working for the CIA and also for Qaddafi. This was after Libya had been placed on the State Sponsors of Terrorism list. "They framed a guilty man," said journalist David Corn.

The Eugene Tafoya trial gave Green Berets a bad name. Reports of other Special Forces operators working as assassins for Muammar Qaddafi were published in newspapers around the country. No one else was ever charged. Billy Waugh knew that his classified work for the CIA against Muammar Qaddafi and military targets in Libya was to remain hidden. It was best for him to lay low. He was given an assignment on the other side of the world, 7,000 miles from Washington, DC, on an atoll in the middle of the Pacific Ocean called Kwajalein. His cover was as chief of security at the U.S. Kwajalein Missile Range.

In the Marshall Islands, the Defense Department was testing a highly classified missile system outfitted with a ten-nuclear-warhead payload, called a MIRV (multiple independently targetable reentry vehicle). The Soviets wanted one. Waugh was tasked with training and overseeing one hundred military security officers who were in charge of surveillance of the twenty-five islands and atolls near and around Kwajalein.

The missiles were launched from Vandenberg Air Force Base in California. They were programmed to hit a target five thousand miles away, sometimes just a buoy on the ocean near Kwajalein. Ever on the prowl, Soviet submarines would quickly surface the moment the MIRV became visible on reentry, then dispatch a small Zodiac boat loaded with Russian amphibious special forces called Spetsnaz Delfin. If the Russians were to capture a piece of a missile or a MIRV it would be a counterintelligence coup d'état. Day in and day out, floating on the open sea in his own Zodiac, Billy Waugh scanned the horizon for a sign of Soviet infiltration. When he spotted one of their Zodiacs, he'd charge toward it, ready to grab a Soviet operator and bring him in for interrogation.

"I never got a Russian, but the Russians never got a MIRV," says Waugh.

PART III

1981

CHAPTER SEVENTEEN

Reagan's Preemptive Neutralization

On the morning of January 28, 1981, a CIA motorcade pulled up to the Jefferson Hotel in Washington, DC, to collect a passenger code-named the Baron. The man's real name was William J. Casey, and he was the new director of the CIA. Age sixty-seven, this was the Bill Casey who used to run Special Operations behind enemy lines for the OSS, the man who found a loophole that allowed General Eisenhower to sign off on a plot to kill Hitler using Nazis who'd been turned. With his signature thick-lensed glasses, jowled chin, and expensive but wrinkled suit, Bill Casey climbed into the backseat of an Oldsmobile outfitted with anti-mine plating and bulletproof windows that couldn't be rolled down. The chase car behind Casey carried four security agents with Uzis. In the advance car, a paramilitary operator sat shotgun, a .357 Magnum on his hip and a submachine gun on his lap.

The convoy drove to CIA headquarters in Langley, twelve miles away, breezing past security, around the boulder barriers, and through a grove of pine trees. The CIA's campus was beautiful, its sloping terrain dotted with white and gray buildings that had an air of grandeur. After a short drive, the motorcade pulled up to the entrance of the headquarters building and Bill Casey climbed out, surrounded by his entourage. He intended to arrive this way, and to convey a message: the power of the CIA was soon to be restored. There was a new sheriff in town and he was it.

Bill Casey made his way through the marble foyer, past the CIA memorial wall, up a short set of stairs, and into the key-operated elevator reserved for Senior Intelligence Service staff. He exited on the seventh floor and walked into the director's conference room to meet with his team. "Casey then told these people what they needed and wanted to hear most," explains his biographer, Joseph Persico, "that the indictment made against them during the seventies was a bum rap." CIA officers and operators simply carry out the wishes of the American presidents they serve.

The CIA Bill Casey took over in 1981 had been decimated by the Ford and Carter administrations, a period staff historians refer to as the Time of Troubles. Under Ford, there were the Church and Pike Committee hearings. Under Carter, director Stansfield Turner eliminated 820 clandestine positions, gutting analysis and special operations capabilities. "With the people fired, driven out, or lured into retirement, our analysis wasn't at all sharp, forward-looking, or relevant," recalls Robert Gates, Turner's young executive assistant, who would become director of Central Intelligence in 1991. "Our paramilitary capability was clinically dead," Gates said. Now, Bill Casey was about to change all that, starting with a robust rebuilding of covert operations.

Bill Casey worked from three ideas. The world was a dangerous place; the Soviets were responsible for most of the danger; the CIA must never be weak. The director of Central Intelligence, the president, and his inner circle of advisors needed to plan and oversee foreign policy—to include covert action—as a team. "Khrushchev told us in 1961 that the communists would not win through nuclear war," Casey told his staff. "But through national liberation wars in Africa, Asia, and Latin America." To do this, the communists as well as rogue states like Libya and Iran were financing proxy armies to bring about the downfall of the United States—it was why the world was so wrought with violence. "Not exactly new in history," said Casey, citing how the ancient Romans used men from conquered countries to fight their enemies abroad. But the biggest emerging threat the CIA needed to confront, Casey warned, was that these countries "also operate camps for training terrorists and insurgents to be sent around the world to practice and foment revolutionary violence." In 1981, these were prescient words.

With the intention of fighting fire with fire, Casey asked five top deputies from the clandestine service to provide him with "a clear-cut articulation of the Agency's paramilitary role, how it relates to Delta Force [and] Green Berets, and exactly what is needed to make the Agency capable of playing that role" again. He wanted the CIA to reassert itself in hidden-hand operations around the world, starting with a "statement of clandestine paramilitary doctrine." "It's called for at this point," Casey said, "because so many people [at the CIA] have forgotten where and how a clandestine paramilitary capability can be important."

The problem for hidden-hand operations was a Congress that wanted them curtailed. After Bill Casey finished reading the 130-page paper on Church Commission guidelines for covert operations, he threw it on the table. "This kind of crap is smothering us," he shouted at his staff. "I'm throwing this thing out. You practically have to take a lawyer with you on a mission." Covert action was meant to serve as the president's hidden hand, not the town crier. Assassination as a threat to U.S. national security did not change with the Church and Pike Commissions' investigations into the concept, Casey maintained.

The way to reaffirm presidential authority was to create a new committee inside the executive branch to plan and oversee covert operations. Where Eisenhower had the Special Group and Johnson the 303 Committee, President Ronald Reagan's inner circle of advisors was called the National Security Planning Group (NSPG). It met at the

White House, sometimes weekly. Casey, one of its nine members, wanted closer full-time proximity than Langley to the president and the NSPG. So he arranged to keep a second office next door to the White House, in the Executive Office Building. It was here, on the morning of March 30, that he sat reading from a tall pile of papers when a call from the CIA operations center came in, upending his world.

The worst possible coded message in the repertoire of the U.S. Secret Service had just sounded across the White House communications system.

"AOP! AOP!" AOP is the acronym for attack on principal; principal is another word for president. Ronald Reagan had been shot by an assassin outside the Washington Hilton Hotel. Casey needed to get over to the West Wing of the White House.

When the director of Central Intelligence finally arrived at the White House Situation Room, one question consumed everyone present: Was the assassin a terrorist with ties to the Soviet Union, Libya, or Iran? Bill Casey had no idea.

Ronald Reagan was coming out of the Washington Hilton Hotel when an assassin fired six .22-caliber bullets in his and his security team's direction in less than two seconds. The first bullet hit White House press secretary James Brady in the head, paralyzing him. The second bullet hit DC police officer Thomas Delahanty in the neck, near the brain stem. The third bullet, aimed directly at the president, missed its target and traveled across the street, where it hit a window. U.S. Secret Service special agent Tim McCarthy took the fourth bullet in the abdomen as he shielded the president. The fifth bullet hit the armor-plated limousine. The sixth bullet ricocheted off the armored side of the vehicle and hit the president in the left underarm, entered his body, grazed his upper rib, penetrated into the lung, and stopped 2.52 centimeters from his heart.

Secret Service agents Jerry Parr and Ray Shaddick pushed Reagan into the limousine, which sped off toward George Washington

University Hospital. The president was in great pain but didn't yet realize he'd been shot. He thought that Parr broke his rib pushing him into the limousine. As Parr checked for gunshot wounds, Reagan coughed. Out of his mouth came bright red blood, which frothed. Four minutes later, they pulled into the hospital. With no stretcher available, President Reagan insisted on walking on his own power. All the while, the military attaché carrying the nation's nuclear football remained at his side. In the lobby, Reagan grew short of breath. His left leg buckled and he fell to one knee.

For reasons of national security, the incident was being reported as non-life-threatening, when in fact President Ronald Reagan was perilously close to death. Ingrained in the psyche of every person in the national-security apparatus is a fundamental: the center of power must never go down. An incapacitated president gives the enemy a dangerous window of opportunity to strike. How that can happen is exemplified in what occurred next.

Once the president was inside the emergency room, the hospital staff began cutting off his suit. The FBI confiscated everything in the pockets, including his wallet, inside of which were the Gold Codes: the gamma-classified launch codes for a nuclear weapons attack, printed on a business-sized card. The FBI took these items back to headquarters. For the next forty-eight hours the FBI, not the commander in chief, had the Gold Codes. U.S. nuclear weapons doctrine rests upon the concept of mutual assured destruction, the idea that no nuclear-armed nation would be crazy enough to launch a nuclear attack against the United States because the president would launch a retaliatory attack, thereby annihilating everyone on both sides. But for forty-eight hours in March 1981, this launch-code authority was in limbo.

The president was physically in shock. His systolic blood pressure was 60, down from the normal 140. Emergency room doctors administered intravenous fluids, oxygen, and tetanus toxoids. When his vitals finally stabilized, the president was wheeled into surgery, where he would spend the next 105 minutes undergoing a thoracotomy, a procedure to open the chest cavity to gain access to the heart and lungs and then remove the bullet.

He had been in surgery for almost an hour when the FBI shared with hospital administrators a horrifying discovery. While searching the assassin's hotel room, agents with the Bureau of Alcohol, Tobacco and Firearms found a box of bullets called Devastators, whose hollow-point tip was reengineered with a flammable powder charge to explode on impact. The Devastator bullets in the assassin's Röhm revolver failed to explode when they hit the president, but there was still a chance they could, during surgery—threatening more lives in the operating room. The doctors and nurses chose to continue and the surgery was a success.

U.S. Secret Service special agent Lew Merletti was in New York City when the assassin struck. He'd been assigned to the field office there when he heard the news. "We were all just stunned," he remembers. "That the shooter was able to get off six shots in [roughly] two seconds.... The Secret Service was like, whoa." The assassin was a delusional loner named John Hinckley Jr., a stray-dog or lone-wolf killer: someone who was violent and dangerous but acted alone, without backup or support, or formal training. That a singleton like Hinckley could unleash this kind of lethality made clear what the consequences could be in the event of an orchestrated attack by a Black September–type terrorist organization. The general feeling at the Secret Service, says Merletti, was, "We need to rethink our protection philosophy."

Before the Reagan assassination attempt, agents assigned to the Presidential Protective Division (PPD) focused on shielding the president from an attack or a threat. While traveling, the president rode in a sedan accompanied by five or six special agents carrying submachine guns, hidden in briefcases. The American public got its first glimpse of these weapons after Reagan was shot and photographs of special agent Robert Wanko waving an Uzi submachine gun outside the Hilton were published in newspapers around the world. The reaction on the part of the Secret Service agents had been just as protocol dictated at the time. "Secret Service agents are trained to step into the line of fire. Cover and evacuate," says Merletti. "You're covering the president with flesh and bone and evacuating him." In the chaos and uncertainty, the fail-safe was the sole action of special agent Tim McCarthy, who threw himself in front of the president, as Clint Hill did with Mrs. Kennedy in 1963. "Tim McCarthy really stuck himself right in the line of fire and took that bullet that would have hit Reagan," says Merletti. The event was a cautionary tale and would transform the U.S. Secret Service.

In the aftermath, the Secret Service began to refocus and rebuild, to shift its mind-set from defense to offense. "It became all about the asymmetric threat," says Merletti of how the U.S. Secret Service would metamorphose. "And these were lessons learned in Vietnam."

A covert paramilitary unit called the Counter Assault Team (CAT) would now shadow the president twenty-four hours a day, seven days a week. "They have nothing to do with cover and evacuate," Merletti says of the CAT team. "They're not stepping into the line of fire. Their job is shooting. They are shooters." CAT members would be unconventional-warfare experts, capable of repelling a coordinated multi-shooter attack with crippling aggression, determination, and speed. The new philosophy was not simply to defend against an assassin but to have a guerrilla warfare corps of the Secret Service always there, anticipating an attack, as if the president were forever in a hostile environment. As if they were all behind enemy lines.

When Reagan was shot, there were roughly five part-time CAT teams already in existence, units that worked with the PPD during high-profile presidential events. "Following the assassination attempt on Reagan," says Merletti, "the Secret Service decided periodic coverage by a Counter Assault Team was not enough." All existing CAT members were transferred to Washington, DC, to be with the president and vice president every day, all the time. Because Lew Merletti had served as a Green Beret in combat, he'd already been selected as a member of CAT by the time Reagan was shot. Each team member was assigned a number, starting with 001, and because Merletti was the seventh member of the Counter Assault Team, his CAT number was 007. Other members joked that he was like James Bond.

Team members were individually selected from the ranks of the Secret Service, identified for high levels of motivation, physical strength, and a paramilitary mind-set. They would go through seven weeks of training in irregular-warfare tactics: close-quarters combat, counterambush, counterassault. "We trained with Delta Force, British SAS, Navy SEALs," recalls Merletti. "When it came to shooting, we were right there with them all, standing shoulder to shoulder." At their classified training facility in Beltsville, Maryland, Counter Assault Team members shot close to a thousand rounds a month just to stay sharp.

Now transferred to Washington, DC, Lew Merletti excelled. "On [CAT], you have to think that an ambush could happen at any moment," he says. "Because of what I experienced in Vietnam, I could bring that [concept] to protection. I always did. We used to say we were 'on a war footing.'" Agents were hypervigilant, never allow-ing their minds to wander, never daydreaming about a ball game or a beer. The concept of speed, surprise, and violence of action under-girded every move. If Merletti ever experienced a particularly rough challenge, something that threatened to derail his focus, a single thought could make everything clear for him. "I'd think to myself, hey—Mike Kuropas doesn't have this problem today." Honoring his brothers killed in the service of the nation propelled him forward.

For Lew Merletti, the assassination attempt against President Reagan was a transformative, life-changing event. He would go from an outer-ring member of the U.S. Secret Service assigned to a remote field office, to serving as an elite member of the Counter Assault Team. "The president's personal detail is the inner perime-ter," Merletti explains. "On the Counter Assault Team we were like the middle perimeter. Meaning real close, but not right on top of him." With the new philosophy firmly in place, were anyone to fire a shot in the vicinity of the president, "we would shoot out a wall of steel between the president and whoever was doing the shooting," Merletti explains. In this protective capacity, Lew Merletti excelled. After a little over two years, he was transferred to President Reagan's detail. He was in the inner ring now.

That the assassin John Hinckley was mentally ill, and not an agent of a foreign government, did not mean that assassination threats from foreign governments did not exist. Bill Casey, a practicing Catholic, was particularly worried about the pope. "John Paul [is] a very controversial figure, and a fanatic could try and kill him," he told colleagues. Moscow's fear of the Polish pope's power as a religious figure was of particular concern to Casey. The pope wielded great influence among Catholics in his homeland, and the Kremlin rightly worried that this sway could have a domino effect across the entire Eastern bloc — that it could lead to the collapse of communism.

"I told [the pope] we had no hard evidence [that] he was in danger," Casey said. Still, he asked officers with the Technical Services Division to share with the Vatican their designs for a specially fitted flak jacket that the pope could wear under his white silk cassock. But the pope opposed the idea of wearing a bulletproof vest. It went against everything his papacy stood for, he said. For this reason, the pope was not wearing a flak jacket on the afternoon of May 13, 1981, when shots rang out in St. Peter's Square.

It was 5:18, and the pope had just kissed a little girl and was handing her back to her mother when an assassin's bullet struck him in his stomach, penetrating his small intestine. Blood spurted out of the bullet hole, causing his white cassock to become stained with bright red blood. As he began to collapse, a second bullet struck his right hand, and then a third bullet tore into his arm. An aid flung himself over John Paul, shielding the pope with his own body.

"Drive!" shouted one of the papal bodyguards.

"The pope has been shot!" wailed someone in the crowd.

With far too many people in St. Peter's Square, the popemobile, a Fiat, could not go any faster than two miles per hour. After several agonizing minutes, the Fiat finally arrived at an ambulance that had been positioned in advance near the Vatican basilica's bronze doors. Once inside the vehicle, the pope began praying aloud, calling out, "Mary, my mother. Mary, my mother!" After six hours of surgery he emerged alive.

During months of recovery, the pope became preoccupied with trying to find out who had ordered his assassination. The man who shot him, a Turkish national named Mehmet Agca, fingered a second man, Sergei Antonov, the manager of a Bulgarian airline in Rome, suggesting a conspiracy. Bulgaria's secret services maintained close ties with the KGB. It was understood at the CIA that when Moscow needed a "wet op," a euphemism for assassination derived from the KGB's directorate of liquid affairs, it turned to Bulgarian or Romanian security services. In 1981, the theory being developed by analysts on the CIA's Russia desk was that the Bulgarian intelligence service had hired Agca to assassinate the pope on behalf of the Kremlin—an attempt to subvert the pope's influence in Warsaw and beyond.

The rift between the Vatican and the Soviet Union widened. For the first time since the 1950s, Russian state-run news media attacked the pope publicly through its press agency, TASS. But it would be twenty-five years before an Italian parliamentary investigation, the Mitrokhin commission, concluded "beyond any reasonable doubt" that the Soviet Union had ordered the assassination of John Paul II in 1981. "This commission believes, beyond any reasonable doubt, that the leaders of the Soviet Union took the initiative to eliminate the pope Karol Wojtyla," it reported, using Pope John Paul's Polish birth name. The Mitrokhin report also stated that it was Soviet military intelligence, the GRU, that had orchestrated the assassination plot, not the KGB. In 2007, Russia's foreign intelligence service spokesman called the accusation "absurd."

As Muammar Qaddafi continued to dispatch assassins around the globe, the CIA compiled intelligence reports in an effort to identify these killers. In a dossier entitled "Libyan Assassination Teams, Some Patterns," analysts noted that "a common modus operandi has been for a two-man hit squad to kill the victims," and that these squads were made up of "professional assassins, presumably belonging to the Libyan Intelligence Services." But there were exceptions to the rule. For example, when a former Libyan intelligence officer was strangled in Rome, and then a former officer of the Libyan Army was decapitated in Athens, Greece, the CIA surmised that "strangulation and decapitation suggests amateurs rather than professional killers." The lack of a clear profile made Qaddafi's assassins even more dangerous in their potential ability to strike inside the United States.

"There were persistent threats by Qaddafi," Lew Merletti says of this time, not only against President Reagan but also aimed at Vice President George H. W. Bush, CIA director Bill Casey, Secretary of State Alexander Haig, and several members of Congress. While the Secret Service improved its precautionary measures, the CIA devised a plan to eliminate Qaddafi. Max Hugel, CIA deputy director of operations (the new name for the clandestine service), was dispatched to the House Permanent Select Committee on Intelligence with a plan to overthrow the Libyan leader, but the committee shot the plan down and sent a strongly worded letter of protest to the president.

The State Department was also concerned. Qaddafi's ire was not limited to the United States. "There is evidence of Libyan-backed assassination plots against Arab leaders," Foreign Service officers were told, and this included "President Nimeiry of the Sudan, Jordan's King Hussein and Iraq's Saddam Hussein." But the person at the top of Qaddafi's hit list for the Arab world was President Anwar Sadat of Egypt.

Sadat was a traitor to the Arab world, Qaddafi said. As a result of President Carter's historic Camp David Accords, the president of Egypt had signed a peace deal with the prime minister of Israel. In response, Qaddafi issued a standing offer of one million dollars to anyone who would assassinate Sadat. In a news conference, Sadat called Qaddafi "a vicious criminal, one hundred percent sick and possessed of a demon." President Nimeiry of Sudan claimed that Qaddafi had "a split personality, both of them evil." Even Yasser Arafat called Qaddafi a "madman." But Qaddafi's threats were to be taken seriously. By the summer of 1981, his hit teams had assassinated more than a dozen Libyan émigrés living abroad.

In July 1981, death threats directed against Sadat caused Austrian Chancellor Bruno Kreisky to cancel a visit from the Egyptian president. Kreisky had already once been the subject of an international terrorism crisis, during the 1975 OPEC oil siege. He was not going to land in the crosshairs of madmen once again. The intelligence warning was provided to Kreisky from Mossad. "I was forced to ask Egyptian President Sadat at the time to postpone the trip to Salzburg because I could not guarantee his security," Kreisky told the Associated Press. During an interview with the Libyan president, *Washington Post* columnist Jack Anderson asked Qaddafi about reports that he was trying to orchestrate Anwar Sadat's murder.

"Sadat will be eliminated by the Egyptian people," Qaddafi replied. Which is what happened on October 6, 1981, in Cairo, during a military parade.

President Anwar Sadat and a group of dignitaries had gathered in a 1,000-person military stand in Cairo to celebrate the eighth anniversary of the Yom Kippur War. Security was intense, with four layers of military guards positioned in an outer perimeter, and eight bodyguards in Sadat's inner ring. Sadat, in full military dress, sat in the front row behind a five-foot-thick cinderblock barrier. As the ceremony began, Egyptian air force Mirage jets flew overhead and a convoy of military trucks passed by the stands. Inside one of them, an Egyptian Army lieutenant named Khalid Islambouli put a gun to the driver's head and ordered the man to stop. With three hand grenades concealed under his helmet, Islambouli leapt out of the vehicle and approached the president. Several gunmen with AK–47s hurried along behind Islambouli.

"The president thought the killers were part of the show," Sadat's nephew told CNN. As the men approached the stands, Sadat stood and saluted them. Islambouli threw a grenade and the gunmen opened fire. It took Sadat's bodyguards forty seconds to respond, suggesting a conspiracy.

The attack lasted two full minutes. Anwar Sadat was riddled with bullets and fatally wounded. By the time he arrived at the hospital he was dead. Eleven men seated near him were killed, including the Cuban ambassador, a general from Oman, a Coptic bishop, and an Egyptian government bureaucrat. Twenty-eight people were wounded, including Egypt's vice president, Hosni Mubarak, Ireland's minister of defense, and four U.S. military liaison officers. The assassins were carrying out a fatwa, or religious decree, issued by a radical Egyptian cleric named Omar Abdel Rahman, who went by the nom de guerre the Blind Sheik.

The CIA watched anti-American governments and their proxy armies rejoice. In Iran, Ayatollah Khomeini declared Khalid Islambouli a hero and a martyr. The state issued a stamp in his honor, showing the assassin shouting behind prison bars. "I am very proud that my son killed Anwar al-Sadat," the assassin's mother said in an interview with the Associated Press. "Some call him a terrorist. [Sadat] sold out the country to the Jews...[My son] admired Iran." In Beirut, Lebanon, militia groups gathered to celebrate, firing their weapons in the air and chanting "Allahu Akbar," God is great. Across Libya, celebrations broke out in the streets. One of the last remaining diplomats in Libya described what he witnessed as "ghastly jubilation." On the state-run radio in Tripoli, the government called for a revolt by the Egyptian masses and encouraged the military to overthrow the government. It was a terrible example of the power of assassination as a political tool. Peace in the Middle East was off the table.

Two days later, in Washington, DC, a former CIA officer named Cord Meyer took to the airwaves to express his opinion. "If Libya had been taken care of two years ago, last year, this year, Sadat would probably be alive today," he said. In an editorial for the *Wall Street Journal,* Meyer suggested that the CIA should be "unleashed." The statement underscored a concept that was being secretly developed as a national-security tool for the president, one that would have a ripple effect moving forward.

At the White House, the president's National Security Planning Group began discussing the concept of "pre-emptive neutralization." Of killing a would-be assassin or member of a terrorist organization before he had the opportunity to strike. Preemptive neutralization moved covert-action counterterrorism policy from a defense position (as in waiting to be shot at) to an offensive one (as in striking first). If assassination was illegal as per the Hague resolutions, preemptive neutralization would now be a legal extension of Article 51 of the United Nations Charter, the inherent right of self-defense.

President Anwar Sadat's funeral took place on October 11, 1981. Just hours before, the White House issued a statement explaining that President Reagan would not attend. There were reports that Qaddafi planned to assassinate Reagan at the funeral.

It was a solemn affair, thinly attended. Former presidents Carter, Nixon, and Ford were there, with Alexander Haig standing in for the president. Also in attendance was the prime minister of Israel, Menachem Begin, corecipient with Sadat of the 1978 Nobel Peace Prize. The president of Sudan, the sultan of Oman, and the president of Somalia were the sole Arab leaders present. No one wanted to poke the bear that was Arab terrorism. Except Bill Casey.

In less than sixty days, President Ronald Reagan signed Executive Order 12333, reiterating the already existing ban on U.S. intelligence agencies from sponsoring or carrying out an assassination, but with new language. "No person employed by or acting on behalf of the United States Government shall engage in, or conspire to engage in, assassination," the president decreed. The fine print of the new executive order spent many paragraphs clarifying specific words used in the earlier assassination bans issued by Presidents Ford and Carter. But the word "assassination" was not one of the words defined. Major Tyler J. Harder, of the Judge Advocate General's Corps, U.S. Army, suggests why. "That an ambiguously broad term like 'assassination' would go undefined tends to support a conclusion that a definition of assassination was intentionally omitted." The proscription against assassination was evolving into an allowance for preemptive neutralization.

To argue his position, Bill Casey referenced one of the covert actions that had been authorized by President Carter, a large-scale operation to supply weapons to anti-Soviet holy warriors, called mujahedin, in Afghanistan. "We're arming the Afghans, right?" Casey argued. "Every time a mujahedin rebel kills a Soviet rifleman, are we engaged in assassination? This is a rough business. If we're afraid to hit the terrorists because somebody's going to yell 'assassination,' it'll never stop. The terrorists will own the world. They'll know nobody is going to raise a finger against them."

From December 4, 1981, on out, there would be great flexibility in how targeted killing could be undertaken, and in what circumstances, so that it was not assassination. As he had done with the OSS operational plot to kill Adolf Hitler, Bill Casey had again found his legal loophole.

In the fall of 1982 an angry, pious twenty-year-old Lebanese militant from a poor Shia family was going around Beirut looking for a large quantity of explosives. His name was Imad Mugniyah. He was known locally as "the boss of a gang of thugs enforcing Islamic laws and modest conduct on the streets of Beirut," says journalist Ronen Bergman, who notes that around this same time, Israeli intelligence began receiving reports from local assets of "an extremist, uninhibited psychopath" who was kneecapping hookers and drug dealers around the city. In 1982, the CIA had not yet heard of him, but over the next twenty-five years, Imad Mugniyah would have more impact on U.S. presidential policy regarding assassination than any other individual in history, including Osama bin Laden.

Four years earlier, Mugniyah had been recruited into the Palestine Liberation Organization by Black September's Ali Hassan Salameh, the Red Prince. Mugniyah, an excellent young sniper, was assigned to Force 17, Yasser Arafat's security detail and the elite force of the PLO's Fatah Party. Salameh took Mugniyah under his wing, until Mossad assassinated Salameh in 1979. After Salameh and four of his bodyguards were killed by a car bomb, Mugniyah shifted his allegiance over to Iran. It is not known if Mugniyah was aware of the fact that his mentor also worked for the CIA.

For Mugniyah and violent radicals like him, it was becoming clear that Iran's Ayatollah Khomeini had the best interests of Shia Muslims like Mugniyah in mind. Yasser Arafat sought gains mostly for himself and the PLO. Iran wielded far greater power; look what they'd done to the United States in Tehran in 1979. The Americans had been humiliated by the U.S. embassy takeover, the world reminded of its impotence for 444 days as Iran held Americans hostage. Recently, at the behest of Ayatollah Khomeini, the Iranian Islamic Revolutionary Guard Corps had created a proxy army, or hidden-hand army, to carry out covert operations in Lebanon and elsewhere. This proxy army would become known as Hezbollah, the Party of God, although they still used a variety of pseudonyms, including Islamic Amal and Islamic Jihad. After the death of Salameh, Mugniyah sought a rise to power within the terrorist group, which is why he was out looking for explosives in the fall of 1982.

"He wanted some explosives and wondered whether I had some for him. I laughed and thought he was crazy. Who would want to blow themselves up?" Bilal Sharara, a well-known member of Fatah, told journalist Nicholas Blanford in 2009.

Mugniyah knew who, exactly: teenagers following the orders of Ayatollah Khomeini. In the early days of the Iran-Iraq war, thousands of these young children were sent to their deaths by the ayatollah as suicide bombers — ordered to clear land mines with their own bodies so as to make way for Iranian infantry troops and advance Iran's front line into Iraq. Years later, *New York Times* reporter Terence Smith interviewed survivors of these human-wave assaults, and learned of frightened Iranian children being drugged with an opiate drink called "martyr's syrup," bound together in groups of twenty with machine guns at their back, ordered to keep moving forward, to walk to their deaths. Across their child-sized uniforms a message had been stenciled: "I have the special permission of the Imam to enter heaven." This appears to be the first reporting of modern-day suicide bombers, unwilling participants ensnared in a wicked irregular-warfare tactic designed by Ayatollah Khomeini.

Hatred of the enemy was a motivator, and Imad Mugniyah told Arafat's deputy he had a seventeen-year-old friend named Ahmed Qassir who was willing to sacrifice himself in the struggle against Israel. The delivery of explosives was arranged, and on November 11, Ahmed Qassir drove a Peugeot packed with 2,000 pounds of explosives up to the Israeli Army headquarters in Tyre, Lebanon. The teenager fingered a triggering device and detonated himself, destroying the building and killing seventy-five Israeli soldiers, policemen, and intelligence agents with the Shin Bet, the Israel Security Agency. The dead teenager's handler, Imad Mugniyah, had made his mark and would now advance to operations chief for Hezbollah. Mugniyah's next target was the United States, a bold and unprecedented move. Hezbollah had never before directly targeted the United States with a mass casualty attack.

It was midday on April 18, 1983, and the staff at the U.S. embassy in Beirut were going about their business when a GMC pickup truck sped into the crescent-shaped driveway, swerving to miss the U.S. ambassador's armored limousine. In the back of the truck, hidden under a tarp, were 2,000 pounds of explosives. The driver of the truck, seen smoking a cigarette and wearing a leather jacket, stepped on the gas pedal, raced up a set of steps, crashed through a set of glass doors, and landed in the central lobby of the building that housed the embassy and the CIA station. The suicide bomber detonated, collapsing part of the building. Sixty-three people were killed, including seventeen Americans, most of them from the CIA. Lebanese pedestrians, motorists, and visa applicants were also killed. In the days that followed, body parts and pieces of skin kept washing up on the beach.

Among the dead was CIA case officer and Near East director Bob Ames. One of his hands was found floating a mile out at sea, his wedding band still on his ring finger. Herein lay the stark reality of covert-action operations. Bob Ames had been Ali Hassan Salameh's case officer and handler before the Red Prince was assassinated by Mossad. Now, Salameh's terrorist protégé, Imad Mugniyah, had succeeded in killing the CIA's Bob Ames. With the majority of its staff wiped out, the CIA dispatched a paramilitary officer named William Francis Buckley to take over as the new station chief in Beirut.

Bill Buckley, 56, had worked for the CIA since the Korean War. Most details of his work remain classified. In Vietnam, Buckley served as deputy chief of a Provincial Reconnaissance Unit (PRU), the lethal direct-action arm of the Phoenix program. He was quintessential CIA, mild-mannered and unassuming on the surface, but brave, bold, and determined, say his friends. Buckley was comfortable in chaotic, dangerous places. After Vietnam, he ran covert operations in Zaire, Pakistan, and Egypt, where he trained Anwar Sadat's bodyguards in close-quarters combat. Unmarried, Buckley was known to volunteer for postings in many of the most dangerous CIA stations in the world. He'd served in the Beirut station several years prior but was forced to leave after his cover was blown. Going back into a war zone like Beirut without the cover of anonymity was dangerous, but Bill Casey appealed personally to Buckley. They both knew that Iran's proxy army, later identified as Hezbollah, had to be stopped. Bill Buckley's assignment was to rebuild for the CIA the asset base that Imad Mugniyah's mass-casualty attack had destroyed.

But the Hezbollah terrorists had only just begun. Six months after the U.S. embassy and CIA station in Beirut were blown up, two suicide bombers struck again, this time with explosive-laden trucks. One crashed into the U.S. Marine Corps barracks compound at Beirut Airport, killing 241 U.S. servicemen. Minutes later, a second suicide truck drove into the French paratroop barracks two miles away, killing 58. Imad Mugniyah is said to have watched the bombings through binoculars from the balcony of a high-rise down the street. Five months later, on March 16, 1984, Hezbollah operatives kidnapped Bill Buckley off the streets of Beirut. Mugniyah personally oversaw the torture that Buckley was subjected to for the next nineteen months.

John Rizzo knew firsthand. "I had first met Bill Buckley in 1980 when he was heading the counterterrorism 'group' at CIA Headquarters," Rizzo later wrote in his memoir, *Company Man,* "which in those days numbered only a handful of people." A thirty-four-year career lawyer at the CIA, Rizzo spent decades writing covert-action findings for U.S. presidents. After Bill Buckley was kidnapped, he was called into a meeting with Casey. "There were just three or four of us in the room," remembers Rizzo. "They played a tape of Buckley being tortured. I was a lawyer for the clandestine service, but I also knew him personally [and] was there to confirm identity, through his voice." In an interview for this book, Rizzo said, "I was told by our courterterrorism analysts sometime later that Mugniyah was doing the torturing.... It still haunts me today."

At the CIA, the level of anguish among Buckley's colleagues was palpable. The quest to rescue him became Bill Casey's personal crusade. "Casey ordered that all the stops be pulled out to locate him—wiretaps, bribes, satellite surveillance," explains Rizzo. "I gave immediate legal approval for everything Casey wanted."

It was a tipping point at the CIA. As director of Central Intelligence, Casey would now aggressively upend how the CIA dealt with terrorists. Assassination, or "pre-emptive neutralization," was about to become presidential policy. On April 3, 1984, just three weeks after Buckley's kidnapping, President Reagan signed National Security Decision Directive 138, authorizing the CIA to develop "capabilities for the pre-emptive neutralization of anti-American terrorist groups which plan, support, or conduct hostile terrorist acts against U.S. citizens, interests, and property overseas." The goal, read the directive, was to "eliminate the threat of terrorism to our way of life." The order allowed the CIA to "develop a clandestine service capability, using all lawful means, for effective response overseas." All covert-action plans were to be submitted directly to the president's National Security Planning Group.

To maximize this direct-action capability, the Defense Department created something not seen since MACV-SOG: its own guerrilla warfare corps, called the Joint Special Operations Agency (JSOA), to operate out of Fort Bragg. When the *New York Times* learned of JSOA's creation, it ran a page-one article, describing the group as a "secret commando unit…whose purpose was to support Central Intelligence Agency covert operations." This "raised concern in Congress" that the CIA was back in the business of overthrowing foreign governments and plotting to kill leaders, as it had done before the Church Committee hearings. Intelligence officials told the newspaper that no such risk existed, that "the new special operations forces constituted a resource for intelligence operations" only, and that any use of JSOA would be directed by the CIA and properly reported to Congress.

Despite redoubling their efforts, the CIA was unable to locate Bill Buckley. No commando force was sent to rescue him. In the end, Mugniyah and his men tortured Bill Buckley to death. "He was the first CIA employee I knew who was murdered in the line of duty," says Rizzo.

In October 1985, after Imad Mugniyah's Islamic Jihad Organization—a cover name for Hezbollah—announced it had killed Buckley, the CIA began developing a covert-action operation to kill or capture Mugniyah. The State Department objected. "We used to have arguments within the executive branch between those who advocated assassinations" and those who insisted it was "illegal," recalls Ambassador Robert Oakley, the State Department coordinator for counterterrorism at the time. It was Ambassador Oakley's view that assassination was like the mythical beast, the hydra. If you cut off the head of the snake, ten more snake heads grew.

Bill Casey disagreed, and took the issue directly to the president. "The CIA believed [Mugniyah] to be in Paris," Oakley later wrote. Oakley argued against the CIA taking action against the terrorist. "While I was briefing the Secretary [of State], he got a call from Bud McFarlane of the NSC [National Security Council]. Bud said that the President had approved Director of Central Intelligence [Bill] Casey's recommendation to kidnap Mugniyah off the streets of Paris." Paramilitary operators raided the hotel room where Mugniyah was believed to be staying. "They found a fifty-year-old Spanish tourist, not a twenty-five-year-old Lebanese terrorist," Oakley recalled.

From the perspective of the CIA, it was time to formalize operations, to have a center at the CIA dedicated to combating terrorism. On February 2, 1986, the CIA's first Counterterrorist Center (CTC) opened its doors (it was renamed the Counterterrorism Center in 2005). Counterterrorist Center officers would work with paramilitary operators and Special Forces soldiers from JSOA. The Center would employ scientists and engineers from the Directorate of

Science and Technology and analysts from the Directorate of Intelligence. It would be a new kind of place, said its first director, Duane "Dewey" Clarridge. A "fusion center."

Vincent Cannistraro, a member of the National Security Council at the time and a future chief of operations at the CTC, explained the thinking in 1986. "Bill Casey saw the Counterterrorism Center as basically an all-capability center to stop terrorists. That we would go out and snatch terrorists and hit them before they could act." Who to go after—the targets—would be determined by CTC analysts pulling data from all available sources: human, signals, imagery. "But this center would also have the capability of actually being an action element to go out there," Cannistraro says, to go out and kill or capture enemies of the United States before they had a chance to strike. "Casey's original conception for a counterterrorism center at the CIA was to give it a paramilitary capability, an intelligence capability, and an analytical capability—to put it all together in one package. The paramilitary capability would be used to go after known terrorists, to kidnap them and render them to U.S. justice." Advocates of CIA kill-or-capture missions in the modern era point out how prescient Bill Casey's thinking was in 1986. Critics say Casey helped create a monster, a multiheaded hydra. That for every head it severed, ten new heads would grow.

One of the radical ideas at the CTC in 1986, to preemptively neutralize threats, was to build and use an unmanned aerial vehicle (UAV), also called a drone. With a budget of seven million dollars, Dewey Clarridge initiated the Eagle Program, which he foresaw being used against targets in difficult to get to places, like Libya or Iran. Two months after the Counterterrorist Center opened its doors, a powerful bomb went off inside La Belle discothèque in West Berlin, a place known to be popular with American soldiers stationed at a U.S. military base down the street. Three people were killed; two were American soldiers. Two hundred twenty-nine were injured. After the National Security Agency intercepted telex messages sent from Tripoli to the Libyan embassy in East Berlin, congratulating its personnel on a "job well done," the CIA laid blame on Muammar Qaddafi personally as well as on Libya's governing body, the Revolutionary Command Council.

At the Counterterrorist Center, Dewey Clarridge proposed killing Qaddafi with the CTC's Eagle Program drone. "Pack it with explosives or engineer it to carry a rocket and fly it into Qaddafi's tent," he said. Clarridge's idea was shut down. Instead, President Ronald Reagan ordered air strikes against Tripoli and Benghazi. The massive, Defense Department–led operation involved sixty-six U.S. aircraft. Qaddafi's residential compound took a direct hit, allegedly killing his fifteen-month-old daughter, Hana. At least thirty soldiers and seventy civilians were killed. In a nationally televised speech, President Reagan defended his actions: "When our citizens are attacked or abused anywhere in the world on the direct orders of hostile regimes, we will respond so long as I'm in this office." Anyone who dared suggest the United States had tried to assassinate Qaddafi was wrong, the president said, that America was simply exercising its right to self-defense as defined by Article 51 of the United Nations Charter.

At the CIA, Dewey Clarridge cried false virtue. It was "hypocritical," he said, to use massive air power to take out a single dictator—killing more than one hundred people—simply because it looked better than a lethal direct-action strike targeting one man. "Why is an expensive military raid with heavy collateral damage to our allies and to innocent children okay—more morally acceptable than a bullet to the head?"

The question was far from answered.

CHAPTER EIGHTEEN

Parachute Assassins, Saddam Hussein, and Osama bin Laden

Every day, Lew Merletti thought about how someone might try to assassinate the new president of the United States, George Herbert Walker Bush. Merletti was always on the lookout for a chink in the armor of the U.S. Secret Service. "The assassination of the President of the United States is, quite literally, a cataclysmic event in world history," Merletti told the Justice Department. "It is also the worst possible incident that can occur on the Secret Service's watch. For this reason, it is the practice of the Secret Service to review and assess all assassination attempts, wherever and whenever they occur."

In reviewing gruesome assassination tapes, it was impossible for Merletti not to think about ambush scenarios he'd witnessed in Vietnam. His mind was always working to find places where presidential protection could improve, something ingrained in him by his highly motivated boss, John Magaw. One day, Magaw approached Merletti with an idea for a radical AOP—attack on principal—training exercise. Did Merletti have any trusted contacts with Delta Force, owing to his time in Special Forces? Magaw asked. Merletti said he did.

John Magaw sent Lew Merletti down to Fort Bragg to meet

secretly with the Delta Force commander. Delta Force, the 1st Special Forces Operational Detachment-Delta (1st SFOD-D), is a classified unit whose existence the army will neither confirm nor deny. (During the war on terror, Delta's name was changed to Combat Applications Group.) With counterterrorism and hostage rescue its primary missions, Delta operators are trained as a direct-action strike force and are arguably the most elite of all Tier One U.S. military operators. Merletti presented Delta Force with a challenge, direct from the Secret Service. They were to come up with the most devastating small-footprint ambush they could conceive of—to plan and train for an AOP targeting the White House.

There were specific ground rules in place. "The Delta operators were not allowed to use their clearances to get classified information to devise the ambush," says Merletti. "They had to use recon only, and use publicly available information. Figure out the weak point in our defense system and try and breach it. We told them, if we catch you in the [White House] tour line, it's a point for us." The Delta commander accepted the challenge and began devising an AOP operation.

The chosen Delta Force unit trained for six to eight weeks. Even John Magaw and Lew Merletti remained in the dark regarding the AOP that Delta Force would attempt: to have a team of parachute assassins try and infiltrate the White House via high-altitude low-opening (HALO) infiltration. The operation has never been reported before.

On the night of October 14, 1990, President George H. W. Bush was taken to Camp David, the presidential retreat in Catoctin Mountain Park in Maryland. Live ammunition was collected from the Secret Service special agents on duty, an indicator that something was going on. One of the agents on duty that night, a sniper on the White House roof, recalls what happened. "All of a sudden, there were these Delta guys on the lawn. It was that fast. It was a 'holy shit' moment for everybody involved."

"The Delta operators did a low-level HALO pull," explains Billy Waugh. "They came in free-falling [at terminal velocity], and pulled just a few hundred feet above the deck. This is very difficult to defend against, unless you're prepared."

At the time of the AOP training exercise, there was a radar system installed at National Airport, five miles from the White House, designed to pick up any aircraft flying in the vicinity. There was also a direct phone line from National to the White House, hardwired into the U.S. Secret Service communications office. "It rang several times a week," recalls Merletti, always reporting anything that was even remotely unusual. But on the night of the AOP exercise, it didn't even ring. Delta Force outfoxed it. How the team did it remains highly classified.

With this weakness in the White House defense system thus revealed, a microwave Doppler system was installed on the roof. Then Delta conducted a second AOP training raid. This time the Doppler radar picked up the parachute assassins. The Delta Force commander gave Lew Merletti an infrared photograph of one of the Delta operators, in a harness, as he was landing on the White House lawn. Merletti taped the photo to a wall in his office at the White House with the words "No Comment" written underneath. One hole had been plugged, but there was always another one to think about.

The following year, in January 1991, America went to war for the first time since Vietnam. The conflict began in August 1990 when Iraqi president Saddam Hussein ordered his military forces to invade neighboring Kuwait. The United States feared that Saudi Arabia was next—that the kingdom was at risk of an Iraqi invasion. In September 1990, a meeting took place at the Riyadh palace of Crown Prince Sultan bin Abdul Aziz, the Saudi Arabian minister of defense. Prince Sultan was meeting with an unusual group of visitors regarding a delicate matter that needed to be handled with the utmost sensitivity. The leader of the group was a wealthy thirty-three-year-old Saudi national named Osama bin Laden.

With bin Laden were a group of friends and colleagues, Afghan mujahedin. This group had spent the past decade fighting Russian infantry forces following the Soviet Union's invasion of Afghanistan in 1979. It was a classic irregular-warfare scenario. A much smaller rebel force, the mujahedin, had managed to defeat one of the largest armies in the world, the Russians, using guerrilla warfare tactics. Training, weapons, and funding for the mujahedin came from the United States, Saudi Arabia, England, Pakistan, and China. In 1989 the Russians left, defeated. At the CIA, analysts called it Russia's Vietnam. Now restless and without purpose, the mujahedin were looking for the next jihad, or holy war. It was why bin Laden was here, he told the Saudi minister of defense.

Osama bin Laden handed Prince Sultan a five-page proposal. The document detailed how his mujahedin fighters would protect the kingdom from what looked like certain invasion by Saddam Hussein. The secular hypocrite Iraqi leader must be stopped, bin Laden warned. His presence anywhere near the two Muslim holy places Mecca and Medina was an insult to Islam. Iraq had a powerful army: 900,000 soldiers in sixty-three divisions, which made it the fourth largest army in the world. Saddam Hussein's Republican Guard included some of the best-trained fighters in the Middle East. Bin Laden and the prince were both aware of the reality of the Saudi Army. In 1990, it consisted of 58,000 poorly trained soldiers, largely because the kingdom relied on technology to stop an attack. Saudi Arabia owned and maintained a $50 billion air defense system, supported by a fleet of British-made fighter-bomber aircraft. But as far as ground operations were concerned, the only thing between Saddam's infantry soldiers and Saudi Arabia's oil fields were a few thousand Saudi national guard soldiers who'd been sent to the front line.

According to a witness in the room named Mohammad din Mohammad, bin Laden made a pitch for a partnership. Pulling out a map, he proposed to dig a massive ditch in the desert sands along the border between Saudi Arabia and Iraq. His group of fighters would use earth-moving equipment supplied by his family's Saudi Binladin

Group. The Afghan mujahedin would supplement the big ditch with lots of little ones, using shovels, he said. In this manner, they'd create all kinds of sand traps—into which Saddam Hussein's 5,700-tank armored cavalry corps would fall.

"I am ready to prepare one hundred thousand fighters with good combat capability within three months," bin Laden reportedly told the prince.

But the prince wasn't interested in what bin Laden was trying to sell. He thanked him, and said he appreciated the fact that his family and bin Laden's family had "always been loyal friends." But he did not need Osama bin Laden's military assistance in fighting Saddam Hussein. Bin Laden's face turned "black with anger," Mohammad din Mohammad recalled.

The prince was uninterested because he already had a partner and a deal in place. Just weeks before, a billion-dollar defense contract had been signed with the Americans. President George H. W. Bush's secretary of defense, Dick Cheney, met personally in Jeddah with Saudi king Fahd to secure this deal. Cheney's advisors on the trip included General Norman Schwarzkopf, commander in chief, U.S. Central Command. General Schwarzkopf would lead all coalition forces in the forthcoming Gulf War. The Americans had state-of-the-art satellite images, including ones that showed how many of Saddam Hussein's tanks were lined up on the border. Osama bin Laden had hand-drawn maps.

General Schwarzkopf told King Fahd, "Tanks being deployed far forward is an indication of offensive action." It meant that Saddam Hussein appeared ready to strike. The general shared with the king the latest imagery intelligence and geospatial intelligence to make his point. The U.S. military was prepared to send fighter squadrons and U.S. troops to defend Saudi Arabia against an invasion by Iraq. All they needed was King Fahd's okay.

"Okay," the king said.

"We did a double-take," Schwarzkopf later recalled.

"So, you agree?" Defense Secretary Cheney asked.

The king said, "Yes, I agree."

Ambassador Charles Freeman, who was also present and who spoke Arabic, confirmed that the king had indeed given his okay.

"When do you expect the first planes to arrive?" the king asked Cheney.

Cheney told the king, "Within twelve hours, they'll be here."

Of course Osama bin Laden knew none of this. But he'd heard palace rumors that the Americans might be involved. It was why he was here in Prince Sultan's home.

"You don't need Americans," bin Laden is said to have told Prince Sultan. "You don't need any other non-Muslim troops. We will be enough."

Prince Sultan considered what bin Laden was saying. "There are no caves in Kuwait," he told him. "What will you do when [Saddam Hussein] lobs missiles at you with chemical and biological weapons?"

"We will fight him with faith," bin Laden said.

But the prince's message was clear: he was not interested in what bin Laden was selling. If bin Laden didn't yet know for certain that he'd lost the contract to the U.S. Department of Defense, he'd learn soon enough, when the first of nearly 500,000 American soldiers began arriving in the kingdom, along with 1,500 international journalists who would broadcast news of the American-Saudi partnership to the world. When the war began, on January 16, 1991, the Americans were already firmly planted on sacred soil. War, the president's second option after diplomacy, had not been authorized by Congress in twenty-seven years—not since the Gulf of Tonkin Resolution approving U.S. military action in Vietnam.

Bin Laden was outraged. He moved to Khartoum and began plotting jihad against the United States. Within months, the CIA sent Billy Waugh there to run reconnaissance on him.

★   ★   ★

Khartoum was a lawless, brutish place in 1991, ruined by decades of civil war that had engulfed the country ever since Sudan gained independence from the United Kingdom in 1956. It had been seventeen years since U.S. ambassador Cleo Noel, U.S. embassy chargé d'affaires Curt Moore, and Belgian diplomat Guy Eid were taken hostage and assassinated by Black September during the attack on the Saudi embassy in 1973. When Billy Waugh first arrived, in the spring of 1991, Sudan remained a hornet's nest of terrorist activity.

The president of Sudan was Brigadier General Omar Hassan al-Bashir, a warlord who took power by military coup. But the real reins of power were held by al-Bashir's secretary general, a Sorbonne-educated Islamist named Hassan al-Turabi. Publicly, Turabi maintained cordial relations with the United States. Privately, he was virulently anti-American. "America incarnates the devil for all Muslims in the world," he told local commanders.

Through NSA signals intelligence (SIGINT) intercepts, the CIA learned that Turabi was in contact with numerous high-ranking leaders of Hezbollah, Abu Nidal Organization, and Palestinian Islamic Jihad, and with individual terrorists, criminals, and rogues wanted by Interpol and the FBI. Turabi offered them sanctuary in Khartoum in exchange for cash. Many took him up on his offer, and by 1991, the CIA understood these terrorists to be freely moving around Khartoum, out of reach of law enforcement and plotting the demise of the West. In April, Turabi hosted the Arab Islamic People's Congress in an effort to unify Afghan mujahedin and other radical players, all of whom opposed Saudi dominance. Attendees included Yasser Arafat; Ayman al-Zawahiri, of Egyptian Islamic Jihad; Khaled Mashal, of Hamas; and Imad Mugniyah. Osama bin Laden may or may not have attended. CIA officers and counterterrorism experts differ in their opinions about when, precisely, bin Laden arrived in Sudan.

The CIA sent Billy Waugh to Khartoum on a covert operation, to conduct surveillance on these shadowy figures, many of whom maintained multiple aliases and noms de guerre to keep their identities hidden. One notable exception was bin Laden, who went by the same name he'd been given at birth.

"In the very early 1990s bin Laden was a nobody to us," recalls Waugh, "but Sudan was an anything-goes cesspool of a place." Few people had ever heard of bin Laden, who was just becoming known to Western intelligence agencies. He was on the CIA's radar, however, because he'd recently cofounded an organization called Al-Qaeda, or the Base.

Bin Laden's base was made up of Afghan mujahedin and any other foreign fighters willing to wage a holy war against the West. With the Berlin wall down and the communist threat reduced nearly to nil, the CIA was gathering intelligence on potential threats. A political-religious system rooted in early Middle Ages thinking seemed conspicuously anachronistic. Bin Laden and his mujahedin called it global jihad.

In 1989, after the Afghan war ended, the stateless mujahedin sought an alliance with the Islamist cleric Hassan al-Turabi, who'd recently helped stage a military coup in Sudan. They were like-minded individuals. In Turabi's eyes, the failure of Arab governments was rooted in a reluctance to enforce sharia law. Turabi became the first Muslim cleric to successfully implement sharia across an entire nation. Bin Laden and his followers respected that. The CIA took note and began to monitor the jihadists in Khartoum.

When Billy Waugh arrived in Khartoum, piles of concrete rubble lay interspersed with crumbling buildings and plywood shacks across the city. Government soldiers patrolled the streets. Armed militia manned makeshift checkpoints at the edges of town. The secret police, the Political Security Organization (PSO), arrested people at whim, mostly on grounds they'd violated sharia law. Eighty-five percent of Sudanese citizens lived without any social or civil services. Khartoum was a challenging place for an athletic sixty-three-year-old white man like Billy Waugh to conduct a covert operation for the CIA. Of medium height, he stood out among the majority population, Dinka tribesmen, many of whom were over six feet tall. But he approached his work there the way he approached any Special Forces military operation, or CIA covert action, he says. "Prepare, rehearse, engage the target." And find good cover.

Waugh was in Sudan as an independent contractor, or IC, for the CIA, not a full-time employee on payroll—that would be a blue badger. Rather, he was a green badger, his contracts individually written and renewed. However, the black diplomatic passport he carried, provided to him by the Agency, identified him as an employee of the U.S. Department of State. In the event he was arrested by the PSO, he'd be afforded diplomatic immunity in the form of a single get-out-of-jail-free card. But getting arrested would also mean the end of his CIA career. "I had a serious interest in wanting to keep my job. There was no way I was going to allow myself to get arrested. No way."

One of the advantages of traveling in Sudan on a diplomatic passport, not with civilian cover, was that he could use a diplomatic pouch to get camera equipment in. "The government had outlawed cameras and developing supplies," Waugh says, fearing photographs would portray the desolate state of affairs inside the country and make obvious the failure of Turabi's imposition of sharia law.

"People were starving to death in the streets," remembers Waugh. "They'd get picked up [by police] and transported to areas outside the city, left to die in a less obvious place." Making photography illegal was the government's solution to this problem.

How was he going to use his camera around Khartoum without getting caught by the secret police? "I had an idea about how to circumvent the problem," he remembers. "I suggested that I use jogging as a cover. Start running around the city with the idea I was a stubborn old American on a fitness craze." The Khartoum chief of station said he'd think about it. He came back to Waugh with an idea that headquarters liked better. "They asked me to conduct surveillance against terrorist targets wearing a disguise that made me look like a black African."

The Technical Services Division created a Dinka disguise, which included a rubber facemask, arms, and hands. The concept had been dreamed up and designed by Anthony Mendez, a technical operations officer who was a legend inside the Agency for having exfiltrated six American diplomats from Iran during the peak of the U.S. embassy hostage crisis. (In 2016, Mendez would become famous to the public as the lead character portrayed in the Hollywood film *Argo*.) A Hollywood prop house did the mask molding and building.

The problem was, the mask didn't really fit, says Waugh. "Its lips were too big, and in order to see through the windshield while I was driving, I had to tilt my head in such a way that my mouth was nearly touching the steering wheel." There was legitimate concern he'd draw attention to himself driving around Khartoum like that. The problems did not end there. The mask made him sweat in Sudan's oppressive heat; summer temperatures hovered around 120 degrees Fahrenheit. The gloves that came with the mask extended from Waugh's fingertips to his shoulders, where they tied at the back with strings. The thick rubber finger-sleeves made holding forbidden camera equipment dangerous and difficult.

Following orders, Waugh donned the mask and drove around Khartoum in a battered Russian-made sedan given to him courtesy of the CIA. "Like just about everything in Sudan," recalls Waugh, "my car was a wreck. It was missing a big piece of the floor, and when I drove around town, usually at seventy kilometers an hour, huge clouds of dust blew up through the open floorboards."

One hot day, a new deputy chief of station (name still classified) came to town. Waugh was given the assignment of showing his new superior around Khartoum. The deputy chief wanted to be shown escape routes out of town and into the desert, roads Billy Waugh had already mastered while conducting surveillance detection routes— necessary tradecraft in the event you had to ditch a tail. During the outing, the deputy chief of station also wore a Dinka mask that had been specially designed for him, complete with gloves and arms. Waugh recalls his colleagues' deep discomfort with the lawlessness of Khartoum, heightened by the discomfort of wearing a mask.

Waugh and the deputy chief set out driving. "It was hot as hell and I drove really fast, showing him the Saharan scenery without wasting any time. He was quiet for a while. Seemed miserable, or at least tense."

At one point he asked Waugh, "Do you always drive this fast?"

Waugh recalls making a joke. "Yes, sir, I do," he said.

"My passenger did not think that was very funny," remembers Waugh.

"Where's the floor of your car?" the deputy chief asked Waugh.

"Some of it's missing," he said. "If the Agency wants to get me a new vehicle, that'll be fine, too."

The deputy chief rode along in silence. At the edge of the town, where the city road meets the desert, Waugh's old Russian car was forced to a stop by a mob of armed militia. One of the men stuck the muzzle of his AK-47 through the window. Waugh knew how to bargain with these people; he always carried cartons of cigarettes he could use for a bribe. After a bit of negotiation, the militia waved Waugh through.

"I heard a muffled sound coming from my passenger, a kind of light gagging noise," he recalls. Suddenly, the whole car smelled of vomit. Waugh realized that the deputy chief of station had thrown up inside his mask.

"He was angry and embarrassed, but he couldn't take off the mask for fear of blowing our cover," remembers Waugh. They drove on, headed back to Khartoum.

"It's your fault," the deputy chief said after a while. "The way you're driving the car caused me to throw up."

The men continued in silence. Outside, Khartoum rolled by. Waugh showed the deputy chief numerous escape routes, shortcuts into the desert, and checkpoints to avoid. Finally, they arrived back at headquarters. Once inside the building, they were met by the chief of station. By now, both men had taken off their sweaty Dinka masks. The chief of station pointed at the deputy's face and hair, which were covered in dried vomit.

"What the hell happened to you?" he asked.

"The deputy chief was furious," Waugh recalls. "He fired off a litany of angry excuses, ending with, 'I can't put up with this shit.'" He didn't have to for long. Just a few months later, he was transferred out of Sudan. The chief of station agreed to let Waugh jog around Khartoum now, as a means of conducting surveillance and reconnaissance on Osama bin Laden.

Billy Waugh worked best alone. To be assigned a mission and to get it done, by any means possible, was what he was best at. Accomplishing a task that others could not accomplish made him feel alive, and gave him meaning and purpose—fulfilled his boyhood dreams of feeling like he was needed in the nation's defense. Each day he'd run an eight-mile loop around the al-Riyadh section of Khartoum, employing the old-school espionage techniques of ground surveillance. His first task was to locate a decent place to set up an observation post, or OP, in agency parlance. Bin Laden's private residence was a pink three-story house on the old French Embassy Road. It was surrounded by high walls. Armed guards kept watch over the place, usually six or eight mujahedin dressed like they were still fighting the Afghan jihad. "Visitors to his home would drive up to the compound with drapes covering the car windows," remembers Waugh. "He had four wives and more than a dozen children but I never saw any of them. If they were there, they stayed inside."

At the time, the CIA did not know much about Osama bin Laden. Waugh was assigned to profile his actions so that a portrait of the man and his pattern of life could emerge. In his jogging excursions, Waugh pieced together bin Laden's daily routine. The man prayed early in the morning, before sunrise. At 9:00 a.m. sharp he left the house, climbed into his white Mercedes sedan, license plate number 0990, and drove himself to the Arab Bank on Latif Street. For noon prayers, he would drive to another building he owned, down on South Riyadh Road, where some of his staff lived. Finally, he made a trip a few blocks to the north. It was here that bin Laden's construction company, al-Hijira, owned a warehouse full of construction equipment.

Through the construction company, bin Laden was building a series of new roads in a country that almost entirely lacked infrastructure. This included a road from Khartoum to Port Sudan, a distance of 520 miles. What machinery Osama bin Laden lacked he would import from Russia, through another of his companies, al-Qadurat. Often the government of Sudan was unable to pay bin Laden for his road work and construction projects, so he agreed to accept large plots of land as barter. In this way, Osama bin Laden acquired the Gash River Delta, a massive plot of land near the Ethiopian border, as well as a huge farm in Gedaref. At one point, he was rumored to be the largest landowner in Sudan.

In Khartoum, Waugh figured out that bin Laden owned at least four buildings. One of them stood near the Palestinian embassy, west of his private residence. The property butted up against Runway 340 at the Khartoum International Airport, giving Waugh a solid viewing perspective of goods being unloaded on the tarmac. But it was while he was observing activities at bin Laden's building on South Riyadh Road that he got his first real break in the case. Directly across the street was a safe house owned by the U.S. intelligence community. This safe house, it turned out, was being used by an ultrasecret U.S. Army SIGINT unit called Intelligence Support Activity, and that went by the codename Gray Fox. Created as a Reagan-era response to the Iranian hostage rescue attempt, one of Gray Fox's primary tasks was to collect intelligence in advance of a paramilitary operation. As Waugh understood it, Gray Fox was listening to activities going on in an Iranian safe house nearby. This Gray Fox facility presented itself as the perfect place for Waugh to set up an observation post and take the CIA's first proprietary photographs of Osama bin Laden.

"One of the most important elements of warfare and of spying is the ability to look down on your target," says Waugh. In Khartoum, this general truth proved both a problem and a solution. Because it was so hot outside, many of the locals slept on the rooftops of their buildings at night. Waugh would use this activity as a cover story. He constructed a bamboo structure, designed to look like a sleeping shack, up on top of the roof of the Gray Fox building. He set up his camera equipment inside the sleep shack and waited. It was from here that he took what are considered to be the first CIA surveillance photographs of Osama bin Laden and his followers. They have never been released to the public, says Waugh. The photographs show bin Laden seated cross-legged and facing his followers. "There were twenty or twenty-five of them, and they sat there mesmerized by him, listening with their mouths open. They hung on his every word."

With Gray Fox as support, and while jogging around the neighborhood, Waugh was able to plant additional devices for gathering signals intelligence. But his singleton operation came with an unforeseen threat. Osama bin Laden unleashed guard dogs. "He had six or eight big white desert dogs," recalls Waugh. "They were meaner than snakes." They would run up to Waugh as he jogged by, threatening to sink their teeth into his bare legs. To counter the threat, Waugh began running with a lead pipe. "A couple of smacks on the snout and the dogs decided I wasn't worth the trouble," he recalls.

Most of the time, Osama bin Laden's Afghan bodyguards let Waugh jog by. Sometimes they'd tail him. "They followed me in a vehicle, staying about twenty feet behind me as I jogged. I ran like I was a boxer training for a fight. After a point, the guards would lose interest, get tired, and go home." Finally, he was able to get photographs from close in, while jogging by the compound.

Waugh left Sudan and returned months later. In February 1993, he observed the tail end of an assassination attempt against bin Laden at the mosque in Omdurman, on the western banks of the Nile, where the Al-Qaeda leader and his followers were known to pray. A gunman leapt out of a car, sprayed the worshippers with gunfire, and sped away. Nineteen people inside the mosque were killed, another fifteen worshippers injured. Waugh was at the Gray Fox safe house at the time. "The two would-be assassins sped across the White Nile Bridge and drove all the way to bin Laden's house, more than twenty-five miles away," he recalls. "They were never stopped by the police." From Waugh's rooftop perch on al-Riyadh Street, he "heard a flurry of gunfire from the direction of bin Laden's residence. Two of bin Laden's bodyguards waxed the assassins, but bin Laden escaped unharmed." So it went in Khartoum.

The local papers reported the arrest of an "Islamist of Libyan origin who'd fought in Afghanistan" who was tried and convicted of the crime. Was it true? Had one of bin Laden's former fighters tried to kill him? "Hard to say," says Waugh. Three months later, the man was executed. The assassination attempt got Waugh thinking.

"In my capacity, I was never in [a position] to make planning decisions," Waugh explains. "But sometimes people asked what I thought was the best thing to do. So in this particular instance, I drew up a plan to kill bin Laden," he says.

It was a transitional time for the CIA in Khartoum. The chief of station, code-named Blackjack, had just left the post. An intruder had broken into his home through a window in his wife's bedroom, and in self-defense he had shot and killed him. The story never made it into the local press, but Blackjack had his cover blown, and he was replaced by a forty-three-year-old longtime veteran of the clandestine service named Cofer Black.

As a teenager at the Canterbury Preparatory School, in Connecticut, Cofer Black first became enamored with the concept of espionage. In an interview for this book, he remembers how he and his friends stayed up late one night trying to imagine the most exciting, most dangerous job in the world. "I came up with CIA officer," recalls Black. A decade later, when he was pursuing a PhD in international relations at the University of Southern California, he decided to leave school and join the CIA.

"As a new recruit in 1975," says Black, "I was assigned the job of watch officer, monitoring foreign cables as they came in from overseas. I learned about the fall of Saigon in real time, sitting there in the operations center of the CIA. It had to have been my first month on the job."

The event had a profound effect on him, he says, as he watched so many evacuees clamoring to get out. "I will never forget the moment. It was total collapse. All our efforts, sucked away to nil. I thought to myself, *This should never happen again*." Black vowed to be the most effective clandestine service officer he could be.

He adapted well to Khartoum. "If you are a counterterrorist, Khartoum was the Super Bowl," says Black. "Hezbollah, Hamas, Islamic Jihad, they were all there in the early 1990s. I'd been doing this kind of work for a long time. [Before Sudan] I administered field operations in Angola for the CIA, with mercenaries. When I arrived in Khartoum, I had operational experience."

When Billy Waugh presented Cofer Black with the photographs he took of Osama bin Laden, Black was impressed by the clarity and the proximity. "Billy's never afraid of putting his personal safety in jeopardy to get the job done," explained Black. Waugh recalls being asked his opinion regarding what might be done next with Osama bin Laden. "I said we should kill him," remembers Waugh, "then take his body and throw it over the wall of the Iranian embassy. Set off a few flash grenades to draw a whole bunch of attention to the Iranians, make people show up and see what was going on." Waugh sat down, wrote up his plan, and gave it to Cofer Black to submit to the director of Central Intelligence.

There are two differing versions of what happened next, one from Cofer Black and the other from Billy Waugh. "Billy's conversational remarks about UBL [Osama bin Laden] were never put to [sic] writing and [never] sent forward to Washington," says Black. "This was a bad idea for so many reasons I won't go further."

Waugh tells a different story. "The proposal went all the way to the desk of President Clinton. I was told he read it, thought about it, and replied in a memorandum that went to the director of the CIA. The president's reply said, and I'm [paraphrasing], 'We will not do this. And please do not suggest this kind of thing to me ever again.'"

Waugh was a ground operator and an expert in irregular warfare. He played by many of the same rules of war as the enemy, the most important being *there are no rules*. Surprise, kill, vanish. Terrorists like Osama bin Laden lived in a den of snakes filled with rogues, assassins, and double-crossers. Waugh believes in tyrannicide, in cutting off the head of the snake.

He left Sudan for another mission. This one involved teaching the nineteen sons of HRH Sheikh Zayed bin Sultan Al Nahyan, founder of United Arab Emirates (UAE), how to parachute-jump. But soon Waugh would once again return to Sudan. In 1994, Turabi is said to have hosted another conference of rogues, albeit much smaller than the conference held in 1991. Egyptian double agent Ali Mohamed, who worked for bin Laden in Khartoum while also double-crossing the U.S. Army Special Forces, says he personally set up this meeting, which was attended by bin Laden and Imad Mugniyah. It is believed that during this meeting, Mugniyah shared with bin Laden techniques for how to build truck bombs to be used in mass casualty attacks against U.S. embassies. By then, the U.S. State Department had placed Sudan on its State Sponsors of Terrorism list.

In 1995, Osama bin Laden began planning the assassination of

CIA station chief Cofer Black. The plot advanced to the point where bin Laden's fighters rehearsed the ambush on the streets of Khartoum. CIA officers determined the time and place of the assassination, on a small road near the U.S. embassy. Things escalated. One day, after being aggressively tailed, a CIA paramilitary team drew guns on a group of Osama bin Laden's men.

Through the U.S. ambassador to Sudan, the CIA lodged an official complaint and warned Hassan al-Turabi against carrying out the assassination. At Langley, the CIA created a unit dedicated to gathering intelligence on Osama bin Laden. It was called Alec Station. There was a long, dangerous road ahead. Bin Laden vowed to attack the United States from the land, the sea, and the air. He would succeed on every front.

CHAPTER NINETEEN

Operation Love Storm

George H. W. Bush had been out of the White House for less than three months when, in April 1993, he traveled to Kuwait on an official visit. He was there to receive the Mubarak the Great medal, the nation's highest civilian award, for having pushed the Persian Gulf War Resolution of 1991 through Congress, authorizing the use of U.S. military force against Iraq, then occupying Kuwait. The result had been Operation Desert Storm.

It was a lavish celebration resplendent with swordsmen, drummers, and hundreds of cheering children waving flags. The Kuwaiti press called the three-day affair Operation Love Storm. The emir of Kuwait, Sheik Jaber al-Ahmed al-Sabah, thanked the former president for the 541,000 U.S. military personnel who'd helped free Kuwait the year before. "This award [is] in gratitude and appreciation for your enormous efforts in liberating Kuwait and your services toward world peace," said the emir. George H. W. Bush responded in kind. "Mere words cannot express how proud I feel to be here with you on the hallowed ground of Kuwait," he said. The emir then knighted the former president and presented him with the Mubarak the Great medal, named for Kuwait's founder, who famously assassinated two of his half-brothers—political rivals—to ascend the throne.

All went well during the festivities. The emir neglected to mention to any U.S. official that a team of sixteen assassins had tried to assassinate former president Bush with a powerful car bomb. Not for another two weeks would the Clinton White House learn about the alleged plot. Richard Clarke, special assistant to the president, later wrote that he was the first person to hear about it. "I was reading headlines from an Arab-language newspaper," says Clarke, when "I saw a subject line that grabbed my eye." *Ash Sharq Al Awsat* was reporting that a band of Iraqi assassins had tried to kill Bush when he was in Kuwait. "There had been no such report from the Secret Service, FBI, CIA, or the embassy," Clarke insists. Alarmed by this news, Clarke telephoned the U.S. ambassador in Kuwait, Ryan Crocker.

Did Crocker know anything about an attempted assassination of former president Bush, Clarke asked? Had he seen the article in *Ash Sharq Al Awsat*? The ambassador said no, that this near attack was news to him. Clarke then called Anthony Lake, President Clinton's national-security advisor.

"Saddam tried to kill Bush," he said.

"The next morning there was a sealed envelope on my desk," remembers Clarke, "a message so sensitive that it could not be sent to me electronically from the Situation Room." Clarke learned that seventeen men accused of being the assassins were presently being held in a Kuwaiti prison. The more the White House staff learned about the plot, the crazier it seemed to get. Two of the prisoners, both Iraqi nationals, had implicated the Iraqi intelligence service, suggesting a conspiracy. Clarke advised Anthony Lake to have the State Department put pressure on Kuwait to find out what, exactly, was going on. Why had the Kuwaitis told a newspaper about the conspiracy before they'd shared information with their friends in the United States?

"They have to come clean with us," Clarke recalls Lake telling him. The fact that the Clinton White House was just now learning about this assassination attempt made the new president look weak.

Ambassador Crocker telephoned Kuwait's minister of defense. "Details of the plot were not supplied at the time because President Bush was on his way home and the plot had been thwarted," the defense minister said. He told Crocker that the government of Kuwait was moving forward with a trial.

The White House demanded immediate access to all the prisoners. Because the attack was against a former U.S. president, the CIA and FBI had to be allowed to conduct their own independent criminal investigations, the White House said. On April 29, 1993, CIA officers from the Counterterrorist Center and FBI agents arrived in Kuwait City to interview suspects and examine evidence. From there, a narrative emerged.

The group of assassins and accomplices included four Iraqis, one Kuwait-born Iraqi national, and twelve stateless Bedouins. The information the CIA found most credible came from the group's ringleader, a former military officer turned nurse, Wali al-Ghazali. The CIA accessed his records and learned he'd been trained to use explosives as a member of Iraq's national guard. In 1993, he was working at Al-Najaf Hospital outside Basra, he said, when military intelligence service agents, the Mukhabarat, informed him he was being sent on a mission he could not refuse: "to assassinate the former president [Bush as] revenge for the devastation caused by Coalition forces during Operation Desert Storm." The Mukhabarat, also known as the Department of General Intelligence, was the most heavy-handed instrument of Iraq's state security system. With its multiple divisions, or directorates, the organization was fundamental to Saddam Hussein's preservation of autocratic rule. Like most Iraqi citizens, al-Ghazali knew better than to challenge a request. Fearing retribution against his family, he agreed to take part in the Mukhabarat's assassination operation.

Taking advantage of the porous Kuwait-Iraq border, he was told to pose as a whiskey smuggler and infiltrate Kuwait with a car bomb: he was to park the vehicle on a busy Kuwait City street and then detonate the bomb remotely, as President Bush's motorcade drove by. The Mukhabarat provided al-Ghazali with a Land Cruiser pre-fitted with explosive devices that had been soldered into the side panels. He was given two Browning pistols with suppressors, two land mines, two hand grenades, an AK-47, a passport from the UAE, a case of contraband whiskey, $1,100 in cash, and a suicide belt. If the car bomb failed to detonate, al-Ghazali was to walk to Kuwait University, get as close to President Bush as possible, and detonate the explosives belt as a fedayeen, or suicide bomber. Directions understood, Wali Al-Ghazali set off into the night, accompanied by the stateless Bedouins.

The assassins crossed the border into Kuwait and drove the Land Cruiser to a predesignated rendezvous point in a town called Al-Jahra. There, they hid in a goat barn belonging to an uncle of one of the Bedouins. The men drank some of the whiskey they were given and fell asleep. When they awoke, the goat barn was surrounded by Kuwaiti police. Al-Ghazali said that he and two others escaped, stole a vehicle, and sped toward Iraq. But their car broke down and they were forced to abandon it on the side of the road. As they walked into the desert, they were spotted by local bird hunters and reported and arrested by a Kuwaiti police patrol.

It's impossible to know if the testimony was fabricated through coercion, or a genuine account of an actual assassination plot. The declassified findings by the FBI forensics team were equally vague. "The car bomb found in Kuwait closely resembles the corresponding components of Iraqi-made bombs that were recovered in February 1991 during Operation Desert Storm," the report indicates, with details redacted. FBI agents warranted that the bomb's fusing system, face plates, and radio-controlled receiving devices, as well as the type of circuit boards used, gave agents what they felt was "a recognizable signature" to a known Iraqi bomb maker affiliated with the Mukhabarat. "The wires ran under the on-off switch and were soldered to the circuit board in a uniquely expert way, proving that the same person was responsible." After pages rife with redactions, the FBI forensics team reached a conclusion: "Examination of other components used in the explosive devices recovered in Kuwait, together with a comparison of the techniques used to assemble them, once again provided ample proof of direct Iraqi responsibility." Ample proof is hardly the same as beyond a reasonable doubt, but the trial was being held in Kuwait, not the United States.

CIA officers with the CTC included Saddam Hussein's long history of assassinations and summary executions in its report for President Clinton. Since assuming power in the late 1970s, Saddam Hussein had ordered the killings of political rivals and people he felt had betrayed him. Religious clerics, Kurdish Peshmerga leaders, and scientists who attempted to defect had been shot, strangled, and blown up by the Mukhabarat.

After the Gulf War, Saddam Hussein became more emboldened with his plots, CTC officers wrote, exemplified in an assassination attempt against Danielle Mitterrand, the wife of the French president, nine months before. On July 6, 1992, Mrs. Mitterrand was traveling in a diplomatic convoy through the town of Sulaimaniya, in northern Iraq, when a parked Toyota Land Cruiser exploded into a sixty-foot-high fireball. She escaped injury, but four members of her security detail were killed and nineteen others wounded—mostly people who'd gathered to wave as she passed by. This brazen attack, wrote the CIA, "demonstrated [Saddam Hussein's] willingness to disregard international opinion and possible military retaliation."

There were other warning signs, wrote CTC analysts, including Ba'ath Party threats against President Bush. Shortly before the plot unfolded, Iraqi government officials hinted at a forthcoming attack. "Bush will be killed based on a universal judicial system," Saddam's press secretary told a reporter for *Al-Thawrah*, one "that goes beyond the law of the jungle." Another Ba'ath Party official promised, "This [President] will be cursed, along with his ancestors, until the day of judgment"—that "he and others would be hunted down and punished...held personally responsible for each drop of blood spilled on Iraqi soil."

What to do? President Clinton called his advisors to the Oval Office. Secretary of State Warren Christopher said, "A plot to kill a former president is an attack against our nation." President Clinton agreed. He ordered the Joint Chiefs of Staff and the CIA to develop a target list. The targets would include the headquarters building of the Mukhabarat. The strike should occur at night, the Joint Chiefs of Staff said, to minimize casualties. Colin Powell suggested cruise missiles launched from a destroyer in the Red Sea.

On June 26, 1993, twenty-three Tomahawk cruise missiles were launched at Baghdad, leveling much of the Iraqi intelligence head-quarters and killing a night watchman. Three of the missiles missed their targets and exploded in a nearby residential neighborhood, killing eight civilians. Among the dead were the director of the Sad-dam Hussein Center for the Arts, a painter named Leila al-Attar, her husband, and their housekeeper. The couple's son and daughter were both seriously injured. Al-Attar was reportedly a close friend of Sad-dam's; her home had been hit by a missile in the Persian Gulf War, and she had suffered a serious wound to her leg. Now she was dead.

In a nationally televised speech, President Clinton called the assassination plot against former president Bush "particularly loath-some and cowardly" and "revenge by a tyrant." But the U.S. response was not an attempt to kill Saddam Hussein, he said, rather a means to prevent future attacks. It was two days later that the twenty-three cruise missiles were fired. Madeleine Albright, U.S. ambassador to the United Nations, citing Article 51 of the United Nations Charter, said that America was exercising its legal right to self-defense.

In Baghdad, anti-American crowds held demonstrations in the streets. "Revenge to America!" they chanted. "Shame on America! Glory to the martyrs of Iraq." They issued a warning to America's new president: "Clinton, pay attention; we are the people who top-pled Bush!"

★   ★   ★

It was the fall of 1993, and Lew Merletti sat at his desk inside the Treasury building, surrounded by piles of paperwork. He was no longer on the Presidential Protective Division and on rare occasions would stop to wonder how on earth he'd wound up in a place doing exactly the opposite of what he excelled at. For more than a decade he had been in the president's inner circle; now he was being asked to serve as a bureaucrat. "It was the job I was assigned to do, and I accepted that. But it was really depressing," Merletti recalls. He felt like Billy Waugh did when he was working at the post office after Vietnam.

Everything had been going so well back in 1992. As the assistant to the special agent in charge of the president during the Gulf War, Merletti had been entrusted with tremendous responsibility. When President Bush and General Schwarzkopf traveled to the Middle East during Operation Desert Storm, Merletti was in charge of their security. Because of his combat experiences as a Green Beret in Vietnam, he felt entirely confident in the role. His missions had all been a success. And now, twenty months later, here he was sitting at a desk, loaded down by paperwork.

Prior to the presidential election of 1992, Merletti was selected by the Secret Service to assume the top position in the Presidential Protective Division—were George H. W. Bush to be reelected. When Bill Clinton won the election instead, Merletti was assigned to the Treasury Department, the organization that governed the U.S. Secret Service.

At Treasury, he had been asked to lead the team investigating what went wrong in Waco, Texas, when federal agents raided the compound of a religious cult suspected of stockpiling illegal weapons, and seventy-six people died. The fiasco would become known as the Waco siege. Merletti's official title summed up the labyrinthine world into which he'd been pulled. He was the deputy director of the review team for the Report of the Department of the

Treasury on the Bureau of Alcohol, Tobacco and Firearms Investigation of Vernon Wayne Howell, also known as David Koresh.

The work was laborious and painstaking. It was not pleasant investigating where fellow civil servants went wrong. Because the investigation was such a high-profile event, as the top law enforcement officer on the team, Merletti was unwittingly shoved into the limelight. When it came time to report the findings to Congress, his situation went from bad to worse. "The Treasury Department's top law enforcement officer has told federal firearms administrators that a probe into their Feb. 28 raid uncovered 'serious errors in agents' judgment,' and that some officials had knowingly made misleading statements about the raid to their superiors and to the media," reported the *Washington Post.* "People lost their jobs," Merletti explains. Then a very strange thing happened.

"At the congressional hearing, under oath, a congressman said to me, 'I'd like to meet the individual who was in charge of this report,'" Merletti recalls. The initial tone of the congressman, a fellow Republican, at first led Merletti to believe that he was expressing appreciation for the truth. Most Republicans seemed to want blame laid at the feet of President Clinton, which the Treasury Report had determined should not happen.

"I wrote the report," Merletti told the congressman.

"He looked at me," recalls Merletti, "and his tone switched. He said, 'I just had to meet the person who wrote this pack of lies.'"

Merletti was stunned. "So you're a Clinton guy," the congressman said, smirking. In that moment, Merletti understood "it was all politics."

As a Secret Service agent, Lew Merletti was trained to leave politics out of the job. "The office of the president is what matters," he explains. "There is an institution to uphold. We used to have a sign on the wall in the White House [field] office that said, 'You elect 'em, we'll protect 'em.' We all worked with that concept in mind."

That Merletti was no longer on the Presidential Protective Division had nothing to do with politics, he told himself; it had to do with circumstance. He reported the Waco failings he'd discovered because it was the truth, not because he was a Democrat—which he wasn't.

Several days later, he received word that President Clinton wanted to see him in the Oval Office.

"I went into his office," Merletti recalls. "I was told to bring a copy of the report. The president gave me a compliment regarding the work. He pointed to the report and asked to autograph it for me."

There was a long pause, Merletti recalled. Then the president spoke candidly. "He said something to the effect of, 'You did a good job up there,' meaning on Capitol Hill. He said that he [and his staff] knew the investigation was going to be politicized and they were [aware] that I [probably] had no idea my testimony was going to be about that." The president was thanking Lew Merletti for being apolitical. The meeting was over, and Merletti went home to his family.

Perhaps President Clinton said something to the director of the Secret Service, or to the special agent in charge of the Presidential Protective Division, or maybe what happened next was circumstantial. Either way, Merletti's life was about to change.

On September 12, 1994, seventy miles north of the White House, near Aberdeen, Maryland, an unemployed truck driver named Frank Eugene Corder spent the evening with his brother, drinking alcohol and smoking crack cocaine. Around midnight, Corder asked his brother to drop him off near a small airport in Churchville. Once there, Corder somehow managed to scale the fence, drop down onto the tarmac, and steal a Cessna aircraft. High on drugs, he taxied down the runway and took off into the night sky.

Corder was not a licensed pilot but had taken a few Cessna lessons the summer before, apparently learning enough to allow him to fly the stolen craft over Pennsylvania and Maryland for roughly forty minutes. At 1:06 a.m., FAA radar systems at Baltimore/Washington International Airport detected the aircraft and noted that it was 6.5

miles north of the White House, flying at an altitude of 2,700 feet. The plane dropped by 1,000 feet, turned around, and headed south. At 1:48, it entered the prohibited airspace of the White House complex and began descending rapidly. With its wing flaps up and its throttle position in full-forward, Corder crashed the Cessna onto the lawn, skidded across the grass, struck a magnolia tree, and slammed into the first floor of the White House, killing himself. President Clinton and his family were across Pennsylvania Avenue at Blair House for the night.

It was a calamitous security breach, made worse by an interview the Secret Service gave to *Newsweek* magazine. "National [airport] shuts down at 11:00 p.m. and controllers in the tower were absorbed in other duties," an official spokesman said. When the reporter asked how that was even possible, why the FAA hadn't detected the security breach, the official said, "The FAA isn't really in the business of protecting the president from flying suicides." To which the *Newsweek* reporter responded, "That leaves the real question: who is?"

The entire event was a disaster. To Lew Merletti's eye, presidential protection was contingent on three fundamentals that never changed. The world is a dangerous place; it doesn't matter who's to blame, only that you defend against it; the U.S. Secret Service must never appear weak. An attack could come from anywhere, including a lone wolf, a terrorist organization, or a foreign government.

Because Merletti had foreseen this kind of attack from above—the Presidential Protective Division had trained for it during the Delta Force HALO assassin AOP exercise—he was called to the White House. Secret Service director Eljay B. Bowron asked him how security could be tightened. These details, like all Secret Service protocols, are classified. Bowron also asked Merletti to come to the Secret Service team room in the White House, to talk to the PPD agents about what it meant to protect the president. The speech is classified, but Lew Merletti says he wrote it with his old friend Mike Kuropas in mind. Bowron transferred Merletti back to the

White House PPD. He would now serve as deputy special agent in charge, which meant he was the number two in charge of the safety and security of the president of the United States.

In the middle of October, President Clinton called Lew Merletti into his office to tell him to prepare for travel to Syria, Jordan, Egypt, and Israel. This was one of the most difficult and dangerous parts of the world in which to protect the president of the United States against assassination attempts.

Lew Merletti was ready for the job.

CHAPTER TWENTY

Carlos the Jackal

I t was Christmastime when Billy Waugh was summoned to his CIA reporting site in northern Virginia. He was being sent on a Top Secret gamma-classified mission as the senior operator on a four-person reconnaissance and surveillance team. During the classified briefing, Waugh learned that the target was Ilich Ramirez Sanchez, nom de guerre Carlos the Jackal, the mastermind behind the spectacular 1975 OPEC siege. Unseen for years and believed by many to be dead, he was now hiding out in Khartoum. CIA chief of station Cofer Black was determined to get him.

The CIA didn't want to kill Carlos the Jackal—they wanted to capture him. For eighteen years he'd been in hiding, able to function out of reach of Interpol, the CIA, the FBI, Mossad, and France's General Directorate for External Security (DGSE). Each had placed a significant bounty on information leading to his arrest. The Jackal moved around the globe as the guest of one state sponsor of terror (official and unofficial) after the next: Libya, Syria, Cuba, Iraq, Hungary, Romania. For the CIA, learning what his quid pro quo was with these countries would help the Counterterrorist Center better understand how the global terrorist network worked—how assassins operated and who pulled the strings.

"Carlos the Jackal was a dangerous killer who'd machine-gunned down people who were after him," Cofer Black explained in 2017. "Billy Waugh was the perfect person" to conduct a hidden-hand operation to capture him.

On December 13, 1993, Waugh flew from Dulles Airport to Frankfurt to Khartoum. His diplomatic passport said he worked for the U.S. Department of State. Looking down over Khartoum as he flew in, he observed the White River and the Blue Nile. The dirt streets. The ramshackle houses made of mud and tin, all barely visible through a thick brown haze that hung like fog. "Being in Sudan was like being behind enemy lines," Waugh recalls. "It's a nonpermissive environment. Every step must be taken with great care."

At the airport, he showed his credentials. A Dinka woman examined his passport and marked his travel bags with white chalk, indicating he was a diplomat and could not be searched. Inside the bags were chemicals necessary to develop film.

By the time Waugh got to his embassy-owned villa, it was past curfew. He'd been stopped by soldiers, called Jundis, on the way in and had given them a carton of cigarettes as a bribe. The U.S. sanctions against Sudan had made money even tighter, and everyone was looking for a bribe. At the safe house, Waugh's teammates were waiting up for him. They all had last-name aliases and would use their regular first names: Billy, Greg, Don, Santos. The team talked for hours. First thing in the morning, Waugh acclimated himself to the city by heading out for a jog, the quickest way to reestablish area familiarization.

Back to the villa, the team climbed into their Land Cruiser and headed to the U.S. embassy complex on Abdel Latif Avenue. The pace of the Sudanese intelligence services had picked up since the bin Laden job, Waugh noted. The vehicle they were driving in was almost immediately tailed. A white Toyota pickup truck filled with soldiers carrying AK-47s followed along a few cars back in a signature show of force.

The Land Cruiser crossed the railroad bridge and headed into

Khartoum City and over to the U.S. embassy compound. In the parking lot there, the guards, Dinka tribesmen and marine corps commanders, kept diligent watch. The team passed through heavy security and traveled up to the third floor, where the CIA station was then located, next to the Regional Security Office, the State Department's law enforcement agency responsible for all in-country personnel. They made their way through an entry lock, past the passcode panel, and through several more doors before they were finally inside.

Cofer Black led the meeting. Everybody wanted Carlos the Jackal, he said. Mossad wanted him. France wanted him. The FBI wanted him. The CIA was going to get him. But the first part of the equation had been the most difficult to date: identifying who Carlos the Jackal actually was. No one could say for sure, since there had not been a photograph taken of Ilich Ramirez Sanchez in roughly eight years. In 1985, the Hungarian security services had secretly made a video of him meeting with their chief of security. Looking fat, slovenly, and unshaven, Carlos the Jackal pleaded that he not be forced to leave Hungary. The image was all the team had to go on for now. The Jackal was a heavy drinker and smoker, a partier in declining health. But how to find a single, debauched-looking white man—who happened to be a most wanted person—in a chaotic, lawless city of over a million people? This was the first critical part of the job: photograph the Jackal to establish proof of life.

It was the Jordanian General Intelligence Directorate (GID), Jordan's equivalent of the CIA, that had provided the initial intelligence that indicated the Jackal had moved to Khartoum. Under the pretense of being a Muslim, Ilich Ramirez Sanchez had married a second time, a twenty-six-year-old Jordanian named Lana Abdel Salem Jarrar. GID tracked the two of them to Khartoum. Jordanian intelligence provided the CIA with a photograph of Jarrar. In Khartoum, the Jackal started making mistakes.

"It was his lack of discipline that would lead to his downfall," recalls Waugh. His first mistake was getting drunk and starting a fight. "He got into an argument with a shopkeeper and pulled a gun on the man, which landed him in jail. Local police do not take kindly to foreigners. He had to call Turabi, President al-Bashir's secretary general, to come get him out." That was only the first mistake, says Waugh. "He decided it was time to get himself a foreign bodyguard. That was the fatal move."

Carlos the Jackal made an international call to one of his old associates from the days of the Black September terrorist attacks. The Israeli Intelligence Corps picked up the signals intelligence. The man, believed to be an Iraqi national, went by the alias Tarek. Mossad provided the CIA with this first real break in the case. They had photographs of Tarek, which were sent to the CIA's Khartoum station via secure fax.

"We all studied the photographs carefully," remembers Waugh. "What was unusual about Tarek was that he looked Caucasian, with white wavy hair. He was around forty years old and fit. He had big muscles, like a bodybuilder on steroids."

Waugh was assigned the job of photographing Tarek when he arrived at Khartoum International Airport. But Carlos the Jackal had friends in high places. A state-sponsored handler met Tarek before he entered the public area and covertly escorted him away, through an airport side door.

On January 20, 1994, Waugh and Greg went to the Meridian Hotel on a reconnaissance mission. Carlos the Jackal frequented international hotels—alcohol was served—and it made sense he'd send his new bodyguard to case these places in advance. Disguised as businessmen eating dinner, Waugh and Greg spotted Tarek sitting on a couch in the lobby, doing a crossword puzzle. Hotel clerks were known to be on the payroll of the secret police, the Political Security Organization. Hanging out doing surveillance was not an option, so Waugh and Greg finished their dinner, went outside, and sat in their parked vehicle. With a solid view of the front exit, they waited.

After some time, Tarek sauntered out. He walked up to a white

1990 Toyota Cressida, license plate 1049, and climbed inside. This was a tremendous lead. Now it was time to follow him. Tarek pulled out of the lot and drove toward the Blue Nile River. He made an immediate U-turn, tradecraft for how to lose a tail. Waugh and Greg followed him for a few blocks, but after a few more U-turns it was time to drop the surveillance. Back at the CIA station, Waugh and Greg shared their findings with Cofer Black. "The search was narrowing in focus, which meant it was gaining momentum," says Waugh.

Over the next few weeks the team divided up, each man spending sixteen hours a day searching for the white Cressida, license plate 1049. Each member of the team had a portable radio that was linked back to a comm system at the CIA station. This enabled them to track one another's whereabouts at all times and to communicate with the Khartoum station in real time. Transmissions were encrypted. "Anyone trying to listen in to what we were doing would hear nothing but loud noise, like howling wind," recalls Waugh.

Each man had a specific talent, just as in Special Forces operations. Team member Don, a former police officer, was a rare genius in vehicle searches, says Waugh. He had a remarkable ability to recognize vehicles and identify plates from great distances, almost a sixth sense. With a list of the places Carlos the Jackal was most likely to visit, they waited and watched. The Meridian Hotel, the Hilton Hotel, and the Diplomatic Club were the three top spots. Every Thursday night, the Diplomatic Club threw a huge party, complete with disco dancing and a full bar. It was located fifteen miles outside the city center. On the first Thursday in February, the Cressida was spotted in the parking lot.

Waugh picked up the car as it left the disco and headed north. Traffic was crazy out here in the suburbs, with cars, trucks, and donkey carts all fighting for a space on the dirt road. There were no lights and lots of tall people meandering across the road. He lost the car in no time and headed back to the Khartoum station. The excitement of locating the Cressida wore off, followed by a long period of surveillance. They were back to ground zero, the hunt for the vehicle. After days of searching, excitement gave way to monotony. They searched the city in vain, eighteen hours a day. Most of the apartment complexes in Khartoum were surrounded by ten-foot-tall mud walls. Trying to find Tarek felt like searching for a needle in a haystack.

When he wasn't out conducting surveillance, Waugh practiced his photo-developing skills in the CIA photographic laboratory located in the U.S. embassy compound, on the sixth floor. Developing film in Khartoum was challenging. The water came out of the pipes somewhere around 90 degrees Fahrenheit. To get a proper water bath cooled down to between the requisite 68 to 70 degrees Fahrenheit involved the skillful use of ice cubes. Waugh and Greg were inside the film lab when the encrypted radio sprang to life. Don had spotted the Cressida in Khartoum's New Addition neighborhood. It had just pulled up to Ibn Khaldoun Hospital, on Nineteenth Street. Waugh told Don to take up a surveillance position. If the car moved, he said, follow it.

Waugh and Greg hurried out of the lab, down the embassy's private elevator, and out into the parking lot. The two PSO intelligence officers assigned to tail them had fallen asleep in their pickup truck. Waugh and Greg climbed into their Land Cruiser and began driving fast, headed toward the hospital. Waugh told Greg to open the lockbox that was welded to the floor, take out the camera, a 35mm Canon F-80 with a 300mm lens, and assemble it.

Five minutes later, they were at the hospital. Waugh spotted Don's car, drove past it, and pulled his vehicle into a spot twenty meters away from the Cressida. From his back window, he now had a clear shot of Tarek's car. "Less than ten minutes before, we'd been in the lab at the embassy, mixing chemicals."

Two white men sitting in a car would surely get the attention of the ever-present PSO. Waugh told Greg the plan. On the dirt shoulder of the road, there was a vendor selling wares. Greg should go over there and consider buying something. Hang out. Wait until Carlos the Jackal exited the hospital. Then make some kind of commotion to get attention.

Waugh got out of the Land Cruiser and opened the hood. Feigning engine trouble, he fiddled around inside. Then, leaving the hood open, he climbed back inside and set up the camera, using the space between the front seat and its headrest as a platform for the long lens. He focused the lens on the hospital exit doors. "As I was adjusting the lens, the face of a pretty woman came into focus," he recalls. "It was Lana, Carlos's second wife." He quickly snapped four or five pictures he believed were properly focused and framed. As Lana Jarrar walked toward the Cressida, there was a sudden outburst near where the vendor was selling his wares, on the dirt shoulder of the road.

"You've cheated me!" Greg shouted at the vendor. Agitated, like he was willing to fight. Waugh watched as the man stood up. "He was about seven feet tall," recalls Waugh. He towered over Greg.

Greg continued to play the role of the customer who'd been cheated. Waugh kept his lens trained on the hospital door. A man emerged. "Caucasian, in his forties. Well groomed, with reddish hair, combed back. A mustache. Fat: forty or fifty pounds overweight," recalls Waugh. He carried a small weapons bag over one shoulder. "I spotted a leg holster near his right ankle. He wore a shooter's vest. Sleeveless and with pockets in the front. Behind him, a black African man was carrying a large manila envelope in one hand." Following the Jackal to his car.

Greg continued arguing with the tall Dinka vendor. "The situation had escalated to such a degree," recalls Waugh, that it had the attention of "the fat man who'd emerged from the hospital."

Click. Click. Click. Waugh took photographs of Carlos the Jackal. One photograph after the next, until he'd used the entire roll of film. Lana Jarrar climbed into the driver's seat and started the car. Carlos climbed into the passenger seat as the hospital technician set the large manila envelope inside the car, on the backseat. X-rays, thought Waugh. There was a quick exchange between Waugh and Greg. Time to close down the operation, Waugh said. Greg pulled a large bill from his wallet and paid the unwitting Dinka vendor for his troubles. It was time to get out of there, fast. The Cressida pulled out of its parking spot. Ahead, Waugh watched Don pull out of his spot and follow along. Waugh and Greg headed back to the embassy.

"We tried getting Cofer Black on the encrypted radio, but he was nowhere to be found." At the embassy, they rushed into the photo lab. "It was the most important roll of film I'd handled to date," recalls Waugh.

Under the glow of the red lightbulb, Waugh worked patiently to get the water bath to the precise temperature. A few degrees off and he could ruin the film. It was quiet in the lab. The smell of the German photographic chemicals filled his senses. When he was confident the elements were correct, he developed the film. Was this Carlos the Jackal? The pictures were sharp. Clear. "The target jumps out at you," remembers Waugh. "And for a minute, it's like you've already captured him."

Right after the film was developed, Don called. He'd tailed the Cressida to an apartment complex in a residential area, where the car was now parked behind a gate. He'd observed the man and the woman walk up a flight of stairs and head inside. It was very likely that this was where Carlos the Jackal lived. Waugh continued developing the film. Waugh and Greg couldn't wait to tell Cofer Black. More than two hours had passed and they still hadn't heard from him.

"Screw it," thought Waugh. "I decided to break protocol and drive to Cofer's house myself."

Waugh and Greg drove out of the embassy, down along the Blue Nile River, past the Chinese embassy, past Turabi's home, past where the aspiring terrorist Osama bin Laden lived. They drove over to the eastern side of the al-Riyadh neighborhood where Cofer Black resided. "We said hello to the guard, who rang the bell." Cofer Black emerged in running attire.

"I'd been exercising in my home," Black recalls. "I asked them what in hell they wanted. What was so important it couldn't wait."

Billy Waugh handed Cofer Black an envelope containing the photographs.

"Jesus Christ, Billy," Black recalls telling Waugh. "This is Carlos's goddamn wife."

"Keep looking," Billy said.

They moved inside the house, where Black spread the photographs out across his dining room table. "Who the hell took these?" he asked.

Greg said Waugh did. Two hours before, outside Ibn Khaldoun Hospital. Time to get the photos to CIA headquarters in DC, Cofer Black said. At 2:00 a.m., a lieutenant colonel with the U.S. Department of State diplomatic staff boarded a Lufthansa flight to Frankfurt, continuing on to Dulles Airport in Virginia. Two CIA officers met the lieutenant colonel at the plane.

"Cofer sometimes said I took actions without bothering to think of the possible repercussions, which was sometimes true," Waugh recalled in 2017. "That's what it means to be an independent contractor. A singleton. You can do the job. Get it done, without having the CIA monitor your every move. It involves risk. You can't make a mistake or your bacon gets kicked out. When it pays off, it pays off big-time."

The photographs went to the seventh floor at CIA headquarters at Langley. There, two division chiefs gave their opinions. Next, an agency operative flew the pictures back the other way to Amman, where Jordanian intelligence confirmed that this was Ilich Ramirez Sanchez. The CIA wanted to capture him. The paramilitary operation needed to move fast, but not too fast. There were spies everywhere. If the Jackal got wind of the fact that the Agency had located him and would now create a plan to capture him, he'd get out of Khartoum fast.

Shortly after the Jordanians confirmed the Jackal's identity, a local asset told his handler that Carlos was moving to Cyprus, transiting through Cairo. Waugh and a team were sent to the Africa terminal of Cairo International Airport to conduct surveillance. For six days, they watched the terminal. Carlos never showed up. "Covert action is not all action. Sometimes you sit around bored out of your mind. A lot of your time is spent running down a bad tip," says Waugh. In March, Cofer Black authorized a team to watch the house that Don had identified. They located a dilapidated six-story apartment building across the street. The apartment on the top floor had a direct line of sight to Carlos's building. It was perfect.

"It was a hellhole," recalls Waugh. "Filthy beyond what you can imagine. Ceilings crumbling down. Holes in the wall. No running water, no toilet. But it had a direct view of the entrance and exit. And the Toyota Cressida parked right out front."

Waugh and Santos told the building manager that they were surveyors working for the U.S. government. "Sensing money, he asked for seven hundred dollars a month," recalls Waugh, an exorbitant amount in Sudan, where the average income was about three hundred dollars a year. "He also asked for three months up front. In a place like Sudan, you can't hide the fact that you're American. Some of the money is keep-your-mouth-shut money. He didn't report us to the PSO because he wanted the fourth month's rent."

The next challenge was getting the surveillance equipment into the apartment. To avoid drawing attention to themselves, Waugh and Santos worked at night. The camera equipment included several camera bodies and an assortment of lenses and tripods that together weighed several hundred pounds. The lens that was hardest to conceal was a 4,000mm Questar, 24 inches in diameter and 140 pounds. It was secreted into Khartoum via diplomatic pouch, in a case the size of a footlocker.

Inside the observation post (OP), they had two folding cots, blackout curtains, and a Bunsen burner for boiling water and cooking rice. Creating a fast way out of the OP in the event of a raid by the security police was key to success as well as peace of mind. "If we were caught in the OP, we were told we would almost certainly be shot on sight," says Waugh. "So we devised an escape route using rappelling ropes. We located the sturdiest pipes, then rigged up a system with ropes. We left a pair of rappelling gloves in an air vent on the roof." With the OP set up, they began surveillance. For this, Waugh fashioned a large chart on the wall, onto which he would document who came and who went, and when.

Waugh was intrigued by how reckless, pathetic, and debauched Carlos was, and yet how predictable was his routine. "He was a drunken partier. He went out, drank, came home, slept, went out again. His security detail were all Arabs. Their style appeared to be modeled after the U.S. Secret Service," says Waugh. They kept perimeter guard around the house. "Before a visitor arrived, they'd open the gate, look around for an ambush, then go back and get Carlos or Lana, then get them into the car." It was the same every day, Waugh says. "But one thing they forgot to do was ever look up. They never saw our OP. That was their big mistake." Plans for a capture mission were being drawn up.

One day at the embassy, Cofer Black told Billy Waugh that he wanted a shot of the Jackal that was really, really close. Billy used the Questar lens and took a photograph of Carlos's teeth.

"He happened to have a toothpick in his mouth," recalls Waugh.

"What the hell is this?" Cofer Black asked when Waugh showed him a photograph that, at first glance, looked more like postmodern art than a surveillance photograph.

"It's a toothpick balanced between Carlos the Jackal's teeth," said Waugh.

Black chuckled and got back to work.

Waugh photographed everyone who visited the Jackal's apartment. "It was a parade of bad guys," Waugh says. For the Counterterrorist Center at Langley, this was an intelligence gold mine.

One week, the CIA chief of station in Paris, Richard Holm,

visited. Dick Holm was a legend at the CIA. He'd served as a covert-action operator in Laos, as had Waugh, although the two men had not worked together. Later, stationed in Congo, Holm had been surveilling military targets from a two-seater T-28 when his plane crashed into rebel-held territory. He survived but suffered third-degree burns over 35 percent of his body. He lived only because he was rescued and taken care of by local Azande tribesmen who dug bugs out of his wounds using a knife and covered him in a homeo-pathic blue-black paste, made of snake oil and tree bark, to keep his burns from becoming infected. Another CIA pilot also on the mission that day, a man named Tunon, was captured by a different group of tribesmen, the Simbas, who killed and ate him, according to reports by local missionaries. "The Simbas believed that if you eat the flesh and vital organs of your enemy you gain strength," Holm explained in an oral history. The world of covert action was peril-ous; it made no sense who lived and who died.

Dick Holm had been tracking Carlos the Jackal since the early 1980s. He would now act as the liaison between DGSE and the CIA. The man in the lead on the French side was Philippe Rondot, a spe-cial services investigator who'd been tracking the Jackal even longer, back to when the terrorist had killed two French intelligence offi-cers before the OPEC siege. Waugh briefed both men on what he'd seen from the observation post. The two senior officers chose not to share with Waugh details about the snatch-and-grab capture mission they were planning.

On August 12, 1994, Waugh watched Carlos the Jackal and Lana Jarrar leave the house at the usual time. He photographed them exit-ing, as he always did. Then something unusual happened. They didn't return after the disco closed, as was customary. All night Waugh waited and watched. Then, into the following day. He was surprised. Had Carlos the Jackal gotten away?

"I got a call from Cofer Black over the encrypted commo. 'Come on in, Billy,'" was all he said.

Anxious to learn what was happening, Waugh drove fast over to the U.S. embassy. Pulling into the driveway, he was surprised to see the U.S. ambassador, Donald Peterson, standing out front. Waugh parked his vehicle and climbed out. Peterson walked toward him, his hand extended. "The ambassador said, 'Great work, Billy,' and as he shook my hand, he said, 'Carlos the Jackal has been captured.'"

Inside the CIA station, the staff celebrated with champagne. It was a big day. In the snack bar, on the overhead television set, Waugh watched the Air France network present a news broadcast. The French had captured Carlos the Jackal in Khartoum, an announcer said. The terrorist was on his way to Paris, where he would face justice for a myriad of attacks and crimes. The role of the CIA in this mission remained entirely hidden.

For several days, news crews gathered around the apartment complex formerly inhabited by Ilich Ramirez Sanchez. By the third day, they were gone. At 3:00 a.m., Waugh went out for a last jog. He passed by the old OP one last time. Running down Riyadh Road toward Airport Road, he spotted traffic in front of Carlos the Jackal's apartment building. *What the hell is going on?* he wondered. It was the middle of the night, hours before dawn.

"There were a number of vehicles. A few station wagons and a large truck with the engine running. There were twenty or so policemen. They'd created a perimeter around the building." Waugh recognized a man from photographs he'd viewed during Agency intelligence briefings.

"He was large and had very black skin," recalls Waugh. "He wore a crisp white turban and a crisp, clean white robe." There was a large security presence around the man. "I realized it was Sudan's number two, Hassan al-Turabi. In the flesh." Waugh stopped jogging and took cover. He called Santos on the portable radio he kept tied to his body at all times, in case of emergency.

"I woke him up. I told him to get up and look out the window of the OP."

Santos did as instructed. "Use the night lens and get some photographs," Waugh said. "Use high-speed night film." If Santos could get photographs of Turabi, the CIA would have evidence linking Carlos the Jackal to his state sponsor, Sudan. From where Waugh hid in the bushes, he watched Lana Jarrar exit the building. "She was carrying a suitcase and crying," he recalls. "Hassan al-Turabi comforted her like they were old friends." Lana climbed into the backseat of a police vehicle and was driven away.

In the morning, Waugh called Cofer Black to tell him about the new photos.

"What in hell were you doing outside at 3:00 a.m.?" Cofer asked.

"Staying fit, boss," Waugh said.

At the embassy, Waugh learned what had happened to the Jackal after he was captured. "They jabbed him with sodium pentothal," says Waugh. "They put a bag over his head and said, 'Start answering questions'—or he'd be turned over to Mossad. No one wants to be turned over to Mossad. Carlos the Jackal sang like a bird." According to Billy Waugh, the CIA got the intelligence it hoped for, and more. The CIA files on Ilich Ramirez Sanchez remain classified. He was taken to France, where he was tried, convicted, and sentenced by an antiterrorism court to serve multiple life terms in a French prison. There he remains.

CHAPTER TWENTY-ONE

The Engineer

As deputy special agent in charge of security for President Clinton, Lew Merletti prepared for travel—to Israel, Syria, Egypt, Jordan, Saudi Arabia, and Kuwait. It was October 19, 1994. The focus of the trip was peace in the Middle East, but all Merletti could think about were assassination attempts and potential mass casualty attacks against his protectees.

No fan of CIA covert operations, President Clinton was pursuing diplomacy instead—always the first option for a commander in chief. The centerpiece of this trip was the historic signing of the Israel-Jordan peace treaty, set to take place on October 26 in a tiny border town between the two warring nations. If successful, the signing ceremony would be a step toward peace in the Middle East—progress not seen since the Camp David Accords of 1978. Then, in advance of the visit, the Shin Bet updated the Secret Service with escalated threat information. It involved a Hamas bomb maker who went by the nom de guerre the Engineer.

The Palestinian terror organization Hamas had recently declared war against Israel, setting off a wave of guerrilla warfare tactics including hit-and-run killings, assassinations, and now suicide bombings. Since its official establishment in 1987, Hamas maintained a hit squad, called Majmouath Jihad u-Dawa, a strike force trained to kill Palestinians suspected of cooperating with Israel. Hamas called these traitors "moral deviants" and made their deaths public, to serve as a warning to others. "Israel, as the Jewish state, must disappear from the map," declared Sheikh Ahmed Yassin, the nearly blind, quadriplegic founder of Hamas—wheelchair-bound since a wrestling accident at the age of twelve. Palestine was and would always be Islamic land, Sheikh Yassin said, "consecrated for future Muslim generations until Judgment Day."

After the end of the Gulf War in 1991, and with rumblings that Yasser Arafat was considering making peace with Israel, Hamas vowed to take power from the PLO. The Hamas assassination squad was folded into the group's military wing, the Ezzedeen al-Qassam Brigades. Without a standing army, the organization relied on guerrilla warfare tactics. Suicide bombings became the new focus for Hamas, the work of a shy electrical engineer from Bir Zeit University in the West Bank named Yahya Ayyash, also known as the Engineer. To date, he'd built four suicide bombs that killed fifteen people and injured thirty-nine.

The lethality of a suicide bomb attack is contingent upon the size of the bomb. In 1994, the master bomb makers in the Middle East were with Hezbollah, Shia Muslims. Hamas was an organization made up of Sunni Muslims. Because militants from these two branches of Islam were engaged in their own sectarian wars, terrorists from Hezbollah and Hamas did not generally mix. When Sudan hosted a terror conference, the Arab Islamic People's Congress, in April 1991, the CIA feared this calculus might change. Hamas leader Khaled Mashal attended, and so had Imad Mugniyah, Hezbollah operations chief. Now the Shin Bet had information suggesting that a pernicious new partnership between these two organizations might be under way.

Yahya Ayyash had been on the run. He and other Hamas members were said to be living in a refugee camp in Lebanon, just over the border from Israel. The place was built into a hillside and difficult to get to, with Lebanese media reporting that convoys of donkeys and mules were bringing supplies in to the Hamas fighters living here, including weatherproof tents, food, clothes, and supplies. "Then came the military and terrorism instructors" from Hezbollah, says Ronen Bergman. "[Imad] Mugniyah himself came to the camp to talk with Ayyash and some of his comrades." Were Hamas and Hezbollah working together? With Imad Mugniyah's training, the power of the Engineer's bombs could grow exponentially more lethal.

In Washington, Lew Merletti, bags packed, was preparing to leave for the Middle East when the deadliest suicide bombing in Israel's history rocked the center of Tel Aviv, just a few blocks from where President Clinton's motorcade was scheduled to travel. The bomb had been built by the Engineer.

It was morning rush hour, and the No. 5 passenger bus was heading down Rothschild Boulevard toward Dizengoff Street, the Champs-Élysées of Tel Aviv. Approaching the heart of the café district, a tall, thin twenty-seven-year-old Arab man from the West Bank boarded the bus, sat down in an aisle seat, and placed a small brown bag at his feet. A thin wire ran out of the bag through a hole in the man's trousers, up his leg, and into his pocket. There, it connected to an electrical switch, which connected to an improvised explosive device (IED) containing 20 kilograms of military-grade TNT and wrapped in nails and screws.

At 8:56, the suicide bomber in the aisle seat flipped the electrical switch in his pocket. The heat and blast produced a fireball so intense, it separated the vehicle's cabin from its chassis, melted the fiberglass frame, crushed a nearby car, and shattered windows all down the street. In a flash, twenty-two people were ripped apart, their limbs hurled across the street, where they landed on café floors and up in the branches of the chinaberry trees. Dazed and in shock, a young hairdresser who'd been riding the bus to work miraculously survived. "I saw fire," she told a journalist. "I saw a woman without a face." Orthodox men in long black cloaks appeared on the scene, carrying plastic bags and tweezers, which they used to pick up fingers, toes, and pieces of skin. Even the most hardened Israeli counterterrorism officers found the carnage too much to bear. A uniformed soldier vomited in the street. "How much more can we take?" screamed a young girl, her face and hands covered in blood. Twenty-two people were dead, fifty injured.

Reporters took to the streets, seeking opinions on whether or not the peace treaty could survive. "If peace comes only from one side, ours, it isn't peace," store owner Moshe Bar told a journalist with a camera, emphasizing the word *ours*. Susana Halperin, a passenger on the bus who had been hospitalized for burns, shared a different opinion. "I want the peace process to continue," she said. "I want my children to live in peace." But as the hours wore on, the ancient, archetypal desire for revenge reemerged. "Death to the Arabs!" shouted the growing crowd, as Kevlar-clad security forces worked to quell riots. In Gaza and the West Bank, vendors took to the streets, selling T-shirts emblazoned with the image of the Engineer. To many Palestinians, Yahya Ayyash was the new face of the revolution. For the Shin Bet, he was the most wanted man in Israel.

Lew Merletti traveled to Andrews Air Force Base, accompanied by a military aide and several staffers. They boarded a ten-person aircraft and flew to the Middle East, with Merletti now leading the advance trip for President Clinton's security. "Typically the DSAIC [deputy special agent in charge] and the SAIC [special agent in charge] travel with the president, but the threat associated with this trip" was unprecedented, Merletti explains. "I would [now] visit each of the country's top security officials for six or eight hours. We would go over security" and then fly to the next country. "It was my job to make sure [each of] the host nations understood without any hesitation what was required of them by us," Merletti says. The first stop was Tel Aviv.

"I was focused on the threat," he remembers. "We were aware of the Engineer." To protect the president inside the United States has its challenges, Merletti explains, but the Secret Service is a highly efficient security machine. Counter snipers with shoot-to-kill orders are positioned atop buildings, prepared to neutralize anyone who takes aim at the president. Counter Assault Teams are ready to repel an attack with overwhelming force. "Protection of the president overseas is an entirely different ball game," says Merletti. "We just don't take that lightly." While the team was airborne, President Clinton issued a statement on the Hamas bombing, calling it "an outrage against the conscience of the world," and vowed it would have no impact on his diplomatic efforts "toward a real and lasting peace in the Middle East."

After landing in Tel Aviv, Merletti and his team traveled to the King David Hotel, in Jerusalem, and checked in. Merletti had with him an eighteen-point security plan, which he intended to share with his Shin Bet counterpart, Benny Lahav. "All eighteen requirements had to be met," Merletti would insist. "We couldn't settle for anything less." Not in this environment.

Israel was a particularly dangerous place at this moment in time. Hamas's mass casualty attack against the No. 5 passenger bus the day before had likely emboldened them. With their expressly stated goal of stopping the peace process, Hamas saw President Clinton as a high-value target (HVT). While in Israel, Clinton's security detail would be jointly run by the U.S. Secret Service and the Shin Bet. On two separate occasions the president would be out in the open, says Merletti, the most challenging environment to defend against.

After a partial night's sleep, Merletti traveled to Tel Aviv to meet with Benny Lahav, who served as assistant director for the Shin Bet protective division responsible for Prime Minister Yitzhak Rabin's personal security detail. Merletti recalls feeling unsettled during the meeting. "We did not see eye to eye on the eighteen points." A contentious discussion ensued. "Their attitude, as I recall, was to solve problems through use of force.

"I was flabbergasted and frustrated," Merletti says, "but after two hours Lahav conceded seventeen of the eighteen criteria the Secret Service demanded for the visit. The point I didn't get was CAT [Counter Assault Team] coming to Israel. Most foreign countries were very sensitive about allowing CAT in because most foreign countries viewed CAT as a 'military type' unit."

With the meeting over, Merletti headed off on a fast-paced trip, meeting with the heads of security for the leaders of Syria, Egypt, Jordan, Saudi Arabia, and Kuwait. It was a tough few days and he felt the greatest pressure when President Clinton was in Israel. At one point, when "we were out in the open with the president, it was clear to me that a Shin Bet agent named S—— [redacted] was not paying attention" to the degree the U.S. Secret Service requires. "[Agent S——] was not watching his area. Without saying too much about security, I can tell you that arrivals and departures are critical times. In these areas, there can never be lapses or holes." Concerned for the president's safety, Merletti spoke directly to Agent S—— about this issue. "He said something to me along the lines of, 'if any threat [approaches], we're going to spray bullets. Ask questions later.' I was appalled." For U.S. Secret Service agents, "Protecting the president is like going on a mission in the jungle, behind enemy lines. A sniper, a hit-and-run grenade attack, a firefight, an ambush...anything is possible, at any time. You have to accept and prepare for this. That's how we are trained."

On October 25, 1994, with high hopes for peace and security in the Middle East, President Clinton began a six-nation tour, with Lew Merletti always within arm's reach. In Damascus, Clinton met with Hafez al-Assad, the first American president to meet with a president of Syria in more than twenty years. During the visit, Assad lauded Syria's capital as one of the oldest continuously inhabited cities in the world, a region that played a role in the dawn of human civilizations. "Syria [is] committed to the peace process," Assad promised. "We aspire to transform the region from a state of war to a state of peace." In 1994, Syria had been on the U.S. State Department's State Sponsors of Terrorism list longer than any other nation, a record it still holds in 2019.

In Cairo, President Clinton met with President Mubarak and Yasser Arafat. Two weeks prior, Arafat had been awarded the Nobel Peace Prize with Israeli prime minister Yitzhak Rabin and foreign minister Shimon Peres. In King Khalid Military City, Saudi Arabia, Clinton met with King Fahd, who praised "the relentless efforts of President Clinton and his government to move ahead the peace process." In Kuwait City, he met with the emir of Kuwait. It had been only a year since Clinton's predecessor, former president George H. W. Bush, had been the target of an Iraqi assassination plot. In a region wrought by centuries of conflict and bloodshed, could these neighbor nations really put aside their blood feuds and live in peace? President Clinton was the first American president since Carter to pursue peace, not covert action, in the Middle East.

At a border crossing between Jordan and Israel, Lew Merletti stood behind the president in the bright sun while the first-ever peace treaty between Israel and Jordan was signed by Prime Minister Yitzhak Rabin and King Hussein of Jordan, ending forty-six years of enmity. "This vast bleak desert hides great signs of life," said President Clinton. "Peace between Jordan and Israel is no longer a mirage. It is real." Jordan was now the second Arab nation to enter into a peace agreement with Israel. Egypt had been the first, sixteen years earlier, in September 1978. Three years later, Anwar Sadat was assassinated. Was it an auspicious time, or a time of ominous foreboding? No one could predict.

When it came time to leave Israel, Merletti felt compelled to speak out to Benny Lahav of the Shin Bet. "I was standing at the bottom of the steps of Air Force One, about to board. Someone made a remark kind of suggesting I was overzealous. Lahav pointed out that everything had worked out fine. He asked if I had anything else to say about Shin Bet security."

Merletti thought about his experiences in Vietnam and specifically of Mike Kuropas, his friend and fellow soldier who died just after turning twenty-two, before he ever had a chance to really shine. Merletti decided he was unwilling to stay silent. "So I said, 'You're weak on arrivals and departures. And Agent S—— doesn't understand protection. Someone is going to get hurt.' Then I climbed the stairs and boarded Air Force One."

Merletti took his seat, located just a few feet from the door to the private cabin for the president of the United States. For the first time in days, he was able to really sleep.

From a security standpoint the trip was a success, and this was also true from a diplomatic perspective. But not everyone felt triumphant. During the signing of the peace accord, as celebratory balloons were released into the hot desert air, Hezbollah, headquartered in nearby Lebanon and financed by Iran, fired rockets into Israeli villages in northern Galilee. As the details of the treaty emerged, Yasser Arafat became enraged. Anyone dumb enough to abide by it could "drink Gaza seawater," Arafat fumed. At the urging of Hamas and the PLO, more than one million Palestinians went on strike, declaring a "day of mourning" in protest.

But no one could have predicted that the greatest direct threat to the safety and security of Israel's prime minister was not necessarily from Hamas or Hezbollah. Peril was brewing at home, within a group of radical nationalistic right-wing Orthodox Jews. They saw Rabin as a traitor to their hard-line views and took to the streets to burn effigies of him. "Death to Rabin!" they shouted from parades and from podiums where they gathered. One of their members, a twenty-five-year-old Jewish law student named Yigal Amir, had begun experimenting with homemade bullets inside his garage.

★   ★   ★

During the first week of May 1995, Prime Minister Rabin traveled to Washington, DC, where he met with President Clinton at the White House. The Shin Bet agent Benny Lahav led the detail. "We recognized one another immediately," Merletti recalls. "Benny Lahav said to me, 'I'd like you to come have lunch with me over at the hotel we're staying at,'" Lahav had something important to tell Merletti, he said. Over lunch, he asked Merletti if he remembered the argument the two of them had had in Israel over the eighteen points of security the Secret Service strongly requested from the Shin Bet.

Merletti told Lahav that of course he did. The way Merletti recalls the conversation, Lahav then shared with him some thoughts about the American's hypervigilance. "Benny Lahav told me [a man] always has to fight for what [he] believes is right." Lahav said, "'Let me tell you, if Rabin were ever hurt, it would be *my* head. And if Clinton was ever hurt? It would be *your* head.'" Merletti knew Lahav's words were the truth.

Four months later, on September 3, 1995, Lew Merletti was promoted to special agent in charge of the Presidential Protective Division. With the exception of director, this was the highest position a Secret Service agent could hold. When Merletti moved into his new office, he brought with him items that reminded him of what was at stake: gravestone rubbings of his friends who died fighting in Vietnam.

Two months later, on Saturday, November 4, 1995, Lew Merletti was at his son's football game when his pager went off. The message indicated that the situation was urgent. Merletti ran to his car and used his Secret Service–issued cellular telephone. "They said there had been an assassination of a world leader," he remembers. On the drive to the White House, a breaking news story came over the radio. Yitzhak Rabin had been killed in Tel Aviv.

As Merletti sat there stunned, the telephone in his car rang. It was President Clinton calling. "He said to me something along the lines of, 'You heard what happened. I have to go to the funeral. I need to talk to you. I need you to be on board with this.'" Because the funeral was in two days, travel would have to happen in a matter of hours, Merletti remembers. "I said to him, 'If you want to go, we'll go. But we need you to do everything we tell you to do. We're going to go [to Israel] and we'll do what we plan on doing. There can be no side events. And if we determine there's something we can't do, we're not doing it.'" The president agreed.

Merletti went home, changed his clothes, and drove to the White House. "The situation was frenetic. People racing around trying to prepare staff for the trip." There were difficult logistics to sort out. "This was not a normal group of people traveling to the funeral for Yitzhak Rabin," he recalls. There would be three living presidents traveling to Israel on Air Force One: President Clinton, former president Jimmy Carter, and former president George H. W. Bush. Also in the delegation were White House chief of staff Leon Panetta; House minority leader Newt Gingrich; Speaker of the House and Senate majority leader Bob Dole; Senate minority leader Tom Daschle; and others. "Besides the vice president, who stayed in Washington, nearly the entire line of [presidential] succession was on the plane."

On the flight over, Merletti gave a security briefing and took questions. What everyone wanted to know was, "How was Rabin assassinated?" But Merletti had no idea.

The delegation arrived in Tel Aviv, drove up the mountain into Jerusalem, and checked into the King David Hotel.

"A guy came up to me and introduced himself from the Shin Bet," Merletti recalls. "He said, 'The director [Carmi Gillon] wants to meet with you right now.' The first thing that went through my mind was, *Ahhh, there's been another assassination attempt.*" It was almost midnight. The funeral was the following day. Whatever it was had to be important enough that it couldn't wait. Merletti told his deputy he'd be right back. The Shin Bet agents whisked him into a car and drove away. It was dark outside and the streets were narrow. The car moved quickly through what felt like Jerusalem's back alleyways and up to a darkened restaurant that looked closed. The agents got out of the car and motioned for Merletti to follow. One of them tapped on a door. The window blinds separated and a man peeked out. The door opened.

Inside the restaurant the chairs were all up on the tables. The place was definitely closed. Merletti was taken through the front room and into a much smaller room at the back.

"There was a big table in there, with all these men sitting there in a row, under very bright lights." Merletti remembers thinking to himself, *What on earth is going on?*

Carmi Gillon introduced himself. "He said, 'I'm the director of the Shin Bet. Are you Lew Merletti?'" Merletti said he was. Gillon said, "'I was told—so I'm asking you—is this true that last year when you were here, you said the Shin Bet was weak on arrivals and departures and that Agent S—— didn't know what he was doing?'"

Merletti told Gillon yes, that's what he said.

Gillon asked Merletti if he knew how the prime minister was killed. If he was aware of "the details of the assassination of Rabin."

Merletti said no.

"It was on a departure, just as you predicted," Gillon said, and told Merletti that the advance agent was Agent S——. "That Agent S—— was standing next to Rabin when he was shot." Merletti felt sick.

"And do you know who was standing next to Agent S——?" Gillon asked.

"No," Merletti said.

"Benny Lahav," Gillon said.

★   ★   ★

There was a coda to the tragedy. Gillon asked Merletti if the U.S. Secret Service would be willing to train Shin Bet agents on arrivals and departures, as well as other security protocols that remain classified. Merletti said he would introduce Gillon to the appropriate people. The men shook hands and the Shin Bet agents took Merletti back to the King David Hotel.

When Israel's Shamgar Commission released its report on the assassination of Yitzhak Rabin, Shin Bet agent Benny Lahav was singled out and fired. Agent S—— resigned. Carmi Gillon assumed full responsibility for the security failures and resigned.

The state funeral, at Jerusalem's Mount Herzl Cemetery, was a solemn affair. President Clinton read a eulogy that remained focused on peace, which he referenced nine times. After the service ended, the delegation drove back down the mountain, boarded Air Force One, and flew home.

There was a second coda, which, like the first, has never been reported. Rabin's assassination was for many Israeli Jews a time of great suffering and soul-searching. Hamas took advantage of the national despair, upping its irregular-warfare campaign with lethality unmatched in its prior terror campaigns. Over a one-month period in February and March, more than sixty Israelis were killed in a wave of suicide bomb attacks. The explosive devices were built by Yahya Ayyash.

The hunt for the Engineer accelerated, and the Shin Bet asked the U.S. Secret Service for assistance. The exact role of the partnership remains classified, but it involved surveillance equipment used by Gray Fox, the army's classified intelligence unit and CIA partner. This technology was lent to the Shin Bet in its hunt for the Engineer.

Meanwhile, in the United States, a technology development in the private sector was giving the U.S. Secret Service grave concerns. Mobile phones had recently become popular. As special agent in charge of the

PPD, Lew Merletti was having great difficulty making the affable president understand the danger in holding someone else's phone.

On one occasion, recalls Merletti, "an individual in a crowd held out her cell phone and asked the president to say hello to her mom." President Clinton obliged. Merletti suggested to the president that he should not receive any object, including a cell phone, that wasn't approved by the Secret Service first. The president noted the request and seemed to agree. But a few weeks later, a similar situation came to pass. Then it happened a third time.

"I spoke to him in the car," recalls Lew Merletti. "I said, 'Mr. President, you must understand how serious the threat is. You can't take a cell phone from anyone. Not unless it has been approved by us first.' "

Merletti was privy to information about the Engineer that had not yet been made public. Shin Bet operators learned that the Hamas bomb maker would sometimes spend the night in the Gaza City home of a childhood friend named Osama Hamad. In order to speak with Hamas leaders clandestinely, the Engineer would sometimes borrow Osama Hamad's cell phone. The Shin Bet had previously used an uncle of Osama Hamad's, a man named Kamil Hamad, as a paid informant. In the fall of 1995, the Shin Bet blackmailed the uncle into working for them, threatening to tell Hamas of his treachery if he didn't honor a simple request. The Shin Bet gave the uncle a cell phone and told him it needed to be put into the hands of the Engineer. The Shin Bet said it wanted to listen to the Engineer's conversations with Hamas. The uncle was not made privy to the fact that the cell phone was an engineered explosive device, outfitted with fifteen grams of RDX explosives.

On January 5, 1996, while visiting with his childhood friend, the Engineer received a call from his father on Osama Hamad's cell phone. Overhead, an Israeli SIGINT aircraft, equipped with technology provided by the U.S. Secret Service, listened in on the call. When voice recognition software confirmed the caller ID, the Shin

Bet remotely detonated the cell phone bomb, instantly killing the Engineer.

With the Hamas bomb maker assassinated, Lew Merletti requested from his Shin Bet counterparts two postmortem photographs of the Engineer. The Shin Bet obliged.

"I went to see the president," Merletti says. "I set down the photographs on his desk and asked him to take a look. The first was a photograph of the bomber's head, the side opposite from where the cell phone had been." The man was clearly dead, but the gruesome results of the cell phone explosion were not evident. Clinton took note, then moved on to the second photograph. "The second photograph had been taken from the side where the Engineer had been holding the cell phone containing the explosive charge. This side of the Engineer's head was almost entirely destroyed."

Merletti's recollection is that President Clinton never again accepted another cell phone that had not been handed to him by a Secret Service agent.

In the summer of 1996, in Khartoum, Hassan al-Turabi banished Osama bin Laden and his followers from the country. The Al-Qaeda leader and his entourage moved to Afghanistan, where they were given sanctuary by the Taliban, the militant Islamist group who'd recently seized the capital city of Kabul. In a financial arrangement with Taliban leader Mullah Omar, bin Laden began to expand his Al-Qaeda organization by setting up terrorist training camps in Afghanistan where fighters prepared for jihad against the United States. Osama bin Laden's first target, not widely known, was President Clinton.

It was November 24, 1996, and Lew Merletti accompanied President Clinton to the Asia-Pacific Economic Cooperation forum in the Philippines. Security was intense, with an estimated 26,000 police and soldiers assigned to protect visiting dignitaries. The U.S.

State Department warned its citizens to be on alert for a possible terrorist attack. In Manila, President Clinton was scheduled to visit a local politician. The route chosen would take him across a bridge in central Manila.

"As the presidential motorcade began to move," recalled Merletti, he received a "crackly message in one earpiece." Intelligence agents had picked up a message using the words "bridge" and "wedding," which Merletti "interpreted to be terrorist code words for assassination." Merletti ordered the motorcade to change course, something only he had the authority to do. "The motorcade agent Nelson Garabito did a great job rerouting the president under those difficult circumstances," he says, and that agents "discovered a bomb on the bridge." The assassination attempt was not made public. The Secret Service keeps all assassination attempts against a U.S. president classified Top Secret so as not to encourage copycat attacks. The details of the Manila bomb were made known to only a handful of members of the U.S. intelligence community.

The following year, on June 6, 1997, Lew Merletti was sworn in as the nineteenth director of the U.S. Secret Service, the first former Counter Assault Team member to hold the position, and the only director to have served in the U.S. Army Special Forces in Vietnam. Six months into the job, in January 1998, Merletti was driving to the White House one morning when he heard NPR reporters Mara Liasson and Robert Siegel interviewing President Clinton.

"Is there any truth to the allegation of an affair between you and the young woman?" one of the reporters asked. The president was being accused of having conducted an affair with an intern named Monica Lewinsky, and of having asked the Secret Service to help keep it a secret. Merletti was stunned. He was the special agent in charge of the president's security detail at the time this affair was allegedly taking place. He'd never heard a word about it from any of his agents. He hurried back to the White House. "Our chief counsel,

John Kelleher, informed me that we would be getting subpoenas from the [Office of the] Independent Counsel for agents on the President's Protective Detail to testify" in open court. Merletti remembers thinking, "What is this guy Ken Starr thinking? Does he know what this means?" If Secret Service agents were forced to testify against a president, it would rock the foundation of trust and confidence, Merletti believed.

Merletti was summoned to Starr's office on Pennsylvania Avenue to speak with the independent counsel and his deputy, Robert J. Bittman. Merletti told Ken Starr that Secret Service agent Clint Hill was living proof that proximity to the president is critical to the success of the Secret Service. As we learned earlier, on the day that President Kennedy was assassinated in Dallas there were no Secret Service agents riding on the running boards of the president's limousine. This protocol change, authorized by President Kennedy just a few days earlier, put several yards' distance between the president and his protective detail. "Proximity is the difference between life and death to our protectees," Merletti told Starr. "If our protectees cannot trust us, if they believe that they will be called to testify before a grand jury to reveal confidences, the president will not allow us that critical proximity."

Ken Starr seemed unconcerned. "It's like it didn't register," Merletti recalls. "Instead he asked questions about lipstick, hair...other things." Merletti was furious. His job was about protection, not politics. A showdown ensued. In May 1998, a judge scheduled a hearing on Merletti's claim that Secret Service agents should be granted a "protective function" privilege and kept from testifying in open court. Accompanying Merletti was former Secret Service agent Clint Hill. Lawyers for the Secret Service showed the judge rare historical photographs of agents, including Clint Hill jumping off the rear bumper of the presidential limousine to ride in the vehicle behind, on President Kennedy's orders, just minutes before heading toward Dealey Plaza in downtown Dallas on November 22, 1963. The case headed to trial. Immunity deals were negotiated. Secret Service agents were forced to testify in court, revealing under oath that they had not known about the Lewinsky affair and had never helped the president keep it secret. In late July, President Clinton volunteered to testify regarding allegations that he'd committed perjury by covering up the affair.

In the middle of this unfolding drama, on August 7, 1998, suicide bombers drove truck bombs into the U.S. embassies in Tanzania and Kenya. Among the 224 people killed, in nearly simultaneous explosions, were 12 Americans. Another 4,000 people were wounded. The truck bombs were reminiscent of the ones Hezbollah had driven into the U.S. embassy and marine corps barracks and the French paratroop barracks in Beirut fifteen years before. But the East Africa embassy bombings proved to be the work of Al-Qaeda.

Three months before the embassy attacks, in February 1998, Osama bin Laden issued a fatwa against the United States, calling for the murder of any American, anywhere on earth, as the "individual duty for every Muslim who can do it in any country in which it is possible to do it." In May, CIA lawyer John Rizzo drafted a Memorandum of Notification for a snatch-and-grab operation against bin Laden, an updated version of a Reagan-era finding against Hezbollah. "I had drafted the Reagan finding," says Rizzo, "I wrote it in another era, to deal with terrorists in another era," and Clinton had a "very different threshold" of tolerance for covert action than Reagan had, Rizzo says. His guess was that in the course of trying to capture bin Laden, there'd be a firefight, and the Al-Qaeda chief—and maybe some of the women and children around him—would be killed. Rizzo wrote the Memorandum of Notification for the president to sign, but Clinton would not sign it and it was shelved. After the embassy bombings in East Africa, the CIA wanted to kill bin Laden outright—using lethal direct action by a covert-action paramilitary team. President Clinton ordered missile strikes instead.

On August 20, four U.S. Navy ships and a submarine stationed in the Arabian Sea fired between sixty and seventy-five Tomahawk cruise missiles at terrorist training camps in Khost, Afghanistan, and the Al-Shifa pharmaceutical factory allegedly linked to Osama bin Laden in Khartoum. Billy Waugh was in Sudan on a classified mission at the time. "A colleague and I went by the factory to look at the damage inflicted by the Tomahawks," he says. "It was a big pile of rubble. An unnecessary move, if you ask me. Osama bin Laden was thousands of miles away. Still alive as could be." American officials later acknowledged their intelligence on Al-Shifa was thin.

Officers at the CIA's Counterterrorist Center began thinking about how to actually kill Osama bin Laden. John Rizzo drafted another covert-action Memorandum of Notification for President Clinton to sign, one that would allow a team of Afghan assets led by CIA paramilitary operators to go after bin Laden in Afghanistan. But the MON came back "with Clinton's handwritten notes," Rizzo recalls, "not something I'd ever seen a president do before." Before lethal direct action could be taken, Clinton noted, a certain set of conditions had to be met, including the right to self-defense. "There were so many caveats and conditions, it muddied the waters" and became prohibitive, according to Rizzo. CIA director George Tenet took a new draft of Rizzo's MON to attorney general Janet Reno. "The Attorney General informed [Tenet] that she would consider as 'illegal' any CIA operation intended solely to kill bin Laden."

There were additional plans in the works aimed at killing Osama bin Laden. Back in 1986, Dewey Clarridge, one of the CTC's cofounders, had envisioned using a drone in a targeted killing operation. It was his idea to fly an unmanned aerial vehicle loaded with explosives and ball bearings into Muammar Qaddafi's tent. In the wake of the embassy bombings in East Africa, Cofer Black, now chief of the CTC, and his deputy Henry "Hank" Crumpton, had a similar idea.

Black allocated a $5 million budget to the CIA's Special Activities Division, authorizing the development of a UAV called the Predator. Originally conceived as a surveillance drone, the 27-foot-long Predator, with its 55-foot wingspan, had a maximum altitude of 25,000 feet and a maximum speed of 138 mph. More importantly, it could hover above a single target for up to 40 hours at a time, take video, and send it back to the CTC.

In the summer of 2000, the CIA sent a Predator drone over bin Laden's training base in Afghanistan, Tarnak Farms, outside Kandahar. The Predator gathered video data, identified vehicles, and established a pattern of life. One day, with the Predator watching, bin Laden appeared in the driveway—tall, robed, and surrounded by followers. The CIA was certain it was him. The Clinton White House was notified. The CTC was told it would take six hours for the president to sign off on a missile strike against Tarnak Farms.

"Unbelievable," recalls Cofer Black.

Cofer Black and Hank Crumpton again proposed sending a paramilitary team to Tarnak Farms to kill Osama bin Laden. John Rizzo wrote up another MON.

"We were driven by an immediate imperative: find bin Laden. Engage in lethal force," Crumpton explained, in an interview for this book. "To our frustration, the president's covert-action finding included many caveats [stating] we could seek to kill Osama bin Laden only if it was part of a capture mission." The situation struck Crumpton as hypocritical. "There was no apparent problem killing him with a cruise missile."

Cofer Black later gave Crumpton his assessment. "Imagine the pre-9/11 headlines," Black said. "CIA Assassinates Saudi Militant." Assassination was un-American.

"No one had the foresight to understand the consequences" down the road, Crumpton laments. Herein lies the enigma of pre-emptive neutralization.

In 2000, Cofer Black and Hank Crumpton remained determined to kill bin Laden, but unable to act without a MON, or Presidential Finding, from the Clinton White House authorizing lethal direct action. "They all but wanted us to take a lawyer from the Justice Department into Afghanistan on a mission," says Black. "Read bin Laden his rights before arresting him." "Clinton issued no new findings or MONs on counterterrorism from mid-'99 through the end of his administration, not even in the wake of the Al-Qaeda bombings of the USS *Cole* in October 2000," says Rizzo.

Hank Crumpton foresaw a solution. "I realized that arming the Predator was perhaps our only chance of achieving our lethal mission," he says. An armed UAV was more likely to get approval from President Clinton than a covert-action strike involving a bullet to the head or chest. Is it the desire for public approval that makes a president loath to kill a man in close-quarters combat? To instead defend as legitimate a missile strike costing $75 million to $100 million that kills civilians and destroys buildings in its path? And how would Hank Crumpton's armed Predator drone fit into this calculus? It involved a missile, but it was also a lethal direct-action strike, intended to kill a single man. With help from White House National Security Council advisor Richard Clarke, the CIA's Cofer Black, Charlie Allen, and others, Crumpton explains, the development, testing, and deployment of the armed Predator drone would begin.

The pretense of virtue attached to killing someone from a distance is curious. Perhaps dangerous as well. The current laws of war prohibit treacherous killing, and that includes assassination. It is also considered treacherous to shoot the enemy while he is taking a bath. But covert action occurs in the in-between, governed by Title 50 of the national-security code. It is undertaken at the behest of the president and is to remain hidden from the public eye. Do the laws of war need to be updated for guerrilla warfare, seeing as it is the only kind of war America has engaged in since World War II? Can terrorism be defeated by gentleman's rules?

War is wicked, violent, and treacherous. A horror of chaos, anarchy, and revenge. Just ask the covert-action operators who run lethal direct-action missions for the CIA's Special Activities Division, including its Ground Branch, all of which remain classified. I spoke to scores of its operators, some on the condition of anonymity.

"Where the laws of war end," one Ground Branch operator told me, "Ground Branch begins."

PART IV

2001

CHAPTER TWENTY-TWO

War in Afghanistan

Billy Waugh stood in line to draw money at CIA headquarters in Langley, where a clandestine operator goes to get advance money for a trip, usually hundred-dollar bills in banded stacks. It was a bright, sunny day, not a cloud in the sky this second Tuesday in September 2001. Waugh was heading to Kuala Lumpur, Malaysia, for a clandestine meeting with Khun Sa, the notorious Asian drug lord and guerrilla leader of the heroin-financed Shan State Army in Myanmar. Khun Sa was one of the most dangerous men in the world. In the hierarchy of Southeast Asia's Golden Triangle, he was the top tyrant, the Prince of Death. With an estimated personal fortune of $5 billion, he was the world's fifth-richest drug lord on record (four slots behind Pablo Escobar, who was worth $30 billion when killed). Once, the Drug Enforcement Agency calculated that 45 percent of all heroin in the United States came from Khun Sa's empire. The covert-action operation that the CIA was engaging in with Khun Sa in the fall of 2001 remains classified.

Standing in line at CIA headquarters, Waugh kept one eye on an overhead television set. One of the news programs was reporting that a passenger airplane had hit the North Tower of the World Trade Center. A few minutes later, a second airplane hit the South Tower, making clear this was a terrorist attack. An alarm sounded.

Emergency lights began to flash. "In all my years at the Agency I'd never seen or heard that before," remembers Waugh. Over the intercom, a prerecorded voice instructed all employees to exit the building and leave CIA grounds immediately. "Everyone except for Special Activities Division," says Waugh. "We were told to report to the north parking lot and wait there."

Lawyer John Rizzo heard the evacuation order over the CIA's intercom system, too. But standing in his office on the top floor of the original headquarters building, watching hundreds of employees evacuate the grounds, he decided not to leave. Instead he closed his door, sat down at his desk, and pulled out a blank yellow legal pad. "I began writing a list of potential covert actions the CIA might undertake in the coming weeks," Rizzo recalls.

Waugh headed over to the lot. It was filled with many faces that had become familiar to him after forty years of working with the CIA. Nerds in suits, knuckle draggers and bearded guys. For roughly thirty minutes, the group sat in the sun discussing what had happened. Suddenly someone shouted out that a third hijacked aircraft had crashed into the Pentagon. The White House and the Capitol were being evacuated, and U.S. airspace was now shut down. A minute before 10:00, the South Tower of the World Trade Center collapsed. On an average working day, 50,000 people worked there, not including daily visitors. Just a few minutes later a fourth hijacked aircraft crashed into a Pennsylvania field. At 10:28, the North Tower collapsed. "Pretty much everybody was thinking the same thing," says Waugh. "America was going to war."

After a few hours, one of the more senior members of the division came out to the parking lot and addressed the group. "Prepare to RON," he said. Remain overnight. Then he told everyone to go get back to work.

Inside the building, Waugh found a large wooden table in an upstairs conference room, sat down, and began reading everything available on Afghanistan.

That night, around 9:30, CIA director George Tenet met with President Bush and his top advisors inside a bunker beneath the White House. Vice President Dick Cheney, Secretary of Defense Donald Rumsfeld, Secretary of State Colin Powell, and national-security advisor Condoleezza Rice were among those present. Tenet told the president and his inner circle that the Counterterrorist Center had identified Osama bin Laden and Al-Qaeda as being behind the attacks and that a hard-line group of Islamic fundamentalists called the Taliban were providing the terrorist organization with a safe haven inside Afghanistan. The meeting in the White House bunker focused on an incontrovertible reality, Tenet said. The terrorist threat was not a one-country problem.

"We have a sixty-country problem," he said. A follow-up wave of attacks could come at any time, from anywhere around the world.

"Let's pick them off one at a time," the president said.

The following morning, at 8:00, Tenet arrived back at the White House, this time to deliver the President's Daily Brief. He described the CIA's recent covert-action operations in Afghanistan, explaining how the Special Activities Division had spent years developing assets inside anti-Taliban guerrilla groups. The most promising of these fighting forces was the Northern Alliance, but their leader, Ahmed Shah Massoud, had been assassinated by Al-Qaeda three days ago — a strategic preemptive move. The CTC was working around the clock on a plan of action for Afghanistan, and it would be ready for the president to view the following day.

"Whatever it takes," the president said.

On September 14 Cofer Black, chief of the CTC, accompanied George Tenet to the White House to lay out a plan of attack unprecedented in American history. The CIA, not the Defense Department, should lead the attack against Osama bin Laden, Al-Qaeda, and the Taliban in Afghanistan, Tenet said. The CIA's Special Activities Division was best suited to wage an unconventional-warfare campaign in Afghanistan. U.S. special operations forces would augment the CIA paramilitary operations being proposed, but Tenet was very clear about the fact that the CIA would lead.

When it came time for Cofer Black to speak, the room grew quiet. Black was a huge man, six foot three, with energy reserves as big as his frame. A twenty-six-year veteran of the clandestine service, he had spent decades running covert-action operations in war-torn countries and failed states like Angola and Sudan. With the terrorist attacks just a few days old, and the dead still thought to number 10,000, Cofer Black presented his plan of lethal action against Al-Qaeda, springing out of his chair, throwing papers on the floor, and hurling his fist in the air to emphasize his points. Timing was everything, he said. Another attack likely loomed on the horizon. America needed to respond immediately, with a heavy as well as a hidden hand. The CIA's Special Activities Division was fast, flexible, and lethal, Black said, and if given the mission it would destroy Al-Qaeda's leadership. "They'll have flies on their eyeballs," he told the president. After that, Cofer Black became known among the war cabinet as the "flies-on-the-eyeballs guy."

In the days since 9/11, President Bush had been candid about his determination to hunt down and kill the terrorists responsible for the worst attack ever on U.S. soil. Now he was being told by an impassioned CTC chief that there was a way to do this immediately. Everyone in the room knew that the Defense Department would need many months to get boots on the ground inside a hostile, land-locked country like Afghanistan. Just a few hours later, at a National Security Council meeting in the White House Situation Room, the president told his advisors that he was going to approve the CIA proposal and allow the Agency to lead the war in Afghanistan.

The group reconvened the following day at Camp David to discuss what would happen next. Tenet delivered a presentation called "Going to War." The Top Secret proposal called for what the CIA termed the Worldwide Attack Matrix, a hidden-hand antiterrorism campaign that would span eighty countries around the globe. The opening phase of the war would focus on Osama bin Laden, Al-Qaeda, and the Taliban regime in Afghanistan. After that, the scope would widen to include all of the Middle East, much of Asia and Africa, and a host of other nations.

In order to implement the Worldwide Attack Matrix, the president would need to grant the CIA what Agency lawyers called "exceptional authorities." President Bush would have to sign off on a Memorandum of Notification that would allow the CIA to conduct covert-action operations around the world without having to come back for another MON each time a new operation was proposed. This MON would modify and supersede the findings signed by President Reagan and those later amended by President Clinton, which hamstrung the CIA's paramilitary teams under legal constraints. When the meeting ended, President Bush took George Tenet aside to say he was going to approve all of Tenet's requests. All he needed now were documents from the CIA's lawyers.

At CIA headquarters, John Rizzo reviewed the language of the MON he'd been drafting one last time. "I wrote the September 2001 MON," said Rizzo, in an interview for this book. "Lethal direct action was [expressly] stated. So was the authority to capture, detain, interrogate." At the time, there was no way to foresee where this would all go. "How those two [sets] of three words [each] would later be interpreted. This is the tricky thing about MONs," Rizzo explains. Lethal direct action would become known as targeted killing. "Capture, detain, interrogate" would become known as enhanced interrogation, or torture.

In September 2001, John Rizzo was the number two lawyer at the CIA. He'd served eleven CIA directors and seven presidents. "The first MON I ever drafted was during the Iranian hostage" crisis, he explains, and "this [September 2001] Memorandum of Notification was nothing short of extraordinary," he says. As he wrote in *Company Man,* "It was the most comprehensive, most ambitious, most aggressive and most risky Finding, or MON, I was ever involved in." A second document drafted by Rizzo delineated the orders and steps for authorization to be followed and taken by the president's war cabinet. This included financial investigations, diplomatic efforts, military planning, and additional covert actions necessary to go after terrorists around the world. Satisfied with the language, Rizzo had the documents sent over to the White House for signature. Both documents were classified Top Secret. Both remain in effect today.

The Memorandum of Notification was radical in terms of scope, ambition, aggression, and risk. It also contained another authority that would revolutionize the way in which individual people would be targeted and killed. At the CTC, ever since President Clinton had forbidden the CIA from killing Osama Bin Laden with a paramilitary team, Hank Crumpton and Cofer Black had been trying to weaponize the Predator drone. Recently, they'd figured out how to retrofit the airframe with laser-guided missiles to strike a target from 25,000 feet overhead. On 9/11, the CTC had a total of two Predator drones, one of which was armed. This new MON authorized the director of the CIA to pull the trigger on a lethal Predator drone strike. Tenet passed this authority on to the chief of the Directorate of Operations, who passed the job on to Cofer Black.

The following day, President Bush signed the MON and summoned his advisors. "The purpose of this meeting," the president said, "is to assign tasks for the first wave of the war against terrorism. It starts today. I want the CIA to be first on the ground." The CIA, not the Department of Defense, was the lead agency in a war.

Billy Waugh did not want to be left behind. Intent on getting himself on a CIA paramilitary team headed to Afghanistan, he went directly to Cofer Black's office and knocked on the door.

"Come in," Black said.

Billy Waugh stood in the doorframe. Black was inundated with responsibility. Many of his duties approximated those of a military general. Waugh addressed his former boss using Black's old code name from Sudan.

"Crusader," Waugh said, "get me in on this war."

Black remembers how absurd it seemed at the time, what Billy Waugh was asking of him. Waugh was old—he'd fought as an infantry soldier in the Korean War. "I asked him how old he was," Black recalled in 2017. "He said he was about to turn seventy-two. I told him he wasn't going to Afghanistan. He said yes he was. I said he was too old."

Although Billy Waugh was not aware, his legacy at the CIA—his decades-long work as a clandestine operator—loomed large, and not just at the Agency but at the White House. Enrique "Ric" Prado, one of Cofer Black's Senior Intelligence Service advisors and a longtime colleague of Billy Waugh's, was preparing a briefing for Vice President Dick Cheney.

Ric Prado was a rare breed of CIA officer—a man as comfortable operating behind enemy lines in disguise as he was strolling the halls of power in a suit. Having grown up in the Special Activities Division, first as a paramilitary operator and later as an operations officer, he was uniquely familiar with the kind of dangerous work Billy Waugh had done for the CIA over the previous decades. In this time of national crisis, Prado had conceived of how to make use of Waugh's tradecraft. Waugh and a handful of male and female operators like him had managed to photograph the world's most wanted terrorists in the world's most dangerous places. This was a key element of a new way forward, Prado told me in 2018.

The Counterterrorist Center was putting together a list of Al-Qaeda leadership it had identified as potential targets of lethal direct action. Ric Prado's plan was to widen that list and to put additional focus on the mid- to upper-level terrorists—the facilitators that the Al-Qaeda leadership relied upon: bomb makers, weapons traders, money men, recruiters, trainers, commanders, and radical imams. Prado discussed his plan with Cofer Black, who set up a meeting in the White House Situation

Room with Vice President Dick Cheney. Also present at the meeting were Cheney's chief of staff, I. Lewis Libby, White House legal counsel David Addington, and the CIA's John Rizzo.

Ric Prado was considered tough and intimidating by friends and enemies alike. At the CIA, he held the rank of SIS-2, which made him the civilian equivalent of a military major general. In addition to being a strategic thinker, Prado, a former U.S. Air Force Pararescue veteran, was a highly trained warfighter. He was an expert in parachute insertion, scuba exfiltration, evasive driving, knife fighting, and a host of other close-quarters combat skills. With his fourth-degree black belt in martial arts, Prado spent his first ten years at the CIA with the Special Activities Division, some of it as a Ground Branch officer, including nearly four years in the jungles of South America. Over the next decade, he was posted at six CIA stations overseas and served as deputy chief, East Asia Division for the Koreas. In 1996, he returned to Langley to become deputy in charge of Alec Station, the original bin Laden task force. In 2000, he was named chief of station in Khartoum, where—like Waugh—he drove around the city disguised as African, wearing a rubber mask designed by the CIA. In 2001, Prado became chief of operations at the Counterterrorist Center. In a matter of months, he would move into an ultrasecret unit called Special Investigations Group.

Accompanying Ric Prado to the meeting in the White House Situation Room was a colleague from the Latin America Division, Jose Rodriguez, also a larger-than-life figure from the Senior Intelligence Service. Rodriguez had recently been moved over to the CTC to serve as Cofer Black's chief operations officer.

During the meeting at the White House, Ric Prado and Jose Rodriguez showed Vice President Cheney photographs of terrorists taken by singleton operators like Billy Waugh. These photographs were acquired the old-school way, they explained, with a 35mm camera and a long lens. They included pictures of Abdul Qadeer Khan, the rogue nuclear scientist who had developed Pakistan's atomic bomb, and Mamoun Darkazanli, who the CIA called the Dark Man, a member of the Syrian Muslim Brotherhood who joined Al-Qaeda to help finance the 9/11 attacks. The reason for showing the vice president and his advisors the photographs was to demonstrate the obvious: the Special Activities Division had for decades been developing a capacity to get a singleton operator within striking range of a terrorist, close enough to kill the man.

Before 9/11, the Clinton administration's Presidential Findings allowed the CIA to conduct reconnaissance and take photographs but not engage in lethal direct action against terrorists. The September 17, 2001, MON signed by President Bush changed all that. Ric Prado was proposing that the CIA maximize its ability to locate human targets, fix their position, and if necessary, kill them. The concept, derived from Special Forces doctrine developed in Latin America in the 1980s, would later become known at the Defense Department as Find, Fix, Finish. According to three individuals familiar with the program, Vice President Cheney agreed that the CIA should develop this capacity. It was provided for in the MON and was precisely the kind of covert action the Worldwide Attack Matrix required. It called for the expansion of the CIA's paramilitary army.

At the time, says Crumpton, "The CIA paramilitary arm was tiny and weak in terms of raw kinetic firepower." Within days of the 9/11 attack, that changed as the Special Activities Division expanded in unprecedented ways. A new entity inside the Counterterrorist Center called CTC/Special Operations emerged, made up of "more than fifty rabidly dedicated officers scrambling in a disciplined frenzy of duty and revenge." Hank Crumpton would run the internal part of the CIA's war in Afghanistan. Ric Prado would oversee counterterrorism operations around the globe, including those for the bin Laden group, Hamas group, Hezbollah group, and others. "We started recruiting people in the hallways," Prado recalls. "A deliberate mix of officers with a range of disciplines from different parts of the clandestine service and even the larger CIA," Crumpton explains, "personnel from Near East Division, Central Eurasia Division, Africa Division, communications officers, medics, bomb experts, all came together under temporary assignment to CTC/SO."

Roughly fifty percent of the men on the teams deployed into Afghanistan were from the Special Activities Division, Ground Branch. Highly classified and totally deniable, Ground Branch is like a human version of the Predator program: zealous, uncompromising, and deadly when necessary. In 2001, roughly half of its efforts were directed at reconnaissance and surveillance missions, with the other half acting as a lethal direct-action strike force. Over time, Ground Branch—like the Predator drone program—would radically transform.

The day after President Bush signed the CIA's MON, he signed into law the Authorization for Use of Military Force. It was directed against Al-Qaeda and "associated forces." Days earlier, Cofer Black had called a veteran field officer named Gary Schroen into his office and asked him to lead the first of nine Special Activities Division teams into the war zone. Fluent in Dari, the native language of roughly 50 percent of Afghanistan, Schroen had worked covert operations in the region since 1978, including ones involving the recently assassinated rebel leader Ahmed Shah Massoud. During the Taliban years, from 1996 to 2001, when there was no U.S. embassy in Kabul, Schroen served as CIA chief of station, Afghanistan, by working out of an office in Islamabad, Pakistan. With the Agency rank of SIS-4, Gary Schroen was a senior intelligence service officer at the very top of the ladder. And yet he was going to fight in Afghanistan, age sixty. That the CIA was sending Schroen directly into a war zone to lead a direct-action team is nothing short of remarkable. It also demonstrates just how far apart the CIA and the Pentagon are in their thinking, their doctrine, and their moves.

The Defense Department is a war machine: a labyrinth of rules and regulations, field manuals, and chains of command that make up a massive trillion-dollar bureaucracy that prides itself on being the most powerful fighting force in the world. The CIA's covert-action arm lives at the opposite end of the spectrum. Its manuals are mostly unwritten. Agency operatives are taught how to break laws of foreign countries. How to circumvent the rules. No one calls anyone else "sir." The smallness and secrecy of the CIA's paramilitary arm—its light, flexible footprint—is exactly what allows its officers and operators to make quick-thinking life-or-death decisions on the fly. "Men calculatingly reckless with disciplined daring who are trained for aggressive action," was how William Donovan described the unconventional warrior-spies of the OSS Special Operations Branch. The Special Activities Division is the closest thing to an heir.

Covert action was created to act as the president's hidden hand, the third option when military force is inappropriate and diplomacy has failed. The concept of plausible deniability has been built into the very fabric of a covert-action mission since its inception in 1947. When an operation is over, the role of the CIA is to go back to remaining hidden from the world. In Afghanistan, an entirely new hybrid way of war was under way. Part unconventional, part conventional. Part covert, part overt. Part Title 50, part Title 10. How, exactly, was a CIA-led, Pentagon-augmented war going to work?

"Let me explain something," Crumpton told me in 2018. "I didn't really care about the hidden hand. The mission was so immediate, so driven by speed and precision—if something leaked, that was beyond my control. The country was in a panic. Everything was driven by need. Need and speed. Some of our guys carried AKs because of the availability of ammo.... Our teams [were] in constant danger on the ground."

On September 20, 2001, Schroen and the first paramilitary team of the war flew into Tashkent, Uzbekistan, in a CIA cargo plane. Six days later they boarded an old Russian-made Mi-17 helicopter and were inserted into the Panjshir Valley north of Kabul. Flying into Afghanistan in a flashy Black Hawk helicopter was out of the question, because no one wanted to convey the idea that the Americans had arrived.

The CIA personnel were armed with weapons, secure satellite communications gear, GPS mapping equipment, and $10 million in boxed cash, highlighting yet another difference between the CIA and the Defense Department. The U.S. military cannot legally pay cash bribes. The CIA's men were met by guerrilla fighters from the Northern Alliance and taken to the village of Barak. There, they established the first of more than a dozen forward operating bases across Afghanistan. The first order of business was to set up secure comms with the CTC back at Langley for this intelligence-driven war.

If the Pentagon is a war machine, the CIA is an intelligence factory. "Intelligence was the foundation of everything we did," says Crumpton. "We were producing intelligence and we were also a consumer of the intelligence we were producing," he explains. "We could be much more productive that way." The paramilitary teams were on the ground to forge a partnership with Afghan allies and to fight with them, but their ultimate goal was to gather intelligence. "Think of everything you can learn from the pocket litter on a dead Al-Qaeda leader," Crumpton adds.

In the field, Schroen and the paramilitary teams started learning as much as they could about Al-Qaeda and Taliban leadership from local fighters on the ground. "Our Afghan allies described the enemy positions in sharp detail," says Crumpton. "They even knew Taliban commanders by name and sometimes communicated with them. They routinely ran recon teams across [enemy] lines," to learn more. Human identity was at the center of the hunt—potential targets for the CIA's kill-or-capture list. The CIA could not identify these men on its own, because the leaders of terrorist organizations are masters of disguise. Think of Carlos the Jackal, how he was able to live on the run for nearly twenty years, or Imad Mugniyah, the most wanted man in the world until Osama bin Laden took his place.

With the president's Memorandum of Notification in place, the

Special Activities Division would transform how terrorists would be identified, located, and captured, or killed. Technology would be leveraged, and the concept of targeting would undergo a revolution. For that, the CIA would build a new tool called the Magic Box.

In the fall of 2001, Ken Stiles had been working as an overt CIA officer for seventeen years, meaning that he did not have to hide the fact that he worked for the CIA. A geospatial and imagery analyst by training, Stiles was one of those people who could see things in satellite images others didn't know were there. What might look like a black spot to most people, Stiles could identify as the entrance to an underground weapons facility. He was excellent at what he did and never intended to have another job, he explained, in a 2018 interview for this book.

"On October 1, I received a phone call from a person who identified himself as 'Dan' wanting to talk to me," remembers Stiles. "I was taken down to the basement in new headquarters, into this cramped, windowless space filled with computers, copiers, briefing binders, books, maps, and communications gear. I was told, 'Hank Crumpton needs a map.' And not just any map. What Crumpton wanted was a complex, three-dimensional image system," that could accurately represent the battle space in Afghanistan, in real time. In 2019 this is easy to imagine, not that different from a GPS system fused with a video game like *Fortnite*. In 2001, it was groundbreaking.

This map would incorporate layers of information—data on everything from geography to anthropology. From the location of schools and mosques to terrorist training camps and caves. "I was confident I could build it," says Stiles. "I said, 'What Crumpton is looking for is called a geographic information system, GIS.'" At the time, the software already existed in the public domain.

Someone handed Ken Stiles a Post-it note with a telephone number written on one side. "They told me to go give it to my boss, and come right back. Tell the boss I worked for the Counterterrorist

Center, now." Ken Stiles's life would never be the same. In an instant, he went from being a GIS analyst at a desk to being the man responsible for building the CIA's roadmap for its targeted killing program. At the time, he had no idea that one day he'd deploy into the battlefield, wear a flak jacket, carry a 9mm Glock and an M4, ride in a Black Hawk helicopter with a team of paramilitary operators and their Black SOF partners from Delta Force. For now, he was the head nerd working overtime in the basement at the CIA.

By that afternoon Ken Stiles began building CIA's three-dimensional targeting map. One of the first layers of intelligence entered into the system came from hand-drawn battle maps created by Russian Army cartographers after the Soviet invasion of Afghanistan in 1979. "The information was still highly accurate," remembers Stiles. "There hadn't exactly been a construction boom since the Soviets' withdrawal." The CIA invited its National Security Agency partner to Langley to add a layer of signals intelligence into the system, things like the location of cell phone and fax intercepts. The same went for the National Geospatial-Intelligence Agency, whose technicians added satellite imagery. "The combination of layers ran into the scores," remembers Crumpton. "Eventually Ken and his team could calculate and display hundreds of combinations." This new system "enabled a new perspective [on] war for the CIA, military and policy makers," Crumpton later explained.

In Afghanistan, Gary Schroen's team worked with Afghan warlords and rebel armies to send human intelligence back to Langley to be inputted into the system. This included data like locations of existing minefields and Al-Qaeda safe houses, as described by Afghan sources. Now, with the stroke of a computer key, the CTC staff could see these locations. And CIA paramilitary operators could better understand the physical environment from a geospatial point of view. But there were technical difficulties in the field, and the CTC decided to have Ken Stiles personally train one member of each team, usually the communications officer, on how to input data into the system before they deployed. Which is how a Green Beret named Nathan Ross Chapman wound up on a CIA paramilitary team.

"I trained him for a week," remembers Stiles. "We became friends. We shared a passion for hunting and shooting, so we were alike in that way. Nate was very smart and the kind of person who always did an excellent job." A quiet professional with a host of warfighting skills including combat scuba diver, sniper, and parachutist. After a week of working with Ken Stiles in the basement at CIA, Nate Chapman left to be part of a team deployed into Khost, Afghanistan. With the geographic information system up and working, Stiles briefed CIA director Tenet, who briefed President Bush. The system was so impressive, the White House started calling it the Magic Box.

The Counterterrorist Center was growing at a furious pace. By late fall 2001, there were over two thousand CTC employees. The Office of Terrorism Analysis expanded from twenty-five people to more than three hundred. Operations were being driven 24/7 from inside the CIA's Global Response Center, located on the sixth floor of the original headquarters building. The center shared a secure direct line to the Defense Department's Joint Intelligence Operations Center at Central Command, in Tampa, Florida. In Afghanistan, the action on the ground was about to shift gears as the war moved from covert to overt. The CIA's paramilitary teams would now be augmented with special operations forces from the military, mostly Green Berets and Delta Force. And the Pentagon would begin its bombing campaign.

Shortly after midnight on October 7, 2001, fifteen U.S. Air Force bombers, twenty-five strike aircraft, and an unspecified number of U.S. and British ships and submarines fired more than fifty Tomahawk missiles against terrorist targets across Afghanistan. In a press conference, the Defense Department identified the targets hit as the Taliban's defense ministry, its command centers, air defense installations, airfields, electrical grids, and other energy production facilities. The hybrid war—part covert action, part conventional warfare—had begun.

Upstairs at Langley, on the seventh floor, Cofer Black returned from a meeting at the White House to find Billy Waugh in front of his office, stretched out on a cheap folding chair. "The kind you take to the beach," Black recalled in 2017. More CIA paramilitary teams were being put together for Afghanistan, and Waugh had not been chosen for any of them, which infuriated him. Black refused to assign him a spot on a team; Waugh's protest was the beach chair setup. Cofer Black was annoyed. "There was a war going on. I had two secretaries running around. All kinds of people were coming to see me, and every goddamn one of them had to step around Billy Waugh in that cheap folding chair."

Cofer Black went into his office and slammed the door. The demands on him were staggering. He also had Billy Waugh on his mind. It was Waugh's dogged insistence, his never-give-up ferocity in the field, that had helped him achieve so many hidden-hand wins for the CIA, the kind only a handful of people would ever know about. Big victories in places where a less determined operator would have likely been captured, compromised, or killed. Cofer Black thought about how, on numerous occasions, he had directly bene-fited from Waugh's wins. This included the Carlos the Jackal recon-naissance operation and capture—whose success is often attributed to Black.

"Billy leaned his head in my office again and said, 'Goddamnit, Crusader, get me in on this war.' This time I said, 'Fine. Get the hell out of here. Go to Kabul.'"

Four days before Thanksgiving, Billy Waugh departed for Afghan-istan by way of United Arab Emirates. Waiting on the tarmac there was a C-54 piloted by someone Waugh recognized immediately.

"An old clandestine operator who flew covert missions for SOG, in Vietnam and Laos," forty years before. "It is a small, small world," says Waugh. He boarded the aircraft and, together with a half-dozen operators and officers from the CIA's Special Activities Division and its Near East Division, flew to the newly captured Bagram Airfield, outside Kabul.

The tarmac was littered with rusting Soviet-era aircraft. The windowless air traffic control tower was pockmarked with bullet holes, the perimeter of the airfield ringed with unexploded antitank mines. With him, Billy Waugh carried an M4 carbine, an AK-47 assault rifle, a Heckler & Koch 40mm grenade launcher, and a suitcase with $6 million in cash. He was going to war and he was about to turn seventy-two years old.

CHAPTER TWENTY-THREE

Poke the Bear

Billy Waugh made his way the sixty kilometers from Bagram Airfield to the CIA facility in Kabul, which was located inside the Ariana Hotel on Silo Road. The square outside the Ariana was infamous: it was where the Taliban in 1996 had beaten and castrated the last communist president, Mohammad Najibullah, before laying siege to the city and taking control. After tying Najibullah to the back of a pickup truck and dragging his body through Kabul, they had suspended his body from a pole outside the hotel to demonstrate that a new era of Islamic piousness had begun. Najibullah's brother was executed in the same way. For the next five years, Taliban commander Mullah Dadullah conducted public hangings of people deemed "would-be assassins" here. Billy Waugh crossed the square and went into the Ariana Hotel. While checking in, he learned from the clerk that the Taliban's top warlords had taken over the hotel the year of Najibullah's death and lived here right up until their exodus from Kabul two weeks ago. Before the CIA was allowed to move in, it was required to pay the Taliban's overdue hotel bill.

In November 2001, the guests at the Ariana were a sight to behold. The place was filled with Special Activities Division and special operations forces personnel. If you were here, you were the best in your field: Delta Force, Green Berets, U.S. Army Rangers,

Navy SEALs, Air Force Combat Control Teams, Air Force Pararescue, Marine Force Recon, and others. The few who weren't unconventional warfighters were Olympic-level performers in their particular field, be it language, anthropology, signals intelligence, or spycraft. Waugh settled in and did what he always did in a hostile environment, where survival depended on knowing the lay of the land and how to escape if cornered. He went out for a jog. This proved fortuitous when a group of special operations forces arrived to join the CIA paramilitary teams, mistakenly dressed in military fatigues. Waugh knew the route to the local bazaar, where the soldiers were able to buy woolen shawls, caps, and shalwar kameez to blend in with the Afghan partners they'd be fighting alongside.

The Pentagon's original plan for Afghanistan was to put 300,000 infantry troops on the ground, young American soldiers, the majority of whom had never seen combat before. Instead, the CIA sent 115 veteran Special Activities Division officers and operators to lead the charge, augmented by what would total around 2,000 special operations forces. Each team consisted of eight or nine men: a team chief, a deputy chief, an operations officer, someone with local language skills, a paramilitary officer, a communications expert, a medic, and one or two tactical weapons experts. Each unit was made up of eight to twelve men, mostly Green Berets and Delta Force. Attached to each team was an air force combat controller to call in tactical air strikes.

The CIA teams spread out across the country. Schroen's team had been leading the ground war up north alongside General Abdul Rashid Dostum, a warlord of questionable repute. Team Alpha had already been made famous for riding into battle on horseback, something American soldiers had not done since World War I. Team Bravo deployed into Mazar-e-Sharif up north. Team Charlie was assigned to central western Afghanistan, to link up with warlord Ismail Khan and fight all the way to the Iranian border. Team Delta was in Bamyan Province to fight alongside a Hazara tribe, Shia

Muslims who claimed ancestry with Genghis Khan. Team Echo was led by Greg Vogle, considered by many to be one of the most competent paramilitary fighters in SAD. Echo was tasked with securing the Taliban stronghold of Kandahar and fighting alongside a guerrilla force assembled by Hamid Karzai, the soon-to-be future president of Afghanistan. Team Foxtrot, led by Duane Evans, went south to occupy Takhteh-Pol. Team Hotel was in charge of securing Afghanistan's porous eastern border with Pakistan. Team Romeo, Waugh's team, would insert into Logar Province. Team Juliet would fight Al-Qaeda in Tora Bora, the place from which bin Laden got away.

After three days in Kabul there was already bad news, including a Taliban prisoner uprising up north that occurred during a covert operation near Mazar-e-Sharif. In preparing for a covert war, the CIA had overlooked the issue of what to do with POWs captured on the battlefield. Agency lawyers neglected to create a postcapture writ. In the fog of war, each paramilitary team's default position was to turn the captured Taliban fighters over to their Afghan allies, in this case to the warlord General Dostum.

The move proved deadly. Declassified State Department intelligence reports reveal that General Dostum ordered his men to herd the surrendered Taliban into metal shipping containers, without ventilation or water, then close and lock the doors. While waiting to be trucked to a prison facility, 1,500 Taliban POWs suffocated to death. Those who tried to escape were shot by Dostum's men. The bodies were buried in a mass grave under a stretch of desert outside Shibarghan. Photographs were included in the State Department report.

Roughly one hundred captured Taliban prisoners lived, American John Walker Lindh among them. General Dostum transported these prisoners to a medieval fortress called Qala-i-Jangi, outside Mazar-e-Sharif. Dostum's men failed to search the surrendered men for weapons and instead herded them into the basement of the citadel. When CIA paramilitary operations officer John "Mike" Spann went inside to gather intel, he was ambushed, shot, and killed. A second CIA paramilitary officer identified as David fought his way outside, where he met a German film crew, who lent him a satellite phone to call the CIA. The Qala-i-Jangi prison uprising became an international news story, Spann being the first CIA officer to die in the war. His death marked the moment that the CIA's paramilitary presence in Afghanistan became known publicly.

The following week, Waugh and Team Romeo were inserted into Logar Province, southeast of Kabul. Logar was a Taliban stronghold and Al-Qaeda safe haven. There was a cave complex in the mountains that served as sleeping quarters for Al-Qaeda, and where four of the 9/11 hijackers trained. The team's helicopter was met by a Special Forces unit led by Colonel John Mulholland, commander of the 5th Special Forces Group. They set up camp in an abandoned schoolhouse, alongside a fighting force of sixty heavily armed Hazaras. The cash Waugh carried was used to buy allegiance, security, and information—a similar bargain that was being struck by CIA paramilitary teams across Afghanistan.

"The foundation for the alliance was simple," Hank Crumpton insists. "The CIA wanted Al-Qaeda. Our Afghan allies wanted their country back."

Back to what? When the Taliban took over in Afghanistan in 1996, the goal of the Islamists was to put an end to the anarchy, violence, and revenge killing among warring tribes that had plagued society since the Soviet withdrawal, in 1989. The Taliban made things worse. By the time of the U.S. invasion in 2001, less than 6 percent of the country had electricity. Eighty-five percent of the population was illiterate. Infant mortality was the highest in the world. Women were routinely beaten by their husbands, boys routinely raped by older men. Afghanistan, a five-thousand-year-old civilization, was the *Mad Max* of the modern world, a dystopian nightmare. How was any of this going to work? After a few weeks in country, a Ground Branch operator, call sign Shark, remembers thinking, "No wonder Alexander the Great lost his mind here."

Nothing was simple in Afghanistan. No one person could pretend to have any idea what the Afghan definition of allegiance was. "You can never buy the loyalty of an Afghan, only rent it," a British officer of the Great Game once famously said. And who should be the rightful ruler of a country made up of a patchwork quilt of warring ethnic groups? In Logar Province, Waugh and the CIA paramilitary team met with assets, gathered intelligence, and made assessments about who and what they encountered. "I didn't trust any of them," Waugh recalls. "From the look in their eyes, I knew they'd just as easily cut my heart out as they'd offer me tea. It was whatever their warlord told them to do."

Over time, shifting allegiances would threaten every team. One of the warlords working with Schroen's team, General Fahim, demanded an outrageous sum of money, to be paid in cash every month. A warlord in Logar Province charged the CIA a fifty-dollar-a-head toll every time its operators drove down the town's only street. Guerrilla fighters working alongside Team Delta pulled guns on the team in Tora Bora, just a thousand yards from where Osama bin Laden and his Al-Qaeda commanders were hiding in a cave. One of the Delta Force operators working with the CIA team that day later told *Sixty Minutes* he was convinced that holdup allowed Osama bin Laden to vanish into Pakistan.

The CIA and the military were faced yet again with the central question of guerrilla warfare: Can the United States ever really buy loyalty from the foreign fighters it pays to arm and equip? The conundrum has plagued seasoned spies and soldiers for as long as wars have been waged. After World War II, during the Korean War, Russell Volckmann, Aaron Bank, and John Singlaub fought over this unanswerable question. And here, now, in Afghanistan, CIA paramilitary officers and operators, and their Defense Department counterparts, were facing the same conundrum yet again. Should America be fighting an unconventional war in a foreign land in the first place—after so many grave missteps and failures in Vietnam? Or was the president's third option, these hidden-hand operations, going to be a wise and fruitful way forward?

When Al-Qaeda attacked the United States on 9/11, U.S. air force lieutenant general Michael Hayden had been director of the NSA for more than two years. After 9/11, he became an advocate of the find, fix, finish approach to counterterrorism. As director of the NSA, Hayden also served as chief of the NSA's Central Security Service, which was in charge of providing combat support for the Defense Department. The war on terror "was an intelligence-driven war," Hayden told colleagues. "All wars are, of course, but this one especially." A career soldier, he had spent much of his professional life fighting the Cold War. "The enemy was pretty easy to find" when the Soviets were the enemy, he says, meaning Russian tank armies and Soviet intercontinental ballistic missile fields in Siberia were visible in satellite imagery. "Just hard to kill," he adds. In this new war against terrorists, the calculus had been inverted. "This [war] was different," Hayden said. "This enemy was relatively easy to kill. He was just very, very hard to find." Hayden and his intelligence community partners were determined to change that.

One night in the fall of 2001, Michael Hayden recalls having dinner with U.S. air force lieutenant general Charles Holland, the commander of Special Operations Command (SOCOM), at Holland's home. The two men had known each other for years. That night, over dessert, they discussed the central problem facing the CIA and Special Forces direct-action teams in Afghanistan. That the enemy was proving impossible to find, let alone fix and finish. The CIA had killed Al-Qaeda military chief Mohammad Atef, but Hayden pointed out that there had been no significant kills since.

Holland dropped his fist on the table. "I need actionable intelligence!" he said. The reason Al-Qaeda leadership wasn't being killed or captured en masse was an intelligence problem, not a combat one, according to Holland.

The way Hayden recalls the story, in this moment he was finally able to convey to SOCOM Commander Charlie Holland what he believed was the way to win an unconventional war. The concept was as old as hunting, killing, and spying, Hayden said. It involved the act of provocation.

"Let me give you another way of thinking about this," Hayden proposed. "You give me a little action and I'll give you a lot more intelligence."

In other words, Hayden explained, "We need operational moves to poke at the enemy, make him move and communicate, so we [can] learn more about him." U.S. special operations forces and CIA Special Activities Division teams needed to aggressively poke the bear.

A six-year veteran of Ground Branch explained it this way: "You work with a bad guy and let him think you think he's a good guy. Doesn't matter. He'll go home and make contact with another bad guy, who will make contact with another bad guy, going right up the chain of command." The reason this system works, they both say, is because the NSA can listen in. "To everything, everywhere," says a third Ground Branch operator, a former team leader. "We'd put ears on a person," he says, referring in a general way to the classified technique that allows the NSA to pull electronic data from an enemy fighter's cell phone and other electronic devices, and from his land line and fax machine. "The goal would evolve—to get the actionable intelligence to send a Ground Branch team in."

Often it worked well—as in the case of Taliban intelligence chief Qari Amadullah in December 2001. Through Afghan intermediaries, the CIA's Team Delta got a message to Amadullah. Much to the CIA's surprise, Amadullah said that he wanted to broker a deal for himself in exchange for information on several top Al-Qaeda leaders. But the NSA had listened in on him for months and told its CIA partners that it suspected the man could not be trusted. Tony, the deputy team leader of the CIA team, was told to set up a meeting.

In 2001 it was dangerous to meet with anyone in Ghazni Province, Al-Qaeda-controlled territory. The team headed in, first by vehicle and then on foot. The CIA's two Predator drones were each assigned missions elsewhere in Afghanistan, which meant that the CTC did not have eyes on the target; nor did the paramilitary operators have air support. As happens with many Special Activities Division missions, the team was on its own.

Qari Amadullah did not show up at the safe house, as agreed. Instead, he sent a subordinate. When the team arrived, the room was filled with hostile Taliban fighters. Weapons were drawn. On Tony's signal, the team overpowered the Taliban fighters. The men were flex-cuffed, bound, and left on the dirt floor. The emissary for the Taliban's intelligence chief was rolled up into a large Afghan carpet, carried out of the house this way, taken down the mountainside, and loaded into a Ground Branch vehicle.

"Within twenty-four hours of his capture, the Taliban prisoner revealed Al-Qaeda and Taliban command posts and other positions along the Pakistan border," says Hank Crumpton.

Based on this new information, the CIA moved its Predator drone into position over new targets obtained from the source. The building was larger than could be eliminated by the Predator's Hellfire missiles, so the CIA asked the Defense Department for an air strike, turning the enemy compound into piles of rubble and rock. At the CTC, Hank Crumpton recalls watching the operation through the viewfinder of the Predator drone, hovering 25,000 feet above the target site. After the dust from the air strike cleared, says Crumpton, "The Predator picked up one individual fleeing on foot. He made it to a motorbike and tried to escape. He did not get far. He disappeared in a fiery blast." Intelligence later confirmed that the man trying to flee on the bike was Qari Amadullah. "He should have taken our offer," Crumpton says.

The pairing of technology and human intelligence did not always work in sync, and sometimes the results were deadly. On December 5, 2001, near Shah Wali Kot, outside Kandahar, Team Echo was inputting bombing coordinates into the geographic information system when the operator's batteries went dead. In changing them, he didn't realize he was erasing the enemy coordinates he had just loaded into the system, replacing those bombing coordinates with his own current location as the system rebooted. A B-52 Stratofortress bomber flew into the battle space and dropped a 2,000-pound bomb on Team Echo. Captain Jason Amerine, a Green Beret attached to the team, was studying a map on a nearby hill when the bomb hit. Amerine was wounded. Killed in the debacle were twenty-seven Afghan soldiers and three Green Berets: Master Sergeant Jefferson Davis, Sergeant First Class Dan Petithory, and Staff Sergeant Brian Prosser.

When the bomb hit, team leader Greg Vogle was talking with a tribal leader named Hamid Karzai in a building nearby. As the room exploded, Vogle threw his body over Karzai's body, likely saving his life. The dust settled, and Vogle's satellite phone rang. It was a United Nations delegation calling from Bonn, Germany—asking to speak with Hamid Karzai. There was news regarding the Bonn Agreement, the international agreement on Afghanistan, the caller said. Hamid Karzai had just been named the head of state of Afghanistan. It was official: the Taliban regime had been overthrown. The CIA's hybrid war was being hailed as a success.

In the last days of December 2001, Team Hotel was infiltrated into Khost Province, along the porous border with Pakistan. The operators came in on a Russian-made Mi-17 belonging to the CIA. On board was Nate Chapman, the Green Beret communications expert who'd been trained by Ken Stiles, in the basement of the CIA, on how to collect intel and input the data into the geographic information system. After flying ninety miles from Bagram Airfield outside Kabul, the team would recon the area, set up a forward operating base, and secure the old airfield here in Khost, abandoned by the Soviets ten years before.

Located twenty-five miles from the Pakistan border, Khost had served as the epicenter of Osama bin Laden's terrorist planning and operations for years. With its plunging valleys, mile-high mountains, and warren of sandstone caves, Khost was a garrison town and a guerrilla army's dream. When the Soviets tried, and failed, to rule Afghanistan, they are said to have fired every weapon in their arsenal at Khost, except for a nuclear bomb. In August 1998, after bin Laden bombed the two U.S. embassies in East Africa, President Clinton hit Khost with dozens of Tomahawk cruise missiles. This effort aimed to kill bin Laden without looking like it was trying to kill him. The strike cost U.S. taxpayers tens of millions of dollars.

Now Nate Chapman was part of a CIA paramilitary team here in Khost, on a covert operation to gather intelligence on enemy fighters in the area—to input data into the geographic information system that would help build up the CIA's kill-or-capture list. On the morning of January 4, 2002, at a meeting with regional warlords already being handsomely paid by the CIA, things went dangerously awry. Shortly after the team arrived, there was a heated argument. Guns were drawn and then set aside, recalls team member Scott Satterlee, in an interview for this book. Then came the tea. Finally, amiable terms were agreed upon. After more tea and more talk, the team was able to get what it had come for: information from the tribe. The warlords identified a building on the outskirts of town as being an Al-Qaeda safe house. Local Afghans, armed with weapons and knowledge about the location, agreed to be hired to take the CIA paramilitary team to this target.

The operators climbed into four Toyota pickup trucks and

headed out of town, down a single-lane dirt road. As was the case all over Afghanistan, the road that got you in was the same road you needed to travel on to get out. In this four-vehicle convoy, Nate Chapman had been assigned a spot in the last pickup truck. It was harsh winter weather, and the road was mostly frozen mud. The first three trucks moved quickly down the muddy, rutted road, but the fourth truck, the one carrying Chapman, got stuck.

Nate Chapman was sitting in the back of the flatbed truck, fiddling with the antenna on his satellite comms, when bullets struck. From roughly thirty feet away, three men with AK-47s had opened fire from a grove of trees. One of the paramilitary officers in the vehicle took a bullet to the chest, but fortunately he was wearing body armor, which protected him from being killed. Nate Chapman was struck by a bullet in the pelvis, severing his femoral artery. Bleeding heavily, Chapman fired back until the magazine on his M4 carbine was empty. Then he passed out from loss of blood.

The team's Afghan driver raced back to the schoolhouse while the operators worked hard to keep Nate Chapman alive. Everyone knew that the Air Branch helicopter was on its way down from Kabul, but the flight took forty-five minutes, and by the time the helicopter landed in the wheat field outside the old Russian schoolhouse, Nate Chapman was dead. Because the mission was a classified covert-action operation, Chapman would not be officially identified for another thirteen years as having worked for the CIA.

Over in Logar Province, Billy Waugh's tour of duty in Afghanistan was coming to an end. His last order was to travel to the CIA base in Kabul and pack up Nate Chapman's things.

"He was a young soldier," recalls Waugh. "A Green Beret, tasked to the Agency, just like me." Packing up the belongings of a young man killed in battle was something Billy Waugh had done countless times, across fifty years of covert-action operations and war. "Some people die, others do not," Waugh reflects. "There's no explanation for any of this. Never has been, never will be."

The classified CIA forward operating base at Khost was named FOB Chapman, in honor of Nate Chapman. In eight years' time, this otherwise secret facility would become known to the world. In December 2009, FOB Chapman was the scene of the deadliest attack against CIA employees since Imad Mugniyah planned and executed the truck bombing of the U.S. embassy in Beirut in 1983. At Khost, an Al-Qaeda suicide bomber wearing an explosives-laden vest, and erroneously believed to be a spy working for the CIA, would kill seven CIA officers and contract personnel, including the chief of base and the base security chief. A Jordanian intelligence officer and an Afghan security chief were also killed in the blast.

But it was January 2002, and this hybrid war in Afghanistan was just getting started. Just hours after Nate Chapman was killed in Khost, at CIA headquarters in Langley, Ken Stiles was told to pack a bag. He was being sent to Afghanistan to set up a geographic information system for the CIA station chief in Kabul, part of an expanding new effort called "targeting." The CIA was doubling down on its plans to kill or capture Al-Qaeda and Taliban leaders. Targeting would become the new way forward, the practice of identifying an individual for placement on the kill-or-capture list. From there, the goal was to find that person, secure his location, and kill him— either with a Predator drone or a Ground Branch team.

Three hundred analysts, called "targeters," were now working at the CTC, leveraging information in the geographic information system, then pushing targeting packages back out to CIA paramilitary teams. "[Targeters] spend all their time looking at one target, [a terrorist] with one name," explains Phil Mudd, deputy director of the CTC from 2003 to 2005. "Their whole goal in life [was] following one human being," tracking that person until he is captured or dead.

"Everything was happening so fast," says Ken Stiles of this time at the CIA. Before September 11, he spent his days behind a desk at Langley, providing geospatial analysis for CIA reports and briefings.

Here he was now, just four months later, heading into the war theater. In Afghanistan, he remembers walking down the hallway at a classified facility in Kabul, just moments after arriving, when he spotted something that took his breath away. "Nate Chapman's belongings," he recalls. "His personal effects there on the floor, packed up in a pile." These were the last things Chapman carried before he was killed. Now they were being sent home with his body, to a grieving wife and two fatherless children, ages one and two years old.

The Special Activities Division had begun its transformation from the small secret strike force at the CIA to a paramilitary army of such profound significance it would soon move into its own center, at CIA headquarters in Virginia. Under Title 50 authority, the Special Activities Center would begin using its Ground Branch arm to run covert-action operations not just in Afghanistan but around the world. First there would be another war.

CHAPTER TWENTY-FOUR

War in Iraq

I t was the fall of 2002, a year after 9/11, and the Pentagon was secretly preparing to go to war in Iraq. The CIA was assigned a more traditional role in the lead-up to this war: to prepare the battlefield with hidden-hand operations including sabotage, subversion, and assassination, OSS-style.

An unmarked aircraft filled with eighty anti-Saddam guerrilla fighters from Iraq crossed into Nevada airspace and made its way toward a classified facility within the Nevada Test Site, a secret test and training facility known as Area 51. This newly created foreign paramilitary force, code-named the Scorpions, was commanded by General Mohammad Abdullah al-Shahwani, exiled arch-nemesis of Iraqi president Saddam Hussein. The aircraft curtains were closed on approach so no one inside the airplane could identify the training facility or leak information. Plausible deniability was essential; Americans had no idea the White House was laying plans for another war.

The Scorpion guerrilla warfare corps was one element of a CIA covert-action operation code-named DB/Anabasis. DB was the Agency's cryptonym for Iraq. Anabasis referred to the soldier-historian Xenophon's epic masterpiece *Anabasis,* the story of an army of Greek mercenaries who tried to seize the Persian throne around 401 BC but failed. "One of the great adventures in human history," remarked historian Will Durant of the effort. The planners of DB/Anabasis had equally high hopes for their program, which presaged one of the most egregious wrongs in American military history. The two men in charge of the program were Luis Rueda, chief of Iraq operations, and John Maguire, deputy chief.

"I know Iraq," said Maguire, in a 2018 interview for this book. He had run operations in the country since 1991. "I still have a home in Baghdad, which I visit." The pair brought range and experience to the table. Rueda, a Cuban American, came from a family of free-dom fighters and spies. His father was a member of Brigade 2506, which stormed the beach at the Bay of Pigs. Enamored with para-military operations since childhood, Luis Rueda joined the CIA after college and spent years working covert operations in Latin America and the Middle East. He'd served as chief of station in Delhi, India, and was now a member of the elite Senior Intelligence Service. From his office on the seventh floor at Langley, Rueda would oversee DB/Anabasis plans. The fieldwork would be handled by Maguire, a legendary paramilitary operations officer whose areas of expertise included explosives and sabotage.

Maguire was old-school and proud of it, trained in the Director-ate of Operations under Bill Casey. "Bush wanted an Iraqi version of the OSS Jedburghs," says Maguire. "He was already thinking about this when I was called back to Washington on September twelfth." Maguire believed in the effectiveness of OSS Special Operations Branch–style operations, he says. He discussed this in a meeting at the White House during the first week after the 9/11 attacks.

Maguire saw counterterrorism operations through a historical lens. "I worked on the issue even before there was a Counterterrorist Center" at the CIA, he remembers, including when Bill Casey, taking a page from Mossad's book, drafted the original plan to train Leba-nese hit squads to eliminate Hezbollah terrorists. "Casey's thinking was way ahead of his time," Maguire insists. With President Bush's signature on the September 17 Memorandum of Notification, "the CIA got what Bill Casey envisioned two decades before," he adds.

In 2002, the concept of using kill-or-capture missions as a primary means of combating terrorism was in its first official year. How to use a rebel army of foreign fighters to augment these lethal direct-action operations gave way to the Scorpions, the first of many war-on-terror partnerships to come. But out at Area 51, problems with these Iraqi émigrés began almost immediately. The unit was supposed to be made up of elite commandos, many of whom claimed to have previously worked for Saddam Hussein's paramilitary army, the Fedayeen Saddam (Saddam's Men of Sacrifice), before defecting. But one of the U.S. paramilitary operators assigned to train these Iraqi nationals complained to headquarters that an unusual number of the Scorpion fighters appeared to lack even the most basic military skills. John Maguire acknowledged the concern but was not worried, he says. The Scorpions' commander, General Mohammad Abdullah al-Shahwani, was a longtime trusted ally of the CIA.

General Shahwani had a complex backstory. In 1984, during Iraq's war with Iran, Shahwani led a successful helicopter attack against an Iranian stronghold in northern Iraq, elevating him to national hero status. But this popularity was a curse, causing the paranoid and jealous Saddam Hussein to view the general as a threat. Shahwani was arrested and jailed on suspicion of plotting a coup. He was questioned and released without charge, but the experience led him to defect to England, where he began working with the CIA. With Agency backing, Shahwani plotted another coup, this time from outside the country. Before the coup happened, he was betrayed as a co-conspirator. In revenge, Saddam's Mukhabarat rounded up eighty-five men suspected of working with General Shahwani and executed them. Shahwani's three sons, all still living in Iraq, were arrested and tortured to death. "I fight to avenge my sons," Shahwani told *Time* magazine in 2004. "I [will do] whatever is required."

Out in the Nevada desert in the fall of 2002, General Shahwani's

Scorpions were trained in unconventional warfare, ambush, hit-and-run operations, and helicopter insertion. They learned how to use explosives to blow up railway lines and power plants inside Iraq. They trained in close-quarters combat and long-range sniper assassination. "Were they good soldiers?" a paramilitary operator who worked with the Scorpions asked rhetorically, in an interview for this book. "No comment. Were they wild? Yes. Very wild," he says. "But General Moe [Mohammad Shahwani] was in charge of them. He kept them in control."

To understand how the general's paramilitary unit came to be, it's necessary to back up to February 16, 2002, just five months after the 9/11 terrorist attacks. President Bush signed a Presidential Finding authorizing DB/Anabasis in Iraq. The CIA's lawyers were concerned that Title 50 operations in Iraq would not be covered under the September 17 Memorandum of Notification, because no link between Saddam Hussein's Iraq and Osama bin Laden's Al-Qaeda had been found. The Presidential Finding was to grant the CIA the authority to make certain a rebel fighting force was in place when the war the White House was now planning came to pass.

An argument over which rebel group inside Iraq was best suited to work on DB/Anabasis ensued. Some people within the Iraq operations group believed that the most competent and loyal anti-Saddam fighters were the Peshmerga, a guerrilla army of Kurdish fighters from northern Iraq. The Peshmerga had been oppressed by Saddam Hussein's Ba'ath Party for decades. In 1988, Iraq's military used mustard gas and nerve agents, including sarin and VX, on Kurdish civilians living in Halabja, killing 5,000 people in the largest chemical weapons attack in history. But the Peshmerga, whose name translates as "those who face death," had their own internecine problems and were presently divided into two rival groups. In April 2002, John Maguire flew to Iraqi Kurdistan to meet separately with the regional Kurdish leaders of these groups: Massoud Barzani, president of the Kurdish Democratic Party, and Jalal Talabani, president of the Patriotic Union of Kurdistan.

"Barzani and Talabani were very skeptical of what we had planned," remembers Maguire. "They'd heard this kind of proposal from us before. I told them, 'This time, it's for real.'" After listening to Maguire's briefing on operations being planned under DB/Anabasis, Barzani and Talabani each expressed wariness. The efforts would be threefold, said Maguire: locate assets inside Saddam Hussein's regime who could be turned; sabotage existing Iraqi infrastructure; and assassinate Mukhabarat officials. There was risk involved, he added. The hit-and-run operations against the Mukhabarat would almost certainly result in retaliatory attacks. Rivals Barzani and Talabani agreed to set aside their differences and work with the CIA to fight their common enemy, Saddam Hussein.

Before leaving Iraqi Kurdistan, Maguire asked to be taken in behind enemy lines. He wanted to observe an Iraqi military base for himself, he says. If Maguire were captured, he'd likely be executed on the spot, or put on trial for being the spy that he was. As a disguise, Maguire's Peshmerga hosts outfitted him in the stolen uniform of an Iraqi Army colonel, complete with red stripes on the shoulders. In a car favored by Iraqi colonels—a four-door Toyota sedan, like an American police cruiser—the Peshmerga took Maguire to the outskirts of an Iraqi Army base, where he observed through binoculars soldiers keeping guard. "They were sitting around in shorts and flip-flops," Maguire recalls. "I was looking at the Iraqi V Corps, and they looked entirely unprepared for war." Mission accomplished, Maguire headed back to Langley.

Upon his return, Vice President Cheney requested a personal briefing on DB/Anabasis. The meeting took place in a conference room on the seventh floor of CIA headquarters. Rueda and Maguire shared with the vice president their plans for covert-action operations in Iraq.

"Cheney asked many questions," recalls Maguire. "There was a lot of back-and-forth. We answered his questions, he listened, then asked more questions. He was interested in...who we were working with. We said the Kurds. He wanted to know specifics. He was very involved."

There was another problem that needed to be addressed, an issue Maguire insists he'd brought up the last time he'd briefed the vice president. "Four days after 9/11," says Maguire. The meeting had been at the White House. "The issue was Iran. Iran, Iraq, Syria. The three were tied, we said. If you pull one brick out, the whole region could collapse. We tried building this into our thinking. Iran, Syria, Iraq."

Maguire was not alone in his assessment. In Israel, Mossad had been tracking a devil's bargain made recently between Syria and Iran involving Hezbollah, Iran's guerrilla army corps. For decades, Syrian president Hafez al-Assad had allowed the Iranians to fly weapons into Damascus, then disperse them to Hezbollah terrorists in the region via trucks. In exchange for passage, President Assad received cash and anonymity, meaning Syria's involvement remained hidden. In 2000 he died, and his son Bashar became the new president of Syria and renegotiated with Iran the terms of the secret bargain with Hezbollah.

According to Mossad, a year and a half into his presidency, in early 2002, Bashar al-Assad struck a new deal with the Iranians. "Assad opened his own army's armories to Hezbollah, providing the organization with modern Russian weaponry that even Iran lacked," explains Ronen Bergman. Iran, Hezbollah, and Syria had formed an alliance that posed an existential threat to Israel. Mossad called this triumvirate the Radical Front. Maguire says he told Vice President Cheney that if Iraq were to become destabilized, the Radical Front could take advantage of this weakness, move its hidden-hand forces into Iraq, and take ground.

Cheney did not need to be convinced of Iran's intent to harm the West. In a speech at the Nixon Library two months before, he had called Iran "a leading exporter of terror." But during the DB/Anabasis briefing at the CIA, Maguire says the potential for Iran to meddle in a weakened Iraq was not further discussed, that "Cheney was focused on Iraq." The briefing ended. The vice president expressed his approval for the CIA's covert-action operations with the Peshmerga. "He told us, 'You have my full support,'" says Maguire.

Maguire returned to his office. He picked up the telephone and spoke to a veteran officer from the Near East Division named Charles "Sam" Faddis, giving Faddis the go-ahead to lead covert operations inside northern Iraq. Faddis had three months to prepare.

Sam Faddis had been a clandestine case officer at the CIA since 1988. He spoke fluent Turkish and conversational Arabic, had a degree in political science, and was also trained as a military lawyer with the Judge Advocate General's Corps, or JAG. In the months since 9/11, Faddis had been working clandestine operations in Pakistan, along its lawless frontier border with Afghanistan. Now he would be leading a CIA paramilitary team into Iraqi Kurdistan to work with Peshmerga rebels.

Orders in hand, Faddis put together the most experienced spies, soldiers, and combat veterans he could find, experts in reconnaissance, surveillance, covert operations, and warfare. Among them they spoke Arabic, Turkish, Farsi, and Kurdish. Two had served in Afghanistan, fighting in Kabul and Tora Bora. One had been at the Qala-i-Jangi prisoner uprising and fought alongside Mike Spann. In northern Iraq, the plan was for the teams to eventually be augmented with operators from Delta Force, Green Berets, U.S. Army Rangers, and other special operations forces.

On July 7, 2002, Faddis and a CIA paramilitary team arrived in Incirlik, Turkey, where regional politics were growing increasingly complex. The Kurds had a long-standing feud with the Turks and it took several days of bargaining before the CIA team was allowed in. Once approved, they climbed into jeeps loaded with weapons and ammunition and drove 425 miles to a border crossing along the Kharbur River in northern Iraq, just north of a Kurdish village called Zakho. Once inside Iraqi Kurdistan, they were met by Peshmerga fighters who brought them to meet separately with Massoud Barzani and Jalal Talabani, as John Maguire had done three months before.

From Barzani and Talabani, the teams were briefed on a developing situation along the border with Iran. Islamist fighters aligned with Al-Qaeda had moved into the mountains there, Peshmerga leaders said. They'd set up a training camp and were running guerrilla warfare operations in a narrow set of hills that rose up from the Halabja plain. "The Peshmerga had captured dozens of these guerrilla fighters," recalls Faddis. This Islamist army, which numbered between 200 and 1,000 men, had taken over several Kurdish towns. Local villagers described brutish, Taliban-like restrictions and said the foreign fighters destroyed local Sufi shrines. The radical group called themselves Ansar al-Islam, Defenders of Islam. There were local Kurds in their ranks but mostly they were nonlocals, said to have journeyed here from Afghanistan.

There was open source information supporting these eyewitness accounts. Earlier that winter, in January 2002, the *Kurdistan Observer* reported on a document found in Kabul that called upon Sunni Kurds to "join Al-Qaeda and create a Little Tora Bora" in northern Iraq. The goal was to create a fighting force to "expel Jews and Christians from Kurdistan, join the way of jihad, [and] rule every piece of land with Islamic Sharia rule." By summer of 2002 the fighting had begun. Ansar al-Islam attacked and killed 103 Peshmerga in an ambush. They tried to assassinate a Peshmerga military commander in Sulaymaniyah, but killed his office manager and four bodyguards instead.

Faddis asked to be taken to the front lines, to view the training camps and interview captured POWs. Dressed like Peshmerga fighters and armed with Peshmerga weapons, the CIA team was taken to the lawless border region with Iran. "We got eyes on Al-Qaeda and Ansar al-Islam," recalls Faddis. "Their heavy machine-gun positions and mortar sites [were] hidden inside medieval castles" across the region. The team interrogated prisoners and determined that the fighters were Al-Qaeda who'd escaped from Afghanistan. They'd journeyed across Iran, using ancient smugglers' routes, and were rebuilding an army to fight American soldiers in the coming war in Iraq.

In the second week of August 2002, says Faddis, "we put together a plan to attack and destroy the Ansar enclave." He sent CIA headquarters a list of weapons required to arm the Peshmerga rebels. "Five hundred 120mm mortars; 2,000 Kalashnikov rifles; 50,000 7.62mm rounds," the cable read. Washington's answer shocked Faddis. "The White House decided that they would not approve us standing up a Kurdish force to fight with us against Ansar. The president had decided to place the priority on invading Iraq instead." This was a radical change of plans, he says. "The White House [now] wanted an Arab face." The rebels needed to be Iraqi Arabs, not Kurdish Peshmerga, he was told, and that General Shahwani's Iraqi Scorpions were to be his Arab face. "They were not to be used against Ansar; they were to be used against Saddam."

After finishing training in the Nevada desert, the Scorpions were flown to a second training base, in Jordan. By the time they arrived in northern Iraq, the group numbered several hundred. To Faddis, the idea of working covert operations behind enemy lines with men he had no proven relationship with seemed unwise. He discussed his concerns with a team member, call sign Doc, the medic who'd been at Qala-i-Jangi when Mike Spann was ambushed and killed. Faddis says Doc agreed that they should conduct additional vetting on their own. They would screen General Shahwani's paramilitary force individually before agreeing to work with them.

A neutral facility was chosen, inside a hotel near Shaqlawa, Iraq. Each member of the Scorpions was stripped of his weapons and interviewed. "Most of them were common criminals," according to Faddis. "No military background whatsoever. General Shahwani got paid per person he supplied to the CIA." After screening more than one hundred men, the CIA team agreed that there were just twenty-five of the Iraqi Scorpions they were willing to fight alongside. But with close-quarters combat training, Faddis says a complex new set of unforeseen problems arose.

"The Scorpions were raping each other during training," says Faddis, "which possesses its own set of problems, including medical ones. What do you do when people start committing felonies during paramilitary training, at a black site? They're committing felonies but officially they don't exist, and neither does the program." Faddis had spent more than a decade engaged in covert operations across the Near and Middle East. "Man-on-man sex is not unusual in this culture," he says. "It's not frowned upon. It occurs. The [fighters] go home to their wives, if they have them." But as the leader of the highly classified DB/Anabasis operation, being privy to rape presented Faddis with an ethical and operational conundrum. "What I was dealing with was nonconsensual sex among the fighters sent by Washington."

The ongoing rapes among the Scorpion fighters were reported to the Iraqi Operations Group at Langley. Headquarters sent veteran Special Activities Division officer Greg Vogle to Kurdistan to assess the situation. It was Greg Vogle who'd saved Hamid Karzai's life in the bombing incident in Kandahar in December 2001. Vogle went by the code name Snake. "Snake declared the Scorpions unfit for combat," according to Faddis. They were undisciplined, unskilled fighters now committing criminal acts. "He told headquarters that the Scorpions were unable to perform any of the missions they'd been trained for."

"We are going to get good men killed for no reason," Snake warned.

But the plan to use the Scorpion fighters moved forward despite protestations from the CIA paramilitary team in the field. General Shahwani was supplied with Russian Mi-17 helicopters, "millions of dollars' worth of air assets," recalls Faddis, "all painted with scorpion logos, all bright and shiny and brand-new." In *At the Center of the Storm,* his memoir, CIA director George Tenet praised the Scorpions, identifying them as an Agency-sponsored paramilitary group that "produced extraordinary successes." General Shahwani, Tenet wrote, served as "one of the U.S. government's most critical partners working against Saddam's regime." He was "a born leader with a significant following, someone who commanded the respect of everyone who worked with him." Michael Hayden, who became CIA director in 2005, also praised Shahwani in his memoir, *Playing to the Edge,* calling him "a friend" who was "clearly talented and courageous." The discrepancy in opinion between the covert-action operators on the ground and the top brass at the CIA is puzzling. According to Faddis, "Washington wanted the Iraqi Jedburgh story." What they got "was an unmitigated disaster."

As Sam Faddis focused his operations in partnership with the Peshmerga rebels, Saddam Hussein sent Mukhabarat hit squads to try to assassinate them, Faddis says. The assassins also included Islamists from Ansar al-Islam. In February 2003, CIA liaison Shawkat Hajji Mushir, a Peshmerga guerrilla commander and Patriotic Union of Kurdistan government official, was shot in the head at close range by a man posing as a peace negotiator. The Peshmerga pushed back against Ansar al-Islam, while the CIA team focused their attention on the Mukhabarat assassination teams dispatched to eliminate them.

Iraq's state-run intelligence organization was notorious for torturing and killing its enemies. Its staff numbered roughly four thousand. Like the CIA, the Mukhabarat was responsible for international intelligence collection and analysis, but it also performed paramilitary, or hidden-hand, operations inside Iraq. The unit responsible for assassinations was called Directorate 9, Secret Operations. As part of DB/Anabasis, the CIA sought to turn a Mukhabarat assassin into a Special Activities Division asset.

"On three occasions," recalls Faddis, "we set up...meetings in locations we could control and then captured [members of] Mukhabarat assassination teams." The operators found the double agent they were looking for in a lieutenant colonel who worked for the Mukhabarat office in Mosul. From this asset, the team learned that Saddam Hussein also wanted to capture an American alive, "to put him on trial in Baghdad, get CNN and BBC world coverage [and] then hang him."

The Mukhabarat officer agreed to act as a double agent in exchange for a large quantity of American cash. First, the CIA team created a scenario whereby this lieutenant colonel appeared to have succeeded in assassinating an American. They dressed one of their own in the uniform of a U.S. Army colonel, put him in a ditch on the side of a mountain road, covered him with mock blood, and photographed him as if he'd been assassinated. The asset brought the pictures to the Mukhabarat field office in Mosul. The branch chief was pleased, and forwarded the photographs on to Baghdad, to be shown to Saddam Hussein. The reply was high praise. The asset brought Faddis a memo he'd received that read, "You've killed a high-ranking American Special Forces Operations commander. Now get one alive."

The CIA paramilitary team sought to lure a Mukhabarat snatch-and-grab team to a meeting point in Erbil, where they could ambush the team. Messages were exchanged by courier. But at the last minute, the asset's branch chief in Mosul requested a cell phone call with the asset before he sent the unit to Erbil. The call was arranged, with the CIA listening in. "You could almost feel sorry for that Mukhabarat [chief] in Mosul," remembers Faddis. "You could almost hear exactly what was going on in his head...to pull this off and be a great hero" in the eyes of Saddam. "On the other hand, you could also hear that he was not an idiot." In the world of espionage and betrayal, nuance is key. The CIA interpreter listened carefully to the Arabic subtleties in the words spoken. When the call ended, the interpreter told the case officer that he believed the team's Mukhabarat asset had been made. The mission was called off. "The case officer was right," says Faddis. "We never heard from the Mukhabarat officer in Mosul again. But they heard from us. In response for all the times the Mukhabarat tried to kill us, we had a team build a satchel charge in a briefcase which [one of] our Kurdish asset[s] took into Mosul."

Faddis was referring to a World War II–era demolition device made of dynamite or C-4 plastic explosive and designed to look like a simple courier bag. The asset walked it into the Mukhabarat head-quarters in Mosul, placed it on the ground floor, and quickly left. "It blew the shit out of most of the building," remembers Faddis. "The ensuing fire destroyed the rest of the structure—burned it down to the ground."

That there was pressure from Washington, DC, to find a pretext for military action was increasingly impossible to ignore. The White House was determined to go to war in Iraq regardless of the evidence at hand. In February 2003, Secretary of State Colin Powell went before the United Nations citing information provided by DB/Anabasis that Ansar al-Islam was training terrorists in the mountains of northern Iraq. Then came the untruthful twist on the facts. "Baghdad has an agent in the most senior levels of the radical organization," Powell said, insisting that Saddam Hussein was working with Ansar al-Islam. The speech would prove disastrous for Powell, who would later call it a "blot" on his record of national service. It eventually became entwined with the false foundations upon which the Iraq war was built. This is an example of the dark side of covert action, how operations designed to remain hidden can so easily be deliberately manipulated or contrived. The construct of plausible deniability can be used by a president and his advisors to build a house of cards.

As the United States prepared to invade Iraq in 2003, the CIA paramilitary team watched Ansar al-Islam fighters who'd been holed up in the mountains pack up and move out. And on the eve of the war, they watched the Scorpion guerrilla warfare corps commit mutiny and vanish. "They simply disappeared," Faddis maintains.

In the early morning hours of March 21, sixty-four Tomahawk cruise missiles were fired against the Ansar al-Islam terrorist training camp in Iraqi Kurdistan. Paramilitary officers with the Special Activities Division, alongside Green Berets, infantry soldiers from the 10th Mountain Division, and more than 1,000 Peshmerga fighters fought a ten-hour battle with the terrorists, with orders to kill or capture anyone left alive. From the dead, the team pulled passports identifying the fighters as having answered the call to jihad from as far away as Somalia, in Africa, and Dhaka, in Bangladesh. Among the prisoners captured, six were deemed Al-Qaeda enemy combatants and sent to the U.S. prison complex at Guantanamo Bay.

The opening salvo in the Pentagon's war in Iraq began with a display of shock-and-awe force meant to paralyze Ba'ath Party infrastructure and destroy the will of Saddam Hussein's fighters — to get them to surrender. Susan Hasler, a CTC analyst and early member of Alec Station, saw the writing on the wall. "Shock and awe does not end wars on terrorism. It only creates more terrorism," she says. During the 1990s, Hasler sometimes edited the President's Daily Brief and on occasion wrote portions of Clinton's counterterrorism speeches. Uniquely familiar with covert operations against terrorist organizations, she considers hidden-hand operations to be the most effective way to combat terrorism in the modern world. Big military operations encourage more terrorism, she says. "Money starts to flow to terrorist groups. People become more radicalized. Wars on terror should be fought under the radar, as quietly as possible. But counterterrorist operations are, by their nature, not very satisfying to a frightened public." After a mass casualty attack like 9/11, the public becomes enraged and unnerved, and thinks they want revenge.

★ ★ ★

After Baghdad fell to U.S. forces, on April 9, 2003, Saddam Hussein's Mukhabarat was disbanded. The U.S.-led Multi-National Force released Order 69, establishing a charter for a new Iraqi National Intelligence Service, or INIS. CIA strongman General Shahwani, commanding general of the mutinied Scorpion paramilitary team, was ●med Iraq's new intelligence chief. Shahwani was installed in Baghdad and presented by the Pentagon to news outlets covering the war as being a "nonsectarian force [able to] recruit its officers and agents from all of Iraq's religious communities." His credentials for impartiality were listed as his being a Sunni from Mosul married to a Shiite woman, whose deputy hailed from Kurdistan.

But privately it was a different story. Revenge-based justice began to undergird the narrative: *lex talionis,* the law of retaliation, as it was called in the ancient world. From Mosul to Najaf, vengeance was the new normal, and assassination became a law enforcement tool. Muwaffak al-Rubaie, Iraq's new national-security advisor, told *Time* magazine, "[General] Al-Shahwani calls for a mix of aggressive tactics, reinstating Saddam-era Mukhabarat intelligence professionals and carefully picking fights that can be won." Newly appointed local officials began making public threats, and encouraged violence: "Be ruthless. Either they kill you or you kill them," and "With them, there can be no mercy"—the "them" being those who'd held power before. A kill-or-be-killed approach emerged. Iraq's new prime minister, Ayad Allawi, echoed the call for retaliation-based justice. "I say that we will hunt them down to give them their just punishment," Allawi said of the old regime.

One of General Shahwani's first moves as chief of the Iraqi National Intelligence Service was to create his own paramilitary units to exact revenge and assassinate former enemies. By July, *Time* reported the general had graduated "at least five classes" from the Special Tactics Unit (STU), allegedly a new national paramilitary force. In fact, its members were trained and overseen by Special Activities Division, Ground Branch, teams. In time, STU would number five thousand men. Soon thereafter, the *Washington Post*'s David Ignatius reported that Iran had entered the conflict and was engaging General Shahwani in tit-for-tat assassinations. "Shahwani's operatives discovered the Iranians had a hit list," he wrote, "drawn from an old Ministry of Defense payroll document that identified the names and home addresses of senior officers who served under the former regime. Shahwani himself was among those targeted for assassination by the Iranians."

The situation spiraled out of control. "The CIA had hoped that Shahwani's INIS could be an effective national force and a deterrent to Iranian meddling...to mount effective operations against the Iranians," the *Post* reported in a second article. But the fact that General Shahwani had recruited the chief of the anti-Iran branch of the Saddam-era Mukhabarat "made the Iranians and their Shiite allies nervous." The Radical Front—Syria, Iran, and Hezbollah—began to move fighters into the chaos that was now Iraq.

Farid al-Khazen, a Christian Lebanese lawmaker allied with Hezbollah, explains how Iran was able to step in and conduct operations in Iraq. "The big story [became] Iraq," he says of the Americans' unforeseen mistake. "In their invasion in 2003, the Americans unwittingly opened it up for the Iranians. The stakes are much higher in Iraq," he explains. In Iraq, "there is a Shiite majority, oil, the shrine cities and borders with Saudi Arabia." This was an opportunity Iran and its proxy army Hezbollah were unwilling to overlook.

Sheikh Naim Qassem, Hezbollah's deputy secretary general, acknowledged his organization's efforts to pass experience along to other Iranian-aligned forces. "Every group anywhere in the world that works as we work, with our ideas, is a win for the party," Qassem told the *New York Times*. "It is natural: All who are in accordance with us in any place in the world, that is a win for us because they are part of our axis and a win for everyone in our axis."

Sam Faddis returned to Washington. A new team of Special Activities Division officers and Ground Branch operators were inserted into Mosul. "We started getting targeted for assassination by operatives from Iran," says a Ground Branch sniper, call sign Zeus. "We had targets on our backs. These were long-range snipers. Well trained. We were told they were from Hezbollah." A rumor started to swirl. Imad Mugniyah was directing the operations himself. So untouchable and elusive was Mugniyah that his nickname was Father of Smoke.

Billy Waugh was sent to Iraq. The missions he was assigned remain classified, but photographs show him working out of Uday Hussein's former palace in Baghdad. From there, Waugh was sent on a singleton mission to the Balkans, where he received an extraordinary call.

"I was in Zagreb, Croatia," remembers Waugh, when "someone showed up and gave me a new passport," with a new identity. A new travel visa. "It was a fast, 'go-now' operation," says Waugh. "To Saudi Arabia."

In forty years of covert operations for the CIA, Waugh had worked in sixty-four countries around the globe, but never Saudi Arabia. "I didn't know who the target was," he says. He'd learn why when he got there.

Waugh landed in Riyadh. He traveled to the U.S. embassy, where the CIA station employed roughly one hundred clandestine service officers and operators. "There was a Navy SEAL who'd gathered a lot of intelligence on the target. He knew where the target lived. But the SEAL didn't want to go after the target," says Waugh.

The target needed to be photographed, not killed, but the SEAL told Waugh he was unwilling to pull out a camera and start taking pictures on a Riyadh street. He had concerns he'd be captured by Saudi intelligence. Being captured in Saudi Arabia was a fate worse than death, says Waugh. "They'd torture you. Probably lock you up and throw away the key."

When it came time to learn the identity of the target, even Waugh, a battle-hardened clandestine operator, recalls being surprised.

"The target was Imad Mugniyah," he says. Father of Smoke. A die-hard Hezbollah operative for Iran who loathed Saudi Arabia. "What the hell was Imad Mugniyah doing in Saudi Arabia?" Waugh wondered. Before 9/11, Imad Mugniyah was the most wanted man in the world. Now Billy Waugh was on a mission to do what no CIA singleton operator had been able to do in more than twenty years: get an identifiable photograph of him. Without getting killed, captured, or made to disappear.

CHAPTER TWENTY-FIVE

Imad Mugniyah

Billy Waugh gave himself twenty-four hours to get the job done and get out. The Saudi intelligence apparatus, renowned for its brutality, reported directly to the king. "Whatever Mugniyah was doing there," says Waugh, "it had to have been strictly a blackmail deal." Waugh theorized that the Saudis had something on Mugniyah that was so tarnishing of his reputation within Hezbollah that he'd become susceptible to blackmail. "What goes on at the top level is a whole bunch of dirty shit. It was our opportunity to get in on that."

To prepare to photograph Mugniyah, Waugh studied geographical intelligence and satellite images of the city and its streets. He had the target's address, and he studied the roads in and the roads out of the area. From the Navy SEAL at the embassy whose operation he was taking over, Waugh learned everything he could about the target's pattern of life. He became familiar with the Agency camera he'd be using, a digital Canon with a 200mm lens and a 2-gigabyte SD card. To rehearse his movements, he tied and retied everything to his body in case he had to run.

Early the next morning, just after the first call to prayer, a CIA driver took Waugh on a driving lesson around Riyadh. Confident he'd learned the Saudi road system well enough to drive on his own,

Waugh told his driver to take the rest of the day off and leave the vehicle with him.

Waugh drove to the southeastern part of the city, to the address he'd been given. As fortune would have it, across the street from the target's apartment was a Sudanese restaurant, a busy establishment where he could conduct decent surveillance. He parked a few blocks away, walked to the restaurant, and sat down at a table. "There were a bunch of people inside. Black. Seven foot tall. Meant one thing," recalls Waugh. "They were from the Dinka tribe."

Waugh ordered a Sudanese coffee. "I started shooting the shit about Khartoum. Drank more coffee, talked a little more, got the Dinka to reminisce about the home country. Even conversed a little in the native Dinka tongue." Chatting with the Sudanese tribesmen, Waugh kept an eye on the target's address across the street as he began to formulate in his mind where he might best position himself in order to photograph the man. "There was a Dempsey Dumpster right out front. It was good cover." The distance from the Dumpster to the front door of the building was about 250 feet. Waugh paid for his coffee. Bade the Dinka good day and left.

The following morning, around 7:30, Waugh returned to the target area. He parked the vehicle and walked down the street toward the Sudanese restaurant. Concealed by his jacket was the Agency camera equipment. Confident no one was watching, he climbed into the Dumpster and waited.

After some time, recalls Waugh, "the front door of the house where the target lived opened and he stepped out. He was carrying what appeared to be a set of clean clothes, covered by a see-through cover from a dry cleaner. He was a mean-looking son of a bitch, a little on the fat side." In front of the building were ten wide steps leading down from the entrance to the street. "This meant he had to walk slowly down the steps, with his body at an angle so he didn't fall." And it made getting nice, clear photographs of the target relatively easy for Billy Waugh.

As the man walked down the steps, Waugh took photographs in rapid succession. "Mugniyah was alone, carrying the clothes. He reached his vehicle, opened the door, and hung the clothes in the back." Waugh took several more photographs. He climbed out of the Dumpster, walked back to his car, and drove to the U.S. embassy building in Riyadh.

Once inside the CIA station, Waugh slid the camera's SD card into an Agency computer and examined the photographs he'd taken from the Dumpster. Excellent. "They were of identification quality," he remembers. He brought them to the chief of station, who stared silently at them for some time. It was Mugniyah, the chief said. "They satisfied the chief of station in Riyadh."

Waugh prepared to leave the kingdom immediately. There was still a chance he could be stopped, arrested, and disappeared. An Agency employee drove him to the airport. Using the false identity and visa provided to him by the CIA, Billy Waugh vanished from the kingdom of Saudi Arabia, never to return.

Billy Waugh's photographs confirmed the existence and location of Imad Mugniyah. Now the ultrasecret U.S. Army unit formerly known as Gray Fox, later renamed Orange, could gather SIGINT. Hezbollah's chief of operations could be fixed and ultimately finished. The United States and Israel had individually been trying to kill or capture Imad Mugniyah for decades. Now they would join forces to accomplish the task. Or maybe they already were: "Mossad can't operate freely in Saudi," says Waugh. "It's probably the only place they don't have a major [footprint]." A secret arrangement was made. Provided it remain the hidden hand, the United States would assist Mossad in fixing and finishing Imad Mugniyah.

Just a few weeks after Waugh took the photograph of Mugniyah in Riyadh, on July 19, 2004, a senior Hezbollah commander named Ghalib Awali was killed by a car bomb in the suburbs of Beirut.

Awali was getting into his car when the vehicle exploded. Hezbollah leader Hassan Nasrallah accused Israel of assassinating Awali and vowed to "cut off the hands" of the killers. To honor their martyred brother, Hezbollah's propaganda wing created a memorial film about Awali, dispersing copies to its operatives in the region. Mossad got hold of it and screened it for members of a combat intelligence team, Unit 8200, Israel's equivalent of the NSA.

Unit 8200 collects SIGINT and decrypts codes. Its analysts, technicians, and field operators have reach and power. "They are highly focused on what they look at," says Peter Roberts, director of military sciences at the Royal United Services Institute, the oldest defense science think tank in the world, "certainly more focused than the NSA, and they conduct their operations with a degree of tenacity and passion that you don't experience elsewhere."

For years, Unit 8200 operated without a name or an insignia. Its members are highly skilled level-five riflemen who have undergone extensive special forces training. From a classified base in the Negev Desert, which is one of the largest listening bases in the world, members of Unit 8200 follow targets using SIGINT. They monitor phone calls, emails, and other electronic communications to collect and decode. Unit 8200's Arabist linguists assigned to the Mugniyah operation were shown Hezbollah's martyr film about Ghalib Awali. In one of the images, Hassan Nasrallah is seen viewing electronic maps on a computer screen. Behind him stands a bearded man wearing glasses and a cap. In the photographs of Mugniyah taken by Billy Waugh, a key identification marker was obtained, namely the size of the target's earlobes and the distance between them. This may have helped confirm to intelligence officers that the man in Hezbollah's martyr film was indeed Mugniyah. Unit 8200 confirmed Mugniyah's identity by his voice.

There was a disagreement about how and when to move. If Mossad didn't act swiftly, one group feared that Mugniyah would vanish into thin air. Mossad chief Meir Dagan had the final word.

"Don't worry," he reportedly told his operatives. "His day will come." Here began a clandestine joint effort between the intelligence services of the United States and Israel to track down Mugniyah and kill him.

A new form of intelligence emerged called HUGINT, the synthesis of human intelligence and signals intelligence. It is said to have been invented at Mossad, with credit for its development going to an officer named Yossi Cohen. He had worked for Mossad's Junction Unit, a special operations team that oversees asset recruitment around the world. Yossi Cohen became the director of Mossad in 2016.

Israeli press describes Yossi Cohen as someone belonging in a Le Carré novel—a master linguist, soldier, and spy. In addition to his native tongue he is said to speak flawless English, French, and Arabic. He runs marathons and is called "the Model," owing to his good looks and stylish dress. For years, when he was undercover, he went by the moniker "Y." At Mossad, the discipline of HUGINT requires the acquisition of the most private, scandalous details about enemies, for the purpose of blackmailing them and turning them into assets. To this end, Mossad collects information on infidelities, illicit sexual encounters, drug use, porn habits, the taking of bribes, and anything else that compromises the reputations of allegedly pious members of terrorist organizations, including Hezbollah and Hamas. Leaked documents indicate such "vulnerabilities, if exposed, would likely call into question a radicalizer's devotion to the jihadist's cause, leading to the degradation or loss of his authority." Unit 8200 tapped phone lines and undersea cables, planted electronic monitoring devices, and used mini-drones and other surveillance platforms equipped with electronic devices to listen in. Owing to HUGINT, Mossad was able to turn operators inside Hezbollah and Iran's Islamic Revolutionary Guard into assets.

After Waugh photographed Mugniyah in Saudi Arabia, Mugniyah returned to Lebanon, where he was assigned by Iranian commanders to undermine U.S. forces in Iraq. "Hezbollah [had] developed a dedicated unit to train Iraqi Shia militia under Imad Mugniyah and several of his key deputies," says Matthew Levitt, an expert on Hezbollah. General David Petraeus, U.S. commander of forces in Iraq, told Congress that Iran was arming, training, and directing fighters into a "Hezbollah-like force to serve [Iran's] interests and fight a proxy war against the Iraqi state and coalition forces." He said that it was Iran that was supplying armor-piercing IEDs called explosively formed projectiles to the Mahdi Army—Iran's action arm in Iraq. These explosive devices had already killed more than two hundred U.S. soldiers in 2004. A declassified Defense Intelligence Agency report identified a Hezbollah-funded assassination unit, called Unit 3800, that provided "training, tactics and technology to conduct kidnappings [and] small unit tactical operations... to bleed the United States militarily." To the U.S. intelligence community, it was time to kill Imad Mugniyah.

Meir Dagan met with CIA director Michael Hayden; the minutes of the meeting remain classified. After completing a wave of regional assassinations in Lebanon, Mugniyah moved to Damascus in 2006. Damascus was one of the most difficult and dangerous places for Mossad to operate. But the United States maintained an embassy there. CIA Director Hayden met with President Bush, who signed off on a Presidential Finding that allowed the CIA to use its Title 50 authority to kill Mugniyah. If there was backlash, if the hidden hand were revealed, the White House would cite Article 51 of the UN Charter, the right to self-defense. General Petraeus had testified that a "Hezbollah-like force" was sending assassins into Iraq who'd been targeting and killing U.S. military personnel.

There were conditions, President Bush is said to have told Hayden. There could be no collateral damage. No civilians passing by could be injured or killed. The targeted killing operation had to be precise. Kill Imad Mugniyah, and Mugniyah alone.

In 2007, a team of Agency operators traveled to the Syrian capital and began tracking Mugniyah's movements. For some time, Mossad had considered using a cell-phone bomb, similar to the one that killed Hamas bomb maker Yahya Ayyash, the Engineer. That idea was ruled out after Unit 8200 determined that Mugniyah too often changed out cell phones. One version of the events is that the United States now took the lead in engineering the device: at the Harvey Point Defense Testing Activity, in North Carolina, a team of explosives experts designed, built, and test-fired an array of devices. When engineers felt confident that they'd developed one with a blast radius precise enough to kill a single man only, they turned the device over to Mossad. Another version of events is that Mossad built the bomb. But according to numerous sources interviewed for this book, both organizations were involved. "This was a gigantic, multi-force operation, with crazy resources invested by both countries," said a Mossad commander involved in the operation. "To the best of my knowledge, the most ever invested to kill a lone individual."

On the evening of February 12, 2008, Imad Mugniyah met with senior Hezbollah commanders and members of the Radical Front in a building in the Kfar Sousa neighborhood of Damascus. Shortly after 10:30, he exited the building. As he walked toward his 2006 Mitsubishi Pajero 4×4, parked in a lot down the street, two CIA paramilitary operators and a local asset had eyes on him.

The explosion detonated around 10:45. A massive fireball engulfed the car, incinerating Imad Mugniyah. It is said to have been detonated remotely by Mossad officers watching in Tel Aviv. Dozens of people rushed to the location, including several of the Hezbollah commanders with whom Mugniyah had just met. The CIA operators on the street took photographs, and these images would be uploaded into Agency databases for future use.

"We were shocked to learn that he was killed in Syria," Mugniyah's aunt told Agence France-Presse. "We thought he was safe there."

For seven years, the United States remained the hidden hand

in this operation. Then, in January 2015, five former intelligence officials confirmed with *Washington Post* reporters Adam Goldman and Ellen Nakashima that the United States had built the bomb that killed Mugniyah. The CIA declined to comment. Mark Regev, chief spokesman for Israeli prime minister Benjamin Netanyahu, told reporters, "We have nothing to add at this time." Meir Dagan told *60 Minutes,* "I'm not sorry to see the fact that he was perished from this world."

The U.S. ban on assassination again came to the fore, with the oft-repeated statement "Executive Order 12333 prohibits assassination" printed and reprinted around the world. Michael Hayden, as director of the CIA, acknowledged the less palatable truth.

"Assassination," said Hayden, is defined as forbidden lethal acts "against political enemies." Terrorists are not political leaders. They do not run sovereign states. "U. S. targeted killings against Al-Qaeda are against members of an opposing armed enemy force," Hayden clarified. "This is war. This [targeted killing of Mugniyah] is under the laws of armed conflict." As for the reports that the operation was a joint effort with Mossad, he said, "Israel is probably the only other country in the world who thinks like the United States — that what we do there [that is, in this calculus] is legal."

"The Americans remember," Dagan said of Mugniyah's attacks against the United States. He was referring to those killed in the U.S. embassy and the marine corps barracks in Beirut, in 1983; to the kidnapping, torture, and killing of station chief Bill Buckley, in 1985; and to the deaths of hundreds of soldiers in Iraq. "They appear to be liberals [merciful], but they are far from that."

One of the most curious footnotes to Mugniyah's assassination is that there were no immediate retaliatory attacks by Hezbollah, neither against Israel nor the United States. No assassinations. No bombing attacks or kidnappings of prominent people in revenge. Perhaps Billy Waugh was right, that blackmail really is the name of the game at the top; that whatever Mugniyah was doing in Saudi Arabia involved "a blackmail deal," the details of which, if released to the public, would make the martyr Mugniyah appear shockingly treacherous. But there was much more going on than has been reported before. It would be another ten years before a radical truth about the CIA's hidden-hand operation would become known, through my reporting in this book.

CHAPTER TWENTY-SIX

The Moral Twilight Zone

It was the late fall of 2007, and a group of Special Activities Division, Ground Branch, operators sat around a firepit at a classified CIA facility in Kandahar called Gecko base, wondering what to do about someone on their team, an Afghan fighter who they suspected was a double agent for the Taliban. Some of the Ground Branch operators felt that their lives were in danger.

They were taking a vote on whether or not they should kill this indigenous fighter, who went by the name of Saif Mohammad. The Ground Branch team called him Saif the Snake. Although this proposed killing had not been initiated from higher up, to an outside observer the scenario feels reminiscent of the 1969 Green Beret Affair in Vietnam.

In the six years since the CIA had first deployed its paramilitary teams into Afghanistan, one element had significantly changed. "The teams got Ground Branch heavy," a Senior Intelligence Service office who oversaw this expansion clarified for this book. The emphasis in Afghanistan and elsewhere was now on lethal direct action, which is what Ground Branch does best.

Few people have ever gone on record to discuss Ground Branch activities. That Ground Branch trains indigenous fighters to go on kill-or-capture missions with them is an even more closely guarded secret. These soldiers were not part of the Afghan National Army, meaning that they did not appear on any official books. They were paid by the CIA in cash, every two weeks, according to the Ground Branch operators who relayed this story.

In 2010, reporter Bob Woodward first identified these CIA-led indigenous force units as Counterterrorism Pursuit Teams, but almost nothing substantive has been written about them since. No Ground Branch operations have appeared in any classified documents stolen by whistle-blowers and leakers (and subsequently published online). At most, occasionally one finds a reference to "OGA": Other Government Agency, a euphemism for the CIA. The idea of having indigenous soldiers fight alongside CIA paramilitary operators is a direct descendant of the Civilian Irregular Defense Group in Vietnam. Billy Waugh and others spent years teaching South Vietnamese indigs to sabotage, subvert, and kill Vietcong. The goal was to train local fighters how to push back against the communists trying to take over their country, so the Americans could leave.

In Afghanistan, the paradigm was the same. The Ground Branch operators were here to train the Afghan indigs to sabotage, subvert, and kill Taliban who were trying to take over the country, so the Americans could leave. But the indigs were also a White House mandate, meant to serve as the so-called Afghan face, similar to how the Scorpions were meant to serve as the Arab face in Iraq. When a Ground Branch team raided a home or compound in search of a high-value target on a kill-or-capture list, the idea was that local civilians they ran into along the way would feel as if their own people were fighting this war—not the American CIA.

At Gecko, many problems got solved around the firepit. The pit was located just a few dozen yards away from where the Ground Branch operators lived, each man inside his own Conex shipping container, stacked two high. The Afghans lived separately, in barracks down the road. Saif the Snake was one of eighty or so indigs assigned to the unit. If the Taliban were to insert a mole inside a Counterterrorism Pursuit Team at Gecko base, the result would be catastrophic.

The team could get ambushed on the way to or from a mission, or the base could get blown up with an IED.

Part of the problem here at Gecko was the provenance of the indig fighters. On most other CIA bases around Afghanistan, the indigs were independently screened before employment. But at Gecko, the Afghan soldiers were supplied to the CIA by Hamid Karzai's notoriously corrupt half-brother, Ahmed Wali Karzai, a former restaurant owner who'd been living in America—in Chicago—until his brother became president. A neighbor in Chicago who owned the hot dog stand next to Ahmed Wali Karzai's restaurant recalls seeing him standing on a street corner the week the Taliban fell in December 2001. Ahmed Wali Karzai was carrying a suitcase and waiting for the bus.

"Where are you going?" the neighbor asked.

"Afghanistan," he replied. "My brother is president."

Now, six years later, Ahmed Wali Karzai was in charge of Kandahar, the second-largest city in Afghanistan.

Since December 2001, Ahmed Wali Karzai had been living in Kandahar as a kind of Mafia boss. His official title was chairman of the Kandahar Provincial Council, but everyone knew him to be emperor. Local newspapers called him the "Little President." To American infantry soldiers he was "the Godfather." In a leaked classified State Department cable, the ambassador's office informed Washington: "As the kingpin in Kandahar, the President's younger half-brother Ahmed Wali Karzai (AWK) dominates access to economic resources, patronage and protection.... The overriding purpose that unifies his political roles as Chairman of the Kandahar Provincial Council and as the President's personal representative in the south is the enrichment, extension, and perpetuation of the Karzai clan."

In Kandahar, it was the same old story repeating itself: Ahmed Wali Karzai was a corrupt, treacherous bad guy, but he was our bad guy. Like President Trujillo or the shah. Like the corrupt Diem brothers who'd been propped up by the CIA and the Defense

Department in South Vietnam forty-five years before. Ground Branch operators recall seeing Ahmed Wali Karzai drop by the Gecko base, always with a posse of local bodyguards, sometimes as often as two or three times a week. "He always left with a suitcase full of cash," says a Ground Branch operator, call sign Hatchet.

"We were absolutely convinced that AWK was the source of all evil" in Kandahar, Lieutenant Colonel Ketti Davison, U.S. military intelligence chief for the Kandahar division, said in an interview with the *Washington Post*. But at the CIA's Gecko base, the State Department and the Defense Department were to accept what the CIA was attempting to accomplish with its hidden hand.

Around the firepit, the Ground Branch operators wondered what to do about the possible traitor, Saif the Snake?

He's called the *Snake,* one of the operators, call sign Shark, emphasized. Shark suggested that this was downright biblical.

"That's just what we call him," someone else reminded Shark. And that they all used made-up call signs on a black program.

The CIA chief of base at Gecko had been brought into the loop; Saif the Snake had been identified to him as a possible double agent. Two of the Ground Branch operators caught Saif sitting on a rooftop inside the compound sketching a map of the base. "Entrances and exits. Who lived where. The location of the armory." When Saif was formally questioned, he said he liked to draw.

There was more. Saif had been caught with a list of names of the Americans on base, as well as "the vehicle count, with numbers identifying each vehicle attached to the teams." He'd been seen with a cell phone on a mission. Cell phones were not allowed on missions; a traitor could phone in the team's location for an ambush. But the CIA's rules of engagement stated that you couldn't search the indigenous Afghan soldiers, "same as you can't shoot a bad guy in the back, even if he's running away from the gunfight you were just having with him." On the operation where Saif Mohammad was seen with a phone, the team was ambushed. Two Afghan soldiers got blown up with an IED and lost limbs. One Ground Branch operator had been shot in the chest, his life saved by his body armor. All three soldiers were medevaced out and survived.

"Circumstantial evidence," one of the team guys said of Saif's cell phone.

There was another operator at Gecko who was concerned, a Ground Branch officer named Brian Ray Hoke. Hoke was young for Ground Branch, just thirty-three. He was a kind of Renaissance man, a philosopher-poet and warfighter in one. He had studied oceanography at the U.S. Naval Academy. Ran marathons. Played the violin. After college, he passed Hell Week and became an officer with the Navy SEALs, deployed to Europe and into the war theater in the Middle East.

In 2004, Brian Hoke retired from the Navy SEALs and joined the clandestine service of the CIA, becoming a paramilitary operations officer in the Special Activities Division. He had a wife and three children at home in Virginia. He wanted to get home to see his kids. He'd been on a mission with Shark a few months back where Saif the Snake had simply disappeared in the middle of a gunfight. Later they found him sitting in one of the Ground Branch trucks. He said he was cold.

A Ground Branch operator with the call sign Stingray was unconvinced Saif was a bad guy. "No way," he insisted. Stingray had been at Gecko longer than anyone else on the team. He'd also been on missions with Saif the Snake. *He may not be the best fighter,* Stingray said. *Hardly any of the Afghans were.* But he was loyal.

Shark remained unconvinced. "This is not a tough one to figure out," he insisted. Saif Mohammad was a traitor who needed to be dealt with. There was too much to lose.

Saif had already been reported to the National Directorate of Security (NDS), Afghanistan's equivalent of the CIA. He'd been questioned, released, and returned to Gecko base. "Everyone knows NDS is a kangaroo court," said another operator, call sign Axe. Besides, he'd been supplied to the CIA by Ahmed Wali Karzai, so he was protected.

The Ground Branch operators had to wait it out. For now.

★   ★   ★

Training the Afghan soldiers for the Counterterrorism Pursuit Teams was its own secret nightmare, starting with the general incompatibility of the two groups' codes of conduct. Ground Branch operators are among the most qualified and experienced Tier One and Tier Two paramilitary operators in the United States. They have near-impeccable service records, no blemishes or black marks. The men must regularly pass a polygraph test. Must be accountable to the CIA. If you fail your polygraph, you're out of Ground Branch for good.

Ground Branch officers and operators are high-level problem-solving warriors who operate in the most radical, nonpermissive combat environments in the world. They must think clearly and act flawlessly in a 360-degree gunfight; in close-quarters combat; in ambush, hit-and-run, snatch-and-grab, and rescue operations. To infiltrate a target, they must be able to fast-rope out of helicopters, perform HALO and high-altitude high-opening (HAHO) jumps out of airplanes, walk twelve kilometers or more behind enemy lines, carrying seventy-five pounds of gear or a wounded soldier. All of this must be performed in any terrain or temperature, on the top of a 10,000-foot mountain or in subsurface underwater environments such as an ocean or a river, from subzero freezing to 122-degree Fahrenheit heat. The operators need Olympian confidence and stamina when they go on kill-or-capture missions and rescue operations.

"You must be completely amoral and completely moral at the same time," says a Ground Branch operator, call sign Lightning. Amoral meaning "unconcerned with the rightness or the wrongness of something because the laws, rules and codes you are operating inside have been already set by others." By lawmakers in the United States.

"You are doing what you are doing on the orders of POTUS," the president of the United States, says an operator, call sign Cheetah. Amoral must not be confused with immoral, Hatchet clarifies. "Immoral means in violation of your moral code."

*   *   *

The early days of the Taliban begin right here in Kandahar, at Gecko base. When the Taliban took over Kabul, in 1996, the CIA started keeping a file on the group's founder and supreme leader, a one-eyed mujahid from the Soviet war named Mullah Mohammad Omar. "Not much is known about Mullah Omar," deputy chief of mission John C. Holzman wrote in a classified cable to Langley. "He formed the Taliban in late 1994 as a reaction against 'immoral' local commanders" who had raped several girls in their village outside Kandahar, Holzman wrote.

Like many guerrilla warfare leaders before him, Mullah Omar's stated purpose was to rid the land of a corrupting and evil force. The way the narrative goes, Mullah Omar and several friends ambushed the suspected warlord-rapist, executed him on the spot, then suspended his corpse from a tank barrel parked in the town square. Mullah Omar commandeered the town's radio and explained to the villagers why he and his friends had done what they'd done.

"The religion of Allah is being stepped on! The people are openly displaying evil. They steal the people's money, they attack their honor on the main street," Mullah Omar cried. "They kill people and put them against the rocks on the side of the road, and the cars pass by and see the dead body." This was a horrible crime against Islam — and it was exactly what Mullah Omar had just done to his victim's body, the suspected warlord-rapist. Clearly the Taliban was not suggesting any kind of Golden Rule to begin with, the Golden Rule being *Do unto others as you would do unto yourself.* Omar's group claimed it would "stand up against this corruption."

Mullah Omar became popular. He took risks. Once, during a public speech on a rooftop, a gathering of the faithful in Kandahar, he pulled a holy relic, the cloak said to be worn by the Prophet Mohammad 1,400 years before, from a sacred holding place and draped it over his own shoulders, declaring himself the emir of all

Muslims. "People in the crowds threw up their turbans to be blessed by it," observed a BBC reporter on hand to film the event. "It was like being in some great religious ceremony in the Middle Ages." The action marked the beginning of Mullah Omar's rise to power. In less than two years, the Taliban seized Kabul.

A spokesman for the Taliban attributed Mullah Omar's greatness to three traits regarded by the fundamental Islamists as admirable: "his religious piety, his reputation for incorruptibility, and his bravery in the jihad." Under his supreme rule, the Taliban famously banned music, football, and kite flying. They cut off the hands of thieves and the fingers of women wearing nail polish. They cut off the heads of infidels, adulterers, and anyone caught carrying "objectionable literature." Homosexuals were thrown off rooftops or tortured to death by a medieval practice of being buried under a mud-and-wattle wall until death comes by suffocation.

Mullah Omar was renowned for his piety. He was said to sleep on cement floors and consume only broth and dry bread. But it did not take long for the supreme leader to become corrupt. Soon he was driving around Afghanistan in a Land Rover and living in a garish palace, the one where the Ground Branch operators now lived. These luxuries—the fancy cars and the palace—were gifts given to Mullah Omar by his benefactor Osama bin Laden.

After bin Laden was kicked out of Sudan and arrived in Afghanistan in 1996, the Al-Qaeda leader moved his family to Kandahar and pledged loyalty to Mullah Omar. In exchange, bin Laden was allowed to operate his terrorist training camps in the country, including one called Tarnak Farms, in Kandahar, and another called the Lion's Den, in Khost.

The Kandahar palace that bin Laden built for Mullah Omar was a tawdry affair. It had gold-plated chandeliers and murals of waterfalls and mud-hut villages painted on its cheap Formica walls. Canadian soldiers who fought alongside Ground Branch operators called it Graceland, for its Elvis-level kitsch. There was a private mosque with a mirrored minaret, stables for horses and camels, a water fountain, and a swimming pool.

Mullah Omar occupied it until sometime before October 19, 2001, when an unusually large, thirty-man Delta Force team conducted an airborne assault on the palace, with the intent of killing or capturing Mullah Omar. Four Chinook helicopters set down inside the palace walls and unloaded the Delta operators, several all-terrain vehicles (ATVs), and sixty U.S. Army Rangers assigned to secure the perimeter. The palace compound was huge, roughly five kilometers in diameter, and the ATVs unloaded from the Chinooks helped the Delta operators quickly secure the compound. The fortress had been built up against a mountain, into which a warren of caves had been carved. Some had showers and squat toilets, U.S. forces discovered.

The original assault on the compound was a Defense Department operation. After a four-hour search of the palace, the Delta operators and the rangers were ambushed by Taliban armed with rocket-propelled grenades and were extracted from the compound under fire. An American was injured during the firefight, reportedly losing a foot to an RPG, and one of the Chinooks lost a piece of its landing gear after getting hit. Mullah Omar was nowhere to be found. The CIA later learned that the one-eyed leader of the Taliban, together with his top commanders, had fled into Pakistan to regroup.

The Taliban government that boasted piety, incorruptibility, and bravery left behind in its wake one of the most immoral, corrupt, criminal, debauched societies the modern world has ever known. Civil order had been destroyed. "Adults [left] traumatized and brutalized," writes Pakistani journalist Ahmed Rashid, in *Taliban*. "Children rootless without identity or reason to live except to fight." In the words of Lakhdar Brahimi, a former United Nations diplomat, "We are dealing with a failed state which looks like an infected wound. You don't even know where to begin cleaning it."

Now, six years later, in late 2007, very little had changed. Michael

Hayden, as director of the CIA, audaciously called Afghanistan "still the good war" despite everything that was known about how dire the situation was—how security for Afghans had gotten worse, not better. In six years, the Americans had set up the Karzai government in Kabul and established the NATO-led International Security Assistance Force (ISAF) to train Afghan National Security Forces (ANSF). The ANSF was supposed to assist in rebuilding key government institutions while fighting the Taliban insurgency. But in reality, by the time 2007 came to a close, civil society had devolved into anarchy and terror that rivaled what it was like before the Americans arrived.

Improvised explosive devices were introduced into the pandemonium, detonated in mosques, at schools, on roads, and at sporting events. The year 2007 marked the most violent year in Afghanistan since the Americans had arrived, with 1,120 IED attacks in Kandahar alone. The birthplace of the Taliban was now the most violent province in the country.

For the Ground Branch operators, the violence was one element, but two issues that no one ever talks about kept getting in the way. These were moral-center issues, says Axe, using a decidedly Western term.

"Moral wounds of war," says an operator, call sign Spear.

"Things no one wants to discuss," adds Cheetah.

Cutting to the chase, says another operator, call sign Sampson, "Afghanistan is a moral twilight zone." A mix of horror, psychological thriller, suspense, and things so strange it feels like science fiction. "All usually end up with a macabre, dark, and evil twist."

"There are new episodes daily," Cheetah recalls. "You never have to watch reruns."

"It's like the *Alice in Wonderland* book I read to my kids," says Hawk. He quotes Lewis Carroll: "If you don't know where you're going, all roads will lead you there."

"Hello darkness, my old friend," says Axe, recalling a lyric from the sixties.

"In Afghanistan, you are confronted with evil situations you think can't be outperformed, but then they are," explains Shark. There's the moral twilight zone outside the wire and inside the wire, he says. But sometimes the evil and wickedness showed up directly at the front gate. Shark relays the story of an indigenous Afghan soldier named Assadallah who requested three days off to walk to a wedding twelve kilometers away. The CIA chief of base said fine.

"Assadallah came back. In two separate pieces," recalls Shark. "His head had been separated from his body. They left him at the front gate." Shark volunteered to go get the body. Accompanying him was a medic who'd graduated from West Point. "The medic wanted to do an autopsy. Find out how Assadallah died. I said, 'Isn't it obvious? They cut off his head.'"

Shark found the moral twilight zone unbearable at times. "Sometimes you can deal with it, other times you cannot." A twenty-seven-year veteran of the U.S. Special Forces—with nearly a decade spent on a Tier One team—Shark's Spartan warrior values sometimes brought him into conflict with the behavior and actions of the Afghan soldiers he was training. Yes, some were exceptionally brave soldiers, he says. Of the five to six hundred fighters Shark trained and fought alongside over a five-year period in Afghanistan, three of the soldiers were like brothers to him.

By 2007, when the meeting took place around the firepit, Shark and a colleague had already been awarded one of the CIA's highest medals, for a voluntary act of courage performed under hazardous conditions and with grave risk to one's own life. During an ambush by the Taliban, the two operators had saved the life of an Afghan teammate whose limb had been blown off by a grenade. Honored for courage under fire, Shark and his colleague had been flown back to the United States to receive the award. All they had were their operator clothes. Shark's ex-wife FedExed a suit to his hotel. The two Ground Branch operators had their pictures taken, were given their medals, and were told that everything would be locked away in a vault until some future date. There was always the question when, or if, programs would get declassified. MACV-SOG operators had to wait more than thirty years for it to happen. "By then," says Axe, "the public has forgotten. And the real issues are no longer anyone's concern." Cheetah points out that headlines appear in the U.S. press occasionally referring to assassination teams being run by the CIA. "We operate under Title 50 rules," says Hatchet. "The indigs we train, and the bad guys we kill, live in a world where there are no rules except 'kill.'"

Outstanding Afghan fighters were rare among those trained for joint indig–CIA operations. Most of them are high on opium a lot of the time, a fact reiterated by every Ground Branch operator interviewed for this book. Eight out of ten soldiers were illiterate. Many had trouble counting beyond thirty. When it came time to train indigenous bodyguards for President Karzai's security detail (he objected to having CIA and Delta Force operators only, concerned it made him look bad), each applicant was required to fill out a questionnaire. According to the *Washington Post*'s Joshua Partlow, all but one of the Afghan recruits handed the paper back blank. Only one in the entire group of applicants could read. Karzai's recruiter sought to hire the man, but the others in the group objected. "He's our teacher in the village," they told Karzai's recruiter. "If we give him to you, we won't have anyone to teach our children."

On occasion, during heavy snows, when some of the CIA's more remote forward operating bases got snowed in, Shark tried teaching math to the indigenous fighters. "This was not math 101," he says. "This was first-grade math." Once, in an effort to explain conceptually how big numbers and long distances work, Shark took a group of soldiers outside to look at the full moon rising up over the Hindu Kush mountains. "I said to them, 'So the moon is 250,000 miles away.' And while I was on the subject, I said, 'By the way, we landed there fifty years ago; the missions were called Apollo.' One of the soldiers said, 'That's impossible.' He pointed to the moon and said, 'The moon's too small to land people on.'"

Welcome to the twilight zone.

"A lot of them were so stoned so much of the time it looked like they'd been swimming in a heavily chlorinated pool," says Spear.

"A few hours before we'd go out on a mission, I'd personally go into their barracks and confiscate their pipes," says Shark. "Make them turn over their drugs until we were done fighting."

"Fighting bad guys high on drugs is a really bad idea," says Axe.

"They do it," says Hatchet. "We're told to accept it. It's how it is."

The other problem, says Shark, "was that they seemed to spend all their free time raping each other in their barracks," a fact confirmed with ten Ground Branch operators interviewed. "We had a code. If I needed them, I'd knock loud on the door to indicate they needed to wrap it up and knock it off, but they ignored that."

"It's disgusting," says Hatchet. "They do it. We had to accept it. We're told, 'It's how it is.' Some of them rape underage boys."

Ken Stiles, who set up the CIA's geographic information system for Hank Crumpton in the basement of Langley in the first weeks of the war, confirmed that rape was said to be a "cultural norm." Stiles was sent to Kabul to set up an in-country electronic targeting system for the CIA. On occasion, he was flown to FOBs in the war zone. "I once asked an Afghan soldier why he joined special forces as opposed to the regular army," recalls Stiles. "He said, 'Because in special forces you get raped less.'"

Why was this not reported more thoroughly in the press? Four months after the war started, the *New York Times* ran an article entitled "Kandahar Journal; Shhh, It's an Open Secret: Warlords and Pedophilia." Then, the press went silent for almost fifteen years. The raping problem was endemic to all Afghan military forces, it would later be revealed, not just within the indigenous forces being trained by the CIA. By 2007, ISAF consisted of approximately 55,100 personnel from thirty-nine countries, including 23,220 troops from the United States. And yet conspicuously missing from the constant rush of war reports were any about Afghan soldiers raping each other and raping and enslaving young boys.

Not until 2018 would the U.S. inspector general produce a devastating report exposing 5,753 cases of "gross human rights abuses by Afghan forces," including the "routine enslavement and rape of underage boys by Afghan commanders." What about the Leahy Amendment, which cuts off U.S. aid to foreign military units that commit human rights abuses? Erica Gaston, of the nonprofit organization Afghanistan Analysts Network, explains: "There is a blanket 'waiver' in the DoD version that allow[s] the Secretary of Defense to waive the Leahy law in 'extraordinary circumstances,' implicitly where serious national security interests are invoked." As an example, Gaston cites Kandahar.

Are the Ground Branch operators correct in their assessment that Afghanistan is the moral twilight zone? And what does this have to do with assassination as a political tool? In a rare authorized interview in 2011, a Green Beret captain identified as Matt told the *Christian Science Monitor,* "The ugly reality is that if the U.S. wants to prevail against the Taliban and its allies, it must work with Afghan fighters whose behavior insults Western sensibilities. There are no good guys by our standards. There is no standard to begin with. There is no justice system or rule of law to hold people accountable."

No justice system. No rule of law. Nothing to hold people accountable. Two trillion U.S. dollars spent in Afghanistan, in more than seventeen years of war, not including veterans' health costs. Every U.S. president has options. When diplomacy fails and war is not— or is no longer—an option, the president can exercise the third option, the CIA's hidden hand. But to what end?

To understand the rest of this story, what the Ground Branch operators proposed to do about the suspected double agent in the ranks, and to evaluate it objectively, it's important to comprehend how profoundly secret and compartmentalized the world of a Ground Branch operator really is. As specific and singular as this situation may seem, no Ground Branch operations in Afghanistan have been made public.

For Ground Branch operators, secrecy and anonymity override every mission. Ground Branch operators work under pseudonyms and regularly change their aliases. They travel into the war theater using a CIA-engineered second passport that has given them an identity separate from the one with which they were born. The different name, different address, even different parents within the backstory—all are elements and attributes of the CIA's hidden hand. An operator who uses the pseudonym David Smith at Gecko might go by Richard White at Jalalabad or Jeff Hill at Khost. And there is another identity that exists within personnel services at CIA headquarters, a consistent identity that chronologically keeps track of each operator's assignments as they accumulate. This pseudonym usually ascribes a false ethnicity to the operator.

For example, an Irish Catholic Ground Branch operator from Wisconsin might be identified in the central database as Danny Nooradian (as if he's Armenian American) or Peter Andropolis (as if he's Greek American). Billy Waugh's database identity made him sound Chinese American. If a Ground Branch operator who works as a contract employee (a green badger) is audited by the Internal Revenue Service, they must follow stringent protocols to ensure that their true employer, the CIA, is never revealed.

An equally complex problem arises if a gunshot wound, endured in the war theater, gets infected back home. U.S. doctors are required to report gunshot wounds to administrators, and patients are required to truthfully explain how they got their injuries. The general rule among Ground Branch operators with regard to an infected wound is to say to the hospital doctor, "I shot myself hunting," but this becomes a problem when it happens more than once.

If a Ground Branch operator is killed in action overseas, his body is sent to a refrigerator located at the nearest CIA station. There, the dead man waits. Only when the Ground Branch operator's "in true" passport is sent from the CIA can the soldier's physical body be repatriated to the United States. Spouse, children, and other family members are not told the circumstances in which their loved one died. Nate Chapman's family had no idea he was on a Special Activities Division, Ground Branch, team until 2015, when the CIA awarded him a star on its marble Memorial Wall.

Identity in Afghanistan for Afghan nationals is as strange as it is complex. "Having a proper identity is everybody's human right," says Najibullah Hameem, a child protection specialist with UNICEF, in Kabul. "This is something which is lacking in Afghanistan." Less than 1 percent of the population have a birth certificate. Even if the government started issuing birth certificates, the Afghan government is incapable of registering and storing this information, says Hameem. If you ask an Afghan soldier how old he is, says a Ground Branch operator, "everyone will tell you he is twenty-five. Some of the twenty-five-year-olds look eighteen, some of them look fifty. But they're all just twenty-five."

"They don't think of time the way we think of time," says Hatchet. "It's fight, fuck, eat, sleep, fight, fuck, repeat."

"Kind of like us," says Cheetah, half-joking.

Blood is a major issue. Most civilians don't know offhand what their blood type is, but for a combat soldier in the war theater, this information is critical. "Almost everyone needs a blood bag at some point or other," says Axe. For this reason, before each mission Ground Branch operators write their blood type in indelible ink on their body armor and their skin.

"The blood problem is bigger than this," says Shark. "Because of all the [man-on-man] sex, many of the fighters have hep B."

"If someone looked into how much Cipro is given out to Afghan fighters, that would be a story right there," says Cheetah.

Setting aside what anyone thinks about the sexual behavior, says

Shark, the real problem is blood-on-blood contact between fighters on the battlefield. When an Afghan soldier named Taj Mohammad had his leg blown off on a kill-or-capture mission, Shark worked quickly to get a tourniquet on him before he bled out. But Shark had also been hit by grenade frag and was bleeding, meaning that the two soldiers had blood-on-blood contact on the battlefield while Shark was trying to save Taj's life.

According to a declassified government report, the Afghan National Army does not have the supplies or equipment to test for blood and requires that new recruits go to a doctor and pay to have their blood types tested, without reimbursement. Almost no one does this. As a result, "a suspiciously large number of soldiers were reported to have the same blood type." And everybody was twenty-five years old.

What to do about Saif Mohammad, the traitor at Gecko base? The consensus around the firepit was: *Wait*. Gather evidence.

Shark accepted the Ground Branch team's decision. Everything that happened here had to be agreed upon by the team. Then, just a few weeks later, two team members from the Canadian unit brought hard evidence to the Ground Branch team. They had a folder. Inside the folder was a photograph. "In the photograph, there was Saif the Snake, yakking it up with known Taliban [leaders] in Pakistan." Saif Mohammad was most certainly a traitor. Something had to be done.

There was a vote on the table. *Why not just kill him?*

But timing is everything, and before anything could be done about Saif the Snake, the chief of base at Gecko approached the team.

"Something's come up," he said.

Something's come up was a euphemism for "there's a kill-or-capture mission on the board." Everything on these kinds of missions was extremely time-sensitive. Once a high-value target was found and his location had been fixed, the movement to finish the individual had to happen fast. This is how the CIA's action arm has worked since the war on terror began. Direct-action missions were fraught with peril and consequence, potentially good and potentially very bad.

"Potential positive strategic effects of HVT operations include eroding insurgent effectiveness, weakening insurgent will, reducing the level of insurgent support, fragmenting or splitting the insurgent group, altering insurgent strategy," reads a leaked CIA directive on "High-Value Targeting Operations." On the downside, "Potential negative effects of HVT operations include increasing the level of insurgent support...strengthening an armed group's bond with the population...creating a vacuum into which more radical groups can enter, and escalating or deescalating a conflict in ways that favor the insurgents." The devil was always in the details of the mission, as the Ground Branch team at Gecko soon learned.

A top Taliban commander and high-value target was holed up in a compound in Sangin, eighty-seven miles to the northwest of Gecko base. With him were three accomplices, also HVTs. This Taliban commander was responsible for financing, building, and placing IEDs on area roads. Scores of coalition forces and hundreds of Afghan civilians were dead because of his IEDs. Just weeks before, a suicide bomber had blown himself up at a dog-fighting competition in Kandahar, killing eighty people and wounding a hundred, the deadliest attack since the fall of the Taliban in 2001. The commander's location had been fixed. His pattern of life suggested he'd leave Sangin at dawn. "These were the same guys we'd gone after before," recalls Shark. "The fact that they'd popped back up was huge." A decision had to be made to go or not. The team had two hours to decide.

The team gathered in the tactical operations center, a huge room with high ceilings and a sand table. The mission was heavily debated. A consensus had to be reached. The Taliban compound was standard for the region: square, made of mud walls, with several inside rooms, a back courtyard with a variety of vehicles. It was likely that bomb-making materials were stored there. Using GPS coordinates, the team was to travel to a specific location. This would be the vehicle drop-off point. They would exit the vehicles, set security, and send two teams out to assault the target.

They had more than enough Ground Branch guys, augmented with Tier One operators on loan to the CIA. The Canadian operators were on standby as backup, as was a quick reaction force (QRF) in the area. An AC-130 Spectre gunship would be with the team, overhead, for the movement there. There would be a short gap with no coverage, then A-10 Thunderbolts flying overhead on the way home. The gear was set. The QRF was set. The primary negative was that there weren't any helicopters available to infiltrate the target with the Ground Branch team. This meant that the team had to drive to Sangin in a twelve-vehicle convoy on a cratered-out, muddy, ruddy, single-lane road that was hard to navigate due to recent heavy rains. One way in, one way out, on a road notorious for ambushes and IEDs.

Finally, a consensus was reached. The operators agreed to accept the mission. Everyone plugged the coordinates of the target area into their GPS systems. Shark jumped on a motorcycle and headed down to brief the Afghan soldiers at their barracks. "We always gave indigs the edited version of our plan, for our safety," says Ground Branch operator Drew Dwyer. "Never specifics of where we were going." A ten-year veteran of the Special Activities Division, Dwyer's first Ground Branch mission was in 2002, and he has participated in covert-action operations on all five continents.

Using a sandbox, the team showed the Afghan soldiers the basic layout of the target area in Sangin. After the briefing, the soldiers were told to have their vehicles in convoy formation lined up at the gate. They had twenty minutes.

Soon, they would set out through Kandahar. Through the land of IEDs.

CHAPTER TWENTY-SEVEN

Just War

There are lots of ways to describe Sangin, in Helmand Province, Afghanistan, and Ground Branch operators describe it in their own ways. The Heart of Darkness. The bad place. The Taliban's heartland. The sordid matrix of opium poppy production. And then there's this: pure evil. In official Pentagon parlance, Secretary of Defense Robert M. Gates said of Sangin: "This district [is] one of the most dangerous not just in Afghanistan but maybe in the whole world." Over a ten-year period, more American marines and British soldiers would be killed in Sangin than in any of Afghanistan's four hundred other districts.

Now the Ground Branch team from Gecko base was heading here, its twelve-vehicle convoy lumbering along the ambush-prone road. Shark, driving, focused on the taillights on the vehicle in front of him. They'd been painted over with black and covered in tape so operators weren't blinded by the night vision devices they wore. There was a decent outline of the truck ahead, and at the same time, the convoy was hidden from people officials called Taliban, or anti-coalition militia. Ground Branch guys knew them simply as bad guys with guns.

"It was a perfect night, as far as light conditions were concerned," remembers Shark. "Enough moon and stars out that night that the night vision was perfect, and through those devices I looked as far as I could see down Highway One." To Shark, the road "looked like it never ended, and it looked a bit eerie, too. The compounds that were in eyeshot were scattered around and had only smoke coming from within them, very little light. Some small fires were visible. The night was over for them—the villagers who lived there—they had eaten and were getting ready to sleep, most of them were." If it wasn't war, this night might have been a beautiful thing, and for a moment, a very brief, very dangerous moment, Shark thought of his own children back home.

"For a split second, I wondered if my kids were safe," he says.

Then instantly, instinctively, he shut that thought down. In the combat zone, behind enemy lines, "you never think of anything that makes you vulnerable," he says. "It interrupts the forward momentum that's been ingrained in you through training. This is a momentum you must maintain every second of every mission, no matter what."

Suddenly there were flashlights going off. *Flashlights.* Afghans signaling to one another, from just outside their homes. This was optical telegraphing. Shark's first thought: Saif the Snake. The enemy had been informed.

Technically, this was a kill-or-capture mission: four high-value targets, a bomb maker and his three lieutenants. But when someone knows you're coming, capture is off the table. The mission becomes kill or be killed.

"Having Saif the Snake on any mission was very much like putting together a ticking time bomb and bringing it along with you for the ride," says Shark. Driving eighty-seven miles from Gecko base to Sangin seemed to take forever, every curve in the road presenting some fresh danger. Thirty minutes outside the target, the convoy came to a halt. There was a guard tower problem. *A guard tower problem?* An old Soviet-era guard tower that never had anyone in it now suddenly had someone in it. Comms said something about the Afghan national police.

"Every minute you're sitting still on an op[eration] is a very bad minute," says Drew Dwyer.

" 'Sitting ducks' is the term," says Hawk.

Shark adds context. "We had Spooky, the [AC-130] gunship, overhead. And that takes away a lot of concerns, but it doesn't eliminate them altogether."

Finally, the team was cleared to move onto the target. Five minutes out, the pilot broke radio silence to announce that the target area was active—that he could see at least ten personnel in the compound, next to a mosque. The convoy moved the final one hundred meters to the target. It was wet, cold, and muddy.

"The makeshift road was saturated and sloppy," remembers Shark. "The steering wheel felt loose, like there was no traction." His thoughts were interrupted by a *whooosh* sound streaking right by him. So close, it felt like inches. So loud, it sounded like the volume had been turned up. He watched an RPG-7, a rocket-propelled grenade, blast down the halted line of Ground Branch trucks. Then *whooosh,* a second rocket fired by the convoy somehow missing them on a second try. The Taliban don't have night vision, and shooting in the dark means shooting blind. It was one of the advantages a Ground Branch team has, that and Spooky tactical air support. The rocket detonated behind the convoy in an empty space that was supposed to be the entry point into the target area.

"We exited the vehicles," recalls Shark. "Get out of the death box and take cover, return fire."

A volley of fire. Kill or be killed. There's always a firefight when you're Ground Branch. Then, as fast as the ambush started, the shooters were gone. The Taliban were masters of irregular warfare. They knew surprise, kill, vanish like the back of their own hand. In the winter of 2008, Afghanistan had been at war for twenty-nine consecutive years. First with the Russian invaders, starting in 1979; then with themselves after the invaders left, from 1989 until 2001; and now with a coalition of American-led invaders, but invaders nonetheless.

The voice of the pilot flying the AC-130 Spectre overhead came over the comms. "Three in the ditch, heading toward your location," the pilot said. Calm, steady.

Ditch, what ditch? The opium-poppy growing land here in Sangin was zippered with irrigation canals, some filled with water, others with ice. Another update: "Be advised you have eight on foot behind you." Then came the distinct *pffffmmpggggg* sound through Shark's noise-reducing comms. A ripping sound, as the gunship fired down at the enemy from overhead. "Spooky laying waste to whatever threatens your position, in a variety of calibers," said Axe.

The AC-130 Spectre gunship—Spooky—is a heavily armed side-firing aircraft. With its sophisticated network of sensors and navigation and fire-control systems, the gunship provides close air support at night in adverse weather and can loiter in an overhead circle for extended periods of time. The suite of sensors on board allows Spectre pilots to visually discern friendlies from enemies, and to attack two targets simultaneously from above. There's little moral outrage over Spooky. It's a war machine used by the Defense Department, in keeping with the laws of war and the rules of engagement.

The pilot repeated, "Eight on foot behind you...three in the ditch" and began firing. In a matter of seconds, all eleven humans were dead.

Then silence. No more shooting. The compound was straight ahead. The pathway to the target was heavily wooded. Shark walked along. He had eight Afghan soldiers with him, following along in a line. After a few minutes of walking, the area erupted in gunfire once again.

Again the shooting stopped. Shark continued to move forward to the target, his gun trained ahead. The mission was to locate the bomb maker and his lieutenants. The eleven dead were almost certainly foot soldiers, which meant that the four high-value targets were probably hiding somewhere right around here. The compound needed to be cleared. There was work to do. Shark readied to make entry over the compound wall when suddenly it occurred to him that he was alone. Where had the Afghan indigs gone? Alone? How was this possible? Alone is dangerous. Two rules: *Never get in the trunk. And never try to clear a room alone.* But he was here. There was work to do. They'd come all the way to Sangin. Against his better judgment, Shark decided to go at it alone.

He walked across the roof of the compound. He looked down into a hole, like a stairwell minus the stairs. There was a wooden ladder leading down inside. "It came to me that a flamethrower would have been nice," recalls Shark. "I could have cleared the whole room with the flamethrower." But Protocol III of the Convention on Prohibitions or Restrictions on the Use of Certain Conventional Weapons prohibited soldiers from using incendiary weapons, which made little sense if you had just seen what Spooky did to the eleven men. "They used flamethrowers in every other war, so why not here?" Shark wondered. He headed back to the trucks to locate the rest of the team. At the convoy he found that the Afghan soldiers were sitting around, some of them inside a vehicle.

There was more work to be done, Shark said, including the SSE, or sensitive site exploitation, of the compound—a search for materials, paper intelligence, bad guys' cell phones. There were two or three vehicles parked behind the compound that needed to be searched as well. Half the team needed to stay with the sensitive equipment in the trucks. The other half needed to go with him.

Back at the target, a perimeter was set up and the compound was cleared, then searched. The HVTs had long gone. The SSE took four hours. Spooky kept watch overhead. Then it was time to go.

Back at the trucks there was an unbelievable commotion under way. A brand-new truck borrowed from the rangers was upside down in a hole. Sabotage? Had one or more of the Afghan indigs tried driving the truck away? The only thing more dangerous than lingering on infiltration was lingering on exfil. Time to get out of Sangin.

But first, the sensitive communications gear in the vehicle needed to be destroyed. Destroy the entire vehicle — that would do the job. Ground Branch operators poured three jerricans of diesel fuel over the truck, tossed a thermite grenade inside, and watched it burn. The operators piled in the trucks, and the eleven-vehicle convoy inched home across the same dark landscape. The indig fighters whose truck had mysteriously been turned upside down squeezed in beside the Ground Branch team. In each vehicle, a computer screen displayed the bird's-eye view of the journey back to Gecko base, one layer of the geographic information system (GIS) created in the basement of Langley by Ken Stiles and his team six years before. The metadata in the GIS had since been increased by orders of magnitude. Layers of anthropology and geography had been fused with every form of intelligence available. But was there any progress being made here in Afghanistan, any at all? Could America ever win this war? Or was the whole effort like the upside-down truck in Sangin? Expensive, intractable, waiting to be burned to the ground.

After the team got back to Gecko base, all the data gathered in Sangin was inputted into the system, including photos from cell phones recovered, papers found in the compound, pocket litter from dead Taliban. All this information would be used to provide targeters working at a classified CIA facility in Kabul called Eagle base with more information about whom to target and kill next. "We were producing intelligence and we were also a consumer of the intelligence we were producing," Hank Crumpton said of the original intent of covert action in Afghanistan. Now, six years later, all across Afghanistan, Ground Branch teams were still doing the same thing. But the goal, to "become more productive," had arguably not been met. The situation in Afghanistan had gotten a lot worse.

After all the SSE data from the Taliban compound in Sangin got turned over to the CIA chief of Gecko base, the debrief took place. Shark brought up his idea about the flamethrower.

"I explained my reason for it. It was valid, in my eyes—beyond valid—and some of the guys loved it, but not everybody," he recalls. "The boss rolled his eyes and said, 'Let's discuss this offline.' It wasn't received well, and I still don't understand why. We drop bombs on [bad guys]. Fire cannons from the sky, which sets people on fire. Why is a flamethrower so taboo?"

Only a few of the guys made it to the postmission firepit discussion that night. "We just sat there on the homemade wooden benches and pieced together the night. The issue of Saif Mohammad came up, and, why wouldn't he? It was not a normal situation," says Shark. "Having him on a mission felt like inviting suicide."

Now, with the mission to Sangin over, the issue about killing Saif the Snake was back on the table.

"Let's get rid of him," one of the operators said.

Shark suggested they throw him out of a helicopter. "That would fix the problem," he said.

Several of the Ground Branch guys agreed. They were almost at a consensus now. Almost.

"I told the chief what we thought should be done. Take him up on a helicopter, tell him it was a mission, then throw him out when we were up there," remembers Shark. Problem solved.

Shark says the chief of base was horrified. "You can't do that," he said. "The chief of base pulled me aside," recalls Shark. "He asked me if I wanted to talk to a doctor. Said maybe something was wrong with my head. I didn't appreciate that."

Shark headed back to his sleeping quarters at Gecko base, the second-story cargo container inside of which he lived. "I grabbed my Copenhagen [tobacco] and my satellite phone. I had one call to make, the kids would be getting ready to go to bed soon, it was early morning for us. When I found that right spot to call home, a spot where my phone could access the satellites and get a call out, it all seemed very normal to me," he recalls.

"Hello?" It was the voice of his ex-wife, whom he still loved even after their divorce. He always experienced pain and difficulty talking to her. She was an excellent mother, and their children always did whatever it was she instructed them to do. They couldn't make their marriage work; he had to accept that. They both loved their children more than anything in this world.

"Let him say everything first," Shark's ex-wife said to the children, back there in the United States.

"They always started their first volley of conversation with, 'Hi, Daddy,'" Shark recalls, "their soft, safe voices, with a unique twang added depending on what stage of baby teeth coming in or out they were in. Many of the times I would be on the receiving end of the sat phone for an extended period of time, just listening as they told me everything about the day."

This time, like many times, Shark stared down at his own physical body. His boots were covered in someone else's blood.

Six days passed. "I was standing in front of my metal fortress sleeping area speaking with a medic when I heard a call over the base radios," remembers Shark.

"Come to the operations center, there's something to see," Stingray said. He insisted it was important. Inside the team room, one of the guys was grappling with some cables and a huge flat-screen TV that was attached to a concrete wall. After a few adjustments, the TV screen came to life.

Whatever the operators were here to watch, it was from the point of view of a Predator drone. You could see the desert floor through a window of superimposed white crosshairs. A structure came into view. The Predator was hovering high in the sky, directly over a building in Sangin. There was tension in the air. Someone offered an explanation: the four Taliban they'd pursued six days before—the bomb maker and his three lieutenants—had been identified as presently being inside the compound they were now observing through the Predator's viewfinder.

The room was quiet. The image played without any sound. Everyone sat there, enthralled. A few seconds passed. The screen went dark for a brief moment. When an image came back into view, there was a small cloud of smoke. Debris, ash, and fire blanketed the desert floor below. The cloud held strong for a few seconds, until it became clear that all that was left of the compound was a rubble pile. The focus in the room was intense.

Someone said, "Fuck yeah."

Someone else said, "Un-fucking-believable."

"For as dramatic as it was," recalls Shark, "we knew not to celebrate too loud, or too often. It takes away from your readiness. That is what we are taught."

Everyone stood up and started to leave. Then someone said, "Hey, look at that shit." Focus went back to the TV screen.

Out from beneath the pile of rubble, a human being emerged. Stumbling. Wounded. Alive. One of the four high-value targets— the bomb maker or one of his three lieutenants—had survived the drone strike. As the man stood there on the ground, bending over, gathering his senses, the numbers at the bottom center of the Predator's viewfinder began to move.

"Here we go again," thought Shark. He was right.

The screen went black for a moment. Then the rubble pile came back into view. This time, there was no movement on the ground. The fourth high-value target was dead. There were a few high-fives in the room, and then the atmosphere returned to normal.

"We went back to what we were doing," remembers Shark.

Something had to be done about Saif the Snake. In Afghanistan, says Lightning, "you have to be willing to take the long route to an objective and a victory, because the fighters there, the Taliban and the other bad guys with guns, they're unlike anyone else you've gone up against before."

The Ground Branch operators had been forbidden to kill Saif the Snake. "So we came up with the next-best idea, and that was to shame him," says Shark. "Make him lose his stature on the base."

To orchestrate his fall from grace, the Ground Branch operators organized a friendly—or not so friendly—regulation boxing match. A bloodless hidden-hand coup d'état. There would be rules that had to be followed. A boxing ring was built. Regulation headgear and boxing gloves were brought in from the United States. The fighters were drawn randomly from a container of names in a box, says Shark, no funny business allowed. "Except the funny business we factored in so a certain Saif Mohammad would be fighting the biggest man on base." The carefully chosen opponent was the Ground Branch team's Afghan mechanic, a 210-pound heavyweight with teeth so strange he'd been given the nickname Jaws. By luck of the draw, the referee announced over the megaphone, "The fight is between Saif Mohammad and the mechanic!"

Saif the Snake stepped out of the crowd of soldiers and walked into the sandpit, where two American referees waited. "Saif wore a strained smile on his puffy face. He had a full beard and it was well-kept," recalls Shark. "He was shorter than most of the other Afghan soldiers, and it looked like he hadn't been missing any meals." He wore desert camouflage trousers and a large white T-shirt. Jaws, the mechanic, lumbered into the ring. "He was big and slow, like a high school football player who hadn't yet grown into his oversized body," and he was a head taller than his opponent.

The referees gave the fighters instructions, translated through an interpreter. The fight began. Out in the stands, the spectators went wild. "A giddy crowd of soldiers who'd never seen a boxing match before," says Shark. The local day workers on base stopped working and were scattered around in the background, leaning on shovels or squatting down.

The mechanic moved steadily into the center of the ring. Saif the Snake froze. The mechanic moved forward until they were face-to-face. It appeared each man was having second thoughts about the competition. The spectators went quiet. The bodies of the two fighters went tight, "each as if he'd come upon a predator that required total stillness to get out alive," recalls Shark. Then Jaws hurled himself toward his frozen opponent, swinging at Saif with his sixteen-ounce regulation gloves. Saif put up his hands, but the blows came hard and fast. One of the lobs struck him in the side of his head, protected by light headgear.

The audience went wild with excitement. There were cheers and boos at the same time. The mechanic moved his arms, working hard to generate solid punches. Mixed in the fighting was a sloppy combination of slaps and punches, but they were all flying in Saif's direction. He had not moved his gloves from the guard position. He stood there stunned and defenseless in front of the jeering crowd. "His stature in the camp was being denigrated by the minute," recalls Shark. Break. Round Two.

The mechanic raced in and unleashed a barrage of punches. Several went straight into Saif's gut. When Saif reached down to hold his stomach, the mechanic saw the opening and hurled a volley of punches his way. Saif stumbled, tripped, and hit the sand. "Jaws leapt on him, smothering him and making strange jerking movements, like someone was using a shock collar on him. The mechanic engulfed Saif—he was hardly visible anymore." There were several more punches thrown, hard blows to the gut and chest. As Saif Mohammad lay there looking straight up at the sky, Jaws mounted him and began pummeling him, as if he had some training. The mechanic leaned in and began wailing on him, over and over. This was obviously not a regulation move, and the referees moved in. Break. Round Three.

The Ground Branch team had advertised a three-round fight, with the winner receiving a ten-dollar prize. Toward the end, the fighters were getting tired. Interest was fading. "The Afghan soldiers needed a nap," says Shark, "and they probably needed to hit the hookah again, too. They had a routine, and as much as they like anything, it is short-lived and they get bored." The whole point of the fight was to have all the soldiers watch Saif the Snake lose. Then suddenly, just as some of the fighters were beginning to wander off, the mechanic suddenly went at him again, full-bore. Saif didn't try to defend himself this time. "He simply absorbed the blows," recalls Shark. "There was no knockout punch; he just fell over. Legs out, arms up, like he'd raised his hand to ask a question. The referees ended the fight. Saif the Snake lost his stature, and therefore his power. No need for war."

Shark rotated onto another CIA base, where he trained another one hundred Afghan soldiers and led kill-or-capture missions in dark places that felt evil, too. A few fighting seasons later, he was back at Gecko base in Kandahar.

"I figure it was two weeks after I returned that we were called into our oversized coliseum of a meeting room. It was an all-hands meeting," he says. "The room was quiet, there were no terps [interpreters] allowed, it was only us. I wanted someone to tell a joke, to get rid of this quiet, at least talk normally. Something. Then the boss [chief of base] put out that Saif Mohammad was found guilty."

The story was explained: a wide variety of explosives and bullets had gone missing from the arsenal at Gecko base, and were then discovered with Saif and an accomplice. Officials got involved. Saif was sent to the National Directorate of Security. He talked in prison and led investigators to his alleged accomplice, an Afghan supply officer employed by the CIA at Gecko base. NDS located information about a plan to attack the Ground Branch team on base. It was written out in the accomplice's workbook, including sketches and maps.

The plan was to steal a Ground Branch truck, fill it with 2,000 pounds of explosives, then drive it into the area near the Conex boxes and the firepit—where the team guys made satellite phone calls home to their kids. For reasons no one could explain, but everyone understood, Saif Mohammad had been released from the NDS and had simply vanished, at least for now.

After several months fighting in Kandahar, Shark rotated out again. He was transferred to yet another CIA base, where he trained another one hundred Afghan indigs and went out on what by now amounted to hundreds of missions with them.

In 2011, Ahmed Wali Karzai, the president's brother, was assassinated in his home by his closest confidant, a man named Sardar Mohammad. In the ensuing investigation, more information about the Afghan indig fighters at Gecko base surfaced. The unit was called the Kandahar Strike Force, the papers said, and described the fighters as Karzai's personal paramilitary force. These were "highly-trained and elite troops who [underwent] regular physical training, including jogging and calisthenics, target practice and classwork such as lectures on choosing targets for kill-and-capture raids."

Why did Sardar Mohammad kill Ahmed Wali Karzai? Rumors flew. Speculative blame was divided. One theory proposed that Sardar Mohammad was a CIA assassin. Another claimed he was a double agent for the Taliban. A third supposition speaks to life in the moral twilight zone that Ground Branch operators are asked to live in.

In *A Kingdom of Their Own: The Family Karzai and the Afghan Disaster,* Josh Partlow, a *Washington Post* reporter in Afghanistan, described what he learned from senior U.S. military officials about the assassination. "Sardar Mohammad was a pedophile, and his pedophilia had gotten way out of hand and had become an embarrassment," Partlow wrote. A group of fathers whose sons Sardar Mohammad had kidnapped, chained to his bed, and held as captives for raping "had gone to AWK and said, 'You've got to rein this guy in. He's out of control.' AWK decided he was going to fire [Sardar Mohammad] from his security job and give him some other job. He summoned him over there that day to do it. And [Sardar Moham-mad] got wind of it." He shot Ahmed Wali Karzai in the head and chest, killing him instantly.

Nine years after the mission in Sangin with the upside-down truck, five hundred miles to the northeast, in Jalalabad, Brian Ray Hoke and a Ground Branch operator named Nathaniel Delemarre were shot and killed by the Islamic State during a kill-or-capture mission. It was October 2011. The "potential negative effects of HVT opera-tions" warned about in the leaked CIA directive "High-Value Tar-geting Operations" had come true. The lethal direct-action missions conducted against HVTs had resulted in precisely what the directive had forewarned: "creating a vacuum into which more radical groups can enter, and escalating…a conflict in ways that favor the insur-gents." The CIA has not released any further information about the circumstances of either man's death.

In Afghanistan, the violence continued to escalate. With the 2009 inauguration of Barack Obama, there was the widely held expectation that this new president would bring peace to the trou-bled Middle East, that diplomacy would predominate and the two wars America was fighting would end. Nominations for the Nobel Peace Prize occurred just eleven days after Obama took office, and his inclusion on that list was a preemptive move by the Nobel Com-mittee. "We are hoping this may contribute a little bit for what he is trying to do," said its chairman, Thorbjørn Jagland. "The prize is a clear signal to the world…. We have to get the world on the right track again." Publicly, there was hope. Privately, there was the real-ity of *Tertia Optio*.

In his first three days as president, Barack Obama took action on two of the CIA programs he'd inherited from the Bush White House. After reviewing the enhanced interrogation program, also called the torture program, he signed Executive Order 13491, revoking it. He ordered the CIA to shut down its detention and interrogation facilities, also called black sites, and prohibited the Agency from opening new ones. After reviewing the lethal direct-action program, including the drone strike and Ground Branch programs, President Obama ordered these operations to be accelerated. His decision to shut down the enhanced interrogation program was made public, but his decision to accelerate lethal direct-action missions was kept hidden.

On Obama's second day in office, a Ground Branch team conducted a kill-or-capture mission in Khyber Agency, Pakistan. The target was a Saudi Al-Qaeda operative named Zabu ul Taifi, involved in a series of terrorist bombings in London on July 7, 2005.

The kill-or-capture operation was run jointly with indigenous forces, but one of the men involved told Pakistan's *The News* that the mission had been led by the CIA. "The Americans seemed quite excited after capturing the Saudi national and immediately bundled him into their vehicle," the Pakistani soldier said. That same second day in office, President Obama also authorized two drone strikes in Pakistan, killing one Al-Qaeda high-value target and up to two dozen other people. Critics accused the president of solving the torture program problem with a killing program solution.

That fall, on October 9, 2009, the Nobel Committee announced that President Barack Obama had won the Nobel Peace Prize. In December, he traveled to Oslo, Norway, to receive the award. In a speech entitled "A Just and Lasting Peace," President Obama talked mostly about war, evoking the concept of just war theory, a set of ethical principles based in Christian theology and first written about in AD 400. In the sixteen hundred years since, just war theory has been providing leaders with a framework in which to rationalize war by reconciling three juxtaposing ideas: taking human life is seriously wrong; a nation has a duty to defend itself and its citizens; defending moral values can require the use of violence. Morality and warfare have been entwined across history, always with the strongest opinions reserved for assassination. Is assassination that is carried out in the name of defending the country, or the moral values of the country, virtuous or corrupt?

In his acceptance speech, President Obama defended the war in Afghanistan as a "just war," a war of last resort, of self-defense, of proportional force. He said that the goal was to spare civilians from violence. "I understand why war is not popular," he acknowledged, but "peace entails sacrifice." Without mentioning covert action, he reminded those familiar with the construct why it even exists in the first place: to prevent World War III. "Yes, terrible wars have been fought, and atrocities committed," he said. "But there has been no Third World War."

The Nobel Committee in Norway applauded the speech sparingly; the audience gave President Obama a standing ovation at the end. The president skipped the honorary lunch and a concert. He attended the honorary dinner and went home.

CHAPTER TWENTY-EIGHT

The Hidden Hand

President Obama's decision to revoke enhanced interrogation and accelerate targeted killing would have a profound effect on the age-old concept of assassination as a foreign policy tool. Whereas the Bush White House authorized 52 drone strikes outside the war theater in an eight-year period, the Obama White House authorized more than ten times that number, some 542 drone strikes that killed 3,797 people—supposedly from the kill-or-capture list—at least three of whom were U.S. citizens. Reportedly 324 civilians were also killed. But these numbers are just estimates.

President Obama not only embraced and accelerated the use of drones to kill terrorist leaders and their lieutenants; he became the first president in U.S. history to acknowledge that the hidden hand could be used this way. "Yes," Obama advisor John Brennan said on April 30, 2012, "in full accordance with the law, and in order to prevent terrorist attacks on the United States and to save American lives, the United States government conducts targeted strikes against specific Al-Qaeda terrorists, sometimes using remotely piloted aircraft, often referred to publicly as drones."

But the truth was far more ruthless and complex than John Brennan made it out to be. The *Wall Street Journal* had already reported that President Obama's drone program in Pakistan had also been killing fighting-age males without knowing exactly who they were. Officially called "signature strikes," these drone strikes were directed against groups of individuals who had been observed keeping company with known terrorists. In the press, signature strikes quickly became known as "crowd kills." "The joke was that when the C.I.A. sees 'three guys doing jumping jacks,' the agency thinks it is a terrorist training camp," reported the *New York Times,* citing a senior official.

The following year, in a carefully worded speech given at the National Defense University at Fort McNair, in Washington, DC, President Obama further owned his administration's targeted killing program. "America's actions are legal," he said. He'd canceled the signature strike program inherited from the Bush administration, he said, and was working "vigorously to establish a framework that governs our use of force against terrorists—insisting upon clear guidelines, oversight and accountability that is now codified in Presidential Policy Guidance that I signed yesterday." By bringing targeted killing out of the shadows and into the light, President Obama intended to silence his critics—to make American citizens accept that killing leaders and prominent people in certain circumstances was not only legal but moral and therefore just. "So this is a just war," President Obama insisted of the war against terrorists. "Doing nothing is not an option."

There was one person whose targeted killing few Americans objected to. Osama bin Laden was killed in Pakistan in May 2011, not by a drone strike but by a CIA-led paramilitary team. While this lethal direct-action mission is famously credited to the Defense Department's Navy SEALs, the team was acting under CIA authority, as the president's guerrilla warfare corps. Outside a war zone, only the CIA can conduct lethal direct action; its Title 50 authority makes it legal. The operators on the bin Laden raid wore clothing with no markings or identifications—as had the OSS Jedburghs in World War II and the MACV-SOG operators in Vietnam, and as do

Ground Branch operators all around the world today. Plausible deniability is built-in, should things go wrong.

After President Obama announced Osama bin Laden's death on national TV, a crowd of people gathered outside the White House. From Lafayette Square to Pennsylvania Avenue and beyond, thousands of Americans chanted in unison: "Obama, Obama! We fucking killed Osama!" Just war theory tells us not to rejoice in the battlefield deaths of others; that there is no place for vengeance or bloodlust. But what is man, if not flawed?

As significant as was President Obama's normalization of targeted killing, so was the reality that he depoliticized it. Here was a liberal Democrat not only embracing and expanding a foreign policy tool previously associated with conservative Republicans but expressing pride in it as well. "There isn't a president who's taken more terrorists off the field than me, over the last seven and a half years," President Obama told Fox News in his last spring as commander in chief.

"Obama succeeded in making Americans comfortable with drone strikes," says former administration official and drone scholar Micah Zenko, "as they are generally supported by the American public and wildly popular in Congress." There is subtext here: if Congress can't fight a battle on political lines, it acts as if it is not a battle worth fighting for.

How did we end up here, with assassination—but not called assassination—normalized, mechanized, and industrialized? Let's back up to the year before Billy Waugh was born.

One day in the summer of 1928, war became outlawed. Representatives of fifteen nations led by the United States and France gathered inside the French Foreign Ministry in Paris and signed a pact declaring war illegal. The General Treaty for Renunciation of War as an Instrument of National Policy, or the Kellogg-Briand Pact, came a decade after World War I, considered the war to end all wars.

Between the staggering losses—eight million dead, thirty million maimed or wounded—and the appalling barbarity of the weapons used, what glory that had previously existed had been sucked out of war. War had become too mechanized, people said, with horses replaced by tanks, and bombs being dropped from the skies. With the use of chlorine and mustard gas on the front lines, world leaders had betrayed the moral rules of warfare. By the time Kellogg-Briand was ratified in 1929, sixty-four nations including Great Britain, Germany, Italy, Russia, Japan, China, Cuba, and Afghanistan agreed to solve their differences through peaceful means. The treaty soared through the U.S. Congress with a vote of eighty-five to one. To wage war was now a crime.

A few months later, at a White House tea ceremony honoring the antiwar pact, President Herbert Hoover expressed high hopes for a new era. "I dare predict that the influence of the Treaty for the Renunciation of War will be felt in a large proportion of all future international acts," he said. But the peace was short-lived. Just two years later, in the fall of 1931, the Imperial Japanese Army invaded Manchuria, an occupation that would last until the end of World War II. In 1935, Adolf Hitler began military conscription of fighting-age males, the first in a series of aggressive acts that laid the groundwork for World War II.

In 1938, on the tenth anniversary of its signing, the editors of the *New York Times* declared, "the Kellogg pact is dead." The treaty, the editors wrote, "has not abolished war.... It has abolished declarations of war." What was being said and what was being done were in fundamental conflict. The facade lasted another year. On September 1, 1939, Hitler's army invaded Poland. Two days later, Britain and France declared war on Germany. World War II had officially begun.

It was after World War II that the idea of a third option came to be. War and peace were no longer the American president's only two foreign policy tools, the National Security Act of 1947 made clear. Covert action would now function as the president's hidden hand. In the words of former CIA inspector general L. Britt Snider, "Covert actions...that the CIA might undertake in other countries [could] accomplish a U.S. foreign policy objective without the hand of the U.S. government becoming known or apparent to the outside world." The most extreme of all covert-action operations, it was decided secretly, would be assassination. The president's advisors spoke "in riddles" to achieve their plausibly deniable goals, Congress later found. Or, in the words of CIA officer William King Harvey, assassination was to be "the last resort beyond last resort...but never mention [the] word."

For the next twenty-five years, from roughly 1950 to 1975, this is how it worked. The CIA's paramilitary force, with assistance from their special operations partners, armed foreign rebel groups, taught them to sabotage and subvert, how to engineer coups d'état, and if necessary to assassinate. Then came the revelation of these assassinations—including of Generalissimo Trujillo and President Diem and his brother Ngo Dinh Nhu—followed by the Church and Pike Committee hearings and the creation of the Senate Select Committee on Intelligence and the House Permanent Select Committee on Intelligence. Assassination was "incompatible with American principles, international order and morality," said Congress. Now there would be rules.

But Congress didn't create a law against assassination; rather, it left things up to the president and his national-security advisors to decide. Covert-action operations now required a Presidential Finding to be shared with the appropriate intelligence committee "as soon as possible" after issuance, Congress decreed.

And so, for the next twenty-five years, from roughly 1976 to 2001, this is how it worked. The attitudes and actions of Republican presidents Ronald Reagan and George H. W. Bush with respect to lethal direct action tended to be hawkish, while those of Democratic presidents Jimmy Carter and Bill Clinton leaned toward dovish.

Congress oversaw the Presidential Findings/MONs and the actions of the CIA paramilitary operators who were dispatched to the field to carry out the wishes of the president and his closest advisors.

Then came the terrorist attacks of September 11, 2001. It was the September 17 Memorandum of Notification that allowed for the return of killing leaders or prominent people in foreign lands—which if not for legalese would be called assassination—as a foreign policy tool. "It's remarkable when you consider what came out of one short paragraph in that [MON]," former CIA general counsel John Rizzo explained for this book. It was Rizzo who drafted this Memorandum of Notification. "Three words authorized the [terrorist] capture and detention program, another few [words] authorized taking lethal direct action against terrorists." When the MON was delivered to the congressional intelligence committees on September 18, "Republicans and Democrats alike had the same reaction," he says, which was: "Is this enough?"

The floodgates reopened. With the Bush administration, an army of drones called Predators and Reapers took to the skies, and an army of paramilitary operators from the Special Activities Division, and its Ground Branch, moved into action in hostile territory and behind enemy lines. The Obama administration embraced and accelerated targeted killing. The Trump administration further broadened these programs, but with the nation consumed by political battles, the targeted killing programs have become easier to hide. Ground Branch operators and their special operations forces partners presently operate in 138 countries around the world. Not just in Afghanistan, Pakistan, Syria, Yemen, Somalia, and Libya but inside (and in the airspace above) 70 percent of the world's sovereign nations, from Colombia to Mongolia, Albania to Uzbekistan, Nepal to the Gaza Strip. Ground Branch operators interviewed for this book have been helicoptered into Bogotá, Colombia, HALOed onto islands in the Philippines, and HAHOed into remote terrain in Iran. All on the orders of the president of the United States.

Covert action in general and targeted killing in particular are accelerating at a rate that far outpaces public awareness or understanding. The CIA has opened a global center called the Special Activities Center—the Special Activities Division has thus expanded from a paramilitary division to an interdisciplinary center.

Still, the goal of covert action remains what it was in 1947: to prevent or avert a nuclear World War III.

To report this book, I interviewed Billy Waugh for several hundred hours and exchanged more than 1,300 emails with him. A majority of the missions Waugh participated in were born classified—designed to accomplish U.S. foreign policy goals without their ever becoming known to the public. Even when discussing declassified operations he was involved in, Waugh tends to play it close to the vest, speaking in phrases that take time to discern. Once, he answered a written question with a series of dashes and dots, which took me a while to decipher as Morse code.

The more illuminating information often came forth when we were traveling together internationally, including to Vietnam and Cuba. Billy Waugh is a veteran soldier, paramilitary operator, and spy. He is a master of intelligence, surveillance, and reconnaissance—ISR, in covert-action parlance. He has spent his life at the tip of the tip of the spear. Having operated in some sixty-four countries around the world, Waugh, I learned, is most at home on the move: riding in airplanes, waiting in airports, driving in cars, and sitting in international hotel lobbies watching people come and go.

It was inside an airplane, traveling at 36,000 feet over the Russian peninsula near the Sea of Okhotsk, that I learned of the most dangerous lethal covert-action operation perhaps ever designed by the CIA and its military counterparts—an operation Waugh led. Dangerous—by way of unintended consequences that threaten the security and stability not just of the United States but of the entire world. The tactic: parachute assassins carrying a nuclear bomb.

It was the middle of the night, and the aircraft we were traveling in was roughly three-quarters of the way from Los Angeles, California, to Seoul, Korea. I couldn't sleep. The Korean Air A380 had a lounge on the upper deck, and it was there that I found Billy Waugh, seated on a couch drinking a glass of pineapple juice and reading *The Ministry of Ungentlemanly Warfare: Churchill's Mavericks Plotting Hitler's Defeat*. I sat down. We began discussing black entry parachute operations. As part of Operation Grouse, during World War II, the British Special Operations Executive parachuted commandos into remote terrain near the Norsk Hydro plant in Norway, where the Germans were secretly working to build a nuclear bomb.

"The nuclear weapon is the ultimate weapon," said Waugh. After he'd trained to parachute-jump a live nuclear weapon in behind enemy lines on Okinawa in the early 1960s, Waugh said, he and his Green Light Team moved to a classified facility in the United States at the Nevada Test Site, where roughly one hundred nuclear weapons had already been detonated in the desert—mushroom cloud and all. There the team conducted a feasibility test to see if a tactical nuclear weapon could be detonated after being parachuted in from above and armed on the ground.

It was the second week in July 1962, and John F. Kennedy was president. The United States and the Soviet Union were engaged in talks to ban atmospheric nuclear weapons tests. As part of Operation Sunbeam, the Atomic Energy Commission and the Defense Department were now jointly testing four tactical nuclear weapons in and around Area 18 of the Nevada Test Site, located seventy-five miles north of Las Vegas. These were the last four known atmospheric nuclear explosions in U.S. history.

"We started out on an aircraft carrier parked on the Pacific near Catalina Island," recalls Waugh. "Our four-man team was sequestered under the deck. No one said a word to any of us, and we didn't say boo. The nuclear device was made of three plutonium rings. Each one weighed thirty-three pounds. We had forty pounds of commo and a hand-cranked generator, which had its own portable seat."

The Green Light Team loaded their gear and the tactical nuclear weapon—capable of destroying a small city—into a TF-1. "The seats were removed," remembers Waugh.

"We were catapulted off this carrier, flew across California into Nevada, and prepared to jump." The goal was to jump, land, assemble the team, and assemble the nuclear weapon in less than fourteen minutes. "We jumped from down low," recalls Waugh. "Around a thousand feet above the deck [terrain]. When you jump that low, enemy radar can't see jumpers, but it sees the airplane."

For this reason, as many as fifteen aircraft are used in these kinds of parachute-insertion operations. The use of multiple aircraft confuses enemy spotters on the ground. In this operation, the Green Light Team landed, located all four members, assembled the device, and used the commo to send an encrypted message to the commanding officer.

"Instead of firing the device ourselves," says Waugh, "we handed it off to a group of [nuclear weapons] engineers."

The engineers armed the device and set the timer. The Green Light Team was driven to a bunker roughly five kilometers away, recalls Waugh. Each man was given a pair of welder's goggles, and a seat from which to watch the nuclear weapon explode.

"It's a thirty-thousand-degree-centigrade burst," says Waugh. "You watch it and you say to yourself, 'Holy goddamn.'" Good and evil. Sacred and profane.

"What's good about a nuclear bomb?" I asked.

"It scares people," said Waugh. "It should. Have you read *Hiroshima*?" The 1946 book by John Hersey follows survivors of the U.S. bombing. "It should be required reading. In a nuclear blast, people incinerate. They melt and disappear."

The feasibility test at the Nevada Test Site was a success. A nuclear device could be parachuted in by a commando team, armed, and fired in a matter of minutes. "The [Central Intelligence] Agency tries to prevent things from happening," says Waugh. "The military prepares for things that might." I thought of Lew Merletti's Delta Force assassins, who had succeeded in covertly parachuting down onto the White House lawn.

Flying over the Russian peninsula, Waugh recalled how, roughly two hours after the tactical nuclear weapon was detonated, a lieutenant colonel arrived at the bunker in the desert for a debrief. "They told us everything we did right and everything we did wrong." Then on to Nellis Air Force Base, fifty miles east, to spend the night.

"We didn't talk much," remembered Waugh. "You don't sit around and congratulate yourself on a job well done. That's not how you're trained." Waugh still recalls what he ate for dinner that night: "ham and lima beans," U.S. Army–style.

Ten days later, Attorney General Robert Kennedy flew to the Nevada Test Site to observe a tactical nuclear weapon explode. Archival footage shows him sitting on a wooden bench, dressed in casual clothing and wearing welder's goggles as he watches a weapon, fired from a recoilless gun, explode in the distance, 2.17 miles away.

Seated inside the upper deck lounge on our Korean Air flight, Waugh pointed out the window and noted the height, 36,000 feet — roughly the same altitude for a military HALO jump. "I never jumped any part of an atomic weapon by free fall, but I do know this has been accomplished," he said.

The concept of parachute-jumping a nuclear weapon must have remained on Waugh's mind because he brought it up again, two days later, during a meeting in Hanoi. We were at the former home of General Vo Nguyen Giap, the indomitable leader of the North Vietnamese Army during the war — the war Americans call the Vietnam War and Vietnamese call the American War. The purpose of this meeting was to discuss the MACV-SOG mission to kill

General Giap at Oscar Eight, in June 1967, a classified operation for which Waugh led forward observation control. The mission failed and Giap lived to be 102; he died in 2013.

Our host was General Giap's son Vo Dien Bien, the keeper of Giap's legacy. Dien Bien was born in 1954, during the battle of Dien Bien Phu, which his father commanded and for which he is named. We were invited to General Giap's former home, located across the street from the Ho Chi Minh Mausoleum in downtown Hanoi. Inside, large framed portraits of General Giap hung on the walls, with dozens of medals and awards neatly displayed in glass cases. Incense burned. We walked through the garden, where General Giap and his commanders sat long ago, plotting the demise of the United States. We were shown tunnels beneath the home where Ho Chi Minh and his inner circle took shelter during the Nixon administration's bombing of Hanoi.

Joining us was General Giap's former aide-de-camp, Colonel Bon Giong, age ninety-two. During the war, Colonel Giong commanded Brigade 48 of the 320th Division of the North Vietnamese Army. He led operations against U.S. marines at Khe Sanh and orchestrated hit-and-run strikes against MACV-SOG operators during Top Secret cross-border missions into Laos. Colonel Giong's fighters killed Sergeant Delmer Lee Laws and Sergeant Donald Sain; his men booby-trapped Sain and mutilated his body. Giong's fighters killed scores of Waugh's fellow SOG operators, just as Waugh and his colleagues killed scores of Giong's men. The goal of war is to kill in order to win.

"If you told me fifty years ago I'd be in Hanoi one day, I'd never believe you," said Waugh. He certainly never believed he'd be in Hanoi under these unusual circumstances. Here were former sworn enemies speaking without enmity. But to an outside observer, something unspoken hung in the air.

For a while, through a translator, Waugh and Giong discussed the other side's guerrilla warfare tactics—ambush, commo, and infiltration. Constructs they remained curious about, after all these decades had passed. Roughly an hour into the discussion, Waugh brought up his tactical nuclear weapons training.

"I was on a Green Light team that trained in Okinawa," he said, followed by a brief explanation of how the team trained to parachute a nuclear weapon in behind enemy lines, which would most likely be somewhere in eastern Europe in the event of war with the Russians.

"We were considering parachuting a SADM nuclear device into Vietnam," Waugh told our hosts.

The statement took a while to translate accurately, requiring repetition and clarification. Dien Bien and Colonel Giong were stunned by what Waugh was saying. "I want to make [sure] I understand you," Dien Bien said.

Waugh repeated his assertion.

Dien Bien disagreed. "We knew nuclear [use] was not possible for the Americans," he said, then clarified: "The Americans would never use nuclear weapons against" Vietnam.

"Not true," said Waugh. "I was on the team. We were going to drop it on the Mu Gia Pass. I wrote up the recommendation," Waugh said. The mission fell to MACV-SOG. The Mu Gia Pass was a steep mountain roadway that connected Vietnam to Laos. Countless communist fighters, weapons, and supplies moved through this pass each month; it was a choke point along the Ho Chi Minh Trail.

There was a long pause. Dien Bien turned to me. "Did he really just say [the] Americans were [considering] dropping a nuclear bomb on Vietnam?"

Documents kept classified until 2003 reveal this truth. In 1966, Secretary of Defense Robert McNamara ordered a scientific advisory group, the Jason scientists, "to evaluate the military consequences of a U.S. decision to use tactical nuclear weapons [TNW] in Southeast Asia."

Jason scientist Seymour Deitchman explained. "[We were asked] whether it made sense to think about using nuclear weapons to close off the supply routes [along] the Ho Chi Minh Trail....The idea had been discussed at the Pentagon."

To augment the evaluation, the CIA performed a landscape analysis of the Mu Gia Pass and determined that it was "the most vulnerable section" of the trail.

But having a SOG team parachute in a tactical nuclear weapon for use in Vietnam was a very bad idea, the Jason scientists concluded. "A very serious long-range problem would arise," they warned. "Insurgent groups everywhere in the world would take note and would try by all means available to acquire TNW for themselves." Such use presaged a dystopian future in which terrorists could use nuclear weapons in a game of existential extortion, the Jasons warned the secretary of defense.

"A small minority of dissidents with a supply of TNW could blackmail and ultimately destroy any but the most resolute government," the scientists wrote. "If this were to happen, the U.S. would probably be faced with a choice between two evils, either to allow nuclear blackmail to succeed, or to intervene with military force under very unfavorable circumstances." Not only would the use of tactical nuclear weapons open the floodgates, it would open Pandora's box—the mythological source of uncontrollable chaos. Prohibiting the use of nuclear weapons on the battlefield was the ultimate red line in the sand, a barrier that a U.S. president simply could not cross, even if it meant losing a war.

But Waugh told our hosts in Hanoi that he felt differently.

"I wish we'd done that," he said. "It would have ended the war."

There was a long silence. When Dien Bien finally spoke, it was to express shock and disgust.

"This is my homeland you're talking about," he said.

"Fifty-eight thousand of my people died," Waugh said. "Half a million of your people died. A lot of them would still be here."

More silence. Then Colonel Giong said, "Yes, but we might not have won the war."

Every nation wants to win at any cost. Except the cost and consequences of nuclear war.

The closest the world ever came to nuclear war was during the Cuban missile crisis. It was Che Guevara, more so than Fidel Castro, who advocated for nuclear war. "If the people [of Cuba] should disappear from the face of the earth because an atomic war is unleashed in their names," Che told the First Latin American Youth Congress in 1960, "they will feel completely happy and fulfilled." This rhetoric likely contributed to President Johnson's granting the CIA the authority to oversee Che's killing.

In June of 2017, I traveled with Billy Waugh to Cuba, where he was to make a HALO jump with a group of Cuban ex-military parajumpers. Our host was Ernesto Guevara. Ernesto was just a baby when his father famously wrote a letter to be read to his children in the event of his death. "Grow up to be good revolutionaries," Che Guevara implored. "Remember that the Revolution is what is important and that each one of us, on our own, is worthless." Following Che's assassination in Bolivia in 1967, Ernesto was taken in by Fidel Castro and educated in Spain and Russia, he says. During my trip, I learned that Ernesto was not a revolutionary like his father. A lawyer by training, he was now part-owner of a Harley-Davidson-themed motorcycle bar in Old Havana called Chacón 162.

Cuba is a great enigma, the original Cold War menace after the Soviet Union. This book begins with Stalin and the very real threat that communism once posed to the free world, and here I was now, visiting one of the last communist dictatorships on the planet. The island is America's closest nonborder neighbor, located just ninety miles off the coast of Florida. Since the revolution in 1959, Cuba has caused every sitting U.S. president foreign policy dilemmas, great and small. And while the threat of communism has now been reduced to nil, Cuba's role in America's national-security interests remains complex. Traveling to Cuba with Billy Waugh, I wondered if something else might lie behind the recreational HALO jump. If perhaps the hidden hand was in some way involved.

During the Obama administration, relations with Cuba had softened, but under President Trump new restrictions had been put in place. Finally, in June 2017, the U.S. State Department cleared our group for travel.

Our group was unique. Our team leader was a former Green Beret, from a legendary family of Green Berets. I knew from my research that our team leader's father had once taught Jordan's King Hussein how to parachute-jump; that he'd served in MACV-SOG, and later in the CIA's Special Activities Division, as part of Ground Branch, alongside Billy Waugh. Also on the trip were a commercial airline pilot (whose last name happens to be a registered trademark) and a beautiful, buxom woman who'd twice been crowned Miss [state withheld]. She had a background in U.S. Army intelligence and now ran a company that tracked criminals across state lines and turned them over to law enforcement. There was me, the journalist; a businessman who would serve as our interpreter; and Billy Waugh, the former Green Beret who was also one of the longest-serving CIA operators in the Agency's history. Waugh's last CIA mission, he said, had been in the fall of 2011, when he was eighty-two—sent to Libya during the revolution that overthrew Qaddafi to make contact with Qaddafi's former generals. Or maybe that wasn't his last mission. Maybe this was.

On the drive from Havana to Varadero Beach, the number of billboards and other forms of propaganda featuring Che Guevara was remarkable to me. He'd been dead for fifty years and yet his image was everywhere. For every one poster, sign, or billboard featuring Fidel Castro, who ruled Cuba for roughly fifty years and who had died only seven months before, there were eight or ten billboards of Che Guevara promoting La Revolución, some of them the size of apartment buildings.

For the parachute jump over Varadero Beach, on Cuba's north shore, our team would be flying in an old Russian aircraft, an Antonov An-2 biplane from the late 1950s. "The writing on the gauges was in Cyrillic," our group's pilot told me. He paid careful attention to the instrument dials. "Over the years, there [have] been six hundred twenty-two Antonov An-2 accidents, claiming seven hundred seventy-four lives," he said. "At least that's what's officially reported." As the person in the group chronicling the event, I had a choice: watch the jumpers from inside the old Antonov aircraft or from the deck of an amphibious rescue craft. Maybe I'd seen too many spy movies like *The Good Shepherd,* where the unwitting person gets thrown out the aircraft into the ocean. I chose the rescue craft.

Down on the white-sand beach, six shirtless Cuban former paratroop commandos ferried me out onto the azure sea. Through binoculars, I scoured the skies. After about an hour, Waugh and the others came hurtling down from above in a free fall. They looked like ants falling from the sky, tiny dots moving at terminal velocity. Finally, their individual parachutes blossomed and each came floating down to earth. Waugh, 87½, plunged into the ocean, where he was met by fast-swimming Cuban commandos, who made sure his lanyards were swiftly unclipped. Billy Waugh earned his paratrooper wings in 1948, when he was nineteen years old. He'd been jumping into war zones and training grounds and who knows where else, ever since. This was his last parachute jump. I could see the emotion on his expressive face.

At dinner, I asked Ernesto Guevara how he and our team leader, the former Green Beret, first met. The meeting took place at Chacón 162 a few years before, he said. The details came out later while we were driving around with the interpreter.

"A few years back," the interpreter said, "when Fidel was still alive, [the team leader] came into the bar. We knew he was an American. We thought, okay, he's either here to kill Fidel or he's an MMA [mixed martial arts] fighter."

Everyone laughed. The interpreter continued.

"We had the Cuban intelligence services ask [the team leader] a few questions."

More laughter.

"We've all been friends ever since."

One person in the group handed me a business card. It read: Dirección de Inteligencia. Cuban intelligence services. The name of an agent, should I need to call.

In Havana, Ernesto Guevara took us to La Casa del Habano, the legendary cigar manufacturer and smoking club where his father and Castro and their inner circle of advisors would meet to smoke cigars and plot the downfall of the United States. The room's wood-paneled walls were covered with museum-quality photographs, iconic images—including the time when the world came within a hairs-breadth of nuclear war—and was filled with European-style antique furniture, velvet chairs, bronze and marble statues. Rare luxuries in a country where I'd seen people riding horses for transportation, bareback and with ropes, not bridles.

The whiskey began to flow, and in the haze of cigar smoke, a rowdy discussion ensued. Everyone was enjoying themselves. Then the conversation turned to politics. Ernesto Guevara began speaking of the ills of capitalism, and he said that the benefits of socialism were worth fighting for. Waugh, never short on earnest opinions, cried bullshit.

"I fought for the revolution in Angola," Guevara said proudly.

"I spent my entire life in the military and the CIA," Waugh retorted.

Silence. You could hear a pin drop. Fair is fair: Ernesto Guevara has good reason to harbor ill will toward the CIA. The CIA trained the commandos that killed his father.

On the way back to the house where we were staying, our team leader asked Waugh, "What the fuck, Billy? Why'd you have to say that?"

"I'm too goddamn old to hide the obvious," Waugh said. "Besides, he can read all about me on the internet. Google 'William D. Waugh.'"

"They don't have internet in Cuba," said our team leader, shaking his head.

Driving through Havana, I noticed dozens of people gathered in a park, seated on benches around a banyan tree. It was around 1:00 a.m.

"What are they doing?" I asked our driver.

"Wi-Fi hotspot," the driver said, explaining that the Cuban government offers internet access for a brief amount of time, on a certain day of the week, late at night. People who want a censored glimpse of the outside world must really work for it in a communist police state.

Our team was staying at a private home billed as an Airbnb, seemingly implausible in a country where citizens haven't owned private property since 1959. The place was surrounded by concertina wire and made me think of a CIA safe house. A guard sat out front, watching our every move. I asked him what he was protecting.

"Lots of valuable things inside," he said.

In the spring of 2017, I traveled to Billy Waugh's house in Florida for lunch. Lew Merletti, the former director of the U.S. Secret Service, drove up from down south to join us. Waugh and Merletti are old friends, going back to the days of Special Forces, when Merletti was just twenty-one years old and Waugh was already a veteran MACV-SOG warrior whose reputation for ruthless bravery preceded him.

The backbone of the conversation was Special Forces. Each man believes his best qualities are a by-product of training and fighting for the U.S. Army Green Berets. After leaving the military, Lew Merletti spent the rest of his career protecting presidents of the United States from assassination—national-security defense. Billy Waugh spent the rest of his life conducting covert-action operations for presidents of the United States—national-security offense. The two work hand in glove.

On the walls of Billy Waugh's Florida home there are so many medals, framed commendations, awards, and honors that the eye doesn't know where to land. Numerous of these medals and citations are from the CIA, and as my eyes locked in on one of them, I thought about something the former director of the CIA's Counterterrorist Center, Cofer Black, said to me during an interview in Virginia in 2016.

"Good that you're writing about Billy [Waugh]," he said. Then he chuckled.

"What's funny?" I asked. We were eating dinner in an Irish pub just a few miles from CIA headquarters. The feeling I had was that there were spies everywhere.

"You'll only ever know a hundredth of the things Billy accomplished for us," said Black cryptically.

I told him I'd learned more than he might think. In addition to interviewing dozens of Waugh's colleagues and friends, I'd examined thousands of pages of declassified documents at the National Archives and obtained hundreds more through Freedom of Information Act requests.

Cofer Black chuckled again, sphinxlike.

"Most of what Billy Waugh did was never written down," he said. "Almost everything was on verbal [orders] from someone like me, to someone like him."

Things stay hidden this way, Black was saying.

On the walls of Waugh's home, one framed award—perhaps more so than the others—spoke to this truth. I'd seen it before, during an interview I conducted with Waugh at his home in May 2015. It was from the CIA and included the Agency's Seal Medallion, a Citation of Excellence, and an eleven-inch Persian-style knife. It read: "The Assassin: In Thanks for Your Friendship, Professionalism and Protection."

I asked Billy Waugh to tell me more about the award.

"You know I can't do that," he said again.

Waugh can't. Others did. In the fall of 2001—in the chaotic wake of the 9/11 terrorist attacks, and with fear of another attack looming—after reviewing the Memorandum of Notification that gave the CIA unprecedented new direct-action authorities, Congress asked the question: Is this enough? Senior Intelligence Service officers at the CIA made a radical decision at this critical moment in U.S. history. It was time for the CIA to pull from its Office of Strategic Services roots, to develop a team that could scour the globe: to surprise, kill, and vanish as necessary. According to participants, the team regularly discussed the need to be "ruthless, relentless, and remorseless" in facing a Nazi-like enemy.

This idea for this radical unit was drafted into a Memorandum of Notification. Known only to a select few, the unit was informally called the Stalker Team. "The idea was taken to President Bush and he signed off on it," says an individual directly involved. The man chosen to lead the Stalker Team was a veteran of the Special Activities Division, Ground Branch, someone who'd risen up through the ranks at the CIA to a Senior Intelligence Service position of great prestige. He vacated his seventh-floor office at CIA headquarters in Langley so quickly that many coworkers erroneously believed he had resigned.

The Stalker Team had roughly twelve members. Two were women; one of them spoke five languages fluently and became known among the group as the femme fatale. Two CIA targeting officers were assigned to the team and a third targeter was brought over from the National Security Agency to assist. All members used code names.

Orders were concise: "make book" on a set of individual targets around the world, some of whom were hiding out in mud structures inside the Federally Administered Tribal Areas (FATA) in northwestern Pakistan; others were hiding in plain sight, in apartment buildings located inside first-world, NATO-partner countries. Using reconnaissance and surveillance techniques developed and perfected by the CIA over decades, the Stalker Team created dossiers on viable targets: names, pseudonyms, locations, workplaces, routines, habits, and more. The unit then constructed alternative options for when a "go" order was given: compromise (blackmail), snatch-and-grab, sabotage, or preemptive neutralization.

"Our mission was to locate targets and stalk them," a team member told me in 2018. "If called upon, to disrupt their operation by going after them personally. Duct-tape them and carry them off. Capture, detain, question. If necessary, neutralize." Most on the Stalker Team were long-serving members of the Special Activities Division. "In the old days, SAD were knuckle draggers and snake eaters. Second-class citizens as operations officers. Not anymore. The [current] DDO [deputy director of operations] is a former knuckle dragger. So are a lot of guys on the seventh floor—SAD-born and -raised. Came up through the ranks. You know, the Agency used to be gun-phobic. Not anymore. The days of Europe and cocktail parties in Argentina are over. It's a different world now. Terrorism was the catalyst for changing the playing field."

Starting in 2002, the work of the Stalker Team was so secret and compartmented it needed its own cover story inside the CIA, and so an office was constructed behind a series of doors inside Budget and Finance. One day, CIA director George Tenet stopped by to discuss the Stalker Team's hidden-hand operations. He noticed a placard fastened to an exterior door. Enigmatic if not ironic, it read ACCOUNTS PAYABLE.

A discussion ensued. Many of the targets being pursued by the Stalker Team were prominent individuals and leaders in their communities—foreign nationals who'd been planning and orchestrating terror acts against Americans, some since the early 1980s. As far as the unit was concerned, these accounts were now overdue.

The details of the program remain highly classified, and the only known target that the Stalker Team was looking at who is now confirmed dead is Hezbollah's former chief of operations, Imad Mugniyah. The identity and fate of the other targets remain obscured, as intended, because the most successful covert-action operations are designed and orchestrated to be plausibly denied.

ACKNOWLEDGMENTS

I am grateful to all the individuals who contributed to this book—all the spies, soldiers, officers, operators, diplomats, policymakers, and historians who let me interview and quote them, by name or anonymously. If a mark of professional happiness is the breadth of fascinating people one gets to meet and become involved in conversation with, then surely journalism is the best job in the world. Getting to spend so much time with Billy Waugh was an experience I'll never forget. I am particularly grateful to those who shared with me certain personal experiences they did not want made public but were willing to reveal about themselves privately so that I could better understand what made them tick. I have yet to interview at length anyone of ruthless daring who doesn't have an Achilles' heel. More often than not, it is that secret vulnerability that in the darkest hour keeps them alive and striving, I learned.

Reporting a book is like a hunt for crumbs in search of a trail. The journeys into the archives were almost as interesting as the ones that involved HALO jumps out of airplanes; one can learn as much from the dead ends as the fruit-bearing ones. One initial hunt involved searching the record for early American presidents who might have been pro-assassination. I came across a somewhat shocking op-ed in the *Los Angeles Times,* from 1991, written by an obscure political theorist and foreign affairs expert named Ernest W. Lefever (who'd been chosen by President Reagan for a top position at the State Department but whose nomination was rejected by the Senate

Foreign Relations Committee). In this piece, "Death to Saddam Hussein? Let His Own People Decide: Assassination: Even Lincoln Believed that Tyrannicide was Morally Justifiable," Lefever argued that Abraham Lincoln was pro-assassination. "It is ironic," he wrote, "that Lincoln, himself a victim of an assassin's bullet, believed in tyrannicide—the killing of a tyrant." Lefever cited the president's own "collected works" as the repository where he "discover[ed Lincoln's] views on tyrants and tyranny." Unable to locate any of these references myself, I wrote to James M. Cornelius, curator of the Lincoln Collection at the Abraham Lincoln Presidential Library and Museum, for his assistance.

Cornelius wrote back. "The word 'tyrannicide' does not occur in Lincoln's writings or speeches," he assured me. "The 'tyrannicide' quotation or implication from a modern scholar not really involved in Lincoln studies is, in my view, a stretch of the truth.... The spirit of Lincoln's presidential policy was in fact in the opposite direction: he sought mercy, pardon, amnesty, against essentially every rebel leader" during the Civil War.

As an author who writes about American history, I am grateful for such historians to turn to for their expertise. The commitment and generosity of those who work to preserve the record and make it available to the public never cease to amaze me. Thank you, Richard Peuser, David Fort, and Jennifer Dryer, at the National Archives and Records Administration; Michelle Meeks, Information and Privacy Coordinator (FOIA), Central Intelligence Agency; Commander Mason Brayman, U.S. Secret Service; Robert Rodriguez, U.S. Secret Service; Herbert Ragan, William J. Clinton Presidential Library; Michael Pinckney, Ronald Reagan Presidential Library; Darla Thompson, Eisenhower Presidential Library; Liza Talbot, Lyndon Baines Johnson Presidential Library and Museum; Ryan Pettigrew, Richard Nixon Presidential Library and Museum; Jeff Senger, Gerald R. Ford Presidential Library; Stephen Plotkin and

Maryrose Grossman, John F. Kennedy Presidential Library; Mary Finch, George H. W. Bush Presidential Library and Museum; and Steven D. Booth, Barack Obama Presidential Library.

Thank you, Tina Hagemike Lepene, at Fort Bragg; Catherine Karnow, for arranging the meeting with Vo Dien Bien, in Hanoi; Chan and Mike Eiland, for their assistance navigating Vietnam; our hosts in Cuba who asked not to be named; Roxanne Merritt, director, JFK Special Warfare Museum, Fort Bragg, who met me on a Saturday, took me around the museum and the base, and shared her immense knowledge of the largest military installation in the United States, its history, and its people; Joe Callahan, for patiently answering my never-ending questions; Lynn Waugh, Donna Fiore, Jeff Hotujec and Leigh Hotujec, Jake Sopcak, Nolan Dunbar, Dylan Welc, and David Chasteen.

Thank you, Vanessa Mobley, Jim Hornfischer, Steve Younger, Tiffany Ward, Matthew Snyder, Liz Garriga, Janet Byrne, Ben Allen, Sareena Kamath, Ira Boudah, Laura Mamelok, and Allison Warner.

Thank you, Tom Soininen, my English-teacher father, who once returned one of my letters home from boarding school with the errors corrected in red pen and a loving note letting me know that his only intention was to help me become a fine writer. Thank you, Dad. And thank you, Alice Soininen, my mother, who died in between the publication of my last book and this one, and who is now one of the muses. My mom read the galley copies of each book I have written with an eagle's eye that was her signature style. We had a wager: I paid her five dollars for any mistake she could find in a narrative that had already been scoured countless times by many talented people. And yet with her drive and precision, she'd always find one or two errant blunders the rest of us had missed: things like Hawaii is 2,500 miles west, not east, of California. Thank you, Mom. And thank you to Kathleen and Geoffrey Silver, Rio and Frank Morse, Keith Rogers and Marion Wroldsen. And to my fellow writers from group: Kirston Mann, Sabrina Weill, Michelle Fiordaliso, Nicole Lucas Haimes, and Annette Murphy.

The only thing that makes me happier than reporting and writing books is the daily joy, wonder, and surprise I get from Kevin, Finley, and Jett. You guys are my best friends.

BOOKS

Aburish, Saïd K. *Nasser: The Last Arab*. New York: Thomas Dunne Books, 2004.

Ahern Jr., Thomas L. *Vietnam Declassified: The CIA and Counterinsurgency*. Lexington: University Press of Kentucky, 2012.

Anderson, John L. *Che: A Revolutionary Life*. New York: Grove Press, 1997.

Atwan, Bari Abdel. *The Secret History of Al-Qaeda*. Berkeley: University of California Press, 2006.

Bank, Aaron. *From OSS to Green Berets: The Birth of Special Forces*. Novato, CA: Presidio Press, 1986.

Bartholomew-Feis, Dixee. *The OSS and Ho Chi Minh: Unexpected Allies in the War Against Japan*. Lawrence: University Press of Kansas, 2006.

Bartrop, Paul R., and Michael Dickerman. *The Holocaust: An Encyclopedia and Document Collection*, Vol. 1, A–K. Santa Barbara, California: ABC-CLIO, 2017.

Bergman, Ronen. *Rise and Kill First: The Secret History of Israel's Targeted Assassinations*. New York: Random House, 2018.

———. *The Secret War with Iran: The 30-Year Clandestine Struggle Against the World's Most Dangerous Terrorist Power*. New York: Free Press, 2007.

Berntsen, Gary, and Ralph Pezzullo. *Jawbreaker: The Attack on Bin Laden and Al-Qaeda: A Personal Account by the CIA's Key Field Commander*. New York: Crown Publishers, 2005.

Bird, Kai. *The Good Spy: The Life and Death of Robert Ames*. New York: Crown Publishers, 2014.

Birstein, Vadim J. *The Perversion of Knowledge: The True Story of Soviet Science*. Cambridge, MA: Westview Press/Perseus, 2001.

Bissell Jr., Richard M., with Jonathan E. Lewis and Frances T. Pudlo. *Reflections of a Cold Warrior: From Yalta to the Bay of Pigs*. New Haven, CT: Yale University Press, 1996.

Boot, Max. *Invisible Armies: An Epic History of Guerrilla Warfare from Ancient Times to the Present*. New York: Liveright Publishing Corporation, 2013.

Burke, Jason. *Al-Qaeda: Casting a Shadow of Terror*. London: I. B. Tauris, 2003.

———. *Al-Qaeda: The True Story of Radical Islam*. London: I. B. Tauris, 2003.

Burton, Fred, and Samuel M. Katz. *Beirut Rules: The Murder of a CIA Station Chief and Hezbollah's War Against America*. New York: Berkley, 2018.

Clarridge, Duane R. *A Spy for All Seasons: My Life in the CIA*. New York: Scribner, 1997.

Cleverley, Michael J. *Born a Soldier: The Times and Life of Larry Thorne*. Privately published, 2008.

Cline, Ray S. *Secrets, Spies and Scholars: The Essential CIA*. Washington, DC: Acropolis, 1976.

Coll, Steve. *Directorate S: The C.I.A. and America's Secret Wars in Afghanistan and Pakistan*. New York: Penguin, 2018.

———. *Ghost Wars: The Secret History of the CIA, Afghanistan, and Bin Laden, from the Soviet Invasion to September 10, 2001*. New York: Penguin, 2004.

Crumpton, Henry A. *The Art of Intelligence: Lessons from a Life in the CIA's Clandestine Service*. New York: Penguin, 2012.

Darwish, Adel, and Gregory Alexander. *Unholy Babylon: The Secret History of Saddam's War*. New York: St. Martin's, 1991.

Daugherty, William J. *Executive Secrets: Covert Action and the President*. Lexington: University Press of Kentucky, 2004.

Dillard, Douglas C. *Operation AVIARY: Airborne Special Operations—Korea, 1950–1953*. Victoria, British Columbia: Trafford, 2003.

Evans, Duane. *Foxtrot in Kandahar: A Memoir of a CIA Officer in Afghanistan at the Inception of America's Longest War*. El Dorado Hills, California: Savas Beatie, 2017.

Fall, Bernard B. *Street Without Joy: The French Debacle in Indochina*. Mechanicsburg, PA: Stackpole Books, 1961.

Ford, Franklin L. *Political Murder: From Tyrannicide to Terrorism*. Cambridge, MA: Harvard University Press, 1985.

Giaconia, Mark. *Operation Viking Hammer: A Green Beret's Firsthand Account of Unconventional Warfare in Northern Iraq, 2003*. Amazon Digital Services, LLC, 2018.

Gill, Henry A. *Soldier Under Three Flags: Exploits of Special Forces' Captain Larry A. Thorne*. Ventura, CA: Pathfinder Publishing, 1998.

Gormley, Ken. *The Death of American Virtue: Clinton vs. Starr*. New York: Broadway Paperbacks, 2010.

Goulden, Joseph C. *Korea: The Untold Story of the War*. New York: Times Books, 1982.

Gregg, Donald P. *Pod Shards: Fragments of a Life Lived in CIA, the White House, and the Two Koreas*. Washington, DC: New Academia Publishing, 2014.

Grose, Peter. *Gentleman Spy: The Life of Allen Dulles*. Boston: Houghton Mifflin, 1994.

Guardia, Mike. *American Guerrilla: The Forgotten Heroics of Russell W. Volckmann: The Man Who Escaped from Bataan, Raised a Filipino Army Against the Japanese, and Became the True "Father" of Army Special Forces*. Philadelphia: Casemate Publishers, 2010.

Guevara, Ernesto. *Guerrilla Warfare*. New York: Monthly Review Press, 1961.

Hart, John. *The CIA's Russians*. Annapolis, MD: Naval Institute Press, 2003.

Hayden, Michael V. *Playing to the Edge: American Intelligence in the Age of Terror.* New York: Penguin, 2016.

Heikal, Mohamed. *The Inside Story of How the Arabs Prepared for and Almost Won the October 1973 War.* London: William Collins Sons & Co., 1975.

Helms, Richard, with William Hood. *A Look Over My Shoulder: A Life in the Central Intelligence Agency.* New York: Random House, 2003.

Horn, Bernd. *No Ordinary Men: Special Operations Forces Missions in Afghanistan.* Toronto: Dundurn, 2016.

Immerman, Richard H. *The CIA in Guatemala: The Foreign Policy of Intervention.* Austin: University of Texas Press, 1982.

Isikoff, Michael, and David Corn. *Hubris: The Inside Story of Spin, Scandal, and the Selling of the Iraq War.* New York: Crown Publishers, 2006.

Jacobsen, Annie. *The Pentagon's Brain: An Uncensored History of DARPA, America's Top Secret Military Research Agency.* New York: Little, Brown and Company, 2015.

Katz, Samuel M. *Hunt for the Engineer: How Israeli Agents Tracked the Hamas Master Bomber.* New York: Fromm International, 1999.

Kean, Thomas H., and Lee H. Hamilton. *9/11 Commission Report: Fully Updated with Controversial Third Monograph and Never-Before-Published Progress Reports from the 9/11 Commissioners.* New York: Barnes & Noble Publishing, 2006.

Kelly, Francis J. *The Green Berets of Vietnam: The U.S. Army Special Forces 61-71: Warfare in the 20th Century.* Washington, DC: Department of the Army, 1973.

Khokhlov, Nikolai. *In the Name of Conscience.* New York: David McKay Company, 1959.

Kinzer, Stephen. *All the Shah's Men: An American Coup and the Roots of Middle East Terror.* Hoboken, NJ: John Wiley & Sons, 2008.

Kissinger, Henry. *Years of Upheaval.* New York: Little, Brown and Company, 1982.

Korn, David A. *Assassination in Khartoum: An Institute for the Study of Diplomacy Book.* Bloomington: Indiana University Press, 1993.

Lance, Peter. *Triple Cross: How Bin Laden's Master Spy Penetrated the CIA, the Green Berets, and the FBI.* New York: Harper, 2006.

Levitt, Matthew. *Hezbollah: The Global Footprint of Lebanon's Party of God.* Washington, DC: Georgetown University Press, 2015.

Lewis, Bernard. *The Assassins: A Radical Sect in Islam.* London: Weidenfeld and Nicolson, 1967.

Luther, Eric, with Ted Henken, M.A. *Che Guevara.* New York: Penguin, 2001.

Maas, Peter. *Manhunt.* New York: Random House, 1986.

MacDonald, Callum. *The Killing of Reinhard Heydrich: The SS "Butcher of Prague."* Boston: Da Capo Press, 1998.

Maurer, Harry. *Strange Ground: An Oral History of Americans in Vietnam, 1945–1975.* Boston: Da Capo Press, 1998.

Mazzetti, Mark. *The Way of the Knife.* New York: Penguin, 2013.

McMaster, H. R. *Dereliction of Duty: Johnson, McNamara, the Joint Chiefs of Staff, and the Lies That Led to Vietnam.* New York: Harper Perennial, 1998.

McRaven, William H. *Spec Ops: Case Studies in Special Operations Warfare: Theory and Practice.* New York: Presidio Press, 1995.

Meyer, John S. *Across the Fence: The Secret War in Vietnam.* Oceanside, CA: SOG Publishing, 2013.

Milton, Giles. *Churchill's Ministry of Ungentlemanly Warfare: The Mavericks Who Plotted Hitler's Defeat.* New York: Picador, 2016.

Mirak-Weissbach, Muriel. *Madmen at the Helm: Pathology and Politics in the Arab Spring.* Reading, UK: Ithaca Press, 2012.

Montague, Ludwell L. *General Walter Bedell Smith as Director of Central Intelligence, October 1950–February 1953.* University Park: Pennsylvania State University Press, 1992.

Moore, Robin. *The Green Berets: The Amazing Story of the U.S. Army's Elite Special Forces Unit.* New York: Skyhorse Publishing, 1965.

Moravec, František. *Master of Spies.* London: Bodley Head, 1975.

Naftali, Timothy. *Blind Spot: The Secret History of American Counterterrorism.* New York: Basic Books, 2005.

Naylor, Sean. *Relentless Strike.* New York: St. Martin's, 2015.

9/11 Commission Report, https://www.9-11commission.gov/report/911Report.pdf.

Paddock Jr., Alfred H. *U.S. Army Special Warfare: Its Origins.* Lawrence: University Press of Kansas, 2002.

Partlow, Joshua. *A Kingdom of Their Own: The Family Karzai and the Afghan Disaster.* New York: Alfred Knopf, 2016.

Persico, Joseph E. *Casey: The Lives and Secrets of William J. Casey: From the OSS to the CIA.* New York: Viking, 1990.

Plaster, John L. *SOG: A Photo History of the Secret Wars.* Boulder: Paladin Press, 2000.

———. *SOG: The Secret Wars of America's Commandos in Vietnam.* New York: New American Library, 1997.

Prados, John. *Lost Crusader: The Secret Wars of CIA Director William Colby: The True Story of One of America's Most Controversial Spymasters.* Oxford: Oxford University Press, 2003.

Prince, Erik, with Davin Coburn. *Civilian Warriors: The Inside Story of Blackwater and the Unsung Heroes of the War on Terror.* New York: Portfolio/Penguin, 2013.

Quesada, Alejandro. *The Bay of Pigs: Cuba 1961.* Oxford: Osprey Publishing, 2009.

Rashid, Ahmed. *Descent into Chaos: The U.S. and the Disaster in Pakistan, Afghanistan, and Central Asia.* New York: Penguin, 2008.

———. *Taliban: Militant Islam, Oil and Fundamentalism in Central Asia.* New Haven: Yale University Press, 2001.

Raviv, Dan, and Yossi Melman. *Spies Against Armageddon: Inside Israel's Secret Wars.* Sea Cliff, NY: Levant Books, 2012.

Rizzo, John. *Company Man: Thirty Years of Controversy and Crisis in the CIA.* New York: Scribner, 2014.

Rodriguez, Felix I., and John Weisman. *Shadow Warrior: The CIA Hero of a Hundred Unknown Battles.* New York: Simon & Schuster, 1989.

Roosevelt, Kermit. *Countercoup: The Struggle for the Control of Iran.* New York: McGraw-Hill, 1979.

Schroen, Gary. *First In: An Insider's Account of How the CIA Spearheaded the War on Terror in Afghanistan.* New York: Ballantine, 2005.

Shultz Jr., Richard H. *The Secret War Against Hanoi.* New York: HarperCollins, 1999.

Singlaub, John K., with Malcolm McConnell. *Hazardous Duty: An American Soldier in the Twentieth Century.* New York: Summit Books, 1991.

Smith, Lisa. *Faithful Devotion.* Privately published: Raider Publishing International, 2009.

Smith, Michael. *Killer Elite: The Inside Story of America's Most Secret Special Operations Team.* New York: St. Martin's, 2006.

Smith, Walter B. *My Three Years in Moscow.* Philadelphia: J. B. Lippincott Company, 1949.

Stein, Jeff. *A Murder in Wartime: The Untold Spy Story That Changed the Course of the Vietnam War.* New York: St. Martin's, 1992.

St. John, R. B. *Libya: From Colony to Independence.* Oxford: Oneworld Press, 2011.

Tenet, George, with Bill Harlow. *At the Center of the Storm: My Years at the CIA.* New York: HarperCollins, 2007.

Thomas, Evan. *The Very Best Men: The Daring Early Years of the CIA.* New York: Simon & Schuster, 2006.

Thomas, Gordon. *Gideon's Spies: The Secret History of the Mossad.* New York: St. Martin's Griffin, 2012.

Tucker, Mike, and Charles Faddis. *Operation Hotel California: The Clandestine War Inside Iraq.* Guilford, CT: Globe Pequot Press, 2009.

Volodarsky, Boris. *The KGB's Poison Factory: From Lenin to Litvinenko.* Barnsley, UK: Frontline Books, 2009.

Walker, Tony, and Andrew Gowers. *Arafat: The Biography.* London: Virgin Books, 2005.

Warren, James A. *Giap: The General Who Defeated America in Vietnam.* New York: Palgrave Macmillan, 2013.

Waugh, Billy, with Tim Keown. *Hunting the Jackal: A Special Forces and CIA Ground Soldier's Fifty-Year Career Hunting America's Enemies.* New York: HarperCollins, 2004.

Weiner, Tim. *Legacy of Ashes: The History of the CIA.* New York: Anchor Books, 2008.

Wilber, Del Quentin. *Rawhide Down: The Near Assassination of Ronald Reagan.* New York: Henry Holt and Company, 2011.

Woodward, Bob. *Obama's Wars.* New York: Simon & Schuster, 2010.

———. *Veil: The Secret Wars of the CIA, 1981–1987.* New York: Simon & Schuster, 1987.

Wright, Lawrence. *The Looming Tower: Al-Qaeda and the Road to 9/11.* New York: Vintage, 2007.

MONOGRAPHS, PAPERS, AND REPORTS

Ahern Jr., Thomas L. "CIA and Rural Pacification in South Vietnam." Center for the Study of Intelligence, Central Intelligence Agency, August 2001.

———. "CIA and the Government of Ngo Dinh Diem." Center for the Study of Intelligence, Central Intelligence Agency, Winter: 1993.

Baker, Joseph R., and Henry G. Crocker. "The Laws of Land Warfare Concerning the Rights and Duties of Belligerents." Washington, DC: Government Printing Office, 1919.

Barry, James A. "Managing Covert Political Actions: Guideposts from Just War Theory." Center for the Study of Intelligence, Central Intelligence Agency, May 8, 2007.

Behl, Thomas J. "Attempted Assassination of President Reagan on March 30, 1981." U.S. Secret Service, Office of Inspection, CO-1-31-833, May 4, 1981.

Briscoe, Charles H., et al. "Weapon of Choice: U.S. Army Special Operations Forces in Afghanistan." Fort Leavenworth, KS: Combat Studies Institute Press, 2003.

Burian, Michal, Aleš Knížek, Jiří Rajlich, and Eduard Stehlík. "Assassination: Operation Anthropoid, 1941–1942." Prague: Ministry of Defence of the Czech Republic–Avis, 2002.

Byrne, Malcolm. "CIA Confirms Role in 1953 Iran Coup: Documents Provide New Details on Mosaddeq Overthrow and Its Aftermath." National Security Archive, George Washington University, August 19, 2013.

Casey, William J. "OSS: Lessons for Today." Center for the Study of Intelligence, Central Intelligence Agency, Winter 1986.

———. "War Behind the Lines." Center for the Study of Intelligence, Central Intelligence Agency, Winter 1982.

Center for the Study of Intelligence, Central Intelligence Agency. "Beirut Diary." *Studies in Intelligence* 27 (Summer 1983).

———. "CIA Analysis of the Korean War: A Collection of Previously Released and Recently Declassified Intelligence Documents," n.d.

———. "Counterintelligence at CIA: A Brief History." 2018 Featured Story Archive, March 23, 2018.

———. "An Interview with TTIC Director John Brennan." *Studies in Intelligence* 48, no. 4, n.d., declassified September 3, 2014.

———. "Soviet Use of Assassination and Kidnapping: A 1964 View of KGB Methods." *Studies in Intelligence* 19, no. 3, February 29, 1964.

———. "Surprise, Kill, Vanish: The Legend of the Jedburghs." *Studies in Intelligence,* n.d.

Chambers II, John W. "Training for War and Espionage: Office of Strategic Services Training During World War II." Center for the Study of Intelligence, Central Intelligence Agency, *Studies in Intelligence* 54, no. 2 (June 2010).

———. "OSS Training in the National Parks and Service Abroad in World War II." Center for the Study of Intelligence, Central Intelligence Agency, *Studies in Intelligence* 53, no. 4 (January 26, 2010).

Commander, United States Military Assistance Command, Vietnam. *Command History 1967,* vol. 3. Military History Branch, Office of the Secretary, Joint Staff Headquarters, USMACV, Saigon, Vietnam, September 16, 1968.

Cosmas, Graham A. "United States Army in Vietnam: MACV: The Joint Command in the Years of Withdrawal, 1968–1973." Center of Military History, United States Army, Washington, DC, 2006.

Cullather, Nicholas, and CIA History Staff. "Operation PBSUCCESS: The United States and Guatemala, 1952–1954." Center for the Study of Intelligence, Central Intelligence Agency, 1994.

Department of Defense, Office of General Counsel. "Department of Defense Law of War Manual," June 2015.

Doolittle, James H., William B. Franke, Morris Hadley, and William D. Pawley. "Report on the Covert Activities of the Central Intelligence Agency." Special Study Group, Washington, DC, July 1954.

Doyle, Kate, and Peter Kornbluh. "CIA and Assassinations: The Guatemala 1954 Documents." National Security Archive, George Washington University, May 23, 1997.

Dujmovic, Nicholas, and CIA History Staff. "The Significance of Walter Bedell Smith as Director of Central Intelligence, 1950–53." Center for the Study of Intelligence, Central Intelligence Agency, n.d.

Dyson, F. J., et al. "Tactical Nuclear Weapons in Southeast Asia." Study S-266, Institute for Defense Analysis, Jason Division (Formerly Restricted Data, Atomic Energy Act 1954), Advanced Research Projects Agency, March 1967.

Federation of American Scientists. "Public Report of the White House Security Review," esp. "History of Ground and Air Assaults on the White House Complex" (in chapter 4) and "Appendix: Order of the Secretary of the Treasury."

Finlayson, Andrew R. "A Retrospective on Counterinsurgency Operations: The Tay Ninh Provincial Reconnaissance Unit and Its Role in the Phoenix Program, 1969–70." Center for the Study of Intelligence, Central Intelligence Agency, *Studies in Intelligence* 5, no. 2 (2007).

Finnigan, John P. "The Evolution of U.S. Army HUMINT: Intelligence Operations in the Korean War." Center for the Study of Intelligence, Central Intelligence Agency, *Studies in Intelligence* 55, no. 2 (June 2011).

Giap, Vo Nguyen. "People's War, People's Army." Reproduced by the Armed Service Technical Information Agency, Arlington, VA, 1962.

Gubbins, Colin. "The Art of Guerrilla Warfare." G.S.(R.), the War Office, May 1939.

Haines, Gerald K. "CIA and Guatemala Assassination Proposals 1952–1954." CIA History Staff Analysts, Center for the Study of Intelligence, Central Intelligence Agency, June 1995.

———. "Looking for a Rogue Elephant: The Pike Committee Investigations and the CIA." Center for the Study of Intelligence, Central Intelligence Agency, April 14, 2007.

Hansen, Chuck. "The Swords of Armageddon: U.S. Nuclear Weapons Development Since 1945," Chuckelea Publications, Sunnyvale, CA, August 1995.

Hawkins, Colonel J. "Record of Paramilitary Action Against the Castro Government of Cuba, 17 March 1960—May 1961." Center for the Study of Intelligence, Central Intelligence Agency, CS Historical Paper No. 105, May 5, 1961.

Hoffman, Jon. T., ed. "Tip of the Spear: U.S. Army Small-Unit Action in Iraq 2004–2007." Center of Military History, United States Army, Washington, DC, 2009.

Holm, Richard L. "A Close Call in Africa: A Plane Crash, Rescue, and Recovery." Center for the Study of Intelligence, Central Intelligence Agency, *Studies in Intelligence,* Winter 1999–2000.

Irwin, Major Wyman W. "A Special Force: Origin and Development of the Jedburgh Project in Support of Operation Overlord." U.S. Army Command and General Staff College, Fayetteville, NC 1975.

Jaggers, R. C. "The Assassination of Reinhard Heydrich." Center for the Study of Intelligence, Central Intelligence Agency, n.d., declassified September 22, 1993.

Joint Special Operations University (JSOU) and Office of Strategic Services Society. "Irregular Warfare and the OSS Model," Symposium Report of Proceedings. Tampa, FL: JSOU Press, 2010.

Kelly, Francis John. *Vietnam Studies: U.S. Army Special Forces, 1961–1971.* Center for Military History Publication 90-23, Department of the Army, Washington, DC, 1972.

Laurie, Clayton D., and Andres Vaart. "CIA and the Wars in Southeast Asia, 1947–75: A Studies in Intelligence Anthology." Center for the Study of Intelligence, Central Intelligence Agency, August 2016.

Leary, William M. "CIA Air Operations in Laos, 1955–1974: Supporting the 'Secret War.'" Center for the Study of Intelligence, Central Intelligence Agency, April 14, 2007.

Lewin, S. J. et al. "Jedburgh Team Operations in Support of the 12th Army Group, August 1944." Fort Leavenworth, KS: Army Command and General Staff College, 1991.

Lieber, Francis. "General Orders No. 100: The Lieber Code: Instructions for the Government of Armies of the United States in the Field." Adjutant General's Office, 1863. Washington, DC: Government Printing Office, 1898.

———. "Guerrilla Parties Considered with Reference to the Laws and Usages of War." Written at the Request of Major-General Henry W. Halleck, General-in-Chief of the Army of the United States, Ordered by the Department of War, August 1862.

Linderman, Aaron R. "Reclaiming the Ungentlemanly Arts: The Global Origins of SOE and OSS." Texas A&M University, 2012.

Merletti, Lewis C. "Report of the Department of the Treasury on the Bureau of Alcohol, Tobacco and Firearms: Investigation of Vernon Wayne Howell, Also Known as David Koresh," September 1993.

Prado, John, and Arturo Jimenez-Barardi, eds. "Gerald Ford White House Altered Rockefeller Commission Report in 1975; Removed Section on CIA Assassination Plots." National Security Archive, George Washington University, February 29, 2016.

Pribbenow, Merle L. "The Man in the Snow White Cell: Limits to Interrogation." Center for the Study of Intelligence, Central Intelligence Agency, *Studies in Intelligence* 48, no. 1 (April 14, 2007).

Robarge, David S. "Richard Helms: The Intelligence Professional Personified: In Memory and Appreciation." Released by the CIA History Staff, Central Intelligence Agency, February 2008.

Snider, L. Britt. *The Agency and the Hill: CIA's Relationship with Congress, 1946–2004.* Center for the Study of Intelligence, Central Intelligence Agency, 2008.

Sulick, Michael J. "Counterintelligence in the War Against Terrorism." Center for the Study of Intelligence, Central Intelligence Agency, *Studies in Intelligence* 48, no. 4, n.d., declassified September 12, 2014.

Troy, Thomas F. "Donavan's Original Marching Orders." Center for the Study of Intelligence, Central Intelligence Agency, *Studies in Intelligence* 17, no. 2 (September 22, 1993).

———. "Truman on CIA: Examining President Truman's Role in the Establishment of the Agency." Center for the Study of Intelligence, Central Intelligence Agency, *Studies in Intelligence* 20, no. 1, n.d., declassified September 22, 1993.

U.S. Army Special Operations Command, Deputy Chief of Staff G3, Sensitive Activities Division G3X, AOOP-SA. "Unconventional Warfare (Sine Pari) Pocket Guide." Fort Bragg, NC, April 2016.

U.S. Department of Energy. "An Account of the Return to Nuclear Weapons Testing by the United States After the Test Moratorium, 1958–1961." October 1985.

———. Office of the Executive Secretariat, History Division. "The United States Nuclear Weapon Program: A Summary History." DOE/ES-0005 (draft), March 1983.

U.S. Department of War. "Rules of Land Warfare." War Department Field Manual FM27-10, October 1940.

Volckmann, Colonel R. W. "Operations Against Guerrilla Forces," Special Text 31-20-1. The Infantry School, Fort Benning, GA, September 1950.

Warner, Michael, and CIA History Staff. "The Office of Strategic Services: America's First Intelligence Agency." Center for the Study of Intelligence, Central Intelligence Agency, May 2000.

Whaley, Barton. "Soviet Clandestine Communication Nets: Notes for a History of the Structures of the Intelligence Services of the USSR." Advanced Research Projects Agency, Washington, DC, September 1969.

Wilder, Ursula M., Toni L. Hiley, Tracey P., and Peter Garfield. "CIA at War." Center for the Study of Intelligence, Central Intelligence Agency, December 2013.

Wright, Donald P., et al. *A Different Kind of War: The United States Army in Operation Enduring Freedom, October 2001–September, 2005.* Fort Leavenworth, KS: Combat Studies Institute Press, 2010.

ARTICLES AND PRESS RELEASES

Agence France-Presse. "Attack on Mosque in Sudan by Fundamentalists Kills 20." December 10, 2000.

Al Jazeera. "Violence Surrounds Wali Karzai's Funeral." July 12, 2011.

Associated Press. "Iraqis: Hezbollah Trained Shiite Militants." July 2, 2008.

———. "Jewish Avengers Unapologetic for Targeting Nazis after WWII." August 31, 2016.

Babcock, Charles R. "U.S. Tightens Security of Top Officials." *Washington Post,* November 28, 1981.

Balz, Dan, and Bob Woodward. "Afghan Campaign's Blueprint Emerges." *Washington Post,* January 29, 2002.

BBC News. "Iraqi Kurdish Leader Evades Assassins." April 3, 2002.

———. "Three Die in Lebanon Border Clash." July 20, 2004.

Beard, Rick. "The Lieber Codes," *New York Times,* April 24, 2013.

Becker, Jo, and Scott Shane. "Secret 'Kill List' Proves a Test of Obama's Principles and Will." *New York Times,* May 29, 2012.

Borden, Sam. "Long-Hidden Details Reveal Cruelty of 1972 Munich Attackers." *New York Times,* December 1, 2015.

Carlson, Peter. "International Man of Mystery." *Washington Post,* June 22, 2004.

Cavendish, Julius. "After the U.S. Pulls Out, Will CIA Rely More on Afghan Mercenaries?" *Christian Science Monitor,* November 16, 2011.

Chardy, Alfonso. "Florida Opa-Locka Field Was Once the Site of Secret CIA Base." *Miami Herald,* April 22, 2013.

Chivers, C. J. "Threats and Responses: Northern Iraq; Kurdish Leader Is Assassinated in Militant Raid." *New York Times,* February 10, 2003.

Chouvy, Pierre-Arnaud. "Opiate Smuggling Routes from Afghanistan to Europe and Asia." Geopium.org, October 14, 2006.

CNN. "America's New War: President Bush Talks with Reporters at Pentagon." September 17, 2001.

Coburn, Davin, Kyle Barss, and Randolph Smith. Video Report Accompanying "Inside the Killing of Imad Mugniyah." *Washington Post,* January 30, 2015.

Cody, Edward. "Bomb Kills Palestinian on Israeli Wanted List." *Washington Post,* January 23, 1979.

Coll, Steve. "Looking for Mullah Omar." *New Yorker,* January 23, 2012.

Congressional Research Service. "Iran-Iraq Relations." August 13, 2010.

Darnton, John. "Ex-Beret Says He Killed Agent on Orders of C.I.A." *New York Times,* April 4, 1971.

Duffy, Michael. "Keeping It Secret." CNN, May 18, 1998.

Eljahmi, Mohamed. "Libya and the US: Qadhafi Unrepentant." *Middle East Quarterly,* Winter 2006.

Entous, Adam, Siobhan Gorman, and Julian E. Barnes. "US Tightens Drone Rules." *Wall Street Journal,* November 4, 2011.

Farnsworth, Clyde H. "Terrorists Raid OPEC Oil Parley in Vienna, Kill 3." *New York Times,* December 22, 1975.

Filippov, A. "Concerning the Attempt on the Life of John Paul II." *Pravda,* May 15, 1981.

Financial Times. "Former Insiders and Whistle-Blowers Provide a View of the Formidable Military Intelligence Outfit." July 10, 2015.

Fox News. "Exclusive: President Barack Obama on *Fox News Sunday.*" April 10, 2016.

Fuller, Thomas. "Khun Sa, Golden Triangle Drug King, Dies at 73." *New York Times,* November 5, 2007.

Getler, Michael, and Scott Armstrong. "Sadat May Have Had Warning Signs of Assassination Attempt." *Washington Post,* October 7, 1981.

Gerth, Jeff, with Philip Taubman. "US Military Creates Secret Units for Use in Sensitive Tasks Abroad." *New York Times,* June 8, 1984.

Gibbons-Neff, Thomas. "After 13 Years, CIA Honors Fort Lewis Green Beret Killed on Secret Afghanistan Mission." *Washington Post,* April 17, 2016.

Goldberg, Jeffrey. "The Great Terror." *New Yorker,* March 25, 2002.

Goldman, Adam, and Ellen Nakashima. "CIA and Mossad Killed Senior Hezbollah Figure in Car Bombing." *Washington Post,* January 30, 2015.

Guardian. "Israeli Intelligence Veterans Refuse to Serve in Palestinian Territories." September 12, 2014.

Gutcher, Lianne, and Julian Borger. "Ahmed Wali Karzai Killing Sparks Fears of Turmoil in Kandahar." *Guardian,* July 12, 2011.

Haberman, Clyde. "Clinton in the Middle East: The Sacred City; Divisiveness of Shrine Issue Forces Clinton to Drop Tour." *New York Times,* October 8, 1994.

Haj-Yahis, Yosif Mahmoud, et al. "Alleged Palestinian Collaborators with Israel and Their Families: A Study of Victims of Internal Political Violence." Harry S. Truman Research Institute for the Advancement of Peace, Hebrew University of Jerusalem, 1999.

Hansen, Peter, "Bắc Di Cu: Catholic Refugees from the North of Vietnam, and Their Role in the Southern Republic, 1954–1959." *Journal of Vietnamese Studies* 4, no. 3 (Fall 2009).

Harder, Tyler J. "Time to Repeal the Assassination Ban of Executive Order 12,333: A Small Step in Clarifying Current Law." *Military Law Review,* June 2002.

Hersh, Seymour M. "Watergate Days." *New Yorker,* June 13, 2005.

Hoffman, Bruce. "All You Need Is Love: How the Terrorists Stopped Terrorism." *Atlantic Monthly,* December 2001.

Hubbard, Ben. "Iran Out to Remake Mideast with Arab Enforcer: Hezbollah." *New York Times,* August 27, 2017.

Ignatius, David. "A Sectarian Spy Duel in Baghdad." *Washington Post,* June 14, 2007.

Inskeep, Steve. "The Cloak of the Prophet: Religious Artifact at the Heart of Former Taliban Stronghold." National Public Radio, January 10, 2002.

Joffe, Lawrence. "Hassan Al-Turabi Obituary." *Guardian,* March 11, 2016.

Johnson, Scott. "How Arafat Got Away with Murder." *Weekly Standard,* January 29, 2007.

Kazim, Hasnain. "Relatives of Pakistani Drone Victims to Sue CIA." *Der Spiegel,* January 21, 2011.

Khaja, Nagieb. "Fault Lines: This Is Taliban Country." *Al Jazeera,* October 24, 2015.

King, Gilbert. "A Halloween Massacre at the White House." *Smithsonian,* October 25, 2012.

Koenig, Rhoda. "Basket Casey." *New York Magazine,* October 15, 1990.

Kreitner, Ricky. "Is the Taliban Really Responsible for the Karzai Assassination?" *Business Insider,* July 12, 2011.

Lynfield, Ben. "Yossi Cohen: The Israeli Spymaster Straight Out of Le Carré and Ian Fleming Takes Charge of Mossad." *Independent,* December 8, 2015.

Malinarich, Nathalie. "Flashback: The Berlin Disco Bombing." *BBC News,* November 13, 2001.

McCulloch, Frank. "A Believer in Self-Reliance and Elitism." *Life Magazine,* November 14, 1969.

McGeary, Johanna. "Taking Back the Streets." *Time,* July 6, 2004.

McMurray, Kevin. "Cofer Black, Out of the Shadows." *Men's Journal,* November 20, 2013.

Miller, Edward. "Behind the Phoenix Program." *New York Times,* December 29, 2017.

Miller, Greg. "Brennan Speech Is First Obama Acknowledgment of Use of Armed Drones." *Washington Post,* April 30, 2012.

Miller, Marjorie. "Britain Reveals Plot to Kill Hitler." *Los Angeles Times,* July 24, 1998.

Nairobi Roar. "20th Anniversary of the U.S. Embassy Bombings in East Africa: Recollections from Employees and Staff of the U.S. Embassies in Nairobi, Kenya and Dar es Salaam, Tanzania." August 27, 1998.

National Public Radio. "Clinton Interview." *All Things Considered,* January 21, 1998.

———. "Reaction to Obama's Nobel Speech." *All Things Considered,* December 10, 2009.

Nelson, Soraya Sarhaddi. "Afghanistan Strives to Register All Newborns." National Public Radio, July 2, 2008.

New York Times. "Embassy of the U.S. in Libya Is Stormed by a Crowd of 2,000." December 3, 1979.

———. "Ex-Green Beret Is Convicted of Assault on Libyan Student." December 5, 1981.

———. "Then and Now." August 27, 1938.

Orleans, Alexander. "Echoes of Syria: Hezbollah Reemerges in Iraq." Institute for the Study of War, August 1, 2014.

Ottaway, David B. "Child POWs." *Washington Post,* July 16, 1984.

Paddock Jr., Alfred H. "Personal Memories of Operation White Star in Laos, 1961." *Small War Journal,* April 10, 2013.

———. "Robert Alexis McClure: Forgotten Father of Army Special Warfare." *Special Warfare: The Professional Bulletin of the John F. Kennedy Special Warfare Center and School* 12, no. 4 (Fall 1999).

Prouty, L. Fletcher. "Green Berets and the CIA," *New Republic,* August 23 and 30, 1969.

Reed, John. "Former Insiders and Whistle-Blowers Provide a View of the Formidable Military Intelligence Outfit." *Financial Times,* July 10, 2015.

Reza, H. G. "Soldiers' Story: Their Heroism No Longer Secret." *Los Angeles Times,* May 26, 2003.

Risen, James. "US Inaction Seen After Taliban P.O.W.s Died." *New York Times,* July 10, 2009.

Sahadi, Jeanne. "The Financial Cost of 16 Years in Afghanistan." CNN Money, August 22, 2017.

Schanzer, Jonathan. "Ansar Al-Islam: Back in Iraq." *Middle East Quarterly,* Winter 2004.

Scotto, Daniel C. "Pope John Paul II, the Assassination Attempt, and the Soviet Union." *Gettysburg Historical Journal* 6 (2007).

Shah, Taimoor, and Rod Nordland. "Taliban Take an Afghan District, Sangin, That Many Marines Died to Keep." *New York Times,* March 23, 2017.

Shapiro, Ian. "The CIA Acknowledges the Legendary Spy Who Saved Hamid Karzai's Life—and Honors Him by Name." *Washington Post,* September 18, 2017.

Smith, Craig S. "Shh, It's an Open Secret: Warlords and Pedophilia." *New York Times,* February 21, 2002.

Smith, Michael. "Afghan War: The Home Movie." *Times* Online, December 17, 2006.

Smith, Terence. "Details of Green Beret Case Are Reported in Saigon." *New York Times,* August 14, 1969.

———. "Iran: Five Years of Fanaticism." *New York Times Magazine,* February 12, 1984.

Tamayo, Juan O. "The Spy Who Betrayed the Brigade." *Miami Herald,* April 17, 2011.

Thomas, Pierre. "Treasury Official Says ATF Made Mistakes in Waco." *Washington Post,* August 14, 1993.

Time. "The Nation: Scenario of the Shake-Up." November 17, 1975.

Turse, Nick. "American Special Operations Forces Are Deployed to 70 Percent of the World's Countries." *The Nation,* January 5, 2017.

U.S. Department of the Treasury. "Treasury Designates Hizballah [*sic*] Commander Responsible for American Deaths in Iraq." November 19, 2012.

Vaughan, Douglas. "Ex-Green Beret Denies Being a Mercenary." *Washington Post,* November 26, 1981.

Vitelli, Paul. "Obit: Robert Rheault, Green Beret, Ensnared in Vietnam Murder Case, Dies at 87." *New York Times,* November 1, 2013.

Wall, Andru E. "Demystifying the Title 10–Title 50 Debate: Distinguishing Military Operations, Intelligence Activities & Covert Action." Harvard Law School *National Security Journal* 3 (2011).

Washington Post. "America's Chaotic Road to War." January 27, 2002.

———. "Funeral Crowd Demands Revenge." June 28, 1993.

———. "Libya Recalls 4 Envoys Under British Pressure." May 13, 1980.

———. "Opinions on President Obama's Peace Prize Win." October 9, 2009.

Washington Times. "Cheney Hails Bush Restoration of Executive Power." December 21, 2005.

Weiner, Tim. "Afghan Camps, Hidden in Hills, Stymied Soviet Attacks for Year." *New York Times,* August 24, 1998.

Willman, David, and Glenn F. Bunting. "Agent Disputes Boss on Waco Raid Warning." *Los Angeles Times,* July 25, 1995.

Woodward, Bob, and Charles Babcock. "Agency Watched Helplessly: CIA's 'Private Hostage Crisis' Over Buckley Told." *Washington Post,* November 25, 1986.

Zenko, Micah. "Obama's Embrace of Drone Strikes Will Be a Lasting Legacy." *New York Times,* January 12, 2016.

———. "Transferring CIA Drone Strikes to the Pentagon." *Council on Foreign Relations*, April 16, 2013.

Zuhur, Sherifa. "Hamas and Israel: Conflicting Strategies of Group-Based Politics." Defense Technical Information Center, December 2008.

INTERVIEWS
Primary Interviews

The individuals listed below served in numerous capacities in their long careers. I cite titles held that pertained to our interviews. All military and intelligence agency personnel are retired, unless noted.

Colonel Geoff Barker: U.S. Army Green Beret; Provincial Reconnaissance Unit, Vietnam

Ambassador Cofer Black: Ambassador at Large and Coordinator for Counterterrorism, U.S. Department of State; Director of the CIA Counterterrorist Center; CIA Chief of Station, Khartoum, Sudan

Ambassador Hank Crumpton: Ambassador at Large and Coordinator for Counterterrorism, U.S. Department of State; Deputy Chief of Operations, CIA Counterterrorist Center; led the CIA's Afghan campaign from 2001 to 2002

Colonel Sully H. de Fontaine: OSS Jedburgh, trained by the Special Operations Executive; 10th Special Forces Group (Airborne); U.S. Army Green Beret, MACV-SOG

Andrew Dwyer: CIA Special Activities Division, Ground Branch; U.S. Marines

Michael Eiland: First Secretary, U.S. Embassy in Hanoi; U.S. Army Green Beret, MACV-SOG

Charles "Sam" Faddis: CIA Special Activities Division Paramilitary Operations Officer; CIA Near East Division Chief; SAD Team Leader, northern Iraq; Chief of CIA Counterterrorism Center, CTC Weapons of Mass Destruction unit; U.S. Army Armor and JAG officer

Mark Giaconia: U.S. Army Green Beret; liaison to CIA Special Activities Division team, northern Iraq

Colonel Nguyen Boi Giong: General Giap's aide-de-camp; Commander, Brigade 48 of the 320th Division, North Vietnamese Army

Ernesto Guevara: Son of Ernesto "Che" Guevara

Ambassador Husain Haqqani: Pakistan's twenty-fourth Ambassador to the United States

General Oleg Kalugin: Thirty-two-year veteran of the 1st Chief Directorate of the KGB, Chief of Operations in Russia; Deputy Chief of the KGB station at the Soviet embassy in Washington, DC

John Maguire: Twenty-three-year veteran of the CIA; Senior Intelligence Service case officer; Chief of Station, Iraq

Terry McIntosh: U.S. Army Green Beret, Vietnam

Lewis Merletti: Nineteenth Director, U.S. Secret Service; Special Agent in Charge (SAIC), Presidential Protective Division for President Clinton; served on the Presidential Protective Division for Presidents Reagan, Bush, Clinton; Served on the Secret Service Counter Assault Team (CAT); U.S. Army Green Beret

Lester Pace: U.S. Army Green Beret, MACV-SOG

John Plaster: U.S. Army Green Beret, MACV-SOG

Enrique "Ric" Prado: Twenty-five-year veteran of the CIA; Chief of Operations, CIA Counterterrorist Center; Special Activities Division, Ground Branch

John Rizzo: Thirty-four-year veteran of the CIA; Office of General Counsel, CIA

Felix Rodriguez: CIA Special Activities Division, Brigade 2506 Gray Team; Team Leader Ernesto "Che" Guevara mission; Provincial Reconnaissance Unit, Vietnam

Scott Satterlee: CIA Special Activities Division, Team Hotel

Major General John "Jack" Singlaub: OSS Jedburgh; Chief of Air Operations, JACK-CCRACK, Korea; Chief of MACV-SOG

Ken L. Stiles: Twenty-nine-year veteran of the CIA; CIA Imagery Analyst who created the Agency's geographic information system; Chief Targeter, CIA Counterterrorist Center

Billy Waugh: Six-decade veteran of the CIA; CIA Special Activities Division, Combined Studies Division and Ground Branch, operating in sixty-four countries; U.S. Army Green Beret, MACV-SOG

Individuals who spoke using call signs; all are CIA Special Activities Division, Ground Branch

Axe
Cheetah
Hatchet
Hawk
Lightning
Sampson
Shark
Spear
Stingray
Zeus

Former employees from the following organizations spoke on condition of anonymity:

Canadian Special Operations Forces
Central Intelligence Agency
Defense Intelligence Agency
Defense Advanced Research Projects Agency
Department of Energy
Intelligence Advanced Research Projects Agency
Israel Security Agency (Shin Bet)

Israel, Institute for Intelligence and Special Operations (Mossad)
National Geospatial-Intelligence Agency
National Reconnaissance Office
National Security Agency
U.S. Air Force
U.S. Army
U.S. Secret Service

Secondary Interviews

Vo Dien Bien: Son of General Vo Nyugen Giap

Ambassador Nguyen Tam Chien: Chairman of the Vietnam Union of Friendship Organization

Colonel Julian Chesnutt: Defense Clandestine Service (DIA), Defense attaché in Israel and Pakistan

Senior Colonel Tran Ngoc Dan: Director of the External Relations Department, Veterans Association of Vietnam, Hanoi, Vietnam

Donna Fiore: Sister of Michael Kuropas

Rear Admiral Kirk A. Foster: Military drone policy expert, Judge Advocate General Corps and Senior Legal Advisor at U.S. Navy; Department of the Navy Office of Legislative Affairs, Office of the U.S. Defense Representative to Pakistan

Sammy Hernandez: U.S. Army Green Beret, MACV-SOG

Luu Van Hop: Deputy Director, Veterans Association of Vietnam, Hanoi, Vietnam

Jeff Hotujec: U.S. Army Special Forces (Delta Force); Training Specialist, Directorate of Training and Doctrine, U.S. Army John F. Kennedy Special Warfare Center and School; Vice President, Special Forces Association

Matthew Levitt: Washington Institute for Near East Policy

John Stryker Meyer: U.S. Army Green Beret, MACV-SOG

Roxanne M. Merritt: Director, JFK Special Warfare Museum, Fort Bragg, Fayetteville, North Carolina

Brigadier General Charles Moore: Deputy Director, Global Operations J-3, the Joint Staff, the Pentagon; former Chief of Security Assistance, Office of Security Cooperation-Iraq, Baghdad, Iraq

Bui Van Nghi: Deputy Director in Charge, Americas Department, Secretary General, Vietnam-USA Society, Hanoi, Vietnam

Virginia Norton: Wife of Colonel Charles W. Norton, Chief of Command and Control Central, MACV-SOG

Doug Patteson: CIA National Clandestine Service, Case Officer

Ilya Ponomarev (in exile): Chairman of Innovation and Venture Capital Subcommittee, Federal Assembly of the Russian Federation, State Duma

Steve Puthoff: U.S. Army Green Beret

Colonel Leonard Rosanoff: Officer, U.S. Army Green Berets

Colonel Sean Ryan: Officer, U.S. Army Green Berets

Jake Sopcak: U.S. Army Green Beret

HRH Princess Basmah Bint Saud Bin Abdul Aziz Al Souad: Member of the Saudi royal family

Major Mark Smith: U.S. Army Green Beret, Vietnam

Harlow Stevens: U.S. Army Green Beret, Vietnam

Sean P. Sullivan: Paramilitary Officer, CIA Special Activities Division

Colonel Tuan T. Ton (active): U.S. Army Defense and Army Attaché, Embassy of the United States, Hanoi, Vietnam

Selçuk Ünal (active): Turkish Ambassador to Canada; Turkish permanent mission to the UN Security Council

Lynn Waugh: Wife of Billy Waugh

Edward Wolcoff: U.S. Army Green Beret, MACV-SOG

Abbreviations used in notes

ARCHIVES

ADST   Association for Diplomatic Studies and Training. These records constitute the world's largest collection of U.S. diplomatic oral histories.

APP   The American Presidency Project. Curated by the University of California, Santa Barbara, and hosted online, this record set contains more than 130,000 presidential documents.

CIA/CREST   Records of the Central Intelligence Agency, National Archives and Records Administration, CIA Records Search Tool. This series contains documents declassified by the CIA, including through the Freedom of Information Act.

CIA/CSI   Records of the Central Intelligence Agency, Center for the Study of Intelligence. These documents reveal the CIA's role in conducting U.S. foreign policy and include senior leadership studies and describe activities of CIA directorates. They also contain manuals on tradecraft; documentation of U.S. national-security threats; and descriptions of events and operations in which covert action played a role influencing outcomes.

DOE/OSTI   Records of the U.S. Department of Energy, Office of Scientific and Technical Information.

FRUS   Records of the Department of State, Office of the Historian, Foreign Relations of the United States. This series represents the official documentary historical record of major U.S. foreign policy decisions and diplomatic activity. It contains documents from the CIA, the Departments of State and Defense, the National Security Council, presidential libraries, and private papers of government officials.

NARA   National Archives and Records Administration, College Park, Maryland.

SSC/CHURCH Records of the United States Senate Select Committee to Study Government Operations with Respect to Intelligence Activities, 1975. Also called the Church Committee, chaired by Senator Frank Church.

PRESIDENTIAL LIBRARIES

DDE/L   Dwight D. Eisenhower Presidential Library, Museum, and Boyhood Home, Abilene, Kansas

GRF/L   Gerald R. Ford Presidential Library, Grand Rapids, Michigan

HST/L   Harry S. Truman Presidential Library & Museum, Independence, Missouri

JC/L   Jimmy Carter Presidential Library and Museum, Atlanta, Georgia

JFK/L   John F. Kennedy Presidential Library and Museum, Boston, Massachusetts

RR/L   Ronald Reagan Presidential Library and Museum, Simi Valley, California

WJC/L   William J. Clinton Presidential Library and Museum, Little Rock, Arkansas

PROLOGUE

3 president's third option when the first option, diplomacy, is inadequate: *Tertia Optio* is the motto of the CIA's Special Activities Center (thirdoptionfoundation.org).

4 "Surprise, Kill, Vanish": Warner and CIA History Staff, "The Office of Strategic Services: America's First Intelligence Agency," n.p., CIA/CREST. The OSS consisted of three branches: Secret Intelligence (SI), Special Operations, and Morale Operations (MO).

4 killing a leader or prominent person: Presidential Policy Guidance, "Procedures for Approving Direct Action Against Terrorist Targets Located Outside the United States and Areas of Active Hostilities," Top Secret/NOFORN, May 22, 2013 (justice.gov). Alternative terms are used including "direct lethal force," "lethal action," "direct action, lethal and non-lethal force."

4 the construct became "pre-emptive neutralization": National Security Decision Directive 138, "Combatting Terrorism," April 3, 1984, RR/L. President Reagan ordered DCI William Casey to develop "capabilities for the pre-emptive neutralization of anti-American terrorist groups which plan, support, or conduct hostile terrorist acts against U.S. citizens, interests, and property overseas." NSDD 138 was not fully declassified until 2009.

4 advance U.S. foreign policy objectives: Former CIA inspector general L. Britt Snider describes covert actions as "activities that the CIA might undertake in other countries to accomplish a U.S. foreign policy objective without the hand of the U.S. government becoming known or apparent to the outside world." Snider, *The Agency and the Hill,* 259, CIA/CSI.

4 no oversight: In 1975, the Church Committee reported, "There is not now, nor has there ever been, a formal procedure or committee to consider and approve covert action operations." SSC/CHURCH.

5 Presidential Finding, or Memorandum of Notification (MON): "A MON is the same as a Finding in everything but name," says Rizzo. In 1980, Rizzo was directed by White House counsel Lloyd Cutler to create a second name for a Presidential Finding, one "that simply expands or otherwise changes the scope of a preexisting Finding. We came up with a deceptively innocuous term, 'Memorandum of Notification'—MON for short. It was purely a cosmetic move." Rizzo, *Company Man,* 75.

CHAPTER ONE

11 "Listen up": interviews with Billy Waugh, 2015–2019. The majority of Waugh's quotes herein are from our interviews and email correspondence. Some are pulled from his 2004 memoir, a) because they are perfectly stated there, and b) because Waugh regularly uses these summary phrases in lectures for the U.S. Army John F. Kennedy Special Warfare Center and School at Fort Bragg.

12 "It is not right": Shirer, *The Rise and Fall of the Third Reich,* 532.

12 paraglider attack at the Belgian fortress Eben Emael: newsreel footage available on YouTube; McRaven, *Spec Ops,* 29–69.

14 stem from the Lieber Code: Francis Lieber, "General Orders No. 100: The Lieber Code: Instructions for the Government of Armies of the United States in the Field." Dr. Francis Lieber originally presented these ideas in a series of lectures entitled "The Laws and Usages of War," at Columbia Law School. Later, Secretary of War Edward Stanton and General-in-Chief of the Army Henry Halleck asked him to prepare them as a code of uniform conduct for warfighting during the Civil War. See also Rick Beard, "The Lieber Codes," *New York Times,* April 24, 2013.

14 "insidious": Lieber, "Guerrilla Parties Considered with Reference to the Laws and Usages of War," 18.

15 handled jointly: Private Papers of Major General Sir Colin M. Gubbins, KCMG DSO MC, Imperial War Museum, Catalogue Document No. 12618; Moravec, *Master of Spies,* 23.

15 willingness to ruthlessly kill: Burian et al., "Assassination: Operation Anthropoid 1941–1942," 37; Jaggers, "The Assassination of Reinhard Heydrich," n.p., CIA/CSI.

15 "whole art of guerilla [*sic*] warfare": Gubbins, "The Art of Guerilla Warfare," 3. This 22-page manuscript was originally printed as a booklet for SOE, along with the "Partisan's Leader's Handbook." Located in Private Papers of Major General Sir Colin M. Gubbins, KCMG DSO MC. Imperial War Museums, UK.

16 small bomb: Milton, *Ministry,* 183.

16 rushed toward the sharpest point: Burian et al., "Assassination: Operation Anthropoid 1941–1942," 64.

18 Heydrich's spleen: Jaggers, "The Assassination of Reinhard Heydrich," n.p., CIA/CSI.

18 "condemn as stupid and idiotic": MacDonald, *Killing of Reinhard Heydrich*, 117.

19 Five thousand Czechs: Numbers and dates vary. I use Moravec's memoir as the authoritative source.

19 Moravec returned to Prague: Moravec, *Master*, 222–23.

20 "You foot-kissers": Jaggers, "The Assassination of Reinhard Heydrich," n.p., CIA/CSI.

20 wartime predecessor: "Executive Order 9182, Establishing the Office of War Information, June 13, 1942," APP. In 1941, President Roosevelt named Donovan first director of the Office of Coordinator of Information (COI). He was charged with gathering national-security information for the coming war. COI was in turn folded into OSS.

21 partnership with SOE: Chambers, "Training for War and Espionage," 1–18, CIA/CSI.

21 Bank spotted: Bank, *OSS to Green Berets*, 1.

21 Initial training took place at a secret facility: author interviews with Singlaub; see also Chambers, *OSS Training*, chapters 3, 5, 7.

21 "Either you kill": Gubbins quotes are cited in Milton, *Ministry*, 122.

22 "constant jeopardy": David S. Robarge, "Richard Helms: The Intelligence Professional Personified: In Memory and Appreciation," public release February 2008, CIA History Staff, Central Intelligence Agency.

22 How to kill a man: "Close Combat," typed lecture, December 1943, Box 158, OSS Records, RG 226, NARA; Chambers, *OSS Training*, 6.

23 art of self-reliance: Irwin, "A Special Force," 154. "Courage is the word that comes to mind when [considering] the Jedburghs," wrote Major Irwin. He spoke not just of courage in battle but of "the courage of those who challenged traditional military thinking."

23 "My observation": Donovan, "OSS Special Operations Branch History. This Phase of SO," F 4, OSS/RG 226, NARA; Troy, "Donovan's Original Marching Orders," n.p., CIA/CREST.

23 "fight to the death": Milton, *Ministry*, 122. Original source is an audio interview with William Pilkington, Imperial War Museums, Catalogue No. 16854, October 2, 1996.

23 more advanced training: Irwin, "A Special Force," 99–128.

24 STS-51: Bank, *OSS to Green Berets*, 11.

24 commandos jumped: interviews with de Fontaine, June 2017, and Singlaub, November 2016.

24 Team Hugh: Irwin, "A Special Force," 142–43.

24 Billy Waugh learned: author interviews with Waugh.

25 Operation Foxley: "The Hitler Assassination Plan," Sources 1-9 (HS6/624), The National Archives (UK); Marjorie Miller, "Britain Reveals Plot to Kill Hitler," *Los Angeles Times*, July 24, 1998.

26 "treacherous killing": Laws and Customs of War on Land (Hague, IV), Article 23 (b), signed at The Hague, October 18, 1907.

26 "vile assassin": Joseph R. Baker and Henry G. Crocker, "The Laws of Land Warfare Concerning the Rights and Duties of Belligerents," 125.

26 rule regarding uniforms: Persico, *Casey,* 73.

27 OSS had recently captured: Bank, *OSS to Green Berets,* 73–98.

28 "wild thoughts": ibid., 93.

29 president thanked Donovan: "Letter to General William J. Donovan on the Termination of the Office of Strategic Services," September 20, 1945, HST/L. Truman's decision was greatly influenced by Colonel Richard Park's damning assessment of the OSS, "The Park Report," an "informal investigation" requested by Truman in December 1944.

CHAPTER TWO

30 Tempered yet tenacious: Dujmovic, "The Significance of Walter Bedell Smith as Director of Central Intelligence, 1950–53," n.p., CIA/CSI.

30 "I believed": Bedell Smith, *My Three Years in Moscow,* 51.

32 Stalin's personal office building: ibid., 47–51. See also Weiner, *Legacy of Ashes,* 15–17. I first learned of this story in Weiner's book.

32 "His drawings": Bedell Smith, *My Three Years in Moscow,* 51.

34 "How far is Russia going to go?": ibid., 47.

34 act officially established: The National Security Act of 1947—July 26, 1947, Public Law 253, 80th Congress; Chapter 343, 1st Session; S. 758, FRUS. The act authorized the NSC to direct the CIA to take action. The mission of the NSC was to advise and assist the president on national-security matters, and to ensure coordination between the CIA and the military. The NSC staff consisted of seven permanent members: the president; the secretaries of state, defense, the army, the navy, and the air force; and the chairman of the National Security Resources Board. The director of the CIA was not a permanent member but instead served as a resident advisor.

34 guerrilla warfare corps: Kennan's concept came from a State Department proposal prepared for the Joint Chiefs of Staff by former OSS officers Charles Thayer and George Lindsey. After reading the Thayer-Lindsey proposal, Kennan sent Secretary of Defense James Forrestal a now-famous letter stating, "I think we have to face the fact that Russian successes have been gained in many areas by irregular and underground methods. I do not think the American people would ever approve of the policies, which rely fundamentally on similar methods for their effectiveness. I do feel, however, that there are cases where it might be essential to our security to fight fire with fire." Joint Chiefs of Staff Discussion papers, JCS 1807, "Guerrilla," September 5, 1951, RG165/NARA; Paddock, *U.S. Army Special Warfare,* 31, 33.

35 CIA was to coordinate: "CIA Authority to Perform Propaganda and Commando Type Functions," Houston to DCI Hillenkoetter, September 25, 1947,

FRUS. In accordance with NSC 10/2, peacetime covert action was to be the sole responsibility of the CIA. During wartime, covert-action operations—which the military also called guerrilla warfare operations—were to be coordinated with the Pentagon.

35 "plausibly disclaim": NSC 10/2, National Security Council Directive on Office of Special Projects, Document 292, June 18, 1948, FRUS. The full text is: "The National Security Council, taking cognizance of the vicious covert activities of the USSR, its satellite countries and Communist groups to discredit and defeat the aims and activities of the United States and other Western powers, has determined that, in the interests of world peace and U.S. national security, the overt foreign activities of the U.S. Government must be supplemented by covert operations....As used in this directive, 'covert operations' are understood to be...so planned and executed that any U.S. Government responsibility for them is not evident to unauthorized persons and that if uncovered the U.S. Government can plausibly disclaim any responsibility for them. Specifically, such operations shall include any covert activities related to: propaganda, economic warfare; preventive direct action, including sabotage, anti-sabotage, demolition and evacuation measures; subversion against hostile states, including assistance to underground resistance movements, guerrillas and refugee liberation groups, and support of indigenous anti-communist elements in threatened countries of the free world."

36 said George Kennan: There is little dispute that Kennan was the architect of NSC 10/2, making him the father of U.S. covert action and the CIA's guerrilla warfare corps. In testimony for the Church Committee, on October 28, 1975, Kennan called this "the greatest mistake I ever made" but otherwise ignored ownership. "Kennan managed to write more than a thousand pages of memoirs without any mention of his role as the progenitor of covert action," writes Tim Weiner, calling this "a small masterpiece of duplicity." Weiner, *Ashes,* 625.

36 including "guerrilla movements": Weiner, *Ashes,* 33.

CHAPTER THREE

38 "Korea became a testing ground": "Office of Policy Coordination 1948–1952," 17 (56-page typed document), CIA/CREST.

39 "I know nothing": Montague, *General Walter Bedell Smith,* 56.

39 pressure from the FBI: Thomas, *The Very Best Men,* 138.

39 "some insoluble riddle": ibid., 140.

40 enigmatic Hans Tofte: Chambers, "Training for War and Espionage: Office of Strategic Services Training During World War II," 6, CIA/CSI; "CIA and the Firing of Hans Tofte," October 3, 1966, CIA/CREST.

40 classified reasons: "The Identity of Kim Il Song," December 2, 1949, CIA/CREST; "The Korean Labor Party and the Kim Il Song Regime: History of the Party from 1925 to Date," Information Report, CIA, October 1962, CIA/CREST.

41 An assassin had been chosen: Goulden, *Korea,* 472.

42 unvouchered funding authority: "Supplementary Detailed Staff Reports on Foreign and Military Intelligence," Senate Report, 4–41, SSC/CHURCH.

42 set a precedent: "Central Intelligence Agency, Office of Policy Coordination, 1948–1952," Summer 1973, 1–27, CIA/CSI; Cline, *Secrets, Spies and Scholars,* 99–110. The invasion of South Korea by the north greatly affected the CIA's covert-action and paramilitary-operations capabilities. Before the war, in 1949, the Office of Police Coordination had 302 individuals in its ranks, a majority of whom had served in the OSS. During the Korean War, OPC grew to include 2,812 full-time employees and another 3,142 contract personnel. The number of overseas CIA stations expanded from 7 to 47 during this same time frame, while the OPC's budget went from $4.7 million in 1949 to $82 million by 1952. By the end of the Korean War, the CIA would be six times the size it was when it began in 1947, and its clandestine service would become the single largest component of the Agency. Effective August 1, 1952, OPC and the Office of Special Operations ceased to exist, merging into a single organization that would become known as the clandestine service.

42 CIA's parachute infiltration efforts: author interviews with Singlaub.

43 Singlaub would rise to the position: In 1977, President Carter fired Major General Jack Singlaub when he was serving as U.S. chief of staff in South Korea after Singlaub told the *Washington Post* that Carter's plan to withdraw U.S. troops from the peninsula was a mistake that would lead to war.

44 studying cryptanalysis: Gregg, *Pot Shards,* Part II: Intelligence.

44 "Chinese were well aware": author interview with Singlaub; Singlaub and McConnell, *Hazardous Duty,* 184.

46 "military has the inherent responsibility": "Memorandum to the Commanding General, Infantry Center, Subj: Analysis and Suggestions from Lt. Col. Russell W. Volckmann," Army-Chief of Special Warfare, April 9, 1951, RG 319/NARA.

47 "Army should be": "Department of the Army, Office of the Chief of Psychological Warfare, Minutes of the Meeting," September 5, 1951, RG 319/NARA; Paddock, *U.S. Army Special Warfare,* 57, 131.

47 an army organization: Dillard, *Operation AVIARY,* 7, 21, photo inserts: the first six-man team operated under the code name Task Force William Able, later changed to LEOPARD.

47 CIA informed the Department of Defense: OPC, Memorandum for Lt. Gen. A. C. Wedemeyer, OCSA, Subject: Transmittal of OPC response to the Special Section Joint Strategic Plans Group, from Frank G. Wisner, Assistant Director of Policy Coordination, August 1, 1949, CIA/CREST; Paddock, *U.S. Army Special Warfare,* 130.

48 "Psy War 040 CIA": author collection, provided by source. Cited in Paddock, *U.S. Army Special Warfare,* 102n258.

48 joint CIA-army airborne operations: Dillard, *Operation AVIARY,* 12.

49 "rate of return": Finnegan, "The Evolution of U.S. Army HUMINT: Intelligence Operations in the Korean War," 64, CIA/CSI.

49 February 19, 1952: Dillard, *Operation AVIARY*, 39–40.

51 "suicide missions": cited in Weiner, *Ashes*, 61.

52 they understood what was going on: "Report on CIA Installations in the Far East," Frank Wisner, Secret [redacted], 8 pages, March 14, 1952, CIA/CREST.

52 "The results of our investigation": Hart, *CIA's Russians*, 9; "National Security Council report on Current Policies of the Government of the United States Relating to the National Security," November 1, 1952, FRUS. Albert Haney should have been fired. Instead, circumstance favored him. In November 1952, he arranged for the transport of a wounded marine that would ensure his survival at the CIA. The marine's name was Allen Macy Dulles, and he was Allen Dulles's son. Two weeks after his son was injured, Bedell Smith stepped down and Allen Dulles became CIA director. Dulles promoted Haney to head up a new covert-action operation, this one in Guatemala. It would rely heavily on assassination as a national-security tool. It would have a profound effect on foreign policy for the rest of the century and into the next.

52 Smith sent his deputy: Weiner, *Ashes*, 65.

53 "Army/CIA relationship": Paddock, *U.S. Army Special Warfare*, 131.

53 Smith was also concerned: "Deputies' Meeting," Top Secret, June 30, 1952, CIA/CREST; Montague, *General Walter Bedell Smith*, 94–96.

53 "resident spies on the planet Mars": Helms and Hood, *A Look Over My Shoulder*, 124.

54 analysis of its Korean War operations: Central Intelligence Agency, Office of the Director, Memorandum for the Chairman, JCS, Subject: "Overseas CIA Logistical Support Bases," June 6, 1952, CIA/CREST; Weiner, *Ashes*, 639n.

54 enemies from its friends: "Office of Policy Coordination 1948–1952," 15–18, CIA/CREST.

CHAPTER FOUR

57 Waugh was transferred: author interviews with Waugh; "Transfer Discharge Data, William Dawson Waugh," RA 18223349.

58 "modest and austere": "Memorandum, Brg. Gen. Robert A. McClure, Subject: Status of Special Forces Training Center," December 3, 1951, RG 319/NARA.

59 Donovan shared with McClure: Paddock, *U.S. Army Special Warfare*, 140, refers to note 82.

59 first unconventional-warfare unit: Brig. Gen. Robert A. McClure, "Trends in Army Psychological Warfare," *Army Information Digest*, February 1952, 10.

60 "a rough group": Major General Edward Partain, quoted in CCS-SOG.org.

61 Larry Thorne...stands out: The story of Thorne is compiled from interviews with Sully de Fontaine (who operated with Thorne in MACV-SOG and was with him shortly before Thorne was killed in Vietnam). See also Cleverley, *Born a Soldier*, and Gill, *Soldier Under Three Flags*. Incidentally, in *The Green Berets*, Robin Moore's pseudonymous version of Thorne is called Captain Sven Kornie.

61 "He would have been at home": Cleverley, *Born a Soldier*, n.p.

61 Mannerheim Cross: ibid., photograph, 127.

62 transferred to Riihimäki: Cleverley, *Born a Soldier,* 172; the escapes and recaptures are also recounted in Gill, *Soldier Under Three Flags,* 86–92.

62 alias Eino Morsky: Gill, *Soldier Under Three Flags,* 95.

62 to become restless and bored: Thorne regularly drank and fought people in bars, which drew the attention of the FBI. The bureau compiled a large file on him that included information about the wartime operations he participated in for the Nazis, directed against Russian soldiers.

62 wrote his commander: Cleverley, *Born a Soldier,* 207.

63 perilous mission in Iran: "After Action Report, Recovery Mission to Iran," 10th Special Forces Group (Airborne) July 5, 1962, author copy; Cleverley, *Born a Soldier,* 313–14.

63 training guerrilla fighters: author tour of JFK Special Warfare Museum with Roxanne M. Merritt, director.

CHAPTER FIVE

65 "Even the light [aircraft] bombings": Anderson, *Che,* 141.

66 "Here, as elsewhere": George F. Kennan, "Memorandum by the Counselor of the Department to the Secretary of State," March 29, 1950, 2, FRUS.

67 Arbenz promised: Cullather, "Operation PBSUCCESS," 26, 41, CIA/CSI.

67 powerful new advisory committee: "Presidential Directive, April 4, 1951," CIA/CREST; "Coordination and Policy Approval of Covert Operations, A Historical Evolution," February 23, 1967, CIA/CREST.

68 agreement was reached to "develop a paper": "Relationship of the PSB to the NSC," May 24, 1951, CIA/CREST.

68 individuals "to eliminate immediately": Haines, "CIA and Guatemala Assassination Proposals," 3, CIA/CREST. On the list, Haines wrote, were "individuals of tactical importance whose removal for psychological, organizational or other reasons is mandatory for the success of military action." At CIA, officers and operators maintained two general points of view when analyzing the situation. One was that by overthrowing the democratically elected government of President Arbenz, the CIA undermined its mission to emplace a stable, democratic government in Guatemala. The second view was to say the Soviet Union never got a foothold in Latin America, that communism was kept at bay.

69 Top Secret "Report to the President": Gordon Gray, "Report to the President: Psychological Strategy Board," February 22, 1952, 1, CIA/CREST.

69 1949 Guatemalan Army list: Washington Cable [redacted] to [redacted], January 29, 1952, CIA/CREST; Doyle and Kornbluh, "CIA and Assassinations: The Guatemala 1954 Documents," National Security Archive, Electronic Briefing Book No. 4.

69 Clandestine service officers were queried: The CIA's clandestine service is responsible for all covert-action operations. Its official name has changed over the years: It was called the Directorate of Plans from 1951 to 1973; the Directorate of Operations from 1973 to 2005; and the National Clandestine Service

(NCS) as of 2005. It is still referred to as the Directorate of Operations, or the clandestine service. According to a CIA.gov posting updated August 6, 2018, in response to the question "What [will you] do in the CIA's Directorate of Operations?," the answer was: "Be accountable to the President, Congress, and the American public to strengthen national security and foreign policy objectives through the clandestine collection of human intelligence (HUMINT) and by conducting Covert Action as directed by the President."

70 "Castillo Armas readily agreed": Haines, "CIA and Guatemala Assassination Proposals," 3, 5, 6, CIA/CSI.

70 "hit list with the location": Memo to [redacted]: "Liaison between Calligeris [pseudonym for Armas] and General Trujillo of Santo Domingo," September 18, 1952, CIA/CREST. The asset was identified as "Seekford."

71 psychological warfare campaign: Memo to Lincoln, "Nerve War Against Individuals," June 9, 1954, CIA/CREST; Haines, "CIA and Guatemala Assassination Proposals," 3, CIA/CREST.

71 find graffiti painted: "Tactical Incursions (part II)," May 16, 1954, CIA/CREST.

72 learned of the hit list: Haines, "CIA and Guatemala Assassination Proposals," 47 [cites memos N.21 and N.22], CIA/CSI.

72 how-to instruction booklet: "A Study of Assassination" Job 79-01025A, Training File of PBSUCCESS, [handwritten date reads "Early 50's"] 1–9, CIA/CREST.

73 code-named Operation Success: "Timeline," Appendix A, from Cullather, "Operation PBSUCCESS," n.p. [41 pages], CIA/CSI.

74 code-named Lincoln: Alfonso Chardy, "Florida Opa-Locka Field." Dunbar was Albert Haney's pseudonym.

74 Come "D-Day": Memorandum for Chief of Project, Subject: KUHOOK Assessment, April 19, 1954, 3, CIA/CREST.

74 cables were sent: Memorandum, LINCOLN to Headquarters, January 6, 1954; Memorandum, LINCOLN to Headquarters, January 21, 1954; "Calligeris Briefing Notes," February 3, 1954. All from CIA/CREST.

75 Matamoros fortress in downtown Guatemala City bombed: Telegram, "Central Intelligence Agency to the CIA Station in Guatemala," June 24, 1954, Job 79–01025A, CIA/CREST; Bissell, "Operational Immediate; RYBAT; PBSUCCESS," CIA/CREST.

75 "Incredible": Cullather, "Operation PBSUCCESS," 84, CIA/CSI.

76 as many as 200,000: Immerman, The CIA in Guatemala, 138–40.

76 impossible to discern: Doyle and Kornbluh, "CIA and Assassinations," National Security Archive. While CIA historians insist that no one from these lists was actually assassinated, Doyle and Kornbluh doubt this claim. When documents were declassified, in 1997, the names of individuals targeted for assassination were redacted, making it impossible to tell if any of them were killed before, during, or after the coup.

77 armed militia: Anderson, Che, 144.

77 "extraordinary audacity," Che Guevara wrote in his diary: ibid., 155. "Ernesto [Che] was convinced that the American intervention in Guatemala was merely the first skirmish in what would be a global confrontation between the United States and Communism," writes Anderson.

78 "Should we start a file": Grose, *Gentleman Spy,* 383–84.

78 Che Guevara on their kill list: author interviews with Rodriguez.

CHAPTER SIX

79 religious fanatics were particularly dangerous: Central Intelligence Agency, "Information Report, Country: Iran, Subject: Possible Connection of Secret Police with Fedayan-i-Islam [*sic*]," March 22, 1951, CIA/CREST.

79 rid Iran of "corrupting individuals": Central Intelligence Agency, "Information Report, Country: Iran, Subject: Evidence of Tudeh Party Plot to Seize Power in Tehran," February 21, 1949, CIA/CREST; Norouzi and Norouzi, "Iran's Decades of Assassinations, 1946–1955," The Mossadegh Project, January 13, 2011.

80 "If Iran succumbed": Memorandum of Discussion at the 135th Meeting of the National Security Council, March 4, 1953, FRUS.

81 history's original assassins: Lewis, *The Assassins,* 5.

82 2,000 students marched: "Ruler of Iran Is Wounded Slightly by Two Bullets Fired by Assassin," United Press, February 5, 1949; "Iran Beset by Unrest," Associated Press, February 4, 1949. Iran's oil industry is the oldest oil industry in the Middle East.

82 shah appointed: Office of Current Intelligence, Central Intelligence Agency, "Reactions to the assassination of Premier Razmara," 5, March 8, 1951, CIA/CREST. Razmara's platform was anticommunism and he strongly opposed nationalizing Iran's oil. Instead, he reworked the agreement, getting the British to guarantee that Iran's annual royalty payment would not drop below four million pounds. The deal reduced the area where the British could drill, and it promised to train more Iranians for white-collar, administrative-type jobs.

83 back-to-back assassinations: "Premier of Iran Is Shot to Death in a Mosque by a Religious Fanatic, Victim of Assassin," Associated Press, March 8, 1951; "Iran Official Dies from Bullet Wound," Associated Press, March 26, 1951.

83 "favorable to Soviet subversion": "Summary Appraisal of the Current Situation in Iran," Top Secret, n.d., FRUS. Although the paper is undated, it is attached to a working draft dated March 13.

84 "He was our friend": "King Abdullah Assassinated," British Pathe Newsreel, July 1951.

84 medal, pinned to his chest: The story was told to me in 1986, by Prince Ghazi bin Muhammad, King Hussein's nephew, a friend and fellow student at Princeton University. Ghazi and I were in a political science class together, under the direction of Professor Manfred Halpern, and I recall an ongoing classroom debate regarding the legitimacy of the divine right of kings as a political construct—Ghazi being pro-monarchy, myself being fine with rule by kings but disagreeing with the divine-right element of the argument.

84 State Department sent a telegram: "Memorandum Prepared in the Office of National Estimates," Central Intelligence Agency, March 9, 1951, CIA/CREST.

86 downfall of Mohammad Mossadegh: "CIA Confirms Role in 1953 Iran Coup, Documents Provide New Details on Mosaddeq Overthrow and Its Aftermath," National Security Archive Electronic Briefing Book No. 435, August 19, 2013, edited by Malcolm Byrne.

87 help the shah assume absolute power: "Information Report(s) Prepared in the Central Intelligence Agency," September 14, 1953, CIA/CREST. During the coup, the shah fled to Paris. When he returned, he declared himself "a new man. Before August 19, 1953, I was the son of Reza Shah. Now I am the shah in my own right." In a show of support, the CIA sent the shah and his puppet prime minister Zahedi American-made bulletproof vests. Zahedi objected, the shah told his CIA handler, and he said, "This is an order that you must obey." In a CIA report marked "For the President's Eyes Only," "The Shah stated also that he will not make the mistakes he made with Ali Razmara and Mohammad Mossadegh. During their premierships, he kept 'hands off' and let them run the country; he will now take a direct interest in all matters of the state." Furthermore, "all action on Army matters would proceed from [the shah] himself."

87 McClure wrote: Telegram from the Chief of the US Military Mission in Iran (McClure) to the Chief of Staff, United States Army (Ridgway), Tehran, September 6, 1953, CIA/CREST.

88 "unintended consequences": Robarge, "Review of 'All the Shah's Men: An American Coup and the Roots of Middle East Terror,' by Stephen Kinzer," April 14, 2007, CIA/CSI; Roosevelt, *Countercoup,* 8.

88 "stress the 'holy war' aspect": "Memorandum of a Conversation with the President, White House, Washington, September 7, 1957, 10:07 a.m.," FRUS.

88 Nasser conducted: Aburish, *Nasser,* 33–35.

90 machine-gunned to death: NSC Briefing, "Iraq—Background, Anti-US and Anti-British Actions by Qasim Government Since 14 July 1958," April 16, 1959, 3 pages, CIA/CREST; Darwish and Alexander, *Unholy Babylon,* 16–18. The dead included King Faisal II; Crown Prince Abd al-Ilah and his wife Princess Hiyam; Abd al-Ilah's mother, Princess Nafisah; Princess Abadiyah, the king's aunt; and numerous servants.

91 "cut up by shawerma knives": "Middle East: Revolt in Baghdad," *Time,* July 25, 1958. Text beside photograph is translated from Arabic as: "Prince 'Abd al-Ilah hung and cut up by shawerma knives, Pasha Nuri al-Said pulled around."

91 six-man hit squad: Darwish and Alexander, *Unholy Babylon,* 21–23. As dictator, Saddam Hussein's role in the attempted assassination of General Qasim would be rewritten and further mythologized over the decades. State-run Iraqi television aired news stories about Hussein's bravery and iron discipline, claiming he was hit by bullets in a hail of gunfire and saved a wounded comrade before disappearing into the desert to heal. None of it was true.

CHAPTER SEVEN

93 He rang the doorbell: Khokhlov, *Conscience,* 245–46.

95 poison dart gun: photographs, press attaché, High Commissioner of Germany (HICOG), author collection, reprinted in Khokhlov, *Conscience,* insert.

95 assassination of Nazi Generalkommissar Wilhelm Kube: Khokhlov, *Conscience,* 45–79. Note: the only known source for this remarkable story is Khokhlov.

96 Executive Action: "Soviet Use of Assassination and Kidnapping. A 1964 view of KGB methods," n.d., CIA/CSI. "Strictly speaking, the term 'executive action' encompasses diversionary activities (such as sabotage) as well as terroristic activities. This paper, however, discusses only the terroristic aspect of Soviet executive action, namely, kidnaping and assassination," writes the CIA author.

96 Laboratory No. 12: Volodarsky, *KGB's Poison Factory,* 33, 37. See also Birstein, *Perversion of Knowledge,* 97, 113, 235.

98 never to be seen again: "Activities of Soviet Secret Service Testimony of Nikolai Eugeniyevich Khokhlov, Former KGB Agent," U.S. Congress, Senate Internal Security Subcommittee Hearing, transcript, May 21, 1954, 1–48; "The Testimony of a Soviet Secret Agent," Hearing Before the Committee on Un-American Activities, House of Representatives, April 17, 1956, 3,755–89.

99 traveled to Germany: Khokhlov, *Conscience,* 350–65.

99 Pentagon received word: The anticommunist émigrés held a press conference in Frankfurt, which is how the CIA and the Defense Department learned about Khokhlov's poisoning.

99 radioactive thallium: When Khokhlov emerged from a coma he was bald, "so disfigured by scars and spots that those who had known me did not at first recognize me...living proof [of] Soviet science—the science of killing." The similarities between Khokhlov's unsuccessful assassination by poisoning, in 1954, and the successful killing of former Russian spy Alexander Litvinenko in 2006, also by a radioactive substance, are extensive. In the case of Litvinenko, assassins slipped polonium-210 into his tea. This mini-nuclear attack cost an estimated $10 million to execute and was designed to send a clear message to anyone thinking about betraying Russia. Before Litvinenko was assassinated, he told the *New York Times,* "The view inside our agency was that poison is just a weapon, like a pistol."

99 CIA that concluded: Letter to J. Edgar Hoover, Esquire, from Allen W. Dulles, May 19, 1954, CIA/CREST. Two other KGB assassins defected shortly after Khokhlov: Yury Rastvorov, in January 1954, and Petr Deryabin, in February 1954. Khokhlov became a U.S. citizen in 1970. In 1992, Russian president Boris Yeltsin pardoned him.

100 Bohdan Stashinsky, defected: Alexander J. Motyl, "A KGB Assassin Speaks," *World Affairs Journal,* November 18, 2011. Stashinsky, age eighty, told his side of the story to journalist Natalya Prykhodko.

100 Interrogated by an officer named William Hood: "Artichoke Techniques," handwritten notes, July 28, 1961, CIA/CREST; "CIA report: William Hood,"

n.d., CIA/CREST. "After initial Agency interrogation of Stashinsky in Frankfurt on Main in August 1961 ... the conclusion was drawn that he would not be valuable operationally as a double agent, that he was not a bona fide defector and the individual he purported to be."

100 sprayed atomized hydrogen cyanide: Gehlen, *The Service*, 241.

101 Soviet mole: Alexander J. Motyl, "A KGB Assassin Speaks," *World Affairs Journal*, November 18, 2011.

101 KGB opened two new divisions: "Soviet Use of Assassination and Kidnapping. A 1964 View of KGB Methods," n.d., CIA/CSI; Volodarsky, *KGB's Poison Factory*, 37.

CHAPTER EIGHT

102 "It was an atomic weapon": author interview with Waugh, here and throughout the chapter.

102 W54 Special Atomic Demolition Munition: "Feasibility of Studies of Special Purpose Conventional Munitions," ARPA Rundle, ARPA Redit, February 21, 1966, Sandia, DOE/OSTI; Seymour Deitchman, "An Insider's Account: Seymour Deitchman," Nautilus Institute for Security and Sustainability, based on an interview conducted by Peter Hayes, February 25, 2003.

104 constructed bases for its army: Lane Johnston, "Okinawa and the US Military Post, 1945," *Scientific American,* June 19, 2013.

105 disassembled device: "SADM Delivery by Parachutist/A Swimmer," film footage, n.d., circa 1965, Sandia, DOE/CREST (also available on YouTube); Taslo, "An Army View of Nuclear Weapons History," Sandia National Laboratories, slide presentation, January 25, 2011, author collection.

107 Bank's OSS car broke down: Bank, *OSS to Green Berets,* 116. The story of the OSS Deer Team, commanded by U.S. Army major Allison B. Thomas, is told in Maurer, *Strange Ground: Americans in Vietnam, 1945–1975.* See also Bartholomew-Feis, *The OSS and Ho Chi Minh.*

108 American-made howitzers: interview with Plaster (former MACV-SOG); footage of Giap's army of civilians digging trenches around Dien Bien Phu is on YouTube.

108 United States did not come to the aid: Laurie and Vaart, "CIA and the Wars in Southeast Asia, 1947–1975," August 2016, 3, CIA/SCSI.

109 Dulles relayed a simple truth: ibid., 19. French-educated Emperor Bao Dai was a corrupt philanderer, hunter, gambler, and lazy bon vivant. Once the pet monarch of the French, this American puppet represented everything a communist freedom fighter was not: he wore the world's most expensive gold Rolex, hunted tigers, and collected concubines. "He was weak, unpredictable and corrupt," warned the CIA.

109 "[G]uerilla [*sic*] war must multiply": Giap, *People's War, People's Army,* 107–8.

110 Lansdale encouraged Diem: See Stanley Karnow's 1979 interview with Edward Geary Lansdale, from "Vietnam: A Television History; America's Mandarin

(1954–1963)," available online at wgbh.org, part of the Vietnam Collection; Ahern Jr., "CIA and the Government of Ngo Dinh Diem," 41–43.

110 "God Has Gone South": Hansen, "Bắc Di Cu," 182–84.

111 special activity cells: Pribbenow, "The Man in the Snow White Cell: Limits to Interrogation," n.p., CIA/CSI. He cites Nguyen Tai, *Doi Mat Voi* [Face to Face with the CIA], published in Hanoi in 1999. "It is an extraordinary book that describes how [Nguyen Tai] resisted years of unrelenting interrogation by some of the CIA's most skilled, and South Vietnam's most brutal, interrogators," to survive and tell the tale of the communists' special activity cell assassination squads.

112 Pathet Lao: Leary, "CIA Air Operations in Laos, 1955–1974," CIA/CSI. Until the twenty-first-century operation in Afghanistan, the CIA's covert-action program in Laos would become the longest-running and largest paramilitary operation in CIA history.

112 Mobile Training Teams: "White Star Mobile Training Teams, Vientiane, Laos, Subject: Civil Assistance," September 22, 1961, CIA/CREST. During World War II, when Bull Simons was a young U.S. Army Ranger, he participated in the Great Raid at Cabanatuan, in the Philippines, killing hundreds of Japanese soldiers before rescuing 500 POWs and 33 civilians, all survivors of the Bataan Death March. Now a lieutenant colonel with the Special Forces, Bull Simons was in charge of the 107 operators sent to Laos as part of White Star.

113 "insurmountable task": Ken Finlayson, "Operation White Star: Prelude to Vietnam," U.S. Army, Special Warfare Center, June 2002.

113 White Star advisor: Paddock, "Personal Memories of Operation White Star in Laos, 1961," *Small Wars Journal*, April 10, 2013.

114 Laos as a supply route: photo collection, Vietnam Military History Museum, Hanoi, Vietnam (author visit); author interviews with former North Vietnamese Army fighters, February 2016. The Truong Son Strategic Supply Route, as locals call it, was engineered by General Vo Bam and built by the 559th Transportation Unit, named for the month and year construction began.

114 National Security Agency (NSA) report: Robert J. Hanyok, "Spartans in Darkness," Center for Cryptographic History, National Security Agency, 2002, 94; Jacobsen, *The Pentagon's Brain*, 193–94.

CHAPTER NINE

115 plans to assassinate foreign leaders: "Dulles January 1960 Statement to the Special Group," 93; "General Cabell's Remarks to the Special Group in November 1960," 98; "The Question of Knowledge and Authorization Outside the Central Intelligence Agency in the Eisenhower Administration," 109; "Richard Bissell's Testimony," 110; "Testimony of White House Official Gordon Gray," 111; "The Question of Whether Assassination Efforts Were Disclosed in Various Briefings of Administration Officials," 120; "Discussion with Bundy on 'Executive Action' Capability," 121; located in "Alleged Assassination Plots of Foreign Leaders." All sources are from SSC/CHURCH.

115 Planning Coordination Group: "Coordination and Policy Approval of Covert Operations," February 23, 1967, CIA/CREST.

116 "Speaking in riddles": "III Assassination Plans and Plots," 95, SSC/CHURCH.

116 Health Alteration Committee: Memo, Acting Chief N.E. Division to DC/Cl, 2/25/60, N181, SSC/CHURCH.

116 "getting rid of Lumumba": "Plot to Assassinate Lumumba: Summary," 19, SSC/CHURCH.

117 "disappear simultaneously": "Pre-Bay of Pigs Assassination Plot," 117–19, located in "Alleged Assassination Plots of Foreign Leaders" [351 pages], SSC/CHURCH.

117 he executed him: Guevara, "Death of a Traitor," essay, n.d., available online. See discussion in Anderson, Che, 237.

118 Castro declared: Castro speech, Camp Columbia, Cuba, January 9, 1959, available online.

118 executed by firing squad: author interview with museum guard at the prison wall in Havana, Cuba, June 2017.

119 Sovietization of Cuba: Anderson, Che, 474.

119 "doorstep": "Alleged Assassination Plots of Foreign Leaders," Prologue, XIII, SSC/CHURCH.

119 What Mr. Hall discovered: "Memorandum from the Director of the Office of Intelligence Research and Analysis for American Republics (Hall) to the Director of Intelligence and Research," November 18, 1959, FRUS.

120 pros and cons: Unsigned Memorandum, Directorate of Plans, "Covert Action Against Cuba," n.d. [probably February 24 or 25, 1960], Latin America Division, CIA/CREST.

120 declassified minutes: Senate report, 73, SSC/CHURCH.

121 invading paramilitary force: "Analysis of the Cuban Operation," January 18, 1962, CIA/CREST.

121 Brigade 2506: author interview with Rodriguez; Quesada, The Bay of Pigs, 8–17. There are lots of documents on the subject at CIA/CREST, largely still redacted. Quesada interviewed numerous 2506 paramilitary operators and his book is an excellent summary, with original photographs.

122 Rodriguez wanted none of it: author interview with Rodriguez; also see Rodriguez and Weisman, Shadow Warrior, 49, 51–52.

123 unconventional-warfare legend: obituary: Col. Napoleon D. Valeriano, Counterinsurgency Expert, Associated Press, January 22, 1975.

124 New Year's Eve party: author interview with Rodriguez; Rodriguez and Weisman, Shadow Warrior, 65.

124 CIA would assist him: Western Hemisphere Division, "Anti-Castro Resistance in Cuba: Actual and Potential," March 16, 1961, CIA/CREST.

124 Trujillo's daughter Flor: "'You're nothing but a two-bit dictator'—Dealing with the DR's Rafael Trujillo," oral history, Ambassador Joseph Farland, n.d., ADST.

125 "He kept law and order": interview with Consul General Henry Dearborn, Association for Diplomatic Studies and Training, Foreign Affairs Oral History

Project, April 24, 1991, 26, ADST. All Dearborn quotes in this section are from this interview and its 61-page transcript.

125 Bissell…oversaw plans: "Pouching the Machine Guns Approved by Bissell," 202, SSC/CHURCH; Bissell, Lewis, and Pudlo, *Reflections of a Cold Warrior,* 183.

125 Dearborn wrote: "Dearborn Reports Assassination May Be Only Way to Overthrow Trujillo Regime," 195, SSC/CHURCH; "Passing the Carbines," 200, SSC/CHURCH.

126 maintain plausible deniability: Dearborn, oral history, 42–43, ADST.

126 "presight the rifle": author interview with Rodriguez.

127 critical covert-action operations: "Memorandum from Secretary of Defense McNamara to President Kennedy," January 24, 1961, FRUS; "The President's Appointments Thursday, January 19, 1961."

127 "treat it as a combat area": Shultz, *Secret War,* 14.

128 "four thousand civil officers": John F. Kennedy, "Special Message to the Congress on Urgent National Needs," May 25, 1961, APP. According to declassified CIA documents, that number would rise to 9,500 over the next four years.

128 Robert Kennedy…overseeing the CIA's covert operations: "Helms' Perception of Robert Kennedy's Position on Assassination," 150, SSC/CHURCH.

128 top of the list: "The Question of Knowledge and Authorization Outside the Central Intelligence Agency in the Kennedy Administrations," 116; "The August 10 1962 Special Group (Augmented) Meeting," 161, SSC/CHURCH. Note: From November 1961 to October 1962, the Special Group (Augmented), whose membership was the same as Special Group 5412 plus AG Robert Kennedy and Gen. Maxwell D. Taylor (as chairman), maintained authority for Operation Mongoose, the covert-action program to overthrow the Castro regime. Kennedy designated Brigadier General Edward G. Lansdale, assistant for special operations to the secretary of defense, to act as chief of operations, to coordinate Mongoose activities with the CIA, DoD, and State. CIA units in Washington and Miami had primary responsibility for implementing Mongoose operations, which included military, sabotage, political propaganda programs, and assassination. Mongoose was terminated shortly after President Kennedy's assassination.

CHAPTER TEN

131 intense gunfire: Anderson, *Che,* 471.

131 not a message: author interview with unnamed Bulgarian-Cuban intelligence agent, Havana, Cuba, June 2017.

132 Guevara is said to: author interview with Ernesto Guevara, Havana, Cuba, June 2017.

132 Gray Teams: Colonel J. Hawkins, Chief of the Paramilitary Staff Section, Branch 4 ["detailed to the Agency"], CIA/CREST; "Record of Paramilitary Action Against the Castro Regime of Cuba: Diversion Plan," 3, 22–23, CIA/CREST.

133 Air Branch pilots: "Inspector General's Survey of the Cuban Operation, Clandestine Paramilitary Operations—Air," October 1961, 98–110, CIA/CREST.

133 beachhead at Arcos de Canasi: The Gray Team infiltration account is from interviews with Rodriguez as well as his memoir, *Shadow Warrior,* 67–86.

134 Benigno Pérez Vivancos: Juan O. Tamayo, "The Spy Who Betrayed the Brigade," *Miami Herald,* April 17, 2011; Rodriguez and Weisman, *Shadow Warrior,* 60.

134 Castro's government rounded up: "Inspector General's Survey of the Cuban Operation, Security," October 1961, 135, CIA/CREST.

135 unforeseen political card: "Cancel the Strikes! Phase Two, April 16," Taylor Committee Investigation of the Bay of Pigs, vol. IV, 171, 234, CIA/CREST; Quesada, "The Bay of Pigs, Cuba 1961," 19–20.

136 middle of the night: Dearborn, oral history, April 24, 1991, 29–30, ADST.

137 dictator's dead body: Tim Mansel, "I Shot the Cruelest Dictator in the Americas," BBC News, May 28, 2011.

137 Dearborn remembered: Dearborn, oral history, April 24, 1991, 30–31, ADST.

138 "a funny incident": ibid., 32.

139 "he shook hands with me": ibid., 40.

139 Rafael Trujillo was assassinated: "Specific Events Indirectly Linking Dissidents' Assassination Plots," 205; "Special Group Meetings of May 4 and May 8, 1961," 208. Both are from "Alleged Assassination Plots of Foreign Leaders," SSC/CHURCH.

140 Bissell told Senate investigators: "Bissell's Testimony About Moving the Assassination Operation from Planning to Implementation," 36, SSC/CHURCH.

140 unsubtle cryptonym: "ZR/RIFLE" [one page, no markings, no attributions], attached to a cover letter from E. H. Knoche, Assistant to the Director, Central Intelligence Agency, Office of the Director, April 25, 1975, CIA/CREST.

140 system of "plausible denial": "Covert Action as a Vehicle for Foreign Policy Implementation: The Concept of Plausible Deniability," 7–11, 314–316, SSC/CHURCH.

CHAPTER ELEVEN

142 anticommunist plank: Shultz, *Secret War,* 18.

142 Adding insult to injury: Memorandum for the President, Secret, The White House, Subject: Conversation with Commandante Ernesto Guevara of Cuba, August 22, 1961, [signed] Dick Goodwin, FRUS.

142 gutted the existing paramilitary authority at the CIA: National Security Action Memorandum No. 57, "Responsibility for Paramilitary Operations," June 28, 1961, JFK/L.

142 "The fiasco at the Bay of Pigs": John L. Helgerson, Central Intelligence Agency: "CIA Briefings of Presidential Candidates," May 22, 1961, n.p., CIA/CREST.

143 Clifton curtly informed the CIA: "Origins of the President's Intelligence Checklist," n.d., CIA/CREST.

143 "Historians have glossed over": oral history interview with L. Fletcher Prouty, "Understanding the Secret Team Part III," with David T. Ratcliffe, 1989.

144 widening a war: National Security Action Memo (NSAM) No. 55, "Relations of the Joint Chiefs of Staff to the President in Cold War Operations"; NSAM 56, "Evaluation of Paramilitary Requirements," and NASM No. 57, "Responsibility for Paramilitary Operations." On January 18, 1962, Kennedy signed

NASM No. 124, establishing a Special Group (Counter-Insurgency) to plan and coordinate classified paramilitary operations. All JFK/L.

144 Facing certain death: Shultz, *Secret War*, 34.

144 Eisenhower forewarned: "The Laos Crisis, 1960–1963," State Department, OTH, FRUS. The July 23, 1962, International Agreement on the Neutrality of Laos shut down all Military Assistance Advisory Groups operating in Laos.

144 leave Laos alone: Shultz, *Secret War*, 22–26.

145 Now in a subordinate role: In Ahern, *Vietnam Declassified: The CIA and Counterinsurgency*, see all of chapter 5, "Operation Switchback," CIA/CSI.

145 Waugh's group trained: interviews with Waugh. Note the CIA's original program in Vietnam was called the Combined Studies Division, a name chosen for blandness. "It was also called Ground Branch, or GB," says Waugh.

146 "CIDG program was an American project": Kelly, *Vietnam Studies, U.S. Army Special Forces, 1962–1972*, 39–42. Kelly's chapters 2–7 cover CIDG origins and development in great detail.

147 Word came back: never: Karnow, *Vietnam*, 277–79.

147 unique history with several of Diem's generals: "Alleged Assassination Plots of Foreign Leaders," 42–44; "[Section] E. Diem, Summary," 218, N228, SSC/CHURCH.

148 prepared himself for the coup d'état: Karnow, *Vietnam*, 305–7; the unique participant details are largely from Karnow's seminal interviews with Conein, Lodge, and other key players.

148 "deaths…would be welcomed": "The Abortive Coup of August 1963," 217–22, SSC/CHURCH. In footnotes, the committee cites the original CIA documents, "Conein After-Action report, November 1, 1963," as well as Conein's closed-door testimony of June 20, 1975.

149 gilded furniture: Karnow, *Vietnam*, 309.

149 guarded the president's mother-in-law: Testimony of Clinton J. C. Hill, Agent, U.S. Secret Service, Warren Commission Report, Appendix 5, vol. II, 132–54. JFK Assassination Records, NARA. All quotes by Hill come from this testimony.

150 president…didn't want Secret Service agents: author interview with Merletti, nineteenth director of the U.S. Secret Service. See chapter 21 for further discussion.

150 Helms…in charge of the president's Executive Action capability: "Helms and Harvey Did Not Brief McCone about the Assassination Plots," 102; "Evidence Bearing on Knowledge of and Authorization for the Assassination Plots," 148; "Helms' Perception on the Relation of Special Group Controls to Assassination Activity," 152; all from SCI/CHURCH.

151 "If you kill someone else's leaders": "An Interview with Richard Helms," transcript of Helms interview with David Frost, May 22–23, 1978, CIA/CSI.

151 percentage calculus: McMaster, *Dereliction of Duty*, 236–37.

151 Billy Waugh was leading: This section was written from author interviews with Waugh; see also Waugh and Keown, *Jackal*, 4–28. Captain Paris D. Davis

recounts his perspective on the events in Kelly, *Vietnam Studies, U.S. Army Special Forces, 1962–1972*, 78–80. Davis received the Silver Star for his actions.

152 "soon be dead": Obituary: SP4 Robert D. Brown, Veterans Party of Montana, KIA, June 18, 1965, Bong Son, Binh Dinh Province, Vietnam.

153 "mercenaries": author interview with Waugh. The Defense Department objected to the term "mercenary"; officially the indigs were part of the 883rd Vietnamese Regional Force Company.

157 tried discussing: Kelly, *Vietnam Studies, U.S. Army Special Forces, 1962–1972*, 79.

158 250 feet of open terrain: "John E. Reinburg, III, recipient, Distinguished Service Cross," Hall of Valor, Awards and Citations, *Military Times*, n.d.

CHAPTER TWELVE

161 amputee ward: author interview with Waugh, photos, medical records.

162 Green Berets began chatting: author interviews with Waugh.

164 job of SOG reconnaissance men: JCS: MACV-SOG Documentation Study (July 1970) Appendix M., Comments of Command and Control, Records of the Senate Select Committee on POW/MIA Affairs, NARA; Shultz, *Secret War*, 45–69. With General Order No. 6, dated January 24, 1964, Military Assistance Command Vietnam (MACV) in Saigon created the Studies and Observations Group; see also Harvey Saal's four-volume series on SOG.

164 "Nobody knew": author interviews with Plaster.

165 Nung tribesmen: Plaster, *SOG: The Secret Wars*, 29.

165 count enemy troops: Wilder et al., "CIA at War," December 2013, CIA/CSI.

166 SOG's first cross-border mission: Plaster, *SOG: A Photo History*, 31. First five recon teams were RT Iowa, RT Alaska, RT Idaho, RT Kansas, and RT Dakota.

166 manufactured in Japan: author interview with Waugh, observation of Waugh's collection of knives used over the decades; Plaster, *SOG: A Photo History*, 18.

167 "All gave some, some gave all": author interview with Meyer.

167 never heard from again: author interview with de Fontaine; Cleverley, *Born a Soldier*, 272–73.

168 visible from the base: author tour of Khe Sanh with Waugh, February 2017; CIA Directorate of Intelligence, "Construction and Logistic Activities in the Khe Sanh Area," February 7, 1968, CIA/CREST.

168 SOG base at Khe Sanh: author interviews with Waugh; author interview with Singlaub.

169 white tuxedo and a bow tie to prom: Virtual Vietnam Veterans Wall of Faces, Don R. Sain, Date of Birth: January 12, 1943, Honored on Panel 9E, Row 88 of the Vietnam Veterans Memorial photo.

169 Once, during a rescue operation: Plaster, *SOG: A Photo History*, 105–6; author interview with Hernandez, who was twice rescued by Mustachio, once with Waugh.

170 Waugh felt the anger: author interview with Waugh. See also Waugh and Keown, *Jackal,* 40–44.

170 Kilburn, a highly decorated combat veteran: Veteran Tributes, Gerald Kilburn, Lieutenant Colonel, U.S. Army, Korean War, 1950–1953 (POW); Vietnam War 1962, 1963–1964, 1966–1967, 1968–1969, 1970.

CHAPTER THIRTEEN

173 kill General Giap: author interviews with Waugh; "To Assassinate General Vo Nguyen Giap, 1967," 16-slide presentation, used by Waugh in lectures for Special Forces soldiers at Fort Bragg (author copy). See also Waugh and Keown, *Jackal,* 40–44.

179 SOG operator…Charles F. Wilklow: Plaster, *SOG: The Secret Wars,* 73–76. Plaster interviewed Wilklow's children to report the story; I interviewed Plaster. Seeing as the Oscar Eight mission remains officially classified, this is the only narrative source material to date. Technical information comes from Defense Intelligence Agency Reference Notes, U.S. Marine Corps helicopter CH-46A tail number 150955, crash; June 3, 1967 MIA-POW file: 0720. Other personnel listed in this incident: Timothy R. Bodden, Ronald J. Dexter, John G. Gardner, and Billy Ray Laney (all missing); Mr. Ky (Nung Commander, rescued) and Charles F. Wilklow (rescued); Frank E. Cius Jr. (returned POW).

181 Back at the SOG base at Khe Sanh: author interviews with Pace.

182 man whose face had been disfigured: author interview with Plaster. Wilklow told his children that he later learned that this kind of disfigurement was often punishment for a soldier's lying or thievery.

182 "These rescue operations": author interview with Plaster.

185 He never told his family: author interview with Pace.

185 no idea where he was: Walt Rostow, "Memorandum to Mr. President," The White House, Washington, May 11, 1967, JFK/L.

185 "state run profiteers": "The Fall of Che Guevara and the Changing Face of the Cuban Revolution," Directorate of Intelligence, Intelligence Memorandum, October 18, 1965, n.p., CIA/CREST.

185 a call for "nuclear war": Che Guevara, "Revolución," August 17, 1964.

185 communiqué from Leonid Brezhnev: September 1966, CIA FOIA, 3.

185 Che gave his wife, Aleida, a letter: Paco Ignacio Taibo II, "Guevara, Also Known as Che," 233.

186 slaughtered their own horses: Anderson, *Che,* 690.

186 So was the CIA: "The Che Guevara Diary," CIA Weekly Review, December 15, 1967, CIA/CSI.

186 "What's the mission?": author interview with Rodriguez.

186 Rodriguez was flown to Bolivia: Memorandum for Deputy Inspector General, "Statement by Benton H. Mizones [headquarters pseudo for Felix Rodriguez] concerning his assignment in Bolivia in 1967 and his role in the capture of Ernesto 'Che' Guevara de la Serna," May 29, 1975, CIA/CREST.

187 "Papá cansado": Rodriguez, *Shadow Warrior,* 158.

187 Rostow told the president: CIA Intelligence Memorandum, Walt Rostow Memorandum, "Death of Che Guevara," October 11, 1967, CIA/CREST.

187 Joaquin Zenteno Anaya: in May 1976, Zenteno Anaya—then serving as the Bolivian ambassador to France—was assassinated in Paris by a group calling itself the International Che Guevara Brigade. The assassin approached the ambassador as he walked along the Seine, killed him with two shots to the head, and vanished.

187 Rodriguez says he spoke to Che alone: author interview with Rodriguez. See also *Shadow Warrior,* 168.

188 "code numbers 500 and 600": op cit. Memo for Deputy IG, "Statement," May 29, 1975, 4, CIA/CREST.

188 "We embraced": Rodriguez, *Shadow Warrior,* 169.

188 swapped out Che's Rolex: ibid., 170. "The guerrilla's watch, on my own band, was now on my wrist," Rodriguez says.

188 helicopter's skids: Memo for Deputy Inspector General, "Statement," May 29, 1975, 5, CIA/CREST.

188 "The hands were sent to Cuba": author interview with Rodriguez.

189 "Phoenix was": Finlayson, "A Retrospective on Counterinsurgency Operations," n.d. CIA/CSI.

189 "CIA paramilitary": CIA Memorandum, Subject: The Phoenix and Provincial Reconnaissance Unit Program, December 16, 1969, CIA/CREST. "Phoenix is an intelligence and operational effort aimed at identifying, ferreting out and arresting the leaders and key members of the Communist political structure in South Vietnam," the CIA memo states.

190 Rodriguez's cover: author interview with Rodriguez.

190 Witnesses say that the program: Edward Miller, "Behind the Phoenix Program," *New York Times,* December 29, 2017.

CHAPTER FOURTEEN

191 murder versus assassination: author interview with McIntosh.

192 Project Gamma: CIA Intelligence Report, Directorate of Intelligence, "Communism and Cambodia, ESAU LV/72, Secret," May 1972, CIA/CREST.

192 enigmatic CIA case officer: Lisa Smith, *Faithful Devotion* (e-book, n.p.). This is Alvin Smith's widow's account of Smith's life, career, and role in the Green Beret Affair.

193 "It was me, Chuyen, and ten indigenous troops": author interview with McIntosh. Also see "The Green Beret Affair, 1969," McIntosh's essay available online at war-stories.com.

194 In one of the photographs: Stein, *A Murder in Wartime,* photo inserts.

194 Marasco contacted the CIA station: Terence Smith, "Details of Green Beret Case Are Reported in Saigon," *New York Times,* August 14, 1969; John Darnton, "Ex-Beret Says He Killed Agent on Orders of C.I.A.," *New York Times,* April 4, 1971.

195 General Abrams summoned: L. Fletcher Prouty, "Green Berets and the CIA," *New Republic,* August 23 and 30, 1969. They awaited an Article 32 hearing as per the Uniform Code of Military Justice.

196 "life in prison, not a firing squad": statement of Major General George Mabry Jr., quoted in Stein, *Murder in Wartime,* 410.

196 Rheault's eleven-year-old son: Frank McCulloch, "A Believer in Self-Reliance and Elitism," *Life,* November 14, 1969.

197 Nixon wrote: White House Morning News Summary, "CIA regarding the double agent," n.d., 3, RN/L. A copy is reprinted in Stein, *Murder in Wartime,* insert.

197 "double agent executed": Shultz, *Secret War,* 279. This story was first reported by John Plaster in *SOG: The Secret Wars,* 216n.

198 "This war was going on": author interviews with Merletti, 2016–19. Includes all quotes and stories in this chapter attributed to Merletti.

200 to see him off to war: author interview with Donna Fiore, Mike Kuropas's sister.

204 "flight-line at Kontum Air Field": "Dak Seang 15 April 1970," original by Donald Summers, edited by Robert L. Noe, author copy (available online at macvsog.cc).

204 "an unacceptable further loss of life": author interview with Singlaub.

205 Summers remembered: The eyewitness account is from Donald Summers's essay "Dak Seang 15 April 1970." Others recall a different way in which Kuropas is said to have died; author interview with Wolcoff.

205 "Kuropas, Killed in Action": Michael Vincent Kuropas is honored on Panel 11W, Line 7 of the Vietnam Veterans Memorial. Born: January 9, 1948. Died April 15, 1970.

206 exiting an aircraft: For amazing photographs and narrative accounts, see Plaster, *SOG: A Photo History of the Secret Wars,* 245–61, chapter 13, "The Ultimate Infiltration Technique."

207 Ie Shima Island: author interview with Waugh; 8-slide presentation, "HALO preparation," used by Waugh in lectures for Special Forces soldiers at Fort Bragg (author copy).

207 captured and killed: Detailed Report of Investigation of Case 1756, Madison A. Strohlein, Joint Casualty Recovery Center, LOC. Today, HALO jumping is a lead component of Special Forces operations. To read more about the original HALO jumps in Vietnam see Plaster, *SOG: The Secret Wars,* 259–80.

208 Back from Vietnam: Deeply affected by the war and by America's negative reaction to those who fought in Vietnam, Merletti firmly believes it was his Special Forces training that set him on his path and made him a man of character—that is, he believes that some of the most negative experiences positively shaped him. "For the longest time, when we came back, I mean there were no welcome-home [parades]. It was bad. People made little comments, snide comments. Yes, there were true lessons to be learned. There were valuable lessons to be learned. But that this group... this army of young men, much of what we brought back [in personal experience] was suppressed, because the American public tried to shame

us. After everything we did to survive, they shamed us for it. And I don't know— I think a lot of people came back and were like, 'Man. Hey, I survived. I just want to put this thing behind me. I just want to forget.' I myself thought, I don't want to come out and say, 'I thought it was a great experience.' But I took it as a learning experience. It was an absolute doctorate [degree]—it was a PhD in life. And I knew that there were ways to use what I learned there in Vietnam as a civilian here in the United States. That moment was like a bright light going off when I saw a notice on a bulletin board." That said, here are some statistics compiled by SFC (Ret.) David Hack, 1st Infantry Division, Lai Khe, Vietnam (uswings.com).

> 9,087,000 military personnel served on active duty during the official Vietnam era from August 5, 1964 to May 7, 1975.
>
> 2,709,918 Americans served in uniform in Vietnam.
>
> 58,148 were killed in Vietnam over 23.11 years.
>
> 75,000 were severely disabled; 23,214 were 100% disabled; 5,283 lost limbs; 1,081 sustained multiple amputations.
>
> 240 men were awarded the Medal of Honor during the Vietnam War.
>
> Five men killed in Vietnam were only 16 years old. Of those killed, 61% were younger than 21 years old.
>
> 11,465 of those killed were younger than 20 years old. Of those killed, 17,539 were married. The average age of the men killed was 23.1 years.
>
> Two-thirds of the men who served in Vietnam were volunteers.
>
> Approximately 70% of those killed in Vietnam were volunteers.
>
> The oldest man killed was 62 years old.
>
> 91% of Vietnam veterans say they are glad they served.
>
> 97% of Vietnam veterans were honorably discharged.
>
> 74% say they would serve again, even knowing the outcome.

CHAPTER FIFTEEN

211 all hell broke loose: Korn, *Assassination in Khartoum*, 6–10. Korn is a former Foreign Service officer who has written the seminal work on this tragedy. His book, a rigorously sourced page-turner, is rife with shocking twists and turns, including his assertion that Belgian chargé d'affaires Guy Eid socialized with PLO members and may have been working with Black September terrorists before he was executed by them (162–65).

212 "We will do everything": "Hostages in the Sudan," Item 10, White House press room, statement of the president, March 2, 1973, Richard Nixon, public papers, item 10, 157, APP.

212 The policy: U.S. Department of State, Bureau of Diplomatic Security, "History of the Bureau of Diplomatic Security," 216.

212 after hearing this news: "The Terrorist Attack on the Saudi Embassy, Khartoum, 1973," ADST. Interested persons can read interviews with U.S. State Department survivors.

213 Fritts recalled: Foreign Affairs Oral History Project, Robert E. Fritts, Arab Israeli Crisis and War, 1973, 156–58, FRUS.

213 "We've heard there was gunfire": as recalled by Fritts in "The Terrorist Attack on the Saudi Embassy, Khartoum, 1973," n.p., ADST.

213 "Cleo and I will die bravely": Department of State, Secret, "The Seizure of the Saudi Arabian Embassy in Khartoum," n.d., declassified May 4, 2006, FRUS.

213 gunmen were told by their handler: Korn, *Assassination in Khartoum,* 2; Korn's position is that this assertion was fabricated, meant to motivate the terrorists to kill Curt Moore. In my research, I located no declassified report(s) that suggested Moore was a CIA officer.

214 NSA listening post in Cyprus: ibid., 3.

214 Arafat, who planned and ordered: Department of State, Secret, "The Seizure of the Saudi Arabian Embassy in Khartoum," n.d., declassified May 4, 2006, FRUS.

214 Black September... "formed... by Arafat and his closest lieutenants": Bruce Hoffman, "All You Need Is Love: How the Terrorists Stopped Terrorism," *Atlantic,* December 2001.

215 Mossad gave him: Bergman, *Rise and Kill First,* 177.

215 assassination of Wasfi al-Tal, Jordan's prime minister: American Embassy Beirut to DOS, "Tal's Assassination," Beirut 10549, December 1, 1971, RG 59, NARA; Walker and Gowers, *Arafat,* 88–89.

216 "They've killed me!": Intelligence Memorandum, CIA Directorate of Intelligence, Subject: Implication of Wasfi al Tal's Assassination, November 28, 1971, CIA/CREST.

216 this blood-licking act: Paul Martin, "Jordan Prime Minister Is Shot Dead in Cairo," *Times* [London], November 29, 1971.

216 "Create Two, Three, Many Vietnams": Che Guevara, "Revolución," August 17, 1964.

216 kept the most horrific details hidden: Sam Borden, "Long-Hidden Details Reveal Cruelty of 1972 Munich Attackers," *New York Times,* December 1, 2015. Note this article came out 43 years after the event.

216 Nakam: See Bartrop and Dickerman, *The Holocaust: An Encyclopedia and Document Collection,* 361, 372. Thomas, in *Gideon's Spies,* 74–75, writes about Raphael "Rafi" Eitan, a seventeen-year-old assassin in postwar Israel, who told colleagues that he did not know of a single case where the Nokmim (Thomas uses the name of Nakam's predecessor organization) targeted the wrong person. Others disagree.

217 The logic was: "Jewish Avengers Unapologetic for Targeting Nazis after WWII," Associated Press, August 31, 2016, an interview with Joseph Harmatz, one of the few remaining Jewish Avengers.

217 elite assassination unit called Kidon: Bergman, *Rise and Kill First,* 146.

217 unleashed kidon: Noam Shalev, "The Hunt for Black September," BBC, January 24, 2006.

217 murders followed: A team of Mossad agents shot and killed Bouchiki, a Moroccan waiter and pool cleaner living in Norway. He had nothing to do with Black September. Six Mossad Bayonet agents, including two women, were arrested by Lillehammer police and charged with murder. Team leader Michael Harari

escaped. Five of those captured were convicted and imprisoned, then released and returned to Israel in 1975 in what remains a secret arrangement.

218 intended to shoot down Meir's airplane: author interview with former Shin Bet source, Tel Aviv, 2016.

219 State Department kept secret: Department of State, Secret, "The Seizure of the Saudi Arabian Embassy in Khartoum," n.d., declassified May 4, 2006.

219 President Nimeiry commuted: In addition to all the primary source material cited above, an excellent summation is: Scott Johnson, "How Arafat Got Away with Murder," *The Weekly Standard,* January 29, 2007.

219 "personal approval of Yasser Arafat": "Memo from Sec Kissinger from American Embassy Khartoum, Subject BSO Terrorists," dated June 26, 1974, KHARTO 01538 02 OF 02 261234Z, author FOIA; Department of State, Secret, "The Seizure of the Saudi Arabian Embassy in Khartoum," n.d., declassified May 4, 2006, FRUS.

220 Salameh, as a clandestine asset: Kissinger, *Years of Upheaval,* 625. Here, Kissinger deceptively refers to his use of Salameh as "low-level intelligence channels." For a comprehensive study of what this actually involved, to include the CIA's Richard Helms, see Bird, *The Good Spy,* 149–52.

220 two sides of a coin: Bird, *The Good Spy,* 93.

220 Ames's relationship with Salameh had warped: ibid., 173. Bird argues that Salameh did not oversee the Munich murders; he remains largely alone in this assessment. Bird accepts that Salameh orchestrated the murders of the diplomats in Sudan.

221 "gift of a gun": Bird, *The Good Spy,* 173–74.

221 analyst colleague Bruce Riedel: ibid., 174. As per Bird's interview with Riedel, who read fifteen files on MJ/TRUST/2.

221 "PLO security is so good": Thomas, *Gideon's Spies,* 281.

221 car bomb exploded: Edward Cody, "Bomb Kills Palestinian on Israeli Wanted List," *Washington Post,* January 23, 1979.

221 With a CIA handler driving: Bird, *Good Spy,* 181–83.

222 "first time in its history": Snider, *The Agency and the Hill,* 30. Before this, explains Snider, "the Agency had provided information to congressional committees through briefings or by providing documents for review on the Hill.... while the Watergate Committee did not recommend change to the oversight arrangements per se, its final report did recommend that Congress should 'more closely supervise the operations of the intelligence and law enforcement community'...and, in particular, its relations with the White House."

222 Schlesinger sent a memo: James R. Schlesinger, "Memorandum from Director of Central Intelligence Schlesinger to All Central Intelligence Agency Employees," May 9, 1973, FRUS, Public Diplomacy 1973–1975. Schlesinger's now famous memorandum dated May 9, 1973, stated, "I have ordered all senior operating officials of this Agency to report to me immediately on any activities now going on, or that have gone on in the past, which might be construed to be outside the legislative charter of this agency."

222 illegally wiretap reporters: Seymour M. Hersh, "Watergate Days," *New Yorker,* June 13, 2005.

223 "clearly were illegal": Memorandum of Conversation, The White House, Washington, January 4, 1975 (CIA/CREST); "Colby must be brought under control," Kissinger said.

223 "the CIA would be destroyed": Memorandum of Conversation, January 4, 1975, The White House, Washington, CIA/CREST.

225 "CIA never did anything the White House didn't want": Pike, quoted in Haines, "Looking for a Rogue Elephant: The Pike Committee Investigations and the CIA," April 14, 2007, 88, CIA/CSI.

225 Later, Ford expressed regret: "The Nation: Scenario of the Shake-Up," *Time,* November 17, 1975; Gilbert King, "A Halloween Massacre at the White House," *Smithsonian,* October 25, 2012.

225 Ford's new team of advisors failed: Snider, *The Agency and the Hill,* 276, CIA/CSI.

226 undated notes: Richard B. Cheney files, "White House Senior Staff Meeting Notes Files, 1974–1977," GRF/L. The note read: "...best prospect for heading off Congressional efforts to further encroach on the Executive branch." In 2005, Ford's former chief of staff told reporters that "an erosion of presidential power and authority" had emerged during that era but that the pendulum has now "swung back.... We've been able to restore the legitimate authority of the presidency." From "Cheney Hails Bush Restoration of Executive Power," *Washington Times,* December 21, 2005.

226 executive order on assassination and not a new law: Snider, *The Agency and the Hill,* 276–78, CIA/SCI. The congressional committees considered doing away with covert action. "Looking at the cumulative effect of covert action, the committee questioned whether the gains for the United States outweighed the costs," Snider explains, "especially the damage done to [America's] reputation around the world.... Rather, the committee concluded that covert action should be employed only in exceptional cases where vital security interests of the United States were at stake."

227 gunmen stormed: Clyde H. Farnsworth, "Terrorists Raid OPEC Oil Parley in Vienna, Kill 3," *New York Times,* December 22, 1975.

228 Patrice Lumumba University, a breeding ground: SNIE 11/2-81: Soviet Support for International Terrorism and Revolutionary Violence, CIA Control No. TS 815753. Formerly called the People's Friendship University of Russia, the university was renamed to honor Lumumba (an earlier target of a CIA assassination plot) after the Congolese independence leader was killed in a coup.

228 Qaddafi, and a secret agreement: "Gadhadhafi [*sic*] Comments on Talks with Boumediene," December 15, 1975, cable, CIA/CREST.

CHAPTER SIXTEEN

230 For Billy Waugh: author interviews with Waugh.

235 "bases of imperialism": Qaddafi, in a public address on October 16, 1969, as cited in St. John, *Libya,* 141.

235 "a plague": "From the archive, September 8, 1973: Gaddafi and Castro clash over Soviet Union," *Guardian,* September 8, 2015.

236 Billy Waugh landed in Tripoli: author interviews with Waugh. See also Lynn Hughes, "*United States of America vs. Edwin Paul Wilson,* United States District Court, Southern District of Texas, Criminal Case H-82-139, Opinion on Conviction in Ancillary Civil Action H-97-831," October 27, 2003.

236 Major Abdullah Hajazzi: Background on Hajazzi is confirmed in "Sitrep Following June 13 Military Takeover, CINCEUR for POLAD, U.S. Department of State," WikiLeaks.org; Maas, *Manhunt,* 62.

237 Qaddafi wanted to provoke a war with Egypt: Robert Carle, US Chargé d'Affaires, Libya, To: Department of State, August 26, 1976, CIA/CREST.

238 Qaddafi called for Sadat's death: "Libyan Assassination Teams: Some Patterns," For: Frank Farrell, Intelligence Branch, June 18, 1980, CIA/CREST. Michael Getler, Scott Armstrong, "Sadat May Have Had Warning Signs of Assassination Attempt," *Washington Post,* October 7, 1981. Egyptian security forces arrested "six Libyans and four non-Egyptian Arabs who [under interrogation] admitted being sent into Egypt by Colonel Muammar Qaddafi with the mission of assassinating the President," the CIA learned.

238 developing a close working relationship: author interview with Waugh; photograph collection of Waugh; Waugh and Keown, *Jackal,* 92–105.

239 Waugh provided to his CIA handler: CIA Intelligence Memorandum, "The Libyan Hand," n.d., CIA/CREST.

241 locked in a walk-in vault: "Embassy of the US in Libya Is Stormed by a Crowd of 2,000," *New York Times,* December 3, 1979.

241 Liquidation of the Stray Dogs: "Libya's Recent Role as a Patron of Terrorists," May 16, 1980, Intelligence Memorandum Prepared in the Central Intelligence Agency, 308, North Africa 1977–1980, vol. 17, part 3, FRUS.

242 Carter described as "would-be assassins": "Libya Recalls 4 Envoys Under British Pressure," *Washington Post,* May 13, 1980.

243 he claimed to be on a hit list: "Evening Reports (State)": October 1980. Secret, National Security Affairs, Brzezinski Material, Subject File, Box 23, JC/L. Carter initialed the memorandum. For a comprehensive assessment of the Libyan situation, including docs from CIA and State, see "North Africa, 1977–1980," part 3, 328–47, FRUS.

243 Officer Martinez interviewed: Jacy Marmaduke, "Uncover the Mystery of a Notorious Fort Collins Shooting," *Coloradoan,* December 8, 2016.

244 Farida Zagallai told the FBI: "Possible Assassination Attempt of a US Dissident," 339–40. North Africa 1977–1980, vol. 17, part 3, FRUS.

245 "quit breathing.... permanently": ibid.

245 Tafoya told the FBI: Douglas Vaughan, "Ex-Green Beret Denies Being a Mercenary," *Washington Post,* November 26, 1981.

245 jury foreman: William E. Schmidt, "Ex-Green Beret Is Convicted of Assault on Libyan Student," *New York Times,* December 5, 1981.

245 military-grade C-4 explosives: Peter Carlson, "International Man of Mystery," *Washington Post*, June 22, 2004.

245 Judge Lynn Hughes wrote: Hughes, Lynn, "United States of America vs. Edwin Paul Wilson, United States District Court, Southern District of Texas, Criminal Case H-82-139, Opinion on Conviction in Ancillary Civil Action H-97-831," October 27, 2003. "Because the government knowingly used false evidence against him and suppressed favorable evidence, his conviction will be vacated," wrote the judge.

246 "They framed a guilty man": Douglas Martin, "Edwin P. Wilson, the Spy Who Lived It Up, Dies at 84," *New York Times*, September 22, 2012.

CHAPTER SEVENTEEN

251 code-named the Baron: Perisco, *Casey*, 213. Story originally told here.

252 Time of Troubles: "Counterintelligence at CIA: A Brief History," n.p., CIA/SCI.

252 Turner eliminated: ibid., n.p. Of the 820 positions eliminated, 649 jobs were dissolved by attrition, 154 officers were asked to retire involuntarily, and 17 were fired.

252 three ideas: "CIA: Confronting 'Undeclared War': CIA Director William J. Casey," The American Legion, vol. 116, no. 6 (June 1984), 12–15, 35–38, CIA/CREST; William J. Casey, "War Behind the Lines," *Studies in Intelligence* 26/4 (Winter 1982), CIA/SCI; William J. Casey, "OSS: Lessons for Today," *Studies in Intelligence* 30/4 (Winter 1986), CIA/SCI.

253 Casey warned: Remarks of William Casey, Director of Central Intelligence, at Loy Henderson Hall, Department of State, June 12, 1984, CIA/CREST.

253 "clear-cut articulation": Memorandum: "Agency's Paramilitary Role," From: Director of Central Intelligence, William J. Casey, May 15, 1981, CIA/CREST.

253 "This kind of crap": Persico, *Casey*, 290.

253 Reagan's inner circle of advisors: author interview with Rizzo.

254 an assassin fired: Much of the information herein comes from Behl, "Attempted Assassination of President Reagan on March 30, 1981," U.S. Secret Service, Office of Inspection, CO-1-31-833, May 4, 1981 (398 pages).

255 gamma-classified launch codes: Wilber, *Rawhide Down*, 154–55.

256 "We were all just stunned": author interviews with Merletti.

257 crippling aggression: author interview with unnamed CAT member (PPD 1983–2000).

259 worried about the pope: author interview with Maguire; Rhoda Koenig, "Basket Casey," *New York*, October 15, 1990: Casey deeply distrusted all atheistic communists and was known to call communism "the Antichrist."

259 "fanatic could try and kill him," Thomas, *Gideon's Spies*, 224.

260 Bulgaria's secret services: "Bulgaria: A Country in Transition, An Intelligence Assessment," Directorate of Intelligence, March 1984, CIA/CREST.

260 rift...widened: A. Filippov, "Concerning the Attempt on the Life of John Paul II," *Pravda,* May 15, 1981, republished in *Current Digest of the Soviet Press,* June 17, 1981, 18.

260 Mitrokhin commission: Daniel C. Scotto, "Pope John Paul II, the Assassination Attempt, and the Soviet Union," *Gettysburg Historical Journal,* vol. 6, 2007.

261 "professional assassins": "Libyan Assassination Teams: Some Patterns," Intelligence Branch, June 18, 1980, CIA/CREST.

261 overthrow the Libyan leader: Daniel Southerland, "Behind Qaddafi's '81 plot to assassinate President Reagan," *Christian Science Monitor,* December 7, 1982.

261 "President Nimeiry": U.S. Department of State, Department History Report, Libya, January 1986 (1980–1985).

263 The attack lasted: "The Assassination of Anwar Sadat, Part I," ADST.

263 "proud that my son killed Anwar al-Sadat": posted online and translated from the Iranian news organization Ahram.org.

264 Cord Meyer took to the airwaves: Cord Meyer, "Interview with Braden and Buchanan, WRC Radio," October 9, 1981, CIA/CREST.

264 "pre-emptive neutralization": National Security Decision Directive 138, Combatting Terrorism, Top Secret/Sensitive, The White House, Washington, April 3, 1984. Note, it took 2.5 years for Executive Order (EO) 12333 to formalize.

264 Qaddafi planned to assassinate Reagan: Charles R. Babcock, "U.S. Tightens Security of Top Officials," *Washington Post,* November 28, 1981.

265 president decreed: "United States Intelligence Activities, December 4, 1981 (As Amended by Executive Orders 13284 [2003], 13355 [2004] and 13470 [2008])" can all be accessed at CIA.gov.

265 "ambiguously broad term": Major Tyler J. Harder, "Time to Repeal the Assassination Ban of Executive Order 12,333: A Small Step in Clarifying Current Law," *Military Law Review,* vol. 172, June 2002, 16.

265 "We're arming the Afghans, right?": Persico, *Casey,* 428–29.

266 known locally: Bergman, *Rise and Kill First,* 373.

267 Bilal Sharara: Blanford lived in Beirut starting in 1994, and served as a correspondent for the *Christian Science Monitor* starting in 2002.

267 human-wave assaults: Terence Smith, "Iran: Five Years of Fanaticism," *New York Times Magazine,* February 12, 1984.

267 first reporting of modern-day suicide bombers: David B. Ottaway, "Child POWs," *Washington Post,* July 16, 1984.

267 Mugniyah told Arafat's deputy: Bergman, *The Secret War with Iran,* 70.

268 say his friends: author interviews with Rizzo, Maguire, Rodriguez, and others who knew Buckley personally.

269 Mugniyah personally oversaw: author interview with Rizzo; Bob Woodward and Charles Babcock, "Agency Watched Helplessly: CIA's 'Private Hostage Crisis' over Buckley Told," *Washington Post,* November 25, 1986.

269 "I had first met Bill Buckley": Rizzo, *Company Man,* 102.

269 "There were just": author interview with Rizzo.

270 "Casey ordered": Rizzo, *Company Man*, 102.

270 "secret commando unit": Jeff Gerth with Philip Taubman, "US military creates Secret Units for use in Sensitive Tasks Abroad," *New York Times*, June 8, 1984.

271 State Department objected: oral history interview with Ambassador Robert Oakley, "The Failed Attempt to Get a Terrorist Mastermind," ADST.

271 Counterterrorist Center (CTC) opened its doors: "About CIA, Timeline," CIA Museum, author visit; Clarridge, *A Spy for All Seasons*, 320–29.

272 Vincent Cannistraro: "Target America," *Frontline*, PBS, October 2001.

272 La Belle discothèque: Nathalie Malinarich, "Flashback: The Berlin Disco Bombing," BBC News, November 13, 2001.

273 Clarridge proposed killing Qaddafi: Coll, *Ghost Wars*, 521–22.

273 allegedly killing: Photographs and documents recovered in Qaddafi's Bab al-Azizya compound, in 2011, suggest to some that Hana was not killed and is alive and working as a doctor in Tripoli. The German newspaper *Die Welt* broke the story.

273 self-defense as defined by Article 51: Ronald Reagan, "Address to the Nation on the United States Air Strike Against Libya," April 14, 1986, available on YouTube.

273 "Why...more morally acceptable": Coll, *Ghost Wars*, 144.

CHAPTER EIGHTEEN

274 told the Justice Department: "Lewis Merletti, Secret Service Director's Declaration, Justice Department," released May 19, 1998, court filing in opposition to independent counsel Kenneth W. Starr's motion to compel testimony from Secret Service agents.

274 radical AOP—Attack on Principal: author interview with Merletti.

275 Delta's name was changed: Sometime later, the name was apparently again changed to Army Compartmented Element, though most special mission unit operators refer to the unit as Delta or CAG.

275 never been reported before: The mission was referenced in 1994, some of the details correct, others not, says Merletti: "Terror on the South Lawn," *Newsweek*, September 26, 1994.

275 "'holy shit' moment": author interview with U.S. Secret Service special agent.

276 AOP training raid: author interviews with Merletti.

276 Prince Sultan was meeting: Burke, *Al-Qaeda*, 124n265. Burke interviewed Mohammad din Mohammad in October 2002 in Peshawar. Some details come from Wright, *Looming Tower*, 158.

277 Iraq had a powerful army: "Command Concepts, Gulf War," RAND, 58.

278 Mohammad din Mohammad recalled: Burke, *Al-Qaeda*, 136. Also see Ali Soufan, notes, Security Committee, UBL, *9/11 Commission Report*.

278 Cheney, met personally in Jeddah with Saudi king Fahd: "Oral History: Norman Schwarzkopf," The Gulf War, *Frontline* (pbs.org). Also present was U.S. ambassador to Saudi Arabia Charles Freeman. Note the controversy here: the

St. Petersburg Times reported that Russian satellite photos showed no Iraqi buildup, as did the testimony of Peter Zimmerman, Defense Department analyst.

279 Cheney told the king: ibid., Schwarzkopf interview with *Frontline,* February 4, 1997.

279 "You don't need Americans": Wright, *Looming Tower,* 157.

280 "America incarnates the devil": Lawrence Joffe, "Obituary: Hassan al-Turabi," *Guardian,* March 11, 2016.

280 Turabi hosted the Arab Islamic People's Congress: Atwan, *The Secret History of al Qaeda,* 48. Journalist Abdel Bari Atwan says he discussed the event with Osama bin Laden.

281 CIA took note and began to monitor the jihadists: Turabi's vision was to create a Muslim caliphate across Africa and the Middle East, with Sudan as the *ummah,* or headquarters. President Eisenhower had once wondered aloud to his National Security Council if Islamic radicalism could be used as a counterbalance to communism. His idea was that it might bring a curious form of peace to the world's most ungovernable nations. Turabi's Islamic regime in Sudan indicated to the intelligence community that this was no longer a viable foreign policy pursuit.

282 green badger: At the CIA's behest, Waugh became a full-time CIA employee during the 1990s, but he disliked this, he says, mostly because it required him to live in Washington, DC. After a little more than a year, he went back to being a green badger, which is how he did most of his work. Being an independent contractor in the Special Activities Division is nothing like being a so-called defense contractor (such work is typified by the organization formerly known as Blackwater). The CIA paramilitary operators and officers interviewed for this book make clear that defense contractors are not authorized to engage in direct-action missions and do not have Title 50 authority.

283 the mask didn't really fit: author interviews with Waugh. The stories in this section were confirmed with a second source in K-town, in agency parlance. See also Waugh and Keown, *Jackal,* 120–44.

285 fulfilled his boyhood dreams: author interviews with Waugh.

286 largest landowner in Sudan: Wright, *Looming Tower,* 169.

286 Intelligence Support Activity: "Subject HPSCI 'Discovery' of the Army's Intelligence Support Activity (ISA)," from DC/PCS, February 10, 1982, CIA/CREST. Organization founded by Colonel Jerry King.

288 local papers reported: "Attack on Mosque in Sudan by Fundamentalists Kills 20," Agence France-Presse, December 10, 2000.

289 "As a new recruit": author interview with Black.

289 "Khartoum was the Super Bowl": Kevin McMurray, "Cofer Black, Out of the Shadows," *Men's Journal,* November 20, 2013.

290 double agent Ali Mohamed: Service Records of Ali Mohamed, as cited in *USA v. Omar Abdel Rahman et al.,* S(5) 93 Cr. 181 (MBM), and from the closing remarks of defense attorney Roger Stavis, September 11, 1995.

290 Mugniyah shared with bin Laden techniques: ibid.; also see Lance, *Triple Cross,* 140; Wright, *Looming Tower,* 192.

290 planning the assassination: author interview with Black; Coll, *Ghost Wars,* 271. See also Black's *9/11 Commission Report* testimony, September 26, 2002. Not until August 1993 was the first official CIA report on Osama bin Laden—called Usama bin Laden (UBL) by the Agency—released. Written by analyst Gina Bennett, it was called "The Wandering Mujahidin: Armed and Dangerous." Six months prior, in February 1993, jihadists struck the United States, detonating a truck bomb below the North Tower of the World Trade Center in New York City, killing six people and injuring one thousand. The ambitious plan was to weaken the North Tower to the degree that it fell over and crashed into the South Tower, bringing both towers down with the hopes of killing tens of thousands of people. One of the men convicted of conspiracy in the bombing was Omar Abdel-Rahman, the Muslim cleric known as "the blind sheikh," who'd ordered the assassination of Anwar Sadat. "The perception that the U.S. has an anti-Islamic foreign policy agenda raises the likelihood that U.S. interests will increasingly become targets for violence from the former mujahidin," wrote Bennett. "The Arab mujahidin [are] considered highly motivated and prepared to die for the jihad."

CHAPTER NINETEEN

293 "I saw a subject line": Clarke, *Against All Enemies,* 80.

293 "no such report": Though not present for the event, Merletti maintains that the Secret Service knew about the foiled bomb plot as events were unfolding in Kuwait. The public affairs office at the Secret Service would not comment on the matter but sent me two contradictory news articles in response to a written request. In "Clinton Awaits Probe of Bush Death Plot," *Washington Post,* May 9, 1993, Barbara Vobejda wrote, "Bush spokesman Andrew Maner said the former president was told about the assassination plot while he was in Kuwait." In "Bush Says Death Plot Wouldn't Deter Him from Kuwait Trip," *Reuters,* May 24, 1993, Michael Conlon wrote, "George Bush said yesterday that the plot to assassinate him during his recent visit to Kuwait was genuine and that he did not learn about [it] until he returned to the United States."

294 Kuwait was moving forward with a trial: "The Attack That Failed: Iraq's Attempt to Assassinate Former President Bush in Kuwait, April 1993," Secret, NOFORN/ORCON, n.d. (84 pages), 43–44, CIA/CREST.

294 a narrative emerged: ibid., 40–44.

294 he was working: ibid., 2.

295 If the car bomb failed to detonate: ibid., 51.

295 Iraqi-made bombs: ibid., 28.

296 "ample proof of direct Iraqi responsibility": ibid., 30.

296 CIA officers with the CTC: "Iraq: Baghdad Attempts to Assassinate Former President Bush," Directorate of Intelligence, Intelligence Memorandum, Counterterrorist Center, July 12, 1993, 1–4.

296 Land Cruiser exploded: "Mitterrand's Wife Escapes Iraq Bomb Attack," Associated Press, July 7, 1992.

297 she had suffered: "Funeral Crowd Demands Revenge," *Washington Post,* June 28, 1993.

298 "really depressing": author interview with Merletti.

299 report the findings to Congress: Pierre Thomas, "Treasury Official Says ATF Made Mistakes in Waco," *Washington Post,* August 14, 1993; David Willman and Glenn F. Bunting, "Agent Disputes Boss on Waco Raid Warning," *Los Angeles Times,* July 25, 1995.

299 Merletti told the congressman: interview with Merletti. This section comes from my interviews with Merletti as well as: Testimony of Lewis Merletti, Waco Investigation, Day 4, Part 1, July 24, 1995; Joint Subcommittee hearings investigating the failed February 28, 1993; Alcohol, Tobacco and Firearms Bureau raid on the Branch Davidian compound near Waco, Texas.

300 smoking crack cocaine: "History of Ground and Air Assaults on the White House Complex," Public Report of the White House Security Review, Appendix, Secretary of the Treasury, 12–13.

300 Corder was not a licensed pilot: ibid., 3.

301 "protecting the president from flying suicides": Melinda Liu, "Terror on the South Lawn," *Newsweek,* September 26, 1994.

CHAPTER TWENTY

303 summoned to his CIA reporting site: This chapter was reported based on extensive interviews with Waugh, as well as a review of documents and photographs in his personal collection. It is further authenticated by an interview and correspondence with then–Chief of Station, Khartoum, Cofer Black, as well as a Senior Intelligence Service officer who wished to remain anonymous, and who served in Sudan before joining the CTC. See also Waugh and Keown, *Jackal,* chapters 9–11.

303 Jackal moved around the globe: Director of Central Intelligence, National Intelligence Council, For Chief, Counterterrorist Group, CPN/DO, "FBIS Excerpts," September 3, 1985, CIA/CREST. Note: General Nicolae Plesita, the ruthless chief of the Securitate secret police, personally arranged shelter in Romania for Carlos the Jackal. In 1998, General Plesita told court prosecutors on the record that President Nicolae Ceausescu had ordered him to find temporary shelter for the terrorist, in Romania, after the bombing of the Radio Free Europe offices, in Munich in 1981.

304 "Billy Waugh was the perfect person": interview with Black.

309 quickly snapped four or five pictures: author review of Waugh's photos.

311 "what in hell they wanted": author interview with Black.

314 He lived only because: Richard L. Holm, "A Close Call in Africa: A Plane Crash, Rescue, and Recovery," CIA/SCI.

CHAPTER TWENTY-ONE

317 Lew Merletti prepared for travel: This chapter is reported based on interviews with Lew Merletti as well as photographs from his personal collection. Herbert Ragan, the digital archives specialist at the William J. Clinton Presidential Library, provided me with 792 pages of contact sheets—Middle East peace process images taken by White House photographers, comprising some 25,000 images that chronicle the travels discussed here. See also "President Clinton's Daily Schedule," Collection, WJC/L.

317 No fan of CIA covert operations: That President Clinton avoided covert action as a third option was a sentiment shared by a majority of covert-action operators who served during his White House tenure. CIA former general counsel John Rizzo writes in his book that immediately after the election, President-elect Clinton "began sending unmistakable signals. He wasn't interested in, didn't care about, the Agency at all." See Rizzo, *Company Man,* 137; Memorandum, "Subject: Usama bin Ladin-related Activities in Kondoz Province, Afghanistan," October 27, 2000, WJC/L.

317 Hamas maintained a hit squad: Yosif Mahmoud Haj-Yahis et al., "Alleged Palestinian Collaborators with Israel and Their Families: A Study of Victims of Internal Political Violence," Harry S. Truman Research Institute for the Advancement of Peace, Hebrew University of Jerusalem, 18–19.

318 "disappear from the map": Bradley Burston, "Netanyahu Wants Peace, Vows War on Militants," *Reuters,* October 18, 1997, quoting Yassin from his interview with Swedish newspaper *Svenska Dagbladet.*

318 "until Judgment Day": "Sheikh Yassin: Spiritual Figurehead," *BBC News,* March 22, 2004; Sherifa Zuhur, "Hamas and Israel: Conflicting Strategies of Group-Based Politics," Strategic Studies Institute, U.S. Army, December 2008.

318 Yasser Arafat was considering making peace: In the fall of 1991, nine months after the end of the Gulf War, the United States and Russia hosted the Madrid Conference in Spain, designed to revive peace talks between the Israelis and the Palestinians. From the point of view of the U.S. State Department, peace between Israel and its Arab neighbors would stabilize the region and further isolate Iran and Iraq. Hamas perceived this move toward stabilization as a direct threat to its existence and pursued mass-casualty attacks.

318 assassination squad was folded into the group's military wing: Al-Qassam, Ezzedeen Al-Qassam Brigades, Information Office, "About Us," author copy provided by source.

318 the Shin Bet had information: author interview with Shin Bet officer, Jaffa, Israel, 2016.

319 "Mugniyah himself came to the camp": Bergman, *Rise and Kill First,* 421.

320 face and hands covered in blood: "Bomb Rips Bus Apart in Tel Aviv," Associated Press, October 19, 1994.

321 Merletti traveled to Tel Aviv: author interview with Merletti. See also *The*

Gatekeepers, a 2015 documentary film, directed by Dror Moreh, in which six former heads of the Shin Bet go on the public record for the first time.

322 "[Agent S———] was not watching his area": In our interviews, Merletti identified the Shin Bet agent by his last name, which begins "S." Mossad identifies him as Agent Y, his first name being Yuval; I chose to redact the name and go with the first initial of the last name.

323 Clinton met with Hafez al-Assad: "The President's News Conference with President Hafiz al-Asad of Syria in Damascus, October 27, 1994," APP.

323 King Fahd, who praised: U.S. Department of State, *Dispatch,* vol. 5, Supplement No. 10, November 1994, 39.

324 Arafat fumed: Clyde Haberman, "Clinton in the Middle East: The Sacred City; Divisiveness of Shrine Issue Forces Clinton to Drop Tour," *New York Times,* October 8, 1994.

328 Shamgar Commission: "The Assassination of a Prime Minister—The Intelligence Failure That Failed to Prevent the Murder of Yitzhak Rabin," National Security Studies Center of Haifa, Haifa, Israel. As for Agent S———, "He was the commander (4–5 agents) of the advanced unit which was in charge of all the preliminary checks and reconnaissance at the venue before the event [where Rabin was assassinated] and created the second circle of protection during it," *Haaretz* reporter Yossi Melman told me. "He was found guilty of negligence and unprofessional conduct."

329 paid informant: The uncle, Kamil Hamad, promptly disappeared from his Gaza home. According to speculation in the Israeli press, in exchange for betraying the Engineer, Kamil Hamad received $650,000, a new passport, and a visa to the United States.

331 "As the presidential motorcade": author interview with Merletti.

331 interviewing President Clinton: Clinton interview: NPR's *All Things Considered,* January 21, 1998.

332 "What is this guy Ken Starr thinking?": author interview with Merletti.

332 Clint Hill was living proof: "Testimony of Clinton J. Hill, Special Agent, Secret Service." Hearings Before the President's Commission on the Assassination of President John F. Kennedy, vol. II, 61, 132–44. According to Hill, President Kennedy made the protocol change during his visit to Tampa, Florida, on November 18, 1963.

332 Ken Starr seemed unconcerned: author interview with Merletti; Gormley, *The Death of American Virtue,* 422–23.

332 Accompanying Merletti was…Clint Hill: ibid. Using a PowerPoint presentation to demonstrate, Merletti showed Ken Starr a history of the Secret Service that covered the murder of President Kennedy. "Secret Service agents think about assassination every day," he says. "They study the way in which assassinations occur around the world. Keeping the president safe is one of the most significant parts of the national security apparatus." Merletti told Starr: "One could argue it sits at the top. An assassination has grave effects. It's not like any other murder. It's a murder that has worldwide implications."

332 Lawyers for the Secret Service showed the judge: Michael Duffy, "Keeping It Secret," CNN, May 18, 1998.

333 suicide bombers drove: "20th Anniversary of the US Embassy Bombings in East Africa: Recollections from Employees and Staff of the US Embassies in Nairobi, Kenya and Dar es Salaam, Tanzania," *Nairobi Roar,* August 27, 1998, vol. 1, issue 41, with a note from the ambassador, Prudence Bushnell. The number of deaths and casualties varies among sources.

333 bin Laden issued a fatwa: *9/11 Commission Report,* chapter 2, section 2.1, "A Declaration of War."

333 Clinton would not sign it: author interview with Rizzo; Rizzo, *Company Man,* 162.

333 CIA wanted to kill bin Laden outright: author interview with Black.

334 Tomahawk cruise missiles: *9/11 Commission Report,* 116. The commission found, "The argument for hitting al Shifa was that it would lessen the chance of Bin Ladin's having nerve gas for a later attack." Others disagreed, including the National Security Council's Mary McCarthy, who felt that the intel between bin Laden and al Shifa was "rather uncertain at this point." See also Marc Lacey, "Look at the Place! Sudan Says, 'Say Sorry,' but U.S. Won't," *New York Times,* October 20, 2005.

334 Waugh was in Sudan...at the time: author interview with Waugh.

334 "so many caveats and conditions": author interview with Rizzo.

334 "she would consider as 'illegal'": author interview with Rizzo; Rizzo, *Company Man,* 162.

335 "Unbelievable": author interview with Black.

335 Crumpton explained: author interview with Crumpton. The second and third quotes come from Crumpton, *Art of Intelligence,* 155–56.

335 "Imagine the pre-9/11 headlines": Crumpton quoting Black in Crumpton, *Art of Intelligence,* 156. I also discussed this with Black in our interview.

335 "No one had the foresight": author interview with Crumpton.

336 "take a lawyer from the Justice Department": author interview with Black.

CHAPTER TWENTY-TWO

341 to get advance money: author interviews with Waugh. Money is given in exchange for an authorization chit from an operations officer, or handler.

341 Shan State Army: Thomas Fuller, "Khun Sa, Golden Triangle Drug King, Dies at 73," *New York Times,* November 5, 2007.

342 "I began writing": author interview with Rizzo.

342 Waugh headed over to the lot: This section is reported from my interviews with Waugh and four other members of the Special Activities Division who were there that day. "The CIA was considered a target and people were moving fast." The members of SAD watched as thousands of CIA employees hurried out of the parking lot. "There were more than a few fender benders that day."

342 "RON": "This is never a problem if you work for SAD," Waugh says. "You always have a bag with a change of clothes, a flashlight, a toothbrush, and some other things in your trunk."

343 "Let's pick them off one at a time": Dan Balz and Bob Woodward, "America's Chaotic Road to War," *Washington Post,* January 27, 2002.

344 Tenet was very clear: author interview with Black.

344 determination to hunt down: "Bush: There's No Rules," CNN.com, September 17, 2001. The rhetoric around 9/11 would now center around hunting and killing. It would be about justice and revenge. A reporter asked the president, "Do you want bin Laden dead?" "I want justice," the president said, and he cited "an old poster out west... that said, 'Wanted, Dead or Alive.'"

344 president told his advisors: Dan Balz and Bob Woodward, "Afghan Campaign's Blueprint Emerges," *Washington Post,* January 29, 2002.

345 said Rizzo: author interview with Rizzo.

345 "The first MON": The first half of this quote is from our interview; the second half is from Rizzo, *Company Man,* 172.

346 one of which was armed: author interview with Crumpton.

346 Tenet passed this authority... to Cofer Black: Coll, *Directorate S,* 70.

346 "The purpose of this meeting": *9/11 Commission Report,* 333; author interview with Black. The memorandum was ten pages long, with two appendices, and it authorized all the steps proposed by Tenet at Camp David to destroy bin Laden and his network.

347 briefing for Vice President Dick Cheney: author interviews with Prado. This information first reported in Mazzetti, *Way of the Knife,* 122.

348 wearing a rubber mask: author interviews with Prado; Coll, *Directorate S,* 84.

348 meeting in the White House: author interviews with Prado.

349 "CIA paramilitary arm": Crumpton, *Art of Intelligence,* 189.

349 Prado recalls: author interviews with Prado.

349 Crumpton explains: author emails with Crumpton.

350 asked him to lead: Schroen, *First In,* 15.

351 "Let me explain something": author interview with Crumpton.

352 U.S. military cannot legally pay cash bribes: It's worth noting this dollar amount was less than one-seventh of the money the Defense Department spent firing Tomahawk missiles on bin Laden's caves in Khost on a single day in 1998.

352 "We were producing": author interview with Crumpton.

352 "Our Afghan allies": Crumpton, *Art of Intelligence,* 237.

353 "On October 1": author interviews with Stiles.

355 growing at a furious pace: Coll, *Directorate S,* 76.

355 augmented with special operations forces: In the second week in October 2001, Green Berets helicoptered into the Panjshir Valley and linked up with Schroen's team. The Green Berets brought with them a laser targeting system, called SOFLAM, which would interact with information from the Pentagon's system and also the Magic Box. In this way, CIA personnel could access Central Command's bombing encyclopedia, including its list of military targets across Afghanistan.

356 "'Go to Kabul'": author interview with Black. Waugh was given one brief in-country assignment before he left. "I was sent to Fort Bragg to try and

wrangle up as many retired Special Forces operators as I could find," Waugh recalls. He scoured the commissary at Fort Bragg's classified Delta Force base, hidden away off Chicken Street, but there was almost no one available for hire. "The military put a freeze on retirement. Everyone was preparing to go to war. I found one guy from Delta and brought him back to DC with me. That was it."

CHAPTER TWENTY-THREE

358 public hangings: "Afghanistan, The Fall of Kabul 2001," BBC Television, available on YouTube, n.d.

358 the Taliban's overdue hotel bill: author interview with Waugh.

359 Bamyan Province: This was one of the few regions inside Afghanistan known to the outside world: in March 2001, the Taliban blew up three 175-foot-tall statues of Buddha carved into a mountainside there.

360 warlord General Dostum: Crumpton, *Art of Intelligence*, 241.

360 State Department report: James Risen, "US Inaction Seen After Taliban P.O.W.'s Died," *New York Times*, July 10, 2009; Bernstein, *Jawbreaker*, 262–63.

361 where four of the 9/11 hijackers trained: Nagieb Khaja, "Fault Lines: This Is Taliban Country," *Al Jazeera*, October 24, 2015.

362 "Alexander the Great lost his mind here": author interview with Ground Branch operator.

362 a British officer of the Great Game: Smith, *Killer Elite*, 214.

363 "Just hard to kill": Hayden, *Playing to the Edge*, 31–32.

365 Weapons were drawn: author interview with Ground Branch operator.

365 Crumpton recalls watching: author interview with Crumpton.

366 when the bomb hit: Captain Jason Amerine, "Campaign Against Terror, Friendly Fire," *Frontline*, PBS, September 8, 2002.

367 except for a nuclear bomb: Tim Weiner, "Afghan Camps, Hidden in Hills, Stymied Soviet Attacks for Year," *New York Times*, August 24, 1998.

367 without looking like it was trying to kill him: "There will be no sanctuary [in Khost] for terrorists," President Clinton declared in a press conference during a vacation in Martha's Vineyard, Massachusetts. The Executive Action bombings at Khost accomplished almost nothing, save a bill for U.S. taxpayers of more than $100 million (at the time, each Tomahawk missile cost $1.6 million).

367 Guns were drawn: author interview with Satterlee.

368 officially identified: Thomas Gibbons-Neff, "After 13 years, CIA Honors Fort Lewis Green Beret Killed on Secret Afghanistan Mission," *Washington Post*, April 17, 2016.

369 pack a bag: author interview with Stiles.

CHAPTER TWENTY-FOUR

371 Plausible deniability; author interview with Scorpion trainer; author interview with Scorpion team leader in Iraq.

372 "I know Iraq": author interview with Maguire.

372 His father: Isikoff and Corn, *Hubris*, 6.

372 under Bill Casey: Not everyone approved of the covert operations run by John Maguire, which, he is quick to say, are always at the behest of the president. Once, in 1984, the chairman of the Senate Select Committee on Intelligence, Senator Barry Goldwater, wrote to Bill Casey to complain about a covert operation Maguire had recently overseen in Nicaragua. It involved CIA-hired local commandos working from speedboats to mine Nicaraguan ports, thereby cutting off weapons, fuel, and supplies to the leftist Sandinista government, which the CIA was trying to overthrow. "I am [expletive redacted] pissed off!" wrote Goldwater. "Mine the harbors in Nicaragua? This is an act violating international law....It is an act of war." The senator warned the director of Central Intelligence that should "anything like this happen [again], I'm going to raise one hell of a lot of fuss about it in public." The harbor-mining program was aborted. Maguire escaped the Iran-Contra affair unscathed. He continued to work on CIA covert actions throughout the eighties and nineties, including in Iraq and Afghanistan. See text of "Goldwater's Letter to the Head of C.I.A.," *New York Times*, April 11, 1984.

372 "Bush wanted": author interview with Maguire.

373 appeared to lack: author interview with Ground Branch operator; author interviews with Faddis.

373 longtime trusted ally: Ned Parker, "Divided Iraq Has Two Spy Agencies: A Sunni Heads the Official CIA-funded Organization," *Los Angeles Times*, April 15, 2007.

373 Shahwani's three sons: Tenet and Harlow, *Center of the Storm*, 388; Lieutenant Colonel Rick Francona, "A Personal Note on the Execution of Saddam Hussein," *Hardball with Chris Matthews*, MSNBC, December 29, 2006.

373 "I fight to avenge my sons": Johanna McGeary, "Taking Back the Streets," *Time*, July 6, 2004.

374 "Yes. Very wild": author interview with Ground Branch operator.

374 Kurdish civilians living in Halabja: Jeffrey Goldberg, "The Great Terror," *New Yorker*, March 25, 2002.

375 "Barzani and Talabani were very skeptical": author interview with Maguire. See also Isikoff and Corn, *Hubris*.

376 "Cheney asked many questions": author interview with Maguire.

376 Bashar al-Assad struck a new deal: Bergman, *Rise and Kill First*, 569–70.

376 triumvirate the Radical Front: ibid. Syria's reasons for aligning itself with Hezbollah, based in nearby Lebanon, were practical. Assad received considerable funding from Iran for his supporting Hezbollah in Lebanon. Now, there was a movement in Lebanon to rid the country of terrorists and also get the Syrians to leave. There were a number of advocates involved, but leading the charge was two-time Lebanese prime minister Rafik Harari. "Imad Mugniyah, the Hezbollah chief of staff, began to assassinate those figures, one after another, on behalf of the Iranians and the Syrians," says Bergman. The assassinations came

to a climax when, in 2005, Rafik Harari and twenty-two others died in a massive car bomb assassination in Beirut.

377 fought alongside Mike Spann: Extraordinary footage of this event, shot by a German film crew, is available on YouTube (https://www.youtube.com/watch?v=ETa9w4o9vy0).

378 Local villagers described: author interviews with Faddis; Major General John R. Landry, National Intelligence Officer for Conventional Military Issues, "Saddam's Preparations for War: Intentions and Capabilities," Top Secret, October 2002.

378 document found in Kabul: Jonathan Schanzer, "Ansar al-Islam: Back in Iraq," *Middle East Quarterly,* Winter 2004, 41–50.

378 the fighting had begun: "Report," *Kurdistan Newsline,* July 23, 2002; Asharq Al-Awsat, December 6, 2002; "Iraqi Kurdish Leader Evades Assassins," BBC News, April 3, 2002.

378 CIA team was taken: author interview with Faddis; Tucker and Faddis, *Operation Hotel California,* 5, 18. The fighters journeyed across Iran, using smugglers' routes, to Iran's northwestern border into Iraq. The group was called Ansar al-Islam, a merger of Jund al-Islam (Soldiers of Islam) and a splinter group from the Kurdistan Islamic Movement led by the radical cleric Najmeddin Faraj Ahmad, known as Mullah Krekar to his followers.

379 He sent CIA headquarters a list: author interview with Faddis. "The team conducted reconnaissance missions behind enemy lines and charted ten-digit GPS grid locations to establish the location of the terrorist encampments in the mountains of Iraqi Kurdistan. The [CIA] had imagery on all these locations that matched up with our own field intelligence. All we needed was the green light to strike," Faddis says.

380 "Scorpions were raping each other during training": author interview with Faddis. See also Tucker and Faddis, *Operation Hotel California,* 47.

380 Vogle went by the code name Snake: Ian Shapiro, "The CIA Acknowledges the Legendary Spy Who Saved Hamid Karzai's Life—and Honors Him by Name," *Washington Post,* September 18, 2017.

380 "We are going to get good men killed": Tucker and Faddis, *Operation Hotel California,* 45.

381 Tenet praised the Scorpions: Tenet and Harlow, *Center of the Storm,* 389. General Michael Hayden also praised Shahwani and his work; see Hayden, *Playing to the Edge,* 201–3.

381 Shahwani: Hayden, *Playing to the Edge,* 201. Hayden fondly recalls visiting Shahwani at his home in the al-Khark district of Iraq. There, the new head of the Iraqi National Intelligence Service kept a pet gazelle and a dog he'd named Chalabi, "after the Iraqi exile turned politician that CIA loved to hate," Hayden wrote.

381 The assassins also included: author interviews with Faddis; Tucker and Faddis, *Operation Hotel California,* 90; Schanzer, "Ansar al-Islam," 41–50.

381 man posing as a peace negotiator: C. J. Chivers, "Threats and Responses: Northern Iraq; Kurdish Leader Is Assassinated in Militant Raid," *New York Times,* February 10, 2003.

381 Directorate 9, Secret Operations: Saddam Hussein was an alumnus of precursor organization Jihaz al Khas, serving as chief of special apparatus between 1964 and 1966.

382 "Mukhabarat assassination teams": author interview with Faddis.

382 capture an American alive: Tucker and Faddis, *Operation Hotel California,* 91.

383 team watched Ansar al-Islam: author interview with Giaconia. See also Giaconia's excellent *Operation Viking Hammer.*

385 Order 69: L. Paul Bremer, "Order 69: Delegation of Authority Regarding Establishment of the Iraqi National Intelligence Service," Coalition Provisional Authority, April 2004.

386 tit-for-tat assassinations: David Ignatius, "A Sectarian Spy Duel in Baghdad," *Washington Post,* June 14, 2007. The invasion of Iraq toppled the government and unleashed a savagely violent, all-encompassing conflict sectarian war, something that the great majority of Americans had never heard of before. At the center of the conflict was an ancient schism, or ideological division, between Islam's two sects, Shiite Muslims and Sunni Muslims. Saddam Hussein, hardly religious, was a Sunni strongman who crushed anyone who threatened him. Many of his most vicious actions were directed against Shiites and Kurds.

386 "The big story": "Iraqis: Hezbollah Trained Shiite Militants," Associated Press, July 2, 2008.

386 Hezbollah's deputy secretary general, acknowledged: Ben Hubbard, "Iran Out to Remake Mideast with Arab Enforcer: Hezbollah," *New York Times,* August 27, 2017.

CHAPTER TWENTY-FIVE

391 renamed Orange: author interview with Waugh.

391 kill or capture Imad Mugniyah: In 1994, Mossad killed Mugniyah's older brother Fouad, with the intention of trying to draw out Imad—to kill him or photograph him. "Fouad had to die because the Israelis didn't have the slightest idea how else to find Mugniyah, who remained no more than a grainy photograph in their intelligence files," says Ronen Bergman. Fouad was killed with a car bomb parked on the street in front of the Beirut hardware store he ran. The blast destroyed the store, Fouad, and three people walking by. Fifteen others were injured. At the funeral, Mossad scoured the crowds. Imad Mugniyah stayed away.

392 Nasrallah accused Israel: "Three Die in Lebanon Border Clash," BBC News, July 20, 2004.

392 Unit 8200: John Reed, "Former Insiders and Whistle-Blowers Provide a View of the Formidable Military Intelligence Outfit," *Financial Times,* July 10, 2015.

392 size of the target's earlobes: author interview with Israeli SIGINT officer, Tel Aviv, Israel, 2016.

393   "His day will come": Bergman, *Rise and Kill First*, 597.

393   Mossad's Junction Unit: Ben Lynfield, "Yossi Cohen: The Israeli Spymaster Straight out of Le Carré and Ian Fleming Takes Charge of Mossad," *Independent*, December 8, 2015.

393   Mossad collects information: "Israeli Intelligence Veterans Refuse to Serve in Palestinian Territories," *Guardian*, September 12, 2014.

393   "vulnerabilities, if exposed": Unit 8200 document, author copy.

393   assigned by Iranian commanders: "Treasury Designates Hizballah Commander Responsible for American Deaths in Iraq," U.S. Department of the Treasury, November 19, 2012; Alexander Orleans, "Echoes of Syria: Hezbollah Reemerges in Iraq," Institute for the Study of War, August 1, 2014.

394   Iraqi Shia militia under Imad Mugniyah: author interview with Levitt; Davin Coburn, Randolph Smith, and Kyle Barss, video report accompanying "Inside the Killing of Imad Mugniyah," *Washington Post*, January 30, 2015.

394   Unit 3800: Kenneth Katzman, "Iran-Iraq Relations," Congressional Research Service, August 13, 2010.

394   Title 50 authority to kill Mugniyah: author interviews with CIA Senior Intelligence Service officer; author interview with former Mossad officer. Mugniyah was directly connected to the arming and training of Shiite militia who were targeting and killing American servicemen and women in Iraq. The Title 50 authority to kill Mugniyah was approved by the attorney general, the director of national intelligence, the national-security advisor, and the Office of Legal Counsel at the Justice Department. President Bush signed off on this finding.

395   Harvey Point: author interviews with former operators familiar with the facility. This same facility would be used by Navy SEALs, Delta Force, and Ground Branch operators to alternately train for the raid that in 2011 would kill Osama bin Laden.

395   engineers felt confident: author interviews with former intelligence officers familiar with the operation; the other version of events comes from Bergman, *Rise and Kill First*, 500–501.

395   "kill a lone individual": Bergman, *Rise and Kill First*, 599.

396   five former intelligence officials confirmed: Adam Goldman and Ellen Nakashima, "CIA and Mossad Killed Senior Hezbollah Figure in Car Bombing," *Washington Post*, January 30, 2015.

396   "Israel is probably": Bergman, *Rise and Kill First*, 710n. Bergman is the only journalist I am aware of who discussed this operation with Hayden.

CHAPTER TWENTY-SIX

399   Counterterrorism Pursuit Teams: Bob Woodward, *Obama's Wars*, 9.

399   not the American CIA: It's a curious premise because no one is in uniform. The Afghan indigs wear camo-striped shirts and pants provided by the CIA, as do Ground Branch operators, but sometimes they go out fighting direct-action missions in their own clothes.

400 replied Ahmed Wali Karzai: Partlow, *A Kingdom of Their Own*, 137–38. This book is brilliant and tragic and should be read by anyone interested in Afghanistan.

400 "enrichment...of the Karzai clan": U.S. Department of State cable, "Kandahar Politics Complicates US Objectives in Afghanistan," October 3, 2009.

401 "AWK was the source of all evil": Quoted in Partlow, *A Kingdom of Their Own*, 269.

403 Ground Branch operators are: Technically there are three acknowledged Tier One Special Military Units: DELTA Force (CAG, U.S. Army SF-Delta), DEVGRU (Naval Special Warfare Development Group, Seal Team Six), and 24th Special Tactics Squadron (Air Force), with Tier Two including Green Berets (U.S. Army Special Forces), Army Rangers (U.S. Army 75th Ranger Regiment), CCT (USAF Combat Controllers), Marine Force Recon, and others.

404 classified cable to Langley: Memorandum From: Deputy Chief of Mission John C. Holzman. Cable 97, Islamabad, n.d., CIA/CREST.

404 Mullah Omar cried: Quoted in Steve Coll, "Looking for Mullah Omar," *New Yorker,* January 23, 2012.

404 draped it over his own shoulders: The BBC filmed this remarkable event; see Steve Inskeep, "The Cloak of the Prophet: Religious Artifact at the Heart of Former Taliban Stronghold," National Public Radio, January 10, 2002.

405 alongside Ground Branch: author interview with Canadian SOF operator.

406 Delta operators: Wright, *A Different Kind of War,* 95–96. The Defense Department called this mission Objective GECKO; CIA operators later wrote "Firebase Ghecko" on one of its security towers, author photos.

406 Chinooks helped the Delta operators: author interview with former Delta operator.

406 "traumatized and brutalized": Rashid, *Taliban,* 207.

407 "still the good war": Hayden, *Playing to the Edge,* 210.

409 MACV-SOG...wait more than thirty years: H. G. Reza, "Soldiers' Story: Their Heroism No Longer Secret," *Los Angeles Times,* May 26, 2003.

409 "The indigs we train": Per mission ratio of CIA Ground Branch operators to Afghan indigenous soldiers is roughly twenty to one, similar to the Ground Branch/Combined Studies Group operational teams in Vietnam.

409 "He's our teacher in the village": Partlow, *A Kingdom of Their Own,* 63.

410 "get raped less": author interview with Stiles.

410 "Warlords and Pedophilia": Craig S. Smith, "Shh, It's an Open Secret: Warlords and Pedophilia," *New York Times,* February 21, 2002.

410 press went silent: one notable exception is Ben Anderson's documentary *This Is What Winning Looks Like* (Vice News, 2013).

411 Leahy Amendment: Erica Gaston, "The Leahy Law and Human Rights Accountability in Afghanistan: Too Little, Too Late, or a Model for the Future?," Afghanistan Analysts Network, March 5, 2017.

411 "The ugly reality": Julius Cavendish, "After the US Pulls Out, Will CIA Rely More on Afghan Mercenaries?," *Christian Science Monitor,* November 16, 2011.

411 Two trillion U.S. dollars spent: Jeanne Sahadi, "The Financial Cost of 16 Years in Afghanistan," CNNMoney, August 22, 2017.

413 Identity in Afghanistan: Soraya Sarhaddi Nelson, "Afghanistan Strives to Register All Newborns," NPR, July 2, 2008.

414 agreed upon: A Ground Branch operator from Khost told me, "In all my years in Ground Branch, I only saw the team vote 'no' on one mission. That mission involved trying to locate Bowe Bergdahl."

414 high-value target was found: "Best Practices in Counterinsurgency: Making High-Value Targeting Operations an Effective Counterinsurgency Tool," July 7, 2009 (WikiLeaks).

415 dog-fighting competition: "Suicide Bomber Kills 80 at Dog Fighting Competition in Afghanistan," *Independent,* February 17, 2008.

CHAPTER TWENTY-SEVEN

417 Sangin, in Helmand Province: Pierre-Arnaud Chouvy, "Opiate Smuggling Routes from Afghanistan to Europe and Asia," Geopium.org, October 14, 2006; Michael Smith, "Afghan War: The Home Movie," *Times* online, December 17, 2006. See also the documentary film *Armadillo,* directed by Janus Metz (FilmBuff, 2011).

417 Pentagon parlance: Taimoor Shah and Rod Nordland, "Taliban Take an Afghan District, Sangin, That Many Marines Died to Keep," *New York Times,* March 23, 2017.

420 war machine: Spooky's onboard arsenal included two rotary cannons that fired 20mm rounds at an extraordinarily high rate of speed—something like 6,000 rounds per minute. It had at least one 40mm cannon, a multipurpose antiaircraft weapon, and a M102 howitzer. In other words, Spooky killed humans with an extraordinary magnitude of explosive power, all under the Title 10 authority of the Defense Department.

421 Protocol III: Convention on Prohibitions or Restrictions on the Use of Certain Conventional Weapons, United Nations Treaty Series, vol. 1342, 137.

422 "We were producing": author interview with Crumpton.

429 ensuing investigation: Lianne Gutcher and Julian Borger, "Ahmed Wali Karzai Killing Sparks Fears of Turmoil in Kandahar," *Guardian,* July 12, 2011.

429 "kill-and-capture raids": Bashir Ahmad Naadem, "Suspects Arrested in Wali Assassination," pajhwok.com, July 12, 2011; "Violence Surrounds Wali Karzai's Funeral," *Al Jazeera,* July 12, 2011; Partlow, *A Kingdom of Their Own,* 142.

429 A group of fathers: Partlow, *A Kingdom of Their Own,* 313.

430 warned about in the leaked CIA directive: "High-Value Targeting Operations: Best Practices in Counterinsurgency: Making High-Value Targeting Operations an Effective Counterinsurgency Tool," July 7, 2009 (WikiLeaks).

430 preemptive move by the Nobel Committee: "Opinions on President Obama's Peace Prize Win," *Washington Post,* October 9, 2009.

431 just war theory: There are lots of treatises on this. The BBC Ethics guide "Just War—Introduction" is recommended for a brief overview (bbc.co.uk).

432 President Obama defended the war: Barack H. Obama, "A Just and Lasting Peace," Nobel lecture delivered in the Oslo City Hall, December 10, 2009. The

president's words were: "The concept of 'just war' emerged, suggesting that war is justified only when certain conditions were met: if it is waged as a last resort or in self-defense; if the force used is proportional; and if, whenever possible, civilians are spared from violence."

432 applauded the speech sparingly: "Reaction to Obama's Nobel Speech," NPR's *All Things Considered,* December 10, 2009. The observation was from Howard Fineman, editor of *Newsweek.* The Nobel Prize YouTube channel published the speech, including visuals of the audience's reaction, on December 17, 2009.

CHAPTER TWENTY-EIGHT

433 John Brennan said: Remarks of John O. Brennan, "The Ethics and Efficacy of the President's Counterterrorism Strategy," April 30, 2012, released by the White House, Office of the Press Secretary; Greg Miller, "Brennan Speech Is First Obama Acknowledgment of Use of Armed Drones," *Washington Post,* April 30, 2012.

434 "crowd kills": Adam Entous, Siobhan Gorman, and Julian E. Barnes, "U.S. Tightens Drone Rules," *Wall Street Journal,* November 4, 2011 (includes the 1,500 KIA figure).

434 " 'three guys doing jumping jacks' ": Jo Becker and Scott Shane, "Secret 'Kill List' Proves a Test of Obama's Principles and Will," *New York Times,* May 29, 2012. Another official name for a signature strike is terrorist attack disruption strike.

434 "America's actions are legal": Remarks by the president at the National Defense University, Fort McNair, Washington, DC, May 23, 2013.

434 canceled the signature strike: "Background Briefing by Senior Administration Officials on the President's Speech on Counterterrorism," The White House, Office of the Press Secretary, May 23, 2013. The official said: "On the signature strike question that you asked, I don't want to get into the details of any specific strike. What I'd say is, first of all, we indicate a preference to work with partners, first and foremost, to deal with the threat of terrorism. Any action that we do take in terms of direct lethal action is subject to that standard of a continuing and imminent threat to the United States. The context for this is generally our war against al Qaeda and associated forces, but of course in the Afghan war theater, there is a slightly different context in the sense that we take action against high-value al Qaeda targets." See also: Presidential Policy Guidance, "Procedures for Approving Direct Action Against Terrorist Targets Located Outside the United States and Areas of Active Hostilities," May 22, 2013.

434 acting under CIA authority: author interviews with CIA Senior Intelligence Service officer; Andru E. Wall, "Demystifying the Title 10-Title 50 Debate: Distinguishing Military Operations, Intelligence Activities & Covert Action," *Harvard Journal,* 85. Note: "Title 10 and [Title] 50 create mutually supporting, not mutually exclusive, authorities," says Wall, who also served as senior legal advisor for U.S. Special Operations Command. The problem in perception, he suggests, is the fault of Congress. "Congress's stovepiped view of national security operations is legally incongruous and operationally dangerous." That Con-

gress as an oversight body—set up as a result of the Church Committee hearings—feigns ignorance about targeted killing operations to present a moral high ground is also deceptive, says Wall.

434 only the CIA can conduct lethal direct action: As stated earlier, the president can assign Title 50 authority to an individual or group outside the CIA, but according to all those with expertise interviewed on the subject, this has never happened. That a defense contractor has ever been given Title 50 authority is "total bullshit," Ric Prado told me. The veteran paramilitary operator who goes by the call sign Shark agrees: "Blackwater and other security guards have said a lot of bogus shit about what they do and it gets [reported as fact] in the news… but when it comes down to it they're security guards, period." Zeus said of defense contractors who claim to conduct direct-action missions: "They don't have the authority…they never have. They guard our bases, our people, and our trucks. They are security guards."

434 no markings or identifications: Navy SEAL Robert J. O'Neill's combat equipment was on public display for the first time at the Nixon Library in Yorba Linda on Monday, July 3, 2017. The front chest patch that reads "O'Neill" was not in place on the raid. Under CIA director Leon Panetta, operational control of the mission was delegated to U.S. Navy Vice Admiral William H. McRaven (who wrote his postgraduate thesis on the Nazi paraglider attack against the Belgian fortress Eben Emael); see McRaven, "The Theory of Special Operations" (Naval Postgraduate School, Monterey, California, June 1993).

435 "taken more terrorists off the field": "Exclusive: President Barack Obama on *Fox News Sunday,*" Fox News, April 10, 2016, in an interview with Chris Wallace.

435 "Obama succeeded": Micah Zenko, "Obama's Embrace of Drone Strikes Will Be a Lasting Legacy," Opinion Pages, *New York Times,* January 12, 2016; Micah Zenko, "Transferring CIA Drone Strikes to the Pentagon, Council on Foreign Relations," April 16, 2013. Note: The Senate Select Committee on Intelligence is briefed on all Title 50 drone strikes and can request to see video footage. The House Permanent Select Committee on Intelligence reviews both CIA and JSOC drone strikes. A poll conducted in 2013 revealed that 75 percent of Americans support military drone strikes, whereas only 65 percent support CIA drone strikes. Same way of killing, different public opinion.

435 normalized, mechanized, and industrialized: The White House, Office of the Press Secretary, "Fact Sheet: US Policy Standards and Procedures for the Use of Force in Counterterrorism Operations Outside the United States and Areas of Active Hostilities," May 23, 2013; Presidential Policy Guidance, "Procedures for Approving Direct Action Against Terrorist Targets Located Outside the United States and Areas of Active Hostilities," May 22, 2013.

436 "the Kellogg pact is dead": "Then and Now," *New York Times,* August 27, 1938. "It does not carry a feather's weight in the trembling balance of Central Europe. It has not abolished war, yet it has had one extraordinary and paradoxical effect. It has abolished declarations of war."

437   former CIA inspector general: Snider, *The Agency and the Hill,* 259.

437   "the last resort beyond last resort": "Institutionalizing Assassination: The 'Executive Action' Capability," 183, SCI/CHURCH. Cites Harvey's testimony for the committee of June 25, 1975.

437   "incompatible with American principles": "Alleged Assassination Plots Involving Foreign Leaders," 1, SCI/CHURCH.

438   "It's remarkable": author interview with Rizzo. He also discusses this in *Company Man,* 174–75.

438   138 countries around the world: author interviews with Ground Branch operators. See also Turse, "American Special Operations Forces Are Deployed to 70 Percent of the World's Countries," *The Nation,* January 5, 2017.

439   illuminating information: author interviews with Waugh; author interviews with Senior Intelligence Service officers.

440   Defense Department were now jointly testing: "Sandia Corporation Monthly Reports, 1958–1963," LASL Report Library, No 411531, July–September 1962; D. B. Davis, Org 7342, "Drop Tests of XW45 Mod 3," Organization 7300 Environmental Test Report, File XW-45, Sandia, n.d.

442   Archival footage shows him: Nevada Test Site archival footage of Little Feller 1, July 17, 1962, is available on YouTube.

444   Documents kept classified until 2003: F. J. Dyson et al., "Tactical Nuclear Weapons in Southeast Asia" (Study S-266), Institute for Defense Analysis, Jason Division, Restricted Data, Atomic Energy Act 1954, March 1967; Jacobsen, *The Pentagon's Brain,* 195–96.

445   "using nuclear weapons": Seymour Deitchman, "An Insider's Account: Seymour Deitchman," Nautilus Institute for Security and Sustainability, based on an interview conducted by Peter Hayes, February 25, 2003.

446   Colonel Giong said: author interview with Giong.

446   Che Guevara...advocated for nuclear war: Luther and Henken, *Che Guevara,* 145. The speech was for the First Latin American Youth Congress, in Havana, July 1962.

446   Che Guevara implored: Paco Ignacio Taibo II, "Guevara, Also Known as Che," 233.

446   taken in by Fidel: author interview with Guevara, Varadero, Cuba, June 2017.

450   seemingly implausible: On May 24, 2017, a draft of the Conceptualization of the Cuban Economic and Social Model of Socialist Development was published, opening the door for private property ownership. Our group was in Cuba three weeks later.

EPILOGUE

451   "Good that you're writing": author interview with Black at the Old Brogue Pub, March 2017. The CTC changed its name from the Counterterrorist Center to the Counterterrorism Center in 2005.

452   to surprise, kill, and vanish as necessary: According to participants, the team regularly discussed its SOE/OSS roots, notably the need to be "ruthless, relent-

less and remorseless" in facing a Nazi-like enemy. This comes from a discussion in Parliament over the creation of the Special Operations Executive: "When you are fighting for your life against a ruthless opponent, you cannot be governed by the Queensberry rules.... We must have a government which will be ruthless, relentless and remorseless. In short, we want a few more cads in this government." See Milton, *Ministry,* 21–22.

453 directly involved: author interview with said individual; confirmed by a second individual directly involved.

454 "In the old days, SAD were knuckle draggers": author interview with Stalker Team member.

ABOUT THE AUTHOR

ANNIE JACOBSEN is a journalist and the *New York Times* bestselling author of *Area 51, Operation Paperclip, Phenomena,* and *The Pentagon's Brain,* which was a 2016 Pulitzer Prize finalist. She was a contributing editor at the *Los Angeles Times Magazine* and presently writes and produces TV including *Tom Clancy's Jack Ryan.* A graduate of Princeton University, she lives in Los Angeles with her husband and two sons.

Also by Annie Jacobsen

Area 51: An Uncensored History of America's
Top Secret Military Base

"A compelling narrative of fifty years of covert operations by the CIA, the U.S. military, and the mysterious 'Atomic Energy Commission'...Jacobsen's meticulous research makes for a fascinating read."   —Rachael Larimore, *Slate*

Operation Paperclip: The Secret Intelligence Program
That Brought Nazi Scientists to America

"A gripping, always disquieting story of a nation forced to trade principle for power...*Operation Paperclip* takes its place in the annals of Cold War literature, one more proof that moral purity and great power can seldom coexist."
        —Chris Tucker, *Dallas Morning News*

The Pentagon's Brain: An Uncensored History of DARPA,
America's Top Secret Military Research Agency

"A brilliantly researched account of a small but powerful secret government agency whose military research profoundly affects world affairs."
        —Pulitzer Prize Committee

Phenomena: The Secret History of the U.S.
Government's Investigations into Extrasensory
Perception and Psychokinesis

"Richly researched...Jacobsen shows that, in the face of inexplicable events, even 'the most pragmatic, commonsense thinkers found themselves uncertain.'"
        —*The New Yorker*

Back Bay Books
Available wherever books are sold